THE

POETICAL WORKS

OF

JAMES RUSSELL LOWELL

BOSTON AND NEW YORK

HOUGHTON, MIFFLIN AND COMPANY

The Riverside Press, Cambridge

The Riverside Press, Cambridge, Mass., U. S. A.
Printed by H. O. Houghton & Company.

CONTENTS.

———◆———

MISCELLANEOUS POEMS.

THRENODIA.

Gone, gone from us! and shall we
    see
Those sibyl-leaves of destiny,
Those calm eyes, nevermore?
Those deep, dark eyes so warm and
    bright,
Wherein the fortunes of the man
Lay slumbering in prophetic light,
In characters a child might scan?
So bright, and gone forth utterly!
O stern word — Nevermore!

The stars of those two gentle eyes
Will shine no more on earth;
Quenched are the hopes that had their
    birth,
As we watched them slowly rise,
Stars of a mother's fate;
And she would read them o'er and o'er,
Pondering as she sate,
Over their dear astrology,
Which she had conned and conned
    before,
Deeming she needs must read aright
What was writ so passing bright.
And yet, alas! she knew not why,
Her voice would falter in its song,
And tears would slide from out her eye,
Silent, as they were doing wrong.
O stern word — Nevermore!

The tongue that scarce had learned
    to claim
An entrance to a mother's heart
By that dear talisman, a mother's name,
Sleeps all forgetful of its art!
I loved to see the infant soul
(How mighty in the weakness
Of its untutored meekness!)
Peep timidly from out its nest,

His lips, the while,
Fluttering with half-fledged words,
Or hushing to a smile
That more than words expressed,
When his glad mother on him stole
And snatched him to her breast!
O, thoughts were brooding in those
    eyes,
That would have soared like strong-
    winged birds
Far, far, into the skies,
Gladding the earth with song,
And gushing harmonies,
Had he but tarried with us long!
O stern word — Nevermore!

How peacefully they rest,
Crossfolded there
Upon his little breast,
Those small, white hands that ne'er
    were still before,
But ever sported with his mother's hair,
Or the plain cross that on her breast
    she wore!
Her heart no more will beat
To feel the touch of that soft palm,
That ever seemed a new surprise
Sending glad thoughts up to her eyes
To bless him with their holy calm, —
Sweet thoughts! they made her eyes
    as sweet.
How quiet are the hands
That wove those pleasant bands!
But that they do not rise and sink
With his calm breathing, I should think
That he were dropped asleep.
Alas! too deep, too deep
Is this his slumber!
Time scarce can number
The years ere he shall wake again.
O, may we see his eyelids open then!
O stern word — Nevermore!

As the airy gossamere,
Floating in the sunlight clear,
Where'er it toucheth clingeth tightly,
Round glossy leaf or stump unsightly,
So from his spirit wandered out
Tendrils spreading all about,
Knitting all things to its thrall
With a perfect love of all:
O stern word — Nevermore !

He did but float a little way
Adown the stream of time,
With dreamy eyes watching the ripples
    play,
Or hearkening their fairy chime ;
His slender sail
Ne'er felt the gale ;
He did but float a little way,
And, putting to the shore
While yet 't was early day,
Went calmly on his way,
To dwell with us no more !
No jarring did he feel,
No grating on his shallop's keel ;
A strip of silver sand
Mingled the waters with the land
Where he was seen no more :
O stern word — Nevermore !

Full short his journey was ; no dust
Of earth unto his sandals clave ;
The weary weight that old men must,
He bore not to the grave.
He seemed a cherub who had lost his
    way
And wandered hither, so his stay
With us was short, and 't was most meet
That he should be no delver in earth's
    clod,
Nor need to pause and cleanse his feet
To stand before his God :
O blest word — Evermore !

    1839.

———

THE SIRENS.

The sea is lonely, the sea is dreary,
The sea is restless and uneasy ;
Thou seekest quiet, thou art weary,
Wandering thou knowest not whith-
    er ; —
Our little isle is green and breezy,

Come and rest thee ! O come hither
Come to this peaceful home of ours,
    Where evermore
The low west-wind creeps panting up
    the shore
To be at rest among the flowers ;
Full of rest, the green moss lifts,
    As the dark waves of the sea
Draw in and out of rocky rifts,
    Calling solemnly to thee
With voices deep and hollow, —
    " To the shore
    Follow ! O, follow !
To be at rest forevermore !
    Forevermore ! "

Look how the gray old Ocean
From the depth of his heart rejoices,
Heaving with a gentle motion,
When he hears our restful voices ;
List how he sings in an undertone,
Chiming with our melody ;
And all sweet sounds of earth and air
Melt into one low voice alone,
That murmurs over the weary sea,
And seems to sing from everywhere, —
" Here mayst thou harbor peacefully,
Here mayst thou rest from the aching
    oar ;
Turn thy curvèd prow ashore,
And in our green isle rest forevermore !
    Forevermore ! "
And Echo half wakes in the wooded
    hill,
    And, to her heart so calm and deep,
    Murmurs over in her sleep,
Doubtfully pausing and murmuring still
    " Evermore ! "
        Thus, on Life's weary sea,
        Heareth the marinere
        Voices sweet, from far and near,
        Ever singing low and clear,
        Ever singing longingly.

Is it not better here to be,
Than to be toiling late and soon ?
In the dreary night to see
Nothing but the blood-red moon
Go up and down into the sea ;
Or, in the loneliness of day,
    To see the still seals only
Solemnly lift their faces gray,
    Making it yet more lonely ?
Is it not better, than to hear

Only the sliding of the wave
Beneath the plank, and feel so near
A cold and lonely grave,
A restless grave, where thou shalt lie
Even in death unquietly?
Look down beneath thy wave-worn
  bark,
  Lean over the side and see
The leaden eye of the sidelong shark
  Upturnèd patiently,
  Ever waiting there for thee :
Look down and see those shapeless
    forms,
  Which ever keep their dreamless
    sleep
Far down within the gloomy deep,
And only stir themselves in storms,
Rising like islands from beneath,
And snorting through the angry spray,
As the frail vessel perisheth
In the whirls of their unwieldy play ;
  Look down !   Look down !
Upon the seaweed, slimy and dark,
That waves its arms so lank and brown,
  Beckoning for thee !
Look down beneath thy wave-worn
    bark
Into the cold depth of the sea !
  Look down !   Look down !
    Thus, on Life's lonely sea,
    Heareth the marinere
    Voices sad, from far and near,
    Ever singing full of fear,
    Ever singing drearfully.

Here all is pleasant as a dream ;
The wind scarce shaketh down the dew,
The green grass floweth like a stream
    Into the ocean's blue ;
    Listen ! O, listen !
Here is a gush of many streams,
  A song of many birds,
And every wish and longing seems
Lulled to a numbered flow of words, —
    Listen ! O, listen !
Here ever hum the golden bees
Underneath full-blossomed trees,
At once with glowing fruit and flowers
    crowned ; —
So smooth the sand, the yellow sand,
That thy keel will not grate as it touches
    the land ;
All around with a slumberous sound,
The singing waves slide up the strand,

And there, where the smooth, wet peb-
    bles be,
The waters gurgle longingly,
As if they fain would seek the shore,
To be at rest from the ceaseless roar,
To be at rest forevermore, —
    Forevermore.
      Thus, on Life's gloomy sea,
      Heareth the marinere
      Voices sweet, from far and near,
      Ever singing in his ear,
      "Here is rest and peace for thee!"
NANTASKET, July, 1840.

IRENÉ.

HERS is a spirit deep, and crystal-
    clear ;
Calmly beneath her earnest face it lies,
Free without boldness, meek without a
    fear,
Quicker to look than speak its sympa-
    thies ;
Far down into her large and patient
    eyes
I gaze, deep-drinking of the infinite,
As, in the mid-watch of a clear, still
    night,
I look into the fathomless blue skies.

So circled lives she with Love's holy
    light,
That from the shade of self she walketh
    free ;
The garden of her soul still keepeth
    she
An Eden where the snake did never
    enter ;
She hath a natural, wise sincerity,
A simple truthfulness, and these have
    lent her
A dignity as moveless as the centre ;
So that no influence of our earth can stir
Her steadfast courage, nor can take
    away
The holy peacefulness, which, night
    and day,
Unto her queenly soul doth minister.

Most gentle is she ; her large charity
(An all unwitting, childlike gift in her)
Not freer is to give than meek to bear ;

And, though herself not unacquaint
    with care,
Hath in her heart wide room for all
    that be, —
Her heart that hath no secrets of its
    own,
But open is as eglantine full blown.
Cloudless forever is her brow serene,
Speaking calm hope and trust within
    her, whence
Welleth a noiseless spring of patience,
That keepeth all her life so fresh, so
    green
And full of holiness, that every look,
The greatness of her woman's soul re-
    vealing,
Unto me bringeth blessing, and a feel-
    ing
As when I read in God's own holy
    book.

A graciousness in giving that doth
    make
The small'st gift greatest, and a sense
    most meek
Of worthiness, that doth not fear to
    take
From others, but which always fears to
    speak
Its thanks in utterance, for the giver's
    sake ;
The deep religion of a thankful heart,
Which rests instinctively in Heaven's
    clear law
With a full peace, that never can de-
    part
From its own steadfastness ; — a holy
    awe
For holy things, — not those which men
    call holy,
But such as are revealed to the eyes
Of a true woman's soul bent down and
    lowly
Before the face of daily mysteries ; —
A love that blossoms soon, but ripens
    slowly
To the full goldenness of fruitful prime,
Enduring with a firmness that defies
All shallow tricks of circumstance and
    time,
By a sure insight knowing where to
    cling,
And where it clingeth never wither-
    ing ; —

These are Irené's dowry, which no fate
Can shake from their serene, deep-
    builded state.

In-seeing sympathy is hers, which
    chasteneth
No less than loveth, scorning to be
    bound
With fear of blame, and yet which ever
    hasteneth
To pour the balm of kind looks on the
    wound,
If they be wounds which such sweet
    teaching makes,
Giving itself a pang for others' sakes ;
No want of faith, that chills with side-
    long eye,
Hath she ; no jealousy, no Levite pride
That passeth by upon the other side ;
For in her soul there never dwelt a lie.
Right from the hand of God her spirit
    came
Unstained, and she hath ne'er forgotten
    whence
It came, nor wandered far from thence,
But laboreth to keep her still the same,
Near to her place of birth, that she
    may not
Soil her white raiment with an earthly
    spot.

Yet sets she not her soul so steadily
Above, that she forgets her ties to
    earth,
But her whole thought would almost
    seem to be
How to make glad one lowly human
    hearth ;
For with a gentle courage she doth
    strive
In thought and word and feeling so to
    live
As to make earth next heaven ; and
    her heart
Herein doth show its most exceeding
    worth,
That, bearing in our frailty her just
    part,
She hath not shrunk from evils of this
    life,
But hath gone calmly forth into the
    strife,
And all its sins and sorrows hath with-
    stood

With lofty strength of patient woman-
hood :
For this I love her great soul more than
all,
That, being bound, like us, with earthly
thrall,
She walks so bright and heaven-like
therein, —
Too wise, too meek, too womanly, to
sin.

Like a lone star through riven storm-
clouds seen
By sailors, tempest-tost upon the sea,
Telling of rest and peaceful heavens
nigh,
Unto my soul her star-like soul hath
been,
Her sight as full of hope and calm to
me ; —
For she unto herself hath builded high
A home serene, wherein to lay her
head,
Earth's noblest thing, a Woman perfected.
1840.

SERENADE.

FROM the close-shut windows gleams
no spark,
The night is chilly, the night is dark,
The poplars shiver, the pine-trees moan,
My hair by the autumn breeze is blown,
Under thy window I sing alone,
Alone, alone, ah woe ! alone !

The darkness is pressing coldly around,
The windows shake with a lonely sound,
The stars are hid and the night is drear,
The heart of silence throbs in thine ear,
In thy chamber thou sittest alone,
Alone, alone, ah woe ! alone !

The world is happy, the world is wide,
Kind hearts are beating on every side :
Ah, why should we lie so coldly curled
Alone in the shell of this great world ?
Why should we any more be alone ?
Alone, alone, ah woe ! alone !

O, 'tis a bitter and dreary word,
The saddest by man's ear ever heard !

We each are young, we each have a
heart,
Why stand we ever coldly apart ?
Must we forever, then, be alone ?
Alone, alone, ah woe ! alone !
1840.

WITH A PRESSED FLOWER.

THIS little blossom from afar
Hath come from other lands to thine :
For, once, its white and drooping star
Could see its shadow in the Rhine.

Perchance some fair-haired German
maid
Hath plucked one from the self-same
stalk,
And numbered over, half afraid,
Its petals in her evening walk.

" He loves me, loves me not," she
cries ;
" He loves me more than earth or
heaven ! "
And then glad tears have filled her
eyes
To find the number was uneven.

And thou must count its petals well,
Because it is a gift from me ;
And the last one of all shall tell
Something I 've often told to thee.

But here at home, where we were born,
Thou wilt find blossoms just as true,
Down-bending every summer morn,
With freshness of New-England dew.

For Nature, ever kind to love,
Hath granted them the same sweet
tongue,
Whether with German skies above,
Or here our granite rocks among.
1840.

THE BEGGAR.

A BEGGAR through the world am I, —
From place to place I wander by.

Fill up my pilgrim's scrip for me,
For Christ's sweet sake and charity!

A little of thy steadfastness,
Rounded with leafy gracefulness,
Old oak, give me, —
That the world's blasts may round me
    blow,
And I yield gently to and fro,
While my stout-hearted trunk below
And firm-set roots unshaken be.

Some of thy stern, unyielding might,
Enduring still through day and night
Rude tempest - shock and withering
    blight, —
That I may keep at bay
The changeful April sky of chance
And the strong tide of circumstance, —
Give me, old granite gray,

Some of thy pensiveness serene,
Some of thy never-dying green,
Put in this scrip of mine, —
That griefs may fall like snow-flakes
    light,
And deck me in a robe of white,
Ready to be an angel bright, —
O sweetly mournful pine.

A little of thy merriment,
Of thy sparkling, light content,
Give me, my cheerful brook, —
That I may still be full of glee
And gladsomeness, where'er I be,
Though fickle fate hath prisoned me
In some neglected nook.

Ye have been very kind and good
To me, since I 've been in the wood;
Ye have gone nigh to fill my heart;
But good-bye, kind friends, every one,
I 've far to go ere set of sun;
Of all good things I would have part,
The day was high ere I could start,
And so my journey 's scarce begun.

Heaven help me! how could I forget
To beg of thee, dear violet!
Some of thy modesty,
That blossoms here as well, unseen,
As if before the world thou 'dst been,
O, give, to strengthen me.

                    1839.

MY LOVE.

I.

NOT as all other women are
Is she that to my soul is dear;
Her glorious fancies come from far,
Beneath the silver evening-star,
And yet her heart is ever near.

II.

Great feelings hath she of her own,
Which lesser souls may never know;
God giveth them to her alone,
And sweet they are as any tone
Wherewith the wind may choose to
    blow.

III.

Yet in herself she dwelleth not,
Although no home were half so fair;
No simplest duty is forgot,
Life hath no dim and lowly spot
That doth not in her sunshine share.

IV.

She doeth little kindnesses,
Which most leave undone, or despise;
For naught that sets one heart at ease,
And giveth happiness or peace,
Is low-esteemèd in her eyes.

V.

She hath no scorn of common things,
And, though she seem of other birth,
Round us her heart intwines and
    clings,
And patiently she folds her wings
To tread the humble paths of earth.

VI.

Blessing she is: God made her so,
And deeds of week-day holiness
Fall from her noiseless as the snow,
Nor hath she ever chanced to know
That aught were easier than to bless.

VII.

She is most fair, and thereunto
Her life doth rightly harmonize;
Feeling or thought that was not true
Ne'er made less beautiful the blue
Unclouded heaven of her eyes.

VIII.

She is a woman : one in whom
The spring-time of her childish years
Hath never lost its fresh perfume,
Though knowing well that life hath room
For many blights and many tears.

IX.

I love her with a love as still
As a broad river's peaceful might,
Which, by high tower and lowly mill,
Goes wandering at its own will,
And yet doth ever flow aright.

X.

And, on its full, deep breast serene,
Like quiet isles my duties lie ;
It flows around them and between,
And makes them fresh and fair and green,
Sweet homes wherein to live and die.
1840.

SUMMER STORM.

UNTREMULOUS in the river clear,
Toward the sky's image, hangs the im-
aged bridge ;
So still the air that I can hear
The slender clarion of the unseen midge ;
Out of the stillness, with a gathering
creep,
Like rising wind in leaves, which now
decreases,
Now lulls, now swells, and all the while
increases,
The huddling trample of a drove of
sheep
Tilts the loose planks, and then as grad-
ually ceases
In dust on the other side ; life's em-
blem deep,
A confused noise between two silences,
Finding at last in dust precarious peace.
On the wide marsh the purple-blos-
somed grasses
Soak up the sunshine ; sleeps the
brimming tide,
Save when the wedge-shaped wake in
silence passes
Of some slow water-rat, whose sinu-
ous glide
Wavers the sedge's emerald shade
from side to side ;

But up the west, like a rock-shivered
surge,
Climbs a great cloud edged with sun-
whitened spray ;
Huge whirls of foam boil toppling o'er
its verge,
And falling still it seems, and yet it
climbs alway.

Suddenly all the sky is hid
As with the shutting of a lid,
One by one great drops are falling
Doubtful and slow,
Down the pane they are crookedly
crawling,
And the wind breathes low ;
Slowly the circles widen on the river,
Widen and mingle, one and all ;
Here and there the slenderer flowers
shiver,
Struck by an icy rain-drop's fall.

Now on the hills I hear the thunder
mutter,
The wind is gathering in the west ;
The upturned leaves first whiten and
flutter,
Then droop to a fitful rest ;
Up from the stream with sluggish flap
Struggles the gull and floats away ;
Nearer and nearer rolls the thunder-
clap, —
We shall not see the sun go down to-
day :
Now leaps the wind on the sleepy marsh,
And tramples the grass with terrified
feet,
The startled river turns leaden and harsh.
You can hear the quick heart of the
tempest beat.

Look ! look ! that livid flash !
And instantly follows the rattling thun-
der,
As if some cloud-crag, split asunder,
Fell, splintering with a ruinous
crash,
On the Earth, which crouches in silence
under ;
And now a solid gray wall of rain
Shuts off the landscape, mile by mile ;
For a breath's space I see the blue
wood again,

And, ere the next heart-beat, the wind-
    hurled pile,
  That seemed but now a league aloof,
Bursts crackling o'er the sun-parched
    roof ;
Against the windows the storm comes
    dashing,
Through tattered foliage the hail tears
    crashing,
    The blue lightning flashes,
    The rapid hail clashes,
  The white waves are tumbling,
    And, in one baffled roar,
  Like the toothless sea mumbling
    A rock-bristled shore,
    The thunder is rumbling
    And crashing and crumbling, —
Will silence return never more ?

    Hush ! Still as death,
    The tempest holds his breath
  As from a sudden will ;
The rain stops short, but from the eaves
You see it drop, and hear it from the
    leaves,
  All is so bodingly still ;
    Again, now, now, again
Plashes the rain in heavy gouts,
    The crinkled lightning
    Seems ever brightening,
    And loud and long
Again the thunder shouts
    His battle-song, —
    One quivering flash,
    One wildering crash,
Followed by silence dead and dull,
  As if the cloud, let go,
    Leapt bodily below
To whelm the earth in one mad over-
    throw,
    And then a total lull.

    Gone, gone, so soon !
No more my half-dazed fancy there
  Can shape a giant in the air,
  No more I see his streaming hair,
The writhing portent of his form ; —
    The pale and quiet moon
  Makes her calm forehead bare,
And the last fragments of the storm,
Like shattered rigging from a fight at sea,
Silent and few, are drifting over me.
  1839.

LOVE.

TRUE Love is but a humble, low-born
    thing,
And hath its food served up in earthen
    ware ;
It is a thing to walk with, hand in hand,
Through the every-dayness of this work-
    day world,
Baring its tender feet to every rough-
    ness,
Yet letting not one heart-beat go astray
From Beauty's law of plainness and
    content ;
A simple, fireside thing, whose quiet
    smile
Can warm earth's poorest hovel to a
    home ;
Which, when our autumn cometh, as it
    must,
And life in the chill wind shivers bare
    and leafless,
Shall still be blest with Indian-summer
    youth
In bleak November, and, with thank-
    ful heart,
Smile on its ample stores of garnered
    fruit,
As full of sunshine to our aged eyes
As when it nursed the blossoms of our
    spring.
Such is true Love, which steals into the
    heart
With feet as silent as the lightsome
    dawn
That kisses smooth the rough brows
    of the dark,
And hath its will through blissful gen-
    tleness, —
Not like a rocket, which, with savage
    glare,
Whirs suddenly up, then bursts, and
    leaves the night
Painfully quivering on the dazèd eyes ;
A love that gives and takes, that seës
    faults,
Not with flaw-seeking eyes like needle
    points,
But loving-kindly ever looks them
    down
With the o'ercoming faith that still
    forgives ;
A love that shall be new and fresh each
    hour,

As is the sunset's golden mystery,
  Or the sweet coming of the evening
    star,
Alike, and yet most unlike, every day,
And seeming ever best and fairest *now;*
A love that doth not kneel for what it
    seeks,
But faces Truth and Beauty as their
    peer,
Showing its worthiness of noble
    thoughts
By a clear sense of inward nobleness;
A love that in its object findeth not
All grace and beauty, and enough to
    sate
Its thirst of blessing, but, in all of good
Found there, sees but the heaven-
    implanted types
Of good and beauty in the soul of man,
And traces, in the simplest heart that
    beats,
A family-likeness to its chosen one,
That claims of it the rights of brother-
    hood.
For love is blind but with the fleshly
    eye,
That so its inner sight may be more
    clear;
And outward shows of beauty only so
Are needful at the first, as is a hand
To guide and to uphold an infant's
    steps :
Fine natures need them not : their ear-
    nest look
Pierces the body's mask of thin dis-
    guise,
And beauty ever is to them revealed,
Behind the unshapeliest, meanest lump
    of clay,
With arms outstretched and eager face
    ablaze,
Yearning to be but understood and
    loved.
  1840.

  _____

TO PERDITA, SINGING.

THY voice is like a fountain,
  Leaping up in clear moonshine:
Silver, silver, ever mounting,
      Ever sinking,
      Without thinking,
  To that brimful heart of thine

Every sad and happy feeling,
Thou hast had in bygone years,
Through thy lips comes stealing, steal-
    ing,
      Clear and low ;
All thy smiles and all thy tears
  In thy voice awaken,
  And sweetness, wove of joy and woe,
    From their teaching it hath taken:
Feeling and music move together,
Like a swan and shadow ever
Floating on a sky-blue river
  In a day of cloudless weather.

It hath caught a touch of sadness,
  Yet it is not sad ;
It hath tones of clearest gladness,
  Yet it is not glad ;
A dim, sweet twilight voice it is
  Where to-day's accustomed blue
Is over-grayed with memories,
  With starry feelings quivered through.

Thy voice is like a fountain
Leaping up in sunshine bright,
  And I never weary counting
Its clear droppings, lone and single,
Or when in one full gush they mingle,
  Shooting in melodious light.

Thine is music such as yields
Feelings of old brooks and fields,
And, around this pent-up room,
Sheds a woodland, free perfume ;
  O, thus forever sing to me !
  O, thus forever !
The green, bright grass of childhood
    bring to me,
  Flowing like an emerald river,
  And the bright blue skies above !
O, sing them back, as fresh as ever,
  Into the bosom of my love, —
  The sunshine and the merriment,
  T~~   ~~en content,

~~   ~~, like a clear breeze,
~~   ~~went
~~   ~~hrough and through the old time !

Peace sits within thine eyes,
  With white hands crossed in joyful
    rest,
While, through thy lips and face,
    arise

The melodies from out thy breast ;
    She sits and sings,
      With folded wings
    And white arms crost,
    "Weep not for bygone things,
      They are not lost :
The beauty which the summer time
O'er thine opening spirit shed,
The forest oracles sublime
That filled thy soul with joyous dread,
The scent of every smallest flower
That made thy heart sweet for an
    hour,
Yea, every holy influence,
Flowing to thee, thou knewest not
    whence,
In thine eyes to-day is seen,
Fresh as it hath ever been ;
Promptings of Nature, beckonings
    sweet,
Whatever led thy childish feet,
Still will linger unawares
The guiders of thy silver hairs ;
Every look and every word
Which thou givest forth to-day,
Tell of the singing of the bird
Whose music stilled thy boyish
    play."

Thy voice is like a fountain,
Twinkling up in sharp starlight,
When the moon behind the mountain
Dims the low East with faintest
    white,
    Ever darkling,
    Ever sparkling,
We know not if 't is dark or bright ;
But, when the great moon hath rolled
    round,
And, sudden-slow, its solemn power
Grows from behind its black, clear-
    edgèd bound,
No spot of dark the fountain keepeth,
But, swift as opening eyelids, leapeth
Into a waving silver flower.
    1841.

THE MOON.

My soul was like the sea,
Before the moon was made,
Moaning in vague immensity,
Of its own strength afraid,
Unrestful and unstaid.

Through every rift it foamed in vain,
    About its earthly prison,
Seeking some unknown thing in pain,
And sinking restless back again,
    For yet no moon had risen :
Its only voice a vast dumb moan,
    Of utterless anguish speaking,
It lay unhopefully alone,
    And lived but in an aimless seeking.

So was my soul ; but when 't was full
    Of unrest to o'erloading,
A voice of something beautiful
    Whispered a dim foreboding,
And yet so soft, so sweet, so low,
It had not more of joy than woe ;
And, as the sea doth oft lie still,
    Making its waters meet,
As if by an unconscious will,
    For the moon's silver feet,
So lay my soul within mine eyes
When thou, its guardian moon, didst
    rise.

And now, howe'er its waves above
    May toss and seem uneaseful,
One strong, eternal law of Love,
    With guidance sure and peaceful,
As calm and natural as breath,
Moves its great deeps through life and
    death.

REMEMBERED MUSIC.

A FRAGMENT.

THICK-RUSHING, like an ocean vast
    Of bisons the far prairie shaking,
The notes crowd heavily and fast
As surfs, one plunging while the last
    Draws seaward from its foamy break-
      ing.

Or in low murmurs they began,
    Rising and rising momently,
As o'er a harp Æolian
A fitful breeze, until they ran
    Up to a sudden ecstasy.

And then, like minute-drops of rain
    Ringing in water silverly,

They lingering dropped and dropped
        again,
Till it was almost like a pain
    To listen when the next would be.
    1840.

———

SONG.

TO M. L.

A LILY thou wast when I saw thee first,
    A lily-bud not opened quite,
        That hourly grew more pure and
            white,
By morning, and noontide, and evening
        nursed:
    In all of nature thou hadst thy share;
        Thou wast waited on
            By the wind and sun;
    The rain and the dew for thee took care;
        It seemed thou never couldst be more
            fair.

A lily thou wast when I saw thee first,
    A lily-bud; but O, how strange,
        How full of wonder was the change,
When, ripe with all sweetness, thy full
        bloom burst!
    How did the tears to my glad eyes start,
            When the woman-flower
                Reached its blossoming hour,
    And I saw the warm deeps of thy
            golden heart!

Glad death may pluck thee, but never
        before
    The gold dust of thy bloom divine
    Hath dropped from thy heart into
        mine,
To quicken its faint germs of heavenly
        lore:
    For no breeze comes nigh thee but
        carries away
            Some impulses bright
                Of fragrance and light,
    Which fall upon souls that are lone
        and astray,
To plant fruitful hopes of the flower
        of day.

———

ALLEGRA.

I WOULD more natures were like thine,
    That never casts a glance before,

Thou Hebe, who thy heart's bright wine
    So lavishly to all dost pour,
That we who drink forget to pine,
    And can but dream of bliss in store.

Thou canst not see a shade in life;
    With sunward instinct thou dost rise,
And, leaving clouds below at strife,
    Gazest undazzled at the skies,
With all their blazing splendors rife,
    A songful lark with eagle's eyes.

Thou wast some foundling whom the
        Hours
    Nursed, laughing, with the milk of
        Mirth;
Some influence more gay than ours
    Hath ruled thy nature from its birth,
As if thy natal stars were flowers
    That shook their seeds round thee on
        earth.

And thou, to lull thine infant rest,
    Wast cradled like an Indian child;
All pleasant winds from south and west
    With lullabies thine ears beguiled,
Rocking thee in thine oriole's nest,
    Till Nature looked at thee and smiled.

Thine every fancy seems to borrow
    A sunlight from thy childish years,
Making a golden cloud of sorrow,
    A hope-lit rainbow out of tears, —
Thy heart is certain of to-morrow,
    Though 'yond to-day it never peers.

I would more natures were like thine,
    So innocently wild and free,
Whose sad thoughts, even, leap and
        shine,
    Like sunny wavelets in the sea,
Making us mindless of the brine,
    In gazing on the brilliancy.

———

THE FOUNTAIN.

INTO the sunshine,
    Full of the light,
Leaping and flashing
    From morn till night;

Into the moonlight,
    Whiter than snow,

Waving so flower-like
    When the winds blow ;

Into the starlight
    Rushing in spray,
Happy at midnight,
    Happy by day ;

Ever in motion,
    Blithesome and cheery,
Still climbing heavenward,
    Never aweary ;

Glad of all weathers,
    Still seeming best,
Upward or downward,
    Motion thy rest ;

Full of a nature
    Nothing can tame,
Changed every moment,
    Ever the same ;

Ceaseless aspiring,
    Ceaseless content,
Darkness or sunshine
    Thy element ;

Glorious fountain,
    Let my heart be
Fresh, changeful, constant,
    Upward, like thee !

ODE.

I.

In the old days of awe and keen-eyed
        wonder,
    The Poet's song with blood-warm
        truth was rife ;
He saw the mysteries which circle under
    The outward shell and skin of daily life.
Nothing to him were fleeting time and
        fashion,
    His soul was led by the eternal law ;
There was in him no hope of fame, no
        passion,
    But, with calm, godlike eyes he only
        saw.
He did not sigh o'er heroes dead and
        buried,

Chief-mourner at the Golden Age's
        hearse,
Nor deem that souls whom Charon
        grim had ferried
    Alone were fitting themes of epic verse :
He could believe the promise of to-
        morrow,
    And feel the wondrous meaning of to-
        day ;
He had a deeper faith in holy sorrow
    Than the world's seeming loss could
        take away.
To know the heart of all things was his
        duty,
    All things did sing to him to make
        him wise,
And, with a sorrowful and conquering
        beauty,
    The soul of all looked grandly from
        his eyes.
He gazed on all within him and without
        him,
    He watched the flowing of Time's
        steady tide,
And shapes of glory floated all about him
    And whispered to him, and he
        prophesied.
Than all men he more fearless was and
        freer,
    And all his brethren cried with one
        accord, —
"Behold the holy man ! Behold the
        Seer !
    Him who hath spoken with the unseen
        Lord !"
He to his heart with large embrace had
        taken
    The universal sorrow of mankind,
And, from that root, a shelter never
        shaken,
    The tree of wisdom grew with sturdy
        rind.
He could interpret well the wondrous
        voices
    Which to the calm and silent spirit
        come ;
He knew that the One Soul no more
        rejoices
    In the star's anthem than the insect's
        hum.
He in his heart was ever meek and
        humble,
    And yet with kingly pomp his num-
        bers ran,

As he foresaw how all things false
    should crumble
Before the free, uplifted soul of man :
And, when he was made full to over-
    flowing
With all the loveliness of heaven and
    earth,
Out rushed his song, like molten iron
    glowing,
To show God sitting by the humblest
    hearth.
With calmest courage he was ever ready
To teach that action was the truth of
    thought,
And, with strong arm and purpose firm
    and steady,
An anchor for the drifting world he
    wrought.
So did he make the meanest man partaker
Of all his brother-gods unto him gave ;
All souls did reverence him and name
    him Maker,
And when he died heaped temples on
    his grave.
And still his deathless words of light
    are swimming
Serene throughout the great deep in-
    finite
Of human soul, unwaning and undim-
    ming,
To cheer and guide the mariner at
    night.

II.

But now the Poet is an empty rhymer
    Who lies with idle elbow on the grass,
And fits his singing, like a cunning timer,
    To all men's prides and fancies as
    they pass.
Not his the song, which, in its metre holy,
    Chimes with the music of the eternal
    stars,
Humbling the tyrant, lifting up the lowly,
    And sending sun through the soul's
    prison-bars.
Maker no more, — O no ! unmaker
    rather,
    For he unmakes who doth not all put
    forth
The power given by our loving Father
    To show the body's dross, the spirit's
    worth.
Awake ! great spirit of the ages olden !
    Shiver the mists that hide thy starry
    lyre,

And let man's soul be yet again beholden
    To thee for wings to soar to her desire.
O, prophesy no more to-morrow's splen-
    dor,
    Be no more shamefaced to speak out
    for Truth,
Lay on her altar all the gushings tender,
    The hope, the fire, the loving faith of
    youth !
O, prophesy no more the Maker's
    coming,
    Say not his onward footsteps thou
    canst hear
In the dim void, like to the awful hum-
    ming
    Of the great wings of some new-light-
    ed sphere !
O, prophesy no more, but be the Poet !
    This longing was but granted unto thee
That, when all beauty thou couldst feel
    and know it,
    That beauty in its highest thou
    shouldst be
O, thou who moanest tost with sealike
    longings
    Who dimly hearest voices call on thee,
Whose soul is overfilled with mighty
    throngings
    Of love, and fear, and glorious agony,
Thou of the toil-strung hands and iron
    sinews
    And soul by Mother Earth with free-
    dom fed,
In whom the hero-spirit yet continues,
    The old free nature is not chained or
    dead,
Arouse ! let thy soul break in music-
    thunder,
    Let loose the ocean that is in thee
    pent,
Pour forth thy hope, thy fear, thy love,
    thy wonder,
    And tell the age what all its signs
    have meant.
Where'er thy wildered crowd of breth-
    ren jostles,
    Where'er there lingers but a shade of
    wrong,
There still is need of martyrs and
    apostles,
    There still are texts for never-dying
    song :
From age to age man's still aspiring spirit
    Finds wider scope and sees with
    clearer eyes,

And thou in larger measure dost inherit
  What made thy great forerunners free
    and wise.
Sit thou enthronëd where the Poet's
    mountain
Above the thunder lifts its silent peak,
And roll thy songs down like a gather-
    ing fountain,
  They all may drink and find the rest
    they seek.
Sing ! there shall silence grow in earth
    and heaven,
  A silence of deep awe and wondering ;
For, listening gladly, bend the angels,
    even,
  To hear a mortal like an angel sing.

III.

Among the toil-worn poor my soul is
    seeking
  For who shall bring the Maker's name
    to light,
To be the voice of that almighty speaking
  Which every age demands to do it
    right.
Proprieties our silken bards environ ;
  He who would be the tongue of this
    wide land
Must string his harp with chords of
    sturdy iron
  And strike it with a toil-imbrownëd
    hand ;
One who hath dwelt with Nature well
    attended,
  Who hath learnt wisdom from her
    mystic books,
Whose soul with all her countless lives
    hath blended,
  So that all beauty awes us in his looks ;
Who not with body's waste his soul
    hath pampered,
  Who as the clear northwestern wind
    is free,
Who walks with Form's observances
    unhampered,
  And follows the One Will obediently ;
Whose eyes, like windows on a breezy
    summit,
  Control a lovely prospect every way ;
Who doth not sound God's sea with
    earthly plummet,
  And find a bottom still of worthless
    clay ;

Who heeds not how the lower gusts are
    working,
  Knowing that one sure wind blows on
    above,
And sees, beneath the foulest faces
    lurking,
  One God-built shrine of reverence
    and love ;
Who sees all stars that wheel their
    shining marches
  Around the centre fixed of Destiny,
Where the encircling soul serene o'er-
    arches
  The moving globe of being like a sky ;
Who feels that God and Heaven's great
    deeps are nearer
  Him to whose heart his fellow-man is
    nigh,
Who doth not hold his soul's own free-
    dom dearer
  Than that of all his brethren, low or
    high ;
Who to the Right can feel himself the
    truer
  For being gently patient with the
    wrong,
Who sees a brother in the evildoer,
  And finds in Love the heart's-blood
    of his song ; —
This, this is he for whom the world is
    waiting
To sing the beatings of its mighty heart,
Too long hath it been patient with the
    grating
  Of scrannel-pipes, and heard it mis-
    named Art.
To him the smiling soul of man shall
    listen
  Laying awhile its crown of thorns
    aside,
And once again in every eye shall glisten
  The glory of a nature satisfied.
His verse shall have a great command-
    ing motion,
  Heaving and swelling with a melody
Learnt of the sky, the river, and the ocean
  And all the pure, majestic things that
    be.
Awake, then, thou ! we pine for thy
    great presence
  To make us feel the soul once more
    sublime,
We are of far too infinite an essence
  To rest contented with the lies of Time

Then, God, take me! We shall be
  near,
  More near than ever, each to each;
Her angel ears will find more clear
  My heavenly than my earthly speech;
And still, as I draw nigh to thee,
Her soul and mine shall closer be.

1841.

———

THE HERITAGE.

The rich man's son inherits lands,
  And piles of brick, and stone, and
    gold,
And he inherits soft white hands,
  And tender flesh that fears the cold,
  Nor dares to wear a garment old;
A heritage, it seems to me,
One scarce would wish to hold in fee.

The rich man's son inherits cares;
  The bank may break, the factory
    burn,
A breath may burst his bubble shares,
  And soft white hands could hardly
    earn
  A living that would serve his turn;
A heritage, it seems to me,
One scarce would wish to hold in fee.

The rich man's son inherits wants,
  His stomach craves for dainty fare;
With sated heart, he hears the pants
  Of toiling hinds with brown arms
    bare,
  And wearies in his easy-chair;
A heritage, it seems to me,
One scarce would wish to hold in fee.

What doth the poor man's son inherit?
  Stout muscles and a sinewy heart,
A hardy frame, a hardier spirit;
  King of two hands, he does his part
  In every useful toil and art;
A heritage, it seems to me,
A king might wish to hold in fee.

What doth the poor man's son inherit?
  Wishes o'erjoyed with humble things,
A rank adjudged by toil-won merit,
  Content that from employment
    springs,
  A heart that in his labor sings;

A heritage, it seems to me,
A king might wish to hold in fee.

What doth the poor man's son inherit?
  A patience learned of being poor,
Courage, if sorrow come, to bear it,
  A fellow-feeling that is sure
  To make the outcast bless his door;
A heritage, it seems to me,
A king might wish to hold in fee.

O rich man's son! there is a toil
  That with all others level stands;
Large charity doth never soil,
  But only whiten, soft white hands,—
  This is the best crop from thy lands;
A heritage, it seems to me,
Worth being rich to hold in fee.

O poor man's son! scorn not thy state;
  There is worse weariness than thine,
In merely being rich and great;
  Toil only gives the soul to shine,
  And makes rest fragrant and benign;
A heritage, it seems to me,
Worth being poor to hold in fee.

Both, heirs to some six feet of sod,
  Are equal in the earth at last;
Both, children of the same dear God,
  Prove title to your heirship vast
  By record of a well-filled past;
A heritage, it seems to me,
Well worth a life to hold in fee.

———

THE ROSE: A BALLAD.

I.

In his tower sat the poet
  Gazing on the roaring sea,
"Take this rose," he sighed, "and
    throw it
  Where there's none that loveth me.
On the rock the billow bursteth
  And sinks back into the seas,
But in vain my spirit thirsteth
  So to burst and be at ease.
Take, O sea! the tender blossom
  That hath lain against my breast;
On thy black and angry bosom
  It will find a surer rest.
Life is vain, and love is hollow,
  Ugly death stands there behind,

Hate and scorn and hunger follow
  Him that toileth for his kind."
Forth into the night he hurled it,
  And with bitter smile did mark
How the surly tempest whirled it
  Swift into the hungry dark.
Foam and spray drive back to leeward,
  And the gale, with dreary moan,
Drifts the helpless blossom seaward,
  Through the breakers all alone.

II.

Stands a maiden, on the morrow,
  Musing by the wave-beat strand,
Half in hope and half in sorrow,
  Tracing words upon the sand :
"Shall I ever then behold him
  Who hath been my life so long,
Ever to this sick heart fold him,
  Be the spirit of his song?
Touch not, sea, the blessed letters
  I have traced upon thy shore,
Spare his name whose spirit fetters
  Mine with love forevermore ! "
Swells the tide and overflows it,
  But, with omen pure and meet,
Brings a little rose, and throws it
  Humbly at the maiden's feet.
Full of bliss she takes the token,
  And, upon her snowy breast,
Soothes the ruffled petals broken
  With the ocean's fierce unrest.
"Love is thine, O heart ! and surely
  Peace shall also be thine own.
For the heart that trusteth purely
  Never long can pine alone."

III.

In his tower sits the poet,
  Blisses new and strange to him
Fill his heart and overflow it
  With a wonder sweet and dim.
Up the beach the ocean slideth
  With a whisper of delight,
And the moon in silence glideth
  Through the peaceful blue of nigth
Rippling o'er the poet's shoulder
  Flows a maiden's golden hair,
Maiden lips, with love grown bolder,
  Kiss his moon-lit forehead bare.
"Life is joy, and love is power,
  Death all fetters doth unbind,

Strength and wisdom only flower
  When we toil for all our kind.
Hope is truth, — the future giveth
  More than present takes away,
And the soul forever liveth
  Nearer God from day to day."
Not a word the maiden uttered,
  Fullest hearts are slow to speak,
But a withered rose-leaf fluttered
  Down upon the poet's cheek.
  1842.

A LEGEND OF BRITTANY.

PART FIRST.

I.

FAIR as a summer dream was Mar-
    garet, —
  Such dream as in a poet's soul might
    start,
Musing of old loves while the moon
    doth set :
  Her hair was not more sunny than
    her heart,
Though like a natural golden coronet
  It circled her dear head with careless
    art,
Mocking the sunshine, that would fain
    have lent
To its frank grace a richer ornament.

II.

His loved one's eyes could poet ever
    speak,
  So kind, so dewy, and so deep were
    hers,
But, while he strives, the choicest
    phrase, too weak,
  Their glad reflection in his spirit
    blurs ;
As one may see a dream dissolve and
    break
  Out of his grasp when he to tell it
    stirs,
Like that sad Dryad doomed no more
    to bless
The mortal who revealed her loveli-
    ness.

III.

She dwelt forever in a region bright,
  Peopled with living fancies of her
    own,
Where naught could come but visions
    of delight,
  Far, far aloof from earth's eternal
    moan :
A summer cloud thrilled through with
    rosy light,
  Floating beneath the blue sky all
    alone,
Her spirit wandered by itself, and won
A golden edge from some unsetting sun.

IV.

The heart grows richer that its lot is
    poor,
  God blesses want with larger sym-
    pathies,
Love enters gladliest at the humble
    door,
  And makes the cot a palace with his
    eyes :
So Margaret's heart a softer beauty
    wore,
  And grew in gentleness and patience
    wise,
For she was but a simple herdsman's
    child,
A lily chance-sown in the rugged wild.

V.

There was no beauty of the wood or
    field
  But she its fragrant bosom-secret
    knew,
Nor any but to her would freely yield
  Some grace that in her soul took root
    and grew :
Nature to her shone as but now re-
    vealed,
  All rosy-fresh with innocent morning
    dew,
And looked into her heart with dim,
    sweet eyes
That left it full of sylvan memories.

VI.

O, what a face was hers to brighten
    light,
  And give back sunshine with an
    added glow,

To wile each moment with a fresh de-
    light,
  And part of memory's best content-
    ment grow !
O, how her voice, as with an inmate's
    right,
  Into the strangest heart would wel-
    come go,
And make it sweet, and ready to become
Of white and gracious thoughts the
    chosen home !

VII.

None looked upon her but he straight-
    way thought
  Of all the greenest depths of country
    cheer,
And into each one's heart was freshly
    brought
  What was to him the sweetest time
    of year,
So was her every look and motion
    fraught
  With out-of-door delights and forest
    lere :
Not the first violet on a woodland lea
Seemed a more visible gift of Spring
    than she.

VIII.

Is love learned only out of poets' books?
  Is there not somewhat in the drop-
    ping flood,
And in the nunneries of silent nooks,
  And in the murmured longing of the
    wood,
That could make Margaret dream of
    lovelorn looks,
  And stir a thrilling mystery in ,her
    blood
More trembly secret than Aurora's tear
Shed in the bosom of an eglatere ?

IX.

Full many a sweet forewarning hath
    the mind,
  Full many a whispering of vague de-
    sire,
Ere comes the nature destined to unbind
  Its virgin zone, and all its deeps in-
    spire, —
Low stirrings in the leaves, before the
    wind

Wakes all the green strings of the
        forest lyre,
Faint heatings in the calyx, ere the rose
Its warm voluptuous breast doth all un-
        close.

x.

Long in its dim recesses pines the spirit,
    Wildered and dark, despairingly
        alone;
Though many a snape of beauty wan-
        der near it,
    And many a wild and half-remem-
        bered tone
Tremble from the divine abyss to cheer
        it,
    Yet still it knows that there is only
        one
Before whom it can kneel and tribute
        bring,
At once a happy vassal and a king.

xi.

To feel a want, yet scarce know what
        it is,
    To seek one nature that is always new,
Whose glance is warmer than another's
        kiss,
    Whom we can bare our inmost
        beauty to,
Nor feel deserted afterwards, — for
        this
    But with our destined co-mate we
        can do, —
Such longing instinct fills the mighty
        scope
Of the young soul with one mysterious
        hope.

xii.

So Margaret's heart grew brimming
        with the lore
    Of love's enticing secrets; and al-
        though
She had found none to cast it down be-
        fore.
    Yet oft to Fancy's chapel she would
        go
To pay her vows, and count the rosary
        o'er
    Of her love's promised graces: —
        haply so

Miranda's hope had pictured Ferdinand
Long ere the gaunt wave tossed him on
        the strand.

xiii.

A new-made star that swims the lonely
        gloom,
    Unwedded yet and longing for the
        sun,
Whose beams, the bride-gifts of the
        lavish groom,
    Blithely to crown the virgin planet
        run,
Her being was, watching to see the
        bloom
    Of love's fresh sunrise roofing one by
        one
Its clouds with gold, a triumph-arch
        to be
For him who came to hold her heart in
        fee.

xiv.

Not far from Margaret's cottage dwelt
        a knight
    Of the proud Templars, a sworn celi-
        bate,
Whose heart in secret fed upon the light
    And dew of her ripe beauty, through
        the grate
Of his close vow catching what gleams
        he might
    Of the free heaven, and cursing — all
        too late —
The cruel faith whose black walls
        hemmed him in
And turned life's crowning bliss to
        deadly sin.

xv.

For he had met her in the wood by chance,
    And, having drunk her beauty's
        wildering spell,
His heart shook like the pennon of a lance
    That quivers in a breeze's sudden swell,
And thenceforth, in a close-infolded
        trance,
    From mistily golden deep to deep he
        fell;
Till earth did waver and fade far away
Beneath the hope in whose warm arms
        he lay.

XVI.

A dark, proud man he was, whose half-
blown youth
   Had shed its blossoms even in opening,
Leaving a few that with more winning
ruth
   Trembling around grave manhood's
stem might cling,
More sad than cheery, making, in good
sooth,
   Like the fringed gentian, a late
autumn spring :—
A twilight nature, braided light and
gloom,
A youth half-smiling by an open tomb.

XVII.

Fair as an angel, who yet inly wore
   A wrinkled heart foreboding his near
fall ;
Who saw him alway wished to know
him more,
   As if he were some fate's defiant thrall
And nursed a dreaded secret at its core ;
   Little he loved, but power most of all,
And that he seemed to scorn, as one
who knew
By what foul paths men choose to crawl
thereto.

XVIII.

He had been noble, but some great deceit
   Had turned his better instinct to a vice :
He strove to think the world was all a
cheat,
   That power and fame were cheap at
any price,
That the sure way of being shortly great
   Was even to play life's game with
loaded dice,
Since he had tried the honest play and
found
That vice and virtue differed but in sound.

XIX.

Yet Margaret's sight redeemed him
for a space
   From his own thraldom ; man could
never be
A hypocrite when first such maiden grace
   Smiled in upon his heart ; the agony

Of wearing all day long a lying face
   Fell lightly from him, and, a moment
free,
Erect with wakened faith his spirit stood
And scorned the weakness of his demon-
mood.

XX.

Like a sweet wind-harp to him was her
thought,
   Which would not let the common air
come near,
Till from its dim enchantment it had
caught
   A musical tenderness that brimmed
his ear
With sweetness more ethereal than aught
   Save silver-dropping snatches that
while ere
Rained down from some sad angel's
faithful harp
To cool her fallen lover's anguish sharp.

XXI.

Deep in the forest was a little dell
   High overarchèd with the leafy sweep
Of a broad oak, through whose gnarled
roots there fell
   A slender rill that sung itself to sleep,
Where its continuous toil had scooped
a well
   To please the fairy folk ; breathlessly
deep
The stillness was, save when the dream-
ing brook
From its small urn a drizzly murmur
shook.

XXII.

The wooded hills sloped upward all
around
   With gradual rise, and made an even
rim,
So that it seemed a mighty casque un-
bound
   From some huge Titan's brow to
lighten him,
Ages ago, and left upon the ground,
   Where the slow soil had mossed it to
the brim,
Till after countless centuries it grew
Into this dell, the haunt of noontide
dew.

XXIII.

Dim vistas, sprinkled o'er with sun-
    flecked green,
    Wound through the thickset trunks
        on every side,
And, toward the west, in fancy might be
        seen
    A gothic window in its blazing pride,
When the low sun, two arching elms
        between,
    Lit up the leaves beyond, which,
        autumn-dyed
With lavish hues, would into splendor
        start,
Shaming the labored panes of richest art.

XXIV.

Here, leaning once against the old oak's
        trunk,
    Mordred, for such was the young
        Templar's name,
Saw Margaret come ; unseen, the falcon
        shrunk
    From the meek dove ; sharp thrills of
        tingling flame
Made him forget that he was vowed a
        monk,
    And all the outworks of his pride
        o'ercame :
Flooded he seemed with bright delicious
        pain,
As if a star had burst within his brain.

XXV.

Such power hath beauty and frank in-
        nocence :
    A flower bloomed forth, that sunshine
        glad to bless,
Even from his love's long leafless stem ;
        the sense
    Of exile from Hope's happy realm
        grew less,
And thoughts of childish peace, he
        knew not whence,
    Thronged round his heart with many
        an old caress,
Melting the frost there into pearly dew
That mirrored back his nature's morn-
        ing-blue.

XXVI.

She turned and saw him, but she felt no
        dread,
    Her purity, like adamantine mail,

Did so encircle her ; and yet her head
    She drooped, and made her golden
        hair her veil,
Through which a glow of rosiest lustre
        spread,
    Then faded, and anon she stood all
        pale,
As snow o'er which a blush of northern-
        light
Suddenly reddens, and as soon grows
        white.

XXVII.

She thought of Tristrem and of Lancilot,
    Of all her dreams, and of kind fairies'
        might,
And how that dell was deemed a haunt-
        ed spot,
    Until there grew a mist before her
        sight,
And where the present was she half
        forgot,
    Borne backward through the realms
        of old delight, —
Then, starting up awake, she would
        have gone,
Yet almost wished it might not be alone.

XXVIII.

How they went home together through
        the wood,
    And how all life seemed focussed into
        one
Thought-dazzling spot that set ablaze
        the blood,
    What need to tell? Fit language
        there is none
For the heart's deepest things. Who
        ever wooed
    As in his boyish hope he would have
        done ?
For, when the soul is fullest, the hushed
        tongue
Voicelessly trembles like a lute unstrung.

XXIX.

But all things carry the heart's mes-
        sages
    And know it not, nor doth the heart
        well know,
But Nature hath her will ; even as the
        bees,
    Blithe go-betweens, fly singing to and
        fro

With the fruit-quickening pollen ; —
    hard if these
    Found not some all unthought-of
        way to show
Their secret each to each ; and so they
    did,
And one heart's flower-dust into the
    other slid.

XXX.

Young hearts are free ; the selfish world
    it is
    That turns them miserly and cold as
        stone,
And makes them clutch their fingers on
    the bliss
    Which but in giving truly is their
        own ; —
She had no dreams of barter, asked not
    his,
    But gave hers freely as she would
        have thrown
A rose to him, or as that rose gives forth
Its generous fragrance, thoughtless of
    its worth.

XXXI.

Her summer nature felt a need to bless,
    And a like longing to be blest again ;
So, from her sky-like spirit, gentleness
    Dropt ever like a sunlit fall of rain,
And his beneath drank in the bright
    caress
As thirstily as would a parchëd plain,
That long hath watched the showers of
    sloping gray
Forever, ever, falling far away.

XXXII.

How should she dream of ill ? the heart
    filled quite
    With sunshine, like the shepherd's-
        clock at noon,
Closes its leaves around its warm delight ;
    What e'er in life is harsh or out of tune
Is all shut out, no boding shade of blight
    Can pierce the opiate ether of its
        swoon :
Love is but blind as thoughtful justice is,
But naught can be so wanton-blind as
    bliss.

XXXIII.

All beauty and all life he was to her ;
    She questioned not his love, she only
        knew
That she loved him, and not a pulse
        could stir
    In her whole frame but quivered
        through and through
With this glad thought, and was a
        minister
To do him fealty and service true,
Like golden ripples hasting to the land
To wreck their freight of sunshine on
    the strand.

XXXIV.

O dewy dawn of love ! O hopes that are
    Hung high, like the cliff-swallow's
        perilous nest,
Most like to fall when fullest, and that jar
    With every heavier billow ! O unrest
Than balmiest deeps of quiet sweeter far !
    How did ye triumph now in Marga-
        ret's breast,
Making it readier to shrink and start
Than quivering gold of the pond-lily's
    heart !

XXXV.

Here let us pause : O, would the soul
        might ever
    Achieve its immortality in youth,
When nothing yet hath damped its
        high endeavor
    After the starry energy of truth !
Here let us pause, and for a moment sever
    This gleam of sunshine from the sad
        unruth
That sometime comes to all, for it is good
To lengthen to the last a sunny mood.

PART SECOND.

I.

As one who, from the sunshine and the
    green,
    Enters the solid darkness of a cave,
Nor knows what precipice or pit unseen
    May yawn before him with its sudden
        grave,

And, with hushed breath, doth often
　　　forward lean,
　Dreaming he hears the plashing of a
　　　wave
Dimly below, or feels a damper air
From out some dreary chasm, he knows
　not where ; —

II.

So, from the sunshine and the green of
　　　love,
　We enter on our story's darker part ;
And, though the horror of it well may
　　　move
An impulse of repugnance in the heart,
Yet let us think, that, as there 's naught
　　　above
The all-embracing atmosphere of Art,
So also there is naught that falls below
Her generous reach, though grimed
　　　with guilt and woe.

III.

Her fittest triumph is to show that good
　Lurks in the heart of evil evermore,
That love, though scorned, and outcast,
　　　and withstood,
　　Can without end forgive, and yet
　　　have store ;
God's love and man's are of the self-
　　　same blood,
　And He can see that always at the door
Of foulest hearts the angel-nature yet
Knocks to return and cancel all its debt.

IV.

It ever is weak falsehood's destiny
　That her thick mask turns crystal to
　　　let through
The unsuspicious eyes of honesty ;
　　But Margaret's heart was too sincere
　　　and true
Aught but plain truth and faithfulness
　　　to see,
　And Mordred's for a time a little grew
To be like hers, won by the mild reproof
Of those kind eyes that kept all doubt
　aloof.

V.

Full oft they met, as dawn and twilight
　　　meet
　In northern climes ; she full of grow-
　　　ing day

As he of darkness, which before her feet
　Shrank gradual, and faded quite away,
Soon to return ; for power had made
　　　love sweet
　To him, and, when his will had
　　　gained full sway,
The taste began to pall ; for never power
Can sate the hungry soul beyond an hour.

VI.

He fell as doth the tempter ever fall,
　Even in the gaining of his loathsome
　　　end :
God doth not work as man works, but
　　　makes all
　The crooked paths of ill to goodness
　　　tend ;
Let him judge Margaret ! If to be the
　　　thrall
　Of love, and faith too generous to
　　　defend
Its very life from him she loved, be sin,
What hope of grace may the seducer
　win ?

VII.

Grim-hearted world, that look'st with
　　　Levite eyes
　On those poor fallen by too much
　　　faith in man,
She that upon thy freezing threshold
　　　lies,
　Starved to more sinning by thy sav-
　　　age ban, —
Seeking that refuge because foulest vice
　More godlike than thy virtue is,
　　　whose span
Shuts out the wretched only, — is more
　　　free
To enter heaven than thou shalt ever
　be !

VIII.

Thou wilt not let her wash thy dainty
　　　feet
　With such salt things as tears, or
　　　with rude hair
Dry them, soft Pharisee, that sit'st at
　　　meat
　With him who made her such, and
　　　speak'st him fair,
Leaving God's wandering lamb the
　　　while to bleat
　Unheeded, shivering in the pitiless
　　　air :

Thou hast made prisoned virtue show
    more wan
And haggard than a vice to look upon.

IX.

Now many months flew by, and weary
    grew
    To Margaret the sight of happy
      things ;
Blight fell on all her flowers, instead
    of dew :
    Shut round her heart were now the
      joyous wings
Wherewith it wont to soar ; yet not
    untrue,
    Though tempted much, her woman's
      nature clings
To its first pure belief, and with sad
    eyes
Looks backward o'er the gate of Para-
    dise.

X.

And so, though altered Mordred came
    less oft,
    And winter frowned where spring
      had laughed before
In his strange eyes, yet half her sad-
    ness doffed,
    And in her silent patience loved him
      more :
Sorrow had made her soft heart yet
    more soft,
    And a new life within her own she
      bore
Which made her tenderer, as she felt
    it move
Beneath her breast, a refuge for her
    love.

XI.

This babe, she thought, would surely
    bring him back,
    And be a bond forever them between ;
Before its eyes the sullen tempest-rack
    Would fade, and leave the face of
      heaven serene ;
And love's return doth more than fill
    the lack,
    Which in his absence withered the
      heart's green :
And yet a dim foreboding still would
    flit
Between her and her hope to darken it.

XII.

She could not figure forth a happy fate,
    Even for this life from heaven so
      newly come ;
The earth must needs be doubly deso-
    late
    To him scarce parted from a fairer
      home :
Such boding heavier on her bosom sate
    One night, as, standing in the twi-
      light gloam,
She strained her eyes beyond that dizzy
    verge
At whose foot faintly breaks the future's
    surge.

XIII.

Poor little spirit ! naught but shame
    and woe
    Nurse the sick heart whose lifeblood
      nurses thine :
Yet not those only ; love hath tri-
    umphed so,
    As for thy sake makes sorrow more
      divine :
And yet, though thou be pure, the world
    is foe
    To purity, if born in such a shrine ;
And, having trampled it for struggling
    thence,
Smiles to itself, and calls it Providence.

XIV.

As thus she mused, a shadow seemed
    to rise
    From out her thought, and turn to
      dreariness
All blissful hopes and sunny memories,
    And the quick blood would curdle up
      and press
About her heart, which seemed to shut
    its eyes
    And hush itself, as who with shud-
      dering guess
Harks through the gloom and dreads
    e'en now to feel
Through his hot breast the icy slide of
    steel.

XV.

But, at that heart-beat, while in dread
    she was,
    In the low wind the honeysuckles
      gleam,

A dewy thrill flits through the heavy
    grass,
    And, looking forth, she saw, as in a
        dream,
Within the wood the moonlight's shad-
    owy mass:
    Night's starry heart yearning to hers
        doth seem,
And the deep sky, full-hearted with the
    moon,
Folds round her all the happiness of
    June.

XVI.

What fear could face a heaven and earth
    like this?
    What silveriest cloud could hang
        'neath such a sky?
A tide of wondrous and unwonted bliss
    Rolls back through all her pulses
        suddenly,
As if some seraph, who had learned to
    kiss
    From the fair daughters of the world
        gone by,
Had wedded so his fallen light with
    hers,
Such sweet, strange joy through soul
    and body stirs.

XVII.

Now seek we Mordred: he who did
    not fear
    The crime, yet fears the latent con-
        sequence:
If it should reach a brother Templar's
    ear,
    It haply might be made a good pre-
        tence
To cheat him of the hope he held most
    dear:
    For he had spared no thought's or
        deed's expense,
That, by and by might help his wish to
    clip
Its darling bride, — the high grand-
    mastership.

XVIII.

The apathy, ere a crime resolved is
    done,
Is scarce less dreadful than remorse
    for crime;

By no allurement can the soul be
    won
    From brooding o'er the weary creep
        of time:
Mordred stole forth into the happy
    sun,
    Striving to hum a scrap of Breton
        rhyme,
But the sky struck him speechless, and
    he tried
In vain to summon up his callous
    pride.

XIX.

In the courtyard a fountain leaped al-·
    way,
    A Triton blowing jewels through his
        shell
Into the sunshine; Mordred turned
    away,
    Weary because the stone face did not
        tell
Of weariness, nor could he bear to-day,
    Heartsick, to hear the patient sink
        and swell
Of winds among the leaves, or golden
    bees
Drowsily humming in the orange-trees.

XX.

All happy sights and sounds now came
    to him
    Like a reproach: he wandered far
        and wide,
Following the lead of his unquiet whim,
    But still there went a something at
        his side
That made the cool breeze hot, the
    sunshine dim;
    It would not flee, it could not be defied,
He could not see it, but he felt it there,
By the damp chill that crept among
    his hair.

XXI.

Day wore at last: the evening star
    arose,
    And throbbing in the sky grew red
        and set:
Then with a guilty, wavering step he
    goes
    To the hid nook where they so oft
        had met

In happier season, for his heart well
        knows
    That he is sure to find poor Margaret
Watching and waiting there with love-
        lorn breast
Around her young dream's rudely
        scattered nest.

XXII.

Why follow here that grim old chronicle
    Which counts the dagger-strokes and
        drops of blood?
Enough that Margaret by his mad steel
        fell,
    Unmoved by murder from her trust-
        ing mood,
Smiling on him as Heaven smiles on
        Hell,
    With a sad love, remembering when
        he stood
Not fallen yet, the unsealer of her heart,
Of all her holy dreams the holiest part.

XXIII.

His crime complete, scarce knowing
        what he did,
    (So goes the tale,) beneath the altar
        there
In the high church the stiffening corpse
        he hid,
    And then, to 'scape that suffocating air,
Like a scared ghoul out of the porch
        he slid ;
    But his strained eyes saw bloodspots
        everywhere,
And ghastly faces thrust themselves
        between
His soul and hopes of peace with blast-
        ing mien.

XXIV.

His heart went out within him like a
        spark
    Dropt in the sea ; wherever he made
        bold
To turn his eyes, he saw, all stiff and stark,
    Pale Margaret lying dead ; the lavish
        gold
Of her loose hair seemed in the cloudy
        dark
    To spread a glory, and a thousand-
        fold

More strangely pale and beautiful she
        grew :
Her silence stabbed his conscience
        through and through :

XXV.

Or visions of past days,—a mother's eyes
    That smiled down on the fair boy at
        her knee,
Whose happy upturned face to hers
        replies, —
    He saw sometimes : or Margaret
        mournfully
Gazed on him full of doubt, as one who
        tries
    To crush belief that does love injury :
Then she would wring her hands, but
        soon again
Love's patience glimmered out through
        cloudy pain.

XXVI.

Meanwhile he dared not go and steal
        away
    The silent, dead-cold witness of his
        sin ;
He had not feared the life, but that dull
        clay,
    Those open eyes that showed the
        death within,
Would surely stare him mad ; yet all
        the day
    A dreadful impulse, whence his will
        could win
No refuge, made him linger in the aisle,
Freezing with his wan look each greet-
        ing smile.

XXVII.

Now, on the second day there was to be
    A festival in church : from far and
        near
Came flocking in the sunburnt peas-
        antry,
    And knights and dames with stately
        antique cheer,
Blazing with pomp, as if all faërie
    Had emptied her quaint halls, or, as
        it were,
The illuminated marge of some old book,
While we were gazing, life and motion
        took.

XXVIII.

When all were entered, and the roving
        eyes
    Of all were stayed, some upon faces
        bright,
Some on the priests, some on the traceries
    That decked the slumber of a marble
        knight,
And all the rustlings over that arise
    From recognizing tokens of delight,
When friendly glances meet, — then
        silent ease
Spread o'er the multitude by slow de-
        grees.

XXIX.

Then swelled the organ : up through
        choir and nave
    The music trembled with an inward
        thrill
Of bliss at its own grandeur : wave on
        wave
    Its flood of mellow thunder rose, until
The hushed air shivered with the throb
        it gave,
    Then, poising for a moment, it stood
        still,
And sank and rose again, to burst in spray
That wandered into silence far away.

XXX.

Like to a mighty heart the music seemed,
    That yearns with melodies it cannot
        speak,
Until, in grand despair of what it
        dreamed,
    In the agony of effort it doth break,
Yet triumphs breaking ; on it rushed
        and streamed
    And wantoned in its might, as when
        a lake,
Long pent among the mountains, bursts
        its walls
And in one crowding gush leaps forth
        and falls.

XXXI.

Deeper and deeper shudders shook the
        air,
    As the huge bass kept gathering
        heavily,
Like thunder when it rouses in its lair,
    And with its hoarse growl shakes the
        low-hung sky,

It grew up like a darkness everywhere,
    Filling the vast cathedral ; — sud-
        denly,
From the dense mass a boy's clear
        treble broke
Like lightning, and the full-toned choir
    awoke.

XXXII.

Through gorgeous windows shone the
        sun aslant,
    Brimming the church with gold and
        purple mist,
Meet atmosphere to bosom that rich
        chant,
    Where fifty voices in one strand did
        twist,
Their varicolored tones, and left no want
    To the delighted soul, which sank
        abyssed
In the warm music cloud, while, far
        below,
The organ heaved its surges to and fro.

XXXIII.

As if a lark should suddenly drop dead
    While the blue air yet trembled with
        its song,
So snapped at once that music's golden
        thread,
    Struck by a nameless fear that leapt
        along
From heart to heart, and like a shadow
        spread
    With instantaneous shiver through
        the throng,
So that some glanced behind, as half
        aware
A hideous shape of dread were stand-
        ing there.

XXXIV.

As when a crowd of pale men gather
        round,
    Watching an eddy in the leaden deep,
From which they deem the body of one
        drowned
    Will be cast forth, from face to face
        doth creep
An eager dread that holds all tongues
        fast bound
    Until the horror, with a ghastly leap,

Starts up, its dead blue arms stretched
    aimlessly,
Heaved with the swinging of the care-
    less sea, —

XXXV.

So in the faces of all these there grew,
    As by one impulse, a dark, freezing
        awe,
Which, with a fearful fascination drew
    All eyes toward the altar; damp and
        raw
The air grew suddenly, and no man
        knew
    Whether perchance his silent neigh-
        bor saw
The dreadful thing which all were sure
        would rise
To scare the strained lids wider from
    their eyes.

XXXVI.

The incense trembled as it upward sent
    Its slow, uncertain thread of wander-
        ing blue,
As 't were the only living element
    In all the church, so deep the still-
        ness grew;
It seemed one might have heard it, as
        it went,
    Give out an audible rustle, curling
        through
The midnight silence of that awe-struck
        air,
More hushed than death, though so
    much life was there.

XXXVII.

Nothing they saw, but a low voice was
        heard
    Threading the ominous silence of
        that fear,
Gentle and terrorless as if a bird,
    Wakened by some volcano's glare,
        should cheer
The murk air with his song; yet every
        word
    In the cathedral's farthest arch seemed
        near,
As if it spoke to every one apart,
Like the clear voice of conscience in
    each heart.

XXXVIII.

" O Rest, to weary hearts thou art most
        dear !
    O Silence, after life's bewildering din,
Thou art most welcome, whether in the
        sear
    Days of our age thou comest, or we
        win
Thy poppy-wreath in youth! then
        wherefore here
    Linger I yet, once free to enter in
At that wished gate which gentle
        Death doth ope,
Into the boundless realm of strength
    and hope?

XXXIX.

" Think not in death my love could
        ever cease ;
    If thou wast false, more need there
        is for me
Still to be true ; that slumber were not
        peace,
    If 't were unvisited with dreams of
        thee :
And thou hadst never heard such words
        as these,
    Save that in heaven I must ever be
Most comfortless and wretched, seeing
        this
Our unbaptizëd babe shut out from bliss.

XL.

" This little spirit with imploring eyes
    Wanders alone the dreary wild of
        space ;
The shadow of his pain forever lies
    Upon my soul in this new dwelling-
        place ;
His loneliness makes me in Paradise
    More lonely, and, unless I see his
        face,
Even here for grief could I lie down
        and die,
Save for my curse of immortality.

XLI.

" World after world he sees around him
        swim
    Crowded with happy souls, that take
        no heed

Of the sad eyes that from the night's
     faint rim
  Gaze sick with longing on them as
     they speed
With golden gates, that only shut out
     him :
  And shapes sometimes from Hell's
     abysses freed
Flap darkly by him, with enormous
     sweep
Of wings that roughen wide the pitchy
     deep.

XLII.

"I am a mother, — spirits do not shake
  This much of earth from them, —
     and I must pine
Till I can feel his little hands, and take
  His weary head upon this heart of
     mine ;
And, might it be, full gladly for his
     sake
Would I this solitude of bliss resign,
And be shut out of Heaven to dwell
     with him
Forever in that silence drear and dim.

XLIII.

"I strove to hush my soul, and would
     not speak
  At first, for thy dear sake ; a woman's
     love
Is mighty, but a mother's heart is weak,
  And by its weakness overcomes ; I
     strove
To smother bitter thoughts with pa-
     tience meek,
  But still in the abyss my soul would
     rove,
Seeking my child, and drove me here
     to claim
The rite that gives him peace in Christ's
     dear name.

XLIV.

"I sit and weep while blessed spirits
     sing :
  I can but long and pine the while they
     praise,
And, leaning o'er the wall of Heaven,
     I fling
  My voice to where I deem my infant
     strays,

Like a robbed bird that cries in vain to
     bring
  Her nestlings back beneath her wings'
     embrace ;
But still he answers not, and I but know
That Heaven and earth are both alike
     in woe."

XLV.

Then the pale priests, with ceremony
     due,
  Baptized the child within its dread-
     ful tomb
Beneath that mother's heart, whose in-
     stinct true
  Star-like had battled down the triple
     gloom
Of sorrow, love, and death : young
     maidens, too,
  Strewed the pale corpse with many
     a milkwhite bloom,
And parted the bright hair, and on the
     breast
Crossed the unconscious hands in sign
     of rest.

XLVI.

Some said, that, when the priest had
     sprinkled o'er
  The consecrated drops, they seemed
     to hear
A sigh, as of some heart from travail
     sore
  Released, and then two voices sing-
     ing clear,
Misereatur Deus, more and more
  Fading far upward, and their ghastly
     fear
Fell from them with that sound, as
     bodies fall
From souls upspringing to celestial hall.

————

PROMETHEUS.

ONE after one the stars have risen
     and set,
Sparkling upon the hoarfrost on my
     chain :
The Bear, that prowled all night about
     the fold

Of the North-star, hath shrunk into
　　his den,
Scared by the blithesome footsteps of
　　the Dawn,
Whose blushing smile floods all the
　　Orient ;
And now bright Lucifer grows less and
　　less,
Into the heaven's blue quiet deep-with-
　　drawn.
Sunless and starless all, the desert sky
Arches above me, empty as this heart
For ages hath been empty of all joy,
Except to brood upon its silent hope,
As o'er its hope of day the sky doth
　　now.
All night have I heard voices : deeper
　　yet
The deep low breathing of the silence
　　grew,
While all about, muffled in awe, there
　　stood
Shadows, or forms, or both, clear-felt
　　at heart,
But, when I turned to front them, far
　　along
Only a shudder through the midnight
　　ran,
And the dense stillness walled me
　　closer round.
But still I heard them wander up and
　　down
That solitude, and flappings of dusk
　　wings
Did mingle with them, whether of
　　those hags
Let slip upon me once from Hades deep,
Or of yet direr torments, if such be,
I could but guess ; and then toward me
　　came
A shape as of a woman : very pale
It was, and calm ; its cold eyes did not
　　move,
And mine moved not, but only stared
　　on them.
Their fixèd awe went through my brain
　　like ice ;
A skeleton hand seemed clutching at
　　my heart,
And a sharp chill, as if a dank night
　　fog
Suddenly closed me in, was all I felt :
And then, methought, I heard a freez-
　　ing sigh,

A long, deep, shivering sigh, as from
　　blue lips
Stiffening in death, close to mine ear
　　I thought
Some doom was close upon me, and I
　　looked
And saw the red moon through the
　　heavy mist,
Just setting, and it seemed as it were
　　falling,
Or reeling to its fall, so dim and dead
And palsy-struck it looked. Then all
　　sounds merged
Into the rising surges of the pines,
Which, leagues below me, clothing the
　　gaunt loins
Of ancient Caucasus with hairy strength,
Sent up a murmur in the morning
　　wind,
Sad as the wail that from the populous
　　earth
All day and night to high Olympus
　　soars,
Fit incense to thy wicked throne, O
　　Jove !

Thy hated name is tossed once more
　　in scorn
From off my lips, for I will tell thy
　　doom.
And are these tears? Nay, do not tri-
　　umph, Jove !
They are wrung from me but by the
　　agonies
Of prophecy, like those sparse drops
　　which fall
From clouds in travail of the lightning,
　　when
The great wave of the storm high-
　　curled and black
Rolls steadily onward to its thunderous
　　break.
Why art thou made a god of, thou poor
　　type
Of anger, and revenge, and cunning
　　force ?
True Power was never born of brutish
　　Strength,
Nor sweet Truth suckled at the shaggy
　　dugs
Of that old she-wolf. Are thy thunder-
　　bolts,
That quell the darkness for a space, so
　　strong

As the prevailing patience of meek
    Light,
Who, with the invincible tenderness
    of peace,
Wins it to be a portion of herself?
Why art thou made a god of, thou, who
    hast
The never-sleeping terror at thy heart,
That birthright of all tyrants, worse to
    bear
Than this thy ravening bird on which
    I smile?
Thou swear'st to free me, if I will un-
    fold
What kind of doom it is whose omen
    flits
Across thy heart, as o'er a troop of
    doves
The fearful shadow of the kite. What
    need
To know that truth whose knowledge
    cannot save?
Evil its errand hath, as well as Good ;
When thine is finished, thou art known
    no more :
There is a higher purity than thou,
And higher purity is greater strength ;
Thy nature is thy doom, at which thy
    heart
Trembles behind the thick wall of thy
    might.
Let man but hope, and thou art straight-
    way chilled
With thought of that drear silence and
    deep night
Which, like a dream, shall swallow thee
    and thine :
Let man but will, and thou art god no
    more,
More capable of ruin than the gold
And ivory that image thee on earth.
He who hurled down the monstrous
    Titan-brood
Blinded with lightnings, with rough
    thunders stunned,
Is weaker than a simple human thought.
My slender voice can shake thee, as the
    breeze,
That seems but apt to stir a maiden's
    hair,
Sways huge Oceanus from pole to pole :
For I am still Prometheus, and fore-
    know
In my wise heart the end and doom of all.

Yes, I am still Prometheus, wiser
    grown
By years of solitude, — that holds apart
The past and future, giving the soul
    room
To search into itself, — and long com-
    mune
With this eternal silence ; — more a
    god,
In my long-suffering and strength to
    meet
With equal front the direst shafts of
    fate,
Than thou in thy faint-hearted despot-
    ism,
Girt with thy baby-toys of force and
    wrath.
Yes, I am that Prometheus who brought
    down
The light to man, which thou, in selfish
    fear,
Hadst to thyself usurped, — his by sole
    right,
For Man hath right to all save Tyr-
    anny, —
And which shall free him yet from thy
    frail throne.
Tyrants are but the spawn of Igno-
    rance,
Begotten by the slaves they trample on,
Who, could they win a glimmer of the
    light,
And see that Tyranny is always weak-
    ness,
Or Fear with its own bosom ill at ease,
Would laugh away in scorn the sand-
    wove chain
Which their own blindness feigned for
    adamant.
Wrong ever builds on quicksands, but
    the Right
To the firm centre lays its moveless
    base.
The tyrant trembles, if the air but stir
The innocent ringlets of a child's free
    hair,
And crouches, when the thought of
    some great spirit,
With world-wide murmur, like a rising
    gale,
Over men's hearts, as over standing
    corn,
Rushes, and bends them to its own
    strong will.

So shall some thought of mine yet cir-
    cle earth,
And puff away thy crumbling altars,
    Jove !

And, wouldst thou know of my su-
    preme revenge,
Poor tyrant, even now dethroned in
    heart,
Realmless in soul, as tyrants ever are,
Listen ! and tell me if this bitter peak,
This never-glutted vulture, and these
    chains
Shrink not before it ; for it shall befit
A sorrow-taught, unconquered Titan-
    heart.
Men, when their death is on them, seem
    to stand
On a precipitous crag that overhangs
The abyss of doom, and in that depth
    to see,
As in a glass, the features dim and vast
Of things to come, the shadows, as it
    seems,
Of what have been.   Death ever fronts
    the wise ;
Not fearfully, but with clear promises
Of larger life, on whose broad vans up-
    borne,
Their outlook widens, and they see
    beyond
The horizon of the Present and the Past,
Even to the very source and end of
    things.
Such am I now : immortal woe hath made
My heart a seer, and my soul a judge
Between the substance and the shadow
    of Truth.
The sure supremeness of the Beautiful,
By all the martyrdoms made doubly
    sure
Of such as I am, this is my revenge,
Which of my wrongs builds a trium-
    phal arch,
Through which I see a sceptre and a
    throne.
The pipings of glad shepherds on the
    hills,
Tending the flocks no more to bleed for
    thee, —
The songs of maidens pressing with
    white feet
The vintage on thine altars poured no
    more, —

The murmurous bliss of lovers, under-
    neath
Dim grapevine bowers, whose rosy
    bunches press
Not half so closely their warm cheeks,
    unpaled
By thoughts of thy brute lust, — the
    hive-like hum
Of peaceful commonwealths, where
    sunburnt Toil
Reaps for itself the rich earth made its
    own
By its own labor, lightened with glad
    hymns
To an omnipotence which thy mad bolts
Would cope with as a spark with the
    vast sea, —
Even the spirit of free love and peace,
Duty's sure recompense through life
    and death, —
These are such harvests as all master-
    spirits
Reap, haply not on earth, but reap no less
Because the sheaves are bound by hands
    not theirs ;
These are the bloodless daggers where-
    withal
They stab fallen tyrants, this their high
    revenge :
For their best part of life on earth is when,
Long after death, prisoned and pent no
    more,
Their thoughts, their wild dreams even,
    have become
Part of the necessary air men breathe ;
When, like the moon, herself behind a
    cloud,
They shed down light before us on life's
    sea,
That cheers us to steer onward still in
    hope.
Earth with her twining memories ivies
    o'er
Their holy sepulchres ; the chainless
    sea,
In tempest or wide calm, repeats their
    thoughts ;
The lightning and the thunder, all free
    things,
Have legends of them for the ears of men.
All other glories are as falling stars,
But universal Nature watches theirs :
Such strength is won by love of human
    kind.

3

Not that I feel that hunger after fame,
Which souls of a half-greatness are
    beset with ;
But that the memory of noble deeds
Cries shame upon the idle and the vile,
And keeps the heart of Man forever up
To the heroic level of old time.
To be forgot at first is little pain
To a heart conscious of such high intent
As must be deathless on the lips of
    men ;
But, having been a name, to sink and be
A something which the world can do
    without,
Which, having been or not, would
    never change
The lightest pulse of fate,—this is indeed
A cup of bitterness the worst to taste,
And this thy heart shall empty to the
    dregs.
Endless despair shall be thy Caucasus,
And memory thy vulture ; thou wilt find
Oblivion far lonelier than this peak.
Behold thy destiny ! Thou think'st it
    much
That I should brave thee, miserable
    god !
But I have braved a mightier than thou,
Even the sharp tempting of this soar-
    ing heart,
Which might have made me, scarcely
    less than thou,
A god among my brethren weak and
    blind,
Scarce less than thou, a pitiable thing
To be down-trodden into darkness
    soon.
But now I am above thee, for thou art
The bungling workmanship of fear, the
    block
That awes the swart Barbarian ; but I
Am what myself have made, — a nature
    wise
With finding in itself the types of all,
With watching from the dim verge of
    the time
What things to be are visible in the gleams
Thrown forward on them from the
    luminous past,
Wise with the history of its own frail heart,
With reverence and sorrow, and with
    love,
Broad as the world, for freedom and for
    man.

Thou and all strength shall crumble,
    except Love,
By whom, and for whose glory, ye shall
    cease :
And, when thou 'rt but a weary moan-
    ing heard
From out the pitiless glooms of Chaos, I
Shall be a power and a memory,
A name to fright all tyrants with, a light
Unsetting as the pole-star, a great voice
Heard in the breathless pauses of the fight
By truth and freedom ever waged with
    wrong,
Clear as a silver trumpet, to awake
Far echoes that from age to age live on
In kindred spirits, giving them a sense
Of boundless power from boundless
    suffering wrung :
And many a glazing eye shall smile to see
The memory of my triumph (for to meet
Wrong with endurance, and to overcome
The present with a heart that looks
    beyond,
Are triumph), like a prophet eagle, perch
Upon the sacred banner of the Right.
Evil springs up, and flowers, and bears
    no seed,
And feeds the green earth with its swift
    decay,
Leaving it richer for the growth of truth ;
But Good, once put in action or in
    thought,
Like a strong oak, doth from its boughs
    shed down
The ripe germs of a forest. Thou,
    weak god,
Shalt fade and be forgotten ! but this soul,
Fresh-living still in the serene abyss,
I in every heaving shall partake, that grows
From heart to heart among the sons of
    men, —
As the ominous hum before the earth-
    quake runs
Far through the Ægean from roused
    isle to isle, —
Foreboding wreck to palaces and shrines,
And mighty rents in many a cavernous
    error
That darkens the free light to man : —
    This heart,
Unscarred by thy grim vulture, as the
    truth
Grows but more lovely 'neath the beaks
    and claws

Of Harpies blind that fain would soil it,
shall
In all the throbbing exultations share
That wait on freedom's triumphs, and in
all
The glorious agonies of martyr-spirits,
Sharp lightning-throes to split the
jagged clouds
That veil the future, showing them the
end,
Pain's thorny crown for constancy and
truth,
Girding the temples like a wreath of stars.
This is a thought, that, like the fabled
laurel,
Makes my faith thunder-proof; and thy
dread bolts
Fall on me like the silent flakes of snow
On the hoar brows of aged Caucasus:
But, O thought far more blissful, they
can rend
This cloud of flesh, and make my soul
a star!

Unleash thy crouching thunders now,
O Jove!
Free this high heart, which, a poor
captive long,
Doth knock to be let forth, this heart
which still,
In its invincible manhood, overtops
Thy puny godship, as this mountain
doth
The pines that moss its roots. O, even
now,
While from my peak of suffering I look
down,
Beholding with a far-spread gush of
hope
The sunrise of that Beauty, in whose
face,
Shone all around with love, no man
shall look
But straightway like a god he be uplift
Unto the throne long empty for his
sake,
And clearly oft foreshadowed in brave
dreams
By his free inward nature, which nor
thou,
Nor any anarch after thee, can bind
From working its great doom, — now,
now set free
This essence, not to die, but to become

Part of that awful Presence which doth
haunt
The palaces of tyrants, to scare off,
With its grim eyes and fearful whisper-
ings
And hideous sense of utter loneliness,
All hope of safety, all desire of peace,
All but the loathed forefeeling of blank
death, —
Part of that spirit which doth ever brood
In patient calm on the unpilfered nest
Of man's deep heart, till mighty
thoughts grow fledged
To sail with darkening shadow o'er
the world,
Filling with dread such souls as dare
not trust
In the unfailing energy of Good,
Until they swoop, and their pale quarry
make
Of some o'erbloated wrong, — that
spirit which
Scatters great hopes in the seed-field
of man,
Like acorns among grain, to grow and
be
A roof for freedom in all coming time!

But no, this cannot be; for ages yet,
In solitude unbroken, shall I hear
The angry Caspian to the Euxine shout,
And Euxine answer with a muffled roar,
On either side storming the giant walls
Of Caucasus with leagues of climbing
foam
(Less, from my height, than flakes of
downy snow),
That draw back baffled but to hurl again,
Snatched up in wrath and horrible tur-
moil,
Mountain on mountain, as the Titans
erst,
My brethren, scaling the high seat of
Jove,
Heaved Pelion upon Ossa's shoulders
broad
In vain emprise. The moon will come
and go
With her monotonous vicissitude;
Once beautiful, when I was free to walk
Among my fellows, and to interchange
The influence benign of loving eyes,
But now by aged use grown wear-
some; —

False thought! most false! for how
    could I endure
These crawling centuries of lonely woe
Unshamed by weak complaining, but
    for thee,
Loneliest, save me, of all created things,
Mild-eyed Astarte, my best comforter,
With thy pale smile of sad benignity?

    Year after year will pass away and
      seem
To me, in mine eternal agony,
But as the shadows of dumb summer
    clouds,
Which I have watched so often darken-
    ing o'er
The vast Sarmatian plain, league-wide
    at first,
But, with still swiftness, lessening on
    and on
Till cloud and shadow meet and mingle
    where
The gray horizon fades into the sky,
Far, far to northward. Yes, for ages
    yet
Must I lie here upon my altar huge,
A sacrifice for man. Sorrow will be,
As it hath been, his portion; endless
    doom,
While the immortal with the mortal
    linked
Dreams of its wings and pines for what
    it dreams,
With upward yearn unceasing. Better
    so:
For wisdom is stern sorrow's patient
    child,
And empire over self, and all the
    deep
Strong charities that make men seem
    like gods;
And love, that makes them be gods,
    from her breasts
Sucks in the milk that makes mankind
    one blood.
Good never comes unmixed, or so it
    seems,
Having two faces, as some images
Are carved, of foolish gods; one face
    is ill;
But one heart lies beneath, and that is
    good,
As are all hearts, when we explore their
    depths.

Therefore, great heart, bear up! thou
    art but type
Of what all lofty spirits endure, that
    fain
Would win men back to strength and
    peace through love:
Each hath his lonely peak, and on each
    heart
Envy, or scorn, or hatred, tears lifelong
With vulture beak; yet the high soul
    is left;
And faith, which is but hope grown
    wise; and love
And patience, which at last shall over-
    come.

1843.

SONG.

VIOLET! sweet violet!
Thine eyes are full of tears;
    Are they wet
    Even yet
With the thought of other years?
Or with gladness are they full,
For the night so beautiful,
And longing for those far-off spheres?

    Loved one of my youth thou wast,
    Of my merry youth,
      And I see,
      Tearfully,
All the fair and sunny past,
All its openness and truth,
Ever fresh and green in thee
As the moss is in the sea.

    Thy little heart, that hath with love
Grown colored like the sky above,
On which thou lookest ever, —
    Can it know
    All the woe
Of hope for what returneth never,
All the sorrow and the longing
To these hearts of ours belonging?

    Out on it! no foolish pining
      For the sky
    Dims thine eye,
Or for the stars so calmly shining;
Like thee let this soul of mine
Take hue from that wherefor I long.

Self-stayed and high, serene and strong,
Not satisfied with hoping — but divine.
 Violet ! dear violet !
 Thy blue eyes are only wet
With joy and love of Him who sent thee,
And for the fulfilling sense
Of that glad obedience
Which made thee all that Nature meant
 thee !
1841.

ROSALINE.

THOU look'dst on me all yesternight.
Thine eyes were blue, thy hair was bright
As when we murmured our troth-plight
 Beneath the thick stars, Rosaline !
Thy hair was braided on thy head,
As on the day we two were wed,
Mine eyes scarce knew if thou wert
 dead,
 But my shrunk heart knew, Rosaline !

The death-watch ticked behind the wall,
The blackness rustled like a pall,
The moaning wind did rise and fall
 Among the bleak pines, Rosaline !
My heart beat thickly in mine ears :
The lids may shut out fleshly fears,
But still the spirit sees and hears,
 Its eyes are lidless, Rosaline !

A wildness rushing suddenly,
A knowing some ill shape is nigh,
A wish for death, a fear to die,
 Is not this vengeance, Rosaline?
A loneliness that is not lone,
A love quite withered up and gone,
A strong soul ousted from its throne,
 What wouldst thou further, Rosaline?

'Tis drear such moonless nights as these,
Strange sounds are out upon the breeze,
And the leaves shiver in the trees,
 And then thou comest, Rosaline !
I seem to hear the mourners go,
With long black garments trailing slow,
And plumes anodding to and fro,
 As once I heard them, Rosaline !

Thy shroud is all of snowy white,
And, in the middle of the night,
Thou standest moveless and upright,

Gazing upon me, Rosaline !
There is no sorrow in thine eyes,
But evermore that meek surprise, —
 O God ! thy gentle spirit tries
 To deem me guiltless, Rosaline !

Above thy grave the robin sings,
And swarms of bright and happy things
Flit all about with sunlit wings,
 But I am cheerless, Rosaline !
The violets on the hillock toss,
The gravestone is o'ergrown with moss;
For nature feels not any loss,
 But I am cheerless, Rosaline !

I did not know when thou wast dead ;
A blackbird whistling overhead
Thrilled through my brain ; I would
 have fled,
But dared not leave thee, Rosaline !
The sun rolled down, and very soon,
Like a great fire, the awful moon
Rose, stained with blood, and then a
 swoon
 Crept chilly o'er me, Rosaline !

The stars came out; and, one by one,
Each angel from his silver throne
Looked down and saw what I had done :
 I dared not hide me, Rosaline !
I crouched ; I feared thy corpse would cry
Against me to God's silent sky,
I thought I saw the blue lips try
 To utter something, Rosaline !

I waited with a maddened grin
To hear that voice all icy thin
Slide forth and tell my deadly sin
 To hell and heaven, Rosaline !
But no voice came, and then it seemed,
That, if the very corpse had screamed,
The sound like sunshine glad had
 streamed
 Through that dark stillness, Rosaline !

And then, amid the silent night,
I screamed with horrible delight,
And in my brain an awful light
 Did seem to crackle, Rosaline !
It is my curse ! sweet memories fall
From me like snow, and only all
Of that one night, like cold worms, crawl
 My doomed heart over, Rosaline !

Why wilt thou haunt me with thine eyes,
Wherein such blessed memories,
Such pitying forgiveness lies,
Than hate more bitter, Rosaline?
Woe 's me! I know that love so high
As thine, true soul, could never die,
And with mean clay in churchyard lie, —
Would it might be so, Rosaline!

1841.

THE SHEPHERD OF KING ADMETUS.

THERE came a youth upon the earth,
  Some thousand years ago,
Whose slender hands were nothing
    worth,
Whether to plough, or reap, or sow.

Upon an empty tortoise-shell
He stretched some chords, and drew
Music that made men's bosoms swell
Fearless, or brimmed their eyes with
    dew.

Then King Admetus, one who had
  Pure taste by right divine,
Decreed his singing not too bad
To hear between the cups of wine:

And so, well pleased with being soothed
    Into a sweet half-sleep,
Three times his kingly beard he
    smoothed,
And made him viceroy o'er his sheep.

His words were simple words enough,
  And yet he used them so,
That what in other mouths was rough
In his seemed musical and low.

Men called him but a shiftless youth,
  In whom no good they saw;
And yet, unwittingly, in truth,
They made his careless words their law.

They knew not how he learned at all,
  For idly, hour by hour,
He sat and watched the dead leaves fall,
Or mused upon a common flower.

It seemed the loveliness of things
  Did teach him all their use,

For, in mere weeds, and stones, and
    springs,
He found a healing power profuse.

Men granted that his speech was wise,
  But, when a glance they caught
Of his slim grace and woman's eyes,
They laughed, and called him good-for-
    naught.

Yet after he was dead and gone,
  And e'en his memory dim,
Earth seemed more sweet to live upon,
More full of love, because of him.

And day by day more holy grew
  Each spot where he had trod,
Till after-poets saw
Their first-born brother as a god.

1842.

THE TOKEN.

IT is a mere wild rosebud,
  Quite sallow now, and dry,
Yet there 's something wondrous in it, —
  Some gleams of days gone by, —
Dear sights and sounds that are to me
The very moons of memory,
And stir my heart's blood far below
Its short-lived waves of joy and woe.

Lips must fade and roses wither,
  All sweet times be o'er, —
They only smile, and, murmuring
    "Thither!"
  Stay with us no more:
And yet ofttimes a look or smile,
Forgotten in a kiss's while,
Years after from the dark will start,
And flash across the trembling heart.

Thou hast given me many roses,
  But never one, like this,
O'erfloods both sense and spirit
  With such a deep, wild bliss;
We must have instincts that glean up
Sparse drops of this life in the cup,
Whose taste shall give us all that we
Can prove of immortality.

Earth's stablest things are shadows,
  And, in the life to come

Happy some chance-saved trifle
    May tell of this old home :
As now sometimes we seem to find,
In a dark crevice of the mind,
Some relic, which, long pondered o'er,
    Hints faintly at a life before.

AN INCIDENT IN A RAILROAD CAR.

HE spoke of Burns : men rude and
        rough
Pressed round to hear the praise of one
Whose heart was made of manly, simple
        stuff,
    As homespun as their own.

And, when he read, they forward
        leaned,
Drinking, with thirsty hearts and ears,
His brook-like songs whom glory never
        weaned
    From humble smiles and tears.

Slowly there grew a tender awe,
Sun-like, o'er faces brown and hard,
As if in him who read they felt and saw
    Some presence of the bard.

It was a sight for sin and wrong
And slavish tyranny to see,
A sight to make our faith more pure and
        strong
    In high humanity.

I thought, these men will carry hence
Promptings their former life above,
And something of a finer reverence
    For beauty, truth, and love.

God scatters love on every side,
Freely among his children all,
And always hearts are lying open wide,
    Wherein some grains may fall.

There is no wind but soweth seeds
Of a more true and open life,
Which burst, unlooked for, into high-
        souled deeds,
    With wayside beauty rife.

We find within these souls of ours
Some wild germs of a higher birth,
Which in the poet's tropic heart bear
        flowers
    Whose fragrance fills the earth.

Within the hearts of all men lie
These promises of wider bliss,
Which blossom into hopes that cannot
        die,
    In sunny hours like this.

All that hath been majestical
In life or death, since time began,
Is native in the simple heart of all,
    The angel heart of man.

And thus, among the untaught poor,
    Great deeds and feelings find a home,
That cast in shadow all the golden lore
    Of classic Greece and Rome.

O, mighty brother-soul of man,
Where'er thou art, in low or high,
Thy skyey arches with exulting span
    O'er-roof infinity !

All thoughts that mould the age begin
Deep down within the primitive soul,
And from the many slowly upward win
    To one who grasps the whole :

In his wide brain the feeling deep
That struggled on the many's tongue
Swells to a tide of thought, whose surges
        leap
    O'er the weak thrones of wrong.

All thought begins in feeling, — wide
In the great mass its base is hid,
And, narrowing up to thought, stands
        glorified,
    A moveless pyramid.

Nor is he far astray who deems
That every hope, which rises and
        grows broad
In the world's heart, by ordered im-
        pulse streams
    From the great heart of God.

God wills, man hopes : in common souls
Hope is but vague and undefined,

Till from the poet's tongue the message
    rolls
        A blessing to his kind.

Never did Poesy appear
    So full of heaven to me, as when
I saw how it would pierce through pride
    and fear
        To the lives of coarsest men.

It may be glorious to write
    Thoughts that shall glad the two or
    three
High souls, like those far stars that
    come in sight
        Once in a century ; —

But better far it is to speak
    One simple word, which now and then
Shall waken their free nature in the
    weak
        And friendless sons of men ;

To write some earnest verse or line,
    Which, seeking not the praise of art,
Shall make a clearer faith and manhood
    shine
        In the untutored heart.

He who doth this, in verse or prose,
    May be forgotten in his day,
But surely shall be crowned at last with
    those
        Who live and speak for aye.
1842.

———

RHŒCUS.

GOD sends his teachers unto every age,
To every clime, and every race of men,
With revelations fitted to their growth
And shape of mind, nor gives the realm
    of Truth
Into the selfish rule of one sole race :
Therefore each form of worship that
    hath swayed
The life of man, and given it to grasp
The master-key of knowledge, rever-
    ence,
Infolds some germs of goodness and
    of right ;
Else never had the eager soul, which
    loathes

The slothful down of pampered igno-
    rance,
Found in it even a moment's fitful rest.

There is an instinct in the human
    heart
Which makes that all the fables it hath
    coined,
To justify the reign of its belief
And strengthen it by beauty's right
    divine,
Veil in their inner cells a mystic gift,
Which, like the hazel twig, in faithful
    hands,
Points surely to the hidden springs of
    truth.
For, as in nature naught is made in
    vain,
But all things have within their hull of
    use
A wisdom and a meaning which may
    speak
Of spiritual secrets to the ear
Of spirit ; so, in whatsoe'er the heart
Hath fashioned for a solace to itself,
To make its inspirations suit its creed,
And from the niggard hands of false-
    hood wring
Its needful food of truth, there ever is
A sympathy with Nature, which re-
    veals,
Not less than her own works, pure
    gleams of light
And earnest parables of inward lore.
Hear now this fairy legend of old
    Greece,
As full of freedom, youth, and beauty
    still
As the immortal freshness of that grace
Carved for all ages on some Attic frieze.

A youth named Rhœcus, wandering
    in the wood,
Saw an old oak just trembling to its
    fall,
And, feeling pity of so fair a tree,
He propped its gray trunk with admir-
    ing care,
And with a thoughtless footstep loitered
    on.
But, as he turned, he heard a voice be-
    hind
That murmured "Rhœcus !" 'T was
    as if the leaves,

Stirred by a passing breath, had mur-
   mured it,
And, while he paused bewildered, yet
   again
It murmured "Rhœcus!" softer than
   a breeze.
He started and beheld with dizzy eyes
What seemed the substance of a happy
   dream
Stand there before him, spreading a
   warm glow
Within the green glooms of the shad-
   owy oak.
It seemed a woman's shape, yet far too
   fair
To be a woman, and with eyes too meek
For any that were wont to mate with
   gods.
All naked like a goddess stood she
   there,
And like a goddess all too beautiful
To feel the guilt-born earthliness of
   shame.
"Rhœcus, I am the Dryad of this tree,"
Thus she began, dropping her low-
   toned words
Serene, and full, and clear, as drops of
   dew,
"And with it I am doomed to live and
   die;
The rain and sunshine are my caterers,
Nor have I other bliss than simple life;
Now ask me what thou wilt, that I can
   give,
And with a thankful joy it shall be
   thine."

Then Rhœcus, with a flutter at the
   heart,
Yet, by the prompting of such beauty,
   bold,
Answered: "What is there that can
   satisfy
The endless craving of the soul but
   love?
Give me thy love, or but the hope of
   that
Which must be evermore my spirit's
   goal."
After a little pause she said again,
But with a glimpse of sadness in her
   tone,
"I give it, Rhœcus, though a perilous
   gift;

An hour before the sunset meet me
   here."
And straightway there was nothing he
   could see
But the green glooms beneath the shad-
   owy oak,
And not a sound came to his straining
   ears
But the low trickling rustle of the
   leaves,
And far away upon an emerald slope
The falter of an idle shepherd's pipe.

Now, in those days of simpleness and
   faith,
Men did not think that happy things
   were dreams
Because they overstepped the narrow
   bourne
Of likelihood, but reverently deemed
Nothing too wondrous or too beauti-
   ful
To be the guerdon of a daring heart.
So Rhœcus made no doubt that he was
   blest,
And all along unto the city's gate
Earth seemed to spring beneath him as
   he walked,
The clear, broad sky looked bluer than
   its wont,
And he could scarce believe he had not
   wings,
Such sunshine seemed to glitter through
   his veins
Instead of blood, so light he felt and
   strange.

Young Rhœcus had a faithful heart
   enough,
But one that in the present dwelt too
   much,
And, taking with blithe welcome whatsoe'er
Chance gave of joy, was wholly bound
   in that,
Like the contented peasant of a
   vale,
Deemed it the world, and never looked
   beyond.
So, haply meeting in the afternoon
Some comrades who were playing at
   the dice,
He joined them, and forgot all else be
   side.

The dice were rattling at the mer-
    riest,
And Rhœcus, who had met but sorry
    luck,
Just laughed in triumph at a happy
    throw,
When through the room there hummed
    a yellow bee
That buzzed about his ear with down-
    dropped legs
As if to light. And Rhœcus laughed
    and said,
Feeling how red and flushed he was
    with loss,
"By Venus! does he take me for a
    rose?"
And brushed him off with rough, im-
    patient hand.
But still the bee came back, and thrice
    again
Rhœcus did beat him off with growing
    wrath.
Then through the window flew the
    wounded bee,
And Rhœcus, tracking him with angry
    eyes,
Saw a sharp mountain-peak of Thessaly
Against the red disk of the setting
    sun, —
And instantly the blood sank from his
    heart,
As if its very walls had caved away.
Without a word he turned, and, rush-
    ing forth,
Ran madly through the city and the
    gate,
And o'er the plain, which now the
    wood's long shade,
By the low sun thrown forward broad
    and dim,
Darkened wellnigh unto the city's wall.

Quite spent and out of breath he
    reached the tree,
And, listening fearfully, he heard once
    more
The low voice murmur "Rhœcus!"
    close at hand:
Whereat he looked around him, but
    could see
Naught but the deepening glooms be-
    neath the oak.
Then sighed the voice, "O Rhœcus!
    nevermore

Shalt thou behold me or by day or
    night,
Me, who would fain have blessed thee
    with a love
More ripe and bounteous than ever yet
Filled up with nectar any mortal heart:
But thou didst scorn my humble mes-
    senger,
And sent'st him back to me with
    bruisèd wings.
We spirits only show to gentle eyes,
We ever ask an undivided love,
And he who scorns the least of Nature's
    works
Is thenceforth exiled and shut out from
    all.
Farewell! for thou canst never see me
    more."

Then Rhœcus beat his breast, and
    groaned aloud,
And cried, "Be pitiful! forgive me yet
This once, and I shall never need it
    more!"
"Alas!" the voice returned, "'t is
    thou art blind,
Not I unmerciful; I can forgive,
But have no skill to heal thy spirit's eyes;
Only the soul hath power o'er itself."
With that again there murmured
    "Nevermore!"
And Rhœcus after heard no other sound,
Except the rattling of the oak's crisp
    leaves,
Like the long surf upon a distant shore,
Raking the sea-worn pebbles up and
    down.
The night had gathered round him: o'er
    the plain
The city sparkled with its thousand
    lights,
And sounds of revel fell upon his ear
Harshly and like a curse; above, the sky,
With all its bright sublimity of stars,
Deepened, and on his forehead smote
    the breeze:
Beauty was all around him and delight,
But from that eve he was alone on earth.

THE FALCON.

I KNOW a falcon swift and peerless
    As e'er was cradled in the pine;

No bird had ever eye so fearless,
  Or wing so strong as this of mine.

The winds not better love to pilot
  A cloud with molten gold o'errun,
Than him, a little burning islet,
  A star above the coming sun.

For with a lark's heart he doth tower,
  By a glorious upward instinct drawn;
No bee nestles deeper in the flower
  Than he in the bursting rose of dawn.

No harmless dove, no bird that singeth,
  Shudders to see him overhead;
The rush of his fierce swooping bringeth
  To innocent hearts no thrill of dread.

Let fraud and wrong and baseness shiver,
  For still between them and the sky
The falcon Truth hangs poised forever
  And marks them with his vengeful eye.

TRIAL.

I.

WHETHER the idle prisoner through his
      grate
Watches the waving of the grass-tuft
      small,
Which, having colonized its rift i' th'
      wall,
Accepts God's dole of good or evil fate,
And, from the sky's just helmet draws
      its lot
Daily of shower or sunshine, cold or
      hot; —
Whether the closer captive of a creed,
Cooped up from birth to grind out end-
      less chaff,
Sees through his treadmill-bars the
      noonday laugh,
And feels in vain his crumpled pinions
      breed; —
Whether the Georgian slave look up
      and mark,
With bellying sails puffed full, the tall
      cloud-bark
Sink northward slowly, — thou alone
      seem'st good,
Fair only thou, O Freedom, whose desire

Can light in muddiest souls quick seeds
      of fire,
And strain life's chords to the old
      heroic mood.

II.

Yet are there other gifts more fair than
      thine,
Nor can I count him happiest who has
      never
Been forced with his own hand his
      chains to sever,
And for himself find out the way divine;
He never knew the aspirer's glorious
      pains,
He never earned the struggle's priceless
      gains,
O, block by block, with sore and sharp
      endeavor,
Lifelong we build these human natures
      up
Into a temple fit for Freedom's shrine,
And Trial ever consecrates the cup
Wherefrom we pour her sacrificial wine.

A REQUIEM.

AY, pale and silent maiden,
  Cold as thou liest there,
Thine was the sunniest nature
  That ever drew the air,
The wildest and most wayward,
  And yet so gently kind,
Thou seemedst but to body
  A breath of summer wind.

Into the eternal shadow
  That girds our life around,
Into the infinite silence
  Wherewith Death's shore is bound,
Thou hast gone forth, beloved!
  And I were mean to weep,
That thou has left Life's shallows,
  And dost possess the Deep.

Thou liest low and silent,
  Thy heart is cold and still,
Thine eyes are shut forever,
  And Death hath had his will;
He loved and would have taken,
  I loved and would have kept,

We strove, — and he was stronger,
    And I have never wept.

Let him possess thy body,
    Thy soul is still with me,
More sunny and more gladsome
    Than it was wont to be :
Thy body was a fetter
    That bound me to the flesh,
Thank God that it is broken,
    And now I live afresh !

Now I can see thee clearly ;
    The dusky cloud of clay,
That hid thy starry spirit,
    Is rent and blown away :
To earth I give thy body,
    Thy spirit to the sky,
I saw its bright wings growing,
    And knew that thou must fly.

Now I can love thee truly,
    For nothing comes between
The senses and the spirit,
    The seen and the unseen ;
Lifts the eternal shadow,
    The silence bursts apart,
And the soul's boundless future
    Is present in my heart.

————

A PARABLE.

WORN and footsore was the Prophet,
    When he gained the holy hill ;
"God has left the earth," he murmured,
    "Here his presence lingers still.

"God of all the olden prophets,
    Wilt thou speak with men no more ?
Have I not as truly served thee
    As thy chosen ones of yore ?

"Hear me, guider of my fathers,
    Lo ! a humble heart is mine ;
By thy mercy I beseech thee
    Grant thy servant but a sign !"

Bowing then his head, he listened
    For an answer to his prayer ;
No loud burst of thunder followed,
    Not a murmur stirred the air : —

But the tuft of moss before him
    Opened while he waited yet,
And, from out the rock's hard bosom,
    Sprang a tender violet.

"God ! I thank thee," said the
        Prophet ;
    "Hard of heart and blind was I,
Looking to the holy mountain
    For the gift of prophecy.

"Still thou speakest with thy children
    Freely as in eld sublime ;
Humbleness, and love, and patience,
    Still give empire over time.

"Had I trusted in my nature,
    And had faith in lowly things,
Thou thyself wouldst then have sought
        me,
    And set free my spirit's wings.

"But I looked for signs and wonders,
    That o'er men should give me sway ;
Thirsting to be more than mortal,
    I was even less than clay.

"Ere I entered on my journey,
    As I girt my loins to start,
Ran to me my little daughter,
    The belovèd of my heart ; —

"In her hand she held a flower,
    Like to this as like may be,
Which, beside my very threshold,
    She had plucked and brought to me."
            1842.

————

A GLANCE BEHIND THE CUR-
TAIN.

WE see but half the causes of our deeds,
Seeking them wholly in the outer life,
And heedless of the encircling spirit-
        world,
Which, though unseen, is felt, and
        sows in us
All germs of pure and world-wide pur-
        poses.
From one stage of our being to the next
We pass unconscious o'er a slender
        bridge,

The momentary work of unseen hands,
Which crumbles down behind us;
    looking back,
We see the other shore, the gulf be-
    tween,
And, marvelling how we won to where
    we stand,
Content ourselves to call the builder
    Chance,
We trace the wisdom to the apple's fall,
Not to the birth-throes of a mighty
    Truth
Which, for long ages in blank Chaos
    dumb,
Yet yearned to be incarnate, and had
    found
At last a spirit meet to be the womb
From which it might be born to bless
    mankind, —
Not to the soul of Newton, ripe with all
The hoarded thoughtfulness of earnest
    years
And waiting but one ray of sunlight
    more
To blossom fully.

        But whence came that ray?
We call our sorrows Destiny, but ought
Rather to name our high successes so.
Only the instincts of great souls are Fate,
And have predestined sway: all other
    things,
Except by leave of us, could never be.
For Destiny is but the breath of God
Still moving in us, the last fragment left
Of our unfallen nature, waking oft
Within our thought, to beckon us be-
    yond
The narrow circle of the seen and
    known,
And always tending to a noble end,
As all things must that overrule the
    soul,
And for a space unseat the helmsman,
    Will.
The fate of England and of freedom
    once
Seemed wavering in the heart of one
    plain man:
One step of his, and the great dial-
    hand,
That marks the destined progress of
    the world
In the eternal round from wisdom on

To higher wisdom, had been made to
    pause
A hundred years. That step he did
    not take, —
He knew not why, nor we, but only
    God, —
And lived to make his simple oaken
    chair
More terrible and soberly august,
More full of majesty than any throne,
Before or after, of a British king.

Upon the pier stood two stern-vis-
    aged men,
Looking to where a little craft lay
    moored,
Swayed by the lazy current of the
    Thames,
Which weltered by in muddy listless-
    ness.
Grave men they were, and battlings of
    fierce thought
Had trampled· out all softness from
    their brows,
And ploughed rough furrows there be-
    fore their time,
For other crop than such as homebred
    Peace
Sows broadcast in the willing soil of
    Youth.
Care, not of self, but for the common-
    weal,
Had robbed their eyes of youth, and
    left instead
A look of patient power and iron will,
And something fiercer, too, that gave
    broad hint
Of the plain weapons girded at their
    sides.
The younger had an aspect of com-
    mand, —
Not such as trickles down, a slender
    stream,
In the shrunk channel of a great descent,
But such as lies entowered in heart and
    head,
And an arm prompt to do the 'hests of
    both.
His was a brow where gold were out
    of place,
And yet it seemed right worthy of a
    crown
(Though he despised such), were it
    only made

Of iron, or some serviceable stuff
That would have matched his brownly
    rugged face.
The elder, although such he hardly
    seemed
(Care makes so little of some five short
    years),
Had a clear, honest face, whose rough-
    hewn strength
Was mildened by the scholar's wiser
    heart
To sober courage, such as best befits
The unsullied temper of a well-taught
    mind,
Yet so remained that one could plainly
    guess
The hushed volcano smouldering un-
    derneath.
He spoke: the other, hearing, kept his
    gaze
Still fixed, as on some problem in the
    sky.

    "O CROMWELL, we are fallen on
        evil times!
There was a day when England had
    wide room
For honest men as well as foolish kings:
But now the uneasy stomach of the
    time
Turns squeamish at them both. There-
    fore let us
Seek out that savage clime, where men
    as yet
Are free: there sleeps the vessel on
    the tide,
Her languid canvas drooping for the
    wind;
Give us but that, and what need we to
    fear
This Order of the Council? The free
    waves
Will not say No to please a wayward
    king,
Nor will the winds turn traitors at his
    beck:
All things are fitly cared for, and the
    Lord
Will watch as kindly o'er the exodus
Of us his servants now, as in old time.
We have no cloud or fire, and haply
    we
May not pass dry-shod through the
    ocean-stream;

But, saved or lost, all things are in His
    hand."
So spake he, and meantime the other
    stood
With wide gray eyes still reading the
    blank air,
As if upon the sky's blue wall he saw
Some mystic sentence, written by a
    hand,
Such as of old made pale the Assyrian
    king,
Girt with his satraps in the blazing
    feast.

    "HAMPDEN! a moment since, my
        purpose was
To fly with thee,— for I will call it
    flight,
Nor flatter it with any smoother
    name,—
But something in me bids me not to
    go;
And I am one, thou knowest, who, un-
    moved
By what the weak deem omens, yet
    give heed
And reverence due to whatsoe'er my
    soul
Whispers of warning to the inner ear.
Moreover, as I know that God brings
    round
His purposes in ways undreamed by
    us,
And makes the wicked but his instru-
    ments
To hasten on their swift and sudden
    fall,
I see the beauty of his providence
In the King's order: blind, he will not
    let
His doom part from him, but must bid
    it stay
As 't were a cricket, whose enlivening
    chirp
He loved to hear beneath his very
    hearth.
Why should we fly? Nay, why not
    rather stay
And rear again our Zion's crumbled
    walls,
Not, as of old the walls of Thebes were
    built,
By minstrel twanging, but, if need
    should be,

With the more potent music of our
  swords?
Think'st thou that score of men beyond
  the sea
Claim more God's care than all of
  England here?
No: when He moves His arm, it is to
  aid
Whole peoples, heedless if a few be
  crushed,
As some are ever, when the destiny
Of man takes one stride onward nearer
  home.
Believe me, 't is the mass of men He
  loves;
And, where there is most sorrow and
  most want,
Where the high heart of man is trodden
  down
The most, 't is not because He hides
  His face
From them in wrath, as purblind teach-
  ers prate:
Not so: there most is He, for there is
  He
Most needed.   Men who seek for Fate
  abroad
Are not so near His heart as they who
  dare
Frankly to face her where she faces
  them,
On their own threshold, where their
  souls are strong
To grapple with and throw her; as I
  once,
Being yet a boy, did cast this puny
  king,
Who now has grown so dotard as to
  deem
That he can wrestle with an angry
  realm,
And throw the brawned Antæus of
  men's rights.
No, Hampden! they have half-way
  conquered Fate
Who go half-way to meet her, — as
  will I.
Freedom hath yet a work for me to do;
So speaks that inward voice which
  never yet
Spake falsely, when it urged the spirit
  on
To noble emprise for country and mankind.

And, for success, I ask no more than
  this, —
To bear unflinching witness to the
  truth.
All true whole men succeed; for what
  is worth
Success's name, unless it be the
  thought,
The inward surety, to have carried out
A noble purpose to a noble end,
Although it be the gallows or the block?
'T is only Falsehood that doth ever
  need
These outward shows of gain to bolster
  her.
Be it we prove the weaker with our
  swords;
Truth only needs to be for once spoke
  out,
And there 's such music in her, such
  strange rhythm,
As makes men's memories her joyous
  slaves,
And clings around the soul, as the sky
  clings
Round the mute earth, forever beauti-
  ful,
And, if o'erclouded, only to burst forth
More all-embracingly divine and clear:
Get but the truth once uttered, and 't is
  like
A star new-born, that drops into its place,
And which, once circling in its placid
  round,
Not all the tumult of the earth can shake.

"What should we do in that small
  colony
Of pinched fanatics, who would rather
  choose
Freedom to clip an inch more from
  their hair,
Than the great chance of setting Eng-
  land free?
Not there, amid the stormy wilderness,
Should we learn wisdom; or if learned,
  what room
To put it into act, — else worse than
  naught?
We learn our souls more, tossing for an
  hour
Upon this huge and ever-vexëd sea
Of human thought, where kingdoms go
  to wreck

Like fragile bubbles yonder in the
    stream,
Than in a cycle of New England sloth,
Broke only by some petty Indian war,
Or quarrel for a letter more or less
In some hard word, which, spelt in
    either way,
Not their most learnèd clerks can un-
    derstand.
New times demand new measures and
    new men ;
The world advances, and in time out-
    grows
The laws that in our fathers' day were
    best ;
And, doubtless, after us, some purer
    scheme
Will be shaped out by wiser men than
    we,
Made wiser by the steady growth of
    truth.
We cannot hale Utopia on by force :
But better, almost, be at work in sin,
Than in a brute inaction browse and
    sleep.
No man is born into the world whose
    work
Is not born with him ; there is always
    work,
And tools to work withal, for those who
    will ;
And blessèd are the horny hands of toil !
The busy world shoves angrily aside
The man who stands with arms akimbo
    set,
Until occasion tells him what to do ;
And he who waits to have his task
    marked out
Shall die and leave his errand unful-
    filled.
Our time is one that calls for earnest
    deeds :
Reason and Government, like two
    broad seas,
Yearn for each other with outstretchèd
    arms
Across this narrow isthmus of the throne,
And roll their white surf higher every
    day.
One age moves onward, and the next
    builds up
Cities and gorgeous palaces, where stood
The rude log huts of those who tamed
    the wild.

Rearing from out the forests they had
    felled
The goodly framework of a fairer state :
The builder's trowel and the settler's axe
Are seldom wielded by the selfsame
    hand ;
Ours is the harder task, yet not the less
Shall we receive the blessing for our toil
From the choice spirits of the aftertime.
My soul is not a palace of the past,
Where outworn creeds, like Rome's
    gray senate, quake,
Hearing afar the Vandal's trumpet
    hoarse,
That shakes old systems with a thunder-
    fit.
The time is ripe, and rotten-ripe, for
    change ;
Then let it come : I have no dread of
    what
Is called for by the instinct of mankind ;
Nor think I that God's world will fall
    apart
Because we tear a parchment more or
    less.
Truth is eternal, but her effluence,
With endless change is fitted to the
    hour ;
Her mirror is turned forward to reflect
The promise of the future, not the past.
He who would win the name of truly
    great
Must understand his own age and the
    next,
And make the present ready to fulfil
Its prophecy, and with the future merge
Gently and peacefully, as wave with
    wave.
The future works out great men's pur-
    poses ;
The present is enough for common souls,
Who, never looking forward, are indeed
Mere clay, wherein the footprints of
    their age
Are petrified forever : better those
Who lead the blind old giant by the hand
From out the pathless desert where he
    gropes,
And set him onward in his darksome
    way.
I do not fear to follow out the truth,
Albeit along the precipice's edge.
Let us speak plain : there is more force
    in names

Than most men dream of; and a lie
  may keep
Its throne a whole age longer, if it skulk
Behind the shield of some fair-seeming
  name.
Let us call tyrants, *tyrants*, and main-
  tain,
That only freedom comes by grace of
  God,
And all that comes not by his grace
  must fall;
For men in earnest have no time to waste
In patching fig-leaves for the naked
  truth.

  "I will have one more grapple with
    the man
Charles Stuart: whom the boy o'er-
  came,
The man stands not in awe of. I, per-
  chance,
Am one raised up by the Almighty arm
To witness some great truth to all the
  world.
Souls destined to o'erleap the vulgar lot,
And mould the world unto the scheme
  of God,
Have a fore-consciousness of their high
  doom,
As men are known to shiver at the heart
When the cold shadow of some coming
  ill
Creeps slowly o'er their spirits un-
  awares.
Hath Good less power of prophecy than
  Ill?
How else could men whom God hath
  called to sway
Earth's rudder, and to steer the bark of
  Truth,
Beating against the tempest tow'rd her
  port,
Bear all the mean and buzzing griev-
  ances,
The petty martyrdoms, wherewith Sin
  strives
To weary out the tethered hope of Faith?
The sneers, the unrecognizing look of
  friends,
Who worship the dead corpse of old
  king Custom,
Where it doth lie in state within the
  Church,
Striving to cover up the mighty ocean

With a man's palm, and making even
    the truth
Lie for them, holding up the glass re-
  versed,
To make the hope of man seem further
  off?
My God! when I read o'er the bitter
    lives
Of men whose eager hearts were quite
    too great
To beat beneath the cramped mode of
    the day,
And see them mocked at by the world
    they love,
Haggling with prejudice for penny-
    worths
Of that reform which their hard toil
    will make
The common birthright of the age to
    come, —
When I see this, spite of my faith in
    God,
I marvel how their hearts bear up so
    long;
Nor could they but for this same
    prophecy,
This inward feeling of the glorious end.

  "Deem me not fond; but in my
    warmer youth,
Ere my heart's bloom was soiled and
    brushed away,
I had great dreams of mighty things to
    come;
Of conquest, whether by the sword or
    pen
I knew not; but some conquest I would
    have,
Or else swift death: now wiser grown
    in years,
I find youth's dreams are but the flutter-
    ings
Of those strong winds whereon the soul
    shall soar
In aftertime to win a starry throne;
And so I cherish them, for they were lots,
Which I, a boy, cast in the helm of Fate.
Now will I draw them, since a man's
    right hand,
A right hand guided by an earnest soul,
With a true instinct, takes the golden
    prize
From out a thousand blanks. What
    men call luck

4

Is the prerogative of valiant souls,
The fealty life pays its rightful kings.
The helm is shaking now, and I will stay
To pluck my lot forth ; it were sin to
        flee ! "

So they two turned together ; one to
        die,
Fighting for freedom on the bloody
        field :
The other, far more happy, to become
A name earth wears forever next her
        heart ;
One of the few that have a right to rank
With the true Makers : for his spirit
        wrought
Order from Chaos ; proved that right
        divine
Dwelt only in the excellence of truth ;
And far within old Darkness' hostile
        lines
Advanced and pitched the shining
        tents of Light.
Nor shall the grateful Muse forget to
        tell,
That — not the least among his many
        claims
To deathless honor — he was MIL-
        TON's friend,
A man not second among those who
        lived
To show us that the poet's lyre de-
        mands
An arm of tougher sinew than the
        sword.

1843.   ———

SONG.

O MOONLIGHT deep and tender,
    A year and more agone,
Your mist of golden splendor
    Round my betrothal shone !

O elm-leaves dark and dewy,
    The very same ye seem,
The low wind trembles through ye,
    Ye murmur in my dream !

O river, dim with distance,
    Flow thus forever by,
A part of my existence
    Within your heart doth lie !

O stars, ye saw our meeting,
    Two beings and one soul,
Two hearts so madly beating
    To mingle and be whole !

O happy night, deliver
    Her kisses back to me,
Or keep them all, and give her
    A blissful dream of me !

1842.   ———

A CHIPPEWA LEGEND.*

ἀλγεινὰ μέν μοι καὶ λέγειν ἐστὶν τάδε
ἄλγος δὲ σιγᾶν.
            Æschylus, Prom. Vinct. 197.

THE old Chief, feeling now wellnigh
        his end,
Called his two eldest children to his
        side,
And gave them, in few words, his part-
        ing charge !
" My son and daughter, me ye see no
        more ;
The happy hunting-grounds await me,
        green
With change of spring and summer
        through the year :
But, for remembrance, after I am gone,
Be kind to little Sheemah for my sake :
Weakling he is and young, and knows
        not yet
To set the trap, or draw the seasoned
        bow ;
Therefore of both your loves he hath
        more need,
And he, who needeth love, to love hath
        right ;
It is not like our furs and stores of corn,
Whereto we claim sole title by our toil,
But the Great Spirit plants it in our
        hearts,
And waters it, and gives it sun, to be
The common stock and heritage of all :
Therefore be kind to Sheemah, that
        yourselves
May not be left deserted in your need."

* For the leading incidents in this tale, I
am indebted to the very valuable "Algic
Researches" of Henry R. Schoolcraft, Esq.

Alone, beside a lake, their wigwam
    stood,
Far from the other dwellings of their
    tribe ;
And, after many moons, the loneliness
Wearied the elder brother, and he said,
"Why should I dwell here far from
    men, shut out
From the free, natural joys that fit my
    age ?
Lo, I am tall and strong, well skilled
    to hunt,
Patient of toil and hunger, and not yet
Have seen the danger which I dared
    not look
Full in the face ; what hinders me to
    be
A mighty Brave and Chief among my
    kin ? "
So, taking up his arrows and his bow,
As if to hunt, he journeyed swiftly on,
Until he gained the wigwams of his
    tribe,
Where, choosing out a bride, he soon
    forgot,
In all the fret and bustle of new life,
The little Sheemah and his father's
    charge.

Now when the sister found her
    brother gone,
And that, for many days, he came not
    back,
She wept for Sheemah more than for
    herself ;
For Love bides longest in a woman's
    heart,
And flutters many times before he flies,
And then doth perch so nearly, that a
    word
May lure him back to his accustomed
    nest ;
And Duty lingers even when Love is
    gone,
Oft looking out in hope of his return ;
And, after Duty hath been driven forth,
Then Selfishness creeps in the last of
    all,
Warming her lean hands at the lonely
    hearth,
And crouching o'er the embers, to shut
    out
Whatever paltry warmth and light are
    left,

With avaricious greed, from all beside.
So, for long months, the sister hunted
    wide,
And cared for little Sheemah tenderly ;
But, daily more and more, the loneli-
    ness
Grew wearisome, and to herself she
    sighed,
"Am I not fair ? at least the glassy pool,
That hath no cause to flatter, tells me
    so ;
But, O, how flat and meaningless the
    tale,
Unless it tremble on a lover's tongue !
Beauty hath no true glass, except it be
In the sweet privacy of loving eyes."
Thus deemed she idly, and forgot the
    lore
Which she had learned of nature and
    the woods,
That beauty's chief reward is to itself,
And that Love's mirror holds no image
    long
Save of the inward fairness, blurred and
    lost
Unless kept clear and white by Duty's
    care.
So she went forth and sought the
    haunts of men,
And, being wedded, in her household
    cares,
Soon, like the elder brother, quite for-
    got
The little Sheemah and her father's
    charge.

But Sheemah, left alone within the
    lodge,
Waited and waited, with a shrinking
    heart,
Thinking each rustle was his sister's
    step,
Till hope grew less and less, and then
    went out,
And every sound was changed from
    hope to fear.
Few sounds there were : — the drop-
    ping of a nut,
The squirrel's chirrup, and the jay's
    harsh scream,
Autumn's sad remnants of blithe Sum-
    mer's cheer,
Heard at long intervals, seemed but to
    make

The dreadful void of silence silenter.
Soon what small store his sister left was
   gone,
And, through the Autumn, he made
   shift to live
On roots and berries, gathered in much
   fear
Of wolves, whose ghastly howl he
   heard ofttimes,
Hollow and hungry, at the dead of
   night.
But Winter came at last, and, when
   the snow,
Thick-heaped for gleaming leagues o'er
   hill and plain,
Spread its unbroken silence over all,
Made bold by hunger, he was fain to
   glean
(More sick at heart than Ruth, and all
   alone)
After the harvest of the merciless wolf,
Grim Boaz, who, sharp-ribbed and
   gaunt, yet feared
A thing more wild and starving than
   himself;
Till, by degrees, the wolf and he grew
   friends,
And shared together all the winter
   through.

Late in the Spring, when all the ice
   was gone,
The elder brother, fishing in the lake,
Upon whose edge his father's wigwam
   stood,
Heard a low moaning noise upon the
   shore :
Half like a child it seemed, half like a
   wolf,
And straightway there was something
   in his heart
That said, " It is thy brother Sheemah's
   voice."
So, paddling swiftly to the bank, he
   saw,
Within a little thicket close at hand,
A child that seemed fast changing to a
   wolf,
From the neck downward, gray with
   shaggy hair,
That still crept on and upward as he
   looked.
The face was turned away, but well he
   knew

That it was Sheemah's, even his broth-
   er's face.
Then with his trembling hands he hid
   his eyes,
And bowed his head, so that he might
   not see
The first look of his brother's eyes,
   and cried,
"O Sheemah! O my brother, speak
   to me!
Dost thou not know me, that I am thy
   brother ?
Come to me, little Sheemah, thou shalt
   dwell
With me henceforth, and know no care
   or want!"
Sheemah was silent for a space, as if
'T were hard to summon up a human
   voice,
And, when he spake, the voice was as
   a wolf's :
"I know thee not, nor art thou what
   thou say'st ;
I have none other brethren than the
   wolves,
And, till thy heart be changed from
   what it is,
Thou art not worthy to be called their
   kin."
Then groaned the other, with a chok-
   ing tongue,
"Alas ! my heart is changed right bit-
   terly ;
'T is shrunk and parched within me
   even now ! "
And, looking upward fearfully, he saw
Only a wolf that shrank away and ran,
Ugly and fierce, to hide among the
   woods.

STANZAS ON FREEDOM.

MEN ! whose boast it is that ye
Come of fathers brave and free,
If there breathe on earth a slave,
Are ye truly free and brave ?
If ye do not feel the chain,
When it works a brother's pain,
Are ye not base slaves indeed,
Slaves unworthy to be freed ?

Women ! who shall one day bear
Sons to breathe New England air,

If ye hear, without a blush,
Deeds to make the roused blood rush
Like red lava through your veins,
For your sisters now in chains, —
Answer! are ye fit to be
Mothers of the brave and free?

Is true Freedom but to break
Fetters for our own dear sake,
And, with leathern hearts, forget
That we owe mankind a debt?
No! true freedom is to share
All the chains our brothers wear,
And, with heart and hand, to be
Earnest to make others free!

They are slaves who fear to speak
For the fallen and the weak;
They are slaves who will not choose
Hatred, scoffing, and abuse,
Rather than in silence shrink
From the truth they needs must think;
They are slaves who dare not be
In the right with two or three.

COLUMBUS.

THE cordage creeks and rattles in the wind,
With freaks of sudden hush; the reeling sea
Now thumps like solid rock beneath the stern,
Now leaps with clumsy wrath, strikes short, and, falling
Crumbled to whispery foam, slips rustling down
The broad backs of the waves, which jostle and crowd
To fling themselves upon that unknown shore,
Their used familiar since the dawn of time,
Whither this foredoomed life is guided on
To sway on triumph's hushed, aspiring poise
One glittering moment, then to break fulfilled.

How lonely is the sea's perpetual swing,
The melancholy wash of endless waves,

The sigh of some grim monster undescried,
Fear-painted on the canvas of the dark,
Shifting on his uneasy pillow of brine!
Yet night brings more companions than the day
To this drear waste; new constellations burn,
And fairer stars, with whose calm height my soul
Finds nearer sympathy than with my herd
Of earthen souls, whose vision's scanty ring
Makes me its prisoner to beat my wings
Against the cold bars of their unbelief,
Knowing in vain my own free heaven beyond.
O God! this world, so crammed with eager life,
That comes and goes and wanders back to silence
Like the idle wind, which yet man's shaping mind
Can make his drudge to swell the longing sails
Of highest endeavor, — this mad, unthrift world,
Which, every hour, throws life enough away
To make her deserts kind and hospitable,
Lets her great destinies be waved aside
By smooth, lip-reverent, formal infidels,
Who weigh the God they not believe with gold,
And find no spot in Judas, save that he,
Driving a duller bargain than he ought,
Saddled his guild with too cheap precedent.
O Faith! if thou art strong, thine opposite
Is mighty also, and the dull fool's sneer
Hath ofttimes shot chill palsy through the arm
Just lifted to achieve its crowning deed,
And made the firm-based heart, that would have quailed
The rack or fagot, shudder like a leaf
Wrinkled with frost, and loose upon its stem.
The wicked and the weak, by some dark law,

Have a strange power to shut and rivet
   down
Their own horizon round us, to unwing
Our heaven-aspiring visions, and to blur
With surly clouds the Future's gleam-
   ing peaks,
Far seen across the brine of thankless
   years.
If the chosen soul could never be alone
In deep mid-silence, open-doored to God,
No greatness ever had been dreamed
   or done ;
Among dull hearts a prophet never
   grew ;
The nurse of full-grown souls is solitude.

The old world is effete ; there man with
   man
Jostles, and, in the brawl for means to
   live,
Life is trod under-foot, — Life, the one
   block
Of marble that 's vouchsafed wherefrom
   to carve
Our great thoughts, white and godlike,
   to shine down
The future, Life, the irredeemable block,
Which one o'er-hasty chisel-dint oft
   mars,
Scanting our room to cut the features out
Of our full hope, so forcing us to crown
With a mean head the perfect limbs, or
   leave
The god's face glowing o'er a satyr's
   trunk,
Failure's brief epitaph.

              Yes, Europe's world
Reels on to judgment ; there the com-
   mon need,
Losing God's sacred use, to be a bond
'Twixt Me and Thee, sets each one
   scowlingly
O'er his own selfish hoard at bay ; no
   state,
Knit strongly with eternal fibres up
Of all men's separate and united weals,
Self-poised and sole as stars, yet one as
   light,
Holds up a shape of large Humanity
To which by natural instinct every man
Pays loyalty exulting, by which all
Mould their own lives, and feel their
   pulses filled

With the red, fiery blood of the general
   life,
Making them mighty in peace, as now
   in war
They are, even in the flush of victory,
   weak,
Conquering that manhood which should
   them subdue.
And what gift bring I to this untried
   world ?
Shall the same tragedy be played anew,
And the same lurid curtain drop at last
On one dread desolation, one fierce crash
Of that recoil which on its makers God
Lets Ignorance and Sin and Hunger
   make,
Early or late ? Or shall that common-
   wealth
Whose potent unity and concentric force
Can draw these scattered joints and
   parts of men
Into a whole ideal man once more,
Which sucks not from its limbs the life
   away,
But sends it flood-tide and creates itself
Over again in every citizen,
Be there built up ? For me, I have no
   choice ;
I might turn back to other destinies,
For one sincere key opes all Fortune's
   doors ;
But whoso answers not God's earliest
   call
Forfeits or dulls that faculty supreme
Of lying open to his genius
Which makes the wise heart certain of
   its ends.

Here am I ; for what end God knows,
   not I ;
Westward still points the inexorable
   soul :
Here am I, with no friend but the sad
   sea,
The beating heart of this great enterprise,
Which, without me, would stiffen in
   swift death ;
This have I mused on, since mine eye
   could first
Among the stars distinguish and with
   joy
Rest on that God-fed Pharos of the
   north,

On some blue promontory of heaven
    lighted
That juts far out into the upper sea;
To this one hope my heart hath clung
    for years,
As would a foundling to the talisman
Hung round his neck by hands he
    knew not whose;
A poor, vile thing and dross to all beside,
Yet he therein can feel a virtue left
By the sad pressure of a mother's hand,
And unto him it still is tremulous
With palpitating haste and wet with
    tears,
The key to him of hope and human-
    ness,
The coarse shell of life's pearl, Expect-
    ancy.
This hope hath been to me for love and
    fame,
Hath made me wholly lonely on the
    earth,
Building me up as in a thick-ribbed
    tower,
Wherewith enwalled my watching spirit
    burned,
Conquering its little island from the
    Dark,
Sole as a scholar's lamp, and heard
    men's steps,
In the far hurry of the outward world,
Pass dimly forth and back, sounds heard
    in dream
As Ganymede by the eagle was
    snatched up
From the gross sod to be Jove's cup-
    bearer,
So was I lifted by my great design:
And who hath trod Olympus, from his
    eye
Fades not that broader outlook of the
    gods;
His life's low valleys overbrow earth's
    clouds,
And that Olympian spectre of the past
Looms towering up in sovereign mem-
    ory,
Beckoning his soul from meaner heights
    of doom.
Had but the shadow of the Thunder-
    er's bird,
Flashing athwart my spirit, made of
    me
A swift-betraying vision's Ganymede,

Yet to have greatly dreamed precludes
    low ends;
Great days have ever such a morning-
    red,
On such a base great futures are built
    up,
And aspiration, though not put in act,
Comes back to ask its plighted troth
    again,
Still watches round its grave the un-
    laid ghost
Of a dead virtue, and makes other
    hopes,
Save that implacable one, seem thin
    and bleak
As shadows of bare trees upon the
    snow,
Bound freezing there by the unpitying
    moon.

While other youths perplexed their
    mandolins,
Praying that Thetis would her fingers
    twine
In the loose glories of the lover's hair,
And wile another kiss to keep back
    day,
I, stretched beneath the many-centu-
    ried shade
Of some writhed oak, the wood's Lao-
    coön,
Did of my hope a dryad mistress make,
Whom I would woo to meet me privily,
Or underneath the stars, or when the
    moon
Flecked all the forest floor with scat-
    tered pearls.
O days whose memory tames to fawn-
    ing down
The surly fell of Ocean's bristled neck!

I know not when this hope enthralled
    me first,
But from my boyhood up I loved to
    hear
The tall pine-forests of the Apennine
Murmur their hoary legends of the
    sea,
Which hearing, I in vision clear beheld
The sudden dark of tropic night shut
    down
O'er the huge whisper of great watery
    wastes,
The while a pair of herons trailingly

Flapped inland, where some league-
   wide river hurled
The yellow spoil of unconjectured
   realms
Far through a gulf's green silence,
   never scarred
By any but the North-wind's hurrying
   keels.
And not the pines alone; all sights
   and sounds
To my world-seeking heart paid fealty,
And catered for it as the Cretan bees
Brought honey to the baby Jupiter,
Who in his soft hand crushed a violet,
Godlike foremusing the rough thunder's
   gripe;
Then did I entertain the poet's song,
My great Idea's guest, and, passing o'er
That iron bridge the Tuscan built to hell,
I heard Ulysses tell of mountain-chains
Whose adamantine links, his manacles,
The western main shook growling, and
   still gnawed.
I brooded on the wise Athenian's tale
Of happy Atlantis, and heard Björne's
   keel
Crunch the gray pebbles of the Vinland
   shore:
I listened, musing, to the prophecy
Of Nero's tutor-victim; lo, the birds
Sing darkling, conscious of the climb-
   ing dawn.
And I believed the poets; it is they
Who utter wisdom from the central
   deep,
And, listening to the inner flow of things,
Speak to the age out of eternity.

Ah me! old hermits sought for soli-
   tude
In caves and desert places of the earth,
Where their own heart-beat was the
   only stir
Of living thing that comforted the
   year;
But the bald pillar-top of Simeon,
In midnight's blankest waste, were
   populous,
Matched with the isolation dreary and
   deep
Of him who pines among the swarm of
   men,
At once a new thought's king and pris-
   oner,

Feeling the truer life within his life,
The fountain of his spirit's prophecy,
Sinking away and wasting, drop by
   drop,
In the ungrateful sands of sceptic ears.
He in the palace-aisles of untrod woods
Doth walk a king; for him the pent-
   up cell
Widens beyond the circles of the stars,
And all the sceptred spirits of the past
Come thronging in to greet him as their
   peer;
But in the market-place's glare and
   throng
He sits apart, an exile, and his brow
Aches with the mocking memory of its
   crown.
Yet to the spirit select there is no
   choice;
He cannot say, This will I do, or that,
For the cheap means putting Heaven's
   ends in pawn,
And bartering his bleak rocks, the free-
   hold stern
Of destiny's first-born, for smoother
   fields
That yield no crop of self-denying will;
A hand is stretched to him from out
   the dark,
Which grasping without question, he
   is led
Where there is work that he must do
   for God.
The trial still is the strength's comple-
   ment,
And the uncertain, dizzy path that
   scales
The sheer heights of supremest pur-
   poses
Is steeper to the angel than the child.
Chances have laws as fixed as planets
   have,
And disappointment's dry and bitter
   root,
Envy's harsh berries, and the choking
   pool
Of the world's scorn, are the right
   mother-milk
To the tough hearts that pioneer their
   kind,
And break a pathway to those unknown
   realms
That in the earth's broad shadow lie
   enthralled;

Endurance is the crowning quality,
And patience all the passion of great
    hearts ;
These are their stay, and when the
    leaden world
Sets its hard face against their fateful
    thought,
And brute strength, like the Gaulish
    conqueror,
Clangs his huge glaive down in the
    other scale,
The inspired soul but flings his pa-
    tience in,
And slowly that outweighs the ponder-
    ous globe, —
One faith against a whole earth's un-
    belief,
One soul against the flesh of all man-
    kind.

Thus ever seems it when my soul can
    hear
The voice that errs not ; then my tri-
    umph gleams,
O'er the blank ocean beckoning, and
    all night
My heart flies on before me as I sail ;
Far on I see my lifelong enterprise,
That rose like Ganges 'mid the freez-
    ing snows
Of a world's sordidness, sweep broad-
    ening down,
And, gathering to itself a thousand
    streams,
Grow sacred ere it mingle with the sea ;
I see the ungated wall of chaos old,
With blocks Cyclopean hewn of solid
    night,
Fade like a wreath of unreturning mist
Before the irreversible feet of light ; —
And lo, with what clear omen in the
    east
On day's gray threshold stands the
    eager dawn,
Like young Leander rosy from the sea
Glowing at Hero's lattice !

                  One day more
These muttering shoalbrains leave the
    helm to me :
God, let me not in their dull ooze be
    stranded ;
Let not this one frail bark, to hollow
    which

I have dug out the pith and sinewy
    heart
Of my aspiring life's fair trunk, be so
Cast up to warp and blacken in the
    sun,
Just as the opposing wind 'gins whistle
    off
His cheek-swollen mates, and from the
    leaning mast
Fortune's full sail strains forward !

                  One poor day ! —
Remember whose and not how short it
    is !
It is God's day, it is Columbus's.
A lavish day ! One day, with life and
    heart,
Is more than time enough to find a
    world.

1844.

───

AN INCIDENT OF THE FIRE
AT HAMBURG.

THE tower of old Saint Nicholas soared
    upward to the skies,
Like some huge piece of Nature's
    make, the growth of centuries ;
You could not deem its crowding spires
    a work of human art,
They seemed to struggle lightward from
    a sturdy living heart.

Not Nature's self more freely speaks in
    crystal or in oak,
Than, through the pious builder's hand,
    in that gray pile she spoke ;
And as from acorn springs the oak, so,
    freely and alone,
Sprang from his heart this hymn to
    God, sung in obedient stone.

It seemed a wondrous freak of chance,
    so perfect, yet so rough,
A whim of Nature crystallized slowly
    in granite tough ;
The thick spires yearned towards the
    sky in quaint harmonious lines,
And in broad sunlight basked and slept,
    like a grove of blasted pines.

Never did rock or stream or tree lay
    claim with better right

To all the adorning sympathies of
    shadow and of light ;
And, in that forest petrified, as forester
    there dwells
Stout Herman, the old sacristan, sole
    lord of all its bells.

Surge leaping after surge, the fire roared
    onward red as blood,
Till half of Hamburg lay engulfed be-
    neath the eddying flood ;
For miles away the fiery spray poured
    down its deadly rain,
And back and forth the billows sucked,
    and paused, and burst again.

From square to square with tiger leaps
    panted the lustful fire,
The air to leeward shuddered with the
    gasps of its desire ;
And church and palace, which even now
    stood whelmed but to the knee,
Lift their black roofs like breakers lone
    amid the whirling sea.

Up in his tower old Herman sat and
    watched with quiet look ;
His soul had trusted God too long to be
    at last forsook ;
He could not fear, for surely God a
    pathway would unfold
Through this red sea for faithful hearts,
    as once he did of old.

But scarcely can he cross himself, or on
    his good saint call,
Before the sacrilegious flood o'erleaped
    the churchyard wall ;
And, ere a *pater* half was said, 'mid
    smoke and crackling glare,
His island tower scarce juts its head
    above the wide despair.

Upon the peril's desperate peak his
    heart stood up sublime ;
His first thought was for God above, his
    next was for his chime ;
" Sing now and make your voices heard
    in hymns of praise," cried he,
" As did the Israelites of old, safe walk-
    ing through the sea !

" Through this red sea our God hath
    made the pathway safe to shore ;

Our promised land stands full in sight :
    shout now as ne'er before ! "
And as the tower came crushing down,
    the bells, in clear accord,
Pealed forth the grand old German
    hymn, — " All good souls, praise
    the Lord ! "

THE SOWER.

I SAW a Sower walking slow
Across the earth, from east to west ;
His hair was white as mountain snow,
His head drooped forward on his breast.

With shrivelled hands he flung his seed,
Nor ever turned to look behind ;
Of sight or sound he took no heed ;
It seemed he was both deaf and blind.

His dim face showed no soul beneath,
Yet in my heart I felt a stir,
As if I looked upon the sheath
That once had held Excalibur.

I heard, as still the seed he cast,
How, crooning to himself, he sung, —
" I sow again the holy Past,
The happy days when I was young.

" Then all was wheat without a tare,
Then all was righteous, fair, and true ;
And I am he whose thoughtful care
Shall plant the Old World in the New.

" The fruitful germs I scatter free,
With busy hand, while all men sleep ;
In Europe now, from sea to sea,
The nations bless me as they reap."

Then I looked back along his path,
And heard the clash of steel on steel,
Where man faced man, in deadly wrath,
While clanged the tocsin's hurrying peal.

The sky with burning towns flared red,
Nearer the noise of fighting rolled,
And brothers' blood, by brothers shed,
Crept, curdling, over pavements cold.

Then marked I how each germ of truth
Which through the dotard's fingers ran

Was mated with a dragon's tooth
Whence there sprang up an armèd man.

I shouted, but he could not hear;
Made signs, but these he could not see;
And still, without a doubt or fear,
Broadcast he scattered anarchy.

Long to my straining ears the blast
Brought faintly back the words he
    sung :—
"I sow again the holy Past,
The happy days when I was young."

HUNGER AND COLD.

SISTERS two, all praise to you,
With your faces pinched and blue;
To the poor man you 've been true
    From of old :
You can speak the keenest word,
You are sure of being heard,
From the point you 're never stirred,
    Hunger and Cold !

Let sleek statesmen temporize;
Palsied are their shifts and lies
When they meet your bloodshot eyes,
    Grim and bold ;
Policy you set at naught,
In their traps you 'll not be caught,
You 're too honest to be bought,
    Hunger and Cold !

Bolt and bar the palace door ;
While the mass of men are poor,
Naked truth grows more and more
    Uncontrolled ;
You had never yet, I guess,
Any praise for bashfulness,
You can visit sans court-dress,
    Hunger and Cold !

While the music fell and rose,
And the dance reeled to its close,
Where her round of costly woes
    Fashion strolled,
I beheld with shuddering fear
Wolves' eyes through the windows peer;
Little dream they you are near,
    Hunger and Cold !

When the toiler's heart you clutch,
Conscience is not valued much,
He recks not a bloody smutch
    On his gold :
Everything to you defers,
You are potent reasoners,
At your whisper Treason stirs,
    Hunger and Cold !

Rude comparisons you draw,
Words refuse to sate your maw,
Your gaunt limbs the cobweb law
    Cannot hold :
You 're not clogged with foolish pride,
But can seize a right denied :
Somehow God is on your side,
    Hunger and Cold !

You respect no hoary wrong
More for having triumphed long ;
Its past victims, haggard throng,
    From the mould
You unbury : swords and spears
Weaker are than poor men's tears,
Weaker than your silent years,
    Hunger and Cold !

Let them guard both hall and bower;
Through the window you will glower,
Patient till your reckoning hour
    Shall be tolled :
Cheeks are pale, but hands are red,
Guiltless blood may chance be shed,
But ye must and will be fed,
    Hunger and Cold !

God has plans man must not spoil,
Some were made to starve and toil,
Some to share the wine and oil,
    We are told :
Devil's theories are these,
Stifling hope and love and peace,
Framed your hideous lusts to please,
    Hunger and Cold !

Scatter ashes on thy head,
Tears of burning sorrow shed,
Earth ! and be by Pity led
    To Love's fold ;
Ere they block the very door
With lean corpses of the poor,
And will hush for naught but gore,
    Hunger and Cold !

1844.

THE LANDLORD.

WHAT boot your houses and your lands?
  In spite of close-drawn deed and
      fence,
Like water, 'twixt your cheated hands,
  They slip into the graveyard's sands
    And mock your ownership's pretence.

How shall you speak to urge your right,
  Choked with that soil for which you
      lust?
The bit of clay, for whose delight
You grasp, is mortgaged, too ; Death
      might
    Foreclose this very day in dust.

Fence as you please, this plain poor
      man,
  Whose only fields are in his wit,
Who shapes the world, as best he can,
According to God's higher plan,
  Owns you, and fences as is fit.

Though yours the rents, his incomes
      wax
  By right of eminent domain ;
From factory tall to woodman's axe,
All things on earth must pay their tax,
  To feed his hungry heart and brain.

He takes you from your easy-chair,
  And what he plans that you must do ;
You sleep in down, eat dainty fare, —
He mounts his crazy garret-stair
  And starves, the landlord over you.

Feeding the clods your idlesse drains,
  You make more green six feet of soil ;
His fruitful word, like suns and rains,
Partakes the seasons' bounteous pains,
  And toils to lighten human toil.

Your lands, with force or cunning got,
  Shrink to the measure of the grave ;
But Death himself abridges not
The tenures of almighty thought,
  The titles of the wise and brave.

————

TO A PINE-TREE.

FAR up on Katahdin thou towerest,
  Purple-blue with the distance and
      vast ;

Like a cloud o'er the lowlands thou
      lowerest,
  That hangs poised on a lull in the
      blast,
    To its fall leaning awful.

In the storm, like a prophet o'ermad-
      dened,
  Thou singest and tossest thy branch-
      es ;
Thy heart with the terror is gladdened,
  Thou forebodest the dread avalanch-
      es,
    When whole mountains swoop
      valeward.

In the calm thou o'erstretchest the val-
      leys
  With thine arms, as if blessings im-
      ploring,
Like an old king led forth from his
      palace,
  When his people to battle are pour-
      ing
    From the city beneath him.

To the slumberer asleep 'neath thy
      glooming
  Thou dost sing of wild billows in
      motion,
Till he longs to be swung 'mid their
      booming
  In the tents of the Arabs of ocean,
    Whose finned isles are their
      cattle.

For the gale snatches thee for his lyre,
  With mad hand crashing melody
      frantic,
While he pours forth his mighty de-
      sire
  To leap down on the eager Atlantic,
    Whose arms stretch to his play-
      mate.

The wild storm makes his lair in thy
      branches,
  Swooping thence on the continent
      under ;
Like a lion, crouched close on his
      haunches,
  There awaiteth his leap the fierce
      thunder,
    Growling low with impatience.

Spite of winter, thou keep'st thy green
glory,
  Lusty father of Titans past number !
The snow-flakes alone make thee hoary,
  Nestling close to thy branches in
    slumber,
    And thee mantling with silence.

Thou alone know'st the splendor of
  winter,
  'Mid thy snow-silvered, hushed pre-
    cipices,
Hearing crags of green ice groan and
  splinter,
  And then plunge down the muffled
    abysses
    In the quiet of midnight.

Thou alone know'st the glory of sum-
  mer,
  Gazing down on thy broad seas of
    forest,
On thy subjects that send a proud mur-
  mur
  Up to thee, to their sachem, who
    toweréd
    From thy bleak throne to heaven.

SI DESCENDERO IN INFER-
NUM, ADES.

O, WANDERING dim on the extremest
  edge
  Of God's bright providence, whose
    spirits sigh
Drearily in you, like the winter sedge
  That shivers o'er the dead pool stiff
    and dry,
  A thin, sad voice, when the bold wind
    roars by
    From the clear North of Duty, —
Still by cracked arch and broken shaft
  I trace
That here was once a shrine and holy
  place
  Of the supernal Beauty,
  A child's play-altar reared of stones
    and moss,
  With wilted flowers for offering laid
    across,
Mute recognition of the all-ruling Grace.

How far are ye from the innocent, from
  those
  Whose hearts are as a little lane
    serene,
Smooth-heaped from wall to wall with
  unbroke snows,
  Or in the summer blithe with lamb-
    cropped green,
  Save the one track, where naught
    more rude is seen
    Than the plump wain at even
Bringing home four months' sunshine
  bound in sheaves !
How far are ye from those ! yet who
  believes
  That ye can shut out heaven ?
  Your souls partake its influence, not
    in vain
Nor all unconscious, as that silent lane
  Its drift of noiseless apple-blooms re-
    ceives.

Looking within myself, I note how thin
  A plank of station, chance, or pros-
    perous fate,
Doth fence me from the clutching
  waves of sin ;
  In my own heart I find the worst
    man's mate,
  And see not dimly the smooth-hingéd
    gate
Where ye grope darkly, — ye who never
  knew
On your young hearts love's consecrat-
  ing dew,
  Or felt a mother's kisses,
  Or home's restraining tendrils round
    you curled ;
  Ah, side by side with heart's-ease in
    this world
The fatal nightshade grows and bitter
  rue !

One band ye cannot break, — the force
  that clips
  And grasps your circles to the central
    light ;
Yours is the prodigal comet's long el-
  lipse,
  Self-exiled to the farthest verge of
    night ;
  Yet strives with you no less that
    inward might
    No sin hath e'er imbruted

The god in you the creed-dimmed eye
　　eludes;
The Law brooks not to have its solitudes
　　By bigot feet polluted;
Yet they who watch your God-com-
　　pelled return
May see your happy perihelion burn
Where the calm sun his unfledged
　　planets broods.

TO THE PAST.

WONDROUS and awful are thy silent
　　halls,
　　O kingdom of the past!
There lie the bygone ages in their palls,
　　Guarded by shadows vast,—
　　There all is hushed and breathless,
Save when some image of old error falls
Earth worshipped once as deathless.

There sits drear Egypt, 'mid beleaguer-
　　ing sands,
　　Half woman and half beast,
The burnt-out torch within her moul-
　　dering hands
　　That once lit all the East:
　　A dotard bleared and hoary,
There Asser crouches o'er the black-
　　ened brands
Of Asia's long-quenched glory.

Still as a city buried 'neath the sea
　　Thy courts and temples stand;
Idle as forms on wind-waved tapestry
　　Of saints and heroes grand,
Thy phantasms grope and shiver,
Or watch the loose shores crumbling
　　silently
Into Time's gnawing river.

Titanic shapes with faces blank and dun,
　　Of their old godhead lorn,
Gaze on the embers of the sunken sun,
　　Which they misdeem for morn;
　　And yet the eternal sorrow
In their unmonarched eyes says day is
　　done
Without the hope of morrow.

O realm of silence and of swart eclipse,
　　The shapes that haunt thy gloom

Make signs to us and move thy with-
　　ered lips
　　Across the gulf of doom;
　　Yet all their sound and motion
Bring no more freight to us than wraiths
　　of ships
On the mirage's ocean.

And if sometimes a moaning wandereth
　　From out thy desolate halls,
If some grim shadow of thy living death
　　Across thy sunshine falls
　　And scares the world to error,
The eternal life sends forth melodious
　　breath
To chase the misty terror.

Thy mighty clamors, wars, and world-
　　noised deeds
　　Are silent now in dust,
Gone like a tremble of the huddling
　　reeds
　　Beneath some sudden gust;
Thy forms and creeds have vanished,
Tossed out to wither like unsightly
　　weeds
From the world's garden banished.

Whatever of true life there was in thee
　　Leaps in our age's veins;
Wield still thy bent and wrinkled em-
　　pery,
　　And shake thine idle chains;—
　　To thee thy dross is clinging,
For us thy martyrs die, thy prophets see,
　　Thy poets still are singing.

Here, 'mid the bleak waves of our strife
　　and care,
　　Float the green Fortunate Isles
Where all thy hero-spirits dwell, and
　　share
　　Our martyrdoms and toils;
　　The present moves attended
With all of brave and excellent and fair
That made the old time splendid.

TO THE FUTURE.

O LAND of Promise! from what Pis-
　　gah's height
　　Can I behold thy stretch of peaceful
　　bowers,

Thy golden harvests flowing out of sight,
  Thy nestled homes and sun-illumined
      towers?
  Gazing upon the sunset's high-heaped
      gold,
Its crags of opal and of chrysolite,
  Its deeps on deeps of glory, that un-
      fold
      Still brightening abysses,
      And blazing precipices,
Whence but a scanty leap it seems to
      heaven,
      Sometimes a glimpse is given
Of thy more gorgeous realm, thy more
      unstinted blisses.

O Land of Quiet! to thy shore the surf
  Of the perturbed Present rolls and
      sleeps;
Our storms breathe soft as June upon
      thy turf
  And lure out blossoms; to thy bosom
      leaps,
As to a mother's, the o'erwearied heart,
Hearing far off and dim the toiling
      mart,
  The hurrying feet, the curses without
      number,
  And, circled with the glow Elysian
      Of thine exulting vision,
Out of its very cares woos charms for
      peace and slumber.

To thee the earth lifts up her fettered
      hands
  And cries for vengeance; with a pity-
      ing smile
Thou blessest her, and she forgets her
      bands,
  And her old woe-worn face a little
      while
Grows young and noble; unto thee the
      Oppressor
  Looks, and is dumb with awe;
  The eternal law,
Which makes the crime its own blind-
      fold redresser,
Shadows his heart with perilous fore-
      boding,
  And he can see the grim-eyed
      Doom
  From out the trembling gloom
Its silent-footed steeds towards his pal-
      ace goading.

What promises hast thou for Poets'
      eyes,
  Aweary of the turmoil and the wrong!
To all their hopes what overjoyed re-
      plies!
  What undreamed ecstasies for bliss-
      ful song!
Thy happy plains no war-trump's brawl-
      ing clangor
  Disturbs, and fools the poor to hate
      the poor;
The humble glares not on the high with
      anger;
  Love leaves no grudge at less, no
      greed for more;
In vain strives Self the godlike sense to
      smother;
      From the soul's deeps
      It throbs and leaps;
The noble 'neath foul rags beholds his
      long-lost brother.

To thee the Martyr looketh, and his
      fires
  Unlock their fangs and leave his spirit
      free;
To thee the Poet 'mid his toil aspires,
  And grief and hunger climb about his
      knee;
Welcome as children; thou upholdest
  The lone Inventor by his demon
      haunted;
The Prophet cries to thee when hearts
      are coldest,
  And gazing o'er the midnight's
      bleak abyss,
      Sees the drowsed soul awaken at
      thy kiss,
And stretch its happy arms and leap up
      disenchanted.

Thou bringest vengeance, but so lov-
      ing-kindly
  The guilty thinks it pity; taught by
      thee,
Fierce tyrants drop the scourges where-
      with blindly
  Their own souls they were scarring;
      conquerors see
With horror in their hands the accursed
      spear
  That tore the meek One's side on
      Calvary,

And from their trophies shrink with
    ghastly fear;
    Thou, too, art the Forgiver,
The beauty of man's soul to man re-
    vealing;
    The arrows from thy quiver
Pierce Error's guilty heart, but only
    pierce for healing.

O, whither, whither, glory-wingèd
    dreams,
    From out Life's sweat and turmoil
        would ye bear me?
Shut, gates of Fancy, on your golden
    gleams, —
    This agony of hopeless contrast spare
        me!
Fade, cheating glow, and leave me to
    my night!
    He is a coward, who would borrow
    A charm against the present sorrow
From the vague Future's promise of
    delight:
    As life's alarums nearer roll,
    The ancestral buckler calls,
    Self-clanging from the walls
In the high temple of the soul;
Where are most sorrows, there the po-
    et's sphere is,
    To feed the soul with patience,
    To heal its desolations
With words of unshorn truth, with love
    that never wearies.

HEBE.

I SAW the twinkle of white feet,
I saw the flash of robes descending;
Before her ran an influence fleet,
That bowed my heart like barley bend-
    ing.

As, in bare fields, the searching bees
Pilot to blooms beyond our finding,
It led me on, by sweet degrees
Joy's simple honey-cells unbinding.

Those Graces were that seemed grim
    Fates;
With nearer love the sky leaned o'er me;
The long-sought Secret's golden gates
On musical hinges swung before me.

I saw the brimmed bowl in her grasp
Thrilling with godhood; like a lover
I sprang the proffered life to clasp; —
The beaker fell; the luck was over.

The Earth has drunk the vintage up;
What boots it patch the goblet's splin-
    ters?
Can Summer fill the icy cup,
Whose treacherous crystal is but Win-
    ter's?

O spendthrift, haste! await the Gods;
Their nectar crowns the lips of Pa-
    tience;
Haste scatters on unthankful sods
The immortal gift in vain libations.

Coy Hebe flies from those that woo,
And shuns the hands would seize upon
    her;
Follow thy life, and she will sue
To pour for thee the cup of honor.

THE SEARCH.

I WENT to seek for Christ,
    And Nature seemed so fair
That first the woods and fields my youth
    enticed,
    And I was sure to find him there:
    The temple I forsook,
    And to the solitude
Allegiance paid; but Winter came and
    shook
    The crown and purple from my
        wood;
His snows, like desert sands, with
    scornful drift,
    Besieged the columned aisle and pal-
        ace-gate;
My Thebes, cut deep with many a sol-
    emn rift,
    But epitaphed her own sepulchred
        state:
Then I remembered whom I went to
    seek,
And blessed blunt Winter for his coun-
    sel bleak.

    Back to the world I turned,
        For Christ, I said, is King;

So the cramped alley and the hut I
    spurned,
  As far beneath his sojourning:
    'Mid power and wealth I sought,
    But found no trace of him,
And all the costly offerings I had
    brought
  With sudden rust and mould grew
    dim:
I found his tomb, indeed, where, by
    their laws,
  All must on stated days themselves
    imprison,
Mocking with bread a dead creed's
    grinning jaws,
  Witless how long the life had thence
    arisen;
Due sacrifice to this they set apart,
  Prizing it more than Christ's own living
    heart.

    So from my feet the dust
    Of the proud World I shook;
Then came dear Love and shared with
    me his crust,
  And half my sorrow's burden took.
    After the World's soft bed,
    Its rich and dainty fare,
Like down seemed Love's coarse pil-
    low to my head,
    His cheap food seemed as manna
    rare;
Fresh-trodden prints of bare and bleed-
    ing feet,
  Turned to the heedless city whence I
    came,
Hard by I saw, and springs of worship
    sweet
  Gushed from my cleft heart smitten
    by the same;
Love looked me in the face and spake
    no words,
But straight I knew those footprints
    were the Lord's.

    I followed where they led
    And in a hovel rude,
With naught to fence the weather from
    his head,
    The King I sought for meekly stood;
    A naked, hungry child
    Clung round his gracious knee,
And a poor hunted slave looked up and
    smiled

    To bless the smile that set him free;
New miracles I saw his presence do, —
  No more I knew the hovel bare and
    poor,
The gathered chips into a woodpile
    grew,
  The broken morsel swelled to goodly
    store;
I knelt and wept: my Christ no more
    I seek,
His throne is with the outcast and the
    weak.

———

THE PRESENT CRISIS.

WHEN a deed is done for Freedom,
    through the broad earth's aching
    breast
Runs a thrill of joy prophetic, trembling
    on from east to west,
And the slave, where'er he cowers, feels
    the soul within him climb
To the awful verge of manhood, as the
    energy sublime
Of a century bursts full-blossomed on
    the thorny stem of Time.

Through the walls of hut and palace
    shoots the instantaneous throe,
When the travail of the Ages wrings
    earth's systems to and fro;
At the birth of each new Era, with a
    recognizing start,
Nation wildly looks at nation, standing
    with mute lips apart,
And glad Truth's yet mightier man-
    child leaps beneath the Future's
    heart.

So the Evil's triumph sendeth, with a
    terror and a chill,
Under continent to continent, the sense
    of coming ill,
And the slave, where'er he cowers, feels
    his sympathies with God
In hot tear-drops ebbing earthward, to
    be drunk up by the sod,
Till a corpse crawls round unburied,
    delving in the nobler clod.

For mankind are one in spirit, and an
    instinct bears along,
Round the earth's electric circle, the
    swift flash of right or wrong;

Whether conscious or unconscious, yet
    Humanity's vast frame
Through its ocean-sundered fibres feels
    the gush of joy or shame ; —
In the gain or loss of one race all the
    rest have equal claim.

Once to every man and nation comes
    the moment to decide,
In the strife of Truth with Falsehood,
    for the good or evil side ;
Some great cause, God's new Messiah,
    offering each the bloom or blight,
Parts the goats upon the left hand, and
    the sheep upon the right,
And the choice goes by forever 'twixt
    that darkness and that light.

Hast thou chosen, O my people, on
    whose party thou shalt stand,
Ere the Doom from its worn sandals
    shakes the dust against our land ?
Though the cause of Evil prosper, yet
    't is Truth alone is strong,
And, albeit she wander outcast now, I
    see around her throng
Troops of beautiful, tall angels, to en-
    shield her from all wrong.

Backward look across the ages and the
    beacon-moments see,
That, like peaks of some sunk conti-
    tinent, jut through Oblivion's sea ;
Not an ear in court or market for the
    low foreboding cry
Of those Crises, God's stern winnowers,
    from whose feet earth's chaff must
    fly ;
Never shows the choice momentous till
    the judgment hath passed by.

Careless seems the great Avenger ; his-
    tory's pages but record
One death-grapple in the darkness
    'twixt old systems and the Word ;
Truth forever on the scaffold, Wrong
    forever on the throne, —
Yet that scaffold sways the future, and,
    behind the dim unknown,
Standeth God within the shadow, keep-
    ing watch above his own.

We see dimly in the Present what is
    small and what is great,
Slow of faith, how weak an arm may
    turn the iron helm of fate,

But the soul is still oracular ; amid the
    market's din,
List the ominous stern whisper from
    the Delphic cave within, —
"They enslave their children's chil-
    dren who make compromise with
    sin."

Slavery, the earth-born Cyclops, fellest
    of the giant brood,
Sons of brutish Force and Darkness,
    who have drenched the earth with
    blood,
Famished in his self-made desert, blind-
    ed by our purer day,
Gropes in yet unblasted regions for his
    miserable prey ; —
Shall we guide his gory fingers where
    our helpless children play ?

Then to side with Truth is noble when
    we share her wretched crust,
Ere her cause bring fame and profit,
    and 't is prosperous to be just ;
Then it is the brave man chooses, while
    the coward stands aside,
Doubting in his abject spirit, till his
    Lord is crucified,
And the multitude make virtue of the
    faith they had denied.

Count me o'er earth's chosen heroes, —
    they were souls that stood alone,
While the men they agonized for hurled
    the contumelious stone,
Stood serene, and down the future saw
    the golden beam incline
To the side of perfect justice, mastered
    by their faith divine,
By one man's plain truth to manhood
    and to God's supreme design.

By the light of burning heretics Christ's
    bleeding feet I track,
Toiling up new Calvaries ever with the
    cross that turns not back,
And these mounts of anguish number
    how each generation learned
One new word of that grand *Credo*
    which in prophet-hearts hath
    burned
Since the first man stood God-con-
    quered with his face to heaven up-
    turned.

For Humanity sweeps onward : where
    to-day the martyr stands,
On the morrow crouches Judas with the
    silver in his hands ;
Far in front the cross stands ready and
    the crackling fagots burn,
While the hooting mob of yesterday in
    silent awe return
To glean up the scattered ashes into
    History's golden urn.

'T is as easy to be heroes as to sit the
    idle slaves
Of a legendary virtue carved upon our
    fathers' graves,
Worshippers of light ancestral make
    the present light a crime ; —
Was the Mayflower launched by cow-
    ards, steered by men behind their
    time ?
Turn those tracks toward Past or
    Future, that make Plymouth rock
    sublime ?

They were men of present valor, stal-
    wart old iconoclasts,
Unconvinced by axe or gibbet that all
    virtue was the Past's ;
But we make their truth our falsehood,
    thinking that hath made us free,
Hoarding it in mouldy parchments,
    while our tender spirits flee
The rude grasp of that great Impulse
    which drove them across the sea.

They have rights who dare maintain
    them ; we are traitors to our sires,
Smothering in their holy ashes Free-
    dom's new-lit altar fires ;
Shall we make their creed our jailer ?
    Shall we, in our haste to slay,
From the tombs of the old prophets
    steal the funeral lamps away
To light up the martyr-fagots round
    the prophets of to-day ?

New occasions teach new duties ; Time
    makes ancient good uncouth ;
They must upward still, and onward,
    who would keep abreast of Truth;
Lo, before us gleam her camp-fires ! we
    ourselves must Pilgrims be,

Launch our Mayflower, and steer bold-
    ly through the desperate winter
    sea,
Nor attempt the Future's portal with
    the Past's blood-rusted key.
December, 1844.

AN INDIAN-SUMMER REV-
ERIE.

WHAT visionary tints the year puts
    on,
When falling leaves falter through
    motionless air
    Or numbly cling and shiver to be
      gone !
How shimmer the low flats and pas-
    tures bare,
    As with her nectar Hebe Autumn
      fills
    The bowl between me and those
      distant hills,
And smiles and shakes abroad her
    misty, tremulous hair !

No more the landscape holds its
    wealth apart,
Making me poorer in my poverty,
    But mingles with my senses and
      my heart ;
My own projected spirit seems to me
    In her own reverie the world to
      steep ;
    'T is she that waves to sympathetic
      sleep,
Moving, as she is moved, each field
    and hill and tree.

How fuse and mix, with what un-
    felt degrees,
Clasped by the faint horizon's languid
    arms,
    Each into each, the hazy distances !
The softened season all the landscape
    charms ;
    Those hills, my native village that
      embay,
    In waves of dreamier purple roll
      away,
And floating in mirage seem all the
    glimmering farms.

Far distant sounds the hidden
    chickadee
Close at my side ; far distant sound
    the leaves ;
    The fields seem fields of dream,
        where Memory
Wanders like gleaning Ruth ; and as
    the sheaves
    Of wheat and barley wavered in
        the eye
    Of Boaz as the maiden's glow went
        by,
So tremble and seem remote all things
    the sense receives.

The cock's shrill trump that tells
    of scattered corn,
Passed breezily on by all his flapping
    mates,
    Faint and more faint, from barn to
        barn is borne,
Southward, perhaps to far Magellan's
    Straits ;
    Dimly I catch the throb of distant
        flails ;
    Silently overhead the hen-hawk
        sails,
With watchful, measuring eye, and for
    his quarry waits.

The sobered robin, hunger-silent
    now,
Seeks cedar-berries blue, his autumn
    cheer ;
    The chipmunk, on the shingly
        shagbark's bough,
Now saws, now lists with downward
    eye and ear,
    Then drops his nut, and, cheeping,
        with a bound
    Whisks to his winding fastness
        underground ;
The clouds like swans drift down the
    streaming atmosphere.

O'er yon bare knoll the pointed
    cedar shadows
Drowse on the crisp, gray moss ; the
    ploughman's call
    Creeps faint as smoke from black,
        fresh-furrowed meadows ;
The single crow a single caw lets fall ;
    And all around me every bush and
        tree

Says Autumn 's here, and Winter
    soon will be,
Who snows his soft, white sleep and
    silence over all.

The birch, most shy and ladylike
    of trees,
    Her poverty, as best she may, re-
        trieves,
    And hints at her foregone gen-
        tilities
With some saved relics of her wealth
    of leaves ;
    The swamp-oak, with his royal
        purple on,
    Glares red as blood across the sink-
        ing sun,
As one who proudlier to a falling for-
    tune cleaves.

He looks a sachem, in red blanket
    wrapt,
Who, 'mid some council of the sad-
    garbed whites,
    Erect and stern, in his own memo-
        ries lapt,
    With distant eye broods over other
        sights,
    Sees the hushed wood the city's
        flare replace,
    The wounded turf heal o'er the
        railway's trace,
And roams the savage Past of his un-
    dwindled rights.

The red-oak, softer-grained, yields
    all for lost,
And, with his crumpled foliage stiff
    and dry,
    After the first betrayal of the frost,
Rebuffs the kiss of the relenting sky ;
    The chestnuts, lavish of their long-
        hid gold,
    To the faint Summer, beggared
        now and old,
Pour back the sunshine hoarded 'neath
    her favoring eye.

The ash her purple drops forgiv-
    ingly
And sadly, breaking not the general
    hush ;
    The maple-swamps glow like a
        sunset sea,
    Each leaf a ripple with its separate
        flush ;

All round the wood's edge creeps
　　the skirting blaze
Of bushes low, as when, on cloudy
　　days,
Ere the rain fall, the cautious farmer
　　burns his brush.

O'er yon low wall, which guards
　　one unkempt zone,
Where vines, and weeds, and scrub-
　　oaks intertwine
Safe from the plough, whose rough,
　　discordant stone
Is massed to one soft gray by lichens
　　fine,
The tangled blackberry, crossed
　　and recrossed, weaves
A prickly network of ensanguined
　　leaves :
Hard by, with coral beads, the prim
　　black-alders shine.

Pillaring with flame this crumbling
　　boundary,
Whose loose blocks topple 'neath the
　　ploughboy's foot,
Who, with each sense shut fast ex-
　　cept the eye,
Creeps close and scares the jay he
　　hoped to shoot,
The woodbine up the elm's straight
　　stem aspires,
Coiling it, harmless, with autumnal
　　fires ;
In the ivy's paler blaze the martyr oak
　　stands mute.

Below, the Charles — a stripe of
　　nether sky,
Now hid by rounded apple-trees be-
　　tween,
Whose gaps the misplaced sail
　　sweeps bellying by,
Now flickering golden through a
　　woodland screen,
Then spreading out, at his next
　　turn beyond,
A silver circle like an inland
　　pond —
Slips seaward silently through marshes
　　purple and green.

Dear marshes ! vain to him the
　　gift of sight
Who cannot in their various incomes
　　share,
From every season drawn, of shade
　　and light,
Who sees in them but levels brown
　　and bare ;
Each change of storm or sunshine
　　scatters free
On them its largess of variety,
For Nature with cheap means still
　　works her wonders rare.

In Spring they lie one broad ex-
　　panse of green,
O'er which the light winds run with
　　glimmering feet ;
Here, yellower stripes track out
　　the creek unseen,
There, darker growths o'er hidden
　　ditches meet ;
And purpler stains show where the
　　blossoms crowd,
As if the silent shadow of a cloud
Hung there becalmed, with the next
　　breath to fleet.

All round, upon the river's slip-
　　pery edge,
Witching to deeper calm the drowsy
　　tide,
Whispers and leans the breeze-
　　entangling sedge ;
Through emerald glooms the linger-
　　ing waters slide,
Or, sometimes wavering, throw
　　back the sun,
And the stiff banks in eddies melt
　　and run
Of dimpling light, and with the cur-
　　rent seem to glide.

In Summer 't is a blithesome sight
　　to see,
As, step by step, with measured
　　swing, they pass,
The wide-ranked mowers wading
　　to the knee,
Their sharp scythes panting through
　　the wiry grass ;
Then, stretched beneath a rick's
　　shade in a ring,
Their nooning take, while one be-
　　gins to sing
A stave that droops and dies 'neath the
　　close sky of brass.

Meanwhile that devil-may-care, the
    bobolink,
Remembering duty, in mid-quaver
    stops
    Just ere he sweeps o'er rapture's
      tremulous brink,
And 'twixt the winrows most de-
      murely drops,
    A decorous bird of business, who
      provides
For his brown mate and fledglings
    six besides,
And looks from right to left, a farmer
    'mid his crops.

Another change subdues them in
    the Fall,
But saddens not; they still show
    merrier tints,
    Though sober russet seems to cover
      all;
When the first sunshine through their
      dew-drops glints,
    Look how the yellow clearness,
      streamed across,
Redeems with rarer hues the sea-
    son's loss,
As Dawn's feet there had touched and
    left their rosy prints.

Or come when sunset gives its
    freshened zest,
Lean o'er the bridge and let the
    ruddy thrill,
    While the shorn sun swells down
      the hazy west,
Glow opposite; — the marshes drink
      their fill
    And swoon with purple veins, then
      slowly fade
Through pink to brown, as east-
      ward moves the shade,
Lengthening with stealthy creep, of Si-
    mond's darkening hill.

Later, and yet ere Winter wholly
    shuts,
Ere through the first dry snow the
    runner grates,
    And the loath cart-wheel screams
      in slippery ruts,
While firmer ice the eager boy awaits,
    Trying each buckle and strap be-
      side the fire,

And until bedtime plays with his
    desire,
Twenty times putting on and off his
    new-bought skates; —

Then, every morn, the river's banks
    shine bright
With smooth plate-armor, treacher-
    ous and frail,
    By the frost's clinking hammers
      forged at night,
'Gainst which the lances of the sun
      prevail,
    Giving a pretty emblem of the day
    When guiltier arms in light shall
      melt away,
And states shall move free-limbed,
    loosed from war's cramping mail.

And now those waterfalls the ebb-
    ing river
Twice every day creates on either
    side
    Tinkle, as through their fresh-
      sparred grots they shiver
In grass-arched channels to the sun
    denied;
    High flaps in sparkling blue the
      far-heard crow,
    The silvered flats gleam frostily
      below,
Suddenly drops the gull and breaks the
    glassy tide.

But crowned in turn by vying sea-
    sons three,
Their winter halo hath a fuller ring;
    This glory seems to rest immova-
      bly, —
The others were too fleet and vanish-
    ing;
    When the hid tide is at its highest
      flow,
    O'er marsh and stream one breath-
      less trance of snow
With brooding fulness awes and hushes
    everything.

The sunshine seems blown off by
    the bleak wind,
As pale as formal candles lit by day;
    Gropes to the sea the river dumb
    and blind;

The brown ricks, snow-thatched by
    the storm in play,
  Show pearly breakers combing o'er
    their lee,
    White crests as of some just en-
      chanted sea,
Checked in their maddest leap and
    hanging poised midway.

    But when the eastern blow, with
      rain aslant,
From mid-sea's prairies green and
    rolling plains
    Drives in his wallowing herds of
      billows gaunt,
  And the roused Charles remembers
    in his veins
    Old Ocean's blood and snaps his
      gyves of frost,
    That tyrannous silence on the
      shores is tost
In dreary wreck, and crumbling deso-
    lation reigns.

    Edgewise or flat, in Druid-like de-
      vice,
  With leaden pools between or gullies
    bare,
    The blocks lie strewn, a bleak
      Stonehenge of ice ;
No life, no sound, to break the grim
    despair,
    Save sullen plunge, as through the
      sedges stiff
    Down crackles riverward some
      thaw-sapped cliff,
Or when the close-wedged fields of ice
    crunch here and there.

    But let me turn from fancy-pic-
      tured scenes
To that whose pastoral calm before
    me lies :
    Here nothing harsh or rugged in-
      tervenes ;
  The early evening with her misty
    dyes
    Smooths off the ravelled edges of
      the nigh,
    Relieves the distant with her cool-
      er sky,
And tones the landscape down, and
    soothes the wearied eyes.

    There gleams my native village,
      dear to me,
Though higher change's waves each
    day are seen,
    Whelming fields famed in boy-
      hood's history,
Sanding with houses the diminished
    green ;
    There, in red brick, which soften-
      ing time defies,
    Stand square and stiff the Muses'
      factories ; —
How with my life knit up is every well-
    known scene !

    Flow on, dear river ! not alone you
    flow
To outward sight, and through your
    marshes wind ;
    Fed from the mystic springs of
      long-ago,
Your twin flows silent through my
    world of mind :
    Grow dim, dear marshes, in the
      evening's gray !
    Before my inner sight ye stretch
      away,
And will forever, though these fleshly
    eyes grow blind.

    Beyond the hillock's house-bespot-
      ted swell,
  Where Gothic chapels house the
    horse and chaise,
    Where quiet cits in Grecian tem-
      ples dwell,
  Where Coptic tombs resound with
    prayer and praise,
    Where dust and mud the equal
      year divide,
    There gentle Allston lived, and
      wrought, and died,
Transfiguring street and shop with his
    illumined gaze.

    Virgilium vidi tantum, — I have
      seen
But as a boy, who looks alike on all,
    That misty hair, that fine Undine-
    like mien,
Tremulous as down the feeling's
    faintest call ; —
    Ah, dear old homestead ! count it
      to thy fame

That thither many times the Painter came ; —
One elm yet bears his name, a feathery
tree and tall.

Swiftly the present fades in memo-
ry's glow, —
Our only sure possession is the past ;
   The village blacksmith died a
      month ago,
   And dim to me the forge's roaring
      blast ;
      Soon fire-new mediævals we shall
         see
      Oust the black smithy from its
         chestnut-tree,
And that hewn down, perhaps, the bee-
hive green and vast.

How many times, prouder than
   king on throne,
Loosed from the village school-
   dame's A's and B's,
      Panting have I the creaking bel-
         lows blown,
      And watched the pent volcano's red
         increase,
      Then paused to see the ponderous
         sledge, brought down
      By that hard arm voluminous and
         brown,
From the white iron swarm its golden
vanishing bees.

Dear native town ! whose choking
   elms each year
With eddying dust before their time
   turn gray,
   Pining for rain, — to me thy dust is
      dear ;
   It glorifies the eve of summer day,
      And when the westering sun half
         sunken burns,
      The mote-thick air to deepest
         orange turns,
The westward horseman rides through
clouds of gold away,

So palpable, I 've seen those unshorn few,
The six old willows at the causey's
   end

(Such trees Paul Potter never
   dreamed nor drew),
Through this dry mist their checker-
   ing shadows send,
      Striped, here and there, with many
         a long-drawn thread,
      Where streamed through leafy
         chinks the trembling red,
Past which, in one bright trail, the
hangbird's flashes blend.

Yes, dearer far thy dust than all
   that e'er,
Beneath the awarded crown of victory,
   Gilded the blown Olympic chariot-
      eer ;
   Though lightly prized the ribboned
      parchments three,
      Yet *collegisse juvat*, I am glad
      That here what colleging was mine
         I had, —
It linked another tie, dear native town,
   with thee !

Nearer art thou than simply native
   earth,
My dust with thine concedes a deep-
   er tie ;
   A closer claim thy soil may well
      put forth,
   Something of kindred more than
      sympathy ;
      For in thy bounds I reverently laid
         away
      That blinding anguish of forsaken
         clay,
That title I seemed to have in earth
   and sea and sky,

That portion of my life more choice
   to me
(Though brief, yet in itself so round
   and whole)
   Than all the imperfect residue can
      be ; —
   The Artist saw his statue of the soul
      Was perfect ; so, with one regret-
         ful stroke,
      The earthen model into fragments
         broke,
And without her the impoverished
   seasons roll.

THE GROWTH OF THE LEGEND.

A FRAGMENT.

A LEGEND that grew in the forest's hush
Slowly as tear-drops gather and gush,
When a word some poet chanced to say
Ages ago, in his careless way,
Brings our youth back to us out of its
    shroud
Clearly as under yon thunder-cloud
I see that white sea-gull. It grew and
    grew,
From the pine-trees gathering a sombre
    hue,
Till it seems a mere murmur out of the
    vast
Norwegian forests of the past ;
And it grew itself like a true Northern
    pine,
First a little slender line,
Like a mermaid's green eyelash, and
    then anon
A stem that a tower might rest upon,
Standing spear-straight in the waist-
    deep moss,
Its bony roots clutching around and
    across,
As if they would tear up earth's heart
    in their grasp
Ere the storm should uproot them or
    make them unclasp ;
Its cloudy boughs singing, as suiteth
    the pine,
To snow-bearded sea-kings old songs
    of the brine,
Till they straightened and let their
    staves fall to the floor,
Hearing waves moan again on the
    perilous shore
Of Vinland, perhaps, while their prow
    groped its way
'Twixt the frothy gnashed tusks of some
    ship-crunching bay.

So, pine-like, the legend grew, strong-
    limbed and tall,
As the Gypsy child grows that eats
    crusts in the hall ;
It sucked the whole strength of the
    earth and the sky,
Spring, Summer, Fall, Winter, all
    brought it supply ;

'Twas a natural growth, and stood fear-
    lessly there,
A true part of the landscape as sea,
    land, and air ;
For it grew in good times, ere the
    fashion it was
To force up these wild births of the
    woods under glass,
And so, if 't is told as it should be told,
Though 't were sung under Venice's
    moonlight of gold,
You would hear the old voice of its
    mother, the pine,
Murmur sealike and northern through
    every line,
And the verses should hang, self-sus-
    tained and free,
Round the vibrating stem of the melody,
Like the lithe sun-steeped limbs of the
    parent tree.

Yes, the pine is the mother of legends ;
    what food
For their grim roots is left when the
    thousand-yeared wood —
The dim-aisled cathedral, whose tall
    arches spring
Light, sinewy, graceful, firm-set as the
    wing
From Michael's white shoulder — is
    hewn and defaced
By iconoclast axes in desperate waste,
And its wrecks seek the ocean it pro-
    phesied long,
Cassandra-like, crooning its mystical
    song?
Then the legends go with them, — even
    yet on the sea
A wild virtue is left in the touch of the
    tree,
And the sailor's night-watches are
    thrilled to the core
With the lineal offspring of Odin and
    Thor.

Yes, wherever the pine-wood has never
    let in,
Since the day of creation, the light and
    the din
Of manifold life, but has safely conveyed
From the midnight primeval its armful
    of shade,
And has kept the weird Past with its
    child-faith alive

'Mid the hum and the stir of To-day's
    busy hive,
There the legend takes root in the age-
    gathered gloom,
And its murmurous boughs for their
    tossing find room.

Where Aroostook, far-heard, seems to
    sob as he goes
Groping down to the sea 'neath his
    mountainous snows ;
Where the lake's frore Sahara of never-
    tracked white,
When the crack shoots across it, com-
    plains to the night
With a long, lonely moan, that leagues
    northward is lost,
As the ice shrinks away from the tread
    of the frost ;
Where the lumberers sit by the log-fires
    which throw
Their own threatening shadows far
    round o'er the snow,
When the wolf howls aloof, and the
    wavering glare
Flashes out from the blackness the eyes
    of the bear,
When the wood's huge recesses, half-
    lighted, supply
A canvas where Fancy her mad brush
    may try,
Blotting in giant Horrors that venture
    not down
Through the right-angled streets of the
    brisk, whitewashed town,
But skulk in the depths of the measure-
    less wood
'Mid the Dark's creeping whispers that
    curdle the blood,
When the eye, glanced in dread o'er
    the shoulder, may dream,
Ere it shrinks to the camp-fire's com-
    panioning gleam,
That it saw the fierce ghost of the Red
    Man crouch back
To the shroud of the tree-trunk's in-
    vincible black ; —
There the old shapes crowd thick round
    the pine-shadowed camp,
Which shun the keen gleam of the
    scholarly lamp,
And the seed of the legend finds true
    Norland ground,
While the border-tale 's told and the
    canteen flits round.

A CONTRAST.

THY love thou sentest oft to me,
    And still as oft I thrust it back ;
Thy messengers I could not see
    In those who everything did lack, —
    The poor, the outcast, and the black.

Pride held his hand before mine eyes,
    The world with flattery stuffed mine
        ears ;
I looked to see a monarch's guise,
    Nor dreamed thy love would knock
        for years,
    Poor, naked, fettered, full of tears.

Yet, when I sent my love to thee,
    Thou with a smile didst take it in,
And entertain'dst it royally,
    Though grimed with earth, with
        hunger thin,
    And leprous with the taint of sin.

Now every day thy love I meet,
    As o'er the earth it wanders wide,
With weary step and bleeding feet,
    Still knocking at the heart of pride
    And offering grace, though still denied.

EXTREME UNCTION.

Go ! leave me, Priest ; my soul would
        be
    Alone with the consoler, Death ;
Far sadder eyes than thine will see
    This crumbling clay yield up its
        breath ;
These shrivelled hands have deeper
        stains
    Than holy oil can cleanse away, —
Hands that have plucked the world's
        coarse gains
    As erst they plucked the flowers of
        May.

Call, if thou canst, to those gray eyes
    Some faith from youth's traditions
        wrung ;
This fruitless husk which dustward
        dries
    Hath been a heart once, hath been
        young ;

On this bowed head the awful Past
  Once laid its consecrating hands ;
The Future in its purpose vast
  Paused, waiting my supreme com-
    mands.

But look ! whose shadows block the
    door ?
  Who are those two that stand aloof ?
See ! on my hands this freshening gore
  Writes o'er again its crimson proof !
My looked-for death-bed guests are
    met ; —
  There my dead Youth doth wring its
    hands,
And there, with eyes that goad me yet,
  The ghost of my Ideal stands !

God bends from out the deep and says,—
  "I gave thee the great gift of life ;
Wast thou not called in many ways ?
  Are not my earth and heaven at strife ?
I gave thee of my seed to sow,
  Bringest thou me my hundred-fold ? "
Can I look up with face aglow,
  And answer, " Father, here is gold " ?

I have been innocent ; God knows
  When first this wasted life began,
Not grape with grape more kindly
    grows,
  Than I with every brother-man :
Now here I gasp ; what lose my kind,
  When this fast ebbing breath shall
    part ?
What bands of love and service bind
  This being to a brother heart ?

Christ still was wandering o'er the earth
  Without a place to lay his head ;
He found free welcome at my hearth,
  He shared my cup and broke my
    bread :
Now, when I hear those steps sublime,
  That bring the other world to this,
My snake-turned nature, sunk in slime,
  Starts sideway with defiant hiss.

Upon the hour when I was born,
  God said, " Another man shall be,"
And the great Maker did not scorn
  Out of himself to fashion me ;
He sunned me with his ripening looks,

And Heaven's rich instincts in me
    grew,
As effortless as woodland nooks
  Send violets up and paint them blue.

Yes, I who now, with angry tears,
  Am exiled back to brutish clod,
Have borne unquenched for fourscore
    years
  A spark of the eternal God ;
And to what end ? How yield I back
  The trust for such high uses given ?
Heaven's light hath but revealed a track
  Whereby to crawl away from heaven.

Men think it is an awful sight
  To see a soul just set adrift
On that drear voyage from whose night
  The ominous shadows never lift ;
But 't is more awful to behold
  A helpless infant newly born,
Whose little hands unconscious hold
  The keys of darkness and of morn.

Mine held them once ; I flung away
  Those keys that might have open set
The golden sluices of the day,
  But clutch the keys of darkness yet ;—
I hear the reapers singing go
  Into God's harvest ; I, that might
With them have chosen, here below
  Grope shuddering at the gates of
    night.

O glorious Youth, that once wast mine !
  O high Ideal ! all in vain
Ye enter at this ruined shrine
  Whence worship ne'er shall rise
    again ;
The bat and owl inhabit here,
  The snake nests in the altar-stone,
The sacred vessels moulder near,
  The image of the God is gone.

THE OAK.

WHAT gnarled stretch, what depth of
    shade, is his !
  There needs no crown to mark the
    forest's king ;
How in his leaves outshines full sum-
    mer's bliss !

Sun, storm, rain, dew, to him their
    tribute bring,
Which he with such benignant royalty
    Accepts, as overpayeth what is lent ;
All nature seems his vassal proud to
    be,
    And cunning only for his ornament.

How towers he, too, amid the billowed
    snows,
    An unquelled exile from the sum-
        mer's throne,
Whose plain, uncinctured front more
    kingly shows,
    Now that the obscuring courtier
        leaves are flown.
His boughs make music of the winter
    air,
    Jewelled with sleet, like some cathe-
        dral front
Where clinging snow-flakes with quaint
    art repair
    The dints and furrows of time's en-
        vious brunt.

How doth his patient strength the rude
    March wind
    Persuade to seem glad breaths of
        summer breeze,
And win the soil that fain would be un-
    kind,
    To swell his revenues with proud in-
        crease !
He is the gem ; and all the landscape
    wide
    (So doth his grandeur isolate the
        sense)
Seems but the setting, worthless all be-
    side,
    An empty socket, were he fallen
        thence.

So, from oft converse with life's wintry
    gales,
    Should man learn how to clasp with
        tougher roots
The inspiring earth ; — how otherwise
    avails
    The leaf-creating sap that sunward
        shoots ?
So every year that falls with noiseless
    flake
    Should fill old scars up on the storm-
        ward side,

And make hoar age revered for age's
    sake,
    Not for traditions of youth's leafy
        pride.

So, from the pinched soil of a churlish
    fate,
    True hearts compel the sap of stur
        dier growth,
So between earth and heaven stand
    simply great,
    That these shall seem but their at-
        tendants both ;
For nature's forces with obedient zeal
    Wait on the rooted faith and oaken
        will ;
As quickly the pretender's cheat they
    feel,
    And turn mad Pucks to flout and
        mock him still.

Lord ! all thy works are lessons, — each
    contains
    Some emblem of man's all-contain-
        ing soul ;
Shall he make fruitless all thy glorious
    pains,
    Delving within thy grace an eyeless
        mole ?
Make me the least of thy Dodona-
    grove,
    Cause me some message of thy truth
        to bring,
Speak but a word through me, nor let
    thy love
    Among my boughs disdain to perch
        and sing.

AMBROSE.

NEVER, surely, was holier man
Than Ambrose, since the world began ;
With diet spare and raiment thin
He shielded himself from the father of
    sin ;
With bed of iron and scourgings oft,
His heart to God's hand as wax made
    soft.

Through earnest prayer and watchings
    long
He sought to know 'twixt right and
    wrong,

Much wrestling with the blessed Word
To make it yield the sense of the Lord,
That he might build a storm-proof
    creed
To fold the flock in at their need.

At last he builded a perfect faith,
Fenced round about with *The Lord
    thus saith*;
To himself he fitted the doorway's size,
Meted the light to the need of his eyes,
And knew, by a sure and inward sign,
That the work of his fingers was divine.

Then Ambrose said, "All those shall
    die
The eternal death who believe not as
    I";
And some were boiled, some burned in
    fire,
Some sawn in twain, that his heart's
    desire,
For the good of men's souls, might be
    satisfied,
By the drawing of all to the righteous
    side.

One day, as Ambrose was seeking the
    truth
In his lonely walk, he saw a youth
Resting himself in the shade of a tree;
It had never been given him to see
So shining a face, and the good man
    thought
'T were pity he should not believe as
    he ought.

So he set himself by the young man's
    side,
And the state of his soul with questions
    tried;
But the heart of the stranger was hard-
    ened indeed,
Nor received the stamp of the one true
    creed,
And the spirit of Ambrose waxed sore
    to find
Such features the porch of so narrow a
    mind.

"As each beholds in cloud and fire
The shape that answers his own desire,
So each," said the youth, "in the Law
    shall find

The figure and fashion of his mind;
And to each in his mercy hath God al-
    lowed
His several pillar of fire and cloud."

The soul of Ambrose burned with zeal
And holy wrath for the young man's
    weal:
"Believest thou then, most wretched
    youth,"
Cried he, "a dividual essence in Truth?
I fear me thy heart is too cramped with
    sin
To take the Lord in his glory in."

Now there bubbled beside them where
    they stood
A fountain of waters sweet and good;
The youth to the streamlet's brink drew
    near
Saying, "Ambrose, thou maker of
    creeds, look here!"
Six vases of crystal then he took,
And set them along the edge of the
    brook.

"As into these vessels the water I pour,
There shall one hold less, another more,
And the water unchanged, in every
    case,
Shall put on the figure of the vase;
O thou, who wouldst unity make
    through strife,
Canst thou fit this sign to the Water of
    Life?

When Ambrose looked up, he stood
    alone,
The youth and the stream and the vases
    were gone;
But he knew, by a sense of humbled
    grace,
He had talked with an angel face to
    face,
And felt his heart change inwardly,
As he fell on his knees beneath the tree.

ABOVE AND BELOW.

I.

O DWELLERS in the valley-land,
  Who in deep twilight grope and
    cower,

Till the slow mountain's dial-hand
  Shorten to noon's triumphal hour,—
While ye sit idle, do ye think
  The Lord's great work sits idle too?
That light dare not o'erleap the brink
  Of morn, because 't is dark with you?

Though yet your valleys skulk in night,
  In God's ripe fields the day is cried,
And reapers, with their sickles bright,
  Troop, singing, down the mountain-
     side;
Come up, and feel what health there is
  In the frank Dawn's delighted eyes,
As, bending with a pitying kiss,
  The night-shed tears of Earth she
     dries!

The Lord wants reapers: O, mount up,
  Before night comes, and says,—"Too
     late!"
Stay not for taking scrip or cup,
  The Master hungers while ye wait;
'T is from these heights alone your eyes
  The advancing spears of day can see,
Which o'er the eastern hill-tops rise,
  To break your long captivity.

II.

Lone watcher on the mountain-height!
  It is right precious to behold
The first long surf of climbing light
  Flood all the thirsty east with gold;
But we, who in the shadow sit,
  Know also when the day is nigh,
Seeing thy shining forehead lit
  With his inspiring prophecy.

Thou hast thine office; we have ours;
  God lacks not early service here,
But what are thine eleventh hours
  He counts with us for morning
     cheer;
Our day, for Him, is long enough,
  And when he giveth work to do,
The bruisèd reed is amply tough
  To pierce the shield of error through.

But not the less do thou aspire
  Light's earlier messages to preach;
Keep back no syllable of fire,—
  Plunge deep the rowels of thy speech.
Yet God deems not thine aeried sight

More worthy than our twilight
     dim,—
For meek Obedience, too, is Light,
  And following that is finding Him.

THE CAPTIVE.

It was past the hour of trysting,
  But she lingered for him still;
Like a child, the eager streamlet
  Leaped and laughed adown the hill,
Happy to be free at twilight
  From its toiling at the mill.

Then the great moon on a sudden
  Ominous, and red as blood,
Startling as a new creation,
  O'er the eastern hill-top stood,
Casting deep and deeper shadows
  Through the mystery of the wood.

Dread closed vast and vague about
     her,
  And her thoughts turned fearfully
To her heart, if there some shelter
  From the silence there might be,
Like bare cedars leaning inland
  From the blighting of the sea.

Yet he came not, and the stillness
  Dampened round her like a tomb;
She could feel cold eyes of spirits
  Looking on her through the gloom,
She could hear the groping footsteps
  Of some blind, gigantic doom.

Suddenly the silence wavered
  Like a light mist in the wind,
For a voice broke gently through it,
  Felt like sunshine by the blind,
And the dread, like mist in sunshine,
  Furled serenely from her mind.

"Once my love, my love forever,—
  Flesh or spirit, still the same;
If I failed at time of trysting,
  Deem thou not my faith to blame;
I, alas, was made a captive,
  As from Holy Land I came.

"On a green spot in the desert,
  Gleaming like an emerald star,

Where a palm-tree, in lone silence,
    Yearning for its mate afar,
Droops above a silver runnel,
    Slender as a scimitar, —

"There thou 'lt find the humble postern
    To the castle of my foe;
If thy love burn clear and faithful,
    Strike the gateway, green and low,
Ask to enter, and the warder
    Surely will not say thee no."

Slept again the aspen silence,
    But her loneliness was o'er;
Round her soul a motherly patience
    Clasped its arms forevermore;
From her heart ebbed back the sorrow,
    Leaving smooth the golden shore.

Donned she now the pilgrim scallop,
    Took the pilgrim staff in hand;
Like a cloud-shade, flitting eastward,
    Wandered she o'er sea and land;
And her footsteps in the desert
    Fell like cool rain on the sand.

Soon, beneath the palm-tree's shadow,
    Knelt she at the postern low;
And thereat she knocked full gently,
    Fearing much the warder's no;
All her heart stood still and listened,
    As the door swung backward slow.

There she saw no surly warder
    With an eye like bolt and bar;
Through her soul a sense of music
    Throbbed, — and, like a guardian
        Lar,
On the threshold stood an angel,
    Bright and silent as a star.

Fairest seemed he of God's seraphs,
    And her spirit, lily-wise,
Opened when he turned upon her
    The deep welcome of his eyes,
Sending upward to that sunlight
    All its dew for sacrifice.

Then she heard a voice come onward
    Singing with a rapture new,
As Eve heard the songs in Eden,
    Dropping earthward with the dew;
Well she knew the happy singer,
    Well the happy song she knew.

Forward leaped she o'er the threshold,
    Eager as a glancing surf;
Fell from her the spirit's languor,
    Fell from her the body's scurf; —
'Neath the palm next day some Arabs
    Found a corpse upon the turf.

THE BIRCH-TREE.

RIPPLING through thy branches goes
    the sunshine,
Among thy leaves that palpitate for-
    ever;
Ovid in thee a pining Nymph had pris-
    oned,
The soul once of some tremulous in-
    land river,
Quivering to tell her woe, but, ah!
    dumb, dumb forever!

While all the forest, witched with
    slumberous moonshine,
Holds up its leaves in happy, happy
    stillness,
Waiting the dew, with breath and pulse
    suspended,
I hear afar thy whispering, gleamy
    islands,
And track thee wakeful still amid the
    wide-hung silence.

On the brink of some wood-nestled
    lakelet,
Thy foliage, like the tresses of a Dryad,
Dripping round thy slim white stem,
    whose shadow
Slopes quivering down the water's
    dusky quiet,
Thou shrink'st as on her bath's edge
    would some startled Naiad.

Thou art the go-between of rustic lovers;
Thy white bark has their secrets in its
    keeping;
Reuben writes here the happy name of
    Patience,
And thy lithe boughs hang murmuring
    and weeping
Above her, as she steals the mystery
    from thy keeping.

Thou art to me like my beloved maiden,
So frankly coy, so full of trembly confi-
    dences:

Thy shadow scarce seems shade, thy
     pattering leaflets
Sprinkle their gathered sunshine o'er
     my senses,
And Nature gives me all her summer
     confidences.

Whether my heart with hope or sorrow
     tremble,
Thou sympathizest still ; wild and un-
     quiet,
I fling me down ; thy ripple, like river,
Flows valleyward, where calmness is,
     and by it
My heart is floated down into the land
     of quiet.

AN INTERVIEW WITH MILES STANDISH.

I sat one evening in my room,
     In that sweet hour of twilight
When blended thoughts, half light, half
     gloom,
     Throng through the spirit's skylight ;
The flames by fits curled round the bars,
     Or up the chimney crinkled,
While embers dropped like falling stars,
     And in the ashes tinkled.

I sat and mused ; the fire burned low,
     And, o'er my senses stealing,
Crept something of the ruddy glow
     That bloomed on wall and ceiling ;
My pictures (they are very few, —
     The heads of ancient wise men)
Smoothed down their knotted fronts,
     and grew
     As rosy as excisemen.

My antique high-backed Spanish chair
     Felt thrills through wood and leather,
That had been strangers since whilere,
     'Mid Andalusian heather,
The oak that built its sturdy frame
     His happy arms stretched over
The ox whose fortunate hide became
     The bottom's polished cover.

It came out in that famous bark
     That brought our sires intrepid,
Capacious as another ark
     For furniture decrepit ; —

For, as that saved of bird and beast
     A pair for propagation,
So has the seed of these increased
     And furnished half the nation.

Kings sit, they say, in slippery seats :
     But those slant precipices
Of ice the northern voyager meets
     Less slippery are than this is ;
To cling therein would pass the wit
     Of royal man or woman,
And whatsoe'er can stay in it
     Is more or less than human.

I offer to all bores this perch,
     Dear well-intentioned people
With heads as void as week-day church,
     Tongues longer than the steeple ;
To folks with missions, whose gaunt
     eyes
See golden ages rising, —
     Salt of the earth ! in what queer Guys
     Thou 'rt fond of crystallizing !

My wonder, then, was not unmixed
     With merciful suggestion,
When, as my roving eyes grew fixed
     Upon the chair in question,
I saw its trembling arms enclose
     A figure grim and rusty,
Whose doublet plain and plainer hose
     Were something worn and dusty.

Now even such men as Nature forms
     Merely to fill the street with,
Once turned to ghosts by hungry worms,
     Are serious things to meet with ;
Your penitent spirits are no jokes,
     And, though I 'm not averse to
A quiet shade, even they are folks
     One cares not to speak first to.

Who knows, thought I, but he has come,
     By Charon kindly ferried,
To tell me of a mighty sum
     Behind my wainscot buried ?
There is a buccaneerish air
     About that garb outlandish —
Just then the ghost drew up his chair
     And said, " My name is Standish.

" I come from Plymouth, deadly bored
     With toasts, and songs, and speeches,
As long and flat as my old sword,
     As threadbare as my breeches :

They understand us Pilgrims! they,
   Smooth men with rosy faces,
Strength's knots and gnarls all pared
    away,
   And varnish in their places!

"We had some toughness in our grain,
   The eye to rightly see us is
Not just the one that lights the brain
   Of drawing-room Tyrtæuses:
They talk about their Pilgrim blood,
   Their birthright high and holy!—
A mountain-stream that ends in mud
   Methinks is melancholy.

"He had stiff knees, the Puritan,
   That were not good at bending;
The homespun dignity of man
   He thought was worth defending;
He did not, with his pinchbeck ore,
   His country's shame forgotten,
Gild Freedom's coffin o'er and o'er,
   When all within was rotten.

"These loud ancestral boasts of yours,
   How can they else than vex us?
Where were your dinner orators
   When slavery grasped at Texas?
Dumb on his knees was every one
   That now is bold as Cæsar,—
Mere pegs to hang an office on
   Such stalwart men as these are."

"Good sir," I said, "you seem much
    stirred;
   The sacred compromises—"
"Now God confound the dastard word!
   My gall thereat arises:
Northward it hath this sense alone,
   That you, your conscience blinding,
Shall bow your fool's nose to the stone,
   When slavery feels like grinding.

"'Tis shame to see such painted sticks
   In Vane's and Winthrop's places,
To see your spirit of Seventy-six
   Drag humbly in the traces,
With slavery's lash upon her back,
   And herds of office-holders
To shout applause, as, with a crack,
   It peels her patient shoulders.

"*We* forefathers to such a rout!—
   No, by my faith in God's word!"
    6

Half rose the ghost, and half drew out
   The ghost of his old broadsword,
Then thrust it slowly back again,
   And said, with reverent gesture,
"No, Freedom, no! blood should not
    stain
   The hem of thy white vesture.

"I feel the soul in me draw near
   The mount of prophesying;
In this bleak wilderness I hear
   A John the Baptist crying;
Far in the east I see upleap
   The streaks of first forewarning,
And they who sowed the light shall reap
   The golden sheaves of morning.

"Child of our travail and our woe,
   Light in our day of sorrow,
Through my rapt spirit I foreknow
   The glory of thy morrow;
I hear great steps, that through the shade
   Draw nigher still and nigher,
And voices call like that which bade
   The prophet come up higher."

I looked, no form mine eyes could find,
   I heard the red cock crowing,
And through my window-chinks the
    wind
   A dismal tune was blowing;
Thought I, My neighbor Buckingham
   Hath somewhat in him gritty,
Some Pilgrim-stuff that hates all sham,
   And he will print my ditty.

ON THE CAPTURE OF CERTAIN FUGITIVE SLAVES NEAR WASHINGTON.

Look on who will in apathy, and stifle
   they who can,
The sympathies, the hopes, the words,
   that make man truly man;
Let those whose hearts are dungeoned
   up with interest or with ease
Consent to hear with quiet pulse of
   loathsome deeds like these!

I first drew in New England's air, and
   from her hardy breast
Sucked in the tyrant-hating milk that
   will not let me rest;

And if my words seem treason to the
    dullard and the tame,
'T is but my Bay-State dialect, — our
    fathers spake the same !

Shame on the costly mockery of piling
    stone on stone
To those who won our liberty, the
    heroes dead and gone,
While we look coldly on, and see law-
    shielded ruffians slay
The men who fain would win their own,
    the heroes of to-day !

Are we pledged to craven silence?   O,
    fling it to the wind,
The parchment wall that bars us from
    the least of human kind,
That makes us cringe and temporize,
    and dumbly stand at rest,
While Pity's burning flood of words is
    red-hot in the breast !

Though we break our fathers' promise,
    we have nobler duties first ;
The traitor to Humanity is the traitor
    most accursed ;
Man is more than Constitutions ; better
    rot beneath the sod,
Than be true to Church and State while
    we are doubly false to God !

We owe allegiance to the State ; but
    deeper, truer, more,
To the sympathies that God hath set
    within our spirit's core ; —
Our country claims our fealty ; we grant
    it so, but then
Before Man made us citizens, great
    Nature made us men.

He's true to God who's true to man ;
    wherever wrong is done,
To the humblest and the weakest, 'neath
    the all-beholding sun,
That wrong is also done to us ; and
    they are slaves most base,
Whose love of right is for themselves,
    and not for all their race.

God works for all.   Ye cannot hem the
    hope of being free
With parallels of latitude, with moun-
    tain-range or sea.

Put golden padlocks on Truth's lips, be
    callous as ye will,
From soul to soul, o'er all the world,
    leaps one electric thrill.

Chain down your slaves with ignorance,
    ye cannot keep apart,
With all your craft of tyranny, the hu-
    man heart from heart :
When first the Pilgrims landed on the
    Bay State's iron shore,
The word went forth that slavery should
    one day be no more.

Out from the land of bondage 't is de-
    creed our slaves shall go,
And signs to us are offered, as erst to
    Pharaoh ;
If we are blind, their exodus, like Is-
    rael's of yore,
Though a Red Sea is doomed to be,
    whose surges are of gore.

'T is ours to save our brethren, with
    peace and love to win
Their darkened hearts from error, ere
    they harden it to sin ;
But if before his duty man with listless
    spirit stands,
Ere long the Great Avenger takes the
    work from out his hands.

TO THE DANDELION.

DEAR common flower, that grow'st
    beside the way,
Fringing the dusty road with harmless
    gold,
    First pledge of blithesome May,
Which children pluck, and, full of pride,
    uphold,
    High-hearted buccaneers, o'erjoyed
        that they
An Eldorado in the grass have found,
    Which not the rich earth's ample
        round
    May match in wealth, — thou art
        more dear to me
Than all the prouder summer-
    blooms may be.

Gold such as thine ne'er drew the
        Spanish prow
Through the primeval hush of Indian
        seas,
    Nor wrinkled the lean brow
Of age, to rob the lover's heart of ease ;
    'T is the spring's largess, which she
        scatters now
To rich and poor alike, with lavish
        hand,
        Though most hearts never under-
            stand
    To take it at God's value, but pass by
The offered wealth with unrewarded
    eye.

Thou art my tropics and mine Italy ;
To look at thee unlocks a warmer clime ;
        The eyes thou givest me
Are in the heart, and heed not space or
        time :
    Not in mid June the golden-cuirassed
        bee
Feels a more summer-like warm ravish-
        ment
    In the white lily's breezy tent,
    His fragrant Sybaris, than I, when
        first
From the dark green thy yellow
    circles burst.

Then think I of deep shadows on the
        grass,—
Of meadows where in sun the cattle
        graze,
    Where as the breezes pass,
The gleaming rushes lean a thousand
        ways,—
Of leaves that slumber in a cloudy
        mass,
Or whiten in the wind, — of waters
        blue
        That from the distance sparkle
            through
    Some woodland gap, — and of a sky
        above,
    Where one white cloud like a stray
        lamb doth move.

My childhood's earliest thoughts are
        linked with thee ;
The sight of thee calls back the robin's
        song,
    Who, from the dark old tree

Beside the door, sang clearly all day
        long,
    And I, secure in childish piety,
Listened as if I heard an angel sing
        With news from heaven, which he
            could bring
    Fresh every day to my untainted ears
When birds and flowers and I were
    happy peers.

How like a prodigal doth nature seem,
When thou, for all thy gold, so com-
        mon art !
        Thou teachest me to deem
More sacredly of every human heart,
    Since each reflects in joy its scanty
        gleam
Of heaven, and could some wondrous
        secret show,
        Did we but pay the love we owe,
    And with a child's undoubting wis-
        dom look
On all these living pages of God's
    book.

THE GHOST-SEER.

YE who, passing graves by night,
Glance not to the left nor right,
Lest a spirit should arise,
Cold and white, to freeze your eyes,
Some weak phantom, which your doubt
Shapes upon the dark without
From the dark within, a guess
At the spirit's deathlessness,
Which ye entertain with fear
In your self-built dungeon here,
Where ye sell your God-given lives
Just for gold to buy you gyves, —
Ye without a shudder meet
In the city's noonday street,
Spirits sadder and more dread
Than from out the clay have fled,
Buried, beyond hope of light,
In the body's haunted night !

See ye not that woman pale ?
There are bloodhounds on her trail !
Bloodhounds two, all gaunt and lean,—
For the soul their scent is keen, —
Want and Sin, and Sin is last, —
They have followed far and fast ;

Want gave tongue, and, at her howl,
Sin awakened with a growl.
Ah, poor girl! she had a right
To a blessing from the light,
Title-deeds to sky and earth
God gave to her at her birth,
But, before they were enjoyed,
Poverty had made them void,
And had drunk the sunshine up
From all nature's ample cup,
Leaving her a first-born's share
In the dregs of darkness there.
Often, on the sidewalk bleak,
Hungry, all alone, and weak,
She has seen, in night and storm,
Rooms o'erflow with firelight warm,
Which, outside the window-glass,
Doubled all the cold, alas!
Till each ray that on her fell
Stabbed her like an icicle,
And she almost loved the wail
Of the bloodhounds on her trail.
Till the floor becomes her bier,
She shall feel their pantings near,
Close upon her very heels,
Spite of all the din of wheels;
Shivering on her pallet poor,
She shall hear them at the door
Whine and scratch to be let in,
Sister bloodhounds, Want and Sin!

Hark! that rustle of a dress,
Stiff with lavish costliness!
Here comes one whose cheek would
    flush
But to have her garment brush
'Gainst the girl whose fingers thin
Wove the weary broidery in,
Bending backward from her toil,
Lest her tears the silk might soil,
And, in midnight's chill and murk,
Stitched her life into the work,
Shaping from her bitter thought
Heart's-ease and forget-me-not,
Satirizing her despair
With the emblems woven there.
Little doth the wearer heed
Of the heart-break in the brede;
A hyena by her side
Skulks, down-looking, — it is Pride.
He digs for her in the earth,
Where lie all her claims of birth,
With his foul paws rooting o'er
Some long-buried ancestor,

Who, perhaps, a statue won
By the ill deeds he had done,
By the innocent blood he shed,
By the desolation spread
Over happy villages,
Blotting out the smile of peace.

There walks Judas, he who sold
Yesterday his Lord for gold,
Sold God's presence in his heart
For a proud step in the mart;
He hath dealt in flesh and blood, —
At the bank his name is good,
At the bank, and only there,
'T is a marketable ware.
In his eyes that stealthy gleam
Was not learned of sky or stream,
But it has the cold, hard glint
Of new dollars from the mint.
Open now your spirit's eyes,
Look through that poor clay disguise
Which has thickened, day by day,
Till it keeps all light at bay,
And his soul in pitchy gloom
Gropes about its narrow tomb,
From whose dank and slimy walls
Drop by drop the horror falls.
Look! a serpent lank and cold
Hugs his spirit fold on fold;
From his heart, all day and night,
It doth suck God's blessed light.
Drink it will, and drink it must,
Till the cup holds naught but dust;
All day long he hears it hiss,
Writhing in its fiendish bliss;
All night long he sees its eyes
Flicker with foul ecstasies,
As the spirit ebbs away
Into the absorbing clay.

Who is he that skulks, afraid
Of the trust he has betrayed,
Shuddering if perchance a gleam
Of old nobleness should stream
Through the pent, unwholesome room,
Where his shrunk soul cowers in
    gloom, —
Spirit sad beyond the rest
By more instinct for the best?
'T is a poet who was sent
For a bad world's punishment,
By compelling it to see
Golden glimpses of To Be,
By compelling it to hear

Songs that prove the angels near;
Who was sent to be the tongue
Of the weak and spirit-wrung,
Whence the fiery-winged Despair
In men's shrinking eyes might flare.
'T is our hope doth fashion us
To base use or glorious:
He who might have been a lark
Of Truth's morning, from the dark
Raining down melodious hope
Of a freer, broader scope,
Aspirations, prophecies,
Of the spirit's full sunrise,
Chose to be a bird of night,
Which, with eyes refusing light,
Hooted from some hollow tree
Of the world's idolatry.
'T is his punishment to hear
Sweep of eager pinions near,
And his own vain wings to feel
Drooping downward to his heel,
All their grace and import lost,
Burdening his weary ghost:
Ever walking by his side
He must see his angel guide,
Who at intervals doth turn
Looks on him so sadly stern,
With such ever-new surprise
Of hushed anguish in her eyes,
That it seems the light of day
From around him shrinks away,
Or drops blunted from the wall
Built around him by his fall.
Then the mountains, whose white peaks
Catch the morning's earliest streaks,
He must see, where prophets sit,
Turning east their faces lit,
Whence, with footsteps beautiful,
To the earth, yet dim and dull,
They the gladsome tidings bring
Of the sunlight's hastening:
Never can these hills of bliss
Be o'erclimbed by feet like his!

But enough! O, do not dare
From the next the veil to tear,
Woven of station, trade, or dress,
More obscene than nakedness,
Wherewith plausible culture drapes
Fallen Nature's myriad shapes!
Let us rather love to mark
How the unextinguished spark
Still gleams through the thin disguise
Of our customs, pomps, and lies,

And, not seldom blown to flame,
Vindicate its ancient claim.

1844.

———

STUDIES FOR TWO HEADS.

I.

SOME sort of heart I know is hers, —
    I chanced to feel her pulse one night;
A brain she has that never errs,
    And yet is never nobly right;
It does not leap to great results,
    But, in some corner out of sight,
Suspects a spot of latent blight,
And, o'er the impatient infinite,
She bargains, haggles, and consults.

Her eye, — it seems a chemic test
    And drops upon you like an acid;
It bites you with unconscious zest,
    So clear and bright, so coldly placid;
It holds you quietly aloof,
    It holds, — and yet it does not win
        you;
It merely puts you to the proof
    And sorts what qualities are in you;
It smiles, but never brings you nearer,
    It lights, — her nature draws not nigh;
'T is but that yours is growing clearer
    To her assays: — yes, try and try,
    You 'll get no deeper than her eye.

There, you are classified: she 's gone
    Far, far away into herself;
Each with its Latin label on,
Your poor components, one by one,
    Are laid upon their proper shelf
In her compact and ordered mind,
And what of you is left behind
Is no more to her than the wind;
In that clear brain, which, day and night,
    No movement of the heart e'er jos-
        tles,
Her friends are ranged on left and
        right, —
Here, silex, hornblende, sienite;
    There, animal remains and fossils.

And yet, O subtle analyst,
    That canst each property detect
Of mood or grain, that canst untwist
    Each tangled skein of intellect,
And with thy scalpel eyes lay bare

Each mental nerve more fine than
    air, —
  O brain exact, that in thy scales
Canst weigh the sun and never err,
  For once thy patient science fails,
  One problem still defies thy art ; —
Thou never canst compute for her
The distance and diameter
  Of any simple human heart.

II.

HEAR him but speak, and you will feel
  The shadows of the Portico
Over your tranquil spirit steal,
  To modulate all joy and woe
  To one subdued, subduing glow ;
Above our squabbling business-hours,
Like Phidian Jove's, his beauty lowers,
  His nature satirizes ours ;
    A form and front of Attic grace,
  He shames the higgling market-place,
And dwarfs our more mechanic powers.

What throbbing verse can fitly render
  That face, — so pure, so trembling-ten-
      der ?
  Sensation glimmers through its rest,
  It speaks unmanacled by words,
    As full of motion as a nest
That palpitates with unfledged birds ;
  'T is likest to Bethesda's stream,
Forewarned through all its thrilling
    springs,
  White with the angel's coming gleam,
And rippled with his fanning wings.

Hear him unfold his plots and plans,
  And larger destinies seem man's ;
You conjure from his glowing face
  The omen of a fairer race ;
With one grand trope he boldly spans
  The gulf wherein so many fall,
  'Twixt possible and actual ;
His first swift word, talaria-shod,
Exuberant with conscious God,
  Out of the choir of planets blots
The present earth with all its spots.

Himself unshaken as the sky,
His words, like whirlwinds, spin on high
  Systems and creeds pellmell together ;
'T is strange as to a deaf man's eye,
While trees uprooted splinter by,
  The dumb turmoil of stormy weather ;
  Less of iconoclast than shaper,

His spirit, safe behind the reach
  Of the tornado of his speech,
    Burns calmly as a glowworm's taper

So great in speech, but, ah! in act
  So overrun with vermin troubles,
The coarse, sharp-cornered, ugly fact
  Of life collapses all his bubbles :
Had he but lived in Plato's day,
  He might, unless my fancy errs,
Have shared that golden voice's sway
  O'er barefooted philosophers.
Our nipping climate hardly suits
  The ripening of ideal fruits :
His theories vanquish us all summer,
But winter makes him dumb and
      dumber ;
To see him 'mid life's needful things
  Is something painfully bewildering ;
He seems an angel with clipt wings
  Tied to a mortal wife and children,
And by a brother seraph taken
In the act of eating eggs and bacon.
Like a clear fountain, his desire
  Exults and leaps toward the light,
In every drop it says " Aspire ! "
  Striving for more ideal height ;
And as the fountain, falling thence,
  Crawls baffled through the common
      gutter,
So, from his speech's eminence,
  He shrinks into the present tense,
    Unkinged by foolish bread and butter.

Yet smile not, worldling, for in deeds
  Not all of life that's brave and wise is ;
He strews an ampler future's seeds,
  'T is your fault if no harvest rises ;
Smooth back the sneer ; for is it naught
  That all he is and has is Beauty's ?
By soul the soul's gains must be
    wrought,
The Actual claims our coarser thought,
  The Ideal hath its higher duties.

ON A PORTRAIT OF DANTE
BY GIOTTO.

CAN this be thou who, lean and pale,
  With such immitigable eye
Didst look upon those writhing souls in
    bale,
    And note each vengeance, and pass by

Unmoved, save when thy heart by
 chance
Cast backward one forbidden glance,
 And saw Francesca, with child's glee,
 Subdue and mount thy wild-horse
 knee
And with proud hands control its fiery
 prance?

With half-drooped lids, and smooth,
 round brow,
 And eye remote, that inly sees
Fair Beatrice's spirit wandering now
 In some sea-lulled Hesperides,
Thou movest through the jarring street,
 Secluded from the noise of feet
 By her gift-blossom in thy hand,
 Thy branch of palm from Holy
 Land : —
No trace is here of ruin's fiery sleet.

Yet there is something round thy lips
That prophesies the coming doom,
The soft, gray herald-shadow ere the
 eclipse
 Notches the perfect disk with gloom ;
A something that would banish thee,
And thine untamed pursuer be,
 From men and their unworthy fates,
 Though Florence had not shut her
 gates,
And Grief had loosed her clutch and let
 thee free.

Ah ! he who follows fearlessly
 The beckonings of a poet-heart
Shall wander, and without the world's
 decree,
 A banished man in field and mart ;
Harder than Florence' walls the bar
Which with deaf sternness holds him far
 From home and friends, till death's
 release,
 And makes his only prayer for peace,
Like thine, scarred veteran of a lifelong
 war !

ON THE DEATH OF A
 FRIEND'S CHILD.

DEATH never came so nigh to me be-
 fore,
Nor showed me his mild face : oft had
 I mused

Of calm and peace and deep forgetful-
 ness,
Of folded hands, closed eyes, and heart
 at rest,
And slumber sound beneath a flowery
 turf,
Of faults forgotten, and an inner place
Kept sacred for us in the heart of
 friends ;
But these were idle fancies, satisfied
With the mere husk of this great mys-
 tery,
And dwelling in the outward shows of
 things.
Heaven is not mounted to on wings of
 dreams,
Nor doth the unthankful happiness of
 youth
Aim thitherward, but floats from bloom
 to bloom,
With earth's warm patch of sunshine
 well content :
'T is sorrow builds the shining ladder up,
Whose golden rounds are our calami-
 ties,
Whereon our firm feet planting, nearer
 God
The spirit climbs, and hath its eyes un-
 sealed.

True is it that Death's face seems stern
 and cold,
When he is sent to summon those we
 love,
But all God's angels come to us dis-
 guised ;
Sorrow and sickness, poverty and death,
One after other lift their frowning
 masks,
And we behold the seraph's face be-
 neath,
All radiant with the glory and the calm
Of having looked upon the front of
 God.
With every anguish of our earthly part
The spirit's sight grows clearer; this
 was meant
When Jesus touched the blind man's
 lids with clay.
Life is the jailer, Death the angel sent
To draw the unwilling bolts and set us
 free.
He flings not ope the ivory gate of
 Rest, —

Only the fallen spirit knocks at that, —
But to benigner regions beckons us,
To destinies of more rewarded toil.
In the hushed chamber, sitting by the
    dead,
It grates on us to hear the flood of life
Whirl rustling onward, senseless of our
    loss.
The bee hums on; around the blos-
    somed vine
Whirs the light humming-bird; the
    cricket chirps;
The locust's shrill alarum stings the
    ear;
Hard by, the cock shouts lustily; from
    farm to farm,
His cheery brothers, telling of the sun,
Answer, till far away the joyance dies:
We never knew before how God had
    filled
The summer air with happy living
    sounds;
All round us seems an overplus of life,
And yet the one dear heart lies cold and
    still.
It is most strange, when the great mir-
    acle
Hath for our sakes been done, when
    we have had
Our inwardest experience of God,
When with his presence still the room
    expands,
And is awed after him, that naught is
    changed,
That Nature's face looks unacknowl-
    edging,
And the mad world still dances heed-
    less on
After its butterflies, and gives no sign.
'T is hard at first to see it all aright:
In vain Faith blows her trump to sum-
    mon back
Her scattered troop: yet, through the
    clouded glass
Of our own bitter tears, we learn to
    look
Undazzled on the kindness of God's
    face;
Earth is too dark, and Heaven alone
    shines through.

It is no little thing, when a fresh soul
And a fresh heart, with their unmeas-
    ured scope

For good, not gravitating earthward
    yet,
But circling in diviner periods,
Are sent into the world,—no little thing,
When this unbounded possibility
Into the outer silence is withdrawn.
Ah, in this world, where every guiding
    thread
Ends suddenly in the one sure centre,
    death,
The visionary hand of Might-have-been
Alone can fill Desire's cup to the brim!

How changed, dear friend, are thy part
    and thy child's!
He bends above *thy* cradle now, or
    holds
His warning finger out to be thy guide;
Thou art the nursling now; he watches
    thee
Slow learning, one by one, the secret
    things
Which are to him used sights of every
    day;
He smiles to see thy wondering glances
    con
The grass and pebbles of the spirit-
    world,
To thee miraculous; and he will teach
Thy knees their due observances of
    prayer.
Children are God's apostles, day by day
Sent forth to preach of love, and hope,
    and peace;
Nor hath thy babe his mission left un-
    done.
To me, at least, his going hence hath
    given
Serener thoughts and nearer to the
    skies,
And opened a new fountain in my heart
For thee, my friend, and all; and O,
    if Death
More near approaches meditates, and
    clasps
Even now some dearer, more reluctant
    hand,
God, strengthen thou my faith, that I
    may see
That 't is thine angel, who, with loving
    haste,
Unto the service of the inner shrine,
Doth waken thy belovèd with a kiss

                                    1844.

EURYDICE.

HEAVEN'S cup held down to me I drain,
The sunshine mounts and spurs my
  brain ;
Bathing in grass, with thirsty eye
I suck the last drop of the sky ;
With each hot sense I draw to the lees
The quickening out-door influences,
And empty to each radiant comer
A supernaculum of summer :
Not, Bacchus, all thy grosser juice
Could bring enchantment so profuse,
Though for its press each grape-bunch
  had
The white feet of an Oread.

Through our coarse art gleam, now and
  then,
The features of angelic men :
'Neath the lewd Satyr's veiling paint
Glows forth the Sibyl, Muse, or Saint ;
The dauber's botch no more obscures
The mighty master's portraitures.
And who can say what luckier beam
The hidden glory shall redeem,
For what chance clod the soil may
  wait
To stumble on its nobler fate,
Or why, to his unwarned abode,
Still by surprises comes the God ?
Some moment, nailed on sorrow's cross,
May mediate a whole youth's loss,
Some windfall joy, we know not whence,
Redeem a lifetime's rash expense,
And, suddenly wise, the soul may mark,
Stripped of their simulated dark,
Mountains of gold that pierce the sky,
Girdling its valleyed poverty.

I feel ye, childhood's hopes, return,
With olden heats my pulses burn, —
Mine be the self-forgetting sweep,
The torrent impulse swift and wild,
Wherewith Taghkanic's rockborn child
Dares gloriously the dangerous leap,
And, in his sky-descended mood,
Transmutes each drop of sluggish blood,
By touch of bravery's simple wand,
To amethyst and diamond,
Proving himself no bastard slip,
But the true granite-cradled one,
Nursed with the rock's primeval drip,
The cloud-embracing mountain's son !

Prayer breathed in vain ! no wish's
  sway
Rebuilds the vanished yesterday ;
For plated wares of Sheffield stamp
We gave the old Aladdin's lamp ;
'T is we are changed ; ah, whither went
That undesigned abandonment,
That wise, unquestioning content,
Which could erect its microcosm
Out of a weed's neglected blossom,
Could call up Arthur and his peers
By a low moss's clump of spears,
Or, in its shingle trireme launched,
Where Charles in some green inlet
  branched,
Could venture for the golden fleece
And dragon-watched Hesperides,
Or, from its ripple-shattered fate,
Ulysses' chances re-create ?

When, heralding life's every phase,
There glowed a goddess-veiling haze,
A plenteous, forewarning grace,
Like that more tender dawn that flies
Before the full moon's ample rise ?
Methinks thy parting glory shines
Through yonder grove of singing pines ;
At that elm-vista's end I trace
Dimly thy sad leave-taking face,
Eurydice ! Eurydice !
The tremulous leaves repeat to me
Eurydice ! Eurydice !
No gloomier Orcus swallows thee
Than the unclouded sunset's glow ;
Thine is at least Elysian woe ;
Thou hast Good's natural decay,
And fadest like a star away
Into an atmosphere whose shine
With fuller day o'ermasters thine,
Entering defeat as 't were a shrine ;
For us, — we turn life's diary o'er
To find but one word, — Nevermore.

1845.

SHE CAME AND WENT.

As a twig trembles, which a bird
  Lights on to sing, then leaves un-
    bent,
So is my memory thrilled and
    stirred ; —
  I only know she came and went.

As clasps some lake, by gusts unriven,
  The blue dome's measureless con-
    tent,
So my soul held that moment's heav-
    en ; —
  I only know she came and went.

As, at one bound, our swift spring
    heaps
  The orchards full of bloom and scent,
So clove her May my wintry sleeps ; —
  I only know she came and went.

An angel stood and met my gaze,
  Through the low doorway of my tent ;
The tent is struck, the vision stays ; —
  I only know she came and went.

O, when the room grows slowly dim,
  And life's last oil is nearly spent,
One gush of light these eyes will brim,
  Only to think she came and went.

THE CHANGELING.

I HAD a little daughter,
  And she was given to me
To lead me gently backward
  To the Heavenly Father's knee,
That I, by the force of nature,
  Might in some dim wise divine
The depth of his infinite patience
  To this wayward soul of mine.

I know not how others saw her,
  But to me she was wholly fair,
And the light of the heaven she came
    from
  Still lingered and gleamed in her
    hair ;
For it was as wavy and golden,
  And as many changes took,
As the shadows of sun-gilt ripples
  On the yellow bed of a brook.

To what can I liken her smiling
  Upon me, her kneeling lover,
How it leaped from her lips to her eye-
    lids,
  And dimpled her wholly over,
Till her outstretched hands smiled also,
  And I almost seemed to see

The very heart of her mother
  Sending sun through her veins to
    me !

She had been with us scarce a twelve-
    month,
  And it hardly seemed a day,
When a troop of wandering angels
  Stole my little daughter away ;
Or perhaps those heavenly Zingari
  But loosed the hampering strings,
And when they had opened her cage-
    door,
  My little bird used her wings.

But they left in her stead a changeling,
  A little angel child,
That seems like her bud in full blossom,
  And smiles as she never smiled :
When I wake in the morning, I see it
  Where she always used to lie,
And I feel as weak as a violet
  Alone 'neath the awful sky.

As weak, yet as trustful also ;
  For the whole year long I see
All the wonders of faithful Nature
  Still worked for the love of me ;
Winds wander, and dews drip earth-
    ward,
  Rain falls, suns rise and set,
Earth whirls, and all but to prosper
  A poor little violet.

This child is not mine as the first was,
  I cannot sing it to rest,
I cannot lift it up fatherly
  And bliss it upon my breast ;
Yet it lies in my little one's cradle
  And sits in my little one's chair,
And the light of the heaven she 's gone
    to
  Transfigures its golden hair.

THE PIONEER.

WHAT man would live coffined with
    brick and stone,
  Imprisoned from the healing touch
    of air,
And cramped with selfish land-
    marks everywhere,

When all before him stretches, furrow-
less and lone,
The unmapped prairie none can fence
or own?

What man would read and read the
selfsame faces,
And, like the marbles which the
windmill grinds,
Rub smooth forever with the same
smooth minds,
This year retracing last year's, every
year's, dull traces,
When there are woods and un-pen-
folded places?

What man o'er one old thought
would pore and pore,
Shut like a book between its covers thin
For every fool to leave his dog's-
ears in,
When solitude is his, and God forevermore,
Just for the opening of a paltry door?

What man would watch life's oozy
element
Creep Letheward forever, when he
might
Down some great river drift beyond men's sight,
To where the undethroned forest's
royal tent
Broods with its hush o'er half a continent?

What man with men would push and
altercate,
Piecing out crooked means to
crooked ends,
When he can have the skies and
woods for friends,
Snatch back the rudder of his undis-
mantled fate,
And in himself be ruler, church, and
state?

Cast leaves and feathers rot in last
year's nest,
The winged brood, flown thence,
new dwellings plan;
The serf of his own Past is not a
man;

To change and change is life, to move
and never rest; —
Not what we are, but what we hope,
is best.

The wild, free woods make no man
halt or blind;
Cities rob men of eyes and hands
and feet,
Patching one whole of many incomplete;
The general preys upon the individual
mind,
And each alone is helpless as the
wind.

Each man is some man's servant;
every soul
Is by some other's presence quite
discrowned;
Each owes the next through all the
imperfect round,
Yet not with mutual help; each man is
his own goal,
And the whole earth must stop to pay
him toll.

Here, life the undiminished man demands;
New faculties stretch out to meet
new wants;
What Nature asks, that Nature
also grants;
Here man is lord, not drudge, of eyes
and feet and hands,
And to his life is knit with hourly
bands.

Come out, then, from the old thoughts
and old ways,
Before you harden to a crystal cold
Which the new life can shatter, but
not mould;
Freedom for you still waits, still, looking backward, stays,
But widens still the irretrievable
space.

LONGING.

OF all the myriad moods of mind
That through the soul come thronging,
Which one was e'er so dear, so kind,
So beautiful as Longing?

The thing we long for, that we are
  For one transcendent moment,
Before the Present poor and bare
  Can make its sneering comment.

Still, through our paltry stir and strife,
  Glows down the wished Ideal,
And Longing moulds in clay what Life
  Carves in the marble Real;
To let the new life in, we know,
  Desire must ope the portal;
Perhaps the longing to be so
  Helps make the soul immortal.

Longing is God's fresh heavenward will
  With our poor earthward striving;
We quench it that we may be still
  Content with merely living;
But, would we learn that heart's full
    scope
  Which we are hourly wronging,
Our lives must climb from hope to hope
  And realize our longing.

Ah! let us hope that to our praise
  Good God not only reckons
The moments when we tread His ways,
  But when the spirit beckons, —
That some slight good is also wrought
  Beyond self-satisfaction,
When we are simply good in thought,
  Howe'er we fail in action.

ODE TO FRANCE.

FEBRUARY, 1848.

I.

As, flake by flake, the beetling ava-
    lanches
  Build up their imminent crags of
    noiseless snow,
Till some chance thrill the loosened
    ruin launches
  In unwarned havoc on the roofs
    below,
So grew and gathered through the silent
    years
  The madness of a People, wrong by
    wrong.
There seemed no strength in the dumb
    toiler's tears, —
  No strength in suffering; — but the
    Past was strong:

The brute despair of trampled centuries
  Leaped up with one hoarse yell and
    snapped its bands,
  Groped for its right with horny,
    callous hands,
And stared around for God with blood-
    shot eyes.
  What wonder if those palms were all
    too hard
For nice distinctions, — if that mænad
    throng —
  They whose thick atmosphere no bard
Had shivered with the lightning of his
    song,
  Brutes with the memories and desires
    of men,
  Whose chronicles were writ with iron
    pen,
    In the crooked shoulder and the
      forehead low —
    Set wrong to balance wrong,
    And physicked woe with woe?

II.

They did as they were taught; not
    theirs the blame,
If men who scattered firebrands reaped
    the flame:
  They trampled Peace beneath their
    savage feet,
  And by her golden tresses drew
  Mercy along the pavement of the
    street.
O Freedom! Freedom! is thy morn-
    ing-dew
    So gory red? Alas, thy light had
    ne'er
    Shone in upon the chaos of their
    lair!
They reared to thee such symbol as
    they knew,
    And worshipped it with flame and
    blood,
    A Vengeance, axe in hand, that
    stood
Holding a tyrant's head up by the
    clotted hair.

III.

What wrongs the Oppressor suffered,
    these we know;
  These have found piteous voice in
    song and prose;

But for the Oppressed, their darkness
   and their woe,
  Their grinding centuries, — what
   Muse had those?
Though hall and palace had nor eyes
   nor ears,
  Hardening a people's heart to sense-
   less stone,
Thou knowest them, O Earth, that
   drank their tears,
  O Heaven, that heard their inarticu-
   late moan !
They noted down their fetters, link by
   link ;
Coarse was the hand that scrawled, and
   red the ink ;
  Rude was their score, as suits un-
   lettered men, —
Notched with a headsman's axe upon
   a block :
What marvel if, when came the aveng-
   ing shock,
  'T was Atë, not Urania, held the
   pen ?

IV.

With eye averted and an anguished
   frown,
  Loathingly glides the Muse through
   scenes of strife,
Where, like the heart of Vengeance up
   and down,
  Throbs in its framework the blood-
   muffled knife ;
Slow are the steps of Freedom, but her
   feet
  Turn never backward : hers no bloody
   glare ;
Her light is calm, and innocent, and
   sweet,
  And where it enters there is no despair :
Not first on palace and cathedral
   spire
Quivers and gleams that unconsuming
   fire ;
  While these stand black against her
   morning skies,
The peasant sees it leap from peak to
   peak
  Along his hills ; the craftsman's burning eyes
Own with cool tears its influence moth-
   er-meek ;

It lights the poet's heart up like a
   star : —
  Ah ! while the tyrant deemed it still
   afar,
And twined with golden threads his
   futile snare,
  That swift, convicting glow all round
   him ran ;
  'T was close beside him there,
Sunrise whose Memnon is the soul of
   man.

V.

O Broker-King, is this thy wisdom's
   fruit ?
  A dynasty plucked out as 't were a
   weed
  Grown rankly in a night, that leaves
   no seed !
Could eighteen years strike down no
   deeper root ?
But now thy vulture eye was turned
   on Spain ;
A shout from Paris, and thy crown
   falls off,
  Thy race has ceased to reign,
And thou become a fugitive and scoff :
  Slippery the feet that mount by
   stairs of gold,
And weakest of all fences one of
   steel ;
  Go and keep school again like him
   of old,
The Syracusan tyrant ; — thou mayst
   feel
Royal amid a birch-swayed common-
   weal !

VI.

Not long can he be ruler who allows
  His time to run before him ; thou
   wast naught
Soon as the strip of gold about thy
   brows
  Was no more emblem of the People's
   thought ;
Vain were thy bayonets against the
   foe
  Thou hadst to cope with ; thou didst
   wage
War not with Frenchmen merely ; —
   no,
  Thy strife was with the Spirit of the
   Age,

The invisible Spirit whose first breath
        divine
    Scattered thy frail endeavor,
And, like poor last year's leaves,
        whirled thee and thine
    Into the Dark forever !

VII.

    Is here no triumph ? Nay, what
        though
The yellow blood of Trade meanwhile
        should pour
Along its arteries a shrunken flow,
And the idle canvas droop around the
        shore ?
    These do not make a state,
    Nor keep it great ;
    I think God made
The earth for man, not trade ;
And where each humblest human crea-
        ture
Can stand, no more suspicious or
        afraid,
Erect and kingly in his right of nature,
To heaven and earth knit with harmo-
        nious ties, —
    Where I behold the exultation
Of manhood glowing in those eyes
    That had been dark for ages, —
    Or only lit with bestial loves and
        rages —
There I behold a Nation :
    The France which lies
Between the Pyrenees and Rhine
Is the least part of France ;
I see her rather in the soul whose shine
Burns through the craftsman's grimy
        countenance,
    In the new energy divine
    Of Toil's enfranchised glance.

VIII.

    And if it be a dream,
If the great Future be the little Past
'Neath a new mask, which drops and
        shows at last
The same weird, mocking face to
        balk and blast,
Yet, Muse, a gladder measure suits the
        theme,
    And the Tyrtæan harp
    Loves notes more resolute and
        sharp,

Throbbing, as throbs the bosom, hot
        and fast ;
    Such visions are of morning,
    Theirs is no vague forewarning,
The dreams which nations dream come
        true,
    And shape the world anew ;
    If this be a sleep,
    Make it long, make it deep,
O Father, who sendest the harvests
        men reap !
    While Labor so sleepeth
    His sorrow is gone,
    No longer he weepeth,
    But smileth and steepeth
    His thoughts in the dawn ;
He heareth Hope yonder
    Rain, lark-like, her fancies,
His dreaming hands wander
    'Mid heart's-ease and pansies ;
"'T is a dream ! 'T is a vision !"
    Shrieks Mammon aghast ;
"The day's broad derision
    Will chase it at last ;
Ye are mad, ye have taken
    A slumbering kraken
For firm land of the Past !"
    Ah ! if he awaken,
    God shield us all then,
If this dream rudely shaken
    Shall cheat him again !

IX.

Since first I heard our North wind
        blow,
Since first I saw Atlantic throw
On our grim rocks his thunderous
        snow,
I loved thee, Freedom ; as a boy
The rattle of thy shield at Marathon
    Did with a Grecian joy
    Through all my pulses run ;
But I have learned to love thee now
Without the helm upon thy gleaming
        brow,
    A maiden mild and undefiled
Like her who bore the world's redeem-
        ing child ;
    And surely never did thy altars glance
With purer fires than now in France ;
While, in their clear white flashes,
    Wrong's shadow, backward cast,
    Waves cowering o'er the ashes
    Of the dead, blaspheming Past,

O'er the shapes of fallen giants,
      His own unburied brood,
Whose dead hands clench defiance
   At the overpowering Good :
And down the happy future runs a flood
   Of prophesying light ;
It shows an Earth no longer stained
      with blood,
Blossom and fruit where now we see the
      bud
   Of Brotherhood and Right.

ANTI-APIS.

PRAISEST Law, friend ? We, too, love
   it much as they that love it best ;
'Tis the deep, august foundation, where-
   on Peace and Justice rest ;
On the rock primeval, hidden in the
   Past its bases be,
Block by block the endeavoring Ages
   built it up to what we see.

But dig down : the Old unbury ; thou
   shalt find on every stone
That each Age hath carved the symbol
   of what god to them was known.
Ugly shapes and brutish sometimes,
   but the fairest that they knew ;
If their sight were dim and earthward,
   yet their hope and aim were true.

Surely as the unconscious needle feels
   the far-off loadstar draw,
So strives every gracious nature to
   at-one itself with law ;
And the elder Saints and Sages laid
   their pious framework right
By a theocratic instinct covered from
   the people's sight.

As their gods were, so their laws were ;
   Thor the strong could reave and
      steal,
So through many a peaceful inlet tore
   the Norseman's eager keel ;
But a new law came when Christ came,
   and not blameless, as before,
Can we, paying him our lip-tithes, give
   our lives and faiths to Thor.

Law is holy : ay, but what law ? Is
   there nothing more divine
Than the patched-up broils of Congress, — venal, full of meat and
   wine ?
Is there, say you, nothing higher ?
   Naught, God save us ! that transcends
Laws of cotton texture, wove by vulgar
   men for vulgar ends ?

Did Jehovah ask their counsel, or submit to them a plan,
Ere he filled with loves, hopes, longings, this aspiring heart of man ?
For their edict does the soul wait, ere it
   swing round to the pole
Of the true, the free, the God-willed,
   all that makes it be a soul ?

Law is holy ; but not your law, ye who
   keep the tablets whole
While ye dash the Law to pieces, shat-
   ter it in life and soul ;
Bearing up the Ark is lightsome, golden
   Apis hid within,
While we Levites share the offerings,
   richer by the people's sin.

Give to Cæsar what is Cæsar's ? yes,
   but tell me, if you can,
Is this superscription Cæsar's here upon
   our brother man ?
Is not here some other's image, dark
   and sullied though it be,
In this fellow-soul that worships, struggles Godward even as we ?

It was not to such a future that the Mayflower's prow was turned ;
Not to such a faith the martyrs clung,
   exulting as they burned ;
Not by such laws are men fashioned,
   earnest, simple, valiant, great
In the household virtues whereon rests
   the unconquerable state.

Ah ! there is a higher gospel, overhead
   the God-roof springs,
And each glad, obedient planet like a
   golden shuttle sings
Through the web which Time is weaving in his never-resting loom,
Weaving seasons many-colored, bringing prophecy to doom.

Think you Truth a farthing rushlight,
    to be pinched out when you will
With your deft official fingers, and your
    politicians' skill?
Is your God a wooden fetish, to be hid-
    den out of sight
That his block eyes may not see you do
    the thing that is not right?

But the Destinies think not so; to their
    judgment-chamber lone
Comes no noise of popular clamor,
    there Fame's trumpet is not blown;
Your majorities they reck not; — that
    you grant, but then you say
That you differ with them somewhat, —
    which is stronger, you or they?

Patient are they as the insects that
    build islands in the deep;
They hurl not the bolted thunder, but
    their silent way they keep;
Where they have been that we know;
    where empires towered that were
    not just;
Lo! the skulking wild fox scratches in
    a little heap of dust.

1851.

A PARABLE.

SAID Christ our Lord, "I will go and
    see
How the men, my brethren, believe in
    me."
He passed not again through the gate
    of birth,
But made himself known to the chil-
    dren of earth.

Then said the chief priests, and rulers,
    and kings,
"Behold, now, the Giver of all good
    things;
Go to, let us welcome with pomp and
    state
Him who alone is mighty and great."

With carpets of gold the ground they
    spread
Wherever the Son of Man should tread,

And in palace-chambers lofty and rare
They lodged him, and served him with
    kingly fare.

Great organs surged through arches dim
Their jubilant floods in praise of him;
And in church, and palace, and judg-
    ment-hall,
He saw his own image high over all.

But still, wherever his steps they led,
The Lord in sorrow bent down his head,
And from under the heavy foundation-
    stones,
The son of Mary heard bitter groans.

And in church, and palace, and judg-
    ment-hall,
He marked great fissures that rent the
    wall,
And opened wider and yet more wide
As the living foundation heaved and
    sighed.

"Have ye founded your thrones and
    altars, then,
On the bodies and souls of living men?
And think ye that building shall endure,
Which shelters the noble and crushes
    the poor?

"With gates of silver and bars of gold
Ye have fenced my sheep from their
    Father's fold;
I have heard the dropping of their tears
In heaven these eighteen hundred
    years."

"O Lord and Master, not ours the guilt,
We build but as our fathers built;
Behold thine images, how they stand,
Sovereign and sole, through all our land.

'Our task is hard, — with sword and
    flame
To hold thy earth forever the same,
And with sharp crooks of steel to keep
Still, as thou leftest them, thy sheep."

Then Christ sought out an artisan,
A low-browed, stunted, haggard man,
And a motherless girl, whose fingers thin
Pushed from her faintly want and sin-

These set he in the midst of them,
And as they drew back their garment-
    hem,
For fear of defilement, " Lo, here,"
    said he,
" The images ye have made of me !"

ODE

WRITTEN FOR THE CELEBRATION OF
THE INTRODUCTION OF THE COCHIT-
UATE WATER INTO THE CITY OF
BOSTON.

My name is Water : I have sped
    Through strange, dark ways, untried
    before,
By pure desire of friendship led,
    Cochituate's ambassador ;
He sends four royal gifts by me :
Long life, health, peace, and purity.

I 'm Ceres' cup-bearer ; I pour,
    For flowers and fruits and all their kin,
Her crystal vintage, from of yore
    Stored in old Earth's selectest bin,
Flora's Falernian ripe, since God
The wine-press of the deluge trod.

In that far isle whence, iron-willed,
    The New World's sires their bark
    unmoored,
The fairies' acorn-cups I filled
    Upon the toadstool's silver board,
And, 'neath Herne's oak, for Shake-
    speare's sight,
Strewed moss and grass with diamonds
    bright.

No fairies in the Mayflower came,
    And, lightsome as I sparkle here,
For Mother Bay State, busy dame,
    I 've toiled and drudged this many a
    year,
Throbbed in her engines' iron veins,
Twirled myriad spindles for her gains.

I, too, can weave : the warp I set
    Through which the sun his shuttle
    throws,
And, bright as Noah saw it, yet
    For you the arching rainbow glows,

7

A sight in Paradise denied
To unfallen Adam and his bride.

When Winter held me in his grip,
    You seized and sent me o'er the wave,
Ungrateful ! in a prison-ship ;
    But I forgive, not long a slave,
For, soon as summer south-winds blew,
Homeward I fled, disguised as dew.

For countless services I 'm fit,
    Of use, of pleasure, and of gain,
But lightly from all bonds I flit,
    Nor lose my mirth, nor feel a stain ;
From mill and wash-tub I escape,
And take in heaven my proper shape.

So, free myself, to-day, elate
    I come from far o'er hill and mead,
And here, Cochituate's envoy, wait
    To be your blithesome Ganymede,
And brim your cups with nectar true
That never will make slaves of you.

LINES

SUGGESTED BY THE GRAVES OF TWO
ENGLISH SOLDIERS ON CONCORD
BATTLE-GROUND.

THE same good blood that now refills
The dotard Orient's shrunken veins,
The same whose vigor westward thrills,
Bursting Nevada's silver chains,
Poured here upon the April grass,
Freckled with red the herbage new ;
On reeled the battle's trampling mass,
Back to the ash the bluebird flew.

Poured here in vain ; — that sturdy blood
Was meant to make the earth more
    green,
But in a higher, gentler mood
Than broke this April noon serene ;
Two graves are here : to mark the place,
At head and foot, an unhewn stone,
O'er which the herald lichens trace
The blazon of Oblivion.

These men were brave enough, and true
To the hired soldier's bull-dog creed ;
What brought them here they never
    knew,

They fought as suits the English breed;
They came three thousand miles, and
　died,
To keep the Past upon its throne;
Unheard, beyond the ocean tide,
　Their English mother made her moan.

The turf that covers them no thrill
Sends up to fire the heart and brain;
No stronger purpose nerves the will,
No hope renews its youth again:
From farm to farm the Concord glides,
And trails my fancy with its flow;
O'erhead the balanced hen-hawk slides,
　Twinned in the river's heaven below.

But go, whose Bay State bosom stirs,
Proud of thy birth and neighbor's right,
Where sleep the heroic villagers
Borne red and stiff from Concord fight;
Thought Reuben, snatching down his
　gun,
Or Seth, as ebbed the life away,
What earthquake rifts would shoot and
　run
World-wide from that short April fray?

What then? With heart and hand they
　wrought,
According to their village light;
'T was for the Future that they fought,
Their rustic faith in what was right.
Upon earth's tragic stage they burst
Unsummoned, in the humble sock;
Theirs the fifth act; the curtain first
Rose long ago on Charles's block.

Their graves have voices; if they threw
Dice charged with fates beyond their
　ken,
Yet to their instincts they were true,
And had the genius to be men.
Fine privilege of Freedom's host,
Of humblest soldiers for the Right! —
Age after age ye hold your post,
　Your graves send courage forth, and
　might.

———

TO ——

We, too, have autumns, when our leaves
　Drop loosely through the dampened
　air,
When all our good seems bound in
　sheaves,
　And we stand reaped and bare.

Our seasons have no fixed returns,
　Without our will they come and go;
At noon our sudden summer burns,
　Ere sunset all is snow.

But each day brings less summer cheer,
　Crimps more our ineffectual spring,
And something earlier every year
　Our singing birds take wing.

As less the olden glow abides,
　And less the chillier heart aspires,
With drift-wood beached in past spring-
　tides
　We light our sullen fires.

By the pinched rushlight's starving
　beam
　We cower and strain our wasted sight,
To stitch youth's shroud up, seam by
　seam,
　In the long arctic night.

It was not so — we once were young —
　When Spring, to womanly Summer
　turning,
Her dew-drops on each grass-blade
　strung,
　In the red sunrise burning.

We trusted then, aspired, believed
　That earth could be remade to-mor-
　row;
Ah, why be ever undeceived?
　Why give up faith for sorrow?

O thou, whose days are yet all spring,
　Faith, blighted once, is past retriev-
　ing;
Experience is a dumb, dead thing;
　The victory's in believing.

———

FREEDOM.

Are we, then, wholly fallen? Can it be
That thou, North wind, that from thy
　mountains bringest
Their spirit to our plains, and thou,
　blue sea,

Who on our rocks thy wreaths of free-
  dom flingest,
As on an altar, — can it be that ye
Have wasted inspiration on dead ears,
Dulled with the too familiar clank of
  chains?
The people's heart is like a harp for
  years
Hung where some petrifying torrent
  rains
Its slow-incrusting spray: the stiffened
  chords
Faint and more faint make answer to
  the tears
That drip upon them: idle are all words:
Only a golden plectrum wakes the tone
Deep buried 'neath that ever-thicken-
  ing stone.

We are not free: doth Freedom, then,
  consist
In musing with our faces toward the
  Past,
While petty cares, and crawling inter-
  ests, twist
Their spider-threads about us, which at
  last
Grow strong as iron chains, to cramp
  and bind
In formal narrowness heart, soul, and
  mind?
Freedom is recreated year by year,
In hearts wide open on the Godward
  side,
In souls calm-cadenced as the whirling
  sphere,
In minds that sway the future like a tide.
No broadest creeds can hold her, and
  no codes;
She chooses men for her august abodes,
Building them fair and fronting to the
  dawn;
Yet, when we seek her, we but find a
  few
Light footprints, leading morn-ward
  through the dew:
Before the day had risen, she was gone.

And we must follow: swiftly runs she
  on,
And, if our steps should slacken in despair,
Half turns her face, half smiles through
  golden hair,

Forever yielding, never wholly won:
That is not love which pauses in the race
Two close-linked names on fleeting
  sand to trace;
Freedom gained yesterday is no more
  ours;
Men gather but dry seeds of last year's
  flowers;
Still there 's a charm ungranted, still a
  grace,
Still rosy Hope, the free, the unattained,
Makes us Possession's languid hand
  let fall;
'T is but a fragment of ourselves is
  gained,
The Future brings us more, but never
  all.

And, as the finder of some unknown
  realm,
Mounting a summit whence he thinks
  to see
On either side of him the imprisoning
  sea,
Beholds, above the clouds that over-
  whelm
The valley-land, peak after snowy peak
Stretch out of sight, each like a silver
  helm
Beneath its plume of smoke, sublime
  and bleak,
And what he thought an island finds
  to be
A continent to him first oped, — so we
Can from our height of Freedom look
  along
A boundless future, ours if we be strong;
Or if we shrink, better remount our
  ships
And, fleeing God's express design, trace
  back
The hero-freighted Mayflower's pro-
  phet-track
To Europe, entering her blood-red
  eclipse.

BIBLIOLATRES.

Bowing thyself in dust before a Book,
And thinking the great God is thine
  alone,
O rash iconoclast, thou wilt not brook

What gods the heathen carves in wood
    and stone,
As if the Shepherd who from outer cold
Leads all his shivering lambs to one
    sure fold
Were careful for the fashion of his
    crook.

There is no broken reed so poor and
    base,
No rush, the bending tilt of swamp-fly
    blue,
But he therewith the ravening wolf
    can chase,
And guide his flock to springs and
    pastures new ;
Through ways unlooked for, and
    through many lands,
Far from the rich folds built with hu-
    man hands,
The gracious footprints of his love I
    trace.

And what art thou, own brother of the
    clod,
That from his hand the crook wouldst
    snatch away
And shake instead thy dry and sapless
    rod,
To scare the sheep out of the whole-
    some day ?
Yea, what art thou, blind, unconverted
    Jew,
That with thy idol-volume's covers two
Wouldst make a jail to coop the living
    God ?

Thou hear'st not well the mountain
    organ-tones
By prophet ears from Hor and Sinai
    caught,
Thinking the cisterns of those He-
    brew brains
Drew dry the springs of the All-know-
    er's thought,
Nor shall thy lips be touched with liv-
    ing fire,
Who blow'st old altar-coals with sole
    desire
To weld anew the spirit's broken
    chains.

God is not dumb, that he should speak
    no more ;
If thou hast wanderings in the wilder-
    ness

And find'st not Sinai, 't is thy soul is
    poor ;
There towers the mountain of the
    Voice no less,
Which whoso seeks shall find, but he
    who bends,
Intent on manna still and mortal ends,
Sees it not, neither hears its thundered
    lore.

Slowly the Bible of the race is writ,
And not on paper leaves nor leaves of
    stone ;
Each age, each kindred, adds a verse
    to it,
Texts of despair or hope, of joy or
    moan.
While swings the sea, while mists the
    mountains shroud,
While thunder's surges burst on cliffs
    of cloud,
Still at the prophets' feet the nations
    sit.

———

BEAVER BROOK.

Hushed with broad sunlight lies the
    hill,
And, minuting the long day's loss,
The cedar's shadow, slow and still,
Creeps o'er its dial of gray moss.

Warm noon brims full the valley's cup,
The aspen's leaves are scarce astir ;
Only the little mill sends up
Its busy, never-ceasing burr.

Climbing the loose-piled wall that hems
The road along the mill-pond's brink,
From 'neath the arching barberry-
    stems,
My footstep scares the shy chewink.

Beneath a bony buttonwood
The mill's red door lets forth the din ;
The whitened miller, dust-imbued,
Flits past the square of dark within.

No mountain torrent's strength is here
Sweet Beaver, child of forest still,
Heaps its small pitcher to the ear,
And gently waits the miller's will.

Swift slips Undine along the race
Unheard, and then, with flashing bound,
Floods the dull wheel with light and
    grace,
And, laughing, hunts the loath drudge
    round.

The miller dreams not at what cost
The quivering millstones hum and
    whirl,
Nor how for every turn are tost
Armfuls of diamond and of pearl.

But Summer cleared my happier eyes
With drops of some celestial juice,
To see how Beauty underlies,
Forevermore each form of Use.

And more: methought I saw that flood,
Which now so dull and darkling steals,

Thick, here and there, with human
    blood,
To turn the world's laborious wheels.

No more than doth the miller there,
Shut in our several cells, do we
Know with what waste of beauty rare
Moves every day's machinery.

Surely the wiser time shall come
When this fine overplus of might,
No longer sullen, slow, and dumb,
Shall leap to music and to light.

In that new childhood of the Earth
Life of itself shall dance and play,
Fresh blood in Time's shrunk veins
    make mirth,
And labor meet delight half-way.

MEMORIAL VERSES.

KOSSUTH.

A RACE of nobles may die out,
A royal line may leave no heir;
Wise Nature sets no guards about
Her pewter plate and wooden ware.

But they fail not, the kinglier breed,
Who starry diadems attain;
To dungeon, axe, and stake succeed
Heirs of the old heroic strain.

The zeal of Nature never cools,
Nor is she thwarted of her ends;
When gapped and dulled her cheaper
    tools,
Then she a saint and prophet spends.

Land of the Magyars! though it be
The tyrant may relink his chain,
Already thine the victory,
As the just Future measures gain.

Thou hast succeeded, thou hast won
The deathly travail's amplest worth;
A nation's duty thou hast done,
Giving a hero to our earth.

And he, let come what will of woe,
Has saved the land he strove to save;
No Cossack hordes, no traitor's blow,
Can quench the voice shall haunt his
    grave.

"I Kossuth am: O Future, thou
That clear'st the just and blott'st the
    vile,
O'er this small dust in reverence bow,
Remembering what I was erewhile.

"I was the chosen trump wherethrough
Our God sent forth awakening breath;
Came chains? Came death? The strain
    He blew
Sounds on, outliving chains and death."

TO LAMARTINE.
1848.

I DID not praise thee when the crowd,
    'Witched with the moment's in-
        spiration,
Vexed thy still ether with hosannas loud,
    And stamped their dusty adoration;

I but looked upward with the rest,
And, when they shouted Greatest,
    whispered Best.

They raised thee not, but rose to thee,
    Their fickle wreaths about thee
      flinging;
So on some marble Phœbus the swol'n
    sea
      Might leave his worthless seaweed
        clinging,
But pious hands, with reverent care,
Make the pure limbs once more sub-
    limely bare.

Now thou 'rt thy plain, grand self again,
    Thou art secure from panegyric,
Thou who gav'st politics an epic strain,
      And actedst Freedom's noblest
      lyric;
This side the Blessed Isles, no tree
Grows green enough to make a wreath
    for thee.

Nor can blame cling to thee; the snow
    From swinish footprints takes no
      staining,
But, leaving the gross soils of earth
    below,
      Its spirit mounts, the skies regain-
        ing,
And unresenting falls again,
To beautify the world with dews and
    rain.

The highest duty to mere man vouch-
    safed
      Was laid on thee, — out of wild
      chaos,
When the roused popular ocean foamed
    and chafed,
      And vulture War from his Imaus
Snuffed blood, to summon homely
    Peace,
And show that only order is release.

To carve thy fullest thought, what
    though
      Time was not granted? Aye in
      history,
Like that Dawn's face which baffled
    Angelo
      Left shapeless, grander for its
      mystery,
Thy great Design shall stand, and day
Flood its blind front from Orients far
    away.

Who says thy day is o'er? Control,
    My heart, that bitter first emotion
While men shall reverence the steadfast
    soul,
    The heart in silent self-devotion
Breaking, the mild, heroic mien,
Thou 'lt need no prop of marble, La-
    martine.

If France reject thee, 't is not thine,
    But her own, exile that she utters;
Ideal France, the deathless, the divine,
    Will be where thy white pennon
      flutters,
As once the nobler Athens went
With Aristides into banishment.

No fitting metewand hath To-day
    For measuring spirits of thy
      stature, —
Only the Future can reach up to lay
    The laurel on that lofty nature, —
Bard, who with some diviner art
Has touched the bard's true lyre, a
    nation's heart.

Swept by thy hand, the gladdened
    chords,
    Crashed now in discords fierce by
      others,
Gave forth one note beyond all skill of
    words,
    And chimed together, We are
      brothers.
O poem unsurpassed! it ran
All round the world, unlocking man to
    man.

France is too poor to pay alone
    The service of that ample spirit;
Paltry seem low dictatorship and throne,
    Weighed with thy self-renouncing
      merit;
They had to thee been rust and loss;
Thy aim was higher, — thou hast
    climbed a Cross.

TO JOHN G. PALFREY.

THERE are who triumph in a losing
    cause,
Who can put on defeat, as 't were a
    wreath

Unwithering in the adverse popular
  breath,
    Safe from the blasting demagogue's
      applause ;
'T is they who stand for Freedom and
  God's laws.

And so stands Palfrey now, as Marvell
  stood,
    Loyal to Truth dethroned, nor could be
      wooed
      To trust the playful tiger's velvet
        paws :
And if the second Charles brought in
  decay
    Of ancient virtue, if it well might wring
Souls that had broadened 'neath a
  nobler day,
    To see a losel, marketable king
Fearfully watering with his realm's best
  blood
    Cromwell's quenched bolts, that erst
      had cracked and flamed,
Scaring, through all their depths of
  courtier mud,
    Europe's crowned bloodsuckers, —
      how more ashamed
Ought we to be, who see Corruption's
  flood
    Still rise o'er last year's mark, to mine
      away
Our brazen idol's feet of treacherous
  clay !

O utter degradation ! Freedom turned
    Slavery's vile bawd, to cozen and
      betray
    To the old lecher's clutch a maiden
      prey,
If so a loathsome pander's fee be earned!
    And we are silent, — we who daily
      tread
A soil sublime, at least, with heroes'
  graves ! —
    Beckon no more, shades of the noble
      dead !
Be dumb, ye heaven-touched lips of
  winds and waves !
    Or hope to rouse some Coptic dullard,
      hid
Ages ago, wrapt stiffly, fold on fold,
With cerements close, to wither in the
  cold,
    Forever hushed, and sunless pyramid!

Beauty and Truth, and all that these
  contain,
Drop not like ripened fruit about our
  feet ;
    We climb to them through years of
      sweat and pain ;
    Without long struggle, none did e'er
      attain
The downward look from Quiet's blissful seat ;
    Though present loss may be the hero's
      part,
    Yet none can rob him of the victor
      heart
Whereby the broad-realmed future is
  subdued,
    And Wrong, which now insults from
      triumph's car,
    Sending her vulture hope to raven far,
Is made unwilling tributary of Good.

O Mother State, how quenched thy
  Sinai fires !
    Is there none left of thy stanch May-
      flower breed ?
No spark among the ashes of thy sires,
    Of Virtue's altar-flame the kindling
      seed ?
Are these thy great men, these that
  cringe and creep,
    And writhe through slimy ways to
      place and power ? —
How long, O Lord, before thy wrath
  shall reap
    Our frail-stemmed summer prosper-
      ings in their flower ?
O for one hour of that undaunted stock
That went with Vane and Sydney to
  the block !

O for a whiff of Naseby, that would
  sweep,
    With its stern Puritan besom, all this
      chaff
    From the Lord's threshing-floor ! Yet
      more than half
The victory is attained, when one or
  two,
    Through the fool's laughter and the
      traitor's scorn,
    Beside thy sepulchre can abide the
      morn,
Crucified Truth, when thou shalt rise
  anew.

TO W. L. GARRISON.

"Some time afterward, it was reported to
me by the city officers that they had ferreted
out the paper and its editor; that his office
was an obscure hole, his only visible auxiliary
a negro boy, and his supporters a few very
insignificant persons of all colors."—*Letter
of H. G. Otis.*

In a small chamber, friendless and un-
        seen,
    Toiled o'er his types one poor, un-
        learned young man;
The place was dark, unfurnitured, and
        mean;
    Yet there the freedom of a race began.

Help came but slowly; surely no man
        yet
    Put lever to the heavy world with
        less:
What need of help?   He knew how
        types were set,
    He had a dauntless spirit, and a press.

Such earnest natures are the fiery pith,
    The compact nucleus, round which
        systems grow;
Mass after mass becomes inspired there-
        with,
    And whirls impregnate with the cen-
        tral glow.

O Truth! O Freedom! how are ye still
        born
    In the rude stable, in the manger
        nurst!
What humble hands unbar those gates
        of morn
    Through which the splendors of the
        New Day burst!

What! shall one monk, scarce known
        beyond his cell,
    Front Rome's far-reaching bolts, and
        scorn her frown?
Brave Luther answered Yes; that
        thunder's swell
    Rocked Europe, and discharmed the
        triple crown.

Whatever can be known of earth we
        know,
    Sneered Europe's wise men, in their
        snail-shells curled;

No! said one man in Genoa, and that
        No
    Out of the darkness summoned this
        New World.

Who is it will not dare himself to trust?
    Who is it hath not strength to stand
        alone?
Who is it thwarts and bilks the inward
        MUST?
    He and his works, like sand, from
        earth are blown.

Men of a thousand shifts and wiles,
        look here!
    See one straightforward conscience
        put in pawn
To win a world; see the obedient
        sphere
    By bravery's simple gravitation drawn!

Shall we not heed the lesson taught of
        old,
    And by the Present's lips repeated
        still,
In our own single manhood to be bold,
    Fortressed in conscience and impreg-
        nable will?

We stride the river daily at its spring,
    Nor, in our childish thoughtlessness,
        foresee
What myriad vassal streams shall trib-
        ute bring,
    How like an equal it shall greet the
        sea.

O small beginnings, ye are great and
        strong,
    Based on a faithful heart and weari-
        less brain!
Ye build the future fair, ye conquer
        wrong,
    Ye earn the crown, and wear it not in
        vain.

ON THE DEATH OF C. T. TORREY.

Woe worth the hour when it is crime
    To plead the poor dumb bondman's
        cause,

When all that makes the heart sublime,
The glorious throbs that conquer time,
Are traitors to our cruel laws!

He strove among God's suffering poor
One gleam of brotherhood to send;
The dungeon oped its hungry door
To give the truth one martyr more,
Then shut, — and here behold the
end!

O Mother State! when this was done,
No pitying throe thy bosom gave;
Silent thou saw'st the death-shroud
spun,
And now thou givest to thy son
The stranger's charity, — a grave.

Must it be thus forever? No!
The hand of God sows not in vain;
Long sleeps the darkling seed below,
The seasons come, and change, and go,
And all the fields are deep with grain.

Although our brother lie asleep,
Man's heart still struggles, still as-
pires;
His grave shall quiver yet, while deep
Through the brave Bay State's pulses
leap
Her ancient energies and fires.

When hours like this the senses' gush
Have stilled, and left the spirit room,
It hears amid the eternal hush
The swooping pinions' dreadful rush,
That bring the vengeance and the
doom; —

Not man's brute vengeance, such as
rends
What rivets man to man apart, —
God doth not so bring round his ends,
But waits the ripened time, and sends
His mercy to the oppressor's heart.

ELEGY ON THE DEATH OF
DR. CHANNING.

I DO not come to weep above thy pall,
And mourn the dying-out of noble
powers;

The poet's clearer eye should see, in all
Earth's seeming woe, seed of immortal flowers.

Truth needs no champions: in the infinite deep
Of everlasting Soul her strength
abides,
From Nature's heart her mighty pulses
leap,
Through Nature's veins her strength,
undying, tides.

Peace is more strong than war, and
gentleness,
Where force were vain, makes conquest o'er the wave;
And love lives on and hath a power to
bless,
When they who loved are hidden in
the grave.

The sculptured marble brags of death-
strewn fields,
And Glory's epitaph is writ in blood;
But Alexander now to Plato yields,
Clarkson will stand where Wellington
hath stood.

I watch the circle of the eternal years,
And read forever in the storied page
One lengthened roll of blood, and
wrong, and tears,
One onward step of Truth from age
to age.

The poor are crushed; the tyrants link
their chain;
The poet sings through narrow dun-
geon-grates;
Man's hope lies quenched; — and, lo!
with steadfast gain
Freedom doth forge her mail of adverse fates.

Men slay the prophets; fagot, rack, and
cross
Make up the groaning record of the
past;
But Evil's triumphs are her endless loss,
And sovereign Beauty wins the soul
at last.

No power can die that ever wrought for
Truth;
Thereby a law of Nature it became,

And lives unwithered in its blithesome
    youth;
  When he who called it forth is but a
    name.

Therefore I cannot think thee wholly
    gone;
  The better part of thee is with us
    still;
Thy soul its hampering clay aside hath
    thrown,
  And only freer wrestles with the Ill.

Thou livest in the life of all good things;
  What words thou spak'st for Free-
    dom shall not die;
Thou sleepest not, for now thy Love
    hath wings
  To soar where hence thy Hope could
    hardly fly.

And often, from that other world, on
    this
  Some gleams from great souls gone
    before may shine,
To shed on struggling hearts a clearer
    bliss,
  And clothe the Right with lustre more
    divine.

Thou art not idle: in thy higher sphere
  Thy spirit bends itself to loving tasks,
And strength, to perfect what it dreamed
    of here
Is all the crown and glory that it asks.

For sure, in Heaven's wide chambers,
    there is room
  For love and pity, and for helpful
    deeds;
Else were our summons thither but a
    doom
  To life more vain than this in clayey
    weeds.

From off the starry mountain-peak of
    song,
  Thy spirit shows me, in the coming
    time,
An earth unwithered by the foot of
    wrong,
  A race revering its own soul sublime.

What wars, what martyrdoms, what
    crimes, may come,
  Thou knowest not, nor I; but God
    will lead

The prodigal soul from want and sorrow
    home,
  And Eden ope her gates to Adam's
    seed.

Farewell! good man, good angel now!
    this hand
  Soon, like thine own, shall lose its
    cunning too;
Soon shall this soul, like thine, be-
    wildered stand,
  Then leap to thread the free, un-
    fathomed blue:

When that day comes, O, may this hand
    grow cold,
  Busy, like thine, for Freedom and
    the Right;
O, may this soul, like thine, be ever
    bold
  To face dark Slavery's encroaching
    blight!

This laurel-leaf I cast upon thy bier;
  Let worthier hands than these thy
    wreath intwine;
Upon thy hearse I shed no useless
    tear, —
  For us weep rather thou in calm di-
    vine!

    1842.   ———

TO THE MEMORY OF HOOD.

ANOTHER star 'neath Time's horizon
    dropped,
  To gleam o'er unknown lands and
    seas;
Another heart that beat for freedom
    stopped, —
  What mournful words are these!

O Love Divine, that claspest our tired
    earth,
  And lullest it upon thy heart,
Thou knowest how much a gentle soul
    is worth
  To teach men what thou art!

His was a spirit that to all thy poor
  Was kind as slumber after pain:
Why ope so soon thy heaven-deep
    Quiet's door
  And call him home again?

Freedom needs all her poets : it is they
  Who give her aspirations wings,
And to the wiser law of music sway
  Her wild imaginings.

Yet thou hast called him, nor art thou unkind,
  O Love Divine, for 't is thy will
That gracious natures leave their love behind
  To work for Mercy still.

Let laurelled marbles weigh on other tombs,
  Let anthems peal for other dead,

Rustling the bannered depth of minster-glooms
  With their exulting spread.

His epitaph shall mock the short-lived stone,
  No lichen shall its lines efface,
He needs these few and simple lines alone
  To mark his resting-place : —

" Here lies a Poet.   Stranger, if to thee
  His claim to memory be obscure,
If thou wouldst learn how truly great was he,
  Go, ask it of the poor."

SONNETS.

I.

TO A. C. L.

THROUGH suffering and sorrow thou hast passed
To show us what a woman true may be :
They have not taken sympathy from thee,
Nor made thee any other than thou wast,
Save as some tree, which, in a sudden blast,
Sheddeth those blossoms, that are weakly grown,
Upon the air, but keepeth every one
Whose strength gives warrant of good fruit at last :
So thou hast shed some blooms of gayety,
But never one of steadfast cheerfulness ;
Nor hath thy knowledge of adversity
Robbed thee of any faith in happiness,
But rather cleared thine inner eyes to see
How many simple ways there are to bless.

1840.

II.

WHAT were I, Love, if I were stripped of thee,
If thine eyes shut me out whereby I live,
Thou, who unto my calmer soul dost give
Knowledge, and Truth, and holy Mystery,
Wherein Truth mainly lies for those who see
Beyond the earthly and the fugitive,
Who in the grandeur of the soul believe,
And only in the Infinite are free ?
Without thee I were naked, bleak, and bare
As yon dead cedar on the sea-cliff's brow ;
And Nature's teachings, which come to me now,
Common and beautiful as light and air,
Would be as fruitless as a stream which still
Slips through the wheel of some old ruined mill.

1841.

III.

I would not have this perfect love of
    ours
Grow from a single root, a single stem,
Bearing no goodly fruit, but only flow-
    ers
That idly hide life's iron diadem :
It should grow alway like that eastern
    tree
Whose limbs take root and spread forth
    constantly ;
That love for one, from which there
    doth not spring
Wide love for all, is but a worthless thing.
Not in another world, as poets prate,
Dwell we apart above the tide of things,
High floating o'er earth's clouds on
    faery wings ;
But our pure love doth ever elevate
Into a holy bond of brotherhood
All earthly things, making them pure
    and good.
1840.

IV.

" For this true nobleness I seek in vain,
In woman and in man I find it not ;
I almost weary of my earthly lot,
My life-springs are dried up with burn-
    ing pain."
Thou find'st it not ? I pray thee look
    again,
Look *inward* through the depths of
    thine own soul.
How is it with thee ? Art thou sound
    and whole ?
Doth narrow search show thee no earth-
    ly stain ?
Be noble ! and the nobleness that lies
In other men, sleeping, but never
    dead,
Will rise in majesty to meet thine
    own ;
Then wilt thou see it gleam in many
    eyes,
Then will pure light around thy path be
    shed,
And thou wilt nevermore be sad and
    lone.
1840

V.

TO THE SPIRIT OF KEATS.

Great soul, thou sittest with me in my
    room,
Uplifting me with thy vast, quiet eyes,
On whose full orbs, with kindly lustre,
    lies
The twilight warmth of ruddy ember-
    gloom :
Thy clear, strong tones will oft bring
    sudden bloom
Of hope secure, to him who lonely cries,
Wrestling with the young poet's agonies,
Neglect and scorn, which seem a cer-
    tain doom :
Yes ! the few words which, like great
    thunder-drops,
Thy large heart down to earth shook
    doubtfully,
Thrilled by the inward lightning of its
    might,
Serene and pure, like gushing joy of
    light,
Shall track the eternal chords of Des-
    tiny,
After the moon-led pulse of ocean stops.
1841.

VI.

Great Truths are portions of the soul
    of man ;
Great souls are portions of Eternity ;
Each drop of blood that e'er through
    true heart ran
With lofty message, ran for thee and
    me ;
For God's law, since the starry song
    began,
Hath been, and still forevermore must
    be,
That every deed which shall outlast
    Time's span
Must spur the soul to be erect and free ;
Slave is no word of deathless lineage
    sprung ;
Too many noble souls have thought and
    died,
Too many mighty poets lived and sung,
And our good Saxon, from lips purified

With martyr-fire, throughout the world
    hath rung
Too long to have God's holy cause de-
    nied.

1841.

    ———

VII.

I ASK not for those thoughts, that sud-
    den leap
From being's sea, like the isle-seeming
    Kraken,
With whose great rise the ocean all is
    shaken
And a heart-tremble quivers through
    the deep ;
Give me that growth which some per-
    chance deem sleep,
Wherewith the steadfast coral-stems
    uprise,
Which, by the toil of gathering energies,
Their upward way into clear sunshine
    keep,
Until, by Heaven's sweetest influences,
Slowly and slowly spreads a speck of
    green
Into a pleasant island in the seas,
Where, 'mid tall palms, the cane-roofed
    home is seen,
And wearied men shall sit at sunset's
    hour,
Hearing the leaves and loving God's
    dear power.

1841.

    ———

VIII.

TO M. W., ON HER BIRTHDAY.

MAIDEN, when such a soul as thine is
    born,
The morning-stars their ancient music
    make,
And, joyful, once again their song awake,
Long silent now with melancholy scorn ;
And thou, not mindless of so blest a
    morn,
By no least deed its harmony shalt
    break,
But shalt to that high chime thy foot-
    steps take,

Through life's most darksome passes
    unforlorn ;
Therefore from thy pure faith thou shalt
    not fall,
Therefore shalt thou be ever fair and
    free,
And in thine every motion musical
As summer air, majestic as the sea,
A mystery to those who creep and crawl
Through Time, and part it from Eter-
    nity.

1841.

    ———

IX.

MY Love, I have no fear that thou
    shouldst die ;
Albeit I ask no fairer life than this,
Whose numbering-clock is still thy
    gentle kiss,
While Time and Peace with hands en-
    lockèd fly, —
Yet care I not where in Eternity
We live and love, well knowing that
    there is
No backward step for those who feel the
    bliss
Of Faith as their most lofty yearnings
    high :
Love hath so purified my being's core,
Meseems I scarcely should be startled,
    even,
To find, some morn, that thou hadst
    gone before ;
Since, with thy love, this knowledge
    too was given,
Which each calm day doth strengthen
    more and more,
That they who love are but one step
    from Heaven.

1841.

    ———

X.

I CANNOT think that thou shouldst pass
    away,
Whose life to mine is an eternal law,
A piece of nature that can have no flaw,
A new and certain sunrise every day ;
But, if thou art to be another ray
About the Sun of Life, and art to live

Free from what part of thee was fugitive,
The debt of Love I will more fully pay,
Not downcast with the thought of thee
        so high,
But rather raised to be a nobler man,
And more divine in my humanity,
As knowing that the waiting eyes which
        scan
My life are lighted by a purer being,
And ask high, calm-browed deeds,
        with it agreeing.

    1841.

                    ———

XI.

THERE never yet was flower fair in vain,
Let classic poets rhyme it as they will ;
The seasons toil that it may blow again,
And summer's heart doth feel its every
        ill ;
Nor is a true soul ever born for naught ;
Wherever any such hath lived and died,
There hath been something for true
        freedom wrought,
Some bulwark levelled on the evil side:
Toil on, then, Greatness ! thou art in
        the right,
However narrow souls may call thee
        wrong ;
Be as thou wouldst be in thine own
        clear sight,
And so thou wilt in all the world's ere-
        long ;
For worldlings cannot, struggle as they
        may,
From man's great soul one great thought
        hide away.

    1841.

                    ———

XII.

SUB PONDERE CRESCIT.

THE hope of Truth grows stronger, day
        by day ;
I hear the soul of Man around me wak-
        ing,
Like a great sea, its frozen fetters
        breaking,
And flinging up to heaven its sunlit
        spray,

Tossing huge continents in scornful play,
And crushing them, with din of grind-
        ing thunder,
That makes old emptinesses stare in
        wonder ;
The memory of a glory passed away
Lingers in every heart, as, in the shell,
Resounds the bygone freedom of the sea,
And, every hour new signs of promise
        tell
That the great soul shall once again be
        free,
For high, and yet more high, the mur-
        murs swell
Of inward strife for truth and liberty.

    1841.

                    ———

XIII.

BELOVED, in the noisy city here,
The thought of thee can make all tur-
        moil cease ;
Around my spirit, folds thy spirit clear
Its still, soft arms, and circles it with
        peace ;
There is no room for any doubt or fear
In souls so overfilled with love's in-
        crease,
There is no memory of the bygone year
But growth in heart's and spirit's per-
        fect ease :
How hath our love, half nebulous at first,
Rounded itself into a full-orbed sun !
How have our lives and wills (as haply
        erst
They were, ere this forgetfulness begun)
Through all their earthly distances out-
        burst,
And melted, like two rays of light, in
        one !

    1842.   ———

XIV.

ON READING WORDSWORTH'S SON-
NETS IN DEFENCE OF CAPITAL
PUNISHMENT.

As the broad ocean endlessly upheaveth,
With the majestic beating of his heart,
The mighty tides, whereof its rightful
        part

Each sea-wide bay and little weed re-
ceiveth,
So, through his soul who earnestly be-
lieveth,
Life from the universal Heart doth flow,
Whereby some conquest of the eternal
Woe,
By instinct of God's nature, he achiev-
eth :
A fuller pulse of this all-powerful beauty
Into the poet's gulf-like heart doth tide,
And he more keenly feels the glorious
duty
Of serving Truth, despised and cruci-
fied, —
Happy, unknowing sect or creed, to rest
And feel God flow forever through his
breast.

1842.

XV.

THE SAME CONTINUED.

Once hardly in a cycle blossometh
A flower-like soul ripe with the seeds of
song,
A spirit foreordained to cope with
wrong,
Whose divine thoughts are natural as
breath,
Who the old Darkness thickly scattereth
With starry words, that shoot prevail-
ing light
Into the deeps, and wither, with the
blight
Of serene Truth, the coward heart of
Death :
Woe, if such spirit thwart its errand high,
And mock with lies the longing soul of
man !
Yet one age longer must true Culture lie,
Soothing her bitter fetters as she can,
Until new messages of love outstart
At the next beating of the infinite Heart.

XVI.

THE SAME CONTINUED.

The love of all things springs from
love of one ;
Wider the soul's horizon hourly grows,

And over it with fuller glory flows
The sky-like spirit of God ; a hope begun
In doubt and darkness 'neath a fairer
sun
Cometh to fruitage, if it be of Truth ;
And to the law of meekness, faith, and
ruth,
By inward sympathy, shall all be won :
This thou shouldst know, who, from the
painted feature
Of shifting Fashion, couldst thy breth-
ren turn
Unto the love of ever-youthful Nature,
And of a beauty fadeless and eterne ;
And always 't is the saddest sight to see
An old man faithless in Humanity.

XVII.

THE SAME CONTINUED.

A poet cannot strive for despotism ;
His harp falls shattered ; for it still
must be
The instinct of great spirits to be free,
And the sworn foes of cunning barba-
rism :
He, who has deepest searched the wide
abysm
Of that life-giving Soul which men call
fate,
Knows that to put more faith in lies
and hate
Than truth and love is the true atheism :
Upward the soul forever turns her eyes ;
The next hour always shames the hour
before :
One beauty, at its highest, prophesies
That by whose side it shall seem mean,
and poor
No Godlike thing knows aught of less
and less,
But widens to the boundless Perfectness.

XVIII.

THE SAME CONTINUED.

Therefore think not the Past is wise
alone,
For Yesterday knows nothing of the
Best,

And thou shalt love it only as the nest
Whence glory-wingèd things to Heaven
    have flown:
To the great Soul only are all things
    known;
Present and future are to her as past,
While she in glorious madness doth
    forecast
That perfect bud, which seems a flower
    full-blown
To each new Prophet, and yet always
    opes
Fuller and fuller with each day and hour,
Heartening the soul with odor of fresh
    hopes,
And longings high, and gushings of
    wide power,
Yet never is or shall be fully blown
Save in the forethought of the Eternal
    One.

XIX.

THE SAME CONCLUDED.

FAR 'yond this narrow parapet of Time,
With eyes uplift, the poet's soul should
    look
Into the Endless Promise, nor should
    brook
One prying doubt to shake his faith
    sublime;
To him the earth is ever in her prime
And dewiness of morning; he can see
Good lying hid, from all eternity,
Within the teeming womb of sin and
    crime;
His soul should not be cramped by any
    bar,
His nobleness should be so Godlike
    high,
That his least deed is perfect as a star,
His common look majestic as the sky,
And all o'erflooded with a light from far,
Undimmed by clouds of weak mortality.

XX.

TO M. O. S.

MARY, since first I knew thee, to this
    hour,
My love hath deepened, with my wiser
    sense

Of what in Woman is to reverence;
Thy clear heart, fresh as e'er was forest-
    flower,
Still opens more to me its beauteous
    dower;—
But let praise hush,—Love asks no
    evidence
To prove itself well-placed; we know
    not whence
It gleans the straws that thatch its hum-
    ble bower:
We can but say we found it in the
    heart,
Spring of all sweetest thoughts, arch foe
    of blame,
Sower of flowers in the dusty mart,
Pure vestal of the poet's holy flame,—
This is enough, and we have done our
    part
If we but keep it spotless as it came.

1842.

XXI.

OUR love is not a fading, earthly
    flower:
Its wingèd seed dropped down from
    Paradise,
And, nursed by day and night, by sun
    and shower,
Doth momently to fresher beauty
    rise:
To us the leafless autumn is not
    bare,
Nor winter's rattling boughs lack lusty
    green.
Our summer hearts make summer's
    fulness, where
No leaf, or bud, or blossom may be
    seen:
For nature's life in love's deep life doth
    lie,
Love,—whose forgetfulness is beauty's
    death,
Whose mystic key these cells of Thou
    and I
Into the infinite freedom openeth,
And makes the body's dark and narrow
    grate
The wide-flung leaves of Heaven's
    own palace-gate.

1842.

XXII.

IN ABSENCE.

THESE rugged, wintry days I scarce
    could bear,
Did I not know, that, in the early spring,
When wild March winds upon their
    errands sing,
Thou wouldst return, bursting on this
    still air,
Like those same winds, when, startled
    from their lair,
They hunt up violets, and free swift
    brooks,
From icy cares, even as thy clear looks
Bid my heart bloom, and sing, and
    break all care :
When drops with welcome rain the
    April day,
My flowers shall find their April in
    thine eyes,
Save there the rain in dreamy clouds
    doth stay,
As loath to fall out of those happy skies ;
Yet sure, my love, thou art most like to
    May,
That comes with steady sun when April
    dies.

1843.

XXIII.

WENDELL PHILLIPS.

HE stood upon the world's broad
    threshold ; wide
The din of battle and of slaughter rose ;
He saw God stand upon the weaker
    side,
That sank in seeming loss before its
    foes ;
Many there were who made great haste
    and sold
Unto the cunning enemy their swords,
He scorned their gifts of fame, and
    power, and gold,
And, underneath their soft and flowery
    words,
Heard the cold serpent hiss ; therefore
    he went
And humbly joined him to the weaker
    part,

8

Fanatic named, and fool, yet well con-
    tent
So he could be the nearer to God's
    heart,
And feel its solemn pulses sending
    blood
Through all the wide-spread veins of
    endless good.

XXIV.

THE STREET.

THEY pass me by like shadows, crowds
    on crowds,
Dim ghosts of men, that hover to and
    fro,
Hugging their bodies round them like
    thin shrouds
Wherein their souls were buried long
    ago :
They trampled on their youth, and
    faith, and love,
They cast their hope of human-kind
    away,
With Heaven's clear messages they
    madly strove,
And conquered, — and their spirits
    turned to clay :
Lo ! how they wander round the world,
    their grave,
Whose ever-gaping maw by such is fed,
Gibbering at living men, and idly rave,
" We, only, truly live, but ye are dead."
Alas ! poor fools, the anointed eye
    may trace
A dead soul's epitaph in every face !

XXV.

I GRIEVE not that ripe Knowledge
    takes away
The charm that Nature to my child-
    hood wore,
For, with that insight, cometh, day by
    day,
A greater bliss than wonder was before ;
The real doth not clip the poet's
    wings, —
To win the secret of a weed's plain heart

Reveals some clew to spiritual things,
And stumbling guess becomes firm-
    footed art :
Flowers are not flowers unto the poet's
    eyes,
Their beauty thrills him by an inward
    sense ;
He knows that outward seemings are
    but lies,
Or, at the most, but earthly shadows,
    whence
The soul that looks within for truth
    may guess
The presence of some wondrous heav-
    enliness.

XXVI.

TO J. R. GIDDINGS.

GIDDINGS, far rougher names than
    thine have grown
Smoother than honey on the lips of men ;
And thou shalt aye be honorably
    known,
As one who bravely used his tongue
    and pen,
As best befits a freeman, — even for
    those,
To whom our Law's unblushing front
    denies
A right to plead against the life-long
    woes
Which are the Negro's glimpse of
    Freedom's skies :
Fear nothing, and hope all things, as
    the Right
Alone may do securely ; every hour
The thrones of Ignorance and ancient
    Night
Lose somewhat of their long usurpëd
    power,
And Freedom's lightest word can make
    them shiver
With a base dread that clings to them
    forever.

XXVII.

I THOUGHT our love at full, but I did err ;
Joy's wreath drooped o'er mine eyes ;
    I could not see

That sorrow in our happy world must be
Love's deepest spokesman and inter-
    preter ?
But, as a mother feels her child first
    stir
Under her heart, so felt I instantly
Deep in my soul another bond to thee
Thrill with that life we saw depart from
    her ;
O mother of our angel child ! twice
    dear !
Death knits as well as parts, and still,
    I wis,
Her tender radiance shall infold us
    here,
Even as the light, borne up by inward
    bliss,
Threads the void glooms of space with-
    out a fear,
To print on farthest stars her pitying
    kiss.

L'ENVOI.

WHETHER my heart hath wiser grown
    or not,
In these three years, since I to thee
    inscribed,
Mine own betrothed, the firstlings of
    my muse, —
Poor windfalls of unripe experience,
Young buds plucked hastily by child-
    ish hands
Not patient to await more full-blown
    flowers, —
At least it hath seen more of life and
    men,
And pondered more, and grown a shade
    more sad ;
Yet with no loss of hope or settled
    trust
In the benignness of that Providence,
Which shapes from out our elements
    awry
The grace and order that we wonder at,
The mystic harmony of right and
    wrong,
Both working out His wisdom and our
    good :
A trust, Beloved, chiefly learned of thee,
Who hast that gift of patient tenderness,
The instinctive wisdom of a woman's
    heart.

They tell us that our land was made
  for song,
With its huge rivers and sky-piercing
  peaks,
Its sealike lakes and mighty cataracts,
Its forests vast and hoar, and prairies
  wide,
And mounds that tell of wondrous
  tribes extinct.
But Poesy springs not from rocks and
  woods ;
Her womb and cradle are the human
  heart,
And she can find a nobler theme for
  song
In the most loathsome man that blasts
  the sight
Than in the broad expanse of sea and
  shore
Between the frozen deserts of the poles.
All nations have their message from on
  high,
Each the messiah of some central
  thought,
For the fulfilment and delight of Man :
One has to teach that labor is divine ;
Another Freedom ; and another Mind ;
And all, that God is open-eyed and
  just,
The happy centre and calm heart of all.

Are, then, our woods, our mountains,
  and our streams,
Needful to teach our poets how to
  sing ?
O maiden rare, far other thoughts were
  ours,
When we have sat by ocean's foaming
  marge,
And watched the waves leap roaring on
  the rocks,
Than young Leander and his Hero had,
Gazing from Sestos to the other shore.
The moon looks down and ocean wor-
  ships her,
Stars rise and set, and seasons come
  and go
Even as they did in Homer's elder
  time,
But we behold them not with Grecian
  eyes :
Then they were types of beauty and of
  strength,
But now of freedom, unconfined and
  pure,

Subject alone to Order's higher law.
What cares the Russian serf or South-
  ern slave
Though we should speak as man spake
  never yet
Of gleaming Hudson's broad magnifi-
  cence,
Or green Niagara's never-ending roar ?
Our country hath a gospel of her own
To preach and practise before all the
  world, —
The freedom and divinity of man,
The glorious claims of human brother-
  hood, —
Which to pay nobly, as a freeman
  should,
Gains the sole wealth that will not fly
  away, —
And the soul's fealty to none but God.
These are realities, which make the
  shows
Of outward Nature, be they ne'er so
  grand,
Seem small, and worthless, and con-
  temptible.
These are the mountain-summits for
  our bards,
Which stretch far upward into heaven
  itself,
And give such wide-spread and exult-
  ing view
Of hope, and faith, and onward des-
  tiny,
That shrunk Parnassus to a molehill
  dwindles.
Our new Atlantis, like a morning-star,
Silvers the mirk face of slow-yielding
  Night,
The herald of a fuller truth than yet
Hath gleamed upon the upraised face
  of Man
Since the earth glittered in her stain-
  less prime, —
Of a more glorious sunrise than of old
Drew wondrous melodies from Mem-
  non huge,
Yea, draws them still, though now he
  sits waist-deep
In the ingulfing flood of whirling sand,
And look across the wastes of endless
  gray,
Sole wreck, where once his hundred-
  gated Thebes
Pained with her mighty hum the calm,
  blue heaven :

Shall the dull stone pay grateful orisons,
And we till noonday bar the splendor
out,
Lest it reproach and chide our sluggard
hearts,
Warm-nestled in the down of Preju-
dice,
And be content, though clad with an-
gel-wings,
Close-clipped, to hop about from perch
to perch,
In paltry cages of dead men's dead
thoughts?
O, rather, like the skylark, soar and
sing,
And let our gushing songs befit the
dawn
And sunrise, and the yet unshaken dew
Brimming the chalice of each full-blown
hope,
Whose blithe front turns to greet the
growing day !
Never had poets such high call before,
Never can poets hope for higher one,
And, if they be but faithful to their trust,
Earth will remember them with love
and joy,
And O, far better, God will not forget.
For he who settles Freedom's prin-
ciples
Writes the death-warrant of all ty-
ranny ;
Who speaks the truth stabs Falsehood
to the heart,
And his mere word makes despots trem-
ble more
Than ever Brutus with his dagger
could.
Wait for no hints from waterfalls or
woods,
Nor dream that tales of red men, brute
and fierce,
Repay the finding of this Western
World,
Or needed half the globe to give them
birth:
Spirit supreme of Freedom ! not for
this
Did great Columbus tame his eagle soul
To jostle with the daws that perch in
courts ;
Not for this, friendless, on an unknown
sea,

Coping with mad waves and more mu-
tinous spirits,
Battled he with the dreadful ache at
heart
Which tempts, with devilish subtleties
of doubt,
The hermit of that loneliest solitude,
The silent desert of a great New
Thought ;
Though loud Niagara were to-day
struck dumb,
Yet would this cataract of boiling life
Rush plunging on and on to endless
deeps,
And utter thunder till the world shall
cease, —
A thunder worthy of the poet's song,
And which alone can fill it with true
life.
The high evangel to our country granted
Could make apostles, yea, with tongues
of fire,
Of hearts half-darkened back again to
clay !
'T is the soul only that is national,
And he who pays true loyalty to that
Alone can claim the wreath of patriot-
ism.

Beloved ! if I wander far and oft
From that which I believe, and feel,
and know,
Thou wilt forgive, not with a sorrow-
ing heart,
But with a strengthened hope of better
things ;
Knowing that I, though often blind
and false
To those I love, and O, more false than
all
Unto myself, have been most true to
thee,
And that whoso in one thing hath been
true
Can be as true in all. Therefore thy
hope
May yet not prove unfruitful, and thy
love
Meet, day by day, with less unworthy
thanks,
Whether, as now, we journey hand in
hand,
Or, parted in the body, yet are one
In spirit and the love of holy things.

THE VISION OF SIR LAUNFAL.

OVER his keys the musing organist,
Beginning doubtfully and far away,
First lets his fingers wander as they list,
  And builds a bridge from Dreamland
    for his lay :
Then, as the touch of his loved instru-
  ment
  Gives hope and fervor, nearer draws
    his theme,
First guessed by faint auroral flushes
  sent
  Along the wavering vista of his dream.

———

Not only around our infancy
Doth heaven with all its splendors lie ;
Daily, with souls that cringe and plot,
We Sinais climb and know it not.

Over our manhood bend the skies ;
  Against our fallen and traitor lives
The great winds utter prophecies ;
  With our faint hearts the mountain
    strives,
Its arms outstretched, the druid wood
  Waits with its benedicite ,
And to our age's drowsy blood
  Still shouts the inspiring sea.

Earth gets its price for what Earth
    gives us ;
  The beggar is taxed for a corner to
    die in,
The priest hath his fee who comes and
    shrives us,
  We bargain for the graves we lie in ;
At the devil's booth are all things sold,
Each ounce of dross costs its ounce of
    gold ;
  For a cap and bells our lives we
    pay,

Bubbles we buy with a whole soul's
    tasking :
  'T is heaven alone that is given away.
'T is only God may be had for the ask-
    ing,
No price is set on the lavish summer ;
June may be had by the poorest comer.

And what is so rare as a day in June ?
  Then, if ever, come perfect days ;
Then Heaven tries earth if it be in
    tune,
  And over it softly her warm ear lays :
Whether we look, or whether we listen,
We hear life murmur, or see it glisten ;
Every clod feels a stir of might,
  An instinct within it that reaches and
    towers,
And, groping blindly above it for light,
  Climbs to a soul in grass and flowers ;
The flush of life may well be seen
  Thrilling back over hills and valleys ;
The cowslip startles in meadows green,
  The buttercup catches the sun in its
    chalice,
And there 's never a leaf nor a blade
    too mean
To be some happy creature's palace ;
The little bird sits at his door in the sun,
  Atilt like a blossom among the leaves,
And lets his illumined being o'errun
  With the deluge of summer it re-
    ceives ;
His mate feels the eggs beneath her
    wings,
And the heart in her dumb breast flut-
    ters and sings ;
He sings to the wide world, and she to
    her nest, —
In the nice ear of Nature which song is
    the best ?

Now is the high-tide of the year,
  And whatever of life hath ebbed away

Comes flooding back with a ripply cheer,
    Into every bare inlet and creek and
        bay ;
Now the heart is so full that a drop
        overfills it,
We are happy now because God wills
        it ;
No matter how barren the past may
        have been,
'T is enough for us now that the leaves
        are green ;
We sit in the warm shade and feel right
        well
How the sap creeps up and the blos-
        soms swell ;
We may shut our eyes, but we cannot
        help knowing
That skies are clear and grass is grow-
        ing ;
The breeze comes whispering in our ear,
That dandelions are blossoming near,
    That maize has sprouted, that streams
        are flowing,
That the river is bluer than the sky,
That the robin is plastering his house
        hard by ;
And if the breeze kept the good news
        back,
For other couriers we should not lack ;
    We could guess it all by yon heifer's
        lowing, —
And hark ! how clear bold chanticleer,
Warmed with the new wine of the year,
Tells all in his lusty crowing !

Joy comes, grief goes, we know not how ;
Everything is happy now,
    Everything is upward striving ;
'T is as easy now for the heart to be true
As for grass to be green or skies to be
        blue, —
    'T is the natural way of living :
Who knows whither the clouds have
        fled ?
    In the unscarred heaven they leave
        no wake ;
And the eyes forget the tears they have
        shed,
    The heart forgets its sorrow and ache ;
The soul partakes the season's youth,
    And the sulphurous rifts of passion
        and woe
Lie deep 'neath a silence pure and
        smooth,

Like burnt-out craters healed with
        snow.
What wonder if Sir Launfal now
Remembered the keeping of his vow ?

PART FIRST.

I.

" My golden spurs now bring to me,
    And bring to me my richest mail,
For to-morrow I go over land and sea
    In search of the Holy Grail ;
Shall never a bed for me be spread,
Nor shall a pillow be under my head,
Till I begin my vow to keep ;
Here on the rushes will I sleep,
And perchance there may come a vision
        true
Ere day create the world anew."
    Slowly Sir Launfal's eyes grew dim,
    Slumber fell like a cloud on him,
And into his soul the vision flew.

II.

The crows flapped over by twos and
        threes,
In the pool drowsed the cattle up to
        their knees,
    The little birds sang as if it were
    The one day of summer in all the
        year,
And the very leaves seemed to sing on
        the trees :
The castle alone in the landscape lay
Like an outpost of winter, dull and
        gray ;
'T was the proudest hall in the North
        Countree,
And never its gates might opened be,
Save to lord or lady of high degree ;
Summer besieged it on every side,
But the churlish stone her assaults de-
        fied ;
She could not scale the chilly wall,
Though around it for leagues her pa-
        vilions tall
Stretched left and right,
Over the hills and out of sight ;
    Green and broad was every tent,
    And out of each a murmur went
Till the breeze fell off at night.

III.

The drawbridge dropped with a surly
    clang,
And through the dark arch a charger
    sprang,
Bearing Sir Launfal, the maiden knight,
In his gilded mail, that flamed so bright
It seemed the dark castle had gathered
    all
Those shafts the fierce sun had shot
    over its wall
    In his siege of three hundred sum-
        mers long,
And, binding them all in one blazing
    sheaf,
    Had cast them forth : so, young and
        strong,
And lightsome as a locust-leaf,
Sir Launfal flashed forth in his maiden
    mail,
To seek in all climes for the Holy Grail.

IV.

It was morning on hill and stream and
    tree,
    And morning in the young knight's
        heart ;
Only the castle moodily
Rebuffed the gifts of the sunshine free,
    And gloomed by itself apart ;
The season brimmed all other things
    up
Full as the rain fills the pitcher-plant's
    cup.

V.

As Sir Launfal made morn through the
    darksome gate,
    He was 'ware of a leper, crouched
        by the same,
Who begged with his hand and moaned
    as he sate ;
    And a loathing over Sir Launfal
        came ;
The sunshine went out of his soul with
    a thrill,
    The flesh 'neath his armor 'gan
        shrink and crawl,
And midway its leap his heart stood still
    Like a frozen waterfall ;
For this man, so foul and bent of stature,
Rasped harshly against his dainty na-
    ture,

And seemed the one blot on the sum-
    mer morn, —
So he tossed him a piece of gold in
    scorn.

VI.

The leper raised not the gold from the
    dust :
" Better to me the poor man's crust,
Better the blessing of the poor,
Though I turn me empty from his door ;
That is no true alms which the hand
    can hold ;
He gives only the worthless gold
    Who gives from a sense of duty ;
But he who gives a slender mite,
And gives to that which is out of sight,
    That thread of the all-sustaining
        Beauty
Which runs through all and doth all
    unite, —
The hand cannot clasp the whole of his
    alms,
The heart outstretches its eager palms,
For a god goes with it and makes it
    store
To the soul that was starving in dark-
    ness before. ''

PRELUDE TO PART SECOND.

Down swept the chill wind from the
    mountain peak,
    From the snow five thousand sum-
        mers old ;
On open wold and hill-top bleak
    It had gathered all the cold,
And whirled it like sleet on the wan-
    derer's cheek ;
It carried a shiver everywhere
From the unleafed boughs and pastures
    bare ;
The little brook heard it and built a
    roof
'Neath which he could house him, win-
    ter-proof ;
All night by the white stars' frosty
    gleams
He groined his arches and matched his
    beams ;
Slender and clear were his crystal spars
As the lashes of light that trim the
    stars ;

He sculptured every summer delight
In his halls and chambers out of sight ;
Sometimes his tinkling waters slipt
Down through a frost-leaved forest-
   crypt,
Long, sparkling aisles of steel-stemmed
   trees
Bending to counterfeit a breeze ;
Sometimes the roof no fretwork knew
But silvery mosses that downward grew ;
Sometimes it was carved in sharp relief
With quaint arabesques of ice-fern leaf ;
Sometimes it was simply smooth and
   clear
For the gladness of heaven to shine
   through, and here
He had caught the nodding bulrush-
   tops
And hung them thickly with diamond
   drops,
That crystalled the beams of moon and
   sun,
And made a star of every one :
No mortal builder's most rare device
Could match this winter-palace of ice ;
'T was as if every image that mirrored
   lay
In his depths serene through the sum-
   mer day,
Each fleeting shadow of earth and sky,
Lest the happy model should be lost,
Had been mimicked in fairy masonry
By the elfin builders of the frost.

Within the hall are song and laughter,
   The cheeks of Christmas glow red
   and jolly,
And sprouting is every corbel and rafter
   With lightsome green of ivy and
   holly ;
Through the deep gulf of the chimney
   wide
Wallows the Yule-log's roaring tide ;
The broad flame-pennons droop and
   flap
   And belly and tug as a flag in the
   wind ;
Like a locust shrills the imprisoned
   sap,
   Hunted to death in its galleries
   blind ;
And swift little troops of silent sparks,
   Now pausing, now scattering away
   as in fear,

Go threading the soot-forest's tangled
   darks
   Like herds of startled deer.

But the wind without was eager and
   sharp,
Of Sir Launfal's gray hair it makes a
   harp,
   And rattles and wrings
   The icy strings,
Singing, in dreary monotone,
A Christmas carol of its own,
Whose burden still, as he might
   guess,
Was—"Shelterless, shelterless, shel-
   terless !"
The voice of the seneschal flared like a
   torch
As he shouted the wanderer away from
   the porch,
And he sat in the gateway and saw all
   night
   The great hall-fire, so cheery and
   bold,
   Through the window-slits of the cas-
   tle old,
Build out its piers of ruddy light
Against the drift of the cold.

PART SECOND.

I.

THERE was never a leaf on bush or
   tree,
The bare boughs rattled shudderingly ;
The river was numb and could not
   speak,
   For the weaver Winter its shroud
   had spun ;
A single crow on the tree-top bleak
   From his shining feathers shed off
   the cold sun ;
Again it was morning, but shrunk and
   cold,
As if her veins were sapless and old,
And she rose up decrepitly
For a last dim look at earth and sea.

II.

Sir Launfal turned from his own hard
   gate,
For another heir in his earldom sate ;

An old, bent man, worn out and frail,
He came back from seeking the Holy
  Grail;
Little he recked of his earldom's loss,
No more on his surcoat was blazoned
  the cross,
But deep in his soul the sign he wore,
The badge of the suffering and the poor.

III.

Sir Launfal's raiment thin and spare
Was idle mail 'gainst the barbed air,
For it was just at the Christmas time;
So he mused, as he sat, of a sunnier
  clime,
And sought for a shelter from cold and
  snow
In the light and warmth of long-ago;
He sees the snake-like caravan crawl
O'er the edge of the desert, black and
  small,
Then nearer and nearer, till, one by
  one,
He can count the camels in the sun,
As over the red-hot sands they pass
To where, in its slender necklace of
  grass,
The little spring laughed and leapt in
  the shade,
And with its own self like an infant
  played,
And waved its signal of palms.

IV.

"For Christ's sweet sake, I beg an
  alms";—
The happy camels may reach the
  spring,
But Sir Launfal sees only the grewsome
  thing,
The leper, lank as the rain-blanched
  bone,
That cowers beside him, a thing as
  lone
And white as the ice-isles of Northern
  seas
In the desolate horror of his disease.

V.

And Sir Launfal said,—"I behold in
  thee
An image of Him who died on the
  tree;

Thou also hast had thy crown of
  thorns,—
Thou also hast had the world's buffets
  and scorns,—
And to thy life were not denied
The wounds in the hands and feet and
  side:
Mild Mary's Son, acknowledge me;
Behold, through him, I give to thee!"

VI.

Then the soul of the leper stood up in
  his eyes
  And looked at Sir Launfal, and
    straightway he
Remembered in what a haughtier guise
  He had flung an alms to leprosie,
When he girt his young life up in
  gilded mail
And set forth in search of the Holy
  Grail.
The heart within him was ashes and
  dust;
He parted in twain his single crust,
He broke the ice on the streamlet's
  brink,
And gave the leper to eat and drink,
'T was a mouldy crust of coarse brown
  bread,
  'T was water out of a wooden bowl,—
Yet with fine wheaten bread was the
  leper fed,
  And 't was red wine he drank with
    his thirsty soul.

VII.

As Sir Launfal mused with a downcast
  face,
A light shone round about the place;
The leper no longer crouched at his side,
But stood before him glorified,
Shining and tall and fair and straight
As the pillar that stood by the Beauti-
  ful Gate,—
Himself the Gate whereby men can
Enter the temple of God in Man.

VIII.

His words were shed softer than leaves
  from the pine,
And they fell on Sir Launfal as snows
  on the brine,

Which mingle their softness and quiet
      in one
With the shaggy unrest they float down
      upon ;
And the voice that was softer than
      silence said,
"Lo it is I, be not afraid !
In many climes, without avail,
Thou hast spent thy life for the Holy
      Grail ;
Behold, it is here, — this cup which thou
Didst fill at the streamlet for me but
      now ;
This crust is my body broken for me,
This water his blood that died on the
      tree ;
The Holy Supper is kept, indeed,
In whatso we share with another's
      need ;
Not what we give, but what we share,
For the gift without the giver is bare ;
Who gives himself with his alms feeds
      three,
Himself, his hungering neighbor, and
      me."

IX.

Sir Launfal awoke as from a swound : —
"The Grail in my castle here is found !
Hang my idle armor up on the wall,
Let it be the spider's banquet-hall ;
He must be fenced with stronger mail
Who would seek and find the Holy
      Grail."

X.

The castle gate stands open now,
    And the wanderer is welcome to the
      hall
As the hangbird is to the elm-tree
      bough ;

No longer scowl the turrets tall,
The Summer's long siege at last is o'er ;
When the first poor outcast went in at
      the door,
She entered with him in disguise,
And mastered the fortress by surprise ;
There is no spot she loves so well on
      ground,
She lingers and smiles there the whole
      year round ;
The meanest serf on Sir Launfal's land
Has hall and bower at his command ;
And there 's no poor man in the North
      Countree
But is lord of the earldom as much as
      he.

NOTE. — According to the mythology of
the Romancers, the San Greal, or Holy Grail,
was the cup out of which Jesus partook of
the Last Supper with his disciples. It was
brought into England by Joseph of Arima-
thea, and remained there, an object of pil-
grimage and adoration, for many years in
the keeping of his lineal descendants. It
was incumbent upon those who had charge
of it to be chaste in thought, word, and
deed ; but one of the keepers having broken
this condition, the Holy Grail disappeared.
From that time it was a favorite enterprise
of the knights of Arthur's court to go in
search of it. Sir Galahad was at last successful in finding it, as may be read in the
seventeenth book of the Romance of King
Arthur. Tennyson has made Sir Galahad
the subject of one of the most exquisite of
his poems.

The plot (if I may give that name to anything so slight) of the foregoing poem is my
own, and, to serve its purposes, I have enlarged the circle of competition in search of
the miraculous cup in such a manner as to in-
clude, not only other persons than the heroes
of the Round Table, but also a period of
time subsequent to the supposed date of
King Arthur's reign.

READER! *walk up at once (it will soon be too late)*
and buy at a perfectly ruinous rate

A

FABLE FOR CRITICS;

OR, BETTER,

(*I like, as a thing that the reader's first fancy may strike,*
an old-fashioned title-page,
such as presents a tabular view of the volume's contents,)

A GLANCE

AT A FEW OF OUR LITERARY PROGENIES

(*Mrs. Malaprop's word*)

FROM

THE TUB OF DIOGENES;

A VOCAL AND MUSICAL MEDLEY,

THAT IS,

A SERIES OF JOKES

By A Wonderful Quiz,

who accompanies himself with a rub-a-dub-dub, full of spirit and grace,
on the top of the tub.

Set forth in October, the 31st day,
In the year '48, G. P. Putnam, Broadway.

TO

CHARLES F. BRIGGS,

THIS VOLUME IS AFFECTIONATELY INSCRIBED.

IT being the commonest mode of procedure, I premise a few candid remarks

TO THE READER :—

This trifle, begun to please only myself and my own private fancy, was laid on the shelf. But some friends, who had seen it, induced me, by dint of saying they liked it, to put it in print. That is, having come to that very conclusion, I asked their advice when 't would make no confusion. For though (in the gentlest of ways) they had hinted it was scarce worth the while, I should doubtless have printed it.

I began it, intending a Fable, a frail, slender thing, rhyme-ywinged, with a sting in its tail. But, by addings and alterings not previously planned, — digressions chance-hatched, like birds' eggs in the sand, — and dawdlings to suit every whimsy's demand (always freeing the bird which I held in my hand, for the two perched, perhaps out of reach, in the tree), — it grew by degrees to the size which you see. I was like the old woman that carried the calf, and my neighbors, like hers, no doubt, wonder and laugh; and when, my strained arms with their grown burthen full, I call it my Fable, they call it a bull.

Having scrawled at full gallop (as far as that goes) in a style that is neither good verse nor bad prose, and being a person whom nobody knows, some people will say I am rather more free with my readers than it is becoming to be, that I seem to expect them to wait on my leisure in following wherever I wander at pleasure, that, in short, I take more than a young author's lawful ease, and laugh in a queer way so like Mephistopheles, that the Public will doubt, as they grope through my rhythm, if in truth I am making fun *of* them or *with* them.

So the excellent Public is hereby assured that the sale of my book is already secured. For there is not a poet throughout the whole land but will purchase a copy or two out of hand, in the fond expectation of being amused in it, by seeing his betters cut up and abused in it. Now, I find, by a pretty exact calculation, there are something like ten thousand bards in the nation, of that special variety whom the Review and Magazine critics call *lofty* and *true*, and about thirty thousand (*this* tribe is increasing) of the kinds who are termed *full of promise* and *pleasing*. The Public will see by a glance at this schedule, that they cannot expect me to be over-sedulous about courting *them*, since it seems I have got enough fuel made sure of for boiling my pot.

As for such of our poets as find not their names mentioned once in my pages, with praises or blames, let them SEND IN THEIR CARDS, without further DELAY, to my friend G. P. PUTNAM, Esquire, in Broadway, where a LIST will be kept with the strictest regard to the day and the hour of receiving the card. Then, taking them up as I chance to have time (that is, if their names can be twisted in rhyme), I will honestly give each his PROPER POSITION, at the rate of ONE AUTHOR to each NEW EDITION. Thus a PREMIUM is offered sufficiently HIGH (as the magazines say when they tell their best lie) to induce bards to CLUB their resources and buy the balance of every edition, until they have all of them fairly been run through the mill.

One word to such readers (judicious

and wise) as read books with something behind the mere eyes, of whom in the country, perhaps, there are two, including myself, gentle reader, and you. All the characters sketched in this slight *jeu d'esprit*, though, it may be, they seem, here and there, rather free, and drawn from a somewhat too cynical stand-point, are *meant* to be faithful, for that is the grand point, and none but an owl would feel sore at a rub from a jester who tells you, without any subterfuge, that he sits in Diogenes' tub.

A PRELIMINARY NOTE TO THE SECOND EDITION,

though it well may be reckoned, of all composition, the species at once most delightful and healthy, is a thing which an author, unless he be wealthy and willing to pay for that kind of delight, is not, in all instances, called on to write, though there are, it is said, who, their spirits to cheer, slip in a new title-page three times a year, and in this way snuff up an imaginary savor of that sweetest of dishes, the popular favor, — much as if a starved painter should fall to and treat the Ugolino inside to a picture of meat.

You remember (if not, pray turn backward and look) that, in writing the preface which ushered my book, I treated you, excellent Public, not merely with a cool disregard, but downright cavalierly. Now I would not take back the least thing I then said, though I thereby could butter both sides of my bread, for I never could see that an author owed aught to the people he solaced, diverted, or taught ; and, as for mere fame, I have long ago learned that the persons by whom it is finally earned are those with whom *your* verdict weighed not a pin, unsustained by the higher court sitting within.

But I wander from what I intended to say, — that you have, namely, shown such a liberal way of thinking, and so much æsthetic perception of anonymous worth in the handsome reception you gave to my book, spite of some private piques (having bought the first thousand in barely two weeks), that I think, past a doubt, if you measured the phiz of yours most devotedly, Wonderful Quiz, you would find that its vertical section was shorter, by an inch and two tenths, or 'twixt that and a quarter.

You have watched a child playing — in those wondrous years when belief is not bound to the eyes and the ears, and the vision divine is so clear and unmarred, that each baker of pies in the dirt is a bard? Give a knife and a shingle, he fits out a fleet, and, on that little mud-puddle over the street, his fancy, in purest good faith, will make sail round the globe with a puff of his breath for a gale, will visit in barely ten minutes, all climes, and do the Columbus-feat hundreds of times. Or, suppose the young poet fresh stored with delights from that Bible of childhood, the Arabian Nights, he will turn to a crony and cry, "Jack, let 's play that I am a Genius!" Jacky straightway makes Aladdin's lamp out of a stone, and, for hours, they enjoy each his own supernatural powers. This is all very pretty and pleasant, but then suppose our two urchins have grown into men, and both have turned authors, — one says to his brother, "Let 's play we 're the American somethings or other, — say Homer or Sophocles, Goethe or Scott (only let them be big enough, no matter what). Come, you shall be Byron or Pope, which you choose : I 'll be Coleridge, and both shall write mutual reviews." So they both (as mere strangers) before many days, send each other a cord of anonymous bays. Each, piling his epithets, smiles in his sleeve to see what his friend can be made to believe ; each, reading the other's unbiased review, thinks — Here's pretty high praise, but no more than my due. Well, we laugh at them both, and yet make no great fuss when the same farce is acted to benefit us. Even I, who, if asked, scarce a month since, what Fudge meant, should have answered, the dear Public's critical judgment, begin to think sharp-witted Horace spoke sooth when he said, that the Public *sometimes* hit the truth.

In reading these lines, you perhaps have a vision of a person in pretty good health and condition; and yet, since I put forth my primary edition, I have been crushed, scorched, withered, used up and put down (by Smith with the cordial assistance of Brown), in all, if you put any faith in my rhymes, to the number of ninety-five several times, and, while I am writing, — I tremble to think of it, for I may at this moment be just on the brink of it, — Molybdostom, angry at being omitted, has begun a critique, — am I not to be pitied?*

Now I shall not crush *them* since, indeed, for that matter, no pressure I know of could render them flatter; nor wither, nor scorch them, — no action of fire could make either them or their articles drier; nor waste time in putting them down — I am thinking not their own self-inflation will keep them from sinking; for there's this contradiction about the whole bevy, — though without the least weight, they are awfully heavy. No, my dear honest bore, *surdo fabulam narras*, they are no more to me than a rat in the arras. I can walk with the Doctor, get facts from the Don, or draw out the Lambish quintessence of John, and feel nothing more than a half-comic sorrow, to think that they all will be lying to-morrow tossed carelessly up on the waste-paper shelves, and forgotten by all but their half-dozen selves. Once snug in my attic, my fire in a roar, I leave the whole pack of them outside the door. With Hakluyt or Purchas I wander away to the black northern seas or barbaric Cathay; get *fou* with O'Shanter, and sober me then with that builder of brick-kilnish dramas, rare Ben; snuff Herbert, as holy as a flower on a grave; with Fletcher wax tender, o'er Chap-

---

* The wise Scandinavians probably called their bards by the queer-looking title of Scald, in a delicate way, as it were, just to hint to the world the hot water they always get into.

---

man grow brave; with Marlowe or Kyd take a fine poet-rave; in Very, most Hebrew of Saxons, find peace; with Lycidas welter on vext Irish seas; with Webster grow wild, and climb earthward again, down by mystical Browne's Jacob's-ladder-like brain, to that spiritual Pepys (Cotton's version) Montaigne; find a new depth in Wordsworth, undreamed of before, — that marvel, a poet divine who can bore. Or, out of my study, the scholar thrown off, Nature holds up her shield 'gainst the sneer and the scoff; the landscape, forever consoling and kind, pours her wine and her oil on the smarts of the mind. The waterfall, scattering its vanishing gems; the tall grove of hemlocks, with moss on their stems, like plashes of sunlight; the pond in the woods, where no foot but mine and the bittern's intrudes, where pitcher-plants purple and gentians hard by recall to September the blue of June's sky; these are all my kind neighbors, and leave me no wish to say aught to you all, my poor critics, but — pish! I 've buried the hatchet: I 'm twisting an allumette out of one of you now, and relighting my calumet. In your private capacities, come when you please, I will give you my hand and a fresh pipe apiece.

As I ran through the leaves of my poor little book, to take a fond author's first tremulous look, it was quite an excitement to hunt the *errata*, sprawled in as birds' tracks are in some kinds of strata (only these made things crookeder). Fancy an heir, that a father had seen born well-featured and fair, turning suddenly wry-nosed, club-footed, squint-eyed, hair-lipped, wapper-jawed, carrot-haired, from a pride become an aversion, — my case was yet worse. A club-foot (by way of a change) in a verse, I might have forgiven, an *o*'s being wry, a limp in an *e*, or a cock in an *i*, — but to have the sweet babe of my brain served in *pi*! I am not queasy-stomached, but such a Thyestean banquet as that was quite out of the question.

In the edition now issued no pains are neglected, and my verses, as orators say, stand corrected. Yet some blunders remain of the Public's own make, which I wish to correct for my personal sake. For instance, a character drawn in pure fun and condensing the traits of a dozen in one, has been, as I hear, by some persons applied to a good friend of mine, whom to stab in the side, as we walked along chatting and joking together, would not be *my* way. I can hardly tell whether a question will ever arise in which he and I should by any strange fortune agree, but meanwhile my esteem for him grows as I know him, and, though not the best judge on earth of a poem, he knows what it is he is saying and why, and is honest and fearless, two good points which I have not found so rife I can easily smother my love for them, whether on my side or t'other.

For my other *anonymi*, you may be sure that I know what is meant by a caricature, and what by a portrait. There *are* those who think it is capital fun to be spattering their ink on quiet, unquarrelsome folk, but the minute the game changes sides and the others begin it, they see something savage and horrible in it. As for me I respect neither women nor men for their gender, nor own any sex in a pen. I choose just to hint to some causeless unfriends that, as far as I know, there are always two ends (and one of them heaviest, too) to a staff, and two parties also to every good laugh.

A FABLE FOR CRITICS.

Phœbus, sitting one day in a laurel-
tree's shade,
Was reminded of Daphne, of whom it
was made,
For the god being one day too warm in
his wooing,
She took to the tree to escape his pursuing;
Be the cause what it might, from his
offers she shrunk,
And, Ginevra-like, shut herself up in a
trunk;
And, though 't was a step into which he
had driven her,
He somehow or other had never forgiven her;
Her memory he nursed as a kind of a
tonic,
Something bitter to chew when he 'd
play the Byronic,
And I can't count the obstinate nymphs
that he brought over,
By a strange kind of smile he put on
when he thought of her.
" My case is like Dido's," he sometimes remarked;
" When I last saw my love, she was
fairly embarked
In a laurel, as *she* thought — but (ah
how Fate mocks !)
She has found it by this time a very bad
box;
Let hunters from me take this saw when
they need it, —
You 're not always sure of your game
when you 've treed it.
Just conceive such a change taking
place in one's mistress!
What romance would be left? — who
can flatter or kiss trees?
And, for mercy's sake, how could one
keep up a dialogue

With a dull wooden thing that will live
and will die a log, —
Not to say that the thought would forever intrude
That you 've less chance to win her the
more she is wood?
Ah ! it went to my heart, and the memory still grieves,
To see those loved graces all taking
their leaves ;
Those charms beyond speech, so en-
chanting but now,
As they left me forever, each making its
bough !
If her tongue *had* a tang sometimes
more than was right,
Her new bark is worse than ten times
her old bite."

Now, Daphne, — before she was hap-
pily treeified, —
Over all other blossoms the lily had
deified,
And when she expected the god on a
visit
('T was before he had made his intentions explicit),
Some buds she arranged with a vast
deal of care,
To look as if artlessly twined in her hair,
Where they seemed, as he said, when
he paid his addresses,
Like the day breaking through the long
night of her tresses;
So whenever he wished to be quite irre-
sistible,
Like a man with eight trumps in his
hand at a whist-table
(I feared me at first that the rhyme was
untwistable,
Though I might have lugged in an allusion to Cristabel),—

9

He would take up a lily, and gloomily
   look in it,
As I shall at the ——, when they cut
   up my book in it.

Well, here, after all the bad rhyme
   I 've been spinning,
I 've got back at last to my story's be-
   ginning :
Sitting there, as I say, in the shade of
   his mistress,
As dull as a volume of old Chester mys-
   teries,
Or as those puzzling specimens, which,
   in old histories,
We read of his verses — the Oracles,
   namely, —
(I wonder the Greeks should have
   swallowed them tamely,
For one might bet safely whatever he
   has to risk,
They were laid at his door by some an-
   cient Miss Asterisk,
And so dull that the men who retailed
   them out-doors
Got the ill name of augurs, because
   they were bores, —)
First, he mused what the animal sub-
   stance or herb is
Would induce a mustache, for you
   know he 's *imberbis* ;
Then he shuddered to think how his
   youthful position
Was assailed by the age of his son the
   physician ;
At some poems he glanced, had been
   sent to him lately,
And the metre and sentiment puzzled
   him greatly ;
"Mehercle ! I 'd make such proceeding felonious, —
Have they all of them slept in the cave
   of Trophonius ?
Look well to your seat, 't is like taking
   an airing
On a corduroy road, and that out of re-
   pairing ;
It leads one, 't is true, through the
   primitive forest,
Grand natural features, — but, then, one
   has no rest ;
You just catch a glimpse of some ravishing distance,
When a jolt puts the whole of it out of
   existence, —

Why not use their ears, if they happen
   to have any ? "
— Here the laurel-leaves murmured
   the name of poor Daphne.

"O, weep with me, Daphne," he
   sighed, "for you know it 's
A terrible thing to be pestered with
   poets !
But, alas, she is dumb, and the proverb
   holds good,
She never will cry till she 's out of the
   wood !
What would n't I give if I never had
   known of her ?
'T were a kind of relief had I something to groan over :
If I had but some letters of hers, now,
   to toss over,
I might turn for the nonce a Byronic
   philosopher,
And bewitch all the flats by bemoaning
   the loss of her.
One needs something tangible, though,
   to begin on, —
A loom, as it were, for the fancy to spin
   on ;
What boots all your grist ? it can never
   be ground
Till a breeze makes the arms of the
   windmill go round
(Or, if 't is a water-mill, alter the metaphor,
And say it won't stir, save the wheel be
   well wet afore,
Or lug in some stuff about water "so
   dreamily,"—
It is not a metaphor, though, 't is a
   simile) :
A lily, perhaps, would set *my* mill
   a-going,
For just at this season, I think, they
   are blowing.
Here, somebody, fetch one, not very
   far hence
They 're in bloom by the score, 't is
   but climbing a fence ;
There 's a poet hard by, who does nothing but fill his
Whole garden, from one end to t'other,
   with lilies ;
A very good plan, were it not for satiety,
One longs for a weed here and there,
   for variety ;

Though a weed is no more than a flower
  in disguise,
Which is seen through at once, if love
  give a man eyes."

Now there happened to be among
  Phœbus's followers,
A gentleman, one of the omnivorous
  swallowers,
Who bolt every book that comes out of
  the press,
Without the least question of larger or
  less,
Whose stomachs are strong at the ex-
  pense of their head, —
For reading new books is like eating
  new bread,
One can bear it at first, but by gradual
  steps he
Is brought to death's door of a mental
  dyspepsy.
On a previous stage of existence, our
  Hero
Had ridden outside, with the glass be-
  low zero;
He had been, 't is a fact you may safely
  rely on,
Of a very old stock a most eminent
  scion, —
A stock all fresh quacks their fierce
  boluses ply on,
Who stretch the new boots Earth's
  unwilling to try on,
Whom humbugs of all shapes and sorts
  keep their eye on,
Whose hair 's in the mortar of every
  new Zion,
Who, when whistles are dear, go direct-
  ly and buy one,
Who think slavery a crime that we
  must not say fie on,
Who hunt, if they e'er hunt at all, with
  the lion
(Though they hunt lions also, whenever
  they spy one),
Who contrive to make every good fortune a wry one,
And at last choose the hard bed of
  honor to die on,
Whose pedigree, traced to earth's
  earliest years,
Is longer than anything else but their
  ears; —
In short, he was sent into life with the
  wrong key,

He unlocked the door, and stept forth
  a poor donkey.
Though kicked and abused by his bi-
  pedal betters
Yet he filled no mean place in the kingdom of letters;
Far happier than many a literary
  hack,
He bore only paper-mill rags on his
  back
(For it makes a vast difference which
  side the mill
One expends on the paper his labor
  and skill);
So, when his soul waited a new trans-
  migration,
And Destiny balanced 'twixt this and
  that station,
Not having much time to expend upon
  bothers,
Remembering he 'd had some connection with authors,
And considering his four legs had grown
  paralytic, —
She set him on two, and he came forth
  a critic.

Through his babyhood no kind of
  pleasure he took
In any amusement but tearing a book;
For him there was no intermediate stage
From babyhood up to straight-laced
  middle age;
There were years when he did n't wear
  coat-tails behind,
But a boy he could never be rightly de-
  fined;
Like the Irish Good Folk, though in
  length scarce a span,
From the womb he came gravely, a
  little old man;
While other boys' trousers demanded
  the toil
Of the motherly fingers on all kinds of
  soil,
Red, yellow, brown, black, clayey,
  gravelly, loamy,
He sat in the corner and read Viri
  Romæ.
He never was known to unbend or to
  revel once
In base, marbles, hockey, or kick up
  the devil once;
He was just one of those who excite
  the benevolence

Of your old prigs who sound the soul's
        depths with a ledger,
And are on the lookout for some young
        men to "edger-
-cate," as they call it, who won't be too
        costly,
And who'll afterward take to the
        ministry mostly;
Who always wear spectacles, always
        look bilious,
Always keep on good terms with each
        mater-familias
Throughout the whole parish, and man-
        age to rear
Ten boys like themselves, on four hun-
        dred a year:
Who, fulfilling in turn the same fearful
        conditions,
Either preach through their noses, or
        go upon missions.

In this way our Hero got safely to
        college,
Where he bolted alike both his com-
        mons and knowledge;
A reading-machine, always wound up
        and going,
He mastered whatever was not worth
        the knowing,
Appeared in a gown, with black waist-
        coat of satin,
To spout such a Gothic oration in
        Latin
That Tully could never have made out
        a word in it
(Though himself was the model the
        author preferred in it),
And grasping the parchment which gave
        him in fee
All the mystic and-so-forths contained
        in A. B.,
He was launched (life is always com-
        pared to a sea)
With just enough learning, and skill
        for the using it,
To prove he'd a brain, by forever con-
        fusing it.
So worthy St. Benedict, piously burn-
        ing
With the holiest zeal against secular
        learning,
Nesciensque scienter, as writers express
        it,
Indoctusque sapienter a Roma recessit.

'T would be endless to tell you the
        things that he knew,
Each a separate fact, undeniably true,
But with him or each other they'd
        nothing to do;
No power of combining, arranging, dis-
        cerning,
Digested the masses he learned into
        learning;
There was one thing in life he had
        practical knowledge for
(And this, you will think, he need
        scarce go to college for), —
Not a deed would he do, nor a word
        would he utter,
Till he'd weighed its relations to plain
        bread and butter.
When he left Alma Mater, he practised
        his wits
In compiling the journals' historical
        bits, —
Of shops broken open, men falling in fits,
Great fortunes in England bequeathed
        to poor printers,
And cold spells, the coldest for many
        past winters, —
Then, rising by industry, knack, and
        address,
Got notices up for an unbiased press,
With a mind so well poised, it seemed
        equally made for
Applause or abuse, just which chanced
        to be paid for;
From this point his progress was rapid
        and sure,
To the post of a regular heavy reviewer.

And here I must say he wrote ex-
        cellent articles
On Hebraical points, or the force of
        Greek particles;
They filled up the space nothing else
        was prepared for,
And nobody read that which nobody
        cared for;
If any old book reached a fiftieth edition,
He could fill forty pages with safe erudi-
        tion:
He could gauge the old books by the
        old set of rules,
And his very old nothings pleased very
        old fools;
But give him a new book, fresh out of
        the heart,

And you put him at sea without com-
    pass or chart, —
His blunders aspired to the rank of an
    art ;
For his lore was engraft, something
    foreign that grew in him,
Exhausting the sap of the native and
    true in him,
So that when a man came with a soul
    that was new in him,
Carving new forms of truth out of Na-
    ture's old granite,
New and old at their birth, like Le
    Verrier's planet,
Which, to get a true judgment, them-
    selves must create
In the soul of their critic the measure
    and weight,
Being rather themselves a fresh stand-
    ard of grace,
To compute their own judge, and assign
    him his place,
Our reviewer would crawl all about it
    and round it,
And, reporting each circumstance just
    as he found it,
Without the least malice, — his record
    would be
Profoundly æsthetic as that of a flea,
Which, supping on Wordsworth, should
    print, for our sakes,
Recollections of nights with the Bard
    of the Lakes,
Or, lodged by an Arab guide, ventured
    to render a
Comprehensive account of the ruins at
    Denderah.

As I said, he was never precisely
    unkind,
The defect in his brain was just absence
    of mind ;
If he boasted, 't was simply that he was
    self-made,
A position which I, for one, never gain-
    said,
My respect for my Maker supposing a
    skill
In His works which our Hero would an-
    swer but ill ;
And I trust that the mould which he
    used may be cracked, or he,
Made bold by success, may enlarge his
    phylactery,
And set up a kind of a man-manufac-
    tory, —

An event which I shudder to think
    about, seeing
That Man is a moral, accountable be-
    ing.

He meant well enough, but was still
    in the way,
As dunces still are, let them be where
    they may ;
Indeed, they appear to come into ex-
    istence
To impede other folks with their awk-
    ward assistance ;
If you set up a dunce on the very
    North pole,
All alone with himself, I believe, on my
    soul,
He'd manage to get betwixt somebody's
    shins,
And pitch him down bodily, all in his
    sins,
To the grave polar bears sitting round
    on the ice,
All shortening their grace, to be in for
    a slice ;
Or, if he found nobody else there to
    pother,
Why, one of his legs would just trip up
    the other,
For there's nothing we read of in tor-
    ture's inventions,
Like a well-meaning dunce, with the
    best of intentions.

A terrible fellow to meet in society,
Not the toast that he buttered was ever
    so dry at tea ;
There he'd sit at the table and stir in
    his sugar,
Crouching close for a spring, all the
    while, like a cougar ;
Be sure of your facts, of your measures
    and weights,
Of your time, — he's as fond as an Arab
    of dates ;
You'll be telling, perhaps, in your com-
    ical way,
Of something you've seen in the course
    of the day ;
And, just as you're tapering out the
    conclusion,
You venture an ill-fated classic allu-
    sion,
The girls have all got their laughs ready,
    when, whack !

The cougar comes down on your thunder-
struck back !
You had left out a comma, — your
Greek 's put in joint,
And pointed at cost of your story's
whole point.
In the course of the evening, you find
chance for certain
Soft speeches to Anne, in the shade of
the curtain :
You tell her your heart can be likened
to *one* flower,
" And that, O most charming of
women, 's the sunflower,
Which turns" — here a clear nasal
voice, to your terror,
From outside the curtain, says, "That 's
all an error."
As for him, he 's — no matter, he never
grew tender,
Sitting after a ball, with his feet on the
fender,
Shaping somebody's sweet features out
of cigar smoke,
(Though he 'd willingly grant you that
such doings are smoke) ;
All women he damns with *mutabile
semper*,
And if ever he felt something like
love's distemper,
T was tow'rds a young lady who spoke
ancient Mexican,
And assisted her father in making a
lexicon,
Though I recollect hearing him get
quite ferocious
About Mary Clausum, the mistress of
Grotius,
Or something of that sort, — but, no
more to bore ye
With character-painting, I 'll turn to
my story.

Now, Apollo, who finds it convenient
sometimes
To get his court clear of the makers
of rhymes,
The *genus*, I think it is called, *irrita-
bile*,
Every one of whom thinks himself
treated most shabbily,
And nurses a — what is it ? — *immedi-
cabile*,
Which keeps him at boiling-point, hot
for a quarrel,

As bitter as wormwood, and sourer
than sorrel,
If any poor devil but look at a laurel ; —
Apollo, I say, being sick of their riot-
ing
(Though he sometimes acknowledged
their verse had a quieting
Effect after dinner, and seemed to sug-
gest a
Retreat to the shrine of a tranquil
siesta),
Kept our Hero at hand, who, by means
of a bray,
Which he gave to the life, drove the
rabble away ;
And if that would n't do, he was sure
to succeed,
If he took his review out and offered
to read ;
Or, failing in plans of this milder de-
scription,
He would ask for their aid to get up a
subscription,
Considering that authorship was n't a
rich craft,
To print the "American drama of
Witchcraft."
"Stay, I 'll read you a scene," — but
he hardly began,
Ere Apollo shrieked "Help !" and the
authors all ran :
And once, when these purgatives acted
with less spirit,
And the desperate case asked a remedy
desperate,
He drew from his pocket a foolscap
epistle,
As calmly as if 't were a nine-barrelled
pistol,
And threatened them all with the judg-
ment to come,
Of " A wandering Star's first impres-
sions of Rome."
"Stop ! stop !" with their hands o'er
their ears, screamed the Muses,
"He may go off and murder himself, if
he chooses,
'T was a means self-defence only sanc-
tioned his trying,
'T is mere massacre now that the enemy 's flying ;
If he 's forced to 't again, and we happen to be there,
Give us each a large handkerchief
soaked in strong ether."

I called this a " Fable for Critics " ;
  you think it 's
More like a display of my rhythmical
  trinkets ;
My plot, like an icicle, 's slender and
  slippery,
Every moment more slender, and likely
  to slip awry,
And the reader unwilling *in loco desi-
  pere,*
Is free to jump over as much of my frip-
  pery
As he fancies, and, if he 's a provident
  skipper, he
May have like Odysseus control of the
  gales,
And get safe to port, ere his patience
  quite fails ;
Moreover, although 't is a slender re-
  turn
For your toil and expense, yet my pa-
  per will burn,
And, if you have manfully struggled
  thus far with me,
You may e'en twist me up, and just
  light your cigar with me :
If too angry for that, you can tear me
  in pieces,
And my *membra disjecta* consign to
  the breezes,
A fate like great Ratzau's, whom one
  of those bores,
Who beflead with bad verses poor
  Louis Quatorze,
Describes (the first verse somehow ends
  with *victoire*),
As *dispersant partout et ses membres
  et sa gloire ;*
Or, if I were over-desirous of earning
A repute among noodles for classical
  learning,
I could pick you a score of allusions, I
  wis,
As new as the jests of *Didaskalos tis ;*
Better still, I could make out a good
  solid list
From authors recondite who do not ex-
  ist, —
But that would be naughty : at least, I
  could twist
Something out of Absyrtus, or turn your
  inquiries
After Milton's prose metaphor, drawn
  from Osiris ; —

But, as Cicero says he won't say this or
  that
(A fetch, I must say, most transparent
  and flat),
After saying whate'er he could possibly
  think of, —
I simply will state that I pause on the
  brink of
A mire, ankle-deep, of deliberate confusion,
Made up of old jumbles of classic allusion :
So, when you were thinking yourselves
  to be pitied,
Just conceive how much harder your
  teeth you 'd have gritted,
An 't were not for the dulness I 've
  kindly omitted.

I 'd apologize here for my many digressions,
Were it not that I 'm certain to trip into
  fresh ones
('T is so hard to escape if you get in
  their mesh once) ;
Just reflect, if you please, how 't is said
  by Horatius,
That Mæonides nods now and then,
  and, my gracious !
It certainly does look a little bit ominous
When he gets under way with *ton
  d'apameibomenos.*
(Here a something occurs which I 'll
  just clap a rhyme to,
And say it myself, ere a Zoilus have
  time to, —
Any author a nap like Van Winkle's
  may take,
If he only contrive to keep readers
  awake,
But he 'll very soon find himself laid on
  the shelf,
If *they* fall a-nodding when he nods
  himself.)

Once for all, to return, and to stay,
  will I, nill I —
When Phœbus expressed his desire for
  a lily,
Our hero, whose homœopathic sagacity
With an ocean of zeal mixed his drop
  of capacity,
Set off for the garden as fast as the wind

(Or, to take a comparison more to my
    mind,
As a sound politician leaves conscience
    behind),
And leaped the low fence, as a party
    hack jumps
O'er his principles, when something
    else turns up trumps.

He was gone a long time, and Apollo,
    meanwhile,
Went over some sonnets of his with a
    file,
For, of all compositions, he thought
    that the sonnet
Best repaid all the toil you expended
    upon it ;
It should reach with one impulse the
    end of its course,
And for one final blow collect all of its
    force ;
Not a verse should be salient, but each
    one should tend
With a wave-like up-gathering to burst
    at the end ; —
So, condensing the strength here, there
    smoothing a wry kink,
He was killing the time, when up walked
    Mr. —— ;
At a few steps behind him, a small man
    in glasses
Went dodging about, muttering, "Mur-
    derers ! asses !"
From out of his pocket a paper he'd take,
With the proud look of martyrdom tied
    to its stake,
And, reading a squib at himself, he'd
    say, " Here I see
'Gainst American letters a bloody con-
    spiracy,
They are all by my personal enemies
    written ;
I must post an anonymous letter to
    Britain,
And show that this gall is the merest
    suggestion
Of spite at my zeal on the Copyright
    question,
For, on this side the water, 't is pru-
    dent to pull
O'er the eyes of the public their na-
    tional wool,
By accusing of slavish respect to John
    Bull

All American authors who have more
    or less
Of that anti-American humbug — suc-
    cess,
While in private we 're always em-
    bracing the knees
Of some twopenny editor over the
    seas,
And licking his critical shoes, for you
    know 't is
The whole aim of our lives to get one
    English notice ;
My American puffs I would willingly
    burn all
(They 're all from one source, monthly,
    weekly, diurnal)
To get but a kick from a transmarine
    journal !"

So, culling the gibes of each critical
    scorner
As if they were plums, and himself
    were Jack Horner,
He came cautiously on, peeping round
    every corner,
And into each hole where a weasel
    might pass in,
Expecting the knife of some critic as-
    sassin,
Who stabs to the heart with a carica-
    ture,
Not so bad as those daubs of the Sun,
    to be sure,
Yet done with a dagger-o'-type, whose
    vile portraits
Disperse all one's good and condense
    all one's poor traits.

Apollo looked up, hearing footsteps
    approaching,
And slipped out of sight the new rhymes
    he was broaching, —
" Good day, Mr. ——, I 'm happy to
    meet,
With a scholar so ripe, and a critic so
    neat,
Who through Grub Street the soul of
    a gentleman carries ;
What news from that suburb of London
    and Paris
Which latterly makes such shrill claims
    to monopolize
The credit of being the New World
    metropolis ?"

"Why, nothing of consequence, save
     this attack
On my friend there, behind, by some
     pitiful hack,
Who thinks every national author a
     poor one,
That is n't a copy of something that 's
     foreign,
And assaults the American Dick—"

                    "Nay, 't is clear
That your Damon there 's fond of a flea
     in his ear,
And, if no one else furnished them
     gratis, on tick
He would buy some himself, just to
     hear the old click ;
Why, I honestly think, if some fool in
     Japan
Should turn up his nose at the 'Poems
     on Man,'
(Which contain many verses as fine,
     by the bye,
As any that lately came under my eye,)
Your friend there by some inward in-
     stinct would know it,
Would get it translated, reprinted, and
     show it ;
As a man might take off a high stock
     to exhibit
The autograph round his own neck of
     the gibbet ;
Nor would let it rest so, but fire column
     after column,
Signed Cato, or Brutus, or something
     as solemn,
By way of displaying his critical crosses,
And tweaking that poor transatlantic
     proboscis,
His broadsides resulting (this last
     there 's no doubt of)
In successively sinking the craft they 're
     fired out of.
Now nobody knows when an author is hit,
If he have not a public hysterical fit ;
Let him only keep close in his snug
     garret's dim ether,
And nobody 'd think of his foes — or
     of him either ;
If an author have any least fibre of
     worth in him,
Abuse would but tickle the organ of
     mirth in him ;
All the critics on earth cannot crush
     with their ban

One word that 's in tune with the nature
     of man."
  "Well, perhaps so ; meanwhile I
     have brought you a book,
Into which if you 'll just have the good-
     ness to look,
You may feel so delighted (when once
     you are through it)
As to deem it not unworth your while
     to review it,
And I think I can promise your
     thoughts, if you do,
A place in the next Democratic Re-
     view."
  "The most thankless of gods you
     must surely have thought me,
For this is the forty-fourth copy you 've
     brought me,
I have given them away, or at least I
     have tried,
But I 've forty-two left, standing all side
     by side
(The man who accepted that one copy
     died),—
From one end of a shelf to the other
     they reach,
'With the author's respects' neatly
     written in each.
The publisher, sure, will proclaim a
     Te Deum,
When he hears of that order the British
     Museum
Has sent for one set of what books
     were first printed
In America, little or big, — for 't is
     hinted
That this is the first truly tangible hope
     he
Has ever had raised for the sale of a copy.
I 've thought very often 't would be a
     good thing
In all public collections of books, if a
     wing
Were set off by itself, like the seas from
     the dry lands,
Marked *Literature suited to desolate
     islands,*
And filled with such books as could
     never be read
Save by readers of proofs, forced to do
     it for bread, —
Such books as one's wrecked on in
     small country-taverns,
Such as hermits might mortify over in
     caverns,

Such as Satan, if printing had then
     been invented,
As the climax of woe, would to Job
     have presented,
Such as Crusoe might dip in, although
     there are few so
Outrageously cornered by fate as poor
     Crusoe;
And since the philanthropists just now
     are banging
And gibbeting all who 're in favor of
     hanging
(Though Cheever has proved that the
     Bible and Altar
Were let down from Heaven at the end
     of a halter,
And that vital religion would dull and
     grow callous,
Unrefreshed, now and then, with a
     sniff of the gallows), —
And folks are beginning to think it looks
     odd,
To choke a poor scamp for the glory of
     God:
And that He who esteems the Virginia
     reel
A bait to draw saints from their spiritual
     weal,
And regards the quadrille as a far
     greater knavery
Than crushing His African children
     with slavery, —
Since all who take part in a waltz or
     cotillon
Are mounted for hell on the Devil's
     own pillion,
Who, as every true orthodox Christian
     well knows,
Approaches the heart through the door
     of the toes,
That He, I am saying, whose judg-
     ments are stored
For such as take steps in despite of His
     word,
Should look with delight on the ago-
     nized prancing
Of a wretch who has not the least
     ground for his dancing,
While the State, standing by, sings a
     verse from the Psalter
About offering to God on His favorite
     halter,
And, when the legs droop from their
     twitching divergence,

Sells the clothes to a Jew, and the
     corpse to the surgeons; —

Now, instead of all this, I think I
     can direct you all
To a criminal code both humane and
     effectual;—
I propose to shut up every doer of
     wrong
With these desperate books, for such
     term, short or long,
As by statute in such cases made and
     provided,
Shall be by your wise legislators de-
     cided:
Thus: — Let murderers be shut, to grow
     wiser and cooler,
At hard labor for life on the works of
     Miss ——— ;
Petty thieves, kept from flagranter
     crimes by their fears,
Shall peruse Yankee Doodle a blank
     term of years, —
That American Punch, like the Eng-
     lish, no doubt, —
Just the sugar and lemons and spirit
     left out.

"But stay, here comes Tityrus Gris-
     wold, and leads on
The flocks whom he first plucks alive,
     and then feeds on, —
A loud-cackling swarm, in whose feath-
     ers warm-drest,
He goes for as perfect a — swan as the
     rest.

"There comes Emerson first, whose
     rich words, every one,
Are like gold nails in temples to hang
     trophies on,
Whose prose is grand verse, while his
     verse, the Lord knows,
Is some of it pr— No, 't is not even
     prose:
I 'm speaking of metres; some poems
     have welled
From those rare depths of soul that
     have ne'er been excelled;
They 're not epics, but that does n't
     matter a pin,
In creating, the only hard thing 's to
     begin;
A grass-blade 's no easier to make than
     an oak;

If you 've once found the way, you 've
  achieved the grand stroke ;
In the worst of his poems are mines of
  rich matter,
But thrown in a heap with a crush and
  a clatter ;
Now it is not one thing nor another alone
Makes a poem, but rather the general
  tone,
The something pervading, uniting the
  whole,
The before unconceived, unconceivable
  soul,
So that just in removing this trifle or
  that, you
Take away, as it were, a chief limb of
  the statue ;
Roots, wood, bark, and leaves singly
  perfect may be,
But, clapt hodge-podge together, they
  don't make a tree.

  "But, to come back to Emerson
    (whom, by the way,
I believe we left waiting), — his is, we
  may say,
A Greek head on right Yankee shoul-
  ders, whose range
Has Olympus for one pole, for t'other
  the Exchange ;
He seems, to my thinking (although
  I 'm afraid
The comparison must, long ere this,
  have been made),
A Plotinus - Montaigne, where the
  Egyptian's gold mist
And the Gascon's shrewd wit cheek-
  by-jowl coexist ;
All admire, and yet scarcely six con-
  verts he 's got
To I don't (nor they either) exactly
  know what ;
For though he builds glorious temples,
  't is odd
He leaves never a doorway to get in a god.
'T is refreshing to old-fashioned people
  like me
To meet such a primitive Pagan as he,
In whose mind all creation is duly re-
  spected
As parts of himself — just a little pro-
  jected ;
And who 's willing to worship the stars
  and the sun,

A convert to — nothing but Emerson.
So perfect a balance there is in his
  head,
That he talks of things sometimes as
  if they were dead ;
Life, nature, love, God, and affairs of
  that sort,
He looks at as merely ideas ; in short,
As if they were fossils stuck round in a
  cabinet,
Of such vast extent that our earth 's a
  mere dab in it ;
Composed just as he is inclined to con-
  jecture her,
Namely, one part pure earth, ninety-
  nine parts pure lecturer ;
You are filled with delight at his clear
  demonstration,
Each figure, word, gesture, just fits the
  occasion,
With the quiet precision of science he 'll
  sort 'em,
But you can't help suspecting the whole
  a *post mortem*.

  "There are persons, mole-blind to
    the soul's make and style,
Who insist on a likeness 'twixt him and
  Carlyle :
To compare him with Plato would be
  vastly fairer,
Carlyle 's the more burly, but E. is the
  rarer ;
He sees fewer objects, but clearlier,
  truelier,
If C. 's as original, E. 's more peculiar ;
That he 's more of a man you might
  say of the one,
Of the other he 's more of an Emer-
  son ;
C. 's the Titan, as shaggy of mind as
  of limb, —
E. the clear-eyed Olympian, rapid and
  slim ;
The one 's two thirds Norseman, the
  other half Greek,
Where the one 's most abounding, the
  other 's to seek ;
C.'s generals require to be seen in the
  mass, —
E.'s specialties gain if enlarged by the
  glass ;
C. gives nature and God his own fits of
  the blues,

And rims common-sense things with
      mystical hues, —
E. sits in a mystery calm and intense,
And looks coolly around him with sharp
      common sense ;
C. shows you how every-day matters
      unite
With the dim transdiurnal recesses of
      night, —
While E., in a plain, preternatural way,
Makes mysteries matters of mere every
      day ;
C. draws all his characters quite à la
      Fuseli, —
Not sketching their bundles of muscles
      and thews illy,
He paints with a brush so untamed and
      profuse,
They seem nothing but bundles of
      muscles and thews ;
E. is rather like Flaxman, lines strait
      and severe,
And a colorless outline, but full, round,
      and clear ;
To the men he thinks worthy he frankly
      accords
The design of a white marble statue in
      words.
C. labors to get at the centre, and then
Take a reckoning from there of his
      actions and men ;
E. calmly assumes the said centre as
      granted,
And, given himself, has whatever is
      wanted.

"He has imitators in scores, who omit
No part of the man but his wisdom
      and wit, —
Who go carefully o'er the sky-blue of
      his brain,
And, when he has skimmed it once,
      skim it again ;
If at all they resemble him, you may be
      sure it is
Because their shoals mirror his mists
      and obscurities,
As a mud-puddle seems deep as heaven
      for a minute,
While a cloud that floats o'er is reflected
      within it.

"There comes ——, for instance ; to
      see him 's rare sport,

Tread in Emerson's tracks with legs
      painfully short ;
How he jumps, how he strains, and
      gets red in the face,
To keep step with the mystagogue's
      natural pace !
He follows as close as a stick to a rocket,
His fingers exploring the prophet's
      each pocket.
Fie, for shame, brother bard ; with
      good fruit of your own,
Can't you let Neighbor Emerson's or-
      chards alone ?
Besides, 't is no use, you 'll not find
      e'en a core, —
—— has picked up all the windfalls be-
      fore.
They might strip every tree, and E.
      never would catch 'em,
His Hesperides have no rude dragon
      to watch 'em ;
When they send him a dishful, and
      ask him to try 'em,
He never suspects how the sly rogues
      came by 'em ;
He wonders why 't is there are none
      such his trees on,
And thinks 'em the best he has tasted
      this season.

"Yonder, calm as a cloud, Alcott
      stalks in a dream,
And fancies himself in thy groves, Aca-
      deme,
With the Parthenon nigh, and the
      olive-trees o'er him,
And never a fact to perplex him or
      bore him,
With a snug room at Plato's, when
      night comes, to walk to,
And people from morning till midnight
      to talk to,
And from midnight till morning, nor
      snore in their listening ; —
So he muses, his face with the joy of
      it glistening,
For his highest conceit of a happiest
      state is
Where they 'd live upon acorns, and
      hear him talk gratis ;
And indeed, I believe, no man ever
      talked better, —
Each sentence hangs perfectly poised
      to a letter ;

He seems piling words, but there's
    royal dust hid
In the heart of each sky-piercing pyr-
    amid.
While he talks he is great, but goes
    out like a taper,
If you shut him up closely with pen,
    ink, and paper;
Yet his fingers itch for 'em from morn-
    ing till night,
And he thinks he does wrong if he
    don't always write;
In this, as in all things, a lamb among
    men,
He goes to sure death when he goes
    to his pen.

    "Close behind him is Brownson, his
    mouth very full
With attempting to gulp a Gregorian
    bull;
Who contrives, spite of that, to pour
    out as he goes
A stream of transparent and forcible
    prose;
He shifts quite about, then proceeds to
    expound
That 't is merely the earth, not himself,
    that turns round,
And wishes it clearly impressed on your
    mind
That the weathercock rules and not fol-
    lows the wind;
Proving first, then as deftly confuting
    each side,
With no doctrine pleased that's not
    somewhere denied,
He lays the denier away on the shelf,
And then — down beside him lies grave-
    ly himself.
He's the Salt River boatman, who al-
    ways stands willing
To convey friend or foe without charg-
    ing a shilling,
And so fond of the trip that, when
    leisure's to spare,
He'll row himself up, if he can't get
    a fare.
The worst of it is, that his logic's so
    strong,
That of two sides he commonly chooses
    the wrong;
If there *is* only one, why, he'll split it
    in two,

And first pummel this half, then that,
    black and blue.
That white's white needs no proof, but
    it takes a deep fellow
To prove it jet-black, and that jet-black
    is yellow.
He offers the true faith to drink in a
    sieve, —
When it reaches your lips there's
    naught left to believe
But a few silly-(syllo-, I mean,) -gisms
    that squat 'em
Like tadpoles, o'erjoyed with the mud
    at the bottom.

    "There is Willis, all *natty* and jaunty
    and gay,
Who says his best things in so foppish
    a way,
With conceits and pet phrases so thick-
    ly o'erlaying 'em,
That one hardly knows whether to
    thank him for saying 'em;
Over-ornament ruins both poem and
    prose,
Just conceive of a Muse with a ring in
    her nose!
His prose had a natural grace of its own,
And enough of it, too, if he'd let it
    alone;
But he twitches and jerks so, one fairly
    gets tired,
And is forced to forgive where one might
    have admired;
Yet whenever it slips away free and
    unlaced,
It runs like a stream with a musical
    waste,
And gurgles along with the liquidest
    sweep; —
'Tis not deep as a river, but who'd
    have it deep?
In a country where scarcely a village is
    found
That has not its author sublime and
    profound,
For some one to be slightly shallow's
    a duty,
And Willis's shallowness makes half
    his beauty.
His prose winds along with a blithe-
    gurgling error,
And reflects all of Heaven it can see in
    its mirror:

'T is a narrowish strip, but it is not an
artifice;
'T is the true out-of-doors with its
genuine hearty phiz;
It is Nature herself, and there 's something in that,
Since most brains reflect but the crown
of a hat.
Few volumes I know to read under a
tree,
More truly delightful than his A l' Abri,
With the shadows of leaves flowing
over your book,
Like ripple-shades netting the bed of a
brook;
With June coming softly your shoulder
to look over,
Breezes waiting to turn every leaf of
your book over,
And Nature to criticise still as you
read,
The page that bears that is a rare one
indeed.

"He 's so innate a cockney, that had
he been born
Where plain bare-skin 's the only full-
dress that is worn,
He 'd have given his own such an air
that you 'd say
'T had been made by a tailor to lounge
in Broadway.
His nature 's a glass of champagne
with the foam on 't,
As tender as Fletcher, as witty as
Beaumont;
So his best things are done in the flush
of the moment;
If he wait, all is spoiled; he may stir
it and shake it,
But, the fixed air once gone, he can
never remake it.
He might be a marvel of easy delight-
fulness,
If he would not sometimes leave the r
out of sprightfulness;
And he ought to let Scripture alone —
't is self-slaughter,
For nobody likes inspiration-and-wa-
ter.
He 'd have been just the fellow to sup
at the Mermaid,
Cracking jokes at rare Ben, with an
eye to the barmaid,

His wit running up as Canary ran
down, —
The topmost bright bubble on the
wave of The Town.

"Here comes Parker, the Orson of
parsons, a man
Whom the Church undertook to put
under her ban
(The Church of Socinus, I mean), — his
opinions
Being So- (ultra) -cinian, they shocked
the Socinians;
They believed — faith I 'm puzzled —
I think I may call
Their belief a believing in nothing at
all,
Or something of that sort; I know they
all went
For a general union of total dissent:
He went a step farther; without cough
or hem,
He frankly avowed he believed not in
them;
And, before he could be jumbled up or
prevented,
From their orthodox kind of dissent he
dissented.
There was heresy here, you perceive,
for the right
Of privately judging means simply that
light
Has been granted to *me*, for deciding
on *you*;
And in happier times, before Atheism
grew,
The deed contained clauses for cooking
you too.
Now at Xerxes and Knut we all laugh,
yet our foot
With the same wave is wet that mocked
Xerxes and Knut;
And we all entertain a secure private
notion,
That our *Thus far!* will have a great
weight with the ocean.
'T was so with our liberal Christians:
they bore
With sincerest conviction their chairs
to the shore;
They brandished their worn theological
birches,
Bade natural progress keep out of the
Churches

And expected the lines they had drawn
    to prevail
With the fast-rising tide to keep out of
    their pale ;
They had formerly dammed the Pon-
    tifical See,
And the same thing, they thought,
    would do nicely for P. ;
But he turned up his nose at their mum-
    ming and shamming,
And cared (shall I say?) not a d—— for
    their damming ;
So they first read him out of their
    church, and next minute
Turned round and declared he had
    never been in it.
But the ban was too small or the man
    was too big,
For he recks not their bells, books,
    and candles a fig
(He scarce looks like a man who would
    stay treated shabbily,
Sophroniscus' son's head o'er the fea-
    tures of Rabelais) ; —
He bangs and bethwacks them, — their
    backs he salutes
With the whole tree of knowledge torn
    up by the roots ;
His sermons with satire are plenteously
    verjuiced,
And he talks in one breath of Confut-
    zee, Cass, Zerduscht,
Jack Robinson, Peter the Hermit,
    Strap, Dathan,
Cush, Pitt (not the bottomless, *that*
    he 's no faith in),
Pan, Pillicock, Shakespeare, Paul,
    Toots, Monsieur Tonson,
Aldebaran, Alcander, Ben Khorat, Ben
    Jonson,
Thoth, Richter, Joe Smith, Father
    Paul, Judah Monis,
Musæus, Muretus, *hem,* — μ Scor-
    pionis,
Maccabee, Maccaboy, Mac — Mac —
    ah ! Machiavelli,
Condorcet, Count d'Orsay, Conder,
    Say, Ganganelli,
Orion, O'Connell, the Chevalier D'O,
(See the Memoirs of Sully,) το παν, the
    great toe
Of the statue of Jupiter, now made to pass
For that of Jew Peter by good Rom-
    ish brass,

(You may add for yourselves, for I find
    it a bore,
All the names you have ever, or not,
    heard before,
And when you 've done that — why,
    invent a few more.)
His hearers can't tell you on Sunday
    beforehand,
If in that day's discourse they 'll be
    Bibled or Koraned,
For he 's seized the idea (by his mar-
    tyrdom fired)
That all men (not orthodox) *may be*
    inspired ;
Yet though wisdom profane with his
    creed he may weave in,
He makes it quite clear what he *does n't*
    believe in,
While some, who decry him, think all
    Kingdom Come
Is a sort of a, kind of a, species of
    Hum,
Of which, as it were, so to speak, not a
    crumb
Would be left, if we did n't keep care-
    fully mum,
And, to make a clean breast, that 't is
    perfectly plain
That *all* kinds of wisdom are some-
    what profane ;
Now P.'s creed than this may be lighter
    or darker
But in one thing, 't is clear, he has faith,
    namely — Parker ;
And this is what make him the crowd-
    drawing preacher,
There 's a background of god to each
    hard-working feature,
Every word that he speaks has been
    fierily furnaced
In the blast of a life that has struggled
    in earnest :
There he stands, looking more like a
    ploughman than priest,
If not dreadfully awkward, not grace-
    ful at least,
His gestures all downright and same,
    if you will,
As of brown-fisted Hobnail in hoeing
    a drill,
But his periods fall on you, stroke after
    stroke,
Like the blows of a lumberer felling an
    oak,

You forget the man wholly, you 're
    thankful to meet
With a preacher who smacks of the
    field and the street,
And to hear, you 're not over-particular
    whence,
Almost Taylor's profusion, quite Lati-
    mer's sense.

    "There is Bryant, as quiet, as cool,
      and as dignified,
As a smooth, silent iceberg, that never
    is ignified,
Save when by reflection 't is kindled o'
    nights
With a semblance of flame by the chill
    Northern Lights.
He may rank (Griswold says so) first
    bard of your nation
(There 's no doubt that he stands in
    supreme ice-olation),
Your topmost Parnassus he may set
    his heel on,
But no warm applauses come, peal fol-
    lowing peal on, —
He 's too smooth and too polished to
    hang any zeal on :
Unqualified merits, I 'll grant, if you
    choose, he has 'em,
But he lacks the one merit of kindling
    enthusiasm ;
If he stir you at all, it is just, on my
    soul,
Like being stirred up with the very
    North Pole.

    "He is very nice reading in summer,
      but *inter*
Nos, we don't want *extra* freezing in
    winter ;
Take him up in the depth of July, my
    advice is,
When you feel an Egyptian devotion to
    ices.
But deduct all you can, there 's enough
    that 's right good in him,
He has a true soul for field, river, and
    wood in him ;
And his heart, in the midst of brick
    walls, or where'er it is,
Glows, softens, and thrills with the
    tenderest charities —
To you mortals that delve in this trade-
    ridden planet?

No, to old Berkshire's hills, with their
    limestone and granite.
If you 're one who *in loco* (add *foco*
    here) *desipis*,
You will get of his outermost heart (as I
    guess) a piece ;
But you 'd get deeper down if you came
    as a precipice,
And would break the last seal of its in-
    wardest fountain,
If you only could palm yourself off for
    a mountain.
Mr. Quivis, or somebody quite as dis-
    cerning,
Some scholar who 's hourly expecting
    his learning,
Calls B. the American Wordsworth ;
    but Wordsworth
May be rated at more than your whole
    tuneful herd's worth.
No, don't be absurd, he 's an excellent
    Bryant ;
But, my friends, you 'll endanger the
    life of your client,
By attempting to stretch him up into a
    giant :
If you choose to compare him, I think
    there are two per-
-sons fit for a parallel — Thomson and
    Cowper ; *
I don't mean exactly, — there 's some-
    thing of each,
There 's T.'s love of nature, C.'s pen-
    chant to preach ;
Just mix up their minds so that C.'s
    spice of craziness
Shall balance and neutralize T.'s turn
    for laziness,
And it gives you a brain cool, quite
    frictionless, quiet,
Whose internal police nips the buds of
    all riot, —
A brain like a permanent strait-jacket
    put on
The heart that strives vainly to burst
    off a button, —
A brain which, without being slow or
    mechanic,

---

* To demonstrate quickly and easily how per-
-versely absurd 't is to sound this name *Cowper,*
As people in general call him named *super,*
I remark that he rhymes it himself with horse-
    trooper.

Does more than a larger less drilled,
more volcanic ;
He 's a Cowper condensed, with no
craziness bitten,
And the advantage that Wordsworth
before him has written.

"But, my dear little bardlings, don't
prick up your ears
Nor suppose I would rank you and
Bryant as peers ;
If I call him an iceberg, I don't mean
to say
There is nothing in that which is grand
in its way ;
He is almost the one of your poets that
knows
How much grace, strength, and dignity
lie in Repose ;
If he sometimes fall short, he is too
wise to mar
His thought's modest fulness by going
too far ;
'T would be well if your authors should
all make a trial
Of what virtue there is in severe self-
denial,
And measure their writings by Hesiod's
staff,
Which teaches that all has less value
than half.

"There is Whittier, whose swelling
and vehement heart
Strains the strait-breasted drab of the
Quaker apart,
And reveals the live Man, still supreme
and erect,
Underneath the bemummying wrappers
of sect ;
There was ne'er a man born who had
more of the swing
Of the true lyric bard and all that kind
of thing ;
And his failures arise (though he seem
not to know it)
From the very same cause that has
made him a poet, —
A fervor of mind which knows no sep-
aration
'Twixt simple excitement and pure in-
spiration,
As my Pythoness erst sometimes erred
from not knowing

If 't were I or mere wind through her
tripod was blowing ;
Let his mind once get head in its favorite direction
And the torrent of verse bursts the
dams of reflection,
While, borne with the rush of the metre
along,
The poet may chance to go right or go
wrong,
Content with the whirl and delirium of
song ;
Then his grammar's not always correct, nor his rhymes,
And he 's prone to repeat his own
lyrics sometimes,
Not his best, though, for those are
struck off at white-heats
When the heart in his breast like a
trip-hammer beats,
And can ne 'er be repeated again any
more
Than they could have been carefully
plotted before ;
Like old what's-his-name there at the
battle of Hastings
(Who, however, gave more than mere
rhythmical bastings),
Our Quaker leads off metaphorical
fights
For reform and whatever they call hu-
man rights,
Both singing and striking in front of the
war
And hitting his foes with the mallet of
Thor ;
Anne haec, one exclaims, on behold-
ing his knocks,
Vestis filii tui, O leather-clad Fox?
Can that be thy son, in the battle's mid
din,
Preaching brotherly love and then driv-
ing it in
To the brain of the tough old Goliath of
sin,
With the smoothest of pebbles from
Castaly's spring
Impressed on his hard moral sense
with a sling ?

"All honor and praise to the right-
hearted bard
Who was true to The Voice when such
service was hard,

Who himself was so free he dared sing
    for the slave
When to look but a protest in silence
    was brave ;
All honor and praise to the women and
    men
Who spoke out for the dumb and the
    down-trodden then !
It needs not to name them, already for
    each
I see History preparing the statue and
    niche ;
They were harsh, but shall *you* be so
    shocked at hard words
Who have beaten your pruning-hooks
    up into swords,
Whose rewards and hurrahs men are
    surer to gain
By the reaping of men and of women
    than grain ?
Why should *you* stand aghast at their
    fierce wordy war, if
You scalp one another for Bank or for
    Tariff?
Your calling them cut - throats and
    knaves all day long
Does n't prove that the use of hard
    language is wrong ;
While the World's heart beats quicker
    to think of such men
As signed Tyranny's doom with a
    bloody steel-pen,
While on Fourth-of-Julys beardless
    orators fright one
With hints at Harmodius and Aristo-
    geiton,
You need not look shy at your sisters
    and brothers
Who stab with sharp words for the free-
    dom of others ; —
No, a wreath, twine a wreath for the
    loyal and true
Who, for sake of the many, dared stand
    with the few,
Not of blood-spattered laurel for ene-
    mies braved,
But of broad, peaceful oak-leaves for
    citizens saved !

  "Here comes Dana, abstractedly
    loitering along,
Involved in a paulo-post-future of song,
Who 'll be going to write what 'll never
    be written

Till the Muse, ere he thinks of it, gives
    him the mitten, —
Who is so well aware of how things
    should be done,
That his own works displease him be-
    fore they 're begun, —
Who so well all that makes up good
    poetry knows,
That the best of his poems is written
    in prose ;
All saddled and bridled stood Pegasus
    waiting,
He was booted and spurred, but he
    loitered debating ;
In a very grave question his soul was
    immersed, —
Which foot in the stirrup he ought to
    put first ;
And, while this point and that he judi-
    cially dwelt on,
He, somehow or other, had written
    Paul Felton,
Whose beauties or faults, whichsoever
    you see there,
You 'll allow only genius could hit
    upon either.
That he once was the Idle Man none
    will deplore,
But I fear he will never be anything
    more ;
The ocean of song heaves and glitters
    before him,
The depth and the vastness and long-
    ing sweep o'er him,
He knows every breaker and shoal on
    the chart,
He has the Coast Pilot and so on by heart,
Yet he spends his whole life, like the
    man in the fable,
In learning to swim on his library-
    table.

  "There swaggers John Neal, who
    has wasted in Maine
The sinews and cords of his pugilist
    brain,
Who might have been poet, but that, in
    its stead, he
Preferred to believe that he was so al-
    ready ;
Too hasty to wait till Art's ripe fruit
    should drop,
He must pelt down an unripe and
    colicky crop ;

Who took to the law, and had this
    sterling plea for it,
It required him to quarrel, and paid
    him a fee for it ;
A man who 's made less than he might
    have, because
He always has thought himself more
    than he was, —
Who, with very good natural gifts as a
    bard,
Broke the strings of his lyre out by
    striking too hard,
And cracked half the notes of a truly
    fine voice,
Because song drew less instant atten-
    tion than noise.
Ah, men do not know how much
    strength is in poise,
That he goes the farthest who goes far
    enough,
And that all beyond that is just bother
    and stuff.
No vain man matures, he makes too
    much new wood ;
His blooms are too thick for the fruit
    to be good ;
'T is the modest man ripens, 't is he
    that achieves,
Just what 's needed of sunshine and
    shade he receives ;
Grapes, to mellow, require the cool
    dark of their leaves ;
Neal wants balance ; he throws his
    mind always too far,
Whisking out flocks of comets, but
    never a star ;
He has so much muscle, and loves so
    to show it,
That he strips himself naked to prove
    he 's a poet,
And, to show he could leap Art's wide
    ditch, if he tried,
Jumps clean o'er it, and into the hedge
    t'other side.
He has strength, but there 's nothing
    about him in keeping ;
One gets surelier onward by walking
    than leaping ;
He has used his own sinews himself to
    distress,
And had done vastly more had he done
    vastly less ;
In letters, too soon is as bad as too late ;
Could he only have waited he might
    have been great ;

But he plumped into Helicon up to the
    waist,
And muddied the stream ere he took
    his first taste.

"There is Hawthorne, with genius
    so shrinking and rare
That you hardly at first see the strength
    that is there ;
A frame so robust, with a nature so
    sweet,
So earnest, so graceful, so lithe and so
    fleet,
Is worth a descent from Olympus to
    meet ;
'T is as if a rough oak that for ages had
    stood,
With his gnarled bony branches like
    ribs of the wood,
Should bloom, after cycles of struggle
    and scathe,
With a single anemone trembly and
    rathe ;
His strength is so tender, his wildness
    so meek,
That a suitable parallel sets one to
    seek, —
He 's a John Bunyan Fouqué, a Puri-
    tan Tieck ;
When nature was shaping him, clay
    was not granted
For making so full-sized a man as she
    wanted,
So, to fill out her model, a little she
    spared
From some finer-grained stuff for a
    woman prepared,
And she could not have hit a more ex-
    cellent plan
For making him fully and perfectly man.
The success of her scheme gave her so
    much delight,
That she tried it again, shortly after, in
    Dwight ;
Only, while she was kneading and shap-
    ing the clay,
She sang to her work in her sweet child-
    ish way,
And found, when she 'd put the last
    touch to his soul,
That the music had somehow got mixed
    with the whole.

"Here 's Cooper, who 's written six
    volumes to show

He's as good as a lord: well, let's
    grant that he's so;
If a person prefer that description of
    praise,
Why, a coronet's certainly cheaper
    than bays;
But need take no pains to convince us
    he's not
(As his enemies say) the American
    Scott.
Choose any twelve men, and let C.
    read aloud
That one of his novels of which he's
    most proud,
And I'd lay any bet that, without ever
    quitting
Their box, they'd be all, to a man, for
    acquitting.
He has drawn you one character, though,
    that is new,
One wildflower he's plucked that is
    wet with the dew
Of this fresh Western world, and, the
    thing not to mince,
He has done naught but copy it ill ever
    since;
His Indians, with proper respect be it
    said,
Are just Natty Bumpo, daubed over
    with red,
And his very Long Toms are the same
    useful Nat,
Rigged up in duck pants and a sou'-
    wester hat
(Though once in a Coffin, a good
    chance was found
To have slipped the old fellow away
    underground).
All his other men-figures are clothes
    upon sticks,
The *dernière chemise* of a man in a
    fix
(As a captain besieged, when his garri-
    son's small,
Sets up caps upon poles to be seen o'er
    the wall);
And the women he draws from one
    model don't vary,
All sappy as maples and flat as a prai-
    rie.
When a character's wanted, he goes to
    the task
As a cooper would do in composing a
    cask;

He picks out the staves, of their quali-
    ties heedful,
Just hoops them together as tight as is
    needful,
And, if the best fortune should crown
    the attempt, he
Has made at the most something wood-
    en and empty.

"Don't suppose I would underrate
    Cooper's abilities;
If I thought you'd do that, I should
    feel very ill at ease;
The men who have given to *one* char-
    acter life
And objective existence are not very
    rife;
You may number them all, both prose-
    writers and singers,
Without overrunning the bounds of
    your fingers,
And Natty won't go to oblivion quicker
Than Adams the parson or Primrose
    the vicar.

"There is one thing in Cooper I
    like, too, and that is
That on manners he lectures his coun-
    trymen gratis;
Not precisely so either, because, for a
    rarity,
He is paid for his tickets in unpopu-
    larity.
Now he may overcharge his American
    pictures,
But you'll grant there's a good deal
    of truth in his strictures;
And I honor the man who is willing to
    sink
Half his present repute for the freedom
    to think,
And, when he has thought, be his
    cause strong or weak,
Will risk t'other half for the freedom
    to speak,
Caring naught for what vengeance the
    mob has in store,
Let that mob be the upper ten thou-
    sand or lower.

"There are truths you Americans
    need to be told,
And it never'll refute them to swagger
    and scold;

John Bull, looking o'er the Atlantic, in
    choler
At your aptness for trade, says you
    worship the dollar;
But to scorn such eye-dollar-try 's what
    very few do,
And John goes to that church as often
    as you do.
No matter what John says, don't try
    to outcrow him,
'T is enough to go quietly on and out-
    grow him;
Like most fathers, Bull hates to see
    Number One
Displacing himself in the mind of his
    son,
And detests the same faults in himself
    he 'd neglected
When he sees them again in his child's
    glass reflected;
To love one another you 're too like by
    half;
If he is a bull, you 're a pretty stout
    calf,
And tear your own pasture for naught
    but to show
What a nice pair of horns you 're be-
    ginning to grow.

"There are one or two things I
    should just like to hint,
For you don't often get the truth told
    you in print;
The most of you (this is what strikes
    all beholders)
Have a mental and physical stoop in
    the shoulders;
Though you ought to be free as the
    winds and the waves,
You 've the gait and the manners of
    runaway slaves;
Though you brag of your New World,
    you don't half believe in it,
And as much of the Old as is possible
    weave in it;
Your goddess of freedom, a tight, bux-
    om girl,
With lips like a cherry and teeth like
    a pearl,
With eyes bold as Herè's, and hair
    floating free,
And full of the sun as the spray of the sea,
Who can sing at a husking or romp at
    a shearing,

Who can trip through the forests alone
    without fearing,
Who can drive home the cows with a
    song through the grass,
Keeps glancing aside into Europe's
    cracked glass,
Hides her red hands in gloves, pinches
    up her lithe waist,
And makes herself wretched with
    transmarine taste;
She loses her fresh country charm when
    she takes
Any mirror except her own rivers and
    lakes.

    " You steal Englishmen's books and
        think Englishmen's thought,
With their salt on her tail your wild
    eagle is caught;
Your literature suits its each whisper
    and motion
To what will be thought of it over the
    ocean;
The cast clothes of Europe your states-
    manship tries
And mumbles again the old blarneys
    and lies; —
Forget Europe wholly, your veins
    throb with blood,
To which the dull current in hers is
    but mud;
Let her sneer, let her say your experi-
    ment fails,
In her voice there 's a tremble e'en
    now while she rails,
And your shore will soon be in the na-
    ture of things
Covered thick with gilt driftwood of
    castaway kings,
Where alone, as it were in a Longfel-
    low's Waif,
Her fugitive pieces will find themselves
    safe.
O my friends, thank your god, if you
    have one, that he
'Twixt the Old World and you set the
    gulf of a sea;
Be strong-backed, brown-handed, up-
    right as your pines,
By the scale of a hemisphere shape
    your designs,
Be true to yourselves and this new nine-
    teenth age,

As a statue by Powers, or a picture by
    Page,
Plough, sail, forge, build, carve, paint,
    make all over new,
To your own New-World instincts con-
    trive to be true,
Keep your ears open wide to the Fu-
    ture's first call,
Be whatever you will, but yourselves
    first of all,
Stand fronting the dawn on Toil's
    heaven-scaling peaks,
And become my new race of more prac-
    tical Greeks.
Hem! your likeness at present, I shud-
    der to tell o't,
Is that you have your slaves, and the
    Greek had his helot."

    Here a gentleman present, who had
        in his attic
More pepper than brains, shrieked, —
    "The man 's a fanatic,
I 'm a capital tailor with warm tar and
    feathers,
And will make him a suit that 'll serve
    in all weathers;
But we 'll argue the point first, I 'm
    willing to reason 't,
Palaver before condemnation 's but
    decent;
So, through my humble person, Hu-
    manity begs
Of the friends of true freedom a loan
    of bad eggs."
But Apollo let one such a look of his
    show forth
As when ἤιε νύκτι ἐοικώς, and so forth,
And the gentleman somehow slunk out
    of the way,
But, as he was going, gained courage
    to say, —
"At slavery in the abstract my whole
    soul rebels,
I am as strongly opposed to't as any
    one else."
"Ay, no doubt, but whenever I 've
    happened to meet
With a wrong or a crime, it is always
    concrete,"
Answered Phœbus severely; then turn-
    ing to us,
"The mistake of such fellows as just
    made the fuss

Is only in taking a great busy nation
For a part of their pitiful cotton-plan-
    tation. —
But there comes Miranda, Zeus! where
    shall I flee to?
She has such a penchant for bothering
    me too!
She always keeps asking if I don't ob-
    serve a
Particular likeness 'twixt her and
    Minerva;
She tells me my efforts in verse are
    quite clever; —
She 's been travelling now, and will be
    worse than ever;
One would think, though, a sharp-
    sighted noter she 'd be
Of all that 's worth mentioning over
    the sea,
For a woman must surely see well, if
    she try,
The whole of whose being 's a capital I:
She will take an old notion, and make
    it her own,
By saying it o'er in her Sibylline tone,
Or persuade you 't is something tre-
    mendously deep,
By repeating it so as to put you to
    sleep;
And she well may defy any mortal 'o
    see through it,
When once she has mixed up her in-
    finite *me* through it.
There is one thing she owns in her
    own single right,
It is native and genuine — namely, her
    spite:
Though, when acting as censor, she
    privately blows
A censer of vanity 'neath her own nose."

    Here Miranda came up, and said,
        "Phœbus! you know
That the infinite Soul has its infinite
    woe,
As I ought to know, having lived cheek
    by jowl,
Since the day I was born, with the In-
    finite Soul;
I myself introduced, I myself, I alone,
To my Land's better life authors solely
    my own,
Who the sad heart of earth on their
    shoulders have taken,

Whose works sound a depth by Life's
quiet unshaken,
Such as Shakespeare, for instance, the
Bible, and Bacon,
Not to mention my own works; Time's
nadir is fleet,
And, as for myself, I'm quite out of
conceit — "

"Quite out of conceit! I'm enchanted to hear it,"
Cried Apollo aside. "Who'd have
thought she was near it?
To be sure, one is apt to exhaust those
commodities
One uses too fast, yet in this case as
odd it is
As if Neptune should say to his turbots
and whitings,
' I'm as much out of salt as Miranda's
own writings '
(Which, as she in her own happy manner has said,
Sound a depth, for 't is one of the functions of lead).
She often has asked me if I could not
find
A place somewhere near me that suited
her mind;
I know but a single one vacant, which
she,
With her rare talent that way, would
fit to a T.
And it would not imply any pause or
cessation
In the work she esteems her peculiar
vocation,
She may enter on duty to-day, if she
chooses,
And remain Tiring-woman for life to
the Muses."

(Miranda meanwhile has succeeded
in driving
Up into a corner, in spite of their
striving,
A small flock of terrified victims, and
there,
With an I-turn-the-crank-of-the-Uni-
verse air
And a tone which, at least to *my* fancy,
appears
Not so much to be entering as boxing
your ears,

Is unfolding a tale (of herself, I surmise,
For 't is dotted as thick as a peacock's
with I's.)
A propos of Miranda, I'll rest on my
oars
And drift through a trifling digression
on bores,
For, though not wearing ear-rings *in
more majorum,*
Our ears are kept bored just as if we
still wore 'em.
There was one feudal custom worth
keeping, at least,
Roasted bores made a part of each well-
ordered feast,
And of all quiet pleasures the very *ne
plus*
Was in hunting wild bores as the tame
ones hunt us.
Archæologians, I know, who have personal fears
Of this wise application of hounds and
of spears,
Have tried to make out, with a zeal
more than wonted,
'T was a kind of wild swine that our
ancestors hunted;
But I'll never believe that the age
which has strewn
Europe o'er with cathedrals, and otherwise shown
That it knew what was what, could by
chance not have known
(Spending, too, its chief time with its
buff on, no doubt),
Which beast 't would most improve the world
most to thin out.
I divide bores myself, in the manner
of rifles,
Into two great divisions, regardless of
trifles;
There's your smooth-bore and screw-
bore, who do much vary
In the weight of cold lead they respec-
tively carry.
The smooth-bore is one in whose essence the mind
Not a corner nor cranny to cling by can
find;
You feel as in nightmares sometimes,
when you slip
Down a steep slated roof, where there's
nothing to grip;

You slide and you slide, the blank hor-
    ror increases, —
You had rather by far be at once
    smashed to pieces;
You fancy a whirlpool below white and
    frothing,
And finally drop off and light upon —
    nothing.
The screw-bore has twists in him, faint
    predilections
For going just wrong in the tritest di-
    rections;
When he's wrong he is flat, when he's
    right he can't show it,
He'll tell you what Snooks said about
    the new poet,*
Or how Fogrum was outraged by Ten-
    nyson's Princess;
He has spent all his spare time and in-
    tellect since his
Birth in perusing, on each art and
    science,
Just the books in which no one puts
    any reliance,
And though *nemo*, we're told, *horis
    omnibus sapit*,
The rule will not fit him, however you
    shape it,
For he has a perennial foison of sappi-
    ness;
He has just enough force to spoil half
    your day's happiness,
And to make him a sort of mosquito to
    be with,
But just not enough to dispute or agree
    with.

These sketches I made (not to be too
    explicit)
From two honest fellows who made me
    a visit,
And broke, like the tale of the Bear
    and the Fiddle,
My reflections on Halleck short off
    by the middle,
I shall not now go into the subject more
    deeply,
For I notice that some of my readers
    look sleep'ly;

*(If you call Snooks an owl, he will show
    by his looks
    That he's morally certain you're jealous
    of Snooks.)

I will barely remark that, 'mongst civi-
    lized nations,
There's none that displays more ex-
    emplary patience
Under all sorts of boring, at all sorts
    of hours,
From all sorts of desperate persons,
    than ours.
Not to speak of our papers, our State
    legislatures,
And other such trials for sensitive na-
    tures,
Just look for a moment at Congress, —
    appalled,
My fancy shrinks back from the phan-
    tom it called;
Why, there's scarcely a member un-
    worthy to frown
'Neath what Fourier nicknames the
    Boreal crown!
Only think what that infinite bore-
    pow'r could do
If applied with a utilitarian view;
Suppose, for example, we shipped it
    with care
To Sahara's great desert and let it bore
    there;
If they held one short session and did
    nothing else,
They'd fill the whole waste with Arte-
    sian wells.
But 'tis time now with pen phonograph-
    ic to follow
Through some more of his sketches
    our laughing Apollo : —

    "There comes Harry Franco, and,
        as he draws near,
You find that's a smile which you took
        for a sneer;
One half of him contradicts t'other;
        his wont
Is to say very sharp things and do very
        blunt;
His manner's as hard as his feelings
        are tender,
And a *sortie* he'll make when he means
        to surrender;
He's in joke half the time when he
        seems to be sternest,
When he seems to be joking, be sure
        he's in earnest;
He has common sense in a way that's
        uncommon,

Hates humbug and cant, loves his
 friends like a woman,
Builds his dislikes of cards and his
 friendships of oak,
Loves a prejudice better than aught
 but a joke,
Is half upright Quaker, half downright Come-outer,
Loves Freedom too well to go stark
 mad about her,
Quite artless himself, is a lover of Art,
Shuts you out of his secrets and into
 his heart,
And though not a poet, yet all must
 admire
In his letters of Pinto his skill on the
 liar.

 " There comes Poe, with his raven,
  like Barnaby Rudge,
Three fifths of him genius and two
 fifths sheer fudge,
Who talks like a book of lambs and
 pentameters,
In a way to make people of common
 sense damn metres,
Who has written some things quite the
 best of their kind,
But the heart somehow seems all
 squeezed out by the mind,
Who — but hey-day! What 's this?
 Messieurs Mathews and Poe,
You must n't fling mud-balls at Long-
 fellow so,
Does it make a man worse that his
 character 's such
As to make his friends love him (as
 you think) too much?
Why, there is not a bard at this mo-
 ment alive
More willing than he that his fellows
 should thrive;
While you are abusing him thus, even
 now
He would help either one of you out of
 a slough;
You may say that he 's smooth and all
 that till you 're hoarse,
But remember that elegance also is
 force;
After polishing granite as much as you
 will,
The heart keeps its tough old persist-
 ency still;

Deduct all you can that still keeps you
 at bay, —
Why, he 'll live till men weary of Col-
 lins and Gray.
I 'm not over-fond of Greek metres in
 English,
To me rhyme 's a gain, so it be not too
 jinglish,
And your modern hexameter verses are
 no more
Like Greek ones than sleek Mr. Pope
 is like Homer;
As the roar of the sea to the coo of a
 pigeon is,
So, compared to your moderns, sounds
 old Melesigenes;
I may be too partial, the reason, per-
 haps, o't is
That I 've heard the old blind man re-
 cite his own rhapsodies,
And my ear with that music impreg-
 nate may be,
Like the poor exiled shell with the soul
 of the sea,
Or as one can't bear Strauss when his
 nature is cloven
To its deeps within deeps by the stroke
 of Beethoven;
But, set that aside, and 't is truth that I
 speak,
Had Theocritus written in English, not
 Greek,
I believe that his exquisite sense would
 scarce change a line
In that rare, tender, virgin-like pastor-
 al Evangeline.
That 's not ancient nor modern, its
 place is apart
Where time has no sway, in the realm
 of pure Art,
'T is a shrine of retreat from Earth's
 hubbub and strife
As quiet and chaste as the author's own
 life.

 " There comes Philothea, her face
  all aglow,
She has just been dividing some poor
 creature's woe,
And can't tell which pleases her most,
 to relieve
His want, or his story to hear and believe;
No doubt against many deep griefs she
 prevails,

For her ear is the refuge of destitute
    tales ;
She knows well that silence is sorrow's
    best food,
And that talking draws off from the
    heart its black blood,
So she 'll listen with patience and let
    you unfold
Your bundle of rags as 't were pure cloth
    of gold,
Which, indeed, it all turns to as soon
    as she 's touched it,
And (to borrow a phrase from the
    nursery) *muched* it ;
She has such a musical taste, she will go
Any distance to hear one who draws a
    long bow ;
She will swallow a wonder by mere
    might and main,
And thinks it geometry's fault if she 's
    fain
To consider things flat, inasmuch as
    they 're plain ;
Facts with her are accomplished, as
    Frenchmen would say, —
They will prove all she wishes them
    to — either way,
And, as fact lies on this side or that,
    we must try,
If we 're seeking the truth, to find
    where it don't lie ;
I was telling her once of a marvellous aloe
That for thousands of years had looked
    spindling and sallow,
And, though nursed by the fruitfullest
    powers of mud,
Had never vouchsafed e'en so much as
    a bud,
Till its owner remarked (as a sailor,
    you know,
Often will in a calm) that it never
    would blow,
For he wished to exhibit the plant, and
    designed
That its blowing should help him in
    raising the wind ;
At last it was told him that if he should
    water
Its roots with the blood of his unmarried
    daughter
(Who was born, as her mother, a Cal-
    vinist, said,
With William Law's serious caul on
    her head),

It would blow as the obstinate breeze
    did when by a
Like decree of her father died Iphige-
    nia ;
At first he declared he himself would
    be blowed
Ere his conscience with such a foul
    crime he would load,
But the thought, coming oft, grew less
    dark than before,
And he mused, as each creditor knocked
    at his door,
If *this* were but done they would dun
    me no more ;
I told Philothea his struggles and
    doubts,
And how he considered the ins and
    the outs
Of the visions he had, and the dreadful
    dyspepsy,
How he went to the seër that lives at
    Po'keepsie,
How the seër advised him to sleep on
    it first
And to read his big volume in case of
    the worst,
And further advised he should pay him
    five dollars
For writing 𝔥𝔲𝔪, 𝔥𝔲𝔪, on his wrist-
    bands and collars ;
Three years and ten days these dark
    words he had studied
When the daughter was missed, and
    the aloe had budded ;
I told how he watched it grow large
    and more large,
And wondered how much for the show
    he should charge, —
She had listened with utter indifference
    to this, till
I told how it bloomed, and discharging/
    its pistil,
With an aim the Eumenides dictated,
    shot
The botanical filicide dead on the
    spot ;
It had blown, but he reaped not his
    horrible gains,
For it blew with such force as to blow
    out his brains,
And the crime was blown also, be-
    cause on the wad,
Which was paper, was writ 'Visitation
    of God,'

As well as a thrilling account of the
    deed
Which the coroner kindly allowed me
    to read.

" Well, my friend took this story up
    just, to be sure,
As one might a poor foundling that's
    laid at one's door ;
She combed it and washed it and
    clothed it and fed it,
And as if 't were her own child most
    tenderly bred it,
Laid the scene (of the legend, I mean)
    far away a-
-mong the green vales underneath
    Himalaya.
And by artist-like touches, laid on
    here and there,
Made the whole thing so touching, I
    frankly declare
I have read it all thrice, and, perhaps
    I am weak,
But I found every time there were tears
    on my cheek.

" The pole, science tells us, the
    magnet controls,
But she is a magnet to emigrant Poles,
And folks with a mission that nobody
    knows,
Throng thickly about her as bees round
    a rose ;
She can fill up the *carets* in such, make
    their scope
Converge to some focus of rational
    hope,
And, with sympathies fresh as the
    morning, their gall
Can transmute into honey, — but this
    is not all ;
Not only for those she has solace, O,
    say,
Vice's desperate nursling adrift in
    Broadway,
Who clingest, with all that is left of
    thee human,
To the last slender spar from the wreck
    of the woman,
Hast thou not found one shore where
    those tired drooping feet
Could reach firm mother-earth, one full
    heart on whose beat
The soothed head in silence reposing
    could hear

The chimes of far childhood throb back
    on the ear ?
Ah, there's many a beam from the
    fountain of day
That, to reach us unclouded, must pass,
    on its way,
Through the soul of a woman, and hers
    is wide ope
To the influence of Heaven as the blue
    eyes of Hope ;
Yes, a great heart is hers, one that
    dares to go in
To the prison, the slave-hut, the alleys
    of sin,
And to bring into each, or to find there,
    some line
Of the never completely out-trampled
    divine ;
If her heart at high floods swamps her
    brain now and then,
'T is but richer for that when the tide
    ebbs agen,
As, after old Nile has subsided, his
    plain
Overflows with a second broad deluge
    of grain ;
What a wealth would it bring to the
    narrow and sour
Could they be as a Child but for one
    little hour !

" What ! Irving ? thrice welcome,
    warm heart and fine brain,
You bring back the happiest spirit from
    Spain,
And the gravest sweet humor, that
    ever were there
Since Cervantes met death in his gen-
    tle despair ;
Nay, don't be embarrassed, nor look
    so beseeching, —
I sha' n't run directly against my own
    preaching,
And, having just laughed at their
    Raphaels and Dantes,
Go to setting you up beside matchless
    Cervantes ;
But allow me to speak what I honestly
    feel, —
To a true poet-heart add the fun of
    Dick Steele,
Throw in all of Addison, *minus* the
    chill,
With the whole of that partnership's
    stock and good-will,

Mix well, and while stirring, hum o'er, as a spell,
The fine *old* English Gentleman, simmer it well,
Sweeten just to your own private liking, then strain,
That you find the finest and clearest remain,
Let it stand out of doors till a soul it receives
From the warm lazy sun loitering down through green leaves,
And you'll find a choice nature, not wholly deserving
A name either English or Yankee, — just Irving.

"There goes, — but *stet nominis umbra*, — his name
You'll be glad enough, some day or other, to claim,
And will all crowd about him and swear that you knew him
If some English critic should chance to review him
The old *porcos ante ne projiciatis*
MARGARITAS, for him you have verified gratis ;
What matters his name ? Why, it may be Sylvester,
Judd, Junior, or Junius, Ulysses, or Nestor,
For aught *I* know or care ; 't is enough that I look
On the author of 'Margaret,' the first Yankee book
With the *soul* of Down East in't, and things farther East,
As far as the threshold of morning, at least,
Where awaits the fair dawn of the simple and true,
Of the day that comes slowly to make all things new.
'T has a smack of pine woods, of bare field and bleak hill,
Such as only the breed of the Mayflower could till ;
The Puritan's shown in it, tough to the core,
Such as prayed, smiting Agag on red Marston Moor ;
With an unwilling humor, half choked by the drouth

In brown hollows about the inhospitable mouth ;
With a soul full of poetry, though it has qualms
About finding a happiness out of the Psalms ;
Full of tenderness, too, though it shrinks in the dark,
Hamadryad-like, under the coarse, shaggy bark ;
That sees visions, knows wrestlings of God with the Will,
And has its own Sinais and thunderings still."

Here, — " Forgive me, Apollo," I cried, " while I pour
My heart out to my birthplace : O loved more and more
Dear Baystate, from whose rocky bosom thy sons
Should suck milk, strong-will-giving, brave, such as runs
In the veins of old Graylock — who is it that dares
Call thee pedler, a soul wrapped in bank-books and shares ?
It is false ! She's a Poet ! I see, as I write,
Along the far railroad the steam-snake glide white,
The cataract-throb of her mill-hearts I hear,
The swift strokes of trip-hammers weary my ear,
Sledges ring upon anvils, through logs the saw screams,
Blocks swing to their place, beetles drive home the beams : —
It is songs such as these that she croons to the din
Of her fast-flying shuttles, year out and year in,
While from earth's farthest corner there comes not a breeze
But wafts her the buzz of her gold-gleaning bees :
What though those horn hands have as yet found small time
For painting and sculpture and music and rhyme ?
These will come in due order ; the need that pressed sorest
Was to vanquish the seasons, the ocean, the forest,

To bridle and harness the rivers, the steam,
Making that whirl her mill-wheels, this tug in her team,
To vassalize old tyrant Winter, and make
Him delve surlily for her on river and lake ; —
When this New World was parted, she strove not to shirk
Her lot in the heirdom, the tough, silent Work,
The hero-share ever, from Herakles down
To Odin, the Earth's iron sceptre and crown :
Yes, thou dear, noble Mother ! if ever men's praise
Could be claimed for creating heroical lays,
Thou hast won it ; if ever the laurel divine
Crowned the Maker and Builder, that glory is thine !
Thy songs are right epic, they tell how this rude
Rock-rib of our earth here was tamed and subdued ;
Thou hast written them plain on the face of the planet
In brave, deathless letters of iron and granite ;
Thou hast printed them deep for all time ; they are set
From the same runic type-fount and alphabet
With thy stout Berkshire hills and the arms of thy Bay, —
They are staves from the burly old Mayflower lay.
If the drones of the Old World, in querulous ease,
Ask thy Art and thy Letters, point proudly to these,
Or, if they deny these are Letters and Art,
Toil on with the same old invincible heart ;
Thou art rearing the pedestal broad-based and grand
Whereon the fair shapes of the Artist shall stand,
And creating, through labors undaunted and long,

The theme for all Sculpture and Painting and Song !

" But my good mother Baystate wants no praise of mine,
She learned from *her* mother a precept divine
About something that butters no parsnips, her *forte*
In another direction lies, work is her sport
(Though she 'll courtesy and set her cap straight, that she will,
If you talk about Plymouth and red Bunker's hill).
Dear, notable goodwife ! by this time of night,
Her hearth is swept neatly, her fire burning bright,
And she sits in a chair (of home plan and make) rocking,
Musing much, all the while, as she darns on a stocking,
Whether turkeys will come pretty high next Thanksgiving,
Whether flour 'll be so dear, for, as sure as she 's living,
She will use rye-and-injun then, whether the pig
By this time ain't got pretty tolerable big,
And whether to sell it outright will be best,
Or to smoke hams and shoulders and salt down the rest, —
At this minute, she 'd swop all my verses, ah, cruel !
For the last patent stove that is saving of fuel ;
So I 'll just let Apollo go on, for his phiz
Shows I 've kept him awaiting too long as it is."

" If our friend, there, who seems a reporter, is done
With his burst of emotion, why, *I* will go on,"
Said Apollo : some smiled, and, indeed, I must own
There was something sarcastic, perhaps, in his tone ; —

" There 's Holmes, who is matchless among you for wit ;

A Leyden-jar always full-charged, from
  which flit
The electrical tingles of hit after hit;
In long poems 't is painful sometimes,
  and invites
A thought of the way the new Telegraph
  writes,
Which pricks down its little sharp
  sentences spitefully
As if you got more than you 'd title to
  rightfully,
And you find yourself hoping its wild
  father Lightning
Would flame in for a second and give
  you a fright'ning.
He has perfect sway of what *I* call a
  sham metre,
But many admire it, the English pen-
  tameter,
And Campbell, I think, wrote most
  commonly worse,
With less nerve, swing, and fire in the
  same kind of verse,
Nor e'er achieved aught in 't so worthy
  of praise
As the tribute of Holmes to the grand
  Marseillaise.
You went crazy last year over Bulwer's
  New Timon; —
Why, if B., to the day of his dying,
  should rhyme on,
Heaping verses on verses and tomes
  upon tomes,
He could ne'er reach the best point
  and vigor of Holmes.
His are just the fine hands, too, to
  weave you a lyric
Full of fancy, fun, feeling, or spiced
  with satyric
In a measure so kindly, you doubt if
  the toes
That are trodden upon are your own or
  your foes.

  "There is Lowell, who 's striving
    Parnassus to climb
With a whole bale of *isms* tied together
  with rhyme,
He might get on alone, spite of bram-
  bles and boulders,
But he can't with that bundle he has
  on his shoulders,
The top of the hill he will ne'er come
  nigh reaching

Till he learns the distinction 'twixt
    singing and preaching;
His lyre has some chords that would
    ring pretty well,
But he 'd rather by half make a drum
    of the shell,
And rattle away till he 's old as Me-
    thusalem,
At the head of a march to the last new
    Jerusalem.

  "There goes Halleck, whose Fan-
    ny 's a pseudo Don Juan,
With the wickedness out that gave salt
    to the true one,
He 's a wit, though, I hear, of the very
    first order,
And once made a pun on the words
    soft Recorder;
More than this, he 's a very great poet,
    I 'm told,
And has had his works published in
    crimson and gold,
With something they call 'Illustra-
    tions,' to wit,
Like those with which Chapman ob-
    scured Holy Writ,*
Which are said to illustrate, because,
    as I view it,
Like *lucus a non*, they precisely don't
    do it;
Let a man who can write what himself
    understands
Keep clear, if he can, of designing
    men's hands,
Who bury the sense, if there 's any
    worth having,
And then very honestly call it engrav-
    ing.
But, to quit *badinage*, which there
    is n't much wit in,
Halleck 's better, I doubt not, than all
    he has written;
In his verse a clear glimpse you will
    frequently find,
If not of a great, of a fortunate mind,
Which contrives to be true to its natural
    loves
In a world of back-offices, ledgers, and
    stoves.
When his heart breaks away from the
    brokers and banks,

  * (Cuts rightly called wooden, as all must ad-
    mit.)

And kneels in its own private shrine to
give thanks,
There 's a genial manliness in him that
earns
Our sincerest respect (read, for instance, his ' Burns '),
And we can't but regret (seek excuse
where we may)
That so much of a man has been peddled away.

" But what 's that? a mass-meeting?
No, there come in lots
The American Disraelis, Bulwers, and
Scotts,
And in short the American everything-
elses,
Each charging the others with envies
and jealousies ; —
By the way, 't is a fact that displays
what profusions
Of all kinds of greatness bless free in-
stitutions,
That while the Old World has pro-
duced barely eight
Of such poets as all men agree to call
great,
And of other great characters hardly a
score
(One might safely say less than that
rather than more),
With you every year a whole crop is
begotten,
They 're as much of a staple as corn is,
or cotton ;
Why, there 's scarcely a huddle of log-
huts and shanties
That has not brought forth its own
Miltons and Dantes ;
I myself know ten Byrons, one Cole-
ridge, three Shelleys,
Two Raphaels, six Titians, (I think)
one Apelles,
Leonardos and Rubenses plenty as
lichens,
One (but that one is plenty) American
Dickens,
A whole flock of Lambs, any number
of Tennysons, —
In short, if a man has the luck to have
any sons,
He may feel pretty certain that one out
of twain

Will be some very great person over
again.
There is one inconvenience in all this
which lies
In the fact that by contrast we estimate
size,*
And, where there are none except Titans, great stature
Is only the normal proceeding of nature.
What puff the strained sails of your
praise shall you furl at, if
The calmest degree that you know is
superlative ?
At Rome, all whom Charon took into
his wherry must,
As a matter of course, be well *issimus*ed
and *errimus*ed,
A Greek, too, could feel, while in that
famous boat he *tost*,
That his friends would take care he
was ωτοϲεd and ωτατοϲεd,
And formerly we, as through grave-
yards we past,
Thought the world went from bad to
worst fearfully fast ;
Let us glance for a moment, 't is well
worth the pains,
And note what an average graveyard
contains ;
There lie levellers levelled, duns done
up themselves,
There are booksellers finally laid on
their shelves,
Horizontally there lie upright politicians,
Dose-a-dose with their patients sleep
faultless physicians,
There are slave-drivers quietly whipped
underground,
There bookbinders, done up in boards,
are fast bound,
There card-players wait till the last
trump be played,
There all the choice spirits get finally
laid,
There the babe that 's unborn is supplied with a berth,

* That is in most cases we do, but not all
Past a doubt, there are men who are in-
nately small,
Such as Blank, who, without being 'min-
ished a tittle,
Might stand for a type of the Absolute
Little.

There men without legs get their six
feet of earth,
There lawyers repose, each wrapped up
in his case,
There seekers of office are sure of a
place,
There defendant and plaintiff get equally cast,
There shoemakers quietly stick to the
last,
There brokers at length become silent
as stocks,
There stage-drivers sleep without quit-
ting their box,
And so forth and so forth and so forth
and so on,
With this kind of stuff one might end-
lessly go on ;
To come to the point, I may safely assert you
Will find in each yard every cardinal
virtue ; *
Each has six truest patriots : four dis-
coverers of ether,
Who never had thought on't nor men-
tioned it either :
Ten poets, the greatest who ever wrote
rhyme :
Two hundred and forty first men of
their time :
One person whose portrait just gave
the least hint
Its original had a most horrible squint :
One critic, most (what do they call it?)
reflective,
Who never had used the phrase ob- or
subjective :
Forty fathers of Freedom, of whom
twenty bred
Their sons for the rice-swamps, at so
much a head,
And their daughters for — faugh ! thir-
ty mothers of Gracchi :
Non-resistants who gave many a spirit-
ual black-eye :
Eight true friends of their kind, one of
whom was a jailer :
Four captains almost as astounding as
Taylor :

*(And at this just conclusion will surely
arrive,
That the goodness of earth is more dead
than alive.)

Two dozen of Italy's exiles who shoot
us his
Kaisership daily, stern pen-and-ink
Brutuses,
Who, in Yankee back-parlors, with
crucified smile,*
Mount serenely their country's funereal
pile :
Ninety-nine Irish heroes, ferocious re-
beliers
'Gainst the Saxon in cis-marine garrets
and cellars,
Who shake their dread fists o'er the
sea and all that, —
As long as a copper drops into the hat :
Nine hundred Teutonic republicans
stark
From Vaterland's battles just won —
in the Park,
Who the happy profession of martyr-
dom take
Whenever it gives them a chance at a
steak :
Sixty-two second Washingtons : two or
three Jacksons :
And so many everythings-else that it
racks one's
Poor memory too much to continue the
list,
Especially now they no longer exist ; —
I would merely observe that you've
taken to giving
The puffs that belong to the dead to the
living,
And that somehow your trump-of-con-
temporary-doom's tones
Is tuned after old dedications and
tombstones." —

Here the critic came in and a thistle
presented † —
From a frown to a smile the god's features relented,
As he stared at his envoy, who, swelling with pride,
To the god's asking look, nothing
daunted, replied, —

* Not forgetting their tea and their toast,
though, the while.
† Turn back now to page — goodness only
knows what,
And take a fresh hold on the thread of
my plot.

"You're surprised, I suppose, I was
    absent so long,
But your godship respecting the lilies
    was wrong;
I hunted the garden from one end to
    t'other,
And got no reward but vexation and
    bother,
Till, tossed out with weeds in a corner
    to wither,
This one lily I found and made haste
    to bring hither."

" Did he think I had given him a
    book to review?
I ought to have known what the fellow
    would do,"
Muttered Phœbus aside, " for a thistle
    will pass
Beyond doubt for the queen of all
    flowers with an ass;
He has chosen in just the same way as
    he 'd choose
His specimens out of the books he re-
    views;
And now, as this offers an excellent
    text,
I 'll give 'em some brief hints on criti-
    cism next."
So, musing a moment, he turned to the
    crowd,
And, clearing his voice, spoke as fol-
    lows aloud: —

" My friends, in the happier days
    of the muse,
We were luckily free from such things
    as reviews;
Then naught came between with its
    fog to make clearer
The heart of the poet to that of his
    hearer;
Then the poet brought heaven to the
    people, and they
Felt that they, too, were poets in hear-
    ing his lay;
Then the poet was prophet, the past in
    his soul
Precreated the future, both parts of
    one whole;
Then for him there was nothing too
    great or too small,
For one natural deity sanctified all;

Then the bard owned no clipper and
    meter of moods
Save the spirit of silence that hovers
    and broods
O'er the seas and the mountains, the
    rivers and woods;
He asked not earth's verdict, forget-
    ting the clods,
His soul soared and sang to an audi-
    ence of gods;
'T was for them that he measured the
    thought and the line,
And shaped for their vision the perfect
    design,
With as glorious a foresight, a balance
    as true,
As swung out the worlds in the infinite
    blue;
Then a glory and greatness invested
    man's heart,
The universal, which now stands es-
    tranged and apart,
In the free individual moulded, was
    Art;
Then the forms of the Artist seemed
    thrilled with desire
For something as yet unattained, ful-
    ler, higher,
As once with her lips, lifted hands, and
    eyes listening,
And her whole upward soul in her
    countenance glistening,
Eurydice stood — like a beacon un-
    fired.
Which, once touched with flame, will
    leap heav'nward inspired —
And waited with answering kindle to
    mark
The first gleam of Orpheus that pained
    the red Dark.
Then painting, song, sculpture did
    more than relieve
The need that men feel to create and
    believe,
And as, in all beauty, who listens with
    love
Hears these words oft repeated — ' be-
    yond and above,'
So these seemed to be but the visible
    sign
Of the grasp of the soul after things
    more divine;
They were ladders the Artist erected to
    climb

O'er the narrow horizon of space and
     of time,
And we see there the footsteps by
     which men had gained
To the one rapturous glimpse of the
     never-attained,
As shepherds could erst sometimes
     trace in the sod
The last spurning print of a sky-cleav-
     ing god.

"But now, on the poet's dispriva-
     cied moods
With *do this* and *do that* the pert critic
     intrudes ;
While he thinks he 's been barely ful-
     filling his duty
To interpret 'twixt men and their own
     sense of beauty,
And has striven, while others sought
     honor or pelf,
To make his kind happy as he was him-
     self,
He finds he 's been guilty of horrid
     offences
In all kinds of moods, numbers, gen-
     ders, and tenses ;
He 's been *ob* and *sub*jective, what
     Kettle calls Pot,
Precisely, at all events, what he ought
     not,
You have done this, says one judge ;
     done that, says another ;
You should have done this, grumbles
     one ; *that,* says t'other ;
Never mind what he touches, one
     shrieks out *Taboo !*
And while he is wondering what he
     shall do,
Since each suggests opposite topics for
     song,
They all shout together *you 're right !*
     and *you 're wrong !*

"Nature fits all her children with
     something to do,

He who would write and can't write,
     can surely review,
Can set up a small booth as critic and
     sell us his
Petty conceit and his pettier jealousies ;
Thus a lawyer's apprentice, just out of
     his teens,
Will do for the Jeffrey of six magazines ;
Having read Johnson's lives of the po-
     ets half through,
There 's nothing on earth he 's not
     competent to ;
He reviews with as much nonchalance
     as he whistles, —
He goes through a book and just picks
     out the thistles,
It matters not whether he blame or
     commend,
If he 's bad as a foe, he 's far worse as
     a friend :
Let an author but write what 's above
     his poor scope,
He goes to work gravely and twists up
     a rope,
And, inviting the world to see punish-
     ment done,
Hangs himself up to bleach in the wind
     and the sun ;
'T is delightful to see, when a man
     comes along
Who has anything in him peculiar and
     strong,
Every cockboat that swims clear its
     fierce (pop) gundeck at him,
And make as he passes its ludicrous
     Peck at him —"

Here Miranda came up and began,
     "As to that —"
Apollo at once seized his gloves, cane,
     and hat,
And, seeing the place getting rapidly
     cleared,
I, too, snatched my notes and forthwith
     disappeared.

THE BIGLOW PAPERS.

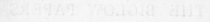

NOTICES OF AN INDEPENDENT PRESS.

[I HAVE observed, reader (bene- or male-volent, as it may happen), that it is customary to append to the second editions of books, and to the second works of authors, short sentences commendatory of the first, under the title of *Notices of the Press.* These, I have been given to understand, are procurable at certain established rates, payment being made either in money or advertising patronage by the publisher, or by an adequate outlay of servility on the part of the author. Considering these things with myself, and also that such notices are neither intended, nor generally believed, to convey any real opinions, being a purely ceremonial accompaniment of literature, and resembling certificates to the virtues of various morbiferal panaceas, I conceived that it would be not only more economical to prepare a sufficient number of such myself, but also more immediately subservient to the end in view to prefix them to this our primary edition rather than await the contingency of a second, when they would seem to be of small utility. To delay attaching the *bobs* until the second attempt at flying the kite would indicate but a slender experience in that useful art. Neither has it escaped my notice, nor failed to afford me matter of reflection, that, when a circus or a caravan is about to visit Jaalam, the initial step is to send forward large and highly ornamented bills of performance to be hung in the bar-room and the post-office. These having been sufficiently gazed at, and beginning to lose their attractiveness except for the flies, and, truly, the boys also (in whom I find it impossible to repress, even during school-hours, certain oral and telegraphic communications concerning the expected show), upon some fine morning the band enters in a gayly painted wagon, or triumphal chariot, and with noisy advertisement, by means of brass, wood, and sheepskin, makes the circuit of our startled village streets. Then, as the exciting sounds draw nearer and nearer, do I desiderate those eyes of Aristarchus, "whose looks were as a breeching to a boy." Then do I perceive, with vain regret of wasted opportunities, the advantage of a pancratic or pantechnic education, since he is most reverenced by my little subjects who can throw the cleanest summerset or walk most securely upon the revolving cask. The story of the Pied Piper becomes for the first time credible to me (albeit confirmed by the Hameliners dating their legal instruments from the period of his exit), as I behold how those strains, without pretence of magical potency, bewitch the pupillary legs, nor leave to the pedagogic an entire self-control. For these reasons, lest my kingly prerogative should suffer diminution, I prorogue my restless commons, whom I also follow into the street, chiefly lest some mischief may chance befall them. After the manner of such a band, I send forward the following notices of domestic manufacture, to make brazen proclamation, not unconscious of the advantage which will accrue, if our little craft, *cymbula sutilis,* shall seem to leave port with a clipping breeze, and to carry, in nautical phrase, a bone in her mouth. Nevertheless, I have chosen, as being more equitable, to prepare some also sufficiently objurgatory, that readers of every taste may find a dish to their palate. I have modelled them upon actually existing specimens, preserved in my own cabinet of natural curiosities. One, in particular, I had copied with tolerable exactness from a notice of one of my own discourses, which, from its superior tone and appearance of vast experience, I concluded to have been written by a man at least three hundred years of age, though I recollected no existing instance of such antediluvian longevity. Nevertheless, I afterwards discovered the author to be a young gentleman preparing for the ministry under the direction of one of my brethren in a neighboring town, and whom I had once instinctively corrected in a Latin quantity. But this I have been forced to omit, from its too great length. — H. W.]

From the Universal Littery Universe.

Full of passages which rivet the attention of the reader. . . . . Under a rustic garb, sentiments are conveyed which should be committed to the memory and engraven on the heart of every moral and social being. . . . . We consider this a *unique* performance. . . . . We hope to see it soon introduced into our common schools. . . . . Mr. Wilbur has performed his duties as editor with excellent taste and judgment. . . . . This is a vein which we hope to see successfully prosecuted. . . . . We hail the appearance of this work as a long stride toward the formation of a purely aboriginal, indigenous, native, and American literature. We rejoice to meet with an author national enough to break away from the slavish deference, too common among us, to English grammar and orthography. . . . . Where all is so good, we are at a loss how to make extracts. . . . . On the whole, we may call it a volume which no library, pretending to entire completeness, should fail to place upon its shelves.

From the Higginbottomopolis Snapping-turtle.

A collection of the merest balderdash and doggerel that it was ever our bad fortune to lay eyes on. The author is a vulgar buffoon, and the editor a talkative, tedious old fool. We use strong language, but should any of our readers peruse the book, (from which calamity Heaven preserve them!) they will find reasons for it thick as the leaves of Vallumbrozer, or, to use a still more expressive

comparison, as the combined heads of author and editor. The work is wretchedly got up. . . . . We should like to know how much *British gold* was pocketed by this libeller of our country and her purest patriots.

From the Oldfogrumville Mentor.

We have not had time to do more than glance through this handsomely printed volume, but the name of its respectable editor, the Rev. Mr. Wilbur, of Jaalam, will afford a sufficient guaranty for the worth of its contents. . . . . The paper is white, the type clear, and the volume of a convenient and attractive size. . . . . In reading this elegantly executed work, it has seemed to us that a passage or two might have been retrenched with advantage, and that the general style of diction was susceptible of a higher polish. . . . . On the whole, we may safely leave the ungrateful task of criticism to the reader. We will barely suggest, that in volumes intended, as this is, for the illustration of a provincial dialect and turns of expression, a dash of humor or satire might be thrown in with advantage. . . . . The work is admirably got up. . . . . This work will form an appropriate ornament to the centre-table. It is beautifully printed, on paper of an excellent quality.

From the Dekay Bulwark.

We should be wanting in our duty as the conductor of that tremendous engine, a public press, as an American, and as a man, did we allow such an opportunity as is presented to us by "The Biglow Papers" to pass by without entering our earnest protest against such attempts (now, alas! too common) at demoralizing the public sentiment. Under a wretched mask of stupid drollery, slavery, war, the social glass, and, in short, all the valuable and time-honored institutions justly dear to our common humanity and especially to republicans, are made the butt of coarse and senseless ribaldry by this low-minded scribbler. It is time that the respectable and religious portion of our community should be aroused to the alarming inroads of foreign Jacobinism, sansculottism, and infidelity. It is a fearful proof of the wide-spread nature of this contagion, that these secret stabs at religion and virtue are given from under the cloak (*credite, posteri!*) of a clergyman. It is a mournful spectacle indeed to the patriot and Christian to see liberality and new ideas (falsely so called, — they are as old as Eden) invading the sacred precincts of the pulpit. . . . . On the whole, we consider this volume as one of the first shocking results which we predicted would spring out of the late French "Revolution"(!).

From the Bungtown Copper and Comprehensive Tocsin (a try-weakly family journal).

Altogether an admirable work. . . . . Full of humor, boisterous, but delicate, — of wit withering and scorching, yet combined with a pathos cool as morning dew, — of satire ponderous as the mace of Richard, yet keen as the scymitar of Saladin. . . . . A work full of "mountain-mirth," mischievous as Puck, and lightsome as Ariel. . . . . We know not whether to admire most the genial, fresh, and discursive concinnity of the author, or his playful fancy, weird imagination, and compass of style, at once both objective and subjective. . . . . . We might indulge in some criticisms, but, were the author other than he is, he would be a different being. As it is, he has a wonderful *pose*, which flits from flower to flower, and bears the reader irresistibly along on its eagle pinions (like Ganymede) to the "highest heaven of invention." . . . . We love a book so purely objective. . . . . Many of his pictures of natural scenery have an extraordinary subjective clearness and fidelity. . . . . In fine, we consider this as one of the most extraordinary volumes of this or any age. We know of no English author who could have written it. It is a work to which the proud genius of our country, standing with one foot on the Aroostook and the other on the Rio Grande, and holding up the star-spangled banner amid the wreck of matter and the crush of worlds, may point with bewildering scorn of the punier efforts of enslaved Europe. . . . . We hope soon to encounter our author among those higher walks of literature in which he is evidently capable of achieving enduring fame. Already we should be inclined to assign him a high position in the bright galaxy of our American bards.

From the Saltriver Pilot and Flag of Freedom.

A volume in bad grammar and worse taste. . . . While the pieces here collected were confined to their appropriate sphere in the corners of obscure newspapers, we considered them wholly beneath contempt, but, as the author has chosen to come forward in this public manner, he must expect the lash he so richly merits. . . . Contemptible slanders. . . . . Vilest Billingsgate. . . . . Has raked all the gutters of our language. . . . . The most pure, upright, and consistent politicians not safe from his malignant venom. . . . . General Cushing comes in for a share of his vile calumnies. . . . . The *Reverend* Homer Wilbur is a disgrace to his cloth. . . . .

From the World-Harmonic-Æolian-Attachment.

Speech is silver: silence is golden. No utterance more Orphic than this. While,

therefore, as highest author, we reverence him whose works continue heroically unwritten, we have also our hopeful word for those who with pen (from wing of goose loud-cackling, or seraph God-commissioned) record the thing that is revealed. . . . . Under mask of quaintest irony, we detect here the deep, storm-tost (nigh shipwracked) soul, thunder-scarred, semiarticulate, but ever climbing hopefully toward the peaceful summits of an Infinite Sorrow. . . . Yes, thou poor, forlorn Hosea, with Hebrew fire-flaming soul in thee, for thee also this life of ours has not been without its aspects of heavenliest pity and laughingest mirth. Conceivable enough! Through coarse Thersites-cloak, we have revelation of the heart, wild-glowing, world-clasping, that is in him. Bravely he grapples with the life-problem as it presents itself to him, uncombed, shaggy, careless of the "nicer proprieties," inexpert of "elegant diction," yet with voice audible enough to whoso hath ears, up there on the gravelly side-hills, or down on the splashy, indiarubber-like salt-marshes of native Jaalam. To this soul also the *Necessity of Creating* somewhat has unveiled its awful front. If not Œdipuses and Electras and Alcestises, then in God's name Birdofredum Sawins! These also shall get born into the world, and filch (if so need) a Zingali subsistence therein, these lank, omnivorous Yankees of his. He shall paint the Seen, since the Unseen will not sit to him. Yet in him also are Nibelungen-lays, and Iliads, and Ulysses-wanderings, and Divine Comedies, — if only once he could come at them! Therein lies much, nay all; for what truly is this which we name *All*, but that which we do *not* possess? . . . . Glimpses also are given us of an old father Ezekiel, not without paternal pride, as is the wont of such. A brown, parchment-hided old man of the geoponic or bucolic species, gray-eyed, we fancy, *queued* perhaps, with much weather-cunning and plentiful September-bergale memories, bidding fair in good time to become the Oldest Inhabitant. After such hasty apparition, he vanishes and is seen no more. . . . . Of "Rev. Homer Wilbur, A. M., Pastor of the First Church in Jaalam," we have small care to speak here. Spare touch in him of his Melesigenes namesake, save, haply, the, — blindness! A tolerably caliginose, nephe-legeretous elderly gentleman, with infinite faculty of sermonizing, muscularized by long practice, and excellent digestive apparatus, and, for the rest, well-meaning enough, and with small private illuminations (somewhat tallowy, it is to be feared) of his own. To him, there, "Pastor of the First Church in Jaalam," our Hosea presents himself as a quite inexplicable Sphinx-riddle. A rich poverty of Latin and Greek, — so far is clear enough, even to eyes peering myopic through horn-lensed editorial spectacles, — but naught farther! O purblind, well-meaning, altogether fuscous

Melesigenes-Wilbur, there are things in him incommunicable by stroke of birch! Did it ever enter that old bewildered head of thine that there was the *Possibility of the Infinite* in him? To thee, quite wingless (and even featherless) biped, has not so much even as a dream of wings ever come? "Talented young parishioner"? Among the Arts whereof thou art *Magister*, does that of *seeing* happen to be one? Unhappy *Artium Magister!* Somehow a Nemean lion, fulvous, torrid-eyed, dry-nursed in broad-howling sand-wildernesses of a sufficiently rare spirit-Libya (it may be supposed) has got whelped among the sheep. Already he stands wild-glaring, with feet clutching the ground as with oak-roots, gathering for a Remus-spring over the walls of thy little fold. In Heaven's name, go not near him with that flybite crook of thine! In good time, thou painful preacher, thou wilt go to the appointed place of departed Artillery-Election Sermons, Right-Hands of Fellowship, and Results of Councils, gathered to thy spiritual fathers with much Latin of the Epitaphial sort; thou, too, shalt have thy reward; but on him the Eumenides have looked, not Xantippes of the pit, snake-tressed, finger-threatening, but radiantly calm as on antique gems; for him paws impatient the winged courser of the gods, champing unwelcome bit; him the starry deeps, the empyrean glooms, and far-flashing splendors await.

From the Onion Grove Phoenix.

A talented young townsman of ours, recently returned from a Continental tour, and who is already favorably known to our readers by his sprightly letters from abroad which have graced our columns, called at our office yesterday. We learn from him, that, having enjoyed the distinguished privilege, while in Germany, of an introduction to the celebrated Von Humbug, he took the opportunity to present that eminent man with a copy of the "Biglow Papers." The next morning he received the following note, which he has kindly furnished us for publication. We prefer to print it *verbatim*, knowing that our readers will readily forgive the few errors into which the illustrious writer has fallen, through ignorance of our language.

"HIGH-WORTHY MISTER!
"I shall also now especially happy starve, because I have more or less a work one those aboriginal Red-Men seen in which have I so deaf an interest ever taken fullworthy on the self shelf with our Gottsched to be upset.
"Pardon my in the English-speech unpractice!
"VON HUMBUG."

He also sent with the above note a copy of his famous work on "Cosmetics," to be pre-sented to Mr. Biglow; but this was taken from our friend by the English custom-house officers, probably through a petty national spite. No doubt, it has by this time found its way into the British Museum. We trust this outrage will be exposed in all our American papers. We shall do our best to bring it to the notice of the State Department. Our numerous readers will share in the pleasure we experience at seeing our young and vigorous national literature thus encouragingly patted on the head by this venerable and world-renowned German. We love to see these reciprocations of good-feeling between the different branches of the great Anglo-Saxon race.

[The following genuine "notice" having met my eye, I gladly insert a portion of it here, the more especially as it contains one of Mr. Biglow's poems not elsewhere printed. — H. W.]

From the Jaalam Independent Blunderbuss.

.... But, while we lament to see our young townsman thus mingling in the heated contests of party politics, we think we detect in him the presence of talents which, if properly directed, might give an innocent pleasure to many. As a proof that he is competent to the production of other kinds of poetry, we copy for our readers a short fragment of a pastoral by him, the manuscript of which was loaned us by a friend. The title of it is "The Courtin'."

ZEKLE crep' up, quite unbeknown,
 An' peeked in thru the winder,
An' there sot Huldy all alone,
 'ith no one nigh to hender.

Agin' the chimbly crooknecks hung,
 An' in amongst 'em rusted
The ole queen's-arm thet gran'ther Young
 Fetched back frum Concord busted.

The wannut logs shot sparkles out
 Towards the pootiest, bless her!
An' leetle fires danced all about
 The chiny on the dresser.

The very room, coz she wuz in,
 Looked warm frum floor to ceilin',
An' she looked full ez rosy agin
 Ez th' apples she wuz peelin'.

She heerd a foot an' knowed it, tu,
 Araspin' on the scraper, —
All ways to once her feelins flew
 Like sparks in burnt-up paper.

He kin' o' l'itered on the mat,
 Some doubtfle o' the seekle;
His heart kep' goin' pitypat,
 But hern went pity Zekle.

An' yet she gin her cheer a jerk
  Ez though she wished him furder
An' on her apples kep' to work
  Ez ef a wager spurred her.

"You want to see my Pa, I spose?"
  "Wal, no; I come designin'—"
"To see my Ma? She's sprinklin' clo'es
  Agin to-morrow's i'nin'."

He stood a spell on one foot fust
  Then stood a spell on tother,
An' on which one he felt the wust
  He could n't ha' told ye, nuther.

Sez he, "I'd better call agin";
  Sez she, "Think likely, *Mister*";
The last word pricked him like a pin,
  An'—wal, he up and kist her.

When Ma bimeby upon 'em slips,
  Huldy sot pale ez ashes,
All kind o' smily round the lips
  An' teary round the lashes.

Her blood riz quick, though, like the tide
  Down to the Bay o' Fundy,
An' all I know is they wuz cried
  In meetin', come nex Sunday.

SATIS multis sese emptores futuros libri professis, Georgius Nichols, Cantabrigiensis, opus emittet de parte gravi sed adhuc neglecta historiæ naturalis, cum titulo sequente, videlicet:

Conatus ad Delineationem naturalem nonnihil perfectiorem Scarabæt Bombilatoris, vulgo dicti HUMBUG, ab HOMERO WILBUR, Artium Magistro, Societatis historico-naturalis Jaalamensis Præside (Secretario, Socioque (eheu!) singulo), multarumque aliarum Societatum eruditarum (sive ineruditarum) tam domesticarum quam transmarinarum Socio — forsitan futuro.

PROEMIUM.

LECTORI BENEVOLO S.

Toga scholastica nondum deposita, quum systemata varia entomslogica, a viris ejus scientiæ cultoribus studiosissimis summa diligentia ædificata, penitus indagâssem, non fuit quin luctuose omnibus in iis, quamvis aliter laude dignissimis, hiatum magni momenti perciperem. Tunc, nescio quo motu superiore impulsus, aut qua captus dulcedine operis, ad eum implendum (Curtius alter) me solemniter devovi. Nec ab isto labore, δαιμονίως imposito, abstinui antequam tractatulum sufficienter inconcinnum lingua vernacula perfeceram. Inde, juveniliter tumefactus, et barathro ineptiæ τῶν βιβλιοπωλῶν (necnon "Publici Legentis") nusquam explorato, me composuisse quod quasi placentas præfervidas (ut sic dicam) homines ingurgitarent credidi. Sed, quum

huic et alio bibliopolæ MSS. mea submisissem et nihil solidius responsione valde negativa in Musæum meum retulissem, horror ingens atque misericordia, ob crassitudinem Lambertianam in cerebris homunculorum istius muneris cœlesti quadam ira infixam, me invasere. Extemplo mei solius impensis librum edere decrevi, nihil omnino dubitans quin "Mundus Scientificus" (ut aiunt) crumenam meam ampliter repleret. Nullam, attamen, ex agro illo meo parvulo segetem demessui, præter gaudium vacuum bene de Republica merendi. Iste panis meus pretiosus super aquas literarias fæculentas præfidenter jactus, quasi Harpyiarum quarundam (scilicet bibliopolarum istorum facinorosorum supradictorum) tactu rancidus, intra perpaucos dies mihi domum rediit. Et, quum ipse tali victu ali non tolerarem, primum in mentem venit pistori (typographo nempe) nihilominus solvendum esse. Animum non idcirco demisi, imo æque ac pueri naviculas suas penes se lino retinent (eo ut e recto cursu delapsas ad ripam retrahant), sic ego Argô meam chartaceam fluctibus laborantem a quæsitu velleris aurei, ipse potius tonsus pelleque exutus, mente solida revocavi. Metaphoram ut mutem, *boomarangam* meam a scopo aberantem retraxi, dum majore vi, occasione ministrante, adversus Fortunam intorquerem. Ast mihi, talia volventi, et, sicut Saturnus ille παιδοβόρος, liberos intellectûs mei depascere fidenti, casus miserandus, nec antea inauditus, supervenit. Nam, ut ferunt Scythas pietatis causa et parsimoniæ, parentes suos mortuos devorâsse, sic filius hic meus primogenitus, Scythis ipsis minus mansuetus, patrem vivum totum e calcitrantem exsorbere enixus est. Nec tamen hac de causa sobolem meam esurientem exheredavi. Sed famem istam pro valido testimonio virilitatis roborisque potius habui, cibumque ad eam satiandam, salva paterna mea carne, petii. Et quia bilem illam scaturientem ad æs etiam concoquendum idoneam esse estimabam, unde æs alienum, ut minoris pretii, haberem, circumspexi. Rebus ita se habentibus, ab avunculo meo Johanne Doolittle, Armigero, impetravi ut pecunias necessarias suppeditaret, ne opus esset mihi universitatem relinquendi antequam ad gradum primum in artibus pervenissem. Tunc ego, salvum facere patronum meum munificum maxime cupiens, omnes libros primæ editionis operis mei non venditos una cum privilegio in omne ævum ejusdem imprimendi et edendi avunculo meo dicto pigneravi. Ex illo, die, atro lapide notando, curae vociferantes familiæ singulis annis crescentis eo usque insultabant ut nunquam tam carum pignus e vinculis istis aheneis solvere possem.

Avunculo vero nuper mortuo, quum inter alios consanguineos testamenti ejus lectionem audiendi causa advenissem, erectis auribus verba talia sequentia accepi : — "Quoniam persuasum habeo meum dilectum nepotem Homerum, longa et intima rerum angustarum domi experientia, aptissimum esse qui divitias tueatur, beneficenterque ac prudenter iis divinis creditis utatur, — ergo, motus hisce cogitationibus, exque amore meo in illum magno, ut, legoque nepoti caro meo supranominato omnes singularesque istas possessiones nec ponderabiles nec computabiles meas quæ sequuntur, scilicet : quingentos libros quos mihi pigneravit dictus Homerus, anno lucis 1792, cum privilegio edendi et repetendi opus istud 'scientificum' (quod dicunt) suum, si sic elegerit. Tamen D. O. M. precor oculos Homeri nepotis mei ita aperiat eumque moveat, ut libros istos in bibliotheca unius e plurimis castellis suis Hispaniensibus tuto abscondat."

His verbis (vix credibilibus) auditis, cor meum in pectore exsultavit. Deində, quoniam tractatus Anglice scriptus spem auctoris fefellerat, quippe quum studium Historiæ Naturalis in Republica nostra inter factionis strepitum languescat, Latine versum edere statui, et eo potius quia nescio quomodo disciplina academica et duo diplomata proficiunt, nisi quod peritos linguarum omnino mortuarum (et damnandarum, ut dicebat iste παvoῦργος Guilielmus Cobbett) nos faciant.

Et mihi adhuc superstes est tota illa editio prima, quam quasi crepitaculum per quod dentes caninos dentibam retineo.

OPERIS SPECIMEN.

(Ad exemplum Johannis Physiophili speciminis Monachologiæ.)

12. S. B. *Militaris,* WILBUR. *Carnifex,* JABLONSK. *Profanus.* DESFONT.

[Male hancce speciem *Cyclopem* Fabricius vocat, ut qui singulo oculo ad quod sui interest distinguitur. Melius vero Isaacus Outis nullum inter S. milit. S.que Belzebul (Fabric. 152) discrimen esse defendit.]

Habitat civitat. Americ. austral.

Aureis lineis sordidus ; plerumque tamen sordidus, utpote lanienas valde frequentans, fœtore sanguinis allectus. Amat quoque insuper septa apricari, neque inde, nisi maxima conatione detrudibur. *Candidatus* ergo populariter vocatus. Caput cristam quasi pennarum ostendit. Pro cibo vaccam publicam callide mulget ; abdomen enorme ; facultas suctus haud facile estimanda. Otiosus, fatuus ; ferox nihilominus, semperque dimicare paratus. Tortuose repit.

Capite sæpe maxima cum cura dissecto, ne illud rudimentum etiam cerebri commune omnibus prope insectis detegere poteram.

Unam de hoc S. milit. rem singularem notavi ; nam S. Guineens. (Fabric. 143) servos facit, et idcirco a multis summa in reverentia habitus, quasi scintillas rationis pæne humanæ demonstrans.

24. S. B. *Criticus,* WILBUR. *Zoilus,* FABRIC. *Pygmæus,* CARLSEN.

[Stultissime Johannes Stryx cum S. punctato (Fabric. 64–109) confundit. Specimina quamplurima scrutationi microscopicæ subjeci, nunquam tamen unum ulla indicia puncti cujusvis prorsus ostendentem inveni.]

Præcipue formidolosus, insectatusque, in proxima rima anonyma sese abscondit, *we, we,* creberrime stridens. Ineptus, segnipes.

Habitat ubique gentium ; in sicco ; nidum suum terebratione indefessa ædificans. Cibus. Libros depascit ; siccos præcipue

MELIBŒUS-HIPPONAX.

THE

𝕭𝖎𝖌𝖑𝖔𝖜 𝕻𝖆𝖕𝖊𝖗𝖘,

EDITED,

WITH AN INTRODUCTION, NOTES, GLOSSARY, AND
COPIOUS INDEX.

BY

HOMER WILBUR, A. M.,

PASTOR OF THE FIRST CHURCH IN JAALAM, AND (PROSPECTIVE) MEMBER OF
MANY LITERARY, LEARNED, AND SCIENTIFIC SOCIETIES,

(*for which see page* 173.)

The ploughman's whistle, or the trivial flute,
Finds more respect than great Apollo's lute.
Quarles's Emblems, B. ii. E. 8.

Margaritas, munde porcine, calcâsti : en, siliquas accipe.
Jac. Car. Fil. ad Pub. Leg. á ĭ.

NOTE TO TITLE-PAGE.

It will not have escaped the attentive eye, that I have, on the title-page, omitted those honorary appendages to the editorial name which not only add greatly to the value of every book, but whet and exacerbate the appetite of the reader. For not only does he surmise that an honorary membership of literary and scientific societies implies a certain amount of necessary distinction on the part of the recipient of such decorations, but he is willing to trust himself more entirely to an author who writes under the fearful responsibility of involving the reputation of such bodies as the *S. Archæol. Dahon.* or the *Acad. Lit. et Scient. Kamtschat.* I cannot but think that the early editions of Shakespeare and Milton would have met with more rapid and general acceptance, but for the barrenness of their respective title-pages ; and I believe, that, even now, a publisher of the works of either of those justly distinguished men would find his account in procuring their admission to the membership of learned bodies on the Continent, — a proceeding no whit more incongruous than the reversal of the judgment against Socrates, when he was already more than twenty centuries beyond the reach of antidotes, and when his memory had acquired a deserved respectability. I conceive that it was a feeling of the importance of this precaution which induced Mr. Locke to style himself "Gent." on the title-page of his Essay, as who should say to his readers that they could receive his metaphysics on the honor of a gentleman.

Nevertheless, finding that, without descending to a smaller size of type than would have been compatible with the dignity of the several societies to be named, I could not compress my intended list within the limits of a single page, and thinking, moreover, that the act would carry with it an air of decorous modesty, I have chosen to take the reader aside, as it were, into my private closet, and there not only exhibit to him the diplomas which I already possess, but also to furnish him with a prophetic vision of those which I may, without undue presumption, hope for, as not beyond the reach of human ambition and attainment. And I am the rather induced to this from the fact that my name has been unaccountably dropped from the last triennial catalogue of our beloved *Alma Mater.* Whether this is to be attributed to the difficulty of Latinizing any of those honorary adjuncts (with a complete list of which I took care to furnish the proper persons nearly a year beforehand), or whether it had its origin in any more culpable motives, I forbear to consider in this place, the matter being in course of painful investigation. But, however this may be, I felt the omission the more keenly, as I had, in expectation of the new catalogue, enriched the library of the Jaalam Athenæum with the old one then in my possession, by which means it has come about that my children will be deprived of a never-wearying winter-evening's amusement in looking out the name of their parent in that distinguished roll. Those harmless innocents had at least committed no —— but I forbear, having intrusted my reflections and animadversions on this painful topic to the safe-keeping of my private diary, intended for posthumous publication. I state this fact here, in order that certain nameless individuals, who are, perhaps, overmuch congratulating themselves upon my silence, may know that a rod is in pickle which the vigorous hand of a justly incensed posterity will apply to their memories.

The careful reader will note, that, in the list which I have prepared, I have included the names of several Cisatlantic societies to which a place is not commonly assigned in processions of this nature. I have ventured to do this, not only to encourage native ambition and genius, but also because I have never been able to perceive in what way distance (unless we suppose them at the end of a lever) could increase the weight of learned bodies. As far as I have been able to extend my researches among such stuffed specimens as occasionally reach America, I have discovered no generic difference between the antipodal *Fogrum Japonicum* and the *F. Americanum* sufficiently common in our own immediate neighborhood. Yet, with a becoming deference to the popular belief that distinctions of this sort are enhanced in value by every additional mile they travel, I have intermixed the names of some tolerably distant literary and other associations with the rest.

I add here, also, an advertisement, which, that it may be the more readily understood by those persons especially interested therein, I have written in that curtailed and otherwise maltreated canine Latin, to the writing and reading of which they are accustomed.

OMNIB. PER TOT. ORB. TERRAR. CATALOG. ACADEM. EDD.

Minim. gent. diplom. ab inclytiss. acad. vest. orans, vir. honorand. opero-siss., at sol. ut sciat. quant. glor. nom. meum (dipl. fort. concess.) catal. vest. temp. futur. affer., ill. subjec., addit. omnib. titul. honorar. qu. adh. non tant. opt. quam probab. put.

₊₊* *Litt. Uncial. distinx. ut Præs. S. Hist. Nat. Jaal.*

HOMERUS WILBUR, Mr., Episc. Jaalam, S. T. D. 1850, et Yal. 1849, et Neo-Cæs. et Brun. et Gulielm. 1852, et Gul. et Mar. et Bowd. et Georgiop. et Viridimont. et Colomb. Nov. Ebor. 1853. et Amherst. et Watervill. et S. Jarlath. Hib. et S. Mar. et S. Joseph. et S. And. Scot. 1854, et Nashvill. et Dart. et Dickins. et Concord. et Wash. et Columbian. et Charlest. et Jeff. et Dubl. et Oxon. et Cantab. et Cæt. 1855, P. U. N. C. H. et J. U. D. Gott. et Osnab. et Heidelb. 1860, et Acad. BORE us. Berolin. Soc., et SS. RR. Lugd. Bat. et Patav. et Lond. et Edinb. et Ins. Feejee. et Null. Terr. et Pekin. Soc. Hon. et S. H. S. et S. P. A. et A. A. S. et S. Humb. Univ. et S. Omn. Rer. Quarund. q. Aliar. Promov. Passamaquod. et H. P. C. et I. O. H. et A. Δ. Φ. et H. K. P. et Φ. B. K. et Peucin. et Erosoph. et Philadelph. et Frat. in Unit. et Σ. T. et S. Archæolog. Athen. et Acad. Scient. et Lit. Panorm. et SS. R. H. Matrit. et Beeloochist. et Caffrar. et Caribb. et M. S. Reg. Paris. et S. Am. Antiserv. Soc. Hon. et P. D. Gott. et LL. D. 1852, et D. C. L. et Mus. Doc. Oxon. 1860, et M. M. S. S. et M. D. 1854, et Med. Fac. Univ. Harv. Soc. et S. pro Convers. Pollywog. Soc. Hon. et Higgl. Piggl. et LL. B. 1853, et S. pro Christianiz. Moschet. Soc., et SS. Ante-Diluv. ubiq. Gent. Soc. Hon. et Civit. Cleric. Jaalam. et S. pro Diffus. General. Tenebr. Secret. Corr.

INTRODUCTION.

WHEN, more than three years ago, my talented young parishioner, Mr. Biglow, came to me and submitted to my animadversions the first of his poems which he intended to commit to the more hazardous trial of a city newspaper, it never so much as entered my imagination to conceive that his productions would ever be gathered into a fair volume, and ushered into the august presence of the reading public by myself. So little are we short-sighted mortals able to predict the event! I confess that there is to me a quite new satisfaction in being associated (though only as sleeping partner) in a book which can stand by itself in an independent unity on the shelves of libraries. For there is always this drawback from the pleasure of printing a sermon, that, whereas the queasy stomach of this generation will not bear a discourse long enough to make a separate volume, those religious and godly-minded children (those Samuels, if I may call them so) of the brain must at first lie buried in an undistinguished heap, and then get such resurrection as is vouchsafed to them, mummy-wrapped with a score of others in a cheap binding, with no other mark of distinction than the word "*Miscellaneous*" printed upon the back. Far be it from me to claim any credit for the quite unexpected popularity which I am pleased to find these bucolic strains have attained unto. If I know myself, I am measurably free from the itch of vanity; yet I may be allowed to say that I was not backward to recognize in them a certain wild, puckery, acidulous (sometimes even verging toward that point which, in our rustic phrase, is termed *shut-eye*) flavor, not wholly unpleasing, nor unwhole-some, to palates cloyed with the sugariness of tamed and cultivated fruit. It may be, also, that some touches of my own, here and there, may have led to their wider acceptance, albeit solely from my larger experience of literature and authorship.*

I was, at first, inclined to discourage Mr. Biglow's attempts, as knowing that the desire to poetize is one of the diseases naturally incident to adolescence, which, if the fitting remedies be not at once and with a bold hand applied, may become chronic, and render one, who might else have become in due time an ornament of the social circle, a painful object even to nearest friends and relatives. But thinking, on a further experience, that there was a germ of promise in him which required only culture and the pulling up of weeds from around it, I thought it best to set before him the acknowledged examples of English composition in verse, and leave the rest to natural emulation. With this view, I accordingly lent him some volumes of Pope and Goldsmith, to the assiduous study of which he promised to devote his evenings. Not long afterward, he brought me some verses written upon that model, a specimen of which I subjoin, having changed some phrases of less elegancy, and a few rhymes objectionable to the cultivated ear. The poem consisted of childish reminiscences, and the sketches which follow

* The reader curious in such matters may refer (if he can find them) to "A Sermon preached on the Anniversary of the Dark Day," "An Artillery Election Sermon," "A Discourse on the Late Eclipse," "Dorcas, a Funeral Sermon on the Death of Madam Submit Tidd, Relict of the late Experience Tidd, Esq.," &c., &c.

will not seem destitute of truth to those whose fortunate education began in a country village. And, first, let us hang up his charcoal portrait of the school-dame.

"Propped on the marsh, a dwelling now, I see
The humble school-house of my A, B, C,
Where well-drilled urchins, each behind his
  tire,
Waited in ranks the wished command to fire,
Then all together, when the signal came,
Dicharged their *a-b abs* against the dame.
Daughter of Danaus, who could daily pour
In treacherous pipkins her Pierian store,
She, 'mid the volleyed learning firm and calm,
Patted the furloughed ferule on her palm,
And, to our wonder, could divine at once
Who flashed the pan, and who was down-
  right dunce.

"There young Devotion learned to climb
  with ease
The gnarly limbs of Scripture family-trees,
And he was most commended and admired
Who soonest to the topmost twig perspired;
Each name was called as many various ways
As pleased the reader's ear on different days,
So that the weather, or the ferule's stings,
Colds in the head, or fifty other things,
Transformed the helpless Hebrew thrice a
  week
To guttural Pequot or resounding Greek,
The vibrant accent skipping here and there,
Just as it pleased invention or despair;
No controversial Hebraist was the Dame;
With or without the points pleased her the
  same;
If any tyro found a name too tough,
And looked at her, pride furnished skill
  enough;
She nerved her larynx for the desperate thing,
And cleared the five-barred syllables at a
  spring.

"Ah, dear old times! there once it was my
  hap,
Perched on a stool, to wear the long-eared
  cap;
From books degraded, there I sat at ease,
A drone, the envy of compulsory bees;
Rewards of merit, too, full many a time,
Each with its woodcut and its moral rhyme,
And pierced half-dollars hung on ribbons gay
About my neck — to be restored next day,
I carried home, rewards as shining then
As those which deck the lifelong pains of
  men,
More solid than the redemanded praise
With which the world beribbons later days.

"Ah, dear old times! how brightly ye return!
How, rubbed afresh, your phosphor traces
  burn!
The ramble schoolward through dewspark-
  ling meads

The willow-wands turned Cinderella steeds;
The impromptu pinbent hook, the deep re-
  morse
O'er the chance-captured minnow's inchlong
  corse;
The pockets, plethoric with marbles round,
That still a space for ball and pegtop found,
Nor satiate yet, could manage to confine
Horsechestnuts, flagroot, and the kite's
  wound twine,
Nay, like the prophet's carpet could take in,
Enlarging still, the popgun's magazine;
The dinner carried in the small tin pail,
Shared with the dog, whose most beseeching
  tail
And dripping tongue and eager ears belied
The assumed indifference of canine pride;
The caper homeward, shortened if the cart
Of Neighbor Pomeroy, trundling from the
  mart,
O'ertook me, — then, translated to the seat
I praised the steed, how stanch he was and
  fleet,
While the bluff farmer, with superior grin,
Explained where horses should be thick,
  where thin,
And warned me (joke he always had in store)
To shun a beast that four white stockings
  wore.
What a fine natural courtesy was his!
His nod was pleasure, and his full bow bliss;
How did his well-thumbed hat, with ardor
  rapt,
Its decorous curve to every rank adapt!
How did it graduate with a courtly ease
The whole long scale of social differences,
Yet so gave each his measure running o'er,
None thought his own was less, his neighbor's
  more;
The squire was flattered, and the pauper
  knew
Old times acknowledged 'neath the thread-
  bare blue!
Dropped at the corner of the embowered
  lane,
Whistling I wade the knee-deep leaves again,
While eager Argus, who has missed all day
The sharer of his condescending play,
Comes leaping onward with a bark elate
And boisterous tail to greet me at the gate;
That I was true in absence to our love
Let the thick dog's-ears in my primer
  prove."

I add only one further extract, which will possess a melancholy interest to all such as have endeavored to glean the materials of revolutionary history from the lips of aged persons, who took a part in the actual making of it, and, finding the manufacture profitable, continued the supply in an adequate proportion to the demand.

"Old Joe is gone, who saw hot Percy goad
  His slow artillery up the Concord road,

A tale which grew in wonder, year by year,
As, every time he told it, Joe drew near
To the main fight, till, faded and grown gray,
The original scene to bolder tints gave way ;
Then Joe had heard the foe's scared double-
    quick
Beat on stove drum with one uncaptured
    stick,
And, ere death came the lengthening tale to
    lop,
Himself had fired, and seen a red-coat drop ;
Had Joe lived long enough, that scrambling
    fight
Had squared more nearly with his sense of
    right,
And vanquished Percy, to complete the tale,
Had hammered stone for life in Concord jail."

I do not know that the foregoing extracts ought not to be called my own
rather than Mr. Biglow's, as, indeed, he
maintained stoutly that my file had left
nothing of his in them. I should not,
perhaps, have felt entitled to take so
great liberties with them, had I not
more than suspected an hereditary vein
of poetry in myself, a very near ancestor
having written a Latin poem in the
Harvard *Gratulatio* on the accession of
George the Third. Suffice it to say,
that, whether not satisfied with such
limited approbation as I could conscientiously bestow, or from a sense of
natural inaptitude, certain it is that my
young friend could never be induced to
any further essays in this kind. He
affirmed that it was to him like writing
in a foreign tongue, — that Mr. Pope's
versification was like the regular tick-
ing of one of Willard's clocks, in which
one could fancy, after long listening, a
certain kind of rhythm or tune, but
which yet was only a poverty-stricken
tick, tick, after all, — and that he had
never seen a sweet-water on a trellis
growing so fairly, or in forms so pleasing to his eye, as a fox-grape over a
scrub-oak in a swamp. He added I
know not what, to the effect that the
sweet-water would only be the more dis-
figured by having its leaves starched
and ironed out, and that Pegasus (so
he called him) hardly looked right with
his mane and tail in curl-papers. These
and other such opinions I did not
long strive to eradicate, attributing
them rather to a defective education
and senses untuned by too long familiarity with purely natural objects, than to
a perverted moral sense. I was the
more inclined to this leniency since
sufficient evidence was not to seek, that
his verses, as wanting as they certainly
were in classic polish and point, had
somehow taken hold of the public ear
in a surprising manner. So, only setting him right as to the quantity of the
proper name Pegasus, I left him to follow the bent of his natural genius.

Yet could I not surrender him wholly
to the tutelage of the pagan (which,
literally interpreted, signifies village)
muse without yet a further effort for his
conversion, and to this end I resolved
that whatever of poetic fire yet burned
in myself, aided by the assiduous bel-
lows of correct models, should be put
in requisition. Accordingly, when my
ingenious young parishioner brought to
my study a copy of verses which he
had written touching the acquisition of
territory resulting from the Mexican
war, and the folly of leaving the question of slavery or freedom to the ad-
judication of chance, I did myself indite
a short fable or apologue after the manner of Gay and Prior, to the end that
he might see how easily even such subjects as he treated of were capable of a
more refined style and more elegant expression. Mr. Biglow's production was
as follows :—

THE TWO GUNNERS,

A FABLE.

Two fellers, Isrel named and Joe,
One Sundy mornin' 'greed to go
Agunnin' soon's the bells wuz done
And meetin' finally begun,
So'st no one would n't be about
Ther Sabbath-breakin' to spy out.

Joe did n't want to go a mite ;
He felt ez though 't warnt skeercely right,
But, when his doubts he went to speak on,
Isrel he up and called him Deacon,
An' kep' apokin' fun like sin
An' then arubbin' on it in,
Till Joe, less skeered o' doin' wrong
Than bein' laughed at, went along.

Past noontime they went trampin' round
An' nary thing to pop at found,
Till, fairly tired o' their spree,
They leaned their guns agin a tree,

An' jest ez they wuz settin' down
To take their noonin', Joe looked roun'
And see (across lots in a pond
That warn't mor'n twenty rod beyond),
A goose that on the water sot
Ez ef awaitin' to be shot.

Isrel he ups and grabs his gun;
Sez he, "By ginger, here 's some fun !"
"Don't fire," sez Joe, "it aint no use,
Thet 's Deacon Peleg's tame wild-goose";
Sez Isrel, "I don't care a cent,
I 've sighted an' I 'll let her went";
Bang ! went queen's-arm, ole gander flopped
His wings a spell, an' quorked, an' dropped.

Sez Joe, "I would n't ha' been hired
At that poor critter to ha' fired,
But, sence it 's clean gin up the ghost,
We 'll hev the tallest kind o' roast ;
I guess our waistbands 'll be tight
'Fore it comes ten o'clock ternight."

"I won't agree to no such bender,"
Sez Isrel, "keep it tell it 's tender ;
'T aint wuth a snap afore it 's ripe."
Sez Joe, "I 'd jest ez lives eat tripe ;
You *air* a buster ter suppose
I 'd eat what makes me hol' my nose ! "

So they disputed to an' fro
Till cunnin' Isrel sez to Joe,
"Don't le's stay here an' play the fool,
Le's wait till both on us git cool,
Jest for a day or two le's hide it
An' then toss up an' so decide it."
"Agreed !" sez Joe, an' so they did,
An' the ole goose wuz safely hid.

Now 't wuz the hottest kind o' weather,
An' when at last they come together,
It did n't signify which won,
Fer all the mischief hed ben done:
The goose wuz there, but, fer his soul,
Joe would n't ha' tetched it with a pole ;
But Isrel kind o' liked the smell on't
An' made *his* dinner very well on't.

My own humble attempt was in manner and form following, and I print it
here, I sincerely trust, out of no vain-
glory, but solely with the hope of doing
good.

LEAVING THE MATTER OPEN.

A TALE.

BY HOMER WILBUR, A. M.

Two brothers once, an ill-matched pair,
Together dwelt (no matter where),
To whom an Uncle Sam, or some one,
Had left a house and farm in common ·
The two in principles and habits
12

Were different as rats from rabbits ;
Stout Farmer North, with frugal care,
Laid up provision for his heir,
Not scorning with hard sun-browned hands
To scrape acquaintance with his lands ;
Whatever thing he had to do
He did, and made it pay him, too ;
He sold his waste stone by the pound,
His drains made water-wheels spin round,
His ice in summer-time he sold,
His wood brought profit when 't was cold,
He dug and delved from morn till night,
Strove to make profit square with right,
Lived on his means, cut no great dash,
And paid his debts in honest cash.

On tother hand, his brother South
Lived very much from hand to mouth,
Played gentleman, nursed dainty hands,
Borrowed North's money on his lands,
And culled his morals and his graces
From cock-pits, bar-rooms, fights, and races;
His sole work in the farming line
Was keeping droves of long-legged swine,
Which brought great bothers and expenses
To North in looking after fences,
And, when they happened to break through,
Cost him both time and temper too,
For South insisted it was plain
He ought to drive them home again,
And North consented to the work
Because he loved to buy cheap pork.

Meanwhile, South's swine increasing fast,
His farm became too small at last,
So, having thought the matter over,
And feeling bound to live in clover
And never pay the clover's worth.
He said one day to Brother North :—

"Our families are both increasing,
And, though we labor without ceasing,
Our produce soon will be too scant
To keep our children out of want ;
They who wish fortune to be lasting
Must be both prudent and forecasting ;
We soon shall need more land ; a lot
I know, that cheaply can be bo't ;
You lend the cash, I 'll buy the acres,
And we 'll be equally partakers."

Poor North, whose Anglo-Saxon blood
Gave him a hankering after mud,
Wavered a moment, then consented,
And, when the cash was paid, repented ;
To make the new land worth a pin,
Thought he, it must be all fenced in,
For, if South 's swine once get the run on't
No kind of farming can be done on't ;
If that don't suit the other side,
'T is best we instantly divide.

But somehow South could ne'er incline
This way or that to run the line,
And always found some new pretence
'Gainst setting the division fence ;
At last he said :—

        "For peace's sake,
Liberal concessions I will make ;
Though I believe, upon my soul,
I 've a just title to the whole,
I 'll make an offer which I call
Gen'rous, — we 'll have no fence at all ;
Then both of us, whene'er we choose,
Can take what part we want to use ;
If you should chance to need it first,
Pick you the best, I 'll take the worst."

"Agreed !" cried North ; thought he, This fall
With wheat and rye I 'll sow it all ;
In that way I shall get the start,
And South may whistle for his part.
So thought, so done, the field was sown,
And, winter having come and gone,
Sly North walked blithely forth to spy,
The progress of his wheat and rye ;
Heavens, what a sight ! his brother's swine
Had asked themselves all out to dine,
Such grunting, munching, rooting, shoving,
The soil seemed all alive and moving,
As for his grain, such work they 'd made on't,
He could n't spy a single blade on't.

Off in a rage he rushed to South,
"My wheat and rye " — grief choked his mouth ;
"Pray don't mind me," said South, "but plant
All of the new land that you want " ;
"Yes, but your hogs," cried North ;

           " The grain
Won't hurt them," answered South again ;
"But they destroy my grain " ;

           " No doubt ;
'T is fortunate you 've found it out ;
Misfortunes teach, and only they,
You must not sow it in their way " ;
"Nay, you," says North, "must keep them out " ;
"Did I create them with a snout?"
Asked South demurely ; "as agreed,
The land is open to your seed,
And would you fain prevent my pigs
From running there their harmless rigs?
God knows I view this compromise
With not the most approving eyes ;
I gave up my unquestioned rights
For sake of quiet days and nights ;
I offered then, you know 't is true,
To cut the piece of land in two."
"Then cut it now," growls North ;

           " Abate
Your heat," says South, "'t is now too late ;
I offered you the rocky corner,
But you, of your own good the scorner,
Refused to take it ; I am sorry ;
No doubt you might have found a quarry,
Perhaps a gold-mine, for aught I know,

Containing heaps of native rhino ;
You can't expect me to resign
My right " —

    "But where," quoth North, "are mine ?"
" *Your* rights," says tother, "well, that 's funny,
I bought the land " —

          " *I* paid the money " ;
"That," answered South, " is from the point,
The ownership, you 'll grant, is joint ;
I 'm sure my only hope and trust is
Not law so much as abstract justice,
Though, you remember, 't was agreed
That so and so — consult the deed ;
Objections now are out of date,
They might have answered once, but Fate
Quashes them at the point we 've got to ;
Obsta principiis, that 's my motto."
So saying, South began to whistle
And looked as obstinate as gristle,
While North went homeward, each brown paw
Clenched like a knot of natural law,
And all the while, in either ear,
Heard something clicking wondrous clear.

To turn now to other matters, there are two things upon which it would seem fitting to dilate somewhat more largely in this place, — the Yankee character and the Yankee dialect. And, first, of the Yankee character, which has wanted neither open maligners, nor even more dangerous enemies in the persons of those unskilful painters who have given to it that hardness, angularity, and want of proper perspective, which, in truth, belonged, not to their subject, but to their own niggard and unskilful pencil.

New England was not so much the colony of a mother country, as a Hagar driven forth into the wilderness. The little self-exiled band which came hither in 1620 came, not to seek gold, but to found a democracy. They came that they might have the privilege to work and pray, to sit upon hard benches and listen to painful preachers as long as they would, yea, even unto thirty-seventhly, if the spirit so willed it. And surely, if the Greek might boast his Thermopylæ, where three hundred men fell in resisting the Persian, we may well be proud of our Plymouth Rock, where a handful of men, women, and children not merely faced, but vanquished, winter, famine, the wilderness, and the yet more invincible *storge* that drew them back to the green island far away. These found no lotus growing upon the surly shore, the taste of which could make them forget their little native Ithaca ; nor were they so wanting to themselves in faith as to burn their ship, but could see the fair west wind belly the homeward sail, and then turn unrepining to grapple with the terrible Unknown.

As Want was the prime foe these hardy exodists had to fortress themselves against, so it is little wonder if that traditional feud is long in wearing out of the stock. The wounds of the old warfare were long a-healing, and an east wind of hard times puts a new ache into every one of them. Thrift was the first lesson in their hornbook, pointed out, letter after letter, by the lean finger of the hard schoolmistress, Necessity. Neither were those plump, rosy-gilled Englishmen that came hither, but a hard-faced, atrabilious, earnest-eyed race, stiff from long wrestling with the Lord in prayer, and who had taught Satan to dread the new Puritan hug. Add two hundred years' influence of soil, climate, and exposure, with its necessary result of idiosyncrasies, and we have the present Yankee, ful. of expedients, half-master of all trades, inventive in all but the beautiful, full of shifts, not yet capable of comfort, armed at all points against the old enemy Hunger, longanimous, good at patching, not so careful for what is best as for what will *do*, with a clasp to his purse and a button to his pocket, not skilled to build against Time, as in old countries, but against sore-pressing Need, accustomed to move the world with no πού στώ but his own two feet, and no lever but his own long forecast. A strange hybrid, indeed, did circumstance beget, here in the New World, upon the old Puritan stock, and the earth never before saw such mystic-practicalism, such niggard-geniality, such calculating-fanaticism, such cast-iron-enthusiasm, such sour-faced-humor, such close-fisted-generosity. This

new *Græculus esuriens* will make a living out of anything. He will invent new trades as well as tools. His brain is his capital, and he will get education at all risks. Put him on Juan Fernandez, and he would make a spelling-book first, and a salt-pan afterward. *In cælum, jusseris, ibit,* — or the other way either, — it is all one, so anything is to be got by it. Yet, after all, thin, speculative Jonathan is more like the Englishman of two centuries ago than John Bull himself is. He has lost somewhat in solidity, has become fluent and adaptable, but more of the original groundwork of character remains. He feels more at home with Fulke Greville, Herbert of Cherbury, Quarles, George Herbert, and Browne, than with his modern English cousins. He is nearer than John, by at least a hundred years, to Naseby, Marston Moor, Worcester, and the time when, if ever, there were true Englishmen. John Bull has suffered the idea of the Invisible to be very much fattened out of him. Jonathan is conscious still that he lives in the world of the Unseen as well as of the Seen. To move John you must make your fulcrum of solid beef and pudding ; an abstract idea will do for Jonathan.

. TO THE INDULGENT READER.

MY friend, the Rev. Mr. Wilbur, having been seized with a dangerous fit of illness, before this Introduction had passed through the press, and being incapacitated for all literary exertion, sent to me his notes, memoranda, &c., and requested me to fashion them into some shape more fitting for the general eye. This, owing to the fragmentary and disjointed state of his manuscripts, I have felt wholly unable to do ; yet, being unwilling that the reader should be deprived of such parts of his lucubrations as seemed more finished, and not well discerning how to segregate these from the rest, I have concluded to send them all to the press precisely as they are.

COLUMBUS NYE,
Pastor of a Church in Bungtown Corner.

It remains to speak of the Yankee dialect. And, first, it may be premised, in a general way, that any one much read in the writings of the early colonists need not be told that the far greater share of the words and phrases now esteemed peculiar to New England, and local there, were brought from the mother country. A person familiar with the dialect of certain portions of Massachusetts will not fail to recognize, in ordinary discourse, many words now noted in English vocabularies as archaic, the greater part of which were in common use about the time of the King James translation of the Bible. Shakespeare stands less in need of a glossary to most New Englanders than to many a native of the Old Country. The peculiarities of our speech, however, are rapidly wearing out. As there is no country where reading is so universal and newspapers are so multitudinous, so no phrase remains long local, but is transplanted in the mail-bags to every remotest corner of the land. Consequently our dialect approaches nearer to uniformity than that of any other nation.

The English have complained of us for coining new words. Many of those so stigmatized were old ones by them forgotten, and all make now an unquestioned part of the currency, wherever English is spoken. Undoubtedly, we have a right to make new words, as they are needed by the fresh aspects under which life presents itself here in the New World; and, indeed, wherever a language is alive, it grows. It might be questioned whether we could not establish a stronger title to the ownership of the English tongue than the mother-islanders themselves. Here, past all question, is to be its great home and centre. And not only is it already spoken here by greater numbers, but with a far higher popular average of correctness than in Britain. The great writers of it, too, we might claim as ours, were ownership to be settled by the number of readers and lovers.

As regards the provincialisms to be met with in this volume, I may say that the reader will not find one which is not (as I believe) either native or imported with the early settlers, nor one which I have not, with my own ears, heard in familiar use. In the metrical portion of the book, I have endeavored to adapt the spelling as nearly as possible to the ordinary mode of pronunciation. Let the reader who deems me over-particular remember this caution of Martial: —

" *Quem recitas, meus est, O Fidentine, libel-*
     lus ;
    Sed male cum recitas, incipit esse tuus."

A few further explanatory remarks will not be impertinent.

I shall barely lay down a few general rules for the reader's guidance.

1. The genuine Yankee never gives the rough sound to the *r* when he can help it, and often displays considerable ingenuity in avoiding it even before a vowel.

2. He seldom sounds the final *g*, a piece of self-denial, if we consider his partiality for nasals. The same of the final *d*, as *han'* and *stan'* for *hand* and *stand.*

3. The *h* in such words as *while, when, where,* he omits altogether.

4. In regard to *a*, he shows some inconsistency, sometimes giving a close and obscure sound, as *hev* for *have, hendy* for *handy, ez* for *as, thet* for *that,* and again giving it the broad sound it has in *father,* as *hânsome* for *handsome.*

5. To the sound *ou* he prefixes an *e* (hard to exemplify otherwise than orally.)

The following passage in Shakespeare he would recite thus: —

" Neow is the winta uv eour discontent
Med glorious summa by this sun o' Yock,
An' all the cleouds thet leowered upun eour
     heouse
In the deep buzzum o' the oshin buried ;
Neow air eour breows beound 'ith victorious
     wreaths ;
Eour breused arms hung up fer monimunce;
Eour starn alarums chinged to merry meet
     ins,
Eour dreffle marches to delighsfle masures

Grim-visaged war heth smeuthed his wrinkled
  front,
Aa' neow, instid o' mountin' barebid steeds
To fright the souls o' ferŝle edverseries,
He capers nimly in a lady's chämber,
To the lascivious pleasin' uv a loot."

6. *Au*, in such words as *daughter*
and *slaughter*, he pronounces *ah.*

7. To the dish thus seasoned add a
drawl *ad libitum.*

[Mr. Wilbur's notes here become entirely
fragmentary. — C. N.]

a. Unable to procure a likeness of
Mr. Biglow, I thought the curious reader might be gratified with a sight of
the editorial effigies. And here a choice
between two was offered, — the one a
profile (entirely black) cut by Doyle,
the other a portrait painted by a native
artist of much promise. The first of
these seemed wanting in expression,
and in the second a slight obliquity of
the visual organs has been heightened
(perhaps from an over-desire of force
on the part of the artist) into too close
an approach to actual *strabismus.* This
slight divergence in my optical apparatus from the ordinary model—however
I may have been taught to regard it in
the light of a mercy rather than a cross,
since it enabled me to give as much of
directness and personal application to
my discourses as met the wants of my
congregation, without risk of offending
any by being supposed to have him or
her in my eye (as the saying is)—
seemed yet to Mrs. Wilbur a sufficient
objection to the engraving of the aforesaid painting. We read of many who
either absolutely refused to allow the
copying of their features, as especially
did Plotinus and Agesilaus among the
ancients, not to mention the more modern instances of Scioppius, Palæottus,
Pinellus, Velserus, Gataker, and others,
or were indifferent thereto, as Cromwell.

β. Yet was Cæsar desirous of concealing his baldness. *Per contra*, my Lord
Protector's carefulness in the matter of
his wart might be cited Men generally more desirous of being *improved* in
their portraits than characters. Shall
probably find very unflattered likeness-
es of ourselves in Recording Angel's
gallery.

γ. Whether any of our national
peculiarities may be traced to our
use of stoves, as a certain close-
ness of the lips in pronunciation, and
a smothered smoulderingness of dis-
position seldom roused to open flame?
An unrestrained intercourse with fire
probably conducive to generosity and
hospitality of soul. Ancient Mexicans
used stoves, as the friar Augustin Ruiz
reports, Hakluyt, III., 468, — but Pop-
ish priests not always reliable authority.
To-day picked my Isabella grapes.
Crop injured by attacks of rose-bug in
the spring. Whether Noah was justifiable in preserving this class of insects?

δ. Concerning Mr. Biglow's pedigree.
Tolerably certain that there was never
a poet among his ancestors. An ordi-
nation hymn attributed to a maternal
uncle, but perhaps a sort of production
not demanding the creative faculty.

His grandfather a painter of the gran-
diose or Michael Angelo school. Seldom painted objects smaller than
houses or barns, and these with uncommon expression.

ε. Of the Wilburs no complete pedi
gree. The crest said to be a *wild boar*,
whence, perhaps, the name.(?) A connection with the Earls of Wilbraham
(*quasi* wild boar ham) might be made
out. This suggestion worth following
up. In 1677, John W. m. Expect ——,
had issue, 1. John, 2. Haggai, 3. Expect, 4. Ruhamah, 5. Desire.

"Hear lyes yᵉ bodye of Mrs Expect Wilber,
  Yᵉ crewell salvages they kil'd her
Together wᵗʰ other Christian soles eleaven,
  October yᵉ ix daye, 1707.
Yᵉ stream of Jordan sh' as crost ore
  And now expeacts me on yᵉ other shore :
I live in hope her soon to join ;
  Her earthlye yeeres were forty and nine."
    From Gravestone in Pekussett, North
      Parish.

This is unquestionably the same John who afterward (1711) married Tabitha Hagg or Ragg.

But if this were the case, she seems to have died early; for only three years after, namely, 1714, we have evidence that he married Winifred, daughter of Lieutenant Tipping.

He seems to have been a man of substance, for we find him in 1696 conveying "one undivided eightieth part of a salt-meadow" in Yabbok, and he commanded a sloop in 1702.

Those who doubt the importance of genealogical studies *fuste potius quam argumento erudiendi.*

I trace him as far as 1723, and there lose him. In that year he was chosen selectman.

No gravestone. Perhaps overthrown when new hearse-house was built, 1802.

He was probably the son of John, who came from Bilham Comit. Salop. circa 1642.

This first John was a man of considerable importance, being twice mentioned with the honorable prefix of *Mr.* in the town records. Name spelt with two *l*-s.

"Hear lyeth yᵉ bod [*stone unhappily broken.*]

Mr. Ihon Willber [Esq.] [*I inclose this in brackets as doubtful. To me it seems clear.*]

Ob't die [*illegible; looks like xviii.*] . . . . .
    iii [*prob.* 1693.]

.   .   .   .   .   paynt
          deseased seinte :
A friend and [fath]er untoe all yᵉ opreast,
Hee gave yᵉ wicked familists noe reast,
When Sat [an bl]ewe his Antinomian blaste,
Wee clong to [Willber as a steadf]ast maste.
[Agaynst yᵉ horrid Qua[kers] . . . . . "

It is greatly to be lamented that this curious epitaph is mutilated. It is said that the sacrilegious British soldiers made a target of this stone during the war of Independence. How odious an animosity which pauses not at the grave! How brutal that which spares not the monuments of authentic history! This is not improbably from the pen of Rev. Moody Pyram, who is mentioned by Hubbard as having been noted for a silver vein of poetry. If his papers be still extant, a copy might possibly be recovered.

THE BIGLOW PAPERS.

No. I.

A LETTER

FROM MR. EZEKIEL BIGLOW OF JAALAM TO THE HON. JOSEPH T. BUCKINGHAM, EDITOR OF THE BOSTON COURIER, INCLOSING A POEM OF HIS SON, MR. HOSEA BIGLOW.

JAYLEM, june 1846.

MISTER EDDYTER :— Our Hosea wuz down to Boston last week, and he see a cruetin Sarjunt a struttin round as popler as a hen with 1 chicking, with 2 fellers a drummin and fifin arter him like all nater. the sarjunt he thout Hosea hed n't gut his i teeth cut cos he looked a kindo 's though he 'd jest com down, so he cal'lated to hook him in, but Hosy wood n't take none o' his sarse for all he hed much as 20 Rooster's tales stuck onto his hat and eenamost enuf brass a bobbin up and down on his shoulders and figureed onto his coat and trousis, let alone wut nater hed sot in his featers, to make a 6 pounder out on.

wal, Hosea he com home considerabal riled, and arter I 'd gone to bed I heern Him a thrashin round like a short-tailed Bull in fli-time. The old Woman ses she to me ses she, Zekle, ses she, our Hosee 's gut the chollery or suthin anuther ses she, don't you Bee skeered, ses I, he 's oney amakin pottery * ses i, he 's ollers on hand at that ere busynes like Da & martin, and shure enuf, cum mornin, Hosy he cum down stares full chizzle, hare on

Aut insanir, aut versos facit. — H. W.

eend and cote tales flyin, and sot rite of to go reed his varses to Parson Wilbur bein he haint aney grate shows o' book larnin himself, bimeby he cum back and sed the parson wuz dreffle tickled with 'em as i hoop you will Be, and said they wuz True grit.

Hosea ses taint hardly fair to call 'em hisn now, cos the parson kind o' slicked off sum o' the last varses, but he told Hosee he did n't want to put his ore in to tetch to the Rest on 'em, bein they wuz verry well As thay wuz, and then Hosy ses he sed suthin a nuther about Simplex Mundishes or sum sech feller, but I guess Hosea kind o' did n't hear him, for I never hearn o' nobody o' that name in this villadge, and I 've lived here man and boy 76 year cum next tater diggin, and thair aint no wheres a kitting spryer 'n I be.

If you print 'em I wish you 'd jest let folks know who hosy's father is, cos my ant Keziah used to say it 's nater to be curus ses she, she aint livin though and he 's a likely kind o' lad.

EZEKIEL BIGLOW.

Thrash away, you 'll hev to rattle
  On them kittle-drums o' yourn, —
'Taint a knowin' kind o' cattle
  Thet is ketched with mouldy corn ;
Put in stiff, you fifer feller,
  Let folks see how spry you be, —
Guess you 'll toot till you are yeller
  'Fore you git ahold o' me !

Thet air flag 's a leetle rotten,
  Hope it aint your Sunday's best ; —

Fact ! it takes a sight o' cotton
  To stuff out a soger's chest :
Sence we farmers hev to pay fer 't,
  Ef you must wear humps like these,
Sposin' you should try salt hay fer 't,
  It would du ez slick ez grease.

'T would n't suit them Southun fellers,
  They 're a dreffle graspin' set,
We must ollers blow the bellers
  Wen they want their irons het ;
May be it 's all right ez preachin',
  But *my* narves it kind o' grates,
Wen I see the overreachin'
  O' them nigger-drivin' States.

Them thet rule us, them slave-traders,
  Haint they cut a thunderin' swarth
(Helped by Yankee renegaders),
  Thru the vartu o' the North !
We begin to think it 's nater
  To take sarse an' not be riled ; —
Who 'd expect to see a tater
  All on eend at bein' biled ?

Ez fer war, I call it murder, —
  There you hev it plain an' flat ;
I don't want to go no furder
  Than my Testyment fer that ;
God hez sed so plump an' fairly,
  It 's ez long ez it is broad,
An' you 've gut to git up airly
  Ef you want to take in God.

'Taint your eppyletts an' feathers
  Make the thing a grain more right ;
'Taint afollerin' your bell-wethers
  Will excuse ye in His sight ;
Ef you take a sword an' dror it,
  An' go stick a feller thru,
Guv'ment aint to answer for it,
  God 'll send the bill to you.

Wut 's the use o' meetin'-goin'
  Every Sabbath, wet or dry,
Ef it 's right to go amowin'
  Feller-men like oats an' rye ?
I dunno but wut it 's pooty
  Trainin' round in bobtail coats, —
But it 's curus Christian dooty
  This 'ere cuttin' folks's throats.

They may talk o' Freedom's airy
  Tell they 're pupple in the face, —

It 's a grand gret cemetary
  Fer the barthrights of our race ;
They jest want this Californy
  So 's to lug new slave-states in
To abuse ye, an' to scorn ye,
  An' to plunder ye like sin.

Aint it cute to see a Yankee
  Take sech everlastin' pains,
All to git the Devil's thankee
  Helpin' on 'em weld their chains ?
Wy, it 's jest ez clear ez figgers,
  Clear ez one an' one make two,
Chaps thet make black slaves o' niggers
  Want to make wite slaves o' you.

Tell ye jest the eend I 've come to
  Arter cipherin' plaguy smart,
An' it makes a handy sum, tu,
  Any gump could larn by heart ;
Laborin' man an' laborin' woman
  Hev one glory an' one shame,
Ev'y thin' thet 's done inhuman
  Injers all on 'em the same.

'Taint by turnin' out to hack folks
  You 're agoin' to git your right,
Nor by lookin' down on black folks
  Coz you 're put upon by wite ;
Slavery aint o' nary color,
  'Taint the hide thet makes it wus,
All it keers fer in a feller
  'S jest to make him fill its pus.

Want to tackle *me* in, du ye ?
  I expect you 'll hev to wait ;
Wen cold lead puts daylight thru ye
  You 'll begin to kal'late ;
S'pose the crows wun't fall to pickin'
  All the carkiss from your bones,
Coz you helped to give a lickin'
  To them poor half-Spanish drones ?

Jest go home an' ask our Nancy
  Wether I 'd be sech a goose
Ez to jine ye, — guess you 'd fancy
  The etarnal bung wuz loose !
She wants me fer home consumption,
  Let alone the hay 's to mow, —
Ef you 're arter folks o' gumption,
  You 've a darned long row to hoe.

Take them editors thet 's crowin'
  Like a cockerel three months old, —

Don't ketch any on 'em goin',
  Though they *be* so blasted bold ;
Aint they a prime lot o' fellers?
  'Fore they think on't guess they'll
    sprout
(Like a peach thet 's got the yellers),
  With the meanness bustin' out.

Wal, go 'long to help 'em stealin'
  Bigger pens to cram with slaves,
Help the men thet 's ollers dealin'
  Insults on your fathers' graves ;
Help the strong to grind the feeble,
  Help the many agin the few,
Help the men thet call your people
  Witewashed slaves an' peddlin' crew!

Massachusetts, God forgive her,
  She 's akneelin' with the rest,
She, thet ough' to ha' clung ferever
  In her grand old eagle-nest ;
She thet ough' to stand so fearless
  Wile the wracks are round her hurled,
Holdin' up a beacon peerless
  To the oppressed of all the world !

Haint they sold your colored seamen?
  Haint they made your env'ys w'iz ?
Wut 'll make ye act like freemen?
  Wut 'll git your dander riz ?
Come, I 'll tell ye wut I 'm thinkin'
  Is our dooty in this fix,
They 'd ha' done 't ez quick ez winkin'
  In the days o' seventy-six.

Clang the bells in every steeple,
  Call all true men to disown
The tradoocers of our people,
  The enslavers o' their own ;
Let our dear old Bay State proudly
  Put the trumpet to her mouth,
Let her ring this messidge loudly
  In the ears of all the South : —

"I 'll return ye good fer evil
  Much ez we frail mortils can,
But I wun't go help the Devil
  Makin' man the cus o' man ;
Call me coward, call me traiter,
  Jest ez suits your mean idees, —
Here I stand a tyrant-hater
  An' the friend o' God an' Peace !"

Ef I 'd *my* way I hed ruther
  We should go to work an' part, —

They take one way, we take t'other, —
  Guess it would n't break my heart ;
Man hed ough' to put asunder
  Them thet God has noways jined ;
An' I should n't gretly wonder
  Ef there 's thousands o' my mind.

[The first recruiting sergeant on record I conceive to have been that individual who is mentioned in the Book of Job as *going to and fro in the earth, and walking up and down in it.* Bishop Latimer will have him to have been a bishop, but to me that other calling would appear more congenial. The sect of Cainites is not yet extinct, who esteemed the first-born of Adam to be the most worthy, not only because of that privilege of primogeniture, but inasmuch as he was able to overcome and slay his younger brother. That was a wise saying of the famous Marquis Pescara to the Papal Legate, that *it was impossible for men to serve Mars and Christ at the same time.* Yet in time past the profession of arms was judged to be κατ' ἐξοχήν that of a gentleman, nor does this opinion want for strenuous upholders even in our day. Must we suppose, then, that the profession of Christianity was only intended for losels, or, at best, to afford an opening for plebeian ambition ? Or shall we hold with that nicely metaphysical Pomeranian, Captain Vratz, who was Count Konigsmark's chief instrument in the murder of Mr. Thynne, that the Scheme of Salvation has been arranged with an especial eye to the necessities of the upper classes, and that " God would consider a *gentleman* and deal with him suitably to the condition and profession he had placed him in"? It may be said of us all, *Exemplo plus quam ratione vivimus.*—H. W.]

No. II.

A LETTER

FROM MR. HOSEA BIGLOW TO THE HON. J. T. BUCKINGHAM, EDITOR OF THE BOSTON COURIER, COVERING A LETTER FROM MR. B. SAWIN, PRIVATE IN THE MASSACHUSETTS REGIMENT.

[This letter of Mr. Sawin's was not originally written in verse. Mr. Biglow, thinking it peculiarly susceptible of metrical adornment, translated it, so to speak, into his own vernacular tongue. This is not the time to consider the question, whether rhyme be a mode of expression natural to the human

race. If leisure from other and more important avocations be granted, I will handle
the matter more at large in an appendix to
the present volume. In this place I will
barely remark, that I have sometimes noticed
in the unlanguaged prattlings of infants a
fondness for alliteration, assonance, and even
rhyme, in which natural predisposition we
may trace the three degrees through which
our Anglo-Saxon verse rose to its culmina-
tion in the poetry of Pope. I would not be
understood as questioning in these remarks
that pious theory which supposes that children, if left entirely to themselves, would
naturally discourse in Hebrew. For this the
authority of one experiment is claimed, and
I could, with Sir Thomas Browne, desire
its establishment, inasmuch as the acquire-
ment of that sacred tongue would thereby be facilitated. I am aware that Herodo-
tus states the conclusion of Psammeticus to
have been in favor of a dialect of the Phry-
gian. But, beside the chance that a trial of
this importance would hardly be blessed to
a Pagan monarch whose only motive was
curiosity, we have on the Hebrew side the
comparatively recent investigation of James
the Fourth of Scotland. I will add to this
prefatory remark, that Mr. Sawin, though
a native of Jaalam, has never been a stated
attendant on the religious exercises of my
congregation. I consider my humble efforts
prospered in that not one of my sheep hath
ever indued the wolf's clothing of war, save
for the comparatively innocent diversion of
a militia training. Not that my flock are
backward to undergo the hardships of *defensive* warfare. They serve cheerfully in
the great array which fights even unto death
pro aris et focis, accoutred with the spade,
the axe, the plane, the sledge, the spelling-
book, and other such effectual weapons
against want and ignorance and unthrift. I
have taught them (under God) to esteem our
human institutions as but tents of a night,
to be stricken whenever Truth puts the bugle
to her lips and sounds a march to the heights
of wider-viewed intelligence and more perfect organization. — H. W.]

MISTER BUCKINUM, the follerin Billet was writ hum by a Yung feller of
our town that wuz cussed fool enuff to
goe atrottin inter Miss Chiff arter a
Drum and fife. it ain't Nater for a
feller to let on that he 's sick o' any
bizness that He went intu off his own
free will and a Cord, but I rather cal'-
late he 's middlin tired o' volunteerin By
this Time. i beleeve u may put depen-
dunts on his statement. For I never
heered nothin bad on him let Alone his
havin what Parson Wilbur cals a *pong-
shong* for cocktales, and he ses it wuz a

soshiashun of idees sot him agoin arter
the Crootin Sargient cos he wore a
cocktale onto his hat.

his Folks gin the letter to me and i
shew it to parson Wilbur and he ses it
oughter Bee printed. send It to mister Buckinum, ses he, i don't ollers
agree with him, ses he, but by Time,*
ses he, I *du* like a feller that aint a
Feared.

I have intusspussed a Few reflech-
shuns hear and thair. We 're kind o'
prest with Hayin.

      Ewers respecfly
        HOSEA BIGLOW.

THIS kind o' sogerin' aint a mite like
    our October trainin',
A chap could clear right out from there
    ef 't only looked liked rainin',
An' th' Cunnles, tu, could kiver up
    their shappoes with bandanners,
An' send the insines skootin' to the
    bar-room with their banners
(Fear o' gittin' on 'em spotted), an' a
    feller could cry quarter
Ef he fired away his ramrod arter tu
    much rum an' water.
Recollect wut fun we hed, you'n' I an'
    Ezry Hollis,
Up there to Waltham plain last fall,
    along o' the Cornwallis? †
This sort o' thing aint *jest* like thet, —
    I wish thet I wuz furder, — ‡
Nimepunce a day fer killin' folks comes
    kind o' low fer murder,
(Wy I 've worked out to slarterin' some
    fer Deacon Cephas Billins,
An' in the hardest times there wuz I
    ollers fetched ten shillins,)

* In relation to this expression, I cannot
but think that Mr. Biglow has been too hasty
in attributing it to me. Though Time be a
comparatively innocent personage to swear
by, and though Longinus in his discourse
Περὶ Ὕψους has commended timely oaths
as not only a useful but sublime figure of
speech, yet I have always kept my lips free
from that abomination. *Odi profanum vul-
gus*, I hate your swearing and hectoring fellows. — H. W.

† i hait the Site of a feller with a muskit as
I du pizn But their *is* fun to a cornwallis I
aint agoin' to deny it. — H. B.

‡ he means Not quite so fur I guess. — H.
B.

There 's sutthin' gits into my throat
  thet makes it hard to swaller,
It comes so nateral to think about a
  hempen collar;
It 's glory, — but, in spite o' all my try-
  in' to git callous,
I feel a kind o' in a cart, aridin' to the
  gallus.
But wen it comes to *bein'* killed, — I
  tell ye I felt streaked
The fust time 't ever I found out wy
  baggonets wuz peaked;
Here 's how it wuz : I started out to go
  to a fandango,
The sentinul he ups an' sez, "Thet 's
  furder 'an you can go."
"None o' your sarse," sez I ; sez he,
  "Stan' back ! " "Aint you a bus-
  ter ? "
Sez I, "I 'm up to all thet air, I guess
  I 've ben to muster ;
I know wy sentinuls air sot ; you aint
  agoin' to eat us ;
Caleb haint no monopoly to court the
  seenoreetas ;
My folks to hum air full ez good ez
  hisn be, by golly ! "
An' so ez I wuz goin' by, not thinkin'
  wut would folly,
The everlastin' cus he stuck his one-
  pronged pitchfork in me
An' made a hole right thru my close ez
  ef I wuz an in'my.

Wal, it beats all how big I felt hooraw-
  in' in ole Funnel
Wen Mister Bolles he gin the sword to
  our Leftenant Cunnle,
(It 's Mister Secondary Bolles,* thet
  writ the prize peace essay ;
Thet 's why he did n't list himself along
  o' us, I dessay,)
An' Rantoul, tu, talked pooty loud, but
  don't put *his* foot in it,
Coz human life 's so sacred thet he 's
  principled agin it, —
Though I myself can't rightly see it 's
  any wus achokin' on 'em,
Than puttin' bullets thru their lights, or
  with a bagnet pokin' on 'em ;

* the ignerant creeter means Sekketary ;
but he ollers stuck to his books like cobbler's
wax to an ile-stone. — H. B.

How dreffle slick he reeled it off (like
  Blitz at our lyceum
Ahaulin' ribbins from his chops so quick
  you skeercely see 'em),
About the Anglo-Saxon race (an' saxons
  would be handy
To du the buryin' down here upon the
  Rio Grandy),
About our patriotic pas an' our star-
  spangled banner,
Our country's bird alookin' on an' sing-
  in' out hosanner,
An' how he (Mister B. himself) wuz
  happy fer Ameriky, —
I felt, ez sister Patience sez, a leetle
  mite histericky.
I felt, I swon, ez though it wuz a dref-
  fle kind o' privilege
Atrampin' round thru Boston streets
  among the gutter's drivelage ;
I act'lly thought it wuz a treat to hear
  a little drummin',
An' it did bonyfidy soem millanyum
  wuz acomin'
Wen all on us got suits (darned like
  them wore in the state prison)
An' every feller felt ez though all Mexico wuz hisn.*

This 'ere 's about the meanest place a
  skunk could wal diskiver
(Saltillo's Mexican, I b'lieve, fer wut
  we call Salt-river) ;
The sort o' trash a feller gits to eat
  doos beat all nater,
I 'd give a year's pay fer a smell o' one
  good blue-nose tater ;
The country here thet Mister Bolles
  declared to be so charmin'
Throughout is swarmin' with the most
  alarmin' kind o' varmin'.

He talked about delishis froots, but
  then it wuz a wopper all,
The holl on 't 's mud an' prickly pears,
  with here an' there a chapparal ;

* it must be aloud that thare 's a streak or
nater in lovin' sho, but it sartinly is 1 of the
curusest things in nater to see a rispecktable
dri goods dealer (deekon off a chutch may-
by) a riggin' himself out in the Weigh they
du and struttin' round in the Reign aspilin'
his trowsis and makin' wet goods of himself.
Ef any thin's foolisher and moor dicklus than
militerry gloary it is milishy gloary. — H. B.

You see a feller peekin' out, an', fust
    you know, a lariat
Is round your throat an' you a copse, 'fore
    you can say, "Wut air ye at?" *
You never see sech darned gret bugs (it
    may not be irrelevant
To say I 've seen a *scarabæus pilula-
    rius* † big ez a year old elephant),
The rigiment come up one day in time
    to stop a red bug
From runnin' off with Cunnle Wright,
    — 't wuz jest a common *cimex
    lectularius.*

One night I started up on eend an'
    thought I wuz to hum agin,
I heern a horn, thinks I it 's Sol the
    fisherman hez come agin, —
His bellowses is sound enough, — ez
    I 'm a livin' creeter,
I felt a thing go thru my leg, — 't wuz
    nothin' more 'n a skeeter !
Then there 's the yaller fever, tu, they
    call it here el vomito, —
(Come, thet wun't du, you landcrab
    there, I tell ye to le' *go* my toe !
My gracious ! it 's a scorpion thet 's
    took a shine to play with 't,
I darsn't skeer the tarnal thing fer fear
    he 'd run away with 't.)
Afore I come away from hum I hed a
    strong persuasion
Thet Mexicans worn't human beans,‡
    — an ourang outang nation,
A sort o' folks a chap could kill an'
    never dream on 't arter,
No more 'n a feller 'd dream o' pigs thet
    he hed hed to slarter ;
I 'd an idee thet they were built arter
    the darkie fashion all,
An' kickin' colored folks about, you
    know, 's a kind o' national ;

But wen I jined I wornt so wise ez thet
    air queen o' Sheby,
Fer, come to look at 'em, they aint
    much diff'rent from wut we be,
An' here we air ascrougin' 'em out o'
    thir own dominions,
Ashelterin' 'em, ez Caleb sez, under
    our eagle's pinions,
Wich means to take a feller up jest by
    the slack o' 's trowsis
An' walk him Spanish clean right out
    o' all his homes an' houses ;
Wal, it doos seem a curus way, but then
    hooraw fer Jackson !
It must be right, fer Caleb sez it 's reg'-
    lar Anglo-saxon.
The Mex'cans don't fight fair, they say,
    they piz'n all the water,
An' du amazin' lots o' things thet is n't
    wut they ough' to ;
Bein' they haint no lead, they make
    their bullets out o' copper
An' shoot the darned things at us, tu,
    wich Caleb sez aint proper ;
He sez they 'd ough' to stan' right up
    an' let us pop 'em fairly
(Guess wen he ketches 'em at thet he 'll
    hev to git up airly),
Thet our nation 's bigger 'n theirn an'
    so its rights air bigger,
An' thet it 's all to make 'em free thet
    we air pullin' trigger,
Thet Anglo Saxondom's idee 's abreak-
    in' 'em to pieces,
An' thet idee 's thet every man doos
    jest wut he damn pleases ;
Ef I don't make his meanin' clear, per-
    haps in some respex I can,
I know thet "every man" don't mean
    a nigger or a Mexican ;
An' there 's another thing I know, an
    thet is, ef these creeturs,
Thet stick an Anglosaxon mask onto
    State-prison feeturs,
Should come to Jaalam Centre fer to
    argify an' spout on 't,
The gals 'ould count the silver spoons
    the minnit they cleared out on 't.

This goin' ware glory waits ye haint
    one agreeable feetur,
An' ef it worn't fer wakin' snakes, I 'd
    home agin short meter ;
O, would n't I be off, quick time, ef 't
    worn't thet I wuz sartin

---

* these fellers are verry proppilly called
Rank Heroes, and the more tha kill the
ranker and more Herowick tha bekum. —
H. B.

† it wuz "tumblebug" as he Writ it, but
the parson put the Latten instid. i sed tother
maid better meeter, but he said tha was ed-
dykated peepl to Boston and tha would n't
stan' it no how. idnow as the *wood* and idnow *as* the wood. — H. B.

‡ he means human beins, that 's wut he
means. i spose he kinder thought tha wuz
human beans ware the Xisle Poles comes
from. — H. B.

They'd let the daylight into me to pay
  me fer desertin'!
I don't approve o' tellin' tales, but jest
  to you I may state
Our ossifers aint wut they wuz afore
  they left the Bay-State;
Then it wuz "Mister Sawin, sir, you're
  middlin' well now, be ye?
Step up an' take a nipper, sir; I'm
  dreffle glad to see ye";
But now it's "Ware's my eppylet?
  here, Sawin, step an' fetch it!
An' mind your eye, be thund'rin' spry,
  or, damn ye, you shall ketch it!"
Wal, ez the Doctor sez, some pork will
  bile so, but by mighty,
Ef I hed some on 'em to hum, I'd give
  'em linkum vity,
I'd play the rogue's march on their
  hides an' other music follerin'—
But I must close my letter here, fer one
  on 'em's ahollerin'
These Anglosaxon ossifers,— wal, taint
  no use ajawin',
I'm safe enlisted fer the war,
    Yourn,
      BIRDOFREDOM SAWIN.

[Those have not been wanting (as, indeed, when hath Satan been to seek for attorneys?) who have maintained that our late in-road upon Mexico was undertaken not so much for the avenging of any national quarrel, as for the spreading of free institutions and of Protestantism. *Capita vix duabus Anticyris medenda!* Verily I admire that no pious sergeant among these new Crusaders beheld Martin Luther riding at the front of the host upon a tamed pontifical bull, as, in that former invasion of Mexico, the zealous Gomara (spawn though he were of the Scarlet Woman) was favored with a vision of St. James of Compostella, skewering the infidels upon his apostolical lance. We read, also, that Richard of the lion heart, having gone to Palestine on a similar errand of mercy, was divinely encouraged to cut the throats of such Paynims as refused to swallow the bread of life (doubtless that they might be thereafter incapacitated for swallowing the filthy gobbets of Mahound) by angels of heaven, who cried to the king and his knights,—*Seigneurs, tuez! tuez!* providentially using the French tongue, as being the only one understood by their auditors. This would argue for the pantoglottism of these celestial intelligences, while, on the other hand, the Devil, *teste* Cotton Mather, is unversed in certain of the Indian dialects. Yet must he be a semeiologist the most expert,

making himself intelligible to every people and kindred by signs; no other discourse, indeed, being needful, than such as the mackerel-fisher holds with his finned quarry, who, if other bait be wanting, can by a bare bit of white rag at the end of a string captivate those foolish fishes. Such piscatorial persuasion is Satan cunning in. Before one he trails a hat and feather, or a bare feather without a hat; before another, a Presidential chair or a tidewaiter's stool, or a pulpit in the city, no matter what. To us, dangling there over our heads, they seem junkets dropped out of the seventh heaven, sops dipped in nectar, but, once in our mouths, they are all one, bits of fuzzy cotton.

This, however, by the way. It is time now *revocare gradum.* While so many miracles of this sort, vouched by eyewitnesses, have encouraged the arms of Papists, not to speak of Echetlæus at Marathon and those *Dioscuri* (whom we must conclude imps of the pit) who sundry times captained the pagan Roman soldiery, it is strange that our first American crusade was not in some such wise also signalized. Yet it is said that the Lord hath manifestly prospered our armies. This opens the question, whether, when our hands are strengthened to make great slaughter of our enemies, it be absolutely and demonstratively certain that this might is added to us from above, or whether some Potentate from an opposite quarter may not have a finger in it, as there are few pies into which his meddling digits are not thrust. Would the Sanctifier and Setter-apart of the seventh day have assisted in a victory gained on the Sabbath, as was one in the late war? Do we not know from Josephus, that, careful of His decree, a certain river in Judæa abstained from flowing on the day of Rest? Or has that day become less an object of his especial care since the year 1697, when so manifest a providence occurred to Mr. William Trowbridge, in answer to whose prayers, when he and all on shipboard with him were starving, a dolphin was sent daily, "which was enough to serve 'em; only on *Saturdays* they still catched a couple, and on the *Lord's Days* they could catch none at all"? Haply they might have been permitted, by way of mortification, to take some few sculpins (those banes of the salt-water angler), which unseemly fish would, moreover, have conveyed to them a symbolical reproof for their breach of the day, being known in the rude dialect of our mariners as *Cape Cod Clergymen.*

It has been a refreshment to many nice consciences to know that our Chief Magistrate would not regard with eyes of approval the (by many esteemed) sinful pastime of dancing, and I own myself to be so far of that mind, that I could not but set my face against this Mexican Polka, though danced to the Presidential piping with a Gubernatorial second. If ever the country should be seized with another such mania *pro propaganda fide*, I think it would be wise to fill our bombshells with alternate copies of the Cambridge Platform and the Thirty-nine Articles, which would produce a mixture of the highest explosive power, and to wrap every one of our cannon-balls in a leaf of the New Testament, the reading of which is denied to those who sit in the darkness of Popery. Those iron evangelists would thus be able to disseminate vital religion and Gospel truth in quarters inaccessible to the ordinary missionary. I have seen lads, unimpregnate with the more sublimated punctiliousness of Walton, secure pickerel, taking their unwary *siesta* beneath the lily-pads too high the surface, with a gun and small shot. Why not, then, since gunpowder was unknown in the time of the Apostles (not to enter here upon the question whether it were discovered before that period by the Chinese), suit our metaphor to the age in which we live, and say *shooters* as well as *fishers* of men?

I do much fear that we shall be seized now and then with a Protestant fervor, as long as we have neighbor Naboths whose wallowings in Papistical mire excite our horror in exact proportion to the size and desirableness of their vineyards. Yet I rejoice that some earnest Protestants have been made by this war, — I mean those who protested against it. Fewer they were than I could wish, for one might imagine America to have been colonized by a tribe of those nondescript African animals the Aye-Ayes, so difficult a word is *No* to us all. There is some malformation or defect of the vocal organs, which either prevents our uttering it at all, or gives it so thick a pronunciation as to be unintelligible. A mouth filled with the national pudding, or watering in expectation thereof, is wholly incompetent to this refractory monosyllable. An abject and herpetic Public Opinion is the Pope, the Anti-Christ, for us to protest against *e corde cordium*. And by what College of Cardinals is this our God's-vicar, our binder and looser, elected? Very like, by the sacred conclave of Tag, Rag, and Bobtail, in the gracious atmosphere of the grog-shop. Yet it is of this that we must all be puppets. This thumps the pulpit-cushion, this guides the editor's pen, this wags the senator's tongue. This decides what Scriptures are canonical, and shuffles Christ away into the Apocrypha. According to that sentence fathered upon Solon, Οὕτω δημόσιον κακὸν ἔρχεται οἰκαδ᾽ ἑκάστῳ. This unclean spirit is skilful to assume various shapes. I have known it to enter my own study and nudge my elbow of a Saturday, under the semblance of a wealthy member of my congregation. It were a great blessing, if every particular of what in the sum we call popular sentiment could carry about the name of its manufacturer stamped legibly upon it. I gave a stab under the fifth rib to that pestilent fallacy, — "Our country, right or wrong," — by tracing its original to a

speech of Ensign Cilley at a dinner of the Bungtown Fencibles. — H. W.

No. III.

WHAT MR. ROBINSON THINKS.

[A FEW remarks on the following verses will not be out of place. The satire in them was not meant to have any personal, but only a general, application. Of the gentleman upon whose letter they were intended as a commentary Mr. Biglow had never heard, till he saw the letter itself. The position of the satirist is oftentimes one which he would not have chosen, had the election been left to himself. In attacking bad principles, he is obliged to select some individual who has made himself their exponent, and in whom they are impersonate, to the end that what he says may not, through ambiguity, be dissipated *tenues in auras*. For what says Seneca? *Longum iter per præcepta, breve et efficace per exempla.* A bad principle is comparatively harmless while it continues to be an abstraction, nor can the general mind comprehend it fully till it is printed in that large type which all men can read at sight, namely, the life and character, the sayings and doings, of particular persons. It is one of the cunningest fetches of Satan, that he never exposes himself directly to our arrows, but, still dodging behind this neighbor or that acquaintance, compels us to wound him through them, if at all. He holds our affections as hostages, the while he patches up a truce with our conscience.

Meanwhile, let us not forget that the aim of the true satirist is not to be severe upon persons, but only upon falsehood, and, as Truth and Falsehood start from the same point, and sometimes even go along together for a little way, his business is to follow the path of the latter after it diverges, and to show her floundering in the bog at the end of it. Truth is quite beyond the reach of satire. There is so brave a simplicity in her, that she can no more be made ridiculous than an oak or a pine. The danger of the satirist is, that continual use may deaden his sensibility to the force of language. He becomes more and more liable to strike harder than he knows or intends. He may be careful to put on his boxing-gloves, and yet forget, that, the older they grow, the more plainly may the knuckles inside be felt. Moreover, in the heat of contest, the eye is insensibly drawn to the crown of victory, whose tawdry tinsel glitters through that dust of the ring which obscures Truth's wreath of simple leaves. I have sometimes thought that my young friend, Mr. Biglow, needed a monitory hand laid on his arm, — *aliquid sufflaminandus erat*. I have never thought it good husbandry to water the tender plants of reform with *aqua fortis*, yet, where so much is to do in the beds, he were a sorry gardener who should wage a whole day's war with an iron scuffle on those ill weeds that make the garden-walks of life unsightly, when a sprinkle of Attic salt will wither them up. *Est ars etiam maledicendi*, says Scaliger, and truly it is a hard thing to say where the graceful gentleness of the lamb merges in downright sheepishness. We may conclude with worthy and wise Dr. Fuller, that "one may be a lamb in private wrongs, but in hearing general affronts to goodness they are asses which are not lions." — H. W.]

GUVENER B. is a sensible man;
　He stays to his home an' looks arter
　　his folks;
He draws his furrer ez straight ez he can,
　An' into nobody's tater-patch pokes;
　　But John P.
　　Robinson he
　Sez he wunt vote fer Guvener B.

My! aint it terrible? Wut shall we du?
　We can't never choose him o' course,
　　— thet 's flat;
Guess we shall hev to come round,
　　(don't you?)
　An' go in fer thunder an' guns, an'
　　all that;
　　Fer John P.
　　Robinson he
　Sez he wunt vote fer Guvener B.

Gineral C. is a dreffle smart man:
　He 's ben on all sides thet give places
　　or pelf;
But consistency still wuz a part of his
　　plan, —
　He 's ben true to *one* party, — an'
　　thet is himself; —
　　So John P.
　　Robinson he
　Sez he shall vote fer Gineral C.

Gineral C. he goes in fer the war;
　He don't vally principle more 'n an
　　old cud;
Wut did God make us raytional cree-
　　turs fer,
　But glory an' gunpowder, plunder an'
　　blood?
　　So John P.
　　Robinson he
　Sez he shall vote fer Gineral C.

We were gittin' on nicely up here to
　　our village,
　With good old idees o' wut 's right
　　an' wut aint,
We kind o' thought Christ went agin
　　war an' pillage,
　An' thet eppyletts worn't the best
　　mark of a saint;
　　But John P.
　　Robinson he
　Sez this kind o' thing 's an ex-
　　ploded idee.

The side of our country must ollers be
　　took,
　An' Presidunt Polk, you know, *he* is
　　our country.
An' the angel thet writes all our sins in
　　a book
　Puts the *debit* to him, an' to us the
　　per contry;
　　An' John P.
　　Robinson he
　Sez this is his view o' the thing to
　　a T.

Parson Wilbur he calls all these argi-
　　munts lies;
　Sez they 're nothin' on airth but jest
　　fee, faw, fum:
An' thet all this big talk of our destinies
　Is half on it ign'ance, an' t'other half
　　rum;
　　But John P.
　　Robinson he
　Sez it aint no sech thing; an', of
　　course, so must we.

Parson Wilbur sez *he* never heerd in
　　his life
　Thet th' Apostles rigged out in their
　　swaller-tail coats,
An' marched round in front of a drum
　　an' a fife,
　To git some on 'em office, an' some
　　on 'em votes;
　　But John P.
　　Robinson he
　Sez they did n't know everythin'
　　down in Judee.

Wal, it 's a marcy we 've gut folks to
　　tell us
　The rights an' the wrongs o' these
　　matters, I vow, —

God sends country lawyers, an' other
          wise fellers,
To start the world's team wen it gits
          in a slough ;
      Fer John P.
      Robinson he
Sez the world 'll go right, ef he hollers
      out Gee !

[The attentive reader will doubtless have
perceived in the foregoing poem an allusion
to that pernicious sentiment,—"Our country,
right or wrong." It is an abuse of language
to call a certain portion of land, much more,
certain personages, elevated for the time
being to high station, our country. I would
not sever nor loosen a single one of those ties
by which we are united to the spot of our
birth, nor minish by a tittle the respect due
to the Magistrate. I love our own Bay State
too well to do the one, and as for the other, I
have myself for nigh forty years exercised,
however unworthily, the function of Justice
of the Peace, having been called thereto by
the unsolicited kindness of that most excellent
man and upright patriot, Caleb Strong. *Pa-
triæ fumus igne alieno luculentior* is best
qualified with this,— *Ubi libertas, ibi patria.*
We are inhabitants of two worlds, and owe
a double, but not a divided allegiance. In
virtue of our clay, this little ball of earth ex-
acts a certain loyalty of us, while, in our capacity as spirits, we are admitted citizens of
an invisible and holier Fatherland. There is
a patriotism of the soul whose claim absolves
us from our other and terrene fealty. Our
true country is that ideal realm which we
represent to ourselves under the names of
religion, duty, and the like. Our terrestrial
organizations are but far-off approaches to
so fair a model, and all they are verily traitors
who resist not any attempt to divert them
from this their original intendment. When,
therefore, one would have us to fling up our
caps and shout with the multitude,— "*Our
country, however bounded !*" he demands of
us that we sacrifice the larger to the less, the
higher to the lower, and that we yield to the
imaginary claims of a few acres of soil our
duty and privilege as liegemen of Truth. Our
true country is bounded on the north and the
south, on the east and the west, by Justice,
and when she oversteps that invisible boun-
dary-line by so much as a hair's-breadth, she
ceases to be our mother, and chooses rather
to be looked upon *quasi noverca.* That is a
hard choice when our earthly love of country
calls upon us to tread one path and our duty
points us to another. We must make as
noble and becoming an election as did Pe-
nelope between Icarius and Ulysses. Veiling
our faces, we must take silently the hand of
Duty to follow her.

Shortly after the publication of the foregoing poem, there appeared some comments
upon it in one of the public prints which
seemed to call for animadversion. I accordingly addressed to Mr. Buckingham, of the
Boston Courier, the following letter.

JAALAM, November 4, 1847.

" *To the Editor of the Courier:*

"RESPECTED SIR,—Calling at the post-
office this morning, our worthy and efficient
postmaster offered for my perusal a paragraph in the Boston Morning Post of the 3d
instant, wherein certain effusions of the pastoral muse are attributed to the pen of Mr.
James Russell Lowell. For aught I know or
can affirm to the contrary, this Mr. Lowell
may be a very deserving person and a youth
of parts (though I have seen verses of his
which I could never rightly understand) ; and
if he be such, he, I am certain, as well as I,
would be free from any proclivity to appropriate to himself whatever of credit (or discredit) may honestly belong to another. I
am confident, that, in penning these few lines,
I am only forestalling a disclaimer from that
young gentleman, whose silence hitherto,
when rumor pointed to himward, has excited
in my bosom mingled emotions of sorrow and
surprise. Well may my young parishioner,
Mr. Biglow, exclaim with the poet,

     'Sic vos non vobis,' &c. ;

though, in saying this, I would not convey
the impression that he is a proficient in the
Latin tongue,—the tongue, I might add, of
a Horace and a Tully.

" Mr. B. does not employ his pen, I can
safely say, for any lucre of worldly gain, or to
be exalted by the carnal plaudits of men,
digito monstrari, &c. He does not wait
upon Providence for mercies, and in his heart
mean *merces.* But I should esteem myself
as verily deficient in my duty (who am his
friend and in some unworthy sort his spiritual
fidus Achates, &c.), if I did not step forward
to claim for him whatever measure of applause might be assigned to him by the judicious.

" If this were a fitting occasion, I might
venture here a brief dissertation touching the
manner and kind of my young friend's poetry.
But I dubitate whether this abstruser sort of
speculation (though enlivened by some apposite instances from Aristophanes) would
sufficiently interest your oppidan readers. As
regards their satirical tone, and their plainness of speech, I will only say, that, in my
pastoral experience, I have found that the
Arch-Enemy loves nothing better than to be
treated as a religious, moral, and intellectual
being, and that there is no *apage Sathanas !*
so potent as ridicule. But it is a kind of
weapon that must have a button of good-
nature on the point of it.

" The productions of Mr. B. have been
stigmatized in some quarters as unpatriotic ;
but I can vouch that he loves his native soil

with that hearty, though discriminating, attachment which springs from an intimate social intercourse of many years' standing. In the ploughing season, no one has a deeper share in the well-being of the country than he. If Dean Swift were right in saying that he who makes two blades of grass grow where one grew before confers a greater benefit on the state than he who taketh a city, Mr. B. might exhibit a fairer claim to the Presidency than General Scott himself. I think that some of those disinterested lovers of the hard-handed democracy, whose fingers have never touched anything rougher than the dollars of our common country, would hesitate to compare palms with him. It would do your heart good, respected Sir, to see that young man mow. He cuts a cleaner and wider swarth than any in this town.

"But it is time for me to be at my Post. It is very clear that my young friend's shot has struck the lintel, for the Post is shaken (Amos ix. 1). The editor of that paper is a strenuous advocate of the Mexican war, and a colonel, as I am given to understand. I presume, that, being necessarily absent in Mexico, he has left his journal in some less judicious hands. At any rate, the Post has been too swift on this occasion. It could hardly have cited a more incontrovertible line from any poem than that which it has selected for animadversion, namely,—

'We kind o' thought Christ went agin war an' pillage.'

"If the Post maintains the converse of this proposition, it can hardly be considered as a safe guide-post for the moral and religious portions of its party, however many other excellent qualities of a post it may be blessed with. There is a sign in London on which is painted,—'The Green Man.' It would do very well as a portrait of any individual who should support so unscriptural a thesis. As regards the language of the line in question, I am bold to say that He who readeth the hearts of men will not account any dialect unseemly which conveys a sound and pious sentiment. I could wish that such sentiments were more common, however uncouthly expressed. Saint Ambrose affirms, that *veritas a quocunque* (why not, then, *quomodocunque?*) *dicatur, a spiritu sancto est.* Digest also this of Baxter: 'The plainest words are the most profitable oratory in the weightiest matters.'

"When the paragraph in question was shown to Mr. Biglow, the only part of it which seemed to give him any dissatisfaction was that which classed him with the Whig party. He says, that, if resolutions are a nourishing kind of diet, that party must be in a very hearty and flourishing condition; for that they have quietly eaten more good ones of their own baking than he could have conceived to be possible without repletion. He has been for some years past (I regret to say)

an ardent opponent of those sound doctrines of protective policy which form so prominent a portion of the creed of that party. I confess, that, in some discussions which I have had with him on this point in my study, he has displayed a vein of obstinacy which I had not hitherto detected in his composition. He is also (*horresco referens*) infected in no small measure with the peculiar notions of a print called the Liberator, whose heresies I take every proper opportunity of combating, and of which, I thank God, I have never read a single line.

"I did not see Mr. B.'s verses until they appeared in print, and there *is* certainly one thing in them which I consider highly improper. I allude to the personal references to myself by name. To confer notoriety on an humble individual who is laboring quietly in his vocation, and who keeps his cloth as free as he can from the dust of the political arena (though *væ mihi si non evangelizavero*), is no doubt an indecorum. The sentiments which he attributes to me I will not deny to be mine. They were embodied, though in a different form, in a discourse preached upon the last day of public fasting, and were acceptable to my entire people (of whatever political views), except the postmaster, who dissented *ex officio*. I observe that you sometimes devote a portion of your paper to a religious summary. I should be well pleased to furnish a copy of my discourse for insertion in this department of your instructive journal. By omitting the advertisements, it might easily be got within the limits of a single number, and I venture to insure you the sale of some scores of copies in this town. I will cheerfully render myself responsible for ten. It might possibly be advantageous to issue it as an *extra*. But perhaps you will not esteem it an object, and I will not press it. My offer does not spring from any weak desire of seeing my name in print; for I can enjoy this satisfaction at any time by turning to the Triennial Catalogue of the University, where it also possesses that added emphasis of Italics with which those of my calling are distinguished.

"I would simply add, that I continue to fit ingenuous youth for college, and that I have two spacious and airy sleeping apartments at this moment unoccupied. *Ingenuas didicisse*, &c. Terms, which vary according to the circumstances of the parents, may be known on application to me by letter, postpaid. In all cases the lad will be expected to fetch his own towels. This rule, Mrs. W. desires me to add, has no exceptions.

"Respectfully, your obedient servant,
"HOMER WILBUR, A. M.

"P. S. Perhaps the last paragraph may look like an attempt to obtain the insertion of my circular gratuitously. If it should appear to you in that light, I desire that you would erase it, or charge for it at the usual rates, and deduct the amount from the proceeds in your hands from the sale of my discourse, when it shall be printed. My circular is much longer and more explicit, and will be forwarded without charge to any who may desire it. It has been very neatly executed on a letter sheet, by a very deserving printer, who attends upon my ministry, and is a creditable specimen of the typographic art. I have one hung over my mantel-piece in a neat frame, where it makes a beautiful and appropriate ornament, and balances the profile of Mrs. W., cut with her toes by the young lady born without arms. H. W."

I have in the foregoing letter mentioned General Scott in connection with the Presidency, because I have been given to understand that he has blown to pieces and otherwise caused to be destroyed more Mexicans than any other commander. His claim would therefore be deservedly considered the strongest. Until accurate returns of the Mexicans killed, wounded, and maimed be obtained, it will be difficult to settle these nice points of precedence. Should it prove that any other officer has been more meritorious and destructive than General S., and has thereby rendered himself more worthy of the confidence and support of the conservative portion of our community, I shall cheerfully insert his name, instead of that of General S., in a future edition. It may be thought, likewise, that General S. has invalidated his claims by too much attention to the decencies of apparel, and the habits belonging to a gentleman. These abstruser points of statesmanship are beyond my scope. I wonder not that successful military achievement should attract the admiration of the multitude. Rather do I rejoice with wonder to behold how rapidly this sentiment is losing its hold upon the popular mind. It is related of Thomas Warton, the second of that honored name who held the office of Poetry Professor at Oxford, that, when one wished to find him, being absconded, as was his wont, in some obscure alehouse, he was counselled to traverse the city with a drum and fife, the sound of which inspiring music would be sure to draw the Doctor from his retirement into the street. We are all more or less bitten with this martial insanity. *Nescio qua dulcedine .... cunctos ducit.* I confess to some infection of that itch myself. When I see a Brigadier-General maintaining his insecure elevation in the saddle under the severe fire of the training-field, and when I remember that some military enthusiasts, through haste, inexperience, or an over-desire to lend reality to those fictitious combats, will sometimes discharge their ramrods, I cannot but admire, while I deplore, the mistaken devotion of those heroic officers. *Semel insanivimus omnes.* I was myself, during the late war with Great Britain, chaplain of a regiment, which was fortunately never called to active military duty. I mention this circumstance with regret rather than pride. Had I been summoned to actual warfare, I trust that I might have been strengthened to bear myself after the manner of that reverend father in our New England Israel, Dr. Benjamin Colman, who, as we are told in Turell's life of him, when the vessel in which he had taken passage for England was attacked by a French privateer, "fought like a philosopher and a Christian, ... and prayed all the while he charged and fired." As this note is already long, I shall not here enter upon a discussion of the question, whether Christians may lawfully be soldiers. I think it sufficiently evident, that, during the first two centuries of the Christian era, at least, the two professions were esteemed incompatible. Consult Jortin on this head.—H. W.]

No. IV.

REMARKS OF INCREASE D. O'PHACE, ESQUIRE, AT AN EXTRUMPERY CAUCUS IN STATE STREET, REPORTED BY MR. H. BIGLOW.

[THE ingenious reader will at once understand that no such speech as the following was ever *totidem verbis* pronounced. But there are simpler and less guarded wits, for the satisfying of which such an explanation may be needful. For there are certain invisible lines, which as Truth successively overpasses, she becomes Untruth to one and another of us, as a large river, flowing from one kingdom into another, sometimes takes a new name, albeit the waters undergo no change, how small soever. There is, moreover, a truth of fiction more veracious than the truth of fact, as that of the Poet, which represents to us things and events as they ought to be, rather than servilely copies them as they are imperfectly imaged in the crooked and smoky glass of our mundane affairs. It is this which makes the speech of Antonius, though originally spoken in no wider a forum than the brain of Shakespeare, more historically valuable than that other which Appian has reported, by as much as the understanding of the Englishman was more comprehensive than that of the Alexandrian. Mr. Biglow, in the present instance, has only made use of a license assumed by all the historians of antiquity, who put into the mouths of various characters such words as seem to them most fitting to the occasion and to the speaker. If it be objected that no such oration could ever have been delivered, I answer, that there are few assemblages for speech-making which do not better deserve the title of *Parliamentum Indoctorum* than did the sixth Parliament of Henry the Fourth, and that men still continue to have as much faith in the Oracle of Fools as ever Pantagruel had. Howell, in his letters, recounts a merry tale of a certain ambassador of Queen Elizabeth, who, having written two letters, — one to her Majesty, and the other to his wife, — directed them at cross-purposes, so that the Queen was beducked and bedeared and requested to send a change of hose, and the wife was beprincessed and otherwise unwontedly besuperlatived, till the one feared for the wits of her ambassador, and the other for those of her husband. In like manner it may be presumed that our speaker has misdirected some of his thoughts, and given to the whole theatre what he would have wished to confide only to a select auditory at the back of the curtain. For it is seldom that we can get any frank utterance from men, who address, for the most part, a Buncombe either in this world or the next. As for their audiences, it may be truly said of our people, that they enjoy one political institution in common with the ancient Athenians : I mean a certain profitless kind of *ostracism*, wherewith, nevertheless, they seem hitherto well enough content. For in Presidential elections, and other affairs of the sort, whereas I observe that the *oysters* fall to the lot of comparatively few, the *shells* (such as the privileges of voting as they are told to do by the *ostrivori* aforesaid, and of huzzaing at public meetings) are very liberally distributed among the people, as being their prescriptive and quite sufficient portion.

The occasion of the speech is supposed to be Mr. Palfrey's refusal to vote for the Whig candidate for the Speakership. — H. W.]

No? Hez he? He haint, though?
  Wut? Voted agin him?
Ef the bird of our country could ketch
    him, she 'd skin him ;
I seem 's though I see her, with wrath
    in each quill,
Like a chancery lawyer, afilin' her bill,
An' grindin' her talents ez sharp ez all
    nater,
To pounce like a writ on the back o'
    the traitor.

Forgive me, my friends, ef I seem to be
    het,
But a crisis like this must with vigor be
    met ;
Wen an Arnold the star-spangled ban-
    ner bestains,
Holl Fourth o' Julys seem to bile in
    my veins.

Who ever 'd ha' thought sech a pison-
    ous rig

Would be run by a chap thet wuz
    chose fer a Wig?
"We knowed wut his princerples wuz
    'fore we sent him "?
Wut wuz there in them from this vote
    to pervent him ?
A marciful Providence fashioned us
    holler
O' purpose thet we might our princer-
    ples swaller ;
It can hold any quantity on 'em, the
    belly can,
An' bring 'em up ready fer use like the
    pelican,
Or more like the kangaroo, who (wich
    is stranger)
Puts her family into her pouch wen
    there 's danger.
Aint princerple precious ? then, who 's
    goin' to use it
Wen there 's resk o' some chap 's gittin'
    up to abuse it ?
I can't tell the wy on 't, but nothin' is
    so sure
Ez thet princerple kind o' gits spiled
    by exposure ; *
A man thet lets all sorts o' folks git a
    sight on 't
Ough' to hev it all took right away,
    every mite on 't ;
Ef he can't keep it all to himself wen
    it 's wise to,
He aint one it 's fit to trust nothin' so
    nice to.

Besides, ther 's a wonderful power in
    latitude
To shift a man's morril relations an'
    attitude ;
Some flossifers think thet a fakkilty 's
    granted

* The speaker is of a different mind from Tully, who, in his recently discovered tractate *De Republica*, tells us, — *Nec vero habere virtutem satis est, quasi artem aliquam, nisi utare*, and from our Milton, who says : "I cannot praise a fugitive and cloistered virtue, unexercised and unbreathed, that never sallies out and sees her adversary, but slinks out of the race where that immortal garland is to be run for, *not without dust and heat*." — *Areop*. He had taken the words out of the Roman's mouth, without knowing it, and might well exclaim with Donatus (if Saint Jerome's tutor may stand sponsor for a curse), *Pereant qui ante nos nostra dixerint !* — H. W.

The minnit it 's proved to be thoroughly wanted,
Thet a change o' demand makes a
change o' condition,
An' thet everythin' 's nothin' except by
position ;
Ez, fer instance, thet rubber-trees fust
begun bearin'
Wen p'litikle conshunces come into
wearin',
Thet the fears of a monkey, whose holt
chanced to fail,
Drawed the vertibry out to a prehensile
tail ;
So, wen one 's chose to Congriss, ez
soon ez he 's in it,
A collar grows right round his neck in
a minnit,
An' sartin it is thet a man cannot be
strict
In bein' himself, wen he gits to the
Deestrict,
Fer a coat thet sets wal here in ole
Massachusetts,
Wen it gits on to Washinton, somehow
askew sets.

Resolves, do you say, o' the Springfield
Convention?
Thet 's percisely the pint I was goin' to
mention ;
Resolves air a thing we most gen'ally
keep ill,
They 're a cheap kind o' dust fer the
eyes o' the people ;
A parcel o' delligits jest get together
An' chat fer a spell o' the crops an' the
weather,
Then, comin' to order, they squabble
awile
An' let off the speeches they 're ferful
'll spile ;
Then — Resolve, — Thet we wunt hev
an inch o' slave territory ;
Thet Presidunt Polk's holl perceedins
air very tory ;
Thet the war is a damned war, an'
them thet enlist in it
Should hev a cravat with a dreffle tight
twist in it ;
Thet the war is a war fer the spreadin'
o' slavery ;
Thet our army desarves our best thanks
fer their bravery ;

Thet we 're the original friends o' the
nation,
All the rest air a paltry an' base fab-
rication ;
Thet we highly respect Messrs. A, B,
an' C,
An' ez deeply despise Messrs. E, F,
an' G.
In this way they go to the eend o' the
chapter,
An' then they bust out in a kind of a
raptur
About their own vartoo, an' folks's
stone-blindness
To the men thet 'ould actilly do 'em a
kindness, —
The American eagle, — the Pilgrims
thet landed, —
Till on ole Plymouth Rock they git
finally stranded.
Wal, the people they listen and say,
" Thet 's the ticket ;
Ez fer Mexico, 't aint no great glory to
lick it,
But 't would be a darned shame to go
pullin' o' triggers
To extend the aree of abusin' the nig-
gers."

So they march in percessions, an' git
up hooraws,
An' tramp thru the mud fer the good o'
the cause,
An' think they 're a kind o' fulfillin' the
prophecies,
Wen they 're on'y jest changin' the
holders of offices ;
Ware A sot afore, B is comf'tably
seated,
One humbug 's victor'ous an' t' other
defeated,
Each honnable doughface gits jest wut
he axes,
An' the people — their annooal soft-
sodder an' taxes.

Now, to keep unimpaired all these
glorious feeturs
Thet characterize morril an' reasonin'
creeturs,
Thet give every paytriot all he can cram,
Thet oust the untrustworthy Presidunt
Flam,
And stick honest Presidunt Sham in
his place,

To the manifest gain o' the holl human race,
An' to some indervidgewals on 't in partickler,
Who love Public Opinion an' know how to tickle her,
I say thet a party with great aims like these
Must stick jest ez close ez a hive full o' bees.

I'm willin' a man should go tollable strong
Agin wrong in the abstract, fer thet kind o' wrong
Is ollers unpop'lar an' never gits pitied,
Because it's a crime no one never com- mitted;
But he mus' n't be hard on partickler sins,
Coz then he'll be kickin' the people's own shins;
On'y look at the Demmercrats, see wut they've done
Jest simply by stickin' together like fun;
They've sucked us right into a mis'able war
Thet no one on airth aint responsible for;
They've run us a hundred cool millions in debt
(An' fer Demmercrat Horners ther's good plums left yet);
They talk agin tayriffs, but act fer a high one,
An' so coax all parties to build up their Zion;
To the people they're ollers ez slick ez molasses,
An' butter their bread on both sides with The Masses,
Half o' whom they've persuaded, by way of a joke,
Thet Washinton's mantelpiece fell upon Polk.

Now all o' these blessin's the Wigs might enjoy,
Ef they'd gumption enough the right means to imploy; *

Fer the silver spoon born in Dermoc- 'acy's mouth
Is a kind of a scringe thet they hev to the South;
Their masters can cuss 'em an' kick 'em an' wale 'em,
An' they notice it less 'an the ass did to Balaam;
In this way they screw into second- rate offices
Wich the slaveholder thinks 'ould sub- stract too much off his ease;
The file-leaders, I mean, du, fer they, by their wiles,
Unlike the old viper, grow fat on their files.
Wal, the Wigs hev been tryin' to grab all this prey frum 'em
An' to hook this nice spoon o' good fortin' away frum 'em,
An' they might ha' succeeded, ez likely ez not,
In lickin' the Demmercrats all round the lot,
Ef it warn't thet, wile all faithful Wigs were their knees on,
Some stuffy old codger would holler out, — "Treason!
You must keep a sharp eye on a dog thet hez bit you once,
An' *I* aint agoin' to cheat my constit- oounts," —
Wen every fool knows thet a man rep- resents
Not the fellers thet sent him, but them on the fence, —
Impartially ready to jump either side
An' make the fust use of a turn o' the tide, —
The waiters on Providunce here in the city,
Who compose wut they call a State Centerl Committy.
Constitoounts air hendy to help a man in,
But arterwards don't weigh the heft of a pin.
Wy, the people can't all live on Uncle Sam's pus,
So they've nothin' to du with 't fer better or wus;
It's the folks thet air kind o' brought up to depend on 't
Thet hev any consarn in 't, an' thet is the end on 't.

---

* That was a pithy saying of Persius, and fits our politicians without a wrinkle. — *Ma- gister artis, ingeniique largitor venter.* — H. W.

Now here wuz New England ahevin'
    the honor
Of a chance at the Speakership show-
    ered upon her ; —
Do you say, — "She don't want no
    more Speakers, but fewer ;
She 's hed plenty o' them, wut she wants
    is a *doer*" ?
Fer the matter o' thet, it 's notorous in
    town
Thet her own representatives du her
    quite brown.
But thet 's nothin' to du with it ; wut
    right hed Palfrey
To mix himself up with fanatical small
    fry ?
'Warn't we gittin' on prime with our hot
    an' cold blowin',
Acondemnin' the war wilst we kep' it
    agoin' ?
We 'd assumed with gret skill a com-
    mandin' position,
On this side or thet, no one could n't
    tell wich one,
So, wutever side wipped, we 'd a chance
    at the plunder
An' could sue fer infringin' our pay-
    tented thunder ;
We were ready to vote fer whoever wuz
    eligible,
Ef on all pints at issoo he 'd stay unin-
    telligible.
Wal, sposin' we hed to gulp down our
    perfessions,
We were ready to come out next morn-
    in' with fresh ones ;
Besides, ef we did, 't was our business
    alone,
Fer could n't we ez we would with
    our own ?
An' ef a man can, wen pervisions hev
    riz so,
Eat up his own words, it 's a marcy it
    is so.

Wy, these chaps frum the North, with
    back-bones to 'em, darn 'em,
'Ould be wuth more 'an Gennle Tom
    Thumb is to Barnum ;
Ther 's enough thet to office on this
    very plan grow,
By exhibitin' how very small a man can
    grow ;

But an M. C. frum here ollers hastens
    to state he
Belongs to the order called inverte-
    braty,
Wence some gret filologists judge primy
    fashy
Thet M. C. is M. T. by paronomashy ;
An' these few exceptions air *loosus
    naytury*
Folks 'ould put down their quarters to
    stare at, like fury.

It 's no use to open the door o' success,
Ef a member can bolt so fer nothin' or
    less ;
Wy, all o' them grand constitootional
    pillers
Our fore-fathers fetched with 'em over
    the billers,
Them pillers the people so soundly hev
    slep' on,
Wile to slav'ry, invasion, an' debt they
    were swep' on,
Wile our Destiny higher an' higher
    kep' mountin'
(Though I guess folks 'll stare wen she
    hends her account in),
Ef members in this way go kicken
    agin 'em,
They wunt hev so much ez a feather left
    in 'em.

An', ez fer this Palfrey,* we thought
    wen we 'd gut him in,
He 'd go kindly in wutever harness we
    put him in ;
Supposin' we *did* know thet he wuz a
    peace man ?
Doos he think he can be Uncle Sam-
    mle's policeman,
An' wen Sam gits tipsy an' kicks up a
    riot,
Lead him off to the lockup to snooze
    till he 's quiet ?
Wy, the war is a war thet true pay/riots
    can bear, ef
It leads to the fat promised land of a
    tayriff ;
We don't go an' fight it, nor aint to be
    driv on,
Nor Demmercrats nuther, thet hev wut
    to live on ;

* There is truth yet in this of Juvenal, —
"Dat veniam corvis, vexat censura columbas."
                                 H. W.

Ef it aint jest the thing thet 's well
   pleasin' to God,
It makes us thought highly on elsewhere abroad ;
The Rooshian black eagle looks blue
   in his eerie
An' shakes both his heads wen he
   hears o' Monteery ;
In the Tower Victory sets, all of a
   fluster,
An' reads, with locked doors, how we
   won Cherry Buster ;
An' old Philip Lewis — thet come an'
   kep' school here
Fer the mere sake o' scorin' his ryalist
   ruler
On the tenderest part of our kings *in
   futuro* —
Hides his crown underneath an old
   shut in his bureau,
Breaks off in his brags to a suckle o'
   merry kings,
How he often hed hided young native
   Amerrikins,
An' turnin' quite faint in the midst of
   his fooleries,
Sneaks down stairs to bolt the front
   door o' the Tooleries.*

You say, — " We 'd ha' scared 'em by
   growin' in peace,
A plaguy sight more then by bobberies
   like these " ?

* Jortin is willing to allow of other miracles besides those recorded in Holy Writ,
and why not of other prophecies? It is granting too much to Satan to suppose him, as
divers of the learned have done, the inspirer
of the ancient oracles. Wiser, I esteem it,
to give chance the credit of the successful
ones. What is said here of Louis Philippe
was verified in some of its minute particulars
within a few months' time. Enough to have
made the fortune of Delphi or Hammon, and
no thanks to Beelzebub neither! That of
Seneca in Medea will suit here : —

   " Rapida fortuna ac levis
Præcepsque regno eripuit, exsilio dedit."

Let us allow, even to richly deserved mis-
fortune, our commiseration, and be not over-
hasty meanwhile in our censure of the French
people, left for the first time to govern themselves, remembering that wise sentence of
Æschylus,

Ἅπας δὲ τραχὺς ὅστις ἂν νέον κρατῇ.

                   H. W.

Who is it dares say thet our naytional
   eagle
Wun't much longer be classed with the
   birds thet air regal,
Coz theirn be hooked beaks, an' she,
   arter this slaughter,
'll bring back a bill ten times longer 'n
   she ough' to " ?
Wut 's your name? Come, I see ye,
   you up-country feller,
You 've put me out severil times with
   your beller ;
Out with it ! Wut? Biglow? I say
   nothin' furder,
Thet feller would like nothin' better 'n
   a murder ;
He 's a traiter, blasphemer, an' wut
   ruther worse is,
He puts all his ath'ism in dreffle bad
   verses ;
Socity aint safe till sech monsters air
   out on it,
Refer to the Post, ef you hev the least
   doubt on it ;
Wy, he goes agin war, agin indirect
   taxes,
Agin sellin' wild lands 'cept to settlers
   with axes,
Agin holdin' o' slaves, though he knows
   it 's the corner
Our libbaty rests on, the mis'able
   scorner !
In short, he would wholly upset with
   his ravages
All thet keeps us above the brute crit-
   ters an' savages,
An' pitch into all kinds o' briles an'
   confusions
The holl of our civilized, free institu-
   tions ;
He writes fer thet ruther unsafe print,
   the Courier,
An' likely ez not hez a squintin' to
   Foorier ;
I 'll be ——, thet is, I mean I 'll be
   blest,
Ef I hark to a word frum so noted a
   pest ;
I sha'n't talk with *him*, my religion 's
   too fervent. —
Good mornin', my friends, I 'm your
   most humble servant.

[Into the question, whether the ability to
express ourselves in articulate language has

been productive of more good or evil, I shall not here enter at large. The two faculties of speech and of speech-making are wholly diverse in their natures. By the first we make ourselves intelligible, by the last unintelligible, to our fellows. It has not seldom occurred to me (noting how in our national legislature everything runs to talk, as lettuces, if the season or the soil be unpropitious, shoot up lankly to seed, instead of forming handsome heads) that Babel was the first Congress, the earliest mill erected for the manufacture of gabble. In these days, what with Town Meetings, School Committees, Boards (lumber) of one kind and another, Congresses, Parliaments, Diets, Indian Councils, Palavers, and the like, there is scarce a village which has not its factories of this description driven by milk-and-water power. I cannot conceive the confusion of tongues to have been the curse of Babel, since I esteem my ignorance of other languages as a kind of Martello-tower, in which I am safe from the furious bombardments of foreign garrulity. For this reason I have ever preferred the study of the dead languages, those primitive formations being Ararats upon whose silent peaks I sit secure and watch this new deluge without fear, though it rain figures (*simulacra*, semblances) of speech forty days and nights together, as it not uncommonly happens. This is my coat, as it were, without buttons by which any but a vernacular wild bore can seize me. Is it not possible that the Shakers may intend to convey a quiet reproof and hint, in fastening their outer garments with hooks and eyes?

This reflection concerning Babel, which I find in no Commentary, was first thrown upon my mind when an excellent deacon of my congregation (being infected with the Second Advent delusion) assured me that he had received a first instalment of the gift of tongues as a small earnest of larger possessions in the like kind to follow. For, of a truth, I could not reconcile it with my ideas of the Divine justice and mercy that the single wall which protected people of other languages from the incursions of this otherwise well-meaning propagandist should be broken down.

In reading Congressional debates, I have fancied, that, after the subsidence of those painful buzzings in the brain which result from such exercises, I detected a slender residuum of valuable information. I made the discovery that *nothing* takes longer in the saying than anything else, for as *ex nihilo nihil fit*, so from one polypus *nothing* any number of similar ones may be produced. I would recommend to the attention of *viva voce* debaters and controversialists the admirable example of the monk Copres, who, in the fourth century, stood for half an hour in the midst of a great fire, and thereby silenced a Manichæan antagonist who had less of the salamander in him. As for those who

quarrel in print, I have no concern with them here, since the eyelids are a divinely granted shield against all such. Moreover, I have observed in many modern books that the printed portion is becoming gradually smaller, and the number of blank or fly-leaves (as they are called) greater. Should this fortunate tendency of literature continue, books will grow more valuable from year to year, and the whole Serbonian bog yield to the advances of firm arable land.

The sagacious Lacedæmonians hearing that Tesephone had bragged that he could talk all day long on any given subject, made no more ado, but forthwith banished him, whereby they supplied him a topic and at the same time took care that his experiment upon it should be tried out of ear-shot.

I have wondered, in the Representatives' Chamber of our own Commonwealth, to mark how little impression seemed to be produced by that emblematic fish suspended over the heads of the members. Our wiser ancestors, no doubt, hung it there as being the animal which the Pythagoreans reverenced for its silence, and which certainly in that particular does not so well merit the epithet *cold-blooded*, by which naturalists distinguish it, as certain bipeds, afflicted with ditch-water on the brain, who take occasion to tap themselves in Faneuil Halls, meeting-houses, and other places of public resort.—H. W.]

No. V.

THE DEBATE IN THE SENNIT.

SOT TO A NUSRY RHYME.

[The incident which gave rise to the debate satirized in the following verses was the unsuccessful attempt of Drayton and Sayres to give freedom to seventy men and women, fellow-beings and fellow-Christians. Had Tripoli, instead of Washington, been the scene of this undertaking, the unhappy leaders in it would have been as secure of the theoretic as they now are of the practical part of martyrdom. I question whether the Dey of Tripoli is blessed with a District Attorney so benighted as ours at the seat of government. Very fitly is he named Key, who would allow himself to be made the instrument of locking the door of hope against sufferers in such a cause. Not all the waters of the ocean can cleanse the vile smutch of the jailer's fingers from off that little Key. *Ahenea clavis*, a brazen Key indeed!

Mr. Calhoun, who is made the chief speaker in this burlesque, seems to think that the light of the nineteenth century is to be put out as soon as he tinkles his little cow-bell curfew. Whenever slavery is touched, he sets up his scarecrow of dissolving the Union. This may do for the North, but I should conjecture that something more than a pumpkin-lantern is required to scare manifest and irretrievable Destiny out of her path. Mr. Calhoun cannot let go the apron-string of the Past. The Past is a good nurse, but we must be weaned from her sooner or later, even though, like Plotinus, we should run home from school to ask the breast, after we are tolerably well-grown youths. It will not do for us to hide our faces in her lap, whenever the strange Future holds out her arms and asks us to come to her.

But we are all alike. We have all heard it said, often enough, that little boys must not play with fire; and yet, if the matches be taken away from us, and put out of reach upon the shelf, we must needs get into our little corner, and scowl and stamp and threaten the dire revenge of going to bed without our supper. The world shall stop till we get our dangerous plaything again. Dame Earth, meanwhile, who has more than enough household matters to mind, goes bustling hither and thither as a hiss or a sputter tells her that this or that kettle of hers is boiling over, and before bedtime we are glad to eat our porridge cold, and gulp down our dignity along with it.

Mr. Calhoun has somehow acquired the name of a great statesman, and, if it be great statesmanship to put lance in rest and run a tilt at the Spirit of the Age with the certainty of being next moment hurled neck and heels into the dust amid universal laughter, he deserves the title. He is the Sir Kay of our modern chivalry. He should remember the old Scandinavian mythus. Thor was the strongest of gods, but he could not wrestle with Time, nor so much as lift up a fold of the great snake which bound the universe together; and when he smote the Earth, though with his terrible mallet, it was but as if a leaf had fallen. Yet all the while it seemed to Thor that he had only been wrestling with an old woman, striving to lift a cat, and striking a stupid giant on the head.

And in old times, doubtless, the giants *were* stupid, and there was no better sport for the Sir Launcelots and Sir Gawains than to go about cutting off their great blundering heads with enchanted swords. But things have wonderfully changed. It is the giants, nowadays, that have the science and the intelligence, while the chivalrous Don Quixotes of Conservatism still cumber themselves with the clumsy armor of a bygone age. On whirls the restless globe through unsounded time, with its cities and its silences, its births and funerals, half light, half shade, but never wholly dark, and sure to swing round into the happy morning at last. With an involuntary smile, one sees Mr. Calhoun letting slip his pack-thread cable with a crooked pin at the end of it to anchor South Carolina upon the bank and shoal of the Past. — H. W.]

TO MR. BUCKENAM.

MR. EDITER, As i wuz kinder prunin round, in a little nussry sot out a year or 2 a go, the Dbait in the sennit cum inter my mine An so i took & Sot it to wut I call a nussry rime. I hev made sum onnable Gentlemun speak that dident speak in a Kind uv Poetikul lie sense the seeson is dreffle backerd up This way

ewers as ushul

HOSEA BIGLOW.

" HERE we stan' on the Constitution,
      by thunder !
    It 's a fact o' wich ther 's bushils o'
      proofs ;
  Fer how could we trample on 't so, I
      wonder,
    Ef 't worn't thet it 's ohers under our
      hoofs ? "
        Sez John C. Calhoun, sez he ;
        " Human rights haint no more
    Right to come on this floor,
        No more 'n the man in the moon,"
        sez he.

" The North haint no kind o' bisness
      with nothin',
    An' you 've no idee how much bother
      it saves ;
  We aint none riled by their frettin' an'
      frothin',
    We 're *used* to layin' the string on
      our slaves,"
        Sez John C. Calhoun, sez he ; —
        Sez Mister Foote,
    " I should like to shoot
    The holl gang, by the gret horn
        spoon ! " sez he.

" Freedom's Keystone is Slavery, thet
      ther 's no doubt on,
    It 's sutthin' thet 's — wha' d' ye call
      it ? — divine, —
  An' the slaves thet we ollers *make* the
      most out on
    Air them north o' Mason an' Dixon's
      line,"
        Sez John C. Calhoun, sez he ; —
        " Fer all thet," sez Mangum,
    " 'T would be better to hang 'em,
        An' so git red on 'em soon," sez he.

"The mass ough' to labor an' we lay
  on soffies,
  That's the reason I want to spread
    Freedom's aree ;
It puts all the cunninest on us in office,
  An' reelises our Maker's orig'nal
    idee,"
    Sez John C. Calhoun, sez he ; —
      "That's ez plain," sez Cass,
      "Ez thet some one 's an ass,
  It's ez clear ez the sun is at noon,"
    sez he.

"Now don't go to say I 'm the friend
  of oppression,
  But keep all your spare breath fer
    coolin' your broth,
Fer I ollers hev strove (at least that 's
  my impression)
  To make cussed free with the rights
    o' the North,"
    Sez John C. Calhoun, sez he ; —
      "Yes," sez Davis o' Miss.,
      "The perfection o' bliss
  Is in skinnin' thet same old coon,"
    sez he.

"Slavery 's a thing thet depends on
  complexion,
  It's God's law thet fetters on black
    skins don't chafe ;
Ef brains wuz to settle it (horrid re-
  flection !)
  Wich of our onnable body 'd be
    safe ?"
    Sez John C. Calhoun, sez he ; —
      Sez Mister Hannegan,
      Afore he began agin,
  "Thet exception is quite opper-
    toon," sez he.

"Gen'nle Cass, Sir, you need n't be
  twitchin' your collar,
  Your merit 's quite clear by the dut
    on your knees,
At the North we don't make no dis-
  tinctions o' color ;
  You can all take a lick at our shoes
    wen you please,"
    Sez John C. Calhoun, sez he ; —
      Sez Mister Jarnagin,
      "They wunt hev to larn agin,
  They all on 'em know the old toon,"
    sez he.

"The slavery question aint no ways
  bewilderin'.
  North an' South hev one int'rest,
    it 's plain to a glance ;
No'thern men, like us patriarchs, don't
  sell their childrin,
  But they du sell themselves, ef they
    git a good chance,"
    Sez John C. Calhoun, sez he ; —
      Sez Atherton here,
      "This is gittin' severe,
  I wish I could dive like a loon," sez
    he.

"It 'll break up the Union, this talk
  about freedom,
  An' your fact'ry gals (soon ez we
    split) 'll make head,
An' gittin' some Miss chief or other to
  lead 'em,
  'll go to work raisin' permiscoous
    Ned,"
    Sez John C. Calhoun, sez he ; —
      "Yes, the North," sez Colquitt,
      "Ef we Southeners all quit,
  Would go down like a busted bal-
    loon," sez he.

"Jest look wut is doin', wut annyky 's
  brewin'
  In the beautiful clime o' the olive an'
    vine,
All the wise aristoxy is tumblin' to ruin,
  An' the sankylots drorin' an' drinkin'
    their wine,"
    Sez John C. Calhoun, sez he ; —
      "Yes," sez Johnson, "in France
      They 're beginnin' to dance
  Beelzebub's own rigadoon," sez he.

"The South 's safe enough, it don't
  feel a mite skeery,
  Our slaves in their darkness an' dut
    air tu blest
Not to welcome with proud hallylugers
    the cry
  Wen our eagle kicks yourn from the
    naytional nest,"
    Sez John C. Calhoun, sez he ; —
      "O," sez Westcott o' Florida,
      "Wut treason is horrider
  Then our priv'leges tryin' tu
    proon ?" sez he.

"It 's 'coz they 're so happy, thet, wen
    crazy sarpints
Stick their nose in our bizness, we git
    so darned riled ;
We think it 's our dooty to give pooty
    sharp hints,
Thet the last crumb of Edin on airth
    sha' n't be spiled,"
    Sez John C. Calhoun, sez he ; —
      "Ah," sez Dixon H. Lewis,
      "It perfectly true is
Thet slavery 's airth's grettest
    boon," sez he.

[It was said of old time, that riches have wings ; and, though this be not applicable in a literal strictness to the wealth of our patriarchal brethren of the South, yet it is clear that their possessions have legs, and an unaccountable propensity for using them in a northerly direction. I marvel that the grand jury of Washington did not find a true bill against the North Star for aiding and abetting Drayton and Sayres. It would have been quite of a piece with the intelligence displayed by the South on other questions connected with slavery. I think that no whip of state was ever freighted with a more veritable Jonah than is this same domestic institution of ours. Mephistopheles himself could not feign so bitterly, so satirically sad a sight as this of three millions of human beings crushed beyond help or hope by this one mighty argument, — *Our fathers knew no better !* Nevertheless, it is the unavoidable destiny of Jonahs to be cast overboard sooner or later. Or shall we try the experiment of hiding our Jonah in a safe place, that none may lay hands on him to make jetsam of him ? Let us, then, with equal forethought and wisdom, lash ourselves to the anchor, and await, in pious confidence, the certain result. Perhaps our suspicious passenger is no Jonah after all, being black. For it is well known that a superintending Providence made a kind of sandwich of Ham and his descendants, to be devoured by the Caucasian race.

In God's name, let all, who hear nearer and nearer the hungry moan of the storm and the growl of the breakers, speak out ! But, alas ! we have no right to interfere. If a man pluck an apple of mine, he shall be in danger of the justice ; but if he steal my brother, I must be silent. Who says this ? Our Constitution, consecrated by the callous consuetude of sixty years, and grasped in triumphant argument by the left hand of him whose right hand clutches the clotted slavewhip. Justice, venerable with the undethronable majesty of countless æons, says, — SPEAK ! The Past, wise with the sorrows and desolations of ages, from amid her shattered fanes and wolf-housing palaces, ech-

oes, — SPEAK ! Nature, through her thousand trumpets of freedom, her stars, her sunrises, her seas, her winds, her cataracts, her mountains blue with cloudy pines, blows jubilant encouragement, and cries, — SPEAK ! From the soul's trembling abysses the still, small voice not vaguely murmurs, — SPEAK ! But, alas ! the Constitution and the Honorable Mr. Bagowind, M. C., say, — BE DUMB !

It occurs to me to suggest, as a topic of inquiry in this connection, whether, on that momentous occasion when the goats and the sheep shall be parted, the Constitution and the Honorable Mr. Bagowind, M. C., will be expected to take their places on the left as our hircine vicars.

Quid sum miser tunc dicturus ?
Quem patronum rogaturus ?

There is a point where toleration sinks into sheer baseness and poltroonery. The toleration of the worst leads us to look on what is barely better as good enough, and to worship what is only moderately good. Woe to that man, or that nation, to whom mediocrity has become an ideal !

Has our experiment of self-government succeeded, if it barely manage to *rub and go* ? Here, now, is a piece of barbarism which Christ and the nineteenth century say shall cease, and which Messrs. Smith, Brown, and others say shall *not* cease. I would by no means deny the eminent respectability of these gentlemen, but I confess, that, in such a wrestling-match, I cannot help having my fears for them.

Discite justitiam, moniti, et non temnere.
                  H. W.]

No. VI.

THE PIOUS EDITOR'S CREED.

[AT the special instance of Mr. Biglow, I preface the following satire with an extract from a sermon preached during the past summer, from Ezekiel xxxiv. 2 : "Son of man, prophesy against the shepherds of Israel." Since the Sabbath on which this discourse was delivered, the editor of the "Jaalam Independent Blunderbuss" has unaccountably absented himself from our house of worship.

"I know of no so responsible position as that of the public journalist. The editor of our day bears the same relation to his time that the clerk bore to the age before the invention of printing. Indeed, the position which he holds is that which the clergyman should hold even now. But the clergyman chooses to walk off to the extreme edge of the world, and to throw such seed as he has clear over into that darkness which he calls the Next Life. As if *next* did not mean *nearest*, and as if any life were nearer than that immediately present one which boils and eddies all around him at the caucus, the ratification meeting, and the polls! Who taught him to exhort men to prepare for eternity, as for some future era of which the present forms no integral part? The furrow which Time is even now turning runs through the Everlasting, and in that must he plant, or nowhere. Yet he would fain believe and teach that we are *going* to have more of eternity than we have now. This *going* of his is like that of the auctioneer, on which *gone* follows before we have made up our minds to bid,—in which manner, not three months back, I lost an excellent copy of Chappelow on Job. So it has come to pass that the preacher, instead of being a living force, has faded into an emblematic figure at christenings, weddings, and funerals. Or, if he exercise any other function, it is as keeper and feeder of certain theologic dogmas, which, when occasion offers, he unkennels with a *staboy!* 'to bark and bite as 't is their nature to,' whence that reproach of *odium theologicum* has arisen.

"Meanwhile, see what a pulpit the editor mounts daily, sometimes with a congregation of fifty thousand within reach of his voice, and never so much as a nodder, even, among them! And from what a Bible can he choose his text,—a Bible which needs no translation, and which no priestcraft can shut and clasp from the laity,—the open volume of the world, upon which, with a pen of sunshine or destroying fire, the inspired Present is even now writing the annals of God! Methinks the editor who should understand his calling, and be equal thereto, would truly deserve that title of ποιμὴν λαῶν, which Homer bestows upon princes. He would be the Moses of our nineteenth century; and whereas the old Sinai, silent now, is but a common mountain stared at by the elegant tourist and crawled over by the hammering geologist, he must find his tables of the new law here among factories and cities in this Wilderness of Sin (Numbers xxxiii. 12) called Progress of Civilization, and be the captain of our Exodus into the Canaan of a truer social order.

"Nevertheless, our editor will not come so far within even the shadow of Sinai as Mahomet did, but chooses rather to construe Moses by Joe Smith. He takes up the crook, not that the sheep may be fed, but that he may never want a warm woollen suit and a joint of mutton.

Immemor, O, fidei, pecorumque oblite tuorum!

For which reason I would derive the name *editor* not so much from *edo*, to publish, as from *edo*, to eat, that being the peculiar profession to which he esteems himself called. He blows up the flames of political discord for no other occasion than that he may thereby handily boil his own pot. I believe there are two thousand of these mutton-loving shepherds in the United States, and of these, how many have even the dimmest perception of their immense power, and the duties consequent thereon? Here and there, haply, one. Nine hundred and ninety-nine labor to impress upon the people the great principles of *Tweedledum*, and other nine hundred and ninety-nine preach with equal earnestness the gospel according to *Tweedledee*."·— H. W.]

I DU believe in Freedom's cause,
   Ez fur away ez Payris is;
I love to see her stick her claws
   In them infarnal Phayrisees;
It 's wal enough agin a king
   To dror resolves an' triggers,—
But libbaty 's a kind o' thing
   Thet don't agree with niggers.

I du believe the people want
   A tax on teas an' coffees,
Thet nothin' aint extravygunt,—
   Purvidin' I 'm in office;
Fer I hev loved my country sence
   My eye-teeth filled their sockets,
An' Uncle Sam I reverence,
   Partic'larly his pockets.

I du believe in *any* plan
   O' levyin' the texes,
Ez long ez, like a lumberman,
   I git jest wut I axes:
I go free-trade thru thick an' thin,
   Because it kind o' rouses
The folks to vote,—an' keeps us in
   Our quiet custom-houses.

I du believe it 's wise an' good
   To sen' out furrin missions,
Thet is, on sartin understood
   An' orthodyx conditions;—
I mean nine thousan' dolls. per ann.,
   Nine thousan' more fer outfit,
An' me to recommend a man
   The place 'ould jest about fit.

I du believe in special ways
   O' prayin' an' convartin';
The bread comes back in many days,
   An' buttered, tu, fer sartin;
I mean in preyin' till one busts
   On wut the party chooses,
An' in convartin' public trusts
   To very privit uses.

I du believe hard coin the stuff
  Fer 'lectioneers to spout on ;
The people's ollers soft enough
  To make hard money out on ;
Dear Uncle Sam pervides fer his,
  An' gives a good-sized junk to all,—
I don't care *how* hard money is,
  Ez long ez mine 's paid punctooal.

I du believe with all my soul
  In the gret Press's freedom,
To pint the people to the goal
  An' in the traces lead 'em ;
Palsied the arm thet forges yokes
  At my fat contracts squintin',
An' withered be the nose thet pokes
  Inter the gov'ment printin'!

I du believe thet I should give
  Wut 's his'n unto Cæsar,
Fer it 's by him I move an' live,
  Frum him my bread an' cheese air ;
I du believe thet all o' me
  Doth bear his superscription, —
Will, conscience, honor, honesty,
  An' things o' thet description.

I du believe in prayer an' praise
  To him thet hez the grantin'
O' jobs, — in every thin' thet pays,
  But most of all in Cantin' ;
This doth my cup with marcies fill,
  This lays all thought o' sin to rest, —
I *don't* believe in princerple,
  But O, I *du* in interest.

I du believe in bein' this
  Or thet, ez it may happen
One way or t'other hendiest is
  To ketch the people nappin' ;
It aint by princerples nor men
  My preudunt course is steadied, —
I scent wich pays the best, an' then
  Go into it baldheaded.

I du believe thet holdin' slaves
  Comes nat'ral to a Presidunt,
Let 'lone the rowdedow it saves
  To hev a wal-broke precedunt ;
Fer any office, small or gret,
  I could n't ax with no face,
uthout I 'd ben, thru dry an' wet,
  Th' unrizzest kind o' doughface.

I du believe wutever trash
  'll keep the people in blindness, —
Thet we the Mexicuns can thrash
  Right inter brotherly kindness,
Thet bombshells, grape, an' powder
  'n' ball
Air good-will 's strongest magnets,
Thet peace, to make it stick at all,
  Must be druv in with bagnets.

In short, I firmly du believe
  In Humbug generally,
Fer it 's a thing thet I perceive
  To hev a solid vally ;
This heth my faithful shepherd ben,
  In pasturs sweet heth led me,
An' this 'll keep the people green
  To feed ez they hev fed me.

[I subjoin here another passage from my
before-mentioned discourse.

" Wonderful, to him that has eyes to see it
rightly, is the newspaper. To me, for example, sitting on the critical front bench of
the pit, in my study here in Jaalam, the advent of my weekly journal is as that of a
strolling theatre, or rather of a puppet-show,
on whose stage, narrow as it is, the tragedy,
comedy, and farce of life are played in little.
Behold the whole huge earth sent to me heb-
domadally in a brown-paper wrapper !

" Hither, to my obscure corner, by wind or
steam, on horseback or dromedary-back, in
the pouch of the Indian runner, or clicking
over the magnetic wires, troop all the famous
performers from the four quarters of the
globe. Looked at from a point of criticism,
tiny puppets they seem all, as the editor sets
up his booth upon my desk and officiates as
showman. Now I can truly see how little
and transitory is life. The earth appears
almost as a drop of vinegar, on which the
solar microscope of the imagination must
be brought to bear in order to make out
anything distinctly. That animalcule there,
in the pea-jacket, is Louis Philippe, just
landed on the coast of England. That other,
in the gray surtout and cocked hat, is Napoleon Bonaparte Smith, assuring France that
she need apprehend no interference from him
in the present alarming juncture. At that
spot, where you seem to see a speck of something in motion, is an immense mass-meeting.
Look sharper, and you will see a mite bran-
dishing his mandibles in an excited manner.
That is the great Mr. Soandso, defining his
position amid tumultuous and irrepressible
cheers. That infinitesimal creature, upon
whom some score of others, as minute as he,
are gazing in open-mouthed admiration, is a
famous philosopher, expounding to a select
audience their capacity for the Infinite.

That scarce discernible pufflet of smoke and dust is a revolution. That speck there is a reformer, just arranging the lever with which he is to move the world. And lo, there creeps forward the shadow of a skeleton that blows one breath between its grinning teeth, and all our distinguished actors are whisked off the slippery stage into the dark Beyond.

"Yes, the little show-box has its solemner suggestions. Now and then we catch a glimpse of a grim old man, who lays down a scythe and hour-glass in the corner while he shifts the scenes. There, too, in the dim background, a weird shape is ever delving. Sometimes he takes up his mattock, and gazes, as a coach whirls by, bearing the newly married on their wedding jaunt, or glances carelessly at a babe brought home from christening. Suddenly (for the scene grows larger and larger as we look) a bony hand snatches back a performer in the midst of his part, and him, whom yesterday two infinities (past and future) would not suffice, a handful of dust is enough to cover and silence forever. Nay, we see the same fleshless fingers opening to clutch the showman himself, and, guess, not without a shudder, that they are lying in wait for spectator also.

"Think of it: for three dollars a year I buy a season-ticket to this great Globe Theatre, for which God would write the dramas (only that we like farces, spectacles, and the tragedies of Apollyon better), whose scene-shifter is Time, and whose curtain is rung down by Death.

"Such thoughts will occur to me sometimes as I am tearing off the wrapper of my newspaper. Then suddenly that otherwise too often vacant sheet becomes invested for me with a strange kind of awe. Look! deaths and marriages, notices of inventions, discoveries, and books, lists of promotions, of killed, wounded, and missing, news of fires, accidents, of sudden wealth and as sudden poverty;— I hold in my hand the ends of myriad invisible electric conductors, along which tremble the joys, sorrows, wrongs, triumphs, hopes, and despairs of as many men and women everywhere. So that upon that mood of mind which seems to isolate me from mankind as a spectator of their puppet-pranks, another supervenes, in which I feel that I, too, unknown and unheard of, am yet of some import to my fellows. For, through my newspaper here, do not families take pains to send me, an entire stranger, news of a death among them? Are not here two who would have me know of their marriage? And, strangest of all, is not this singular person anxious to have me informed that he has received a fresh supply of Dimitry Bruisgins? But to none of us does the Present continue miraculous (even if for a moment discerned as such). We glance carelessly at the sunrise, and get used to Orion and the Pleiades. The wonder wears off, and to-morrow this sheet (Acts x. 11, 12), in which a vision was let down to me from Heaven, shall be the wrappage to a bar of soap or the platter for a beggar's broken victuals."— H. W.]

No. VII.

A LETTER

FROM A CANDIDATE FOR THE PRESIDENCY IN ANSWER TO SUTTIN QUESTIONS PROPOSED BY MR. HOSEA BIGLOW, INCLOSED IN A NOTE FROM MR. BIGLOW TO S. H. GAY, ESQ., EDITOR OF THE NATIONAL ANTI-SLAVERY STANDARD.

[CURIOSITY may be said to be the quality which pre-eminently distinguishes and segregates man from the lower animals. As we trace the scale of animated nature downward, we find this faculty (as it may truly be called) of the mind diminished in the savage, and wellnigh extinct in the brute. The first object which civilized man proposes to himself I take to be the finding out whatsoever he can concerning his neighbors. *Nihil humanum a me alienum puto;* I am curious about even John Smith. The desire next in strength to this (an opposite pole, indeed, of the same magnet) is that of communicating the unintelligence we have carefully picked up.

Men in general may be divided into the inquisitive and the communicative. To the first class belong Peeping Toms, eaves-droppers, navel-contemplating Brahmins, metaphysicians, travellers, Empedocleses, spies, the various societies for promoting Rhinothism, Columbuses, Yankees, discoverers, and men of science, who present themselves to the mind as so many marks of interrogation wandering up and down the world, or sitting in studies and laboratories. The second class I should again subdivide into four. In the first subdivision I would rank those who have an itch to tell us about themselves, — as keepers of diaries, insignificant persons generally, Montaignes, Horace Walpoles, autobiographers, poets. The second includes those who are anxious to impart information concerning other people, — as historians, barbers, and such. To the third belong those who labor to give us intelligence about nothing at all, — as novelists, political orators, the large majority of authors, preachers, lecturers, and the like. In the fourth come those who are communicative from motives of public benevolence, — as finders of mares'-nests and bringers of ill news. Each of us two-legged fowls without feathers embraces all these subdivisions in himself to a greater or less degree. for none of us so much as lays an egg, or incubates a chalk one, but straightway the whole barnyard shall know it by our cackle or our cluck. *Omnibus hoc vitium est.* There are different grades in all these classes. One will turn his telescope toward a back-yard, another toward Uranus; one will tell you that he dined with Smith, another that he supped with Plato. In one particular, all men may be considered as belonging to the first grand division, inasmuch as they all seem equally desirous of discovering the mote in their neighbor's eye.

To one or another of these species every human being may safely be referred. I think it beyond a peradventure that Jonah prosecuted some inquiries into the digestive apparatus of whales, and that Noah sealed up a letter in an empty bottle, that news in regard to him might not be wanting in case of the worst. They had else been super or subter human. I conceive, also, that, as there are certain persons who continually peep and pry at the key-hole of that mysterious door through which, sooner or later, we all make our exits, so there are doubtless ghosts fidgeting and fretting on the other side of it, because they have no means of conveying back to this world the scraps of news they have picked up in that. For there is an answer ready somewhere to every question, the great law of *give and take* runs through all nature, and if we see a hook, we may be sure that an eye is waiting for it. I read in every face I meet a standing advertisement of information wanted in regard to A. B., or that the friends of C. D. can hear something to his disadvantage by application to such a one.

It was to gratify the two great passions of asking and answering that epistolary correspondence was first invented. Letters (for by this usurped title epistles are now commonly known) are of several kinds. First, there are those which are not letters at all,—as letters-patent, letters dimissory, letters enclosing bills, letters of administration, Pliny's letters, letters of diplomacy, of Cato, of Mentor, of Lords Lyttelton, Chesterfield, and Orrery, of Jacob Behmen, Seneca (whom St. Jerome includes in his list of sacred writers), letters from abroad, from sons in college to their fathers, letters of marque, and letters generally, which are in no wise letters of mark. Second, are real letters, such as those of Gray, Cowper, Walpole, Howel, Lamb, D. Y., the first letters from children (printed in staggering capitals), Letters from New York, letters of credit, and others, interesting for the sake of the writer or the thing written. I have read also letters from Europe by a gentleman named Pinto, containing some curious gossip, and which I hope to see collected for the benefit of the curious. There are, besides, letters addressed to posterity,—as epitaphs, for example, written for their own monuments by monarchs, whereby we have lately become possessed of the names

of several great conquerors and kings of kings, hitherto unheard of and still unpronounceable, but valuable to the student of the entirely dark ages. The letter of our Saviour to King Abgarus, that which St. Peter sent to King Pepin in the year of grace 755, that of the Virgin to the magistrates of Messina, that of the Sanhedrim of Toledo to Annas and Caiaphas, A. D. 35, that of Galeazzo Sforza's spirit to his brother Lodovico, that of St. Gregory Thaumaturgus to the D—l, and that of this last-mentioned active police-magistrate to a man of Girgenti, I would place in a class by themselves, as also the letters of candidates, concerning which I shall dilate more fully in a note at the end of the following poem. At present, *sat prata biberunt.* Only, concerning the shape of letters, they are all either square or oblong, to which general figures circular letters and round-robins also conform themselves.— H. W.]

DEER SIR its gut to be the fashun now to rite letters to the candid 8s and i wus chose at a publick Meetin in Jaalam to du wut wus nessary fur that town. i writ to 271 ginerals and gut ansers to 209. tha air called candid 8s but I don't see nothin candid about 'em. this here i wich I send wus thought satty'factory. I dunno as it's ushle to print Poscrips, but as all the ansers I got hed the saim, I sposed it wus best. times has gretly changed. Formaly to knock a man into a cocked hat wus to use him up, but now it ony gives him a chance fur the cheef madgustacry. — H. B.

DEAR SIR, — You wish to know my notions
On sartin pints thet rile the land;
There's nothin' thet my natur so shuns
  Ez bein' mum or underhand;
I'm a straight-spoken kind o' creetur
  Thet blurts right out wut's in his head,
An' ef I've one pecooler feetur,
  It is a nose thet wunt be led.

So, to begin at the beginnin',
  An' come direcly to the pint,
I think the country's underpinnin'
  Is some consid'ble out o' jint;
I aint agoin' to try your patience
  By tellin' who done this or thet,
I don't make no insinooations,
  I jest let on I smell a rat.

Thet is, I mean, it seems to me so,
  But, ef the public think I'm wrong,

I wunt deny but wut I be so, —
    An', fact, it don't smell very strong ;
My mind 's tu fair to lose its balance
    An' say wich party hez most sense ;
There may be folks o' greater talence
    Thet can't set stiddier on the fence.

I 'm an eclectic ; ez to choosin'
    'Twixt this an' thet, I 'm plaguy
        lawth ;
I leave a side thet looks like losin',
    But (wile there 's doubt) I stick to
        both ;
I stan' upon the Constitution,
    Ez preudunt statesmun say, who 've
        planned
A way to git the most profusion
    O' chances ez to *ware* they 'll stand.

Ez fer the war, I go agin it, —
    I mean to say I kind o' du, —
Thet is, I mean thet, bein' in it,
    The best way wuz to fight it thru ;
Not but wut abstract war is horrid,
    - I sign to thet with all my heart, —
But civlyzation *does* git forrid
    Sometimes upon a powder-cart.

About thet darned Proviso matter
    I never hed a grain o' doubt,
Nor I aint one my sense to scatter
    So 'st to one could n't pick it out ;
My love fer North an' South is equil,
    So I 'll jest answer plump an' frank, —
No matter wut may be the sequil, —
    Yes, Sir, I *am* agin a Bank.

Ez to the answerin' o' questions,
    I 'm an off ox at bein' druv,
Though I aint one thet ary test shuns
    'll give our folks a helpin' shove ;
Kind o' permiscuous I go it
    Fer the holl country, an' the ground
I take, ez nigh ez I can show it,
    Is pooty gen'ally all round.

I don't appruve o' givin' pledges ;
    You 'd ough' to leave a feller free,
An' not go knockin' out the wedges
    To ketch his fingers in the tree ;
Pledges air awfle breachy cattle
    Thet preudunt farmers don't turn
        out, —
Ez long 'z the people git their rattle,
    Wut is there fer 'm to grout about ?

Ez to the slaves, there 's no confusion
    In *my* idees consarnin' them, —
I think they air an Institution,
    A sort of — yes, jest so, — ahem :
Do *I* own any ? Of my merit
    On thet pint you yourself may jedge
All is, I never drink no sperit,
    Nor I haint never signed no pledge.

Ez to my princerples, I glory
    In hevin' nothin' o' the sort ;
I aint a Wig, I aint a Tory,
    I 'm jest a candidate, in short ;
Thet 's fair an' square an' parpendicler,
    But, ef the Public cares a fig
To hev me an' thin' in particler,
    Wy, I 'm a kind o' peri-wig.

P. S.

Ez we 're a sort o' privateerin',
    O' course, you know, it 's sheer **an**
        sheer,
An' there is sutthin' wuth your hearin'
    I 'll mention in *your* privit ear ;
Ef you git *me* inside the White House,
    Your head with ile I 'll kin' o' 'nint
By gittin' *you* inside the Light-house
    Down to the eend o' Jaalam Pint.

An' ez the North hez took to brustlin'
    At bein' scrouged frum off the roost,
I 'll tell ye wut 'll save all tusslin'
    An' give our side a harnsome boost, —
Tell 'em thet on the Slavery question
    I 'm RIGHT, although to speak I 'm
        lawth ;
This gives you a safe pint to rest on,
    An' leaves me frontin' South by
        North.

[And now of epistles candidatial, which are
of two kinds, — namely, letters of acceptance, and letters definitive of position. Our
republic, on the eve of an election, may safely enough be called a republic of letters.
Epistolary composition becomes then an epi-
demic, which seizes one candidate after another, not seldom cutting short the thread of
political life. It has come to such a pass,
that a party dreads less the attacks of its op-
ponents than a letter from its candidate.
Litera scripta manet, and it will go hard if
something bad cannot be made of it. General Harrison, it is well understood, was sur-
rounded, during his candidacy, with the *cor-
don sanitaire* of a vigilance committee. No

prisoner in Spielberg was ever more cautiously deprived of writing materials. The soot was scraped carefully from the chimneyplaces; outposts of expert rifle-shooters rendered it sure death for any goose (who came clad in feathers) to approach within a certain limited distance of North Bend; and all domestic fowls about the premises were reduced to the condition of Plato's original man. By these precautions the General was saved. *Parva componere magnis*, I remember, that, when party-spirit once ran high among my people, upon occasion of the choice of a new deacon, I, having my preferences, yet not caring too openly to express them, made use of an innocent fraud to bring about that result which I deemed most desirable. My stratagem was no other than the throwing a copy of the Complete Letter-Writer in the way of the candidate whom I wished to defeat. He caught the infection, and addressed a short note to his constituents, in which the opposite party detected so many and so grave improprieties (he had modelled it upon the letter of a young lady accepting a proposal of marriage), that he not only lost his election, but, falling under a suspicion of Sabellianism and I know not what (the widow Endive assured me that he was a Paralipomenon, to her certain knowledge), was forced to leave the town. Thus it is that the letter killeth.

The object which candidates propose to themselves in writing is to convey no meaning at all. And here is a quite unsuspected pitfall into which they successively plunge headlong. For it is precisely in such cryptographies that mankind are prone to seek for and find a wonderful amount and variety of significance. *Omne ignotum pro mirifico.* How do we admire at the antique world striving to crack those oracular nuts from Delphi, Hammon, and elsewhere, in only one of which can I so much as surmise that any kernel had ever lodged ; that, namely, wherein Apollo confessed that he was mortal. One Didymus is, moreover, related to have written six thousand books on the single subject of grammar, a topic rendered only more tenebrific by the labors of his successors, and which seems still to possess an attraction for authors in proportion as they can make nothing of it. A singular loadstone for theologians, also, is the Beast in the Apocalypse, whereof, in the course of my studies, I have noted two hundred and three several interpretations, each lethiferal to all the rest. *Non nostrum est tantas componere lites*, yet I have myself ventured upon a two hundred and fourth, which I embodied in a discourse preached on occasion of the demise of the late usurper, Napoleon Bonaparte, and which quieted, in a large measure, the minds of my people. It is true that my views on this important point were ardently controverted by Mr. Shearjashub Holden, the then preceptor of our academy,

and in other particulars a very deserving and sensible young man, though possessing a somewhat limited knowledge of the Greek tongue. But his heresy struck down no deep root, and, he having been lately removed by the hand of Providence, I had the satisfaction of reaffirming my cherished sentiments in a sermon preached upon the Lord's day immediately succeeding his funeral. This might seem like taking an unfair advantage, did I not add that he had made provision in his last will (being celibate) for the publication of a posthumous tractate in support of his own dangerous opinions.

I know of nothing in our modern times which approaches so nearly to the ancient oracle as the letter of a Presidential candidate. Now, among the Greeks, the eating of beans was strictly forbidden to all such as had it in mind to consult those expert amphibologists, and this same prohibition on the part of Pythagoras to his disciples is understood to imply an abstinence from politics, beans having been used as ballots. That other explication, *quod videlicet sensus eo cibo obtundi existimaret*, though supported *pugnis et calcibus* by many of the learned, and not wanting the countenance of Cicero, is confuted by the larger experience of New England. On the whole, I think it safer to apply here the rule of intrepretation which now generally obtains in regard to antique cosmogonies, myths, fables, proverbial expressions, and knotty points generally, which is, to find a common-sense meaning, and then select whatever can be imagined the most opposite thereto. In this way we arrive at the conclusion, that the Greeks objected to the questioning of candidates. And very properly, if, as I conceive, the chief point be not to discover what a person in that position is, or what he will do, but whether he can be elected. *Vos exemplaria Græca nocturna versate manu, versate diurna.*

But, since an imitation of the Greeks in this particular (the asking of questions being one chief privilege of freemen) is hardly to be hoped for, and our candidates will answer, whether they are questioned or not, I would recommend that these ante-electionary dialogues should be carried on by symbols, as were the diplomatic correspondences of the Scythians and Macrobii, or confined to the language of signs, like the famous interview of Panurge and Goatsnose. A candidate might then convey a suitable reply to all committees of inquiry by closing one eye, or by presenting them with a phial of Egyptian darkness to be speculated upon by their respective constituencies. These answers would be susceptible of whatever retrospective construction the exigencies of the political campaign might seem to demand, and the candidate could take his position on either side of the fence with entire consistency. Or, if letters must be written, profitable use might be made of the Dighton rock hieroglyphic or the cuneiform script, every fresh decipherer of which is enabled to educe a different meaning, whereby a sculptured stone or two supplies us, and will probably continue to supply posterity, with a very vast and various body of authentic history. For even the briefest epistle in the ordinary chirography is dangerous. There is scarce any style so compressed that superfluous words may not be detected in it. A severe critic might curtail that famous brevity of Cæsar's by two thirds, drawing his pen through the supererogatory *veni* and *vidi*. Perhaps, after all, the surest footing of hope is to be found in the rapidly increasing tendency to demand less and less of qualification in candidates. Already have statesmanship, experience, and the possession (nay, the profession, even) of principles been rejected as superfluous, and may not the patriot reasonably hope that the ability to write will follow? At present, there may be death in pot-hooks as well as pots, the loop of a letter may suffice for a bow-string, and all the dreadful heresies of Antislavery may lurk in a flourish. — H. W.]

No. VIII.

A SECOND LETTER FROM B. SAWIN, ESQ.

[IN the following epistle, we behold Mr. Sawin returning, a *miles emeritus*, to the bosom of his family. *Quantum mutatus!* The good Father of us all had doubtless intrusted to the keeping of this child of his certain faculties of a constructive kind. He had put in him a share of that vital force, the nicest economy of every minute atom of which is necessary to the perfect development of Humanity. He had given him a brain and heart, and so had equipped his soul with the two strong wings of knowledge and love, whereby it can mount to hang its nest under the eaves of heaven. And this child, so dowered, he had intrusted to the keeping of his vicar, the State. How stands the account of that stewardship? The State, or Society (call her by what name you will), had taken no manner of thought of him till she saw him swept out into the street, the pitiful leavings of last night's debauch, with cigar-ends, lemon-parings, tobacco-quids, slops, vile stenches, and the whole loathsome next-morning of the bar-room, — an own child of the Almighty God! I remember him as he was brought to be christened, a ruddy, rugged babe; and now there he wallows, reeking, seething, — the dead corpse, not of a man, but of a soul, — a putrefying lump, horrible for the life that is in it. Comes the wind of heaven, that good Samaritan, and parts the hair upon his forehead, nor is too nice to kiss those parched, cracked lips; the

morning opens upon him her eyes full of pitying sunshine, the sky yearns down to him, — and there he lies fermenting. O sleep! let me not profane thy holy name by calling that stertorous unconsciousness a slumber! By and by comes along the State, God's vicar. Does she say, — "'My poor, forlorn foster-child! Behold here a force which I will make dig and plant and build for me'"? Not so, but, — "Here is a recruit ready-made to my hand, a piece of destroying energy lying unprofitably idle." So she claps an ugly gray suit on him, puts a musket in his grasp, and sends him off, with Gubernatorial and other godspeeds, to do duty as a destroyer.

I made one of the crowd at the last Mechanics' Fair, and, with the rest, stood gazing in wonder at a perfect machine, with its soul of fire, its boiler-heart that sent the hot blood pulsing along the iron arteries, and its thews of steel. And while I was admiring the adaptation of means to end, the harmonious involutions of contrivance, and the never-bewildered complexity, I saw a grimed and greasy fellow, the imperious engine's lackey and drudge, whose sole office was to let fall, at intervals, a drop or two of oil upon a certain joint. Then my soul said within me, See there a piece of mechanism to which that other you marvel at is but as the rude first effort of a child, — a force which not merely suffices to set a few wheels in motion, but which can send an impulse all through the infinite future, — a contrivance, not for turning out pins, or stitching button-holes, but for making Hamlets and Lears. And yet this thing of iron shall be housed, waited on, guarded from rust and dust, and it shall be a crime but so much as to scratch it with a pin; while the other, with his fire of God in it, shall be buffeted hither and thither, and finally sent carefully a thousand miles to be the target for a Mexican cannon-ball. Unthrifty Mother State! My heart burned within me for pity and indignation, and I renewed this covenant with my own soul, — *In aliis mansuetus ero, at, in blasphemiis contra Christum, non ita.* — H. W.]

I SPOSE you wonder ware I be; I can't
    tell, fer the soul o' me,
Exacly ware I be myself, — meanin' by
    thet the holl o' me.
Wen I left hum, I hed two legs, an'
    they worn't bad ones neither,
(The scaliest trick they ever played wuz
    bringin' on me hither,)
Now one on 'em's I dunno ware; —
    they thought I wuz adyin',
An' sawed it off because they said 't wuz
    kin' o' mortifyin';
I'm willin' to believe it wuz, an yit I
    don't see, nuther,

Wy one should take to feelin' cheap a
    minnit sooner 'n t' other,
Sence both wuz equilly to blame ; but
    things is ez they be :
It took on so they took it off, an' thet 's
    enough fer me :
There 's one good thing, though, to be
    said about my wooden new one,—
The liquor can't git into it ez 't used to
    in the true one ;
So it saves drink ; an' then, besides, a
    feller could n't beg
A gretter blessin' then to hev one ollers
    sober peg ;
It 's true a chap 's in want o' two fer
    follerin' a drum,
But all the march I 'm up to now is jest
    to Kingdom Come.

I 've lost one eye, but thet 's a loss it 's
    easy to supply
Out o' the glory that I 've gut, fer thet
    is all my eye ;
An' one is big enough, I guess, by
    diligently usin' it,
To see all I shall ever git by way o' pay
    fer losin' it ;
Offcers, I notice, who git paid fer all
    our thumps an' kickins,
Du wal by keepin' single eyes arter the
    fattest pickins ;
So, ez the eye 's put fairly out, I 'll larn
    to go without it,
An' not allow *myself* to be no gret put
    out about it.
Now, le' me see, thet is n't all ; I used,
    'fore leavin' Jaalam,
To count things on my finger-eends,
    but sutthin' seems to ail 'em :
Ware 's my left hand ? O, darn it, yes,
    I recollect wut 's come on 't ;
I haint no left arm but my right, an'
    thet 's gut jest a thumb on 't ;
It aint so hendy ez it wuz to cal'late a
    sum on 't.
I 've hed some ribs broke, — six (I
    b'lieve), — I haint kep' no ac-
    count on 'em ;
Wen pensions git to be the talk, I 'll
    settle the amount on 'em.
An' now I 'm speakin' about ribs, it
    kin' o' brings to mind
One thet I couldn't never break, — the
    one I lef' behind ;

Ef you should see her, jest clear out the
    spout o' your invention
An' pour the longest sweetnin' in about
    an annooal pension,
An' kin' o' hint (in case, you know, the
    critter should refuse to be
Consoled) I aint so 'xpensive now to
    keep ez wut I used to be ;
There 's one arm less, ditto one eye,
    an' then the leg thet 's wooden
Can be took off an' sot away wenever
    ther 's a puddin'.

I spose you think I 'm comin' back ez
    opperlunt ez thunder,
With shiploads o' gold images an' varus
    sorts o' plunder ;
Wal, 'fore I vullinteered, I thought this
    country wuz a sort o'
Canaan, a reg'lar Promised Land flowin'
    with rum an' water,
Ware propaty growed up like time,
    without no cultivation,
An' gold wuz dug ez taters be among
    our Yankee nation,
Ware nateral advantages were pufficly
    amazin',
Ware every rock there wuz about with
    precious stuns wuz blazin',
Ware mill-sites filled the country up ez
    thick ez you could cram 'em,
An' desput rivers run about abeggin'
    folks to dam 'em ;
Then there were meetinhouses, tu,
    chockful o' gold an' silver
Thet you could take, an' no one couldn't
    hand ye in no bill fer ;
Thet 's wut I thought afore I went,
    thet 's wut them fellers told us
Thet stayed to hum an' speechified an'
    to the buzzards sold us ;
I thought thet gold mines could be gut
    cheaper than Chiny asters,
An' see myself acomin' back like sixty
    Jacob Astors ;
But sech idees soon melted down an'
    did n't leave a grease-spot ;
I vow my holl sheer o' the spiles
    wouldn't come nigh a V spot ;
Although, most anywares we 've ben,
    you need n't break no locks,
Nor run no kin' o' risks, to fill your
    pocket full o' rocks.

I guess I mentioned in my last some o'
    the nateral feeturs
O' this all-fiered buggy hole in th' way
    o' awfle creeturs,
But I fergut to name (new things to
    speak on so abounded)
How one day you'll most die o' thust,
    an' 'fore the next git drownded.

The clymit seems to me jest like a tea-
    pot made o' pewter
Our Preudence hed, thet wouldn't pour
    (all she could du) to suit her;
Fust place the leaves 'ould choke the
    spout, so 's not a drop 'ould dreen
    out,
Then Prude 'ould tip an' tip an' tip,
    till the holl kit bust clean out,
The kiver-hinge-pin bein' lost, tea-
    leaves an' tea an' kiver
'ould all come down *kerswosh!* ez
    though the dam bust in a river.

Jest so 't is here; holl months there
    aint a day o' rainy weather,
An' jest ez th' officers 'ould be alayin'
    heads together
Ez t' how they'd mix their drink at
    sech a milingtary deepot, —
'T 'ould pour ez though the lid wuz off
    the everlastin' teapot.

The cons'quence is, thet I shall take,
    wen I'm allowed to leave here,
One piece o' propaty along, — an' thet's
    the shakin' fever;
It's reggilar employment, though, an'
    thet aint thought to harm one,
Nor 't aint so tiresome ez it wuz with
    t' other leg an' arm on;
An' it's a consolation, tu, although it
    doos n't pay,
To hev it said you've got some gret shakes
    in any kin' o' way.

'T worn't very long, I tell ye wut, I
    thought o' fortin-makin', —
One day a reg'lar shiver-de-freeze, an'
    next ez good ez bakin', —
One day abrilin' in the sand, then
    smoth'rin' in the mashes, —
Git up all sound, be put to bed a mess
    o' hacks an' smashes.
But then, thinks I, at any rate there's
    glory to be hed, —
Thet's an investment, arter all, thet
    may n't turn out so bad;
But somehow, wen we'd fit an' licked,
    I ollers found the thanks

Gut kin' o' lodged afore they come ez
    low down ez the ranks;
The Gin'rals gut the biggest sheer, the
    Cunnles next, an' so on, —
We never gut a blasted mite o' glory
    ez I know on;
An' spose we hed, I wonder how you're
    goin' to contrive its
Division so 's to give a piece to twenty
    thousand privits;
Ef you should multiply by ten the por-
    tion o' the brav'st one,
You wouldn't git more 'n half enough
    to speak of on a grave-stun;
We git the licks, — we're jest the grist
    thet's put into War's hoppers;
Leftenants is the lowest grade thet
    helps pick up the coppers.
It may suit folks thet go agin a body
    with a soul in 't,
An' aint contented with a hide without
    a bagnet hole in 't;
But glory is a kin' o' thing *I* sha'n't
    pursue no furder,
Coz thet's the off'cers parquisite, —
    yourn 's on'y jest the murder.

Wal, arter I gin glory up, thinks I at
    least there's one
Thing in the bills we aint hed yit, an'
    thet's the GLORIOUS FUN;
Ef once we git to Mexico, we fairly
    may persume we
All day an' night shall revel in the halls
    o' Montezumy.
I'll tell ye wut *my* revels wuz, an' see
    how you would like 'em;
We never gut inside the hall — the nigh-
    est ever *I* come
Wuz stan'in' sentry in the sun (an',
    fact, it *seemed* a cent'ry)
A ketchin' smells o' biled an' roast thet
    come out thru the entry,
An' hearin' ez I sweltered thru my
    passes an' repasses,
A rat-tat-too o' knives an' forks, a
    clinkty-clink o' glasses:
I can't tell off the bill o' fare the Gin'-
    rals hed inside;
All I know is, thet out o' doors a pair
    o' soles wuz fried,
An' not a hundred miles away frum
    ware this child wuz posted,
A Massachusetts citizen wuz baked an'
    biled an' roasted;

The on'y thing like revellin' thet ever
    come to me
Wuz bein' routed out o' sleep by thet
    darned revelee.

They say the quarrel 's settled now ; fer
    my part I 've some doubt on 't,
'T'll take more fish-skin than folks think
    to take the rile clean out on 't ;
At any rate, I 'm so used up I can't do
    no more fightin',
The on'y chance thet 's left to me is
    politics or writin' ;
Now, ez the people 's gut to hev a mil-
    ingtray man,
An' I aint nothin' else jest now, I 've
    hit upon a plan ;
The can'idatin' line, you know, 'ould
    suit me to a T,
An' ef I lose, 't wunt hurt my ears to
    lodge another flea ;
So I 'll set up ez can'idate fer any kin'
    o' office,
(I mean fer any thet includes good easy-
    cheers an' soffies ;
Fer ez tu runnin' fer a place ware
    work 's the time o' day,
You know thet 's wut I never did, —
    except the other way ;)
Ef it 's the Presidential cheer fer wich
    I 'd better run,
Wut two legs anywares about could
    keep up with my one ?
There aint no kin' o' quality in can'i-
    dates, it 's said,
So useful ez a wooden leg, — except a
    wooden head ;
There 's nothin' aint so poppylar — (wy,
    it 's a parfect sin
To think wut Mexico hez paid fer Santy
    Anny's pin ;) —
Then I haint gut no princerples, an',
    sence I wuz knee-high,
I never *did* hev any gret, ez you can
    testify ;
I 'm a decided peace-man, tu, an' go
    agin the war, —
Fer now the holl on 't 's gone an' past,
    wut is there to go *for* ?
Ef, wile you 're 'lectioneerin' round,
    some curus chaps should beg
To know my views o' state affairs, jest
    answer WOODEN LEG !

Ef they aint settisfied with thet, an' kin
    o' pry an' doubt
An' ax fer sutthin' deffynit, jest say,
    ONE EYE PUT OUT !
Thet kin' o' talk I guess you 'll find 'll
    answer to a charm,
An' wen you 're druv tu nigh the wall,
    hol' up my missin' arm ;
Ef they should nose round fer a pledge,
    put on a vartuous look
An' tell 'em thet 's percisely wut I
    never gin nor — took !

Then you can call me "Timbertoes,"
    — thet 's wut the people likes ;
Sutthin' combinin' morril truth with
    phrases sech ez strikes ;
Some say the people 's fond o' this, or
    thet, or wut you please, —
I tell ye wut the people want is jest cor-
    rect idees ;
"Old Timbertoes," you see, 's a creed
    it 's safe to be quite bold on,
There 's nothin' in 't the other side can
    any ways git hold on ;
It 's a good tangible idee, a sutthin' to
    embody
Thet valooable class o' men who look
    thru brandy-toddy ;
It gives a Party Platform, tu, jest level
    with the mind
Of all right-thinkin', honest folks thet
    mean to go it blind ;
Then there air other good hooraws to
    dror on ez you need 'em,
Sech ez the ONE-EYED SLARTERER, the
    BLOODY BIRDOFREDUM !
Them 's wut takes hold o' folks thet
    think, ez well ez o' the masses,
An' makes you sartin o' the aid o' good
    men of all classes.

There 's one thing I 'm in doubt about ;
    in order to be Presidunt,
It 's absolutely ne'ssary to be a South-
    ern residunt ;
The Constitution settles thet, an' also
    thet a feller
Must own a nigger o' some sort, jet
    black, or brown, or yeller.
Now I haint no objections agin par-
    ticklar climes,
Nor agin ownin' anythin' (except the
    truth sometimes),

But, ez I haint no capital, up there
   among ye, maybe,
You might raise funds enough fer me to
   buy a low-priced baby,
An' then to suit the No'thern folks,
   who feel obleeged to say
They hate an' cuss the very thing they
   vote fer every day,
Say you 're assured I go full butt fer
   Libbaty's diffusion
An' made the purchis on'y jest to spite
   the Institootion ; —
But, golly ! there 's the currier's hoss
   upon the pavement pawin' !
I 'll be more 'xplicit in my next.
           Yourn,
              BIRDOFREDUM SAWIN.

[We have now a tolerably fair chance of esti-
mating how the balance-sheet stands between our returned volunteer and glory. Supposing the entries to be set down on both
sides of the account in fractional parts of one
hundred, we shall arrive at something like
the following result : —

B. SAWIN, Esq., in account with (BLANK)
              GLORY.

Cr.		Dr.	
By loss of one leg,	20	To one 675th three	
" do. one arm,	15	cheers in Fan-	
" do. four fin-		euil Hall, .	30
gers, . . .	5	" do. do. on	
" do. one eye,	10	occasion of	
" the breaking of		presentation of	
six ribs, . .	6	sword to Col-	
" having served		onel Wright,	25
under Colonel		" one suit of	
Cushing one		gray clothes	
month, . .	44	(ingeniously un-	
		becoming), .	15
		" musical enter-	
		tainments (drum	
		and fife six	
		months), . .	5
		" one dinnerafter	
		return, . .	1
		" chance of pen-	
		sion, . . .	1
		" privilege of	
		drawing long-	
		bow during rest	
		of natural life,	23
	100		100

E. E.

It should appear that Mr. Sawin found the
actual feast curiously the reverse of the bill
of fare advertised in Faneuil Hall and other
places. His primary object seems to have
been the making of his fortune. *Quærenda*

pecunia primum, virtus post nummos. He
hoisted sail for Eldorado, and shipwrecked
on Point Tribulation. *Quid non mortalia
pectora cogis, auri sacra fames ?* The speculation has sometimes crossed my mind, in
that dreary interval of drought which inter-
venes between quarterly stipendiary showers,
that Providence, by the creation of a money-
tree, might have simplified wonderfully the
sometimes perplexing problem of human life.
We read of bread-trees, the butter for which
lies ready-churned in Irish bogs. Milk-trees
we are assured of in South America, and stout
Sir John Hawkins testifies to water-trees in
the Canaries. Boot-trees bear abundantly
in Lynn and elsewhere ; and I have seen, in
the entries of the wealthy, hat-trees with a
fair show of fruit. A family-tree I once cultivated myself, and found therefrom but a
scanty yield, and that quite tasteless and in-
nutritious. Of trees bearing men we are not
without examples ; as those in the park of
Louis the Eleventh of France. Who has
forgotten, moreover, that olive-tree, growing
in the Athenian's back-garden, with its
strange uxorious crop, for the general propagation of which, as of a new and precious
variety, the philosopher Diogenes, hitherto
uninterested in arboriculture, was so zealous ?
In the *sylva* of our own Southern States, the
females of my family have called my attention
to the china-tree. Not to multiply examples,
I will barely add to my list the birch-tree, in
the smaller branches of which has been im-
planted so miraculous a virtue for communicating the Latin and Greek languages, and
which may well, therefore, be classed among
the trees producing necessaries of life, —
venerabile donum fatalis virgæ. That
money-trees existed in the golden age there
want not prevalent reasons for our believing.
For does not the old proverb, when it as-
serts that money does not grow on *every*
bush, imply *a fortiori* that there were certain
bushes which did produce it ? Again, there
is another ancient saw to the effect that
money is the *root* of all evil. From which
two adages it may be safe to infer that the
aforesaid species of tree first degenerated
into a shrub, then absconded underground,
and finally, in our iron age, vanished altogether. In favorable exposures it may be
conjectured that a specimen or two survived
to a great age, as in the garden of the Hesperides ; and, indeed, what else could that
tree in the Sixth Æneid have been, with a
branch whereof the Trojan hero procured
admission to a territory, for the entering of
which money is a surer passport than to a
certain other more profitable and too foreign
kingdom ? Whether these speculations of
mine have any force in them, or whether they
will not rather, by most readers, be deemed
impertinent to the matter in hand, is a
question which I leave to the determination
of an indulgent posterity. That there were,
in more primitive and happier times, shops

where money was sold,—and that, too, on credit and at a bargain,—I take to be matter of demonstration. For what but a dealer in this article was that Æolus who supplied Ulysses with motive power for his fleet in bags? What that Ericus, king of Sweden, who is said to have kept the winds in his cap? what, in more recent times, those Lapland Nornas who traded in favorable breezes? All which will appear the more clearly when we consider, that, even to this day, *raising the wind* is proverbial for raising money, and that brokers and banks were invented by the Venetians at a later period.

And now for the improvement of this digression. I find a parallel to Mr. Sawin's fortune in an adventure of my own. For, shortly after I had first broached to myself the before-stated natural-historical and archæological theories, as I was passing, *hæc negotia penitus mecum revolvens*, through one of the obscure suburbs of our New England metropolis, my eye was attracted by these words upon a sign-board,—CHEAP CASH-STORE. Here was at once the confirmation of my speculations, and the substance of my hopes. Here lingered the fragment of a happier past, or stretched out the first tremulous organic filament of a more fortunate future. Thus glowed the distant Mexico to the eyes of Sawin, as he looked through the dirty pane of the recruiting-office window, or speculated from the summit of that mirage-Pisgah which the imps of the bottle are so cunning to raise up. Already had my Alnaschar-fancy (even during that first half-believing glance) expended in various useful directions the funds to be obtained by pledging the manuscript of a proposed volume of discourses. Already did a clock ornament the tower of the Jaalam meeting-house, a gift appropriately, but modestly, commemorated in the parish and town records, both, for now many years, kept by myself. Already had my son Seneca completed his course at the University. Whether, for the moment, we may not be considered as actually lording it over Barataria with the viceroyalty of which Hope invests us, and whether we are ever so warmly housed as in our Spanish castles, would afford matter of argument. Enough that I found that sign-board to be no other than a bait to the trap of a decayed grocer. Nevertheless, I bought a pound of dates (getting short weight by reason of immense flights of harpy flies who pursued and lighted upon their prey even in the very scales), which purchase I made, not only with an eye to the little ones at home, but also as a figurative reproof of that too frequent habit of my mind, which, forgetting the due order of chronology, will often persuade me that the happy sceptre of Saturn is stretched over this Astræa-forsaken nineteenth century.

Having glanced at the ledger of Glory under the title *Sawin, B.*, let us extend our investigations, and discover if that instructive volume does not contain some charges more personally interesting to ourselves. I think we should be more economical of our resources, did we thoroughly appreciate the fact, that, whenever Brother Jonathan seems to be thrusting his hand into his own pocket, he is, in fact, picking ours. I confess that the late *muck* which the country has been running has materially changed my views as to the best method of raising revenue. If, by means of direct taxation, the bills for every extraordinary outlay were brought under our immediate eye, so that, like thrifty housekeepers, we could see where and how fast the money was going, we should be less likely to commit extravagances. At present, these things are managed in such a huggermugger way, that we know not what we pay for; the poor man is charged as much as the rich; and, while we are saving and scrimping at the spigot, the government is drawing off at the bung. If we could know that a part of the money we expend for tea and coffee goes to buy powder and balls, and that it is Mexican blood which makes the clothes on our backs more costly, it would set some of us athinking. During the present fall, I have often pictured to myself a government official entering my study and handing me the following bill:—

WASHINGTON, Sept. 30, 1848.

REV. HOMER WILBUR to **Uncle Samuel**, *Dr.*

To his share of work done in Mexico on partnership account, sundry jobs, as below.	
" killing, maiming, and wounding about 5,000 Mexicans, . .	$2.00
" slaughtering one woman carrying water to wounded, . . .	.10
" extra work on two different Sabbaths (one bombardment and one assault) whereby the Mexicans were prevented from defiling themselves with the idolatries of high mass, ...	3.50
" throwing an especially fortunate and Protestant bombshell into the Cathedral at Vera Cruz, whereby several female Papists were slain at the altar, ...	.50
" his proportion of cash paid for conquered territory, ...	1.75
" do. do. for conquering do.	1.50
" manuring do. with new superior compost called "American Citizen,"	.50
" extending the area of freedom and Protestantism, ...	.01
" glory, ...	.01
	$9.87

Immediate payment is requested.

N. B. Thankful for former favors, U. S. requests a continuance of patronage. Orders executed with neatness and despatch. Terms as low as those of any other contractor for the same kind and style of work.

I can fancy the official answering my look of horror with, — "Yes, Sir, it looks like a high charge, Sir ; but in these days slaughtering is slaughtering." Verily, I would that every one understood that it was ; for it goes about obtaining money under the false pretence of being glory. For me, I have an imagination which plays me uncomfortable tricks. It happens to me sometimes to see a slaughterer on his way home from his day's work, and forthwith my imagination puts a cocked-hat upon his head and epaulettes upon his shoulders, and sets him up as a candidate for the Presidency. So, also, on a recent public occasion, as the place assigned to the "Reverend Clergy" is just behind that of "Officers of the Army and Navy" in processions, it was my fortune to be seated at the dinner-table over against one of these respectable persons. He was arrayed as (out of his own profession) only kings, court-officers, and footmen are in Europe, and Indians in America. Now what does my over-officious imagination but set to work upon him, strip him of his gay livery, and present him to me coatless, his trowsers thrust into the tops of a pair of boots thick with clotted blood, and a basket on his arm out of which lolled a gore-smeared axe, thereby destroying my relish for the temporal mercies upon the board before me ! — H. W.]

No. IX.

A THIRD LETTER FROM B. SAWIN, ESQ.

[UPON the following letter slender comment will be needful. In what river Selemnus has Mr. Sawin bathed, that he has become so swiftly oblivious of his former loves? From an ardent and (as befits a soldier) confident wooer of that coy bride, the popular favor, we see him subside of a sudden into the (I trust not jilted) Cincinnatus, returning to his plough with a goodly sized branch of willow in his hand ; figuratively returning, however, to a figurative plough, and from no profound affection for that honored implement of husbandry (for which, indeed, Mr. Sawin never displayed any decided predilection), but in order to be gracefully summoned therefrom to more congenial labors. It should seem that the character of the ancient Dictator had become part of the recognized stock of our modern political comedy, though, as our term of office extends to a quadrennial length, the parallel is not so minutely exact as could be desired. It is sufficiently so, however, for purposes of scenic representation. An humble cottage (if built of logs, the better) forms the Arcadian background of the stage. This rustic paradise is labelled Ashland, Jaalam, North Bend, Marshfield, Kinderhook, or Bâton Rouge, as occasion demands. Before the door stands a something with one handle (the other painted in proper perspective), which represents, in happy ideal vagueness, the plough. To this the defeated candidate rushes with delirious joy, welcomed as a father by appropriate groups of happy laborers, or from it the successful one is torn with difficulty, sustained alone by a noble sense of public duty. Only I have observed, that, if the scene be laid at Bâton Rouge or Ashland, the laborers are kept carefully in the background, and are heard to shout from behind the scenes in a singular tone resembling ululation, and accompanied by a sound not unlike vigorous clapping. This, however, may be artistically in keeping with the habits of the rustic population of those localities. The precise connection between agricultural pursuits and statesmanship, I have not been able, after diligent inquiry, to discover. But, that my investigations may not be barren of all fruit, I will mention one curious statistical fact, which I consider thoroughly established, namely, that no real farmer ever attains practically beyond a seat in General Court, however theoretically qualified for more exalted station.

It is probable that some other prospect has been opened to Mr. Sawin, and that he has not made this great sacrifice without some definite understanding in regard to a seat in the cabinet or a foreign mission. It may be supposed that we of Jaalam were not untouched by a feeling of villatic pride in beholding our townsman occupying so large a space in the public eye. And to me, deeply revolving the qualifications necessary to a candidate in these frugal times, those of Mr. S. seemed peculiarly adapted to a successful campaign. The loss of a leg, an arm, an eye, and four fingers, reduced him so nearly to the condition of a *vox et preterea nikil*, that I could think of nothing but the loss of his head by which his chance could have been bettered. But since he has chosen to balk our suffrages, we must content ourselves with what we can get, remembering *lactucas non esse dandas, dum cardui sufficiant.* — H. W.]

I SPOSE you recollect thet I explained
    my gennle views
In the last billet thet I writ, 'way down
    frum Veery Cruze,
Jest arter I'd a kind o' ben spontanously sot up
To run unanimously fer the Presidential
    cup ;

O' course it worn't no wish o' mine,
   't wuz ferfely distressin',
But poppler enthusiasm gut so almighty
   pressin'
Thet, though like sixty all along I
   fumed an' fussed an' sorrered,
There did n't seem no ways to stop
   their bringin' on me forrerd :
Fact is, they udged the matter so, I
   could n't help admittin'
The Father o' his Country's shoes no
   feet but mine 'ould fit in,
Besides the savin' o' the soles fer ages
   to succeed,
Seein' thet with one wannut foot, a pair
   'd be more 'n I need ;
An', tell ye wut, them shoes 'll want a
   thund'rin sight o' patchin',
Ef this 'ere fashion is to last we 've gut
   into o' hatchin'
A pair o' second Washintons fer every
   new election, —
Though, fur ez number one's consarned,
   I don't make no objection.

I wuz agoin' on to say thet wen at fust
   I saw
The masses would stick to 't I wuz the
   Country's father-'n-law,
(They would ha' hed it *Father*, but I
   told 'em 't would n't du,
Coz thet wuz sutthin' of a sort they
   could n't split in tu,
An' Washinton hed hed the thing laid
   fairly to his door,
Nor dars n't say 't worn't his 'n, much
   ez sixty year afore,)
But 't aint no matter ez to thet ; wen I
   wuz nomernated,
'T worn't natur but wut I should feel
   consid'able elated,
An' wile the hoomw o' the thing wuz
   kind o' noo an' fresh,
I thought our ticket would ha' caird the
   country with a resh.

Sence I 've come hum, though, an'
   looked round, I think I seem to
   find
Strong argiments ez thick ez fleas to
   make me change my mind ;
It 's clear to any one whose brain aint
   fur gone in a phthisis,
Thet hail Columby's happy land is goin'
   thru a crisis,

An' 't would n't noways du to hev the
   people's mind distracted
By bein' all to once by sev'ral pop'lar
   names attackted ;
'T would save holl haycartloads o' fuss
   an' three four months o' jaw,
Ef some illustrous paytriot should back
   out an' withdraw ;
So, ez I aint a crooked stick, jest like —
   like ole (I swow,
I dunno ez I know his name)— I 'll
   go back to my plough.

Wenever an Amerikin distinguished
   politishin
Begins to try et wut they call definin'
   his posishin,
Wal, I, fer one, feel sure he aint gut
   nothin' to define ;
It 's so nine cases out o' ten, but jest
   that tenth is mine ;
And 't aint no more 'n is proper 'n'
   right in sech a sitooation
To hint the course you think 'll be the
   savin' o' the nation ;
To funk right out o' p'lit'cal strife aint
   thought to be the thing,
Without you deacon off the toon you
   want your folks should sing ;
So I edvise the noomrous friends thet 's
   in one boat with me
To jest up killick, jam right down their
   hellum hard a lee,
Haul the sheets taut, an', laying out
   upon the Suthun tack,
Make fer the safest port they can, wich,
   I think, is Ole Zack.

Next thing you 'll want to know, I
   spose, wut argiments I seem
To see thet makes me think this ere 'll
   be the strongest team ;
Fust place, I 've ben consid'ble round
   in bar-rooms an' saloons
Agethrin' public sentiment, 'mongst
   Demmercats and Coons,
An' 't aint ve'y offen thet I meet a chap
   but wut goes in
Fer Rough an' Ready, fair an' square,
   hufs, taller, horns, an' skin ;
I don't deny but wut, fer one, ez fur ez
   I could see,
I did n't like at fust the Pheladelphy
   nomernee :

I could ha' pinted to a man thet wuz, I
    guess, a peg
Higher than him, — a soger, tu, an' with
    a wooden leg;
But every day with more an' more o'
    Taylor zeal I'm burnin',
Seein' wich way the tide thet sets to
    office is aturnin';
Wy, into Bellers's we notched the votes
    down on three sticks, —
'T wuz Birdofredum *one*, Cass *aught*,
    an' Taylor *twenty-six*,
An' bein the on'y canderdate thet wuz
    upon the ground,
They said 't wuz no more 'n right thet
    I should pay the drinks all round;
Ef I'd expected sech a trick, I wouldn't
    ha' cut my foot
By goin' an' votin' fer myself like a con-
    sumed coot;
It didn't make no diff'rence, though; I
    wish I may be cust,
Ef Bellers wuzn't slim enough to say
    he wouldn't trust!

Another pint thet influences the minds
    o' sober jedges
Is thet the Gin'ral hezn't gut tied hand
    an' foot with pledges;
He hezn't told ye wut he is, an' so
    there aint no knowin'
But wut he may turn out to be the best
    there is agoin';
This, at the on'y spot thet pinched, the
    shoe directly eases,
Coz every one is free to 'xpercisely
    wut he pleases;
I want free-trade; you don't; the Gin-
    'ral isn't bound to neither; —
I vote my way; you, yourn; an' both
    air sooted to a T there.
Ole Rough an' Ready, tu, 's a Wig, but
    without bein' ultry
(He 's like a holsome hayinday, thet's
    warm, but isn't sultry;
He 's jest wut I should call myself, a
    kin' o' *scratch* ez 't ware,
Thet aint exacly all a wig nor wholly
    your own hair;
I 've ben a Wig three weeks myself,
    jest o' this mod'rate sort,
An' don't find them an' Demmercrats
    so different ez I thought;
They both act pooty much alike, an'
    push an' scrouge an' cus;

They 're like two pickpockets in league
    fer Uncle Samwell's pus;
Each takes a side, an' then they squeeze
    the old man in between 'em,
Turn all his pockets wrong side out an'
    quick ez lightnin' clean 'em;
To nary one on 'em I 'd trust a secon'-
    handed rail
No furder off 'an I could sling a bul-
    lock by the tail.

Webster sot matters right in thet air
    Mashfiel' speech o' his'n; —
"Taylor," sez he, "aint nary ways the
    one thet I 'd a chizzen,
Nor he aint fittin' fer the place, an'
    like ez not he aint
No more 'n a tough ole bullethead, an'
    no gret of a saint;
But then," sez he, "observe my pint,
    he 's jest ez good to vote fer
Ez though the greasin' on him won't
    a thing to hire Choate fer;
Aint it ez easy done to drop a ballot in
    a box
Fer one ez 't is fer t' other, fer the bull-
    dog ez the fox?"
It takes a man like Dannel's, fact, ez
    big ez all ou' doors,
To find out thet it looks like rain arter
    it fairly pours;
I 'gree with him, it aint so dreffle
    troublesome to vote
Fer Taylor arter all, — it 's jest to go
    an' change your coat;
Wen he 's once greased, you 'll swaller
    him an' never know on 't, scurce,
Unless he scratches, goin' down, with
    them 'ere Gin'ral's spurs.
I 've ben a votin' Demmercrat, ez reg-
    'lar as a clock,
But don't find goin' Taylor gives my
    narves no gret 'f a shock;
Truth is, the cutest leadin' Wigs, ever
    sence fust they found
Wich side the bread gut buttered on,
    hev kep' a edgin' round;
They kin' o' slipt the planks frum out
    th' ole platform one by one
An' made it gradooally noo, 'fore folks
    know'd wut wuz done,
Till, fur'z I know, there aint an inch
    thet I could lay my han' on,
But I, or any Demmercrat, feels com-
    f'table to stan' on,

An' ole Wig doctrines act'lly look, their
   occ'pants bein' gone,
Lonesome ez staddles on a mash without no hayricks on.

I spose it 's time now I should give my
   thoughts upon the plan,
Thet chipped the shell at Buffalo, o'
   settin' up ole Van.
I used to vote fer Martin, but, I swan,
   I 'm clean disgusted, —
He aint the man thet I can say is fittin'
   to be trusted ;
He aint half antislav'ry 'nough, nor I
   aint sure, ez some be,
He 'd go in fer abolishin' the Deestrick
   o' Columby ;
An', now I come to recollect, it kin' o'
   makes me sick 'z
A horse, to think o' wut he wuz in
   eighteen thirty-six.
An' then, another thing ; — I guess,
   though mebby I am wrong,
This Buff'lo plaster aint agoin' to dror
   almighty strong ;
Some folks, I know, hev gut th' idee
   thet No'thun dough 'll rise,
Though, 'fore I see it riz an' baked, I
   would n't trust my eyes ;
'T will take more emptins, a long chalk,
   than this noo party 's gut,
To give sech heavy cakes ez them a
   start, I tell ye wut.
But even ef they caird the day, there
   would n't be no endurin'
To stan' upon a platform with sech
   critters ez Van Buren ;
An' his son John, tu, I can't think how
   thet 'ere chap should dare
To speak ez he doos ; wy, they say he
   used to cuss an' swear !
I spose he never read the hymn thet
   tells how down the stairs
A feller with long legs wuz throwed
   thet would n't say his prayers.
This brings me to another pint : the
   leaders o' the party
Aint jest sech men ez I can act along
   with free an' hearty ;
They aint not quite respectable, an'
   wen a feller's morrils
Don't toe the straightest kin' o' mark,
   wy, him an' me jest quarrils.
I went to a free soil meetin' once, an'
   wut d' ye think I see ?

A feller was aspoutin' there thet act'lly
   come to me,
About two year ago last spring, ez nigh
   ez I can jedge,
An' axed me ef I did n't want to sign
   the Temprunce pledge !
He 's one o' them thet goes about an'
   sez you hed n't ough' ter
Drink nothin', mornin', noon, or night,
   stronger 'an Taunton water.
There 's one rule I 've ben guided by,
   in settlin' how to vote, ollers, —
I take the side thet *is n't* took by them
   consarned teetotallers.

Ez fer the niggers, I 've ben South, an'
   thet hez changed my mind ;
A lazier, more ongrateful set you could
   n't nowers find.
You know I mentioned in my last thet
   I should buy a nigger,
Ef I could make a purchase at a pooty
   mod'rate figger ;
So, ez there 's nothin' in the world I 'm
   fonder of 'an gunnin',
I closed a bargain finally to take a fel-
   ler runnin'.
I shou'dered queen's-arm an' stumped
   out, an' wen I come t' th' swamp,
'T worn't very long afore I gut upon
   the nest o' Pomp ;
I come acrost a kin' o' hut, an', playin'
   round the door,
Some little woolly-headed cubs, ez
   many 'z six or more.
At fust I thought o' firin', but *think
   twice* is safest ollers ;
There aint, thinks I, not one on 'em
   but 's wuth his twenty dollars,
Or would be, ef I hed 'em back into a
   Christian land, —
How temptin' all on 'em would look
   upon an auction-stand !
(Not but wut *I* hate Slavery in th' ab-
   stract, stem to starn, —
I leave it ware our fathers did, a privit
   State consarn.)
Soon 'z they see me, they yelled an'
   run, but Pomp wuz out ahoein'
A leetle patch o' corn he hed, or else
   there aint no knowin'
He would n't ha' took a pop at me ; but
   I hed gut the start,
An' wen he looked, I vow he groaned
   ez though he 'd broke his heart :

He done it like a wite man, tu, ez nat'-
  ral ez a pictur,
The imp'dunt, pis'nous hypocrite! wus
  'an a boy constrictur.

"You can't gum *me*, I tell ye now, an'
  so you need n't try,
I 'xpect my eye-teeth every mail, so
  jest shet up," sez I.

"Don't go to actin' ugly now, or else
  I 'll jest let strip,
You 'd best draw kindly, seein' 'z how
  I 've gut ye on the hip;

Besides, you darned ole fool, it aint no
  gret of a disaster
To be benev'lently druv back to a contented master,
Ware you hed Christian priv'ledges you
  don't seem quite aware of,
Or you 'd ha' never run away from bein'
  well took care of;

Ez fer kin' treatment, wy, he wuz so
  fond on ye, he said
He 'd give a fifty spot right out, to git
  ye, 'live or dead;
Wite folks aint sot by half ez much;
  'member I run away,
Wen I wuz bound to Cap'n Jakes, to
  Mattysqumscot Bay;
Don' know him, likely? Spose not;
  wal, the mean ole codger went
An' offered — wut reward, think? Wal,
  it worn't no *less* 'n a cent."

Wal, I jest gut 'em into line, an' druv
  'em on afore me,
The pis'nous brutes, I 'd no idee o' the
  ill-will they bore me;
We walked till som'ers about noon, an'
  then it grew so hot
I thought it best to camp awile, so I
  chose out a spot
Jest under a magnoly tree, an' there
  right down I sot;
Then I unstrapped my wooden leg, coz
  it begun to chafe,
An' laid it down 'long side o' me, supposin' all wuz safe;
I made my darkies all set down around
  me in a ring,
An' sot an' kin' o' ciphered up how
  much the lot would bring;
But, wile I drinked the peaceful cup of
  a pure heart an' mind

(Mixed with some wiskey, now an' then),
  Pomp he snaked up behind,
An' creepin' grad'lly close tu, ez quiet
  ez a mink,
Jest grabbed my leg, and then pulled
  foot, quicker 'an you could wink,
An', come to look, they each on 'em
  hed gut behin' a tree,
An' Pomp poked out the leg a piece,
  jest so ez I could see,
An' yelled to me to throw away my pis-
  tils an' my gun,
Or else thet they 'd cair off the leg, an'
  fairly cut an' run.

I vow I did n't b'lieve there wuz a decent alligatur
Thet hed a heart so destitoot o' common human natur;
However, ez there worn't no help, I
  finally give in
An' heft my arms away to git my leg
  safe back agin.
Pomp gethered all the weapins up, an'
  then he come an' grinned,
He showed his ivory some, I guess, an'
  sez, "You 're fairly pinned;
Jest buckle on your leg agin, an' git
  right up an' come,
'T wun't du fer fammerly men like me to
  be so long from hum."

At fust I put my foot right down an'
  swore I would n't budge.

"Jest ez you choose," sez he, quite
  cool, "either be shot or trudge."
So this black-hearted monster took an'
  act'lly druv me back
Along the very feetmarks o' my happy
  mornin' track,
An' kep' me pris'ner 'bout six months,
  an' worked me, tu, like sin,
Till he hed gut his corn an' his Carliny
  taters in;
He made me larn him readin', tu (although the crittur saw
How much it hut my morril sense to
  act agin the law),
So 'st he could read a Bible he 'd gut;
  an' axed ef I could pint
The North Star out; but there I put
  his nose some out o' jint,
Fer I weeled roun' about sou'west, an',
  lookin' up a bit,
Picked out a middlin' shiny one an' tole
  him thet wuz it.

Fin'lly, he took me to the door, an',
    givin' me a kick,
Sez, — "Ef you know wut 's best fer
    ye, be off, now, double-quick ;
The winter-time 's a comin' on, an',
    though I gut ye cheap,
You 're so darned lazy, I don't think
    you 're hardly wuth your keep ;
Besides, the childrin 's growin' up, an'
    you aint jest the model
I 'd like to hev 'em immertate, an' so
    you 'd better toddle !"

Now is there anythin' on airth 'll ever
    prove to me
Thet renegader slaves like him air fit
    fer bein' free?
D' you think they 'll suck me in to jine
    the Buff 'lo chaps, an' them
Rank infidels that go agin the Scrip-
    tur'l cus o' Shem?
Not by a jugfull ! sooner 'n thet, I 'd
    go thru fire an' water ;
Wen I hev once made up my mind, a
    meet'nhus aint sotter ;
No, not though all the crows thet flies to
    pick my bones wuz cawin', —
I guess we 're in a Christian land, —
    Yourn,
           BIRDOFREDUM SAWIN.

[Here, patient reader, we take leave of each other, I trust with some mutual satisfaction. I say *patient*, for I love not that kind which skims dippingly over the surface of the page, as swallows over a pool before rain. By such no pearls shall be gathered. But if no pearls there be (as, indeed, the world is not without example of books wherefrom the longest-winded diver shall bring up no more than his proper handful of mud), yet let us hope that an oyster or two may reward adequate perseverance. If neither pearls nor oysters, yet is patience itself a gem worth diving deeply for.

It may seem to some that too much space has been usurped by my own private lucubrations, and some may be fain to bring against me that old jest of him who preached all his hearers out of the meeting-house save only the sexton who, remaining for yet a little space, from a sense of official duty, at last gave out also, and, presenting the keys, humbly requested our preacher to lock the doors, when he should have wholly relieved himself of his testimony. I confess to a satisfaction in the self act of preaching, nor do I esteem a discourse to be wholly thrown away even upon a sleeping or unintelligent auditory. I cannot easily believe that the Gos-

pel of Saint John, which Jacques Cartier ordered to be read in the Latin tongue to the Canadian savages, upon his first meeting with them, fell altogether upon stony ground. For the earnestness of the preacher is a sermon appreciable by dullest intellects and most alien ears. In this wise did Episcopius convert many to his opinions, who yet understood not the language in which he discoursed. The chief thing is that the messenger believe that he has an authentic message to deliver. For counterfeit messengers that mode of treatment which Father John de Plano Carpini relates to have prevailed among the Tartars would seem effectual, and, perhaps, deserved enough. For my own part, I may lay claim to so much of the spirit of martyrdom as would have led me to go into banishment with those clergymen whom Alphonso the Sixth of Portugal drave out of his kingdom for refusing to shorten their pulpit eloquence. It is possible, that, having been invited into my brother Biglow's desk, I may have been too little scrupulous in using it for the venting of my own peculiar doctrines to a congregation drawn together in the expectation and with the desire of hearing him.

I am not wholly unconscious of a peculiarity of mental organization which impels me, like the railroad-engine with its train of cars, to run backward for a short distance in order to obtain a fairer start. I may compare myself to one fishing from the rocks when the sea runs high, who, misinterpreting the suction of the undertow for the biting of some larger fish, jerks suddenly, and finds that he has *caught bottom*, hauling in upon the end of his line a trail of various *algæ*, among which, nevertheless, the naturalist may haply find somewhat to repay the disappointment of the angler. Yet have I conscientiously endeavored to adapt myself to the impatient temper of the age, daily degenerating more and more from the high standard of our pristine New England. To the catalogue of lost arts I would mournfully add also that of listening to two-hour sermons. Surely we have been abridged into a race of pygmies. For, truly, in those of the old discourses yet subsisting to us in print, the endless spinal column of divisions and subdivisions can be likened to nothing so exactly as to the vertebræ of the saurians, whence the theorist may conjecture a race of Anakim proportionate to the withstanding of these other monsters. I say Anakim rather than Nephelim, because there seem reasons for supposing that the race of those whose heads (though no giants) are constantly enveloped in clouds (which that name imports) will never become extinct. The attempt to vanquish the innumerable *heads* of one of those aforementioned discourses may supply us with a plausible interpretation of the second labor of Hercules, and his successful experiment with fire affords us a useful *precedent*.

But while I lament the degeneracy of the

age in this regard, I cannot refuse to succumb to its influence. Looking out through my study-window, I see Mr. Biglow at a distance busy in gathering his Baldwins, of which, to judge by the number of barrels lying about under the trees, his crop is more abundant than my own, — by which sight I am admonished to turn to those orchards of the mind wherein my labors may be more prospered, and apply myself diligently to the preparation of my next Sabbath's discourse. — H. W.]

MELIBŒUS-HIPPONAX.

THE

𝕭𝖎𝖌𝖑𝖔𝖜 𝕻𝖆𝖕𝖊𝖗𝖘,

SECOND SERIES.

Εστιν ἄρ' ὁ ἰδιωτισμὸς ἐνίοτε τοῦ κόσμου παραπολὺ ἐμφανιστικώτερον.
LONGINUS.

" J'aimerois mieulx que mon fils apprinst aux tavernes à parler, qu'aux escholes de la parlerie."
MONTAIGNE.

„ Unſer Sprach iſt auch ein Sprach und kan ſo wohl ein Sack nennen als die Latiner saccus."
FISCHART.

" Vim rebus aliquando ipsa verborum humilitas affert."
QUINTILIANUS.

" O ma lengo,
Plantarèy une estèlo à toun froun encrumit ! "
JASMIN.

TO

E. R. HOAR.

"Multos enim, quibus loquendi ratio non desit, invenias, quos curiose potius loqui dixeris quam Latine; quomodo et illa Attica anus Theophrastum, hominem alioqui disertissimum, annotata unius affectatione verbi, hospitem dixit, nec alio se id deprehendisse interrogata respondit, quam quod nimium Attice loqueretur."

QUINTILIANUS.

"Et Anglice sermonicari solebat populo, sed secundum linguam Norfolchie ubi natus et nutritus erat."

CRONICA JOCELINI.

"La politique est une pierre attachée au cou de la littérature, et qui, en moins de six mois la submerge. . . . . Cette politique va offenser mortellement une moitié des lecteurs, et ennuyer l'autre qui l'a trouvée bien autrement spéciale et énergique dans le journal du matin."

HENRI BEYLE.

INTRODUCTION.

THOUGH prefaces seem of late to have fallen under some reproach, they have at least this advantage, that they set us again on the feet of our personal consciousness and rescue us from the gregarious mock-modesty or cowardice of that *we* which shrills feebly throughout modern literature like the shrieking of mice in the walls of a house that has past its prime. Having a few words to say to the many friends whom the "Biglow Papers" have won me, I shall accordingly take the freedom of the first person singular of the personal pronoun. Let each of the good-natured unknown who have cheered me by the written communication of their sympathy look upon this Introduction as a private letter to himself.

When, more than twenty years ago, I wrote the first of the series, I had no definite plan and no intention of ever writing another. Thinking the Mexican war, as I think it still, a national crime committed in behoof of Slavery, our common sin, and wishing to put the feeling of those who thought as I did in a way that would tell, I imagined to myself such an upcountry man as I had often seen at antislavery gatherings, capable of district-school English, but always instinctively falling back into the natural stronghold of his homely dialect when heated to the point of self-forgetfulness. When I began to carry out my conception and to write in my assumed character, I found myself in a strait between two perils. On the one hand, I was in danger of being carried beyond the limit of my own opinions, or at least of that temper with which every man should speak his mind in print, and on the other I feared the risk of seeming to vulgarize a deep and sacred conviction. I needed on occasion to rise above the level of mere *patois,* and for this purpose conceived the Reverend Mr. Wilbur, who should express the more cautious element of the New England character and its pedantry, as Mr. Biglow should serve for its homely common-sense vivified and heated by conscience. The parson was to be the complement rather than the antithesis of his parishioner, and I felt or fancied a certain humorous element in the real identity of the two under a seeming incongruity. Mr. Wilbur's fondness for scraps of Latin, though drawn from the life, I adopted deliberately to heighten the contrast. Finding soon after that I needed some one as a mouthpiece of the mere drollery, for I conceive that true humor is never divorced from moral conviction, I invented Mr. Sawin for the clown of my little puppet-show. I meant to embody in him that half-conscious *un*morality which I had noticed as the recoil in gross natures from a puritanism that still strove to keep in its creed the intense savor which had long gone out of its faith and life. In the three I thought I should find room enough to express, as it was my plan to do, the popular feeling and opinion of the time. For the names of two of my characters, since I have received some remonstrances from very worthy persons who happened to bear them, I would say that they were purely fortuitous, probably mere unconscious memories of signboards or directories. Mr. Sawin's sprang from the accident of a rhyme at the end of his first epistle, and I purposely christened him by the impossible surname of Birdofredum not more to stigmatize him as the incarnation of "Manifest Destiny," in other words, of national recklessness as to right and wrong, than to avoid the chance of wounding any private sensitiveness.

The success of my experiment soon began not only to astonish me, but to make me feel the responsibility of knowing that I held in my hand a weapon instead of the mere fencing-stick I had supposed. Very far from being a popular author under my own name, so far, indeed, as to be almost unread, I found the verses of my pseudonym copied everywhere; I saw them pinned up in workshops; I heard them quoted and their authorship debated; I once even, when rumor had at length caught up my name in one of its eddies, had the satisfaction of overhearing it demonstrated, in the pauses of a concert, that *I* was utterly incompetent to have written anything of the kind. I had read too much not to know the utter worthlessness of contemporary reputation, especially as regards satire, but I knew also that by giving a certain amount of influence it also had its worth, if that influence were used on the right side. I had learned, too, that the first requisite of good writing is to have an earnest and definite purpose, whether æsthetic or moral, and that even good writing, to please long, must have more than an average amount either of imagination or common-sense. The first of these falls to the lot of scarcely one in several generations; the last is within the reach of many in every one that passes; and of this an author may fairly hope to become in part the mouthpiece. If I put on the cap and bells and made myself one of the court-fools of King Demos, it was less to make his majesty laugh than to win a passage to his royal ears for certain serious things which I had deeply at heart. I say this because there is no imputation that could be more galling to any man's self-respect than that of being a mere jester. I endeavored, by generalizing my satire, to give it what value I could beyond the passing moment and the immediate application. How far I have succeeded I cannot tell, but I have had better luck than I ever looked for in seeing my verses survive to pass beyond their nonage.

In choosing the Yankee dialect, I did

not act without forethought. It had long seemed to me that the great vice of American writing and speaking was a studied want of simplicity, that we were in danger of coming to look on our mother-tongue as a dead language, to be sought in the grammar and dictionary rather than in the heart, and that our only chance of escape was by seeking it at its living sources among those who were, as Scottowe says of Major-General Gibbons, "divinely illiterate." President Lincoln, the only really great public man whom these latter days have seen, was great also in this, that he was master — witness his speech at Gettysburg — of a truly masculine English, classic because it was of no special period, and level at once to the highest and lowest of his countrymen. I learn from the highest authority that his favorite reading was in Shakespeare and Milton, to which, of course, the Bible should be added. But whoever should read the debates in Congress might fancy himself present at a meeting of the city council of some city of Southern Gaul in the decline of the Empire, where barbarians with a Latin varnish emulated each other in being more than Ciceronian. Whether it be want of culture, for the highest outcome of that is simplicity, or for whatever reason, it is certain that very few American writers or speakers wield their native language with the directness, precision, and force that are common as the day in the mother country. We use it like Scotsmen, not as if it belonged to us, but as if we wished to prove that we belong to it, by showing our intimacy with its written rather than with its spoken dialect. And yet all the while our popular idiom is racy with life and vigor and originality, bucksome (as Milton used the word) to our new occasions, and proves itself no mere graft by sending up new suckers from the old root in spite of us. It is only from its roots in the living generations of men that a language can be reinforced with fresh vigor for its needs; what may be called a literate dialect grows ever more and more pedantic and foreign, till it becomes at last as unfitting a vehicle for living thought as monkish Latin. That we should all be made to talk like books is the danger with which we are threatened by the Universal Schoolmaster, who does his best to enslave the minds and memories of his victims to what he esteems the best models of English composition, that is to say, to the writers whose style is faultily correct and has no blood-warmth in it. No language after it has faded into *diction*, none that cannot suck up the feeding juices secreted for it in the rich mother-earth of common folk, can bring forth a sound and lusty book. True vigor and heartiness of phrase do not pass from page to page, but from man to man, where the brain is kindled and the lips supplied by downright living interests and by passion in its very throe. Language is the soil of thought, and our own especially is a rich leaf-mould, the slow deposit of ages, the shed foliage of feeling, fancy, and imagination, which has suffered an earth-change, that the vocal forest, as Howell called it, may clothe itself anew with living green. There is death in the dictionary; and, where language is too strictly limited by convention, the ground for expression to grow in is limited also; and we get a *potted* literature, Chinese dwarfs instead of healthy trees.

But while the schoolmaster has been busy starching our language and smoothing it flat with the mangle of a supposed classical authority, the newspaper reporter has been doing even more harm by stretching and swelling it to suit his occasions. A dozen years ago I began a list, which I have added to from time to time, of some of the changes which may be fairly laid at his door. I give a few of them as showing their tendency, all the more dangerous that their effect, like that of some poisons, is insensibly cumulative, and that they are sure at last of effect among a people whose chief reading is the daily paper. I give in two columns the old style and its modern equivalent.

Old Style.	*New Style.*
Was hanged.	Was launched into eternity.
When the halter was put round his neck.	When the fatal noose was adjusted about the neck of the unfortunate victim of his own unbridled passions.
A great crowd came to see.	A vast concourse was assembled to witness.
Great fire.	Disastrous conflagration.
The fire spread.	The conflagration extended its devastating career.
House burned.	Edifice consumed.
The fire was got under.	The progress of the devouring element was arrested.
Man fell.	Individual was precipitated.
A horse and wagon ran against.	A valuable horse attached to a vehicle driven by J. S., in the employment of J. B., collided with.
The frightened horse.	The infuriated animal.
Sent for the doctor.	Called into requisition the services of the family physician.
The mayor of the city in a short speech welcomed.	The chief magistrate of the metropolis, in well-chosen and eloquent language, frequently interrupted by the plaudits of the surging multitude, officially tendered the hospitalities.
I shall say a few words.	I shall, with your permission, beg leave to offer some brief observations.
Began his answer.	Commenced his rejoinder.
Asked him to dine.	Tendered him a banquet.
A bystander advised.	One of those omnipresent characters who, as if in pursuance of some previous arrangement, are certain to be encountered in the vicinity when an accident occurs, ventured the suggestion.

He died.

He deceased, he passed out of existence, his spirit quitted its earthly habitation, winged its way to eternity, shook off its burden, &c.

In one sense this is nothing new. The school of Pope in verse ended by wire-drawing its phrase to such thinness that it could bear no weight of meaning whatever. Nor is fine writing by any means confined to America. All writers without imagination fall into it of necessity whenever they attempt the figurative. I take two examples from Mr. Merivale's "History of the Romans under the Empire," which, indeed, is full of such. "The last years of the age familiarly styled the Augustan were singularly barren of the literary glories from which its celebrity was chiefly derived. One by one the stars in its firmament had been lost to the world; Virgil and Horace, &c., had long since died; the charm which the imagination of Livy had thrown over the earlier annals of Rome had ceased to shine on the details of almost contemporary history; and if the flood of his eloquence still continued flowing, we can hardly suppose that the stream was as rapid, as fresh, and as clear as ever." I will not waste time in criticising the bad English or the mixture of metaphor in these sentences, but will simply cite another from the same author which is even worse. "The shadowy phantom of the Republic continued to flit before the eyes of the Cæsar. There was still, he apprehended, a germ of sentiment existing, on which a scion of his own house, or even a stranger, might boldly throw himself and raise the standard of patrician independence." Now a ghost may haunt a murderer, but hardly, I should think, to scare him with the threat of taking a new lease of its old tenement. And fancy the *scion* of a *house* in the act of *throwing itself* upon a *germ of sentiment* to *raise a standard!* I am glad, since we have so much in the same kind to answer for, that this bit of horticultural rhetoric is from beyond sea. I would not be supposed to condemn truly imaginative prose. There is a simplicity of splendor, no less than of plainness, and prose would be poor indeed if it could not find a tongue for that meaning of the mind which is behind the meaning of the words. It has sometimes seemed to me that in England there was a growing tendency to curtail language into a mere convenience, and to defecate it of all emotion as thoroughly as algebraic signs. This has arisen, no doubt, in part from that healthy national contempt of humbug which is characteristic of Englishmen, in part from that sensitiveness to the ludicrous which makes them so shy of expressing feeling, but in part also, it is to be feared, from a growing distrust, one might almost say hatred, of whatever is supermaterial. There is something sad in the scorn with which their journalists treat the notion of there being such a thing as a national ideal, seeming utterly to have forgotten that even in the affairs of this world the imagination is as much matter-of-fact as the understanding. If we were to trust the impression made on us by some of the cleverest and most characteristic of their periodical literature, we should think England hopelessly stranded on the good-humored cynicism of well-to-do middle-age, and should fancy it an enchanted nation, doomed to sit forever with its feet under the mahogany in that after-dinner mood which follows conscientious repletion, and which it is ill-manners to disturb with any topics more exciting than the quality of the wines. But there are already symptoms that a large class of Englishmen are getting weary of the dominion of consols and divine common-sense, and to believe that eternal three *per cent* is not the chief end of man, nor the highest and only kind of interest to which the powers and opportunities of England are entitled.

The quality of exaggeration has often been remarked on as typical of American character, and especially of American humor. In Dr. Petri's *Gedrängtes Handbuch der Fremdwörter*, we are told that the word *humbug* is commonly used for the exaggerations of the North-Americans. To be sure, one would be tempted to think the dream of Columbus half fulfilled, and that Europe had found in the West a nearer way to Orientalism, at least in diction. But it seems to me that a great deal of what is set down as mere extravagance is more fitly to be called intensity and picturesqueness, symptoms of the imaginative faculty in full health and strength, though producing, as yet, only the raw and formless material in which poetry is to work. By and by, perhaps, the world will see it fashioned into poem and picture, and Europe, which will be hard pushed for originality erelong, may have to thank us for a new sensation. The French continue to find Shakespeare exaggerated because he treated English just as our country-folk do when they speak of a "steep price," or say that they "freeze to" a thing. The first postulate of an original literature is that a people should use their language instinctively and unconsciously, as if it were a lively part of their growth and personality, not as the mere torpid boon of education or inheritance. Even Burns contrived to write very poor verse and prose in English. Vulgarisms are often only poetry in the egg. The late Mr. Horace Mann, in one of his public addresses, commented at some length on the beauty and moral significance of the French phrase *s'orienter*, and called on his young friends to practise upon it in life. There was not a Yankee in his audience whose problem had not always been to find out what was *about east*, and to shape his course accordingly. This charm which a familiar expression gains by being commented, as it were, and set in a new light by a foreign language, is curious and instructive. I cannot help thinking that Mr. Matthew Arnold forgets this

a little too much sometimes when he writes of the beauties of French style. It would not be hard to find in the works of French Academicians phrases as coarse as those he cites from Burke, only they are veiled by the unfamiliarity of the language. But, however this may be, it is certain that poets and peasants please us in the same way by translating words back again to their primal freshness, and infusing them with a delightful strangeness which is anything but alienation. What, for example, is Milton's "*edge of battle*" but a doing into English of the Latin *acies*? *Was die Gans gedacht das der Schwan vollbracht*, what the goose but thought, that the swan full brought (or, to de-Saxonize it a little, what the goose conceived, that the swan achieved), and it may well be that the life, invention, and vigor shown by our popular speech, and the freedom with which it is shaped to the instant want of those who use it, are of the best omen for our having a swan at last. The part I have taken on myself is that of the humbler bird.

But it is affirmed that there is something innately vulgar in the Yankee dialect. M. Sainte-Beuve says, with his usual neatness: "*Je définis un patois une ancienne langue qui a eu des malheurs, ou encore une langue toute jeune et qui n'a pas fait fortune.*" The first part of his definition applies to a dialect like the Provençal, the last to the Tuscan before Dante had lifted it into a classic, and neither, it seems to me, will quite fit a *patois*, which is not properly a dialect, but rather certain archaisms, proverbial phrases, and modes of pronunciation, which maintain themselves among the uneducated side by side with the finished and universally accepted language. Norman French, for example, or Scotch down to the time of James VI., could hardly be called *patois*, while I should be half inclined to name the Yankee a *lingo* rather than a dialect. It has retained a few words now fallen into disuse in the mother country, like *to tarry*, *to progress*, *fleshy*, *fall*, and some others; it has changed the meaning of some, as in *freshet;* and it has clung to what I suspect to have been the broad Norman pronunciation of *e* (which Molière puts into the mouth of his rustics) in such words as *sarvant, parfect, vartoo,* and the like. It maintains something of the French sound of *a* also in words like *chămber, dănger* (though the latter had certainly begun to take its present sound so early as 1636, when I find it sometimes spelt *dainger*). But in general it may be said that nothing can be found in it which does not still survive in some one or other of the English provincial dialects. There is, perhaps, a single exception in the verb to *sleeve.* To *sleeve* silk means to divide or ravel out a thread of silk with the point of a needle till it becomes *floss.* (A.-S. *sléfan,* to *cleave* = divide.) This, I think, explains the "*sleeveless* errand " in " Troilus and Cressida " so inadequately, sometimes so ludicrously darkened by the commentators. Is not a "sleeveless errand" one that cannot be unravelled, incomprehensible and therefore bootless?

I am not speaking now of Americanisms properly so called, that is, of words or phrases which have grown into use here either through necessity, invention, or accident, such as a *carry,* a *one-horse affair,* a *prairie,* to *vamose.* Even these are fewer than is sometimes taken for granted. But I think some fair defence may be made against the charge of vulgarity. Properly speaking, vulgarity is in the thought, and not in the word or the way of pronouncing it. Modern French, the most polite of languages, is barbarously vulgar if compared with the Latin out of which it has been corrupted, or even with Italian. There is a wider gap, and one implying greater boorishness, between *ministerium* and *métier,* or *sapiens* and *sachant,* than between *druv* and *drove,* or *agin* and *against,* which last is plainly an arrant superlative. Our rustic *coverlid* is nearer its French original than the diminutive *coverlet,* into which it has been ignorantly corrupted in politer

speech. I obtained from three cultivated Englishmen at different times three diverse pronunciations of a single word, — *cowcumber, coocumber,* and *çucumber.* Of these the first, which is Yankee also, comes nearest to the nasality of *concombre.* Lord Ossory assures us that Voltaire saw the best society in England, and Voltaire tells his countrymen that *handkerchief* was pronounced *hankercher.* I find it so spelt in Hakluyt and elsewhere. This enormity the Yankee still persists in, and as there is always a reason for such deviations from the sound as represented by the spelling, may we not suspect two sources of derivation, and find an ancestor for *kercher* in *couverture* rather than in *couvrechef?* And what greater phonetic vagary (which Dryden, by the way, called *fegary*) in our *lingua rustica* than this *ker* for *couvre?* I copy from the fly-leaves of my books where I have noted them from time to time a few examples of pronunciation and phrase which will show that the Yankee often has antiquity and very respectable literary authority on his side. My list might be largely increased by referring to glossaries, but to them every one can go for himself, and I have gathered enough for my purpose.

I will take first those cases in which something like the French sound has been preserved in certain single letters and diphthongs. And this opens a curious question as to how long this Gallicism maintained itself in England. Sometimes a divergence in pronunciation has given us two words with different meanings, as in *genteel* and *jaunty,* which I find coming in toward the close of the seventeenth century, and wavering between *genteel* and *jantee.* It is usual in America to drop the *u* in words ending in *our,* — a very proper change recommended by Howell two centuries ago, and carried out by him so far as his printers would allow. This and the corresponding changes in *musique, musick,* and the like, which he also advocated, show that in his time the French accent indicated by the superfluous letters (for French had once nearly as strong an accent as Italian) had gone out of use. There is plenty of French accent down to the end of Elizabeth's reign. In Daniel we have *riches'* and *counsell'*, in Bishop Hall *comet'*, *chapelain*, in Donne *pictures'*, *virtue'*, *presence'*, *mortal'*, *merit'*, *hainous'*, *giant'*, with many more, and Marston's satires are full of them. The two latter, however, are not to be relied on, as they may be suspected of Chaucerizing. Herrick writes *baptime*. The tendency to throw the accent backward began early. But the incongruities are perplexing, and perhaps mark the period of transition. In Warner's "Albion's England" we have *creator'* and *creature'* side by side with the modern *creator* and *creature*. *E'nvy* and *e'nvying* occur in Campion (1602), and yet *envy'* survived Milton. In some cases we have gone back again nearer to the French, as in *rev'enue* for *reven'ue*. I had been so used to hearing *imbecile* pronounced with the accent on the first syllable, which is in accordance with the general tendency in such matters, that I was surprised to find *imbec'ile* in a verse of Wordsworth. The dictionaries all give it so. I asked a highly cultivated Englishman, and he declared for *imbeceel'*. In general it may be assumed that accent will finally settle on the syllable dictated by greater ease and therefore quickness of utterance. *Blas'phemous*, for example, is more rapidly pronounced than *blasphem'ous*, to which our Yankee clings, following in this usage of many of the older poets. *Amer'ican* is easier than *Ameri'can*, and therefore the false quantity has carried the day, though the true one may be found in George Herbert, and even so late as Cowley.

To come back to the matter in hand. Our "uplandish man" retains the soft or thin sound of the *u* in some words, such as *rule*, *truth* (sometimes also pronounced *trüth*, not *trooth*), while he says *noo* for *new*, and gives to *view* and *few* so indescribable a mixture of the two sounds with a slight nasal tincture

that it may be called the Yankee shibboleth. Voltaire says that the English pronounce *true* as if it rhymed with *view*; and this is the sound our rustics give to it. Spenser writes *deow (dew)* which can only be pronounced with the Yankee nasality. In *rule* the least sound of *a* precedes the *u*. I find *reule* in Pecock's "Repressor." He probably pronounced it *rayoolé*, as the old French word from which it is derived was very likely to be sounded at first, with a reminiscence of its original *regula*. Tindal has *rueler*, and the Coventry Plays have *preudent*. In the "Parlyament of Byrdes" I find *reule*. As for *noo*, it may it not claim some sanction in its derivation, whether from *nouveau* or *neuf*, the ancient sound of which may very well have been *noof*, as nearer *novus?* *Beef* would seem more like to have come from *buffe* than from *bœuf*, unless the two were mere varieties of spelling. The Saxon *few* may have caught enough from its French cousin *peu* to claim the benefit of the same doubt as to sound; and our slang phrase *a few* (as "I licked him a few") may well appeal to *un peu* for sense and authority. Nay, might not *lick* itself turn out to be the good old word *lam* in an English disguise, if the latter should claim descent as, perhaps, he fairly might, from the Latin *lambere?* The New England *ferce* for *fierce*, and *perce* for *pierce* (sometimes heard as *fairce* and *pairce*), are also Norman. For its antiquity I cite the rhyme of *verse* and *pierce* in Chapman and Donne, and in some commendatory verses by a Mr. Berkenhead before the poems of Francis Beaumont. Our *pairlous* for *perilous* is of the same kind, and is nearer Shakespeare's *parlous* than the modern pronunciation. One other Gallicism survives in our pronunciation. Perhaps I should rather call it a semi-Gallicism, for it is the result of a futile effort to reproduce a French sound with English lips. Thus for *joint*, *employ*, *royal* we have *jynt*, *emply*, *ryle*, the last differing only from *rile (roil)* in a prolongation of the *y* sound. I find *royal* so pronounced in the "Mirror for Magistrates." In Walter de Biblesworth I find *solives* Englished by *gistes*. This, it is true, may have been pronounced *jeests*, but the pronunciation *jystes* must have preceded the present spelling, which was no doubt adopted after the radical meaning was forgotten, as analogical with other words in *oi*. In the same way after Norman-French influence had softened the *l* out of *would* (we already find *woud* for *veut* in N. F. poems), *should* followed the example, and then an *l* was foisted into *could*, where it does not belong, to satisfy the logic of the eye, which has affected the pronunciation and even the spelling of English more than is commonly supposed. I meet with *eyster* for *oyster* as early as the fourteenth century. I find *viage* in Bishop Hall and Middleton the dramatist, *bile* for *boil* in Donne and Chrononhotonthologos, *line* for *loin* in Hall, *ryall* and *chyse* for *choice*, and *dystrye* for *destroy* in the Coventry Plays. In Chapman's "All Fools" is the misprint of *employ* for *imply*, fairly inferring an identity of sound in the last syllable. Indeed, this pronunciation was habitual till after Pope, and Rogers tells us that the elegant Gray said *naise* for *noise* just as our rustics still do. Our *cornish* (which I find also in Herrick) remembers the French better than *cornice* does. While, clinging more closely to the Anglo-Saxon in dropping the *g* from the end of the present participle, the Yankee now and then pleases himself with an experiment in French nasality in words ending in *n*. It is not, so far as my experience goes, very common, though it may formerly have been more so. *Capting*, for instance, I never heard save in jest, the habitual form being *keppʼn*. But at any rate it is no invention of ours. In that delightful old volume, "Ane Compendious Buke of Godly and Spirituall Songs," in which I know not whether the piety itself or the simplicity of its expression be more charming, I find *burding*, *garding*, and *cousing*, and in the State Trials *uncerting* used by a gentleman. The *n* for *ng* I confess preferring.

Of Yankee preterites I find *risse* and *rize* for *rose* in Beaumont and Fletcher, Middleton and Dryden, *clim* in Spenser, *chees* (*chose*) in Sir John Mandevil, *give* (*gave*) in the Coventry Plays, *shet* (*shut*) in Golding's Ovid, *het* in Chapman and in Weever's Epitaphs, *thriv* and *smit* in Drayton, *quit* in Ben Jonson and Henry More, and *pled* in the fastidious Landor. *Rid* for *rode* was anciently common. So likewise was *see* for *saw*, but I find it in no writer of authority, unless Chaucer's *seie* and Gower's *sigh* were, as I am inclined to think, so sounded. *Shew* is used by Hector Boece, Giles Fletcher, and Drummond of Hawthornden. Similar strong preterites, like *snew*, *thew*, and even *mew*, are not without example. I find *sew* for *sewed* in Piers Ploughman. Indeed, the anomalies in English preterites are perplexing. We have probably transferred *flew* from *flow* (as the preterite of which I have heard it) to *fly* because we had another preterite in *fled*. Of weak preterites the Yankee retains *growed*, *blowed*, for which he has good authority, and less often *knowed*. His *sot* is merely a broad sounding of *sat*, no more inelegant than the common *got* for *gat*, which he further degrades into *gut*. When he says *darst*, he uses a form as old as Chaucer.

The Yankee has retained something of the long sound of the *a* in such words as *axe*, *wax*, pronouncing them *exe*, *wex* (shortened from *aix*, *waix*). He also says *hev* and *hed* (*hăve*, *hăd*) for *have* and *had*. In most cases he follows an Anglo-Saxon usage. In *aix* for *axle* he certainly does. I find *wex* and *aisches* (*ashes*) in Pecock, and *exe* in the Paston Letters. Chaucer wrote *hendy*. Dryden rhymes *can* with *men*, as Mr. Biglow would. Alexander Gill, Milton's teacher, in his "Logonomia" cites *hez* for *hath* as peculiar to Lincolnshire. I find *hayth* in Collier's "Bibliographical Account of Early English Literature" under the date 1584, and Lord Cromwell so wrote it. Sir Christopher Wren wrote *belcony*. Our *fect* is only the O. F. *faict*. *Thaim* for *them* was common in the sixteenth century. We have an example of the same thing in the double form of the verb *thrash, thresh.* While the New-Englander cannot be brought to say *instead* for *instid* (commonly *'stid* where not the last word in a sentence), he changes the *i* into *e* in *red* for *rid, tell* for *till, hender* for *hinder, rense* for *rinse.* I find *red* in the old interlude of "Thersytes," *tell* in a letter of Daborne to Henslowe, and also, I shudder to mention it, in a letter of the great Duchess of Marlborough, Atossa herself! It occurs twice in a single verse of the Chester Plays, which I copy as containing another Yankeeism:—

"*Tell* the day of dome, *tell* the beames *blow.*"

From the word *blow* (in another sense) is formed *blowth,* which I heard again this summer after a long interval. Mr. Wright * explains it as meaning "a blossom." With us a single blossom is a *blow,* while *blowth* means the blossoming in general. A farmer would say that there was a good blowth on his fruit-trees. The word retreats farther inland and away from the railways, year by year. Wither rhymes *hinder* with *slender,* and Shakespeare and Lovelace have *renched* for *rinsed.* In "Gammer Gurton" and "Mirror for Magistrates" is *sence* for *since*; Marlborough's Duchess so writes it, and Donne rhymes *since* with *Amiens* and *patience,* Bishop Hall and Otway with *pretence,* Chapman with *citizens,* Dryden with *providence.* Indeed, why should not *sithence* take that form? Dryden's wife (an earl's daughter) has *tell* for *till,* Margaret, mother of Henry VII., writes *seche* for *such,* and our *ef* finds authority in the old form *yeffe.*

E sometimes takes the place of *u,* as *jedge, tredge, bresh.* I find *tredge* in the interlude of "Jack Jugler," *bresh* in a citation by Collier from "London Cries" of the middle of the seventeenth century, and *resche* for *rush* fifteenth century) in the very valuable "Volume of Vocabularies" edited by Mr. Wright. *Resce* is one of the

* Dictionary of Obsolete and Provincial English.

Anglo-Saxon forms of the word in Bosworth's A. S. Dictionary. The Yankee always shortens the *u* in the ending *ture,* making *ventur, natur, pictur,* and so on. This was common, also, among the educated of the last generation. I am inclined to think it may have been once universal, and I certainly think it more elegant than the vile *vencher, naycher, piekcher,* that have taken its place, sounding like the invention of a lexicographer to mitigate a sneeze. Nash in his "Pierce Pennilesse" has *ventur,* and so spells it, and I meet it also in Spenser, Drayton, Ben Jonson, Herrick, and Prior. Spenser has *tort'rest,* which can be contracted only from *tortur* and not from *torcher.* Quarles rhymes *nature* with *creator,* and Dryden with *satire,* which he doubtless pronounced according to its older form of *satyr.* Quarles has also *torture* and *mortar.* Mary Boleyn writes *kreatur.* I find *pikter* in Izaak Walton's autograph will.

I shall now give some examples which cannot so easily be ranked under any special head. Gill charges the Eastern counties with *kiver* for *cover,* and *ta* for *to.* The Yankee pronounces both *too* and *to* like *ta* (like the *tou* in *touch*) where they are not emphatic. When they are, both become *tu.* In old spelling, *to* is the common (and indeed correct) form of *too,* which is only *to* with the sense of *in addition.* I suspect that the sound of our *too* has caught something from the French *tout,* and it is possible that the old *too-too* is not a reduplication, but a reminiscence of the feminine form of the same word (*toute*) as anciently pronounced, with the *e* not yet silenced. Gill gives a Northern origin to *geaun* for *gown* and *waund* for *wound (vulnus).* Lovelace has *waund,* but there is something too dreadful in suspecting Spenser (who *borealized* in his pastorals) of having ever been guilty of *geaun*! And yet some delicate mouths even now are careful to observe the Hibernicism of *ge-ard* for *guard,* and *ge-url* for *girl.* Sir Philip Sidney (*credite posteri!*) wrote *furr* for *far.* I would hardly have believed it had I not seen it in *fac-simile*. As some consolation, I find *furder* in Lord Bacon and Donne, and Wither rhymes *far* with *cur*. The Yankee, who omits the final *d* in many words, as do the Scotch, makes up for it by adding one in *geound*. The purist does not feel the loss of the *d* sensibly in *lawn* and *yon*, from the former of which it has dropped again after a wrongful adoption (retained in *laundry*), while it properly belongs to the latter. But what shall we make of *git*, *yit*, and *yis?* I find *yis* and *git* in Warner's "Albion's England," *yet* rhyming with *wit*, *admit*, and *fit* in Donne, with *wit* in the "Revenger's Tragedy," Beaumont, and Suckling, with *writ* in Dryden, and latest of all with *wit* in Sir Hanbury Williams. Prior rhymes *fitting* and *begetting*. Worse is to come. Among others, Donne rhymes *again* with *sin*, and Quarles repeatedly with *in*. Ben for *been*, of which our dear Whittier is so fond, has the authority of Sackville, "Gammer Gurton" (the work of a bishop), Chapman, Dryden, and many more, though *bin* seems to have been the common form. Whittier's accenting the first syllable of *rom'ance* finds an accomplice in Drayton among others, and though manifestly wrong, is analogous with *Rom'ans*. Of other Yankeeisms, whether of form or pronunciation, which I have met with I add a few at random. Pecock writes *sowdiers* (*sogers*, *soudoyers*), and Chapman and Gill *sodder*. This absorption of the *l* is common in various dialects, especially in the Scottish. Pecock writes also *biyende*, and the authors of "Jack Jugler" and "Gammer Gurton" *yender*. The Yankee includes "*yon*" in the same category, and says "hither an' yen," for "to and fro." (Cf. German *jenseits*.) Pecock and plenty more have *wrastle*. Tindal has *agynste*, *gretter*, *shett*, *ondone*, *debyté*, and *scace*. "Jack Jugler" has *scacely* (which I have often heard, though *skurce* is the common form), and Donne and Dryden make *great* rhyme with *set*. In the inscription on

Caxton's tomb I find *ynd* for *end*, which the Yankee more often makes *eend*, still using familiarly the old phrase "right anend" for "continuously." His "stret (straight) along" in the same sense, which I thought peculiar to him, I find in Pecock. Tindal's *debyté* for *deputy* is so perfectly Yankee that I could almost fancy the brave martyr to have been deacon of the First Parish at Jaalam Centre. "Jack Jugler" further gives us *playsent* and *sartayne*. Dryden rhymes *certain* with *parting*, and Chapman and Ben Jonson use *certain*, as the Yankee always does, for *certainly*. The "Coventry Mysteries" have *occapied*, *massage*, *nateralle*, *materal* (*material*), and *meracles*,—all excellent Yankeeisms. In the "Quatre fils," Aymon (1504),* is *vertus* for *virtuous*. Thomas Fuller called *volume vollum*, I suspect, for he spells it *volumne*. However, *per contra*, Yankees habitually say *colume* for *column*. Indeed, to prove that our ancestors brought their pronunciation with them from the Old Country, and have not wantonly debased their mother tongue, I need only to cite the words *scriptur*, *Isràll*, *athists*, and *cherfulness* from Governor Bradford's "History." Brampton Gurdon writes *shet* in a letter to Winthrop. So the good man wrote them, and so the good descendants of his fellow-exiles still pronounce them. *Purtend* (*pretend*) has crept like a serpent into the "Paradise of Dainty Devices"; *purvide*, which is not so bad, is in Chaucer. These, of course, are universal vulgarisms, and not peculiar to the Yankee. Butler has a Yankee phrase, and pronunciation too, in "To which these *carr'ings-on* did tend." Langham or Laneham, who wrote an account of the festivities at Kenilworth in honor of Queen Bess, and who evidently tried to spell phonetically, makes *sorrows* into *sororz*. Herrick writes *hollow* for *halloo*, and perhaps pronounced it (*horresco suggerens!*) *hallô*;

* Cited in Collier. (I give my authority where I do not quote from the original book.)

as Yankees do. Why not, when it comes from *holà*? I find *ffelaschyppe* (fellowship) in the Coventry Plays. Spenser and his queen neither of them scrupled to write *afore*, and the former feels even no inelegance in *chaw* and *idee*. *'Fore* was common till after Herrick. Dryden has *do's* for *does*, and his wife spells *worse wosce*. *Afeared* was once universal. Warner has *ery* for *ever a;* nay, he also has *illy*, with which we were once ignorantly reproached by persons more familiar with Murray's Grammar than with English literature. And why not *illy?* Mr. Bartlett says it is "a word used by writers of an inferior class, who do not seem to perceive that *ill* is itself an adverb, without the termination *ly*," and quotes Dr. Messer, President of Brown University, as asking triumphantly, "Why don't you say *welly?*" I should like to have had Dr. Messer answer his own question. It would be truer to say that it was used by people who still remembered that *ill* was an adjective, the shortened form of *evil*, out of which Shakespeare and the translators of the Bible ventured to make *evilly*. This slurred *evil* is "the dram of *eale*" in "Hamlet." I find *illy* in Warner. The objection to *illy* is not an etymological one, but simply that it is contrary to good usage, — a very sufficient reason. *Ill* as an adverb was at first a vulgarism, precisely like the rustic's when he says, "I was treated *bad*." May not the reason of this exceptional form be looked for in that tendency to dodge what is hard to pronounce, to which I have already alluded? If the letters were distinctly uttered, as they should be, it would take too much time to say *ill-ly*, *well-ly*, and it is to be observed that we have avoided *smally** and *tally* in the same way, though we add *ish* to them without hesitation in *smallish* and *tallish*. We have, to be sure, *dully* and *fully*, but for the one we prefer *stupidly*, and the other (though this may have come from eliding the *y* before *as*) is giving way to *full*. The uneducated, whose

utterance is slower, still make adverbs when they will by adding *like* to all manner of adjectives. We have had *big* charged upon us, because we use it where an Englishman would now use *great*. I fully admit that it were better to distinguish between them, allowing to *big* a certain contemptuous quality; but as for authority, I want none better than that of Jeremy Taylor, who, in his noble sermon "On the Return of Prayer," speaks of "Jesus, whose spirit was meek and gentle up to the greatness of the *biggest* example." As for our double negative, I shall waste no time in quoting instances of it, because it was once as universal in English as it still is in the neo-Latin languages, where it does not strike us as vulgar. I am not sure that the loss of it is not to be regretted. But surely I shall admit the vulgarity of slurring or altogether eliding certain terminal consonants? I admit that a clear and sharp-cut enunciation is one of the crowning charms and elegancies of speech. Words so uttered are like coins fresh from the mint, compared with the worn and dingy drudges of long service, — I do not mean American coins, for those look less badly the more they lose of their original ugliness. No one is more painfully conscious than I of the contrast between the rifle-crack of an Englishman's *yes* and *no*, and the wet-fuse drawl of the same monosyllables in the mouths of my countrymen. But I do not find the dropping of final consonants disagreeable in Allan Ramsay or Burns, nor do I believe that our literary ancestors were sensible of that inelegance in the fusing them together of which we are conscious. How many educated men pronounce the *t* in *chestnut?* how many say *pentise* for *penthouse*, as they should? When a Yankee skipper says that he is "boun' for Gloster" (not Gloucëster, with the leave of the Universal Schoolmaster),* he but speaks like Chaucer or an old ballad-singer, though they would have pronounced it *boon*. This is one of the cases where the *d* is surreptitious, and has been

---

* The word occurs in a letter of Mary Boleyn, in Golding, and in Warner. Milton also was fond of the word.

* Though I find Worcëster in the *Mirror for Magistrates*.

added in compliment to the verb *bind*, with which it has nothing to do. If we consider the root of the word (though of course I grant that every race has a right to do what it will with what is so peculiarly its own as its speech), the *d* has no more right there than at the end of *gone*, where it is often put by children, who are our best guides to the sources of linguistic corruption, and the best teachers of its processes. Cromwell, minister of Henry VIII., writes *worle* for *world*. Chapman has *wan* for *wand*, and *lawn* has rightfully displaced *laund*, though with no thought, I suspect, of etymology. Rogers tells us that Lady Bathurst sent him some letters written to William III. by Queen Mary, in which she addresses him as "*Dear Husban.*" The old form *expoun'*, which our farmers use, is more correct than the form with a barbarous *d* tacked on which has taken its place. Of the kind opposite to this, like our *gownd* for *gown*, and the London cockney's *wind* for *wine*, I find *drownd* for *drown* in the "Misfortunes of Arthur" (1584), and in Swift. And, by the way, whence came the long sound of *wind* which our poets still retain, and which survives in "winding" a horn, a totally different word from "winding" a kitestring? We say *behind* and *hinder* (comparative), and yet *to hinder*. Shakespeare pronounced *kind kind*, or what becomes of his play on that word and *kin* in Hamlet? Nay, did he not even (shall I dare to hint it?) drop the final *d* as the Yankee still does? John Lilly plays in the same way on *kindred* and *kindness*. But to come to some other ancient instances. Warner rhymes *bounds* with *crowns*, *grounds* with *towns*, *text* with *sex*, *worst* with *crust*, *interrupts* with *cups*; Drayton, *defects* with *sex*; Chapman, *amends* with *cleanse*; Webster, *defects* with *checks*; Ben Jonson, *minds* with *combines*; Marston, *trust* and *obsequious*, *clothes* and *shows*; Dryden gives the same sound to *clothes*, and has also *minds* with *designs*. Of course, I do not affirm that their ears may not have told them that these were

imperfect rhymes (though I am by no means sure even of that), but they surely would never have tolerated any such had they suspected the least vulgarity in them. Prior has the rhyme *first* and *trust*, but puts it into the mouth of a landlady. Swift has *stunted* and *burnt it*, an intentionally imperfect rhyme, no doubt, but which I cite as giving precisely the Yankee pronunciation of *burned*. Donne couples *after* and *matter*, thus seeming to give to both the true Yankee sound; and it is not uncommon to find *after* and *daughter*. Worse than all, in one of Dodsley's Old Plays we have *onions* rhyming with *minions*, —I have tears in my eyes while I record it. And yet what is viler than the universal *Misses* (Mrs.) for *Mistress?* This was once a vulgarism, and in "The Miseries of Inforced Marriage" the rhyme (printed as prose in Dodsley's Old Plays by Collier),

> "To make my young *mistress*,
> Delighting in *kisses*,"

is put into the mouth of the clown. Our people say *Injun* for *Indian*. The tendency to make this change where *i* follows *d* is common. The Italian *giorno* and French *jour* from *diurnus* are familiar examples. And yet *Injun* is one of those depravations which the taste challenges peremptorily, though it have the authority of Charles Cotton—who rhymes "*Indies*" with "*cringes*" —and four English lexicographers, beginning with Dr. Sheridan, bid us say *invidgeous*. Yet after all it is no worse than the debasement which all our terminations in *tion* and *tience* have undergone, which yet we hear with *resignashun* and *payshunce*, though it might have aroused both *impat-i-ence* and *indigna-ti-on* in Shakespeare's time. When George Herbert tells us that if the sermon be dull,

> "God takes a text and preacheth *pati-ence*,"

the prolongation of the word seems to convey some hint at the longanimity of the virtue. Consider what a poor curtal we have made of Ocean. There was something of his heave and expanse in *o-ce-an*, and Fletcher knew how to use it when he wrote so fine a verse as the second of these, the best deep-sea verse I know, —

" In desperate storms stem with a little rudder
    The tumbling ruins of the ocëan."

Oceanus was not then wholly shorn of his divine proportions, and our modern *oshun* sounds like the gush of small-beer in comparison. Some other contractions of ours have a vulgar air about them. *More 'n* for *more than*, as one of the worst, may stand for a type of such. Yet our old dramatists are full of such obscurations (elisions they can hardly be called) of the *th*, making *whe'r* of *whether*, *where* of *whither*, *here* of *hither*, *bro'r* of *brother*, *smo'r* of *smother*, *mo'r* of *mother*, and so on. And dear Brer Rabbit, can I forget him? Indeed, it is this that explains the word *rare* (which has Dryden's support), and which we say of meat where an Englishman would use *underdone*. I do not believe, with the dictionaries, that it had ever anything to do with the Icelandic *hrár* (*raw*), as it plainly has not in *rareripe*, which means *earlier* ripe. President Lincoln said of a precocious boy that " he was a *rareripe*." And I do not believe it, for this reason, that the earliest form of the word with us was, and the commoner now in the inland parts still is, so far as I can discover, *rare-done*. Golding has " egs *reere-rosted*," which, whatever else it mean, cannot mean *raw*-roasted. I find *rather* as a monosyllable in Donne, and still better, as giving the sound, rhyming with *fair* in Warner. There is an epigram of Sir Thomas Browne in which the words *rather than* make a monosyllable : —

" What furie is 't to take Death's part
    And rather than by Nature, die by Art !"

The contraction *more 'n* I find in the old play " Fuimus Troes," in a verse where the measure is so strongly accented as to leave it beyond doubt, —

" A golden crown whose heirs
    More than half the world subdue."

It may be, however, that the contrac-

tion is in " th' 'orld." It is unmistakable in the " Second Maiden's Tragedy " : —

" It were but folly,
Dear soul, to boast of *more than* I can perform."

Is our *gin* for *given* more violent than *mar'l* for *marvel*, which was once common, and which I find as late as Herrick? Nay, Herrick has *gin* (spelling it *g'en*), too, as do the Scotch, who agree with us likewise in preferring *chimly* to *chimney*.

I will now leave pronunciation and turn to words or phrases which have been supposed peculiar to us, only pausing to pick up a single dropped stitch, in the pronunciation of the word *su'preme*, which I had thought native till I found it in the well-languaged Daniel. I will begin with a word of which I have never met with any example in any English writer of authority. We express the first stage of withering in a green plant suddenly cut down by the verb *to wilt*. It is, of course, own cousin of the German *welken*, but I have never come upon it in literary use, and my own books of reference give me faint help. Graff gives *welhèn, marcescere*, and refers to *weih* (*weak*), and conjecturally to A. S. *hvelan*. The A. S. *wealwian* (*to wither*) is nearer, but not so near as two words in the Icelandic, which perhaps put us on the track of its ancestry, — *velgi, tepefacere*, and *velki*, with the derivative meaning *con-taminare*. *Wilt*, at any rate, is a good word, filling, as it does, a sensible gap between drooping and withering, and the imaginative phrase " he wilted right down," like " he caved right in," is a true Americanism. *Wilt* occurs in English provincial glossaries, but is explained by *wither*, which with us it does not mean. We have a few words such as *cache, cohog, carry* (*portage*), *shoot* (*chute*), *timber* (*forest*), *bush-whack* (to pull a boat along by the bushes on the edge of a stream), *buck-eye* (a picturesque word for the horse-chestnut) ; but how many can we be said to have fairly brought into the language, as Alexander Gill, who first mentions Americanisms, meant it when he said, "*Sed et ab Americanis non-nulla mutuamur ut* MAIZ *et* CANOA"? Very few, I suspect, and those mostly by borrowing from the French, German, Spanish, or Indian.* "The Dipper" for the "Great Bear" strikes me as having a native air. *Bogus*, in the sense of *worthless*, is undoubtedly ours, but is, I more than suspect, a corruption of the French *bagasse* (from low Latin *bagasea*), which travelled up the Mississippi from New Orleans, where it was used for the refuse of the sugar-cane. It is true we have modified the meaning of some words. We use *freshet* in the sense of *flood*, for which I have not chanced upon any authority. Our New England cross between Ancient Pistol and Dugald Dalgetty, Captain Underhill, uses the word (1638) to mean a *current*, and I do not recollect it elsewhere in that sense. I therefore leave it with a *?* for future explorers. *Crick* for *creek* I find in Captain John Smith and in the dedication of Fuller's "Holy Warre," and *run*, meaning a *small stream*, in Waymouth's "Voyage" (1605). *Humans* for *men*, which Mr. Bartlett includes in his "Dictionary of Americanisms," is Chapman's habitual phrase in his translation of Homer. I find it also in the old play of "The Hog hath lost his Pearl." *Dogs* for *andirons* is still current in New England, and in Walter de Biblesworth I find *chiens* glossed in the margin by *andirons*. *Gunning* for *shooting* is in Drayton. We once got credit for the poetical word *fall* for *autumn*, but Mr. Bartlett and the last edition of Webster's Dictionary refer us to Dryden. It is even older, for I find it in Drayton, and Bishop Hall has *autumn fall*. Middleton plays upon the word: "May'st thou have a reasonable good *spring*, for thou art like to have many dangerous foul *falls*." Lord Herbert of Cherbury (more prop-

erly perhaps than even Sidney, the last *preux chevalier*) has "the Emperor's folks" just as a Yankee would say it. *Loan* for *lend*, with which we have hitherto been blackened, I must retort upon the mother island, for it appears so long ago as in "Albion's England." *Fleshy*, in the sense of *stout*, may claim Ben Jonson's warrant, and I find it also so lately as in Francklin's "Lucian." *Chore* is also Jonson's word, and I am inclined to prefer it to *chare* and *char*, because I think that I see a more natural origin for it in the French *jour*—whence it might come to mean a day's work, and thence a job — than anywhere else.* *At onst* for *at once* I thought a corruption of our own, till I found it in the Chester Plays. I am now inclined to suspect it no corruption at all, but only an erratic and obsolete superlative *at onest*. *To progress!* was flung in our teeth till Mr. Pickering retorted with Shakespeare's "doth pro′gress down thy cheeks." I confess that I was never satisfied with this answer, because the accent was different, and because the word might here be reckoned a substantive quite as well as a verb. Mr. Bartlett (in his Dictionary above cited) adds a surrebutter in a verse from Ford's "Broken Heart." Here the word is clearly a verb, but with the accent unhappily still on the first syllable. Mr. Bartlett says that he "cannot say whether the word was used in Bacon's time or not." It certainly was, and with the accent we give to it. Ben Jonson, in the "Alchemist," has this verse,—

"*Progress′* so from extreme unto extreme."

and Sir Philip Sidney,—

"*Progressing* then from fair Turia's golden place.*"

Surely we may now sleep in peace, and our English cousins will forgive us, since we have cleared ourselves from any suspicion of originality in the matter! Even after I had convinced myself that the chances were desperately

---

* This was written twenty years ago, and now (1890) I cannot open an English journal without coming upon an Americanism.

* The Rev. A. L. Mayhew of Wadham College, Oxford, has convinced me that I was astray in this.

against our having invented any of the *Americanisms* with which we are *faulted* and which we are in the habit of *voicing*, there were one or two which had so prevailingly indigenous an accent as to stagger me a little. One of these was "the biggest *thing out*." Alas, even this slender comfort is denied me. Old Gower has

"So harde an herte was none *oute*,"

and

"That such merveile was none *oute*."

He also, by the way, says "a *sighte* of flowres" as naturally as our up-country folk would say it. *Poor* for *lean*, *thirds* for *dower*, and *dry* for *thirsty* I find in Middleton's plays. *Dry* is also in Skelton and in the "World" (1754). In a note on Middleton, Mr. Dyce thinks it needful to explain the phrase *I can't tell* (universal in America) by the gloss *I could not say*. Middleton also uses *snecked*, which I had believed an Americanism till I saw it there. It is, of course, only another form of *snatch*, analogous to *theek* and *thatch* (cf. the proper names Dekker and Thacher), *break* (*brack*) and *breach*, *make* (still common with us) and *match*. *'Long on* for *occasioned by* ("who is this 'long on?'") occurs constantly in Gower and likewise in Middleton. *'Cause why* is in Chaucer. *Raising* (an English version of the French *leaven*) for *yeast* is employed by Gayton in his "Festivous Notes on Don Quixote." I have never seen an instance of our New England word *emptins* in the same sense, nor can I divine its original. Gayton has *limekill*; also *shuts* for *shutters*, and the latter is used by Mrs. Hutchinson in her "Life of Colonel Hutchinson." Bishop Hall, and Purchas in his "Pilgrims," have *chist* for *chest*, and it is certainly nearer *cista*, as well as to its form in the Teutonic languages, whence probably we got it. We retain the old sound from *cist*, but *chest* is as old as Chaucer. Lovelace says *wropt* for *wrapt*. "Musicianer" I had always associated with the militiamusters of my boyhood, and too hastily concluded it an abomination of our own, but Mr. Wright calls it a Norfolk

word, and I find it to be as old as 1642 by an extract in Collier. "Not worth the time of day" had passed with me for native till I saw it in Shakespeare's "Pericles." For *slick* (which is only a shorter sound of *sleek*, like *crick* and the now universal *britches* for *breeches*) I will only call Chapman and Jonson. "That 's a sure card!" and "That 's a stinger!" both sound like modern slang, but you will find the one in the old interlude of "Thersytes" (1537), and the other in Middleton. "Right here" a favorite phrase with our orators and with a certain class of our editors, turns up *passim* in the Chester and Coventry plays. Mr. Dickens found something very ludicrous in what he considered our neologism *right away*. But I find a phrase very like it, and which I would gladly suspect to be a misprint for it, in "Gammer Gurton": —

"Lyght it and bring it *tite away*."

But *tite* is the true word in this case. After all, what is it but another form of *straightway*? *Cussedness*, meaning *wickedness*, *malignity*, and *cuss*, a sneaking, ill-natured fellow, in such phrases as "He done it out o' pure cussedness," and "He is a nateral cuss," have been commonly thought Yankeeisms. To vent certain contemptuously indignant moods they are admirable in their rough-and-ready way. But neither is our own. *Cursydnesse*, in the same sense of malignant wickedness, occurs in the Coventry Plays, and *cuss* may perhaps claim to have come in with the Conqueror. At least the term is also French. Saint Simon uses it and confesses its usefulness. Speaking of the Abbé Dubois he says, "Qui étoit en plein ce qu'un mauvais françois appelle un *sacre*, mais qui ne se peut guère exprimer autrement." "Not worth a cuss," though supported by "not worth a damn," may be a mere corruption, since "not worth a cress" is in "Piers Ploughman." "I don't see it" was the popular slang a year or two ago, and seemed to spring from the soil; but no, it is in Cibber's

"Careless Husband." "*Green sauce*" for *vegetables* I meet in Beaumont and Fletcher, Gayton, and elsewhere. Our rustic pronunciation *sahce* (for either the diphthong *au* was anciently pronounced *ah*, or else we have followed abundant analogy in changing it to the latter sound, as we have in *chance*, *dance*, and so many more) may be the older one, and at least gives some hint at its ancestor *salsa*. *Warn*, in the sense of *notify*, is, I believe, now peculiar to us, but Pecock so employs it. I find *primmer* (*primer*, as we pronounce it) in Beaumont and Fletcher, and a "*square* eater" too (compare our "*square* meal"), *heft* for *weight*, and *muchness* in the "Mirror for Magistrates," *bankbill* in Swift and Fielding, and *as* for *that* I might say *passim*. *To cotton to* is, I rather think, an Americanism. The nearest approach to it I have found is *cotton together*, in Congreve's "Love for Love." To *cotton* or *cotten*, in another sense, is old and common. Our word means to *cling*, and its origin, possibly, is to be sought in another direction, perhaps in A. S. *cvead*, which means *mud*, *clay* (both proverbially clinging), or better yet, in the Icelandic *qvoda* (otherwise *kôd*), meaning *resin* and *glue*, which are κατ' ἐξοχὴν sticky substances. To *spit cotton* is, I think, American, and also, perhaps, *to flax* for *to beat*. *To the halves* still survives among us, though apparently obsolete in England. It means either to let or to hire a piece of land, receiving half the profit in money or in kind (*partibus locare*). I mention it because in a note by some English editor, to which I have lost my reference, I have seen it wrongly explained. The editors of Nares cite Burton. *To put*, in the sense of *to go*, as *Put!* for *Begone!* would seem our own, and yet it is strictly analogous to the French *se mettre à la voie*, and the Italian *mettersi in via*. Indeed, Dante has a verse,

"*Io sarei* [for *mi sarei*] *gia messo per lo sentiero*,"

which, but for the indignity, might be translated,

"I should, ere this, have *put* along the way."

I deprecate in advance any share in General Banks's notions of international law, but we may all take a just pride in his exuberant eloquence as something distinctively American. When he spoke a few years ago of "letting the Union slide," even those who, for political purposes, reproached him with the sentiment, admired the indigenous virtue of his phrase. Yet I find "let the world slide" in Heywood's "Edward IV."; and in Beaumont and Fletcher's "Wit without Money" Valentine says,

"Will you go drink,
And let the world slide?"

In the one case it is put into the mouth of a clown, in the other, of a gentleman, and was evidently proverbial. It has even higher sanction, for Chaucer writes,

"Well nigh all other curẽs *let he slide*."

Mr. Bartlett gives "above one's bend" as an Americanism; but compare Hamlet's "to the top of my bent." *In his tracks* for *immediately* has acquired an American accent, and passes where he can for a native, but is an importation nevertheless; for what is he but the Latin *e vestigio*, or at best the Norman French *eneslespas*, both which have the same meaning? *Hotfoot* (provincial also in England), I find in the old romance of "Tristan,"

"*Si s'en parti* CHAUT PAS."

Like for *as* is never used in New England, but is universal in the South and West. It has on its side the authority of two kings (*ego sum rex Romanorum et supra grammaticam*), Henry VIII. and Charles I. This were ample, without throwing into the scale the scholar and poet Daniel. *Them* was used as a nominative by the majesty of Edward VI., by Sir P. Hoby, and by Lord Paget (in Froude's "History"). I have never seen any passage adduced where *guess* was used as the Yankee uses it. The word was familiar in the mouths of our ancestors, but with a dif ferent shade of meaning from that we have given it, which is something like *rather think*, though the Yankee implies a confident certainty by it when he says, "I guess I *du!*" There are two examples in Otway, one of which ("So in the struggle, I guess the note was lost") perhaps might serve our purpose, and Coleridge's

"I guess 't was fearful there to see"

certainly comes very near. But I have a higher authority than either in Selden, who, in one of his notes to the "Polyolbion," writes, "The first inventor of them (I *guess* you dislike not the addition) was one Berthold Swartz." Here he must mean by it, "I take it for granted." Robert Greene, in his "Quip for an Upstart Courtier," makes Cloth-breeches say, "but I *gesse* your maistership never tried what true honor meant." In this case the word seems to be used with a meaning precisely like that which we give it. Another peculiarity almost as prominent is the beginning sentences, especially in answer to questions, with "well." Put before such a phrase as "How d'e do?" it is commonly short, and has the sound of *wul*, but in reply it is deliberative, and the various shades of meaning which can be conveyed by difference of intonation, and by prolonging or abbreviating, I should vainly attempt to describe. I have heard *ooa-ahl*, *wahl*, *ahl*, *wăl*, and something nearly approaching the sound of the *le* in *able*. Sometimes before "I" it dwindles to a mere *l*, as "'l I dunno." A friend of mine (why should I not please myself, though I displease him, by brightening my page with the initials of the most exquisite of humorists, J. H.?) told me that he once heard five "wells," like pioneers, precede the answer to an inquiry about the price of land. The first was the ordinary *wul*, and the second to custom; the second, the long, perpending *ooahl*, with a falling inflection of the voice; the third, the same, but with the voice rising, as if in despair of a conclusion, into a plaintively nasal whine; the fourth, *wulh*, ending in the aspirate of

a sigh; and then, fifth, came a short, sharp *wal*, showing that a conclusion had been reached. I have used this latter form in the "Biglow Papers," because, if enough nasality be added, it represents most nearly the average sound of what I may call the interjection.

A locution prevails in the Southern and Middle States which is so curious that, though never heard in New England, I will give a few lines to its discussion, the more readily because it is extinct elsewhere. I mean the use of *allow* in the sense of *affirm*, as "I allow that 's a good horse." I find the word so used in 1558 by Anthony Jenkinson in Hakluyt: "Corne they sowe not, neither doe eate any bread, mocking the Christians for the same, and disabling our strengthe, saying we live by eating the toppe of a weede, and drinke a drinke made of the same, *allowing* theyr great devouring of flesh and drinking of milke to be the increase of theyr strength." That is, they undervalued our strength, and affirmed their own to be the result of a certain diet. In another passage of the same narrative the word has its more common meaning of approving or praising: "The said king, much *allowing* this declaration, said." Ducange quotes Bracton *sub voce* ADLO-CARE for the meaning "to admit as proved," and the transition from this to "affirm" is by no means violent. Izaak Walton has "Lebault *allows* waterfrogs to be good meat," and here the word is equivalent to *affirms*. At the same time, when we consider some of the meanings of *allow* in old English, and of *allouer* in old French, and also remember that the verbs *prize* and *praise* are from one root, I think we must admit *allaudare* to a share in the paternity of *allow*. The sentence from Hakluyt would read equally well, "contemning our strengthe, ... and praising (or valuing) their great eating of flesh as the cause of their increase in strength." After all, if we confine ourselves to *allocare*, it may turn out that the word was somewhere and somewhen used for *to bet*, analogously to *put up*, *put down*, *post* (cf. Spanish *apostar*), and the like. I hear boys in the street continually saying, "I bet that 's a good horse," or what not, meaning by no means to risk anything beyond their opinion in the matter.

The word *improve*, in the sense of "to occupy, make use of, employ," as Dr. Pickering defines it, he long ago proved to be no neologism. He would have done better, I think, had he substituted *profit by* for *employ*. He cites Dr. Franklin as saying that the word had never, so far as he knew, been used in New England before he left it in 1723, except in Dr. Mather's "Remarkable Providences," which he oddly calls a "very old book." Franklin, as Dr. Pickering goes on to show, was mistaken. Mr. Bartlett in his "Dictionary" merely abridges Pickering. Both of them should have confined the application of the word to material things, its extension to which is all that is peculiar in the supposed American use of it. For surely "Complete Letter-Writers" have been "*improving*" this opportunity" time out of mind. I will illustrate the word a little further, because Pickering cites no English authorities. Skelton has a passage in his "Phyllyp Sparowe," which I quote the rather as it contains also the word *allowed*, and as it distinguishes *improve* from *employ* : —

"His [Chaucer's] Englysh well alowed,
    So as it is enproved,
    For as it is enployd,
    There is no English voyd."

Here the meaning is *to profit by*. In Fuller's "Holy Warre" (1647), we have "The Egyptians standing on the firm ground, were thereby enabled to *improve* and enforce their darts to the utmost." Here the word might certainly mean *to make use of*. Mrs. Hutchinson (Life of Colonel H.) uses the word in the same way : "And therefore did not *emproove* his interest to engage the country in the quarrell." I find it also in "Strength out of Weakness" (1652), and Plutarch's "Morals" (1714), but I know of only one

example of its use in the purely American sense, and that is, "a very good *improvement* for a mill" in the "State Trials" (Speech of the Attorney-General in the Lady Ivy's case, 1684). Swift in one of his letters says : "There is not an acre of land in Ireland turned to half its advantage; yet it is better *improved* than the people."[*] In the sense of *employ*, I could cite a dozen old English authorities.

In running over the fly-leaves of those delightful folios for this reference, I find a note which reminds me of another word, for our abuse of which we have been deservedly ridiculed. I mean *lady*. It is true I might cite the example of the Italian *donna*[†] (*domina*), which has been treated in the same way by a whole nation, and not, as *lady* among us, by the uncultivated only. It perhaps grew into use in the half-democratic republics of Italy in the same way and for the same reasons as with us. But I admit that our abuse of the word is villanous. I know of an orator who once said in a public meeting where bonnets preponderated, that "the ladies were last at the cross and first at the tomb"! But similar sins were committed before our day and in the mother country. In the "Harleian Miscellany" (vol. v. p. 455) I find "this *lady* is my servant; the hedger's daughter, Ioan." In the "State Trials" I learn of "a *gentlewoman* that lives cook with" such a one, and I hear the Lord High Steward speaking of the wife of a waiter at a bagnio as a *gentlewoman*! From the same authority, by the way, I can state that our vile habit of chewing tobacco had the somewhat unsavory example of Titus Oates, and I know by tradition from an eye-witness that the elegant General Burgoyne partook of the same vice. Howell, in one of his letters (dated 26 August, 1623), speaks thus of another "institution" which many have thought American : "They speak much of that boisterous Bishop of Hal-

---

[*] Swift, letter to Brandorth, O. R. I., 154.
[†] *Dame*, in English, is a decayed gentlewoman of the same family.

rstadt (for so they term him here), that, having taken a place wher ther were two Monasteries of Nuns and Friers, he caus'd divers feather-beds to be rip'd, and all the feathers to be thrown in a great Hall, whither the Nuns and Friers were thrust naked with their bodies oil'd and pitch'd, and to tumble among the feathers." Howell speaks as if the thing were new to him, and I know not if the "boisterous" Bishop was the inventor of it, but I find it practised in England before our Revolution.

Before leaving the subject, I will add a few comments made from time to time on the margin of Mr. Bartlett's excellent "Dictionary," to which I am glad thus publicly to acknowledge my many obligations. "Avails" is good old English, and the *vails* of Sir Joshua Reynolds's porter are famous. *Averse from*, averse *to*, and in connection with them the English vulgarism "different *to*." The corrupt use of *to* in these cases, as well as in the Yankee "he lives to Salem," "to home," and others, must be a very old one, for in the one case it plainly arose from confounding the two French prepositions *à* (from Latin *ad* and *ab*), and in the other from translating the first of them. I once thought "different to" a modern vulgarism, and Mr. Thackeray, on my pointing it out to him in "Henry Esmond," confessed it to be an anachronism. Mr. Bartlett refers to "the old writers quoted in Richardson's Dictionary" for "different to," but in my edition of that work all the examples are with *from*. But I find *to* used invariably by Sir R. Hawkins in Hakluyt. *Banjo* is a negro corruption of O. E. *bandore*. *Bind-weed* can hardly be modern, for *wood-bind* is old and radically right, intertwining itself through *bindan* and *windan* with classic stems. *Bobolink*: is this a contraction for Bob o' Lincoln? I find *bobolynes*, in one of the poems attributed to Skelton, where it may be rendered *giddy-pate*, a term very fit for the bird in his ecstasies. *Cruel* for *great* is in Hakluyt. *Bowling-alley* is

in Nash's "Pierce Pennilesse." *Curious*, meaning nice, occurs continually in old writers, and is as old as Pecock's "Repressor." *Droger* is O. E. *drugger*. *Educational* is in Burke. *Feeze* is only a form of *fizz*. *To fix*, in the American sense, I find used by the Commissioners of the United Colonies so early as 1675, "their arms well *fixed* and fit for service." *To take the foot in the hand* is German: so is to *go under*. *Gundalow* is old: I find *gundelo* in Hakluyt, and *gundello* in Booth's reprint of the folio Shakespeare of 1623. *Gonoff* is O. E. *gnoffe*. *Heap* is in "Piers Ploughman" ("and other names *an heep*"), and in Hakluyt ("seeing such a *heap* of their enemies ready to devour them"). *To liquor* is in the "Puritan" ("call 'em in, and liquor 'em a little"). *To loaf*: this, I think, is unquestionably German. *Laufen* is pronounced *lofen* in some parts of Germany, and I once heard one German student say to another, *Ich lauf* (lofe) *hier bis du wiederkehrest*, and he began accordingly to saunter up and down, in short, to *loaf*. *To mull*, Mr Bartlett says, means "to soften, to dispirit," and quotes from "Margaret," — "There has been a pretty considerable *mullin* going on among the doctors," — where it surely cannot mean what he says it does. We have always heard *mulling* used for *stirring, bustling*, sometimes in an underhand way. It is a metaphor derived probably from *mulling* wine, and the word itself must be a corruption of *mell*, from O. F. *mesler*. *Pair* of stairs is in Hakluyt. *To pull up stakes* is in Curwen's Journal, and therefore pre-Revolutionary. I think I have met with it earlier. *Raise*: under this word Mr. Bartlett omits "to raise a house," that is, the frame of a wooden one, and also the substantive formed from it, a *raisin'*. *Retire* for *go to bed* is in Fielding's "Amelia." *Setting-poles* cannot be new, for I find "some *set* [the boats] with long *poles*" in Hakluyt. *Shoulder-hitters*: I find that *shoulder-striker* is old, though I have lost the reference to my authority. *Snag* is no new word, though perhaps the Western application of it is so ; but I find in Gill the proverb, "A bird in the bag is worth two on the snag." Dryden has *swop* and *to rights*. *Trail* : Hakluyt has "many wayes *traled* by the wilde beastes."

I subjoin a few phrases not in Mr. Bartlett's book which I have heard. *Bald-headed* : "to go it bald-headed" ; in great haste, as where one rushes out without his hat. *Bogue* : "I don't git much done 'thout I *bogue* right in along 'th my men." *Carry* : a *portage*. *Cat-nap* : a short doze. *Cat-stick* : a small stick. *Chowder-head* : a muddle-brain. *Cling-john* : a soft cake of rye. *Cocoa-nut* : the head. *Cohees'* : applied to the people of certain settlements in Western Pennsylvania, from their use of the archaic form *Quo' he*. *Dunnow'z I know* : the nearest your true Yankee ever comes to acknowledging ignorance. *Essence-pedler* : a skunk. *First-rate and a half. Fish-flakes*, for drying fish : O. E. *fleck* (*cratis*). *Gander-party* : a social gathering of men only. *Gawnicus* : a dolt. *Hawkins's whetstone* : rum ; in derision of one Hawkins, a well-known temperance-lecturer. *Hyper* : to bustle : "I mus' *hyper* about an' git tea." *Keeler-tub* : one in which dishes are washed. ("And Greasy Joan doth *keel* the pot.") *Laptea* : where the guests are too many to sit at table. *Last of pea-time* : to be hard up. *Lose-laid* (loose-laid) : a weaver's term, and probably English ; weak-willed. *Malahack* : to cut up hastily or awkwardly. *Moonglade* : a beautiful word for the track of moonlight on the water. *Off-ox* : an unmanageable, cross-grained fellow. *Old Driver, Old Splitfoot* ; the Devil. *Onhitch* : to pull trigger (cf. Spanish *disparar*). *Popular* : conceited. *Rote* : sound of surf before a storm. *Rot-gut* : cheap whiskey ; the word occurs in Heywood's "English Traveller" and Addison's "Drummer," for a poor kind of drink. *Seem* : it is habitual with the New-Englander to put this verb to

strange uses, as, "I can't *seem* to be suited," "I could n't *seem* to know him." *Sidehill*, for *hillside. State-house* : this seems an Americanism, whether invented or derived from the Dutch *Stadhuys*, I know not. *Strike* and *string* : from the game of ninepins ; to make a *strike* is to knock down all the pins with one ball, hence it has come to mean fortunate, successful. *Swampers* : men who break out roads for lumberers. *Tormented* : euphemism for damned, as, "not a tormented cent." *Virginia fence*, *to make a* : to walk like a drunken man.

It is always worth while to note down the erratic words or phrases which one meets with in any dialect. They may throw light on the meaning of other words, on the relationship of languages, or even on history itself. In so composite a language as ours they often supply a different form to express a different shade of meaning as in *viol* and *fiddle*, *thrid* and *thread*, *smother* and *smoulder*, where the *l* has crept in by a false analogy with *would*. We have given back to England the excellent adjective *lengthy*, formed honestly like *earthy*, *drouthy*, and others, thus enabling their journalists to characterize our President's messages by a word civilly compromising between *long* and *tedious*, so as not to endanger the peace of the two countries by wounding our national sensitiveness to British criticism. Let me give two curious examples of the antiseptic property of dialects at which I have already glanced. Dante has *dindi* as a childish or low word for *danari* (money), and in Shropshire small Roman coins are still dug up which the peasants call *dinders*. This can hardly be a chance coincidence, but seems rather to carry the word back to the Roman soldiery. So our farmers say *chuk, chuk*, to their pigs, and *ciacco* is one of the Italian words for *hog*. When a countryman tells us that he "fell *all of a heap*," I cannot help thinking that he unconsciously points to an affinity between our word *tumble*, and the Latin *tumulus*, that is older than most others. I believe that words, or even the mere intonation of them, have an astonishing vitality and power of propagation by the root, like the gardener's pest, quitch-grass,* while the application or combination of them may be new. It is in these last that my countrymen seem to me full of humor, invention, quickness of wit, and that sense of subtle analogy which needs only refining to become fancy and imagination. Prosaic as American life seems in many of its aspects to a European, bleak and bare as it is on the side of tradition, and utterly orphaned of the solemn inspiration of antiquity, I cannot help thinking that the ordinary talk of unlettered men among us is fuller of metaphor and of phrases that suggest lively images than that of any other people I have seen. Very many such will be found in Mr. Bartlett's book, though his short list of proverbs at the end seem to me, with one or two exceptions, as un-American as possible. Most of them have no character at all but coarseness, and are quite too long-skirted for working proverbs, in which language always "takes off its coat to it," as a Yankee would say. There are plenty that have a more native and puckery flavor, seedlings from the old stock often, and yet new varieties. One hears such not seldom among us Easterners, and the West would yield many more. "Mean enough to steal acorns from a blind hog"; "Cold as the north side of a Jenooary gravestone by starlight"; "Hungry as a graven image"; "Pop'lar as a hen with one chicken"; "Quicker 'n greased lightnin'"; "Ther 's sech a thing ez bein' *tu*" (our Yankee paraphrase of μηδὲν ἄγαν); hence the phrase *tooin' round*, meaning a supererogatory activity, like that of flies; "Stingy enough to skim his milk at both eends"; "Hot as the Devil's kitchen"; "Handy as a pocket in a shirt"; "He 's a whole team and the dog under the wagon"; "All

deacons are good, but there 's odds in deacons" (to *deacon* berries is to put the largest atop); "So thievish they hev to take in their stone walls nights"; * may serve as specimens. "I take my tea *barfoot*," said a backwoodsman when asked if he would have cream and sugar. (I find *barfoot*, by the way, in the Coventry Plays.) A man speaking to me once of a very rocky clearing said, "Stone 's got a pretty heavy mortgage on that land," and I overheard a guide in the woods say to his companions who were urging him to sing, "Wal, I *did* sing once, but toons gut invented, an' thet spilt my trade." Whoever has driven over a stream by a bridge made of *slabs* will feel the picturesque force of the epithet *slab-bridged* applied to a fellow of shaky character. Almost every county has some good die-sinker in phrase, whose mintage passes into the currency of the whole neighborhood. Such a one described the county jail (the one stone building where all the dwellings are of wood) as "the house whose underpinnin' come up to the eaves," and called hell "the place where they did n't rake up their fires nights." I once asked a stage-driver if the other side of a hill were as steep as the one we were climbing: "Steep? chain-lightnin' could n' go down it 'thout puttin' the shoe on !" And this brings me back to the exaggeration of which I spoke before. To me there is something very taking in the negro "so black that charcoal made a chalk-mark on him," and the wooden shingle "painted so like marble that it sank in water," as if its very consciousness or its vanity had been over-persuaded by the cunning of the painter. I heard a man, in order to give a notion of some very cold weather, say to another that a certain Joe, who had been taking mercury, found a lump of quicksilver in each boot, when he went home to dinner. This power of rapidly dramatizing a dry fact into flesh and blood,

---

* Which, whether in that form, or under its aliases *witch*-grass and *cooch*-grass, points us back to its original Saxon *quick*.

* And, by the way, the Yankee never says "o' nights," but uses the older adverbial form, analogous to the German *nachts*.

and the vivid conception of Joe as a human thermometer, strike me as showing a poetic sense that may be refined into faculty. At any rate there is humor here, and not mere quickness of wit, — the deeper and not the shallower quality. The *tendency* of humor is always towards overplus of expression, while the very essence of wit is its logical precision. Captain Basil Hall denied that our people had any humor, deceived, perhaps, by their gravity of manner. But this very seriousness is often the outward sign of that humorous quality of the mind which delights in finding an element of identity in things seemingly the most incongruous, and then again in forcing an incongruity upon things identical. Perhaps Captain Hall had no humor himself, and if so he would never find it. Did he always feel the point of what was said to himself? I doubt it, because I happen to know a chance he once had given him in vain. The Captain was walking up and down the veranda of a country tavern in Massachusetts while the coach changed horses. A thunderstorm was going on, and, with that pleasant European air of indirect self-compliment in condescending to be surprised by American merit, which we find so conciliating, he said to a countryman lounging against the door, "Pretty heavy thunder you have here." The other, who had divined at a glance his feeling of generous concession to a new country, drawled gravely, "Waal, we *du*, considerin' the number of inhabitants." This, the more I analyze it, the more humorous does it seem. The same man was capable of wit also, when he would. He was a cabinet-maker, and was once employed to make some commandment-tables for the parish meeting-house. The parson, a very old man, annoyed him by looking into his workshop every morning, and cautioning him to be very sure to pick out "clear mahogany without any *knots* in it." At last, wearied out, he retorted one day: "Wal, Dr. B., I guess ef I was to leave the *nots* out o' some o' the c'man'ments, 't 'ould soot you full ez wal!"

If I had taken the pains to write down the proverbial or pithy phrases I have heard, or if I had sooner thought of noting the Yankeeisms I met with in my reading, I might have been able to do more justice to my theme. But I have done all I wished in respect to pronunciation, if I have proved that where we are vulgar, we have the countenance of very good company. For, as to the *jus et norma loquendi*, I agree with Horace and those who have paraphrased or commented him, from Boileau to Gray. I think that a good rule for style is Galiani's definition of sublime oratory, — "l'art de tout dire sans être mis à la Bastille dans un pays où il est défendu de rien dire." I profess myself a fanatical purist, but with a hearty contempt for the speech-gilders who affect purism without any thorough, or even pedagogic, knowledge of the engendure, growth, and affinities of the noble language about whose *mésalliances* they profess (like Dean Alford) to be so solicitous. If *they* had their way — ! "Doch es sey," says Lessing, "dass jene gothische Höflichkeit eine unentbehrliche Tugend des heutigen Umganges ist. Soll sie darum unsere Schriften eben so schaal und falsch machen als unsern Umgang?" And Drayton was not far wrong in affirming that

> "'T is possible to climb,
> To kindle, or to slake,
>   Although in Skelton's rhyme."

Cumberland in his Memoirs tells us that when, in the midst of Admiral Rodney's great sea-fight, Sir Charles Douglas said to him, "Behold, Sir George, the Greeks and Trojans contending for the body of Patroclus!" the Admiral answered, peevishly, "Damn the Greeks and damn the Trojans! I have other things to think of." After the battle was won, Rodney thus to Sir Charles, "Now, my dear friend, I am at the service of your Greeks and Trojans, and the whole of Homer's Iliad, or as much of it as you please!" I had some such feeling of the impertinence of our pseudo-classicality when I chose our homely dialect to work in. Should we be nothing, because somebody had contrived to be something (and that perhaps in a provincial dialect) ages ago? and to be nothing by our very attempt to be that something,which they had already been, and which therefore nobody could be again without being a bore? Is there no way left, then, I thought, of being natural, of being *naïf*, which means nothing more than native, of belonging to the age and country in which you are born? The Yankee, at least, is a new phenomenon ; let us try to be *that*. It is perhaps a *pis aller*, but is not *No Thoroughfare* written up everywhere else? In the literary world, things seemed to me very much as they were in the latter half of the last century. Pope, skimming the cream of good sense and expression wherever he could find it, had made, not exactly poetry, but an honest, salable butter of worldly wisdom which pleasantly lubricated some of the drier morsels of life's daily bread, and seeing this, scores of harmlessly insane people went on for the next fifty years coaxing his buttermilk with the regular up and down of the pentameter churn. And in our day do we not scent everywhere, and even carry away in our clothes against our will, that faint perfume of musk which Mr. Tennyson has left behind him, or worse, of Heine's *patchouli*? And might it not be possible to escape them by turning into one of our narrow New England lanes, shut in though it were by bleak stone walls on either hand, and where no better flowers were to be gathered than golden-rod and hardhack?

Beside the advantage of getting out of the beaten track, our dialect offered others hardly inferior. As I was about to make an endeavor to state them, I remembered something that the clearsighted Goethe had said about Hebel's *Allemannische Gedichte*, which, making proper deduction for special reference to the book under review, expresses what I would have said far better than I could hope to do : "Allen diesen innern guten Eigenschaften

kommt die behagliche naive Sprache sehr zu statten. Man findet mehrere sinnlich bedeutende und wohlklingende Worte . . . . von einem, zwei Buchstaben, Abbreviationen, Contractionen, viele kurze, leichte Sylben, neue Reime, welches, mehr als man glaubt, ein Vortheil für den Dichter ist. Diese Elemente werden durch glückliche Constructionen und lebhafte Formen zu einem Styl zusammengedrängt der zu diesem Zwecke so grosse Vorzüge hat." Of course I do not mean to imply that *I* have come near achieving any such success as the great critic here indicates, but I think the success is *there*, and to be plucked by some more fortunate hand.

Nevertheless, I was encouraged by the approval of many whose opinions I valued. With a feeling too tender and grateful to be mixed with any vanity, I mention as one of these the late A. H. Clough, who, more than any one of those I have known (no longer living), except Hawthorne, impressed me with the constant presence of that indefinable thing we call genius. He often suggested that I should try my hand at some Yankee Pastorals, which would admit of more sentiment and a higher tone without foregoing the advantage offered by the dialect. I have never completed anything of the kind, but, in this Second Series, both my remembrance of his counsel and the deeper feeling called up by the great interests at stake, led me to venture some passages nearer to what is called poetical than could have been admitted without incongruity into the former series. The time seemed calling to me, with the old poet, —

> " Leave, then, your wonted prattle,
>   The oaten reed forbear ;
> For I hear a sound of battle,
>   And trumpets rend the air ! "

The only attempt I had ever made at anything like a pastoral (if that may be called an attempt which was the result almost of pure accident) was in "The Courtin'." While the introduction to the First Series was going through the press, I received word from the printer that there was a blank page left which must be filled. I sat down at once and improvised another fictitious "notice of the press," in which, because verse would fill up space more cheaply than prose, I inserted an extract from a supposed ballad of Mr. Biglow. I kept no copy of it, and the printer, as directed, cut it off when the gap was filled. Presently I began to receive letters asking for the rest of it, sometimes for the *balance* of it. I had none, but to answer such demands, I patched a conclusion upon it in a later edition. Those who had only the first continued to importune me. Afterward, being asked to write it out as an autograph for the Baltimore Sanitary Commission Fair, I added other verses, into some of which I infused a little more sentiment in a homely way, and after a fashion completed it by sketching in the characters and making a connected story. Most likely I have spoiled it, but I shall put it at the end of this Introduction, to answer once for all those kindly importunings.

As I have seen extracts from what purported to be writings of Mr. Biglow, which were not genuine, I may properly take this opportunity to say, that the two volumes now published contain every line I ever printed under that pseudonyme, and that I have never, so far as I can remember, written an anonymous article (elsewhere than in the *North American Review*, and the *Atlantic Monthly*, during my editorship of it) except a review of Mrs. Stowe's "Minister's Wooing," and, some twenty years ago, a sketch of the anti-slavery movement in America for an English journal.

A word more on pronunciation. I have endeavored to express this so far as I could by the types, taking such pains as, I fear, may sometimes make the reading harder than need be. At the same time, by studying uniformity I have sometimes been obliged to sacrifice minute exactness. The emphasis often modifies the habitual sound.

For example, *for* is commonly *fer* (a shorter sound than *fur* for *far*), but when emphatic it always becomes *for*, as "wut *for ?*" So *too* is pronounced like *to* (as it was anciently spelt), and *to* like *ta* (the sound as in the *tou* of *touch*), but *too*, when emphatic, changes into *tue*, and *to*, sometimes, in similar cases, into *toe*, as, "I did*n'* hardly know wut *toe* du!" Where vowels come together, or one precedes another following an aspirate, the two melt together, as was common with the older poets who formed their versification on French or Italian models. Drayton is thoroughly Yankee when he says "I 'xpect," and Pope when he says "*t'* inspire." *With* becomes sometimes '*ith*, '*üth*, or '*th*, or even disappears wholly where it comes before *the*, as, "I went along th' Square" (along with the Squire), the *are* sound being an archaism which I have noticed also in *choir*, like the old Scottish *quhair*.* (Herrick has, "Of flowers ne'er sucked by th' theeving bee.") *Without* becomes *athout* and '*thout*. *Afterwards* always retains its locative *s*, and is pronounced always *ahterwurds'*, with a strong accent on the last syllable. This oddity has some support in the erratic *towards'* instead of *to'wards*, which we find in the poets and sometimes hear. The sound given to the first syllable of *to'wards*, I may remark, sustains the Yankee lengthening of the *o* in *to*. At the beginning of a sentence, *ahterwurds* has the accent on the first syllable; at the end of one, on the last; as *ah'terwurds* he tol' me," "he tol' me *ahterwurds'*." The Yankee never makes a mistake in his aspirates. *U* changes in many words to *e*, always in *such*, *brush*, *tush*, *hush*, *rush*, *blush*, seldom in *much*, oftener in *trust* and *crust*, never in *mush*, *gust*, *bust*, *tumble*, or (?) *flush*, in the latter case probably to avoid confusion with *flesh*. I have heard *flush* with the *ĕ* sound, however. For the same reason, I suspect, never in *gush* (at least, I

---

* Greene in his *Quip for an Upstart Courtier* says "To square it up and downe the streetes before his mistresse."

never heard it), because we have already one *gesh* for *gash*. *A* and *i* short frequently become *e* short. *U* always becomes *o* in the prefix *un* (except *unto*), and *o* in return changes to *u* short in *uv* for *of*, and in some words beginning with *om*. *T* and *d*, *b* and *p*, *v* and *w*, remain intact. So much occurs to me in addition to what I said on this head in the preface to the former volume.

Of course in what I have said I wish to be understood as keeping in mind the difference between provincialisms properly so called and *slang*. *Slang* is always vulgar, because it is not a natural but an affected way of talking, and all mere tricks of speech or writing are offensive. I do not think that Mr. Biglow can be fairly charged with vulgarity, and I should have entirely failed in my design, if I have not made it appear that high and even refined sentiment may coexist with the shrewder and more comic elements of the Yankee character. I believe that what is essentially vulgar and mean-spirited in politics seldom has its source in the body of the people, but much rather among those who are made timid by their wealth or selfish by their love of power. A democracy can *afford* much better than an aristocracy to follow out its convictions, and is perhaps better qualified to build those convictions on plain principles of right and wrong, rather than on the shifting sands of expediency. I had always thought "Sam Slick" a libel on the Yankee character, and a complete falsification of Yankee modes of speech, though, for aught I know, it may be true in both respects so far as the British Provinces are concerned. To me the dialect was native, was spoken all about me when a boy, at a time when an Irish day-laborer was as rare as an American one now. Since then I have made a study of it so far as opportunity allowed. But when I write in it, it is as in a mother tongue, and I am carried back far beyond any studies of it to long-ago noonings in my father's hay-fields, and to the talk of Sam and Job over their jug of *blackstrap*

under the shadow of the ash-tree which still dapples the grass whence they have been gone so long.

But life is short, and prefaces should be. And so, my good friends, to whom this introductory epistle is addressed, farewell. Though some of you have remonstrated with me, I shall never write any more "Biglow Papers," however great the temptation, — great especially at the present time, — unless it be to complete the original plan of this Series by bringing out Mr. Sawin as an "original Union man." The very favor with which they have been received is a hindrance to me, by forcing on me a self-consciousness from which I was entirely free when I wrote the First Series. Moreover, I am no longer the same careless youth, with nothing to do but live to myself, my books, and my friends, that I was then. I always hated politics, in the ordinary sense of the word, and I am not likely to grow fonder of them, now that I have learned how rare it is to find a man who can keep principle clear from party and personal prejudice, or can conceive the possibility of another's doing so. I feel as if I could in some sort claim to be an *emeritus*, and I am sure that political satire will have full justice done it by that genuine and delightful humorist, the Rev. Petroleum V. Nasby. I regret that I killed off Mr. Wilbur so soon, for he would have enabled me to bring into this preface a number of learned quotations, which must now go a-begging, and also enabled me to dispersonalize myself into a vicarious egotism. He would have helped me likewise in clearing myself from a charge which I shall briefly touch on, because my friend Mr. Hughes has found it needful to defend me in his preface to one of the English editions of the "Biglow Papers." I thank Mr. Hughes heartily for his friendly care of my good name, and were his Preface accessible to my readers here (as I am glad it is not, for its partiality makes me blush), I should leave the matter where he left it. The charge is of profanity, brought in by persons who proclaimed African slavery of Divine institution, and is based (so far as I have heard) on two passages in the First Series, —

> "An' you've gut to git up airly,
>   Ef you want to take in God,"

and,

> "God'll send the bill to you,"

and on some Scriptural illustrations by Mr. Sawin.

Now, in the first place, I was writing under an assumed character and must talk as the person would whose mouthpiece I made myself. Will any one familiar with the New England countryman venture to tell me that he does *not* speak of sacred things familiarly? That Biblical allusions (allusions, that is, to the single book with whose language, from his church-going habits, he is intimate) are *not* frequent on his lips? If so, he cannot have pursued his studies of the character on so many long-ago muster-fields and at so many cattle-shows as I. But I scorn any such line of defence, and will confess at once that one of the things I am proud of in my countrymen is (I am not speaking now of such persons as I have assumed Mr. Sawin to be) that they do not put their Maker away far from them, or interpret the fear of God into being afraid of Him. The Talmudists had conceived a deep truth when they said, that "all things were in the power of God, save the fear of God"; and when people stand in great dread of an invisible power, I suspect they mistake quite another personage for the Deity. I might justify myself for the passages criticised by many parallel ones from Scripture, but I need not. The Reverend Homer Wilbur's note-books supply me with three apposite quotations. The first is from a Father of the Roman Church, the second from a Father of the Anglican, and the third from a Father of Modern English poetry. The Puritan divines would furnish me with many more such. St. Bernard says, *Sapiens nummularius est Deus: nummum fictum non recipiet*; "A cunning money-changer is God: he will take in no base coin." Latimer says, "You shall perceive that

God, by this example, shaketh us by the noses and taketh us by the ears." Familiar enough, both of them, one would say! But I should think Mr. Biglow had verily stolen the last of the two maligned passages from Dryden's "Don Sebastian," where I find

> "And beg of Heaven to charge the bill on me!"

And there I leave the matter, being willing to believe that the Saint, the Martyr, and even the Poet, were as careful of God's honor as my critics are ever likely to be.

J. R. L.

THE COURTIN'.

God makes sech nights, all white an' still
    Fur 'z you can look or listen,
Moonshine an' snow on field an' hill,
    All silence an' all glisten.

Zekle crep' up quite unbeknown
    An' peeked in thru' the winder,
An' there sot Huldy all alone,
    'Ith no one nigh to hender.

A fireplace filled the room 's one side
    With half a cord o' wood in —
There warn't no stoves (tell comfort died)
    To bake 'ye to a puddin'.

The wa'nut logs shot sparkles out
    Towards the pootiest, bless her,
An' leetle flames danced all about
    The chiny on the dresser.

Agin the chimbley crook-necks hung,
    An' in amongst 'em rusted
The ole queen's-arm thet gran'ther Young
    Fetched back from Concord busted.

The very room, coz she was in,
    Seemed warm from floor to ceilin',
An' she looked full ez rosy agin
    Ez the apples she was peelin'.

'T was kin' o' kingdom-come to look
    On sech a blessed cretur,

A dogrose blushin' to a brook
  Ain't modester nor sweeter.

He was six foot o' man, A 1,
  Clean grit an' human natur';
None could n't quicker pitch a ton
  Nor dror a furrer straighter.

He'd sparked it with full twenty gals,
  Hed squired 'em, danced 'em, druv 'em,
Fust this one, an' then thet, by spells —
  All is, he could n't love 'em.

But long o' her his veins 'ould run
  All crinkly like curled maple,
The side she breshed felt full o' sun
  Ez a south slope in Ap'il.

She thought no v'ice hed sech a swing
  Ez hisn in the choir;
My! when he made Ole Hunderd ring,
  She *knowed* the Lord was nigher.

An' she'd blush scarlit, right in prayer,
  When her new meetin'-bunnet
Felt somehow thru' its crown a pair
  O' blue eyes sot upun it.

Thet night, I tell ye, she looked *some* !
  She seemed to 've gut a new soul,
For she felt sartin-sure he'd come,
  Down to her very shoe-sole.

She heered a foot, an' knowed it tu,
  A-raspin' on the scraper, —
All ways to once her feelins flew
  Like sparks in burnt-up paper.

He kin' o' l'itered on the mat,
  Some doubtfle o' the sekle,
His heart kep' goin' pity-pat,
  But hern went pity Zekle.

An' yit she gin her cheer a jerk
  Ez though she wished him furder,

An' on her apples kep' to work,
  Parin' away like murder.

" You want to see my Pa, I s'pose ?"
  " Wal . . . . no . . . . I come da,
    signin' " —
" To see my Ma? She 's sprinklin'
    clo'es
  Agin to-morrer's i'nin'."

To say why gals acts so or so,
  Or don't, 'ould be presumin';
Mebby to mean *yes* an' say *no*
  Comes nateral to women.

He stood a spell on one foot fust,
  Then stood a spell on t'other,
An' on which one he felt the wust
  He could n't ha' told ye nuther.

Says he, " I'd better call agin " ;
  Says she, " Think likely, Mister " ;
Thet last word pricked him like a pin,
  An' . . . . Wal, he up an' kist her.

When Ma bimeby upon 'em slips,
  Huldy sot pale ez ashes,
All kin' o' smily roun' the lips
  An' teary roun' the lashes.

For she was jes' the quiet kind
  Whose naturs never vary,
Like streams that keep a summer mind
  Snowhid in Jenooary.

The blood clost roun' her heart felt
    glued
  Too tight for all expressin',
Tell mother see how metters stood,
  And gin 'em both her blessin'.

Then her red come back like the tide
  Down to the Bay o' Fundy,
An' all I know is they was cried
  In meetin' come nex' Sunday.

THE BIGLOW PAPERS.

No. I.

BIRDOFREDUM SAWIN, ESQ., TO MR. HOSEA BIGLOW.

LETTER FROM THE REVEREND HOMER WILBUR, M. A., ENCLOSING THE EPISTLE AFORESAID.

JAALAM, 15th Nov., 1861.

* * * *

It is not from any idle wish to obtrude my humble person with undue prominence upon the publick view that I resume my pen upon the present occasion. *Juniores ad labores*. But having been a main instrument in rescuing the talent of my young parishioner from being buried in the ground, by giving it such warrant with the world as could be derived from a name already widely known by several printed discourses (all of which I may be permitted without immodesty to state have been deemed worthy of preservation in the Library of Harvard College by my esteemed friend Mr. Sibley), it seemed becoming that I should not only testify to the genuineness of the following production, but call attention to it, the more as Mr. Biglow had so long been silent as to be in danger of absolute oblivion. I insinuate no claim to any share in the authorship (*vix ea nostra voco*) of the works already published by Mr. Biglow, but merely take to myself the credit of having fulfilled toward them the office of taster (*experto crede*), who, having first tried, could afterward bear witness (*credenzen* it was aptly named by the Germans), an office always arduous,

and sometimes even dangerous, as in the case of those devoted persons who venture their lives in the deglutition of patent medicines (*dolus latet in generalibus*, there is deceit in the most of them) and thereafter are wonderfully preserved long enough to append their signatures to testimonials in the diurnal and hebdomadal prints. I say not this as covertly glancing at the authors of certain manuscripts which have been submitted to my literary judgment (though an epick in twenty-four books on the "Taking of Jericho" might, save for the prudent forethought of Mrs. Wilbur in secreting the same just as I had arrived beneath the walls and was beginning a catalogue of the various horns and their blowers, too ambitiously emulous in longanimity of Homer's list of ships, might, I say, have rendered frustrate any hope I could entertain *vacare Musis* for the small remainder of my days), but only the further to secure myself against any imputation of unseemly forthputting. I will barely subjoin, in this connexion, that, whereas Job was left to desire, in the soreness of his heart, that his adversary had written a book, as perchance misanthropically wishing to indite a review thereof, yet was not Satan allowed so far to tempt him as to send Bildad, Eliphaz, and Zophar each with an unprinted work in his wallet to be submitted to his censure. But of this enough. Were I in need of other excuse, I might add that I write by the express desire of Mr. Biglow himself, whose entire winter leisure is occupied, as he assures me, in answering demands for autographs, a labor exacting enough in itself, and egregiously so to him, who, being no ready penman, cannot sign so much as his name without strange contortions of the face (his nose, even, being essential to complete success) and painfully suppressed Saint-Vitus-dance of every muscle in his body. This, with his having been put in the Commission of the Peace by our excellent Governor (*O, si sic omnes!*) immediately on his accession to office, keeps him continually employed. *Haud inexpertus loquor*, having for many years written myself J. P., and being not seldom applied to for specimens of my chirography, a request to which I have sometimes over weakly assented, believing as I do that nothing written of set purpose can properly be called an autograph, but only those unpremeditated sallies and lively runnings which betray the fireside Man instead of the hunted Notoriety doubling on his pursuers. But it is time that I should bethink me of St. Austin's prayer, *libera me a meipso*, if I would arrive at the matter in hand.

Moreover, I had yet another reason for taking up the pen myself. I am informed that the *Atlantic Monthly* is mainly indebted for its success to the contributions and editorial supervision of Dr. Holmes, whose excellent "Annals of America" occupy an honored place upon my shelves. The journal itself I have never seen : but if this be so, it might seem that the recommendation of a brother-clergyman (though *par magis quam similis*) should carry a greater weight. I suppose that you have a department for historical lucubrations, and should be glad, if deemed desirable, to forward for publication my "Collections for the Antiquities of Jaalam," and my (now happily complete) pedigree of the Wilbur family from its *fons et origo*, the Wild Boar of Ardennes. Withdrawn from the active duties of my profession by the settlement of a colleague-pastor, the Reverend Jeduthun Hitchcock, formerly of Brutus Four-Corners, I might find time for further contributions to general literature on similar topicks. I have made large advances towards a completer genealogy of Mrs. Wilbur's family, the Pilcoxes, not, if I know myself, from any idle vanity, but with the sole desire of rendering myself useful in my day and generation. *Nulla dies sine lineâ.* I inclose a meteorological register, a list of the births, deaths, and marriages, and a few *memorabilia* of longevity in Jaalam East Parish for the last half-century. Though spared to the unusual period of more than eighty years, I find no diminution of my faculties or abatement of my natural vigor, except a scarcely sensible decay of memory and a necessity of recurring to younger eyesight or spectacles for the finer print in Cruden. It would gratify me to make some further provision for declining years from the emoluments of my literary labors. I had intended to effect an insurance on my life, but was deterred therefrom by a circular from one of the offices, in which the sudden death of so large a proportion of the insured was set forth as an inducement, that it seemed to me little less than a tempting of Providence. *Neque in summâ inopiâ levis esse senectus potest, ne sapienti quidem.*

Thus far concerning Mr. Biglow; and so much seemed needful (*brevis esse laboro*) by way of preliminary, after a silence of fourteen years. He greatly fears lest he may in this essay have fallen below himself, well knowing that, if exercise be dangerous on a full stomach, no less so is writing on a full reputation. Beset as he has been on all sides, he could not refrain, and would only imprecate patience till he shall again have "got the hang" (as he calls it) of an accomplishment long disused The letter of Mr. Sawin was received some time in last June, and others have followed which will in due season be submitted to the publick. How largely his statements are to be depended on, I more than merely dubitate. He was always distinguished for a tendency to exaggeration,—it might almost be qualified by a stronger term. *Fortiter inentire, aliquid hæret,* seemed to be his favourite rule of rhetorick. That he is actually where he says he is the postmark would seem to confirm; that he was received with the pubiick demonstrations he describes would appear consonant with what we know of the habits of those regions; but further than this I venture not to decide. I have sometimes suspected a vein of humour in him which leads him to speak by contraries; but since, in the unrestrained intercourse of private life, I have never observed in him any striking powers of invention, I am the more willing to put a certain qualified faith in the incidents and the details of life and manners which give to his narratives some portion of the interest and entertainment which characterizes a Century Sermon.

It may be expected of me that I should say something to justify myself with the world for a seeming inconsistency with my well-known principles in allowing my youngest son to raise a company for the war, a fact known to all through the medium of the publick prints. I did reason with the young man, but *expellas naturam furcâ, tamenusque recurrit.* Having myself been a chaplain in 1812, I could the less wonder that a man of war had sprung from my loins. It was, indeed, grievous to send my Benjamin, the child of my old age; but after the discomfiture of Manassas, I with my own hands did buckle on his armour, trusting in the great Comforter and Commander for strength according to my need. For truly the memory of a brave son dead in his shroud were a greater staff of my declining years than a living coward (if those may be said to have lived who carry all of themselves into the grave with them), though his days might be long in the land, and he should get much goods. It is not till our earthen vessels are broken that we find and truly possess the treasure that was laid up in them. *Migravi in animam meam,* I have sought refuge in my own soul; nor would I be shamed by the heathen comedian with his *Ne-*

quam illud verbum, bene vult, nisi bene facit. During our dark days, I read constantly in the inspired book of Job, which I believe to contain more food to maintain the fibre of the soul for right living and high thinking than all pagan literature together, though I would by no means vilipend the study of the classicks. There I read that Job said in his despair, even as the fool saith in his heart there is no God, — "The tabernacles of robbers prosper, and they that provoke God are secure." (*Job* xii. 6.) But I sought farther till I found this Scripture also, which I would have those perpend who have striven to turn our Israel aside to the worship of strange gods: — "If I did despise the cause of my man-servant or of my maid-servant when they contended with me, what then shall I do when God riseth up? and when he visiteth, what shall I answer him?" (*Job* xxxi. 13, 14.) On this text I preached a discourse on the last day of Fasting and Humiliation with general acceptance, though there were not wanting one or two Laodiceans who said that I should have waited till the President announced his policy. But let us hope and pray, remembering this of Saint Gregory, *Vult Deus rogari, vult cogi, vult quâdam importunitate vinci.*

We had our first fall of snow on Friday last. Frosts have been unusually backward this fall. A singular circumstance occurred in this town on the 20th October, in the family of Deacon Pelatiah Tinkham. On the previous evening, a few moments before family-prayers,

* * * *

[The editors of the *Atlantic* find it necessary here to cut short the letter of their valued correspondent, which seemed calculated rather on the rates of longevity in Jaalam than for less favored localities. They have every encouragement to hope that he will write again.]

With esteem and respect,
Your obedient servant,
HOMER WILBUR, A. M.

It 's some consid'ble of a spell sence
  I hain't writ no letters,
An' ther' 's gret changes hez took
  place in all polit'cle metters:
Some canderdates air dead an' gone,
  an' some hez ben defeated,
Which 'mounts to pooty much the
  same; fer it 's ben proved repeated
A betch o' bread thet hain't riz once
  ain't goin' to rise agin,
An' it 's jest money throwed away to
  put the emptins in:
But thet 's wut folks wun't never larn;
  they dunno how to go,
Arter you want their room, no more 'n
  a bullet-headed beau;
Ther' 's ollers chaps a-hangin' roun'
  thet can't see peatime 's past,
Mis'ble as roosters in a rain, heads
  down an' tails half-mast:
It ain't disgraceful bein' beat, when a
  holl nation doos it,
But Chance is like an amberill, — it
  don't take twice to lose it.

I spose you 're kin' o' cur'ous, now, to
  know why I hain't writ.
Wal, I 've ben where a litt'ry taste
  don't somehow seem to git
Th' encouragement a feller 'd think,
  thet 's used to public schools,
An' where sech things ez paper 'n' ink
  air clean agin the rules:
A kind o' vicyvarsy house, built dreffle
  strong an' stout,
So 's 't honest people can't get in, ner
  t'other sort git out,
An' with the winders so contrived,
  you 'd prob'ly like the view
Better alookin' in than out, though it
  seems sing'lar, tu;
But then the landlord sets by ye, can't
  bear ye out o' sight,
And locks ye up ez reg'lar ez an outside door at night.

This world is awfle contrary: the rope
  may stretch your neck
Thet mebby kep' another chap frum
  washin' off a wreck;
An' you may see the taters grow in
  one poor feller's patch,
So small no self-respectin' hen thet
  vallied time 'ould scratch,
So small the rot can't find 'em out, an'
  then agin, nex' door,
Ez big ez wut hogs dream on when
  they 're 'most too fat to snore.
But groutin' ain't no kin' o' use; an' ef
  the fust throw fails,
Why, up an' try agin, thet 's all, — the
  coppers ain't all tails;
Though I *hev* seen 'em when I thought
  they hed n't no more head
Than 'd sarve a nussin' Brigadier thet
  gits some ink to shed.

When I writ last, I 'd ben turned
  loose by thet blamed nigger, Pomp,
Ferlorner than a musquash, ef you 'd
  took an' dreened his swamp:
But I ain't o' the meechin' kind, thet
  sets an' thinks fer weeks
The bottom 's out o' th' univarse coz
  their own gillpot leaks.
I hed to cross bayous an' criks, (wal, it
  did beat all natur',)
Upon a kin' o' corderoy, fust log, then
  alligator:
Luck'ly, the critters warn't sharp-sot;
  I guess 't wuz overruled
They 'd done their mornin's marketin'
  an' gut their hunger cooled;
Fer missionaries to the Creeks an' run-
  aways are viewed
By them an' folks ez sent express to be
  their reg'lar food:
Wutever 't wuz, they laid an' snoozed
  ez peacefully ez sinners,
Meek ez digestin' deacons be at ordi-
  nation dinners;
Ef any on 'em turned an' snapped, I
  let 'em kin' o' taste
My live-oak leg, an' so, ye see, ther'
  warn't no gret o' waste;
Fer they found out in quicker time than
  ef they 'd ben to college
'T warn't heartier food than though 't
  wuz made out o' the tree o' knowledge.
But *I* tell *you* my other leg hed larned
  wut pizon-nettle meant,
An' var'ous other usefle things, afore I
  reached a settlement,
An' all o' me thet wuz n't sore an'
  sendin' prickles thru me

Wuz jest the leg I parted with in lickin'
   Montezumy:
A usefle limb it 's ben to me, an' more
   of a support
Than wut the other hez ben, — coz I
   dror my pension for 't.

Wal, I gut in at last where folks wuz
   civerlized an' white,
Ez I diskivered to my cost afore
   't warn't hardly night ;
Fer 'z I wuz settin' in the bar a-takin'
   sunthin' hot,
An' feelin' like a man agin, all over in
   one spot,
A feller thet sot opposite, arter a squint
   at me,
Lep up an' drawed his peacemaker,
   an', " Dash it, Sir," suz he,
" I 'm doubledashed ef you ain't him
   thet stole my yaller chettle,
(You 're all the stranger thet 's around,)
   so now you 've gut to settle ;
It ain't no use to argerfy ner try to cut
   up frisky,
I know ye ez I know the smell of ole
   chain lightnin' whiskey ;
We 're lor-abidin' folks down here,
   we 'll fix ye so 's 't a bar
Would n' tech ye with a ten-foot pole ;
   (Jedge, you jest warm the tar ;)
You 'll think you 'd better ha' gut among
   a tribe o' Mongrel Tartars,
'Fore we 've done showin' how we raise
   our Southun prize tar-martyrs ;
A moultin' fallen cherubim, ef he
   should see ye, 'd snicker,
Thinkin' he warn't a suckemstance.
   Come, genlemun, le' 's liquor ;
An', Gin'ral, when you 've mixed the
   drinks an' chalked 'em up, tote
   roun'
An' see ef ther' 's a feather-bed (thet 's
   borryable) in town.
We 'll try ye fair, old Grafted-Leg, an'
   ef the tar wun't stick,
Th' ain't not a juror here but wut 'll
   'quit ye double-quick."
To cut it short, I wun't say sweet, they
   gi' me a good dip,
(They ain't *perfessin'* Bahptists here,)
   then give the bed a rip, —
The jury 'd sot, an' quicker 'n a flash
   they hetched me out, a livin'

Extemp'ry mammoth turkey-chick fer
   a Fejee Thanksgivin'.
Thet I felt some stuck up is wut it 's
   nat'ral to suppose,
When poppylar enthusiasm hed fun-
   nished me sech clo'es ;
(Ner 't ain't without edvantiges, this
   kin' o' suit, ye see,
It 's water-proof, an' water 's wut I like
   kep' out o' me ;)
But nut content with thet, they took a
   kerridge from the fence
An' rid me roun' to see the place, en-
   tirely free 'f expense,
With forty-'leven new kines o' sarse
   without no charge acquainted me,
Gi' me three cheers, an' vowed thet I
   wuz all their fahncy painted me ;
They treated me to all their eggs ;
   (they keep 'em I should think,
Fer sech ovations, pooty long, for they
   wuz mos' distinc' ;)
They starred me thick 'z the Milky-
   Way with indiscrim'nit cherity,
Fer wut we call reception eggs air sun-
   thin' of a rerity ;
Green ones is plentifle anough, skurce
   wuth a nigger's getherin',
But your dead-ripe ones ranges high fer
   treatin' Nothun bretherin ;
A spotteder, ringstreakeder child the'
   warn't in Uncle Sam's
Holl farm, — a cross of stripèd pig an'
   one o' Jacob's lambs ;
'T wuz Dannil in the lions' den, new
   an' enlarged edition,
An' everythin' fust-rate o' 'ts kind, the'
   warn't no impersition.
People 's impulsiver down here than
   wut our folks to home be,
An' kin' o' go it 'ith a resh in raisin'
   Hail Columby ;
Thet 's *so :* an' they swarmed out like
   bees, for your real Southun men's
Time is n't o' much more account than
   an ole settin' hen's ;
(They jest work semioccashnally, or
   else don't work at all,
An' so their time an' 'tention both air
   at saci'ty's call.)
Talk about hospatality ! wut Nothun
   town d' ye know
Would take a totle stranger up an' treat
   him gratis so ?

You 'd better b'lieve ther' 's nothin' like
  this spendin' days an' nights
Along 'ith a dependent race fer civer-
  lizin' whites.

But this wuz all prelim'nary; it 's so
  Gran' Jurors here
Fin' a true bill, a handier way than
  ourn, an' not so dear;
So arter this they sentenced me, to
  make all tight 'n' snug,
Afore a reg'lar court o' law, to ten
  years in the Jug.
I did n' make no gret defence: you
  don't feel much like speakin',
When, ef you let your clamshells gape,
  a quart o' tar will leak in:
I *hev* hearn tell o' wingëd words, but
  pint o' fact it tethers
The spoutin' gift to hev your words *tu*
  thick set on with feathers,
An' Choate ner Webster would n't ha'
  made an A ɪ kin' o' speech
Astride a Southun chestnut horse shar-
  per 'n a baby's screech.
Two year ago they ketched the thief,
  'n' seein' I wuz innercent,
They jest uncorked an' le' me run, an'
  in my stid the sinner sent
To see how *he* liked pork 'n' pone
  flavored with wa'nut saplin',
An' nary social priv'ledge but a one-
  hoss, starn-wheel chaplin.
When I come out, the folks behaved
  mos' gen'manly an' harnsome;
They 'lowed it would n't be more 'n
  right, ef I should cuss 'n' darn
  some:
The Cunnle he aperlogized; suz he,
  " I 'll du wut 's right,
I 'll give ye settisfection now by shootin'
  ye at sight,
An' give the nigger (when he 's
  caught), to pay him fer his trickin'
In gittin' the wrong man took up, a
  most H fired lickin'," —
It 's jest the way with all on 'em, the
  inconsistent critters,
They 're most enough to make a man
  blaspheme his mornin' bitters;
I 'll be your frien' thru thick an' thin
  an' in all kines o' weathers,
An' all you 'll hev to pay fer 's jest the
  waste o' tar an' feathers:

A lady owned the bed, ye see, a wid-
  der, tu, Miss Shennon;
It wuz her mite; we would ha' took
  another, ef ther 'd ben one:
We don't make *no* charge for the ride
  an' all the other fixins.
Le' 's liquor; Gin'ral, you can chalk
  our friend for all the mixins."
A meetin' then wuz called, where they
  " RESOLVED, Thet we respec'
B. S. Esquire for quallerties o' heart
  an' intellec'
Peculiar to Columby's sile, an' not to
  no one else's,
Thet makes Européan tyrans scringe
  in all their gilded pel'ces,
An' doos gret honor to our race an'
  Southun institootions" :
(I give ye jest the substance o' the
  leadin' resolootions :)
" RESOLVED, Thet we revere in him a
  soger 'thout a flor,
A martyr to the princerples o' libbaty
  an' lor:
RESOLVED, Thet other nations all, ef
  sot 'longside o' us,
For vartoo, larnin', chivverlry, ain't
  noways wuth a cuss."
They gut up a subscription, tu, but no
  gret come o' *thet*;
I 'xpect in cairin' of it roun' they took
  a leaky hat;
Though Southun genelmun ain't slow
  at puttin' down their name,
(When they can write,) fer in the eend
  it comes to jes' the same,
Because, ye see, 't 's the fashion here
  to sign an' not to think
A critter 'd be so sordid ez to ax 'em for
  the chink :
I did n't call but jest on one, an' *he*
  drawed toothpick on me,
An' reckoned he warn't goin' to stan'
  no sech doggauned econ'my;
So nothin' more wuz realized, 'ceptin'
  the good-will shown,
Than ef 't had ben from fust to last a
  reg'lar Cotton Loan.
It 's a good way, though, come to
  think, coz ye enjy the sense
O' lendin' lib'rally to the Lord, an'
  nary red o' 'xpense :
Sence then I 've gut my name up for a
  gin'rous-hearted man

By jes' subscribin' right an' left on this
　　high-minded plan ;
I 've gin away my thousans so to every
　　Southun sort
O' missions, colleges, an' sech, ner
　　ain't no poorer for 't.

I warn't so bad off, arter all ; I need n't
　　hardly mention
That Guv'ment owed me quite a pile
　　for my arrears o' pension, —
I mean the poor, weak thing we *hed* :
　　we run a new one now,
Thet strings a feller with a claim up ta
　　the nighes' bough,
An' *prectises* the rights o' man, pur-
　　tects down-trodden debtors,
Ner wun't hev creditors about a-
　　scrougin' o' their betters :
Jeff 's gut the last idees ther' is,
　　poscrip', fourteenth edition,
He knows it takes some enterprise to
　　run an opposition :
Ourn 's the fust thru-by-daylight train,
　　with all ou'doors for deepot ;
Yourn goes so slow you 'd think 't wuz
　　drawed by a las' cent'ry teapot ; —
Wal, I gut all on 't paid in gold afore
　　our State seceded,
An' done wal, for Confed'rit bonds
　　warn't jest the cheese I needed :
Nut but wut they 're ez *good* ez gold,
　　but then it 's hard a-breakin' on'em,
An' ignorant folks is ollers sot an'
　　wun't git used to takin' on 'em ;
They 're wuth ez much ez wut they wuz
　　afore ole Mem'nger signed 'em,
An' go off middlin' wal for drinks,
　　when ther' 's a knife behind 'em ;
We *du* miss silver, jes' fer thet an'
　　ridin' in a bus,
Now we 've shook off the desputs thet
　　wuz suckin' at our pus ;
An' it 's *because* the South 's so rich,
　　't wuz nat'ral to expec'
Supplies o' change wuz jes' the things
　　we should n't recollec' ;
We 'd ough' to ha' thought aforehan',
　　though, o' thet good rule o' Crock-
　　ett's,
For 't 's tiresome cairin' cotton-bales
　　an' niggers in your pockets,
Ner 't ain't quite hendy to pass off one
　　o' your six-foot Guineas

An' git your halves an' quarters back
　　in gals an' pickaninnies ;
Wal, 't ain't quite all a feller 'd ax, but
　　then ther' 's this to say,
It 's on'y jest among ourselves thet we
　　expec' to pay ;
Our system would ha' caird us thru in
　　any Bible cent'ry,
'Fore this onscripterl plan come up o'
　　books by double entry ;
We go the patriarkle here out o' all
　　sight an' hearin',
For Jacob warn't a suckemstance to
　　Jeff at financierin' ;
He never 'd thought o' borryin' from
　　Esau like all nater
An' then cornfiscatin' all debts to sech
　　a small pertater ;
There 's p'litickle econ'my, now, com-
　　bined 'ith morril beauty
Thet saycrifices privit eends (your
　　in'my's, tu) to dooty !
Wy, Jeff 'd ha' gin him five an' won
　　his eye-teeth 'fore he knowed it,
An', stid o' wastin' pottage, he 'd ha'
　　eat it up an' owed it.
But I wuz goin' on to say how I come
　　here to dwall : —
'Nough said, thet, arter lookin' roun',
　　I liked the place so wal,
Where niggers doos a double good,
　　with us atop to stiddy 'em,
By bein' proofs o' prophecy an' suckle-
　　atin' medium,
Where a man 's sunthin' coz he 's
　　white, an' whiskey 's cheap ez fleas,
An' the financial pollercy jes' sooted my
　　idees,
Thet I friz down right where I wuz,
　　merried the Widder Shennón,
(Her thirds wuz part in cotton-land,
　　part in the curse o' Canaan,)
An' here I be ez lively ez a chipmunk
　　on a wall,
With nothin' to feel riled about much
　　later 'n Eddam's fall.

Ez fur ez human foresight goes, we
　　made an even trade :
She gut an overseer, an' I a fem'ly
　　ready-made,
(The youngest on 'em 's 'mos' growed
　　up,) rugged an' spry ez weazles,

So 's 't ther' 's no resk o' doctors' bills
    fer hoopin'-cough an' measles.
Our farm 's at Turkey-Buzzard Roost,
    Little Big Boosy River,
Wal located in all respex, — fer 't ain't
    the chills 'n' fever
Thet makes my writin' seem to squirm ;
    a Southuner 'd allow I 'd
Some call to shake, fer I 've jest hed
    to meller a new cowhide.

Miss S. is all 'f a lady ; th' ain't no
    better on Big Boosy
Ner one with more accomplishmunts
    'twixt here an' Tuscaloosy ;
She 's an F. F., the tallest kind, an'
    prouder 'n the gret Turk,
An' never hed a relative thet done a
    stroke o' work ;
Hern ain't a scrimpin' fem'ly sech ez
    you git up Down East,
Th' ain't a growed member on 't but
    owes his thousuns et the least :
She *is* some old ; but then agin ther' 's
    drawbacks in my sheer :
Wut 's left o' me ain't more 'n enough
    to make a Brigadier :
Wust is, thet she hez tantrums ; she 's
    like Seth Moody's gun
(Him thet wuz nicknamed frum his
    limp Ole Dot an' Kerry One) ;
He 'd left her loaded up a spell, an' hed
    to git her clear,
So he onhitched, — Jeerusalem ! the
    middle o' last year
Wuz right nex' door compared to
    where she kicked the critter tu
(Though *jest* where he brought up wuz
    wut no human never knew) ;
His brother Asaph picked her up an'
    tied her to a tree,
An' then she kicked an hour 'n' a half
    afore she 'd let it be :
Wal, Miss S. *does* hev cuttins-up an'
    pourins-out o' vials,
But then she hez her widder's thirds,
    an' all on us hez trials.
My objec', though, in writin' now
    warn't to allude to sech ;
But to another suckemstance more
    dellykit to tech, —
I want thet you should grad'lly break
    my merriage to Jerushy,
An' there 's a heap of argymunts thet 's
    emple to indooce ye :

Fust place, State's Prison, — wal, it 's
    true it warn't fer crime, o' course,
But then it 's jest the same fer her in
    gittin' a divorce ;
Nex' place, my State 's secedin' out hez
    leg'lly lef' me free
To merry any one I please, pervidin'
    it 's a she ;
Fin'lly, I never wun't come back, she
    need n't hev no fear on 't,
But then it 's wal to fix things right fer
    fear Miss S. should hear on 't ;
Lastly, I 've gut religion South, an'
    Rushy she 's a pagan
Thet sets by th' graven imiges o' the
    gret Nothun Dagon ;
(Now I hain't seen one in six munts,
    for, sence our Treashry Loan,
Though yaller boys is thick anough,
    eagles hez kind o' flown ;)
An' ef J. wants a stronger pint than
    them thet I hev stated,
Wy, she 's an aliun in my now, an'
    I 've been cornfiscated,—
For sence we 've entered on th' estate
    o' the late nayshnul eagle,
She hain't no kin o' right but jes' wut
    I allow ez legle :
Wut *does* Secedin' mean, ef 't ain't thet
    nat'rul rights hez riz, 'n'
Thet wut is mine 's my own, but wut's
    another man's ain't his'n ?

Besides, I could n't do no else ; Miss
    S. suz she to me,
"You 've sheered my bed," [thet 's
    when I paid my interduction fee
To Southun rites,] "an' kep' your
    sheer," [wal, I allow it sticked
So 's 't I wuz most six weeks in jail
    afore I gut me picked,]
" Ner never paid no demmiges ; but
    thet wun't do no harm,
Pervidin' thet you 'll ondertake to
    oversee the farm ;
(Myeldes' boy he 's so took up, wut with
    the Ringtail Rangers
An' settin' in the Jestice-Court for wel-
    comin' o' strangers " ;)
[He sot on *me* ;] " an' so, ef you 'll jest
    ondertake the care
Upon a mod'rit sellery, we 'll up an
    call it square ."

But ef you *can't* conclude," suz she,
  an' give a kin' o' grin,
" Wy, the Gran' Jurymen, I 'xpect, 'll
  hev to set agin."

Thet 's the way metters stood at fust;
  now wut wuz I to du,
But jes' to make the best on 't an' off
  coat an' buckle tu ?

Ther' ain't a livin' man thet finds an
  income necessarier
Than me, — bimeby I 'll tell ye how I
  fin'lly come to merry her.

She hed another motive, tu : I mention
  of it here
T' encourage lads thet 's growin' up to
  study 'n' persevere,
An' show 'em how much better 't pays
  to mind their winter-schoolin'
Than to go off on benders 'n' sech, an'
  waste their time in foolin';
Ef 't warn't for studyin' evenin's, I
  never 'd ha' been here
An orn'ment o' society, in my appro-
  prut spear :
She wanted somebody, ye see, o' taste
  an' cultivation,
To talk along o' preachers when they
  stopt to the plantation ;
For folks in Dixie th't read an' rite,
  onless it is by jarks,
Is skurce ez wut they wuz among th'
  origenle patriarchs ;
To fit a feller f' wut they call the soshle
  higherarchy,
All thet you 've gut to know is jes' be-
  yund an evrage darky ;
Schoolin' 's wut they can't seem to
  stan', they 're tu consarned high-
  pressure,
An' knowin' t' much might spile a boy
  for bein' a Seceher.
We hain't no settled preachin' here,
  ner ministeril taxes ;
The min'ster's only settlement 's the
  carpet-bag he packs his
Razor an' soap-brush intu, with his
  hymbook an' his Bible, —
But they *du* preach, I swan to man, it 's
  puf'kly indescrib'le !
They go it like an Ericsson's ten-hoss-
  power coleric ingine,
An' make Ole Split-Foot winch an'
  squirm, for all he 's used to
  singein' ;

Hawkins's whetstone ain't a pinch o'
  primin' to the innards
To hearin' on 'em put free grace t' a lot
  o' tough old sinhards !
But I must eend this letter now : 'fore
  Jong I 'll send a fresh un ;
I 've lots o' things to write about, per-
  ticklerly Seceshun :
I 'm called off now to mission-work, to
  let a leetle law in
To Cynthy's hide : an' so, till death,
  Yourn,

      BIRDOFREDUM SAWIN.

No. II.

MASON AND SLIDELL : A YANKEE IDYLL.

TO THE EDITORS OF THE ATLANTIC MONTHLY.

      JAALAM, 6th Jan., 1862.

GENTLEMEN, — I was highly gratified by the insertion of a portion of my letter in the last number of your valuable and entertaining Miscellany, though in a type which rendered its substance inaccessible even to the beautiful new spectacles presented to me by a Committee of the Parish on New Year's Day. I trust that I was able to bear your very considerable abridgment of my lucubrations with a spirit becoming a Christian. My third granddaughter, Rebekah, aged fourteen years, and whom I have trained to read slowly and with proper emphasis (a practice too much neglected in our modern systems of education), read aloud to me the excellent essay upon "Old Age," the authour of which I cannot help suspecting to be a young man who has never yet known what it was to have snow (*canities morosa*) upon his own roof. *Dissolve frigus, large super foco ligna reponens*, is a rule for the young, whose wood-pile is yet abundant for such cheerful lenitives. A good life behind him is the best thing to keep an old man's shoulders from shivering at every breath of sorrow or ill-fortune. But methinks it were easier for an old man to feel the disadvantages of youth than the advantages of age. Of these latter I reckon one of the chiefest to be this; that we attach a less inordinate value to our own productions, and, distrusting daily more and more our own wisdom (with the conceit whereof at twenty we wrap ourselves away from knowledge as with a garment), do reconcile ourselves with the wisdom of God. I could have wished, indeed, that room might have been made for the residue of the anecdote relating to Deacon Tinkham, which would not only have gratified a natural curiosity on the part of the publick (as I have reason to know from several letters of inquiry already received), but would also, as I think, have largely increased the circulation of your Magazine in this town. *Nihil humani alienum*, there is a curiosity about the affairs of our neighbours which is not only pardonable, but even commendable. But I shall abide a more fitting season.

As touching the following literary effort of Esquire Biglow, much might be profitably said on the topick of Idyllick and Pastoral Poetry, and concerning the proper distinctions to be made between them, from Theocritus, the inventor of the former, to Collins, the latest authour I know of who has emulated the classicks in the latter style. But in the time of Civil War worthy a Milton to defend and a Lucan to sing, it may be reasonably doubted whether the publick, never too studious of serious instruction, might not consider other objects more deserving of present attention. Concerning the title of Idyll, which Mr. Biglow has adopted at my suggestion, it may not be improper to animadvert, that the name properly signifies a poem somewhat rustick in phrase (for, though the learned are not agreed as to the particular dialect employed by Theocritus, they are universanimous both as to its rusticity and its capacity of rising now and then to the level of more elevated sentiments and expressions), while it is also descriptive of real scenery and manners.

Yet it must be admitted that the production now in question (which here and there bears perhaps too plainly the marks of my correcting hand) does partake of the nature of a Pastoral, inasmuch as the interlocutors therein are purely imaginary beings, and the whole is little better than κапνοῦ σκιᾶς ὄναρ. The plot was, as I believe, suggested by the "Twa Briggs" of Robert Burns, a Scottish poet of the last century, as that found its prototype in the "Mutual Complaint of Plainstanes and Causey" by Fergusson, though the metre of this latter be different by a foot in each verse. Perhaps the "Two Dogs" of Cervantes gave the first hint. I reminded my talented young parishioner and friend that Concord Bridge had long since yielded to the edacious tooth of Time. But he answered me to this effect: that there was no greater mistake of an authour than to suppose the reader had no fancy of his own; that, if once that faculty was to be called into activity, it were *better* to be in for the whole sheep than the shoulder; and that he knew Concord like a book,—an expression questionable in propriety, since there are few things with which he is not more familiar than with the printed page. In proof of what he affirmed, he showed me some verses which with others he had stricken out as too much delaying the action, but which I communicate in this place because they rightly define "punkin-seed" (which Mr. Bartlett would have a kind of perch,—a creature to which I have found a rod or pole not to be so easily equivalent in our inland waters as in the books of arithmetic), and because it conveys an eulogium on the worthy son of an excellent father, with whose acquaintance (*eheu, fugaces anni!*) I was formerly honoured.

"But nowadays the Bridge ain't wut they show,
So much ez Em'son, Hawthorne, an' Thoreau.
I know the village, though; was sent there once
A-schoolin', 'cause to home I played the dunce;
An' I 've ben sence a-visitin' the Jedge,

Whose garding whispers with the river's
    edge,
Where I've sot mornin's lazy as the bream,
    Whose on'y business is to head up-stream,
    'We call 'em punkin-seed,) or else in chat
Along 'th the Jedge, who covers with his hat
More wit an' gumption an' shrewd Yankee
    sense
Than there is mosses on an ole stone fence."

Concerning the subject-matter of the
verses, I have not the leisure at present to write so fully as I could wish,
my time being occupied with the preparation of a discourse for the forth-
coming bi-centenary celebration of the
first settlement of Jaalam East Parish.
It may gratify the publick interest to
mention the circumstance, that my investigations to this end have enabled
me to verify the fact (of much historick
importance, and hitherto hotly debated)
that Shearjashub Tarbox was the first
child of white parentage born in this
town, being named in his father's will
under date August 7th, or 9th, 1662. It
is well known that those who advocate
the claims of Mehetable Goings are
unable to find any trace of her existence
prior to October of that year. As respects the settlement of the Mason and
Slidell question, Mr. Biglow has not
incorrectly stated the popular sentiment,
so far as I can judge by its expression
in this locality. For myself, I feel
more sorrow than resentment : for I am
old enough to have heard those talk of
England who still, even after the unhappy estrangement, could not un-
school their lips from calling her the
Mother-Country. But England has
insisted on ripping up old wounds, and
has undone the healing work of fifty
years ; for nations do not reason, they
only feel, and the *spretæ injuria formæ*
rankles in their minds as bitterly as in
that of a woman. And because this is
so, I feel the more satisfaction that our
Government has acted (as all Govern-
ments should, standing as they do between the people and their passions) as
if it had arrived at years of discretion.
There are three short and simple words,
the hardest of all to pronounce in any
language (and I suspect they were no
easier before the confusion of tongues),

but which no man or nation that cannot
utter can claim to have arrived at manhood. Those words are, *I was wrong*,
and I am proud that, while England
played the boy, our rulers had strength
enough from the People below and
wisdom enough from God above to
quit themselves like men.

The sore points on both sides have
been skilfully exasperated by interested and unscrupulous persons, who saw
in a war between the two countries the
only hope of profitable return for
their investment in Confederate stock,
whether political or financial. The always supercilious, often insulting, and
sometimes even brutal tone of British
journals and publick men has certainly
not tended to soothe whatever resentment might exist in America.

" Perhaps it was right to dissemble your love,
    But why did you kick me down stairs?"

We have no reason to complain that
England, as a necessary consequence
of her clubs, has become a great society
for the minding of other people's business, and we can smile good-naturedly
when she lectures other nations on the
sins of arrogance and conceit ; but we
may justly console it a breach of the
political *convenances* which are expected to regulate the intercourse of one
well-bred government with another,
when men holding places in the ministry allow themselves to dictate our domestic policy, to instruct us in our duty,
and to stigmatize as unholy a war for
the rescue of whatever a high-minded
people should hold most vital and most
sacred. Was it in good taste, that I
may use the mildest term, for Earl
Russell to expound our own Constitution to President Lincoln, or to make a
new and fallacious application of an old
phrase for our benefit, and tell us that
the Rebels were fighting for independence and we for empire ? As if all
wars for independence were by nature
just and deserving of sympathy, and
all wars for empire ignoble and worthy
only of reprobation, or as if these easy
phrases in any way characterized this
terrible struggle, — terrible not so truly

in any superficial sense, as from the essential and deadly enmity of the principles that underlie it. His Lordship's bit of borrowed rhetoric would justify Smith O'Brien, Nana Sahib, and the Maori chieftains, while it would condemn nearly every war in which England has ever been engaged. Was it so very presumptuous in us to think that it would be decorous in English statesmen if they spared time enough to acquire some kind of knowledge, though of the most elementary kind, in regard to this country and the questions at issue here, before they pronounced so off-hand a judgment? Or is political information expected to come Dogberry-fashion in England, like reading and writing, by nature?

And now all respectable England is wondering at our irritability, and sees a quite satisfactory explanation of it in our national vanity. *Suave mari magno*, it is pleasant, sitting in the easy-chairs of Downing Street, to sprinkle pepper on the raw wounds of a kindred people struggling for life, and philosophical to find in self-conceit the cause of our instinctive resentment. Surely we were of all nations the least liable to any temptation of vanity at a time when the gravest anxiety and the keenest sorrow were never absent from our hearts. Nor is conceit the exclusive attribute of any one nation. The earliest of English travellers, Sir John Mandeville, took a less provincial view of the matter when he said, "For fro what partie of the erthe that men duellen, other aboven or beneathen, it semethe alweys to hem that duellen that thei gon more righte than any other folke." The English have always had their fair share of this amiable quality. We may say of them still, as the authour of the *Lettres Cabalistiques* said of them more than a century ago, "*Ces derniers disent naturellement qu'il n'y a qu'eux qui soient estimables.*" And, as he also says, "*J'aimerois presque autant tomber entre les mains d'un Inquisiteur que d'un Anglois qui me fait sentir sans cesse combien il s'estime plus que moi,*

et qui ne daigne me parler que pour injurier ma Nation et pour m'ennuyer du récit des grandes qualités de la sienne." Of *this* Bull we may safely say with Horace, *habet fœnum in cornu.* What we felt to be especially insulting was the quiet assumption that the descendants of men who left the Old World for the sake of principle, and who had made the wilderness into a New World patterned after an Idea, could not possibly be susceptible of a generous or lofty sentiment, could have no feeling of nationality deeper than that of a tradesman for his shop. One would have thought, in listening to England, that we were presumptuous in fancying that we were a nation at all, or had any other principle of union than that of booths at a fair, where there is no higher notion of government than the constable, or better image of God than that stamped upon the current coin.

It is time for Englishmen to consider whether there was nothing in the spirit of their press and of their leading public men calculated to rouse a just indignation, and to cause a permanent estrangement on the part of any nation capable of self-respect, and sensitively jealous, as ours then was, of foreign interference. Was there nothing in the indecent haste with which belligerent rights were conceded to the Rebels, nothing in the abrupt tone assumed in the Trent case, nothing in the fitting out of Confederate privateers, that might stir the blood of a people already overcharged with doubt, suspicion, and terrible responsibility? The laity in any country do not stop to consider points of law, but they have an instinctive perception of the *animus* that actuates the policy of a foreign nation; and in our own case they remembered that the British authorities in Canada did not wait till diplomacy could send home to England for her slow official tinder-box to fire the "Caroline." Add to this, what every sensible American knew, that the moral support of England was equal to an army of two hundred thousand men to the Revels, while it insured us another year or two of exhausting war. It was not so much the spite of her words (though the time might have been more tastefully chosen) as the actual power for evil in them that we felt as a deadly wrong. Perhaps the most immediate and efficient cause of mere irritation was the sudden and unaccountable change of manner on the other side of the water. Only six months before, the Prince of Wales had come over to call us cousins; and everywhere it was nothing but "our American brethren," that great offshoot of British institutions in the New World, so almost identical with them in laws, language, and literature, — this last of the alliterative compliments being so bitterly true, that perhaps it will not be retracted even now. To this outburst of long-repressed affection we responded with genuine warmth, if with something of the awkwardness of a poor relation bewildered with the sudden tightening of the ties of consanguinity when it is rumored that he has come into a large estate. Then came the Rebellion, and, *presto!* a flaw in our titles was discovered, the plate we were promised at the family table is flung at our head, and we were again the scum of creation, intolerably vulgar, at once cowardly and overbearing, — no relations of theirs, after all, but a dreggy hybrid of the basest bloods of Europe. Panurge was not quicker to call Friar John his *former* friend. I cannot help thinking of Walter Mapes's jingling paraphase of Petronius, —

"Dummodo sim splendidis vestibus ornatus,
Et multa familia sim circumvallatus,
Prudens sum et sapiens et morigeratus,
Et tuus nepos sum et tu meus cognatus," —

which I may freely render thus : —

So long as I was prosperous, I'd dinners by
    the dozen,
Was well-bred, witty, virtuous, and every-
    body's cousin;
If luck should turn, as well she may, her
    fancy is so flexile,
Will virtue, cousinship, and all return with
    her from exile?

There was nothing in all this to exasperate a philosopher, much to make

him smile rather; but the earth's surface is not chiefly inhabited by philosophers, and I revive the recollection of it now in perfect good-humour, merely by way of suggesting to our *ci-devant* British cousins, that it would have been easier for them to hold their tongues than for us to keep our tempers under the circumstances.

The English Cabinet made a blunder, unquestionably, in taking it so hastily for granted that the United States had fallen forever from their position as a first-rate power, and it was natural that they should vent a little of their vexation on the people whose inexplicable obstinacy in maintaining freedom and order, and in resisting degradation, was likely to convict them of their mistake. But if bearing a grudge be the sure mark of a small mind in the individual, can it be a proof of high spirit in a nation? If the result of the present estrangement between the two countries shall be to make us more independent of British twaddle (*Indomito nec dira ferens stipendia Tauro*), so much the better; but if it is to make us insensible to the value of British opinion, it matters where it gives us the judgment of an impartial and cultivated outsider, if we are to shut ourselves out from the advantages of English culture, the loss will be ours, and not theirs. Because the door of the old homestead has been once slammed in our faces, shall we in a huff reject all future advances of conciliation, and cut ourselves foolishly off from any share in the humanizing influences of the place, with its ineffable riches of association, its heirlooms of immemorial culture, its historic monuments, ours no less than theirs, its noble gallery of ancestral portraits? We have only to succeed, and England will not only respect, but, for the first time, begin to understand us. And let us not, in our justifiable indignation at wanton insult, forget that England is not the England only of snobs who dread the democracy they do not comprehend, but the England of history, of heroes, statesmen, and poets, whose names are dear, and their influence as salutary to us as to her.

Let us strengthen the hands of those in authority over us, and curb our own tongues, remembering that General Wait commonly proves in the end more than a match for General Headlong, and that the Good Book ascribes safety to a multitude, indeed, but not to a mob, of counsellours. Let us remember and perpend the words of Paulus Emilius to the people of Rome ; that, "if they judged they could manage the war to more advantage by any other, he would willingly yield up his charge; but if they confided in him, *they were not to make themselves his colleagues in his office, or raise reports, or criticise his actions, but, without talking, supply him with means and assistance necessary to the carrying on of the war ; for, if they proposed to command their own commander, they would render this expedition more ridiculous than the former.*" (*Vide Plutarchum in Vitâ P. E.*) Let us also not forget what the same excellent authour says concerning Perseus's fear of spending money, and not permit the covetousness of Brother Jonathan to be the good fortune of Jefferson Davis. For my own part, till I am ready to admit the Commander-in-Chief to my pulpit, I shall abstain from planning his battles. If courage be the sword, yet is patience the armour of a nation ; and in our desire for peace, let us never be willing to surrender the Constitution bequeathed us by fathers at least as wise as ourselves (even with Jefferson Davis to help us), and, with those degenerate Romans, *tuta et presentia quam vetera et periculosa malle.*

And not only should we bridle our own tongues, but the pens of others, which are swift to convey useful intelligence to the enemy. This is no new inconvenience ; for, under date, 3d June, 1745, General Pepperell wrote thus to Governor Shirley from Louisbourg : — "What your Excellency observes of the *army's being made acquainted with any plans proposed, until ready to be put in execution,* has

always been disagreeable to me, and I have given many cautions relating to it. But when your Excellency considers that *our Council of War consists of more than twenty members,* I am persuaded you will think it *impossible for me to hinder it,* if any of them will persist in communicating to inferior officers and soldiers what ought to be kept secret. I am informed that the Boston newspapers are filled with paragraphs from private letters relating to the expedition. Will your Excellency permit me to say I think it may be of ill consequence? Would it not be convenient, if your Excellency should forbid the Printers' inserting such news?" Verily, if *tempora mutantur,* we may question the *et nos mutamur in illis ;* and if tongues be leaky, it will need all hands at the pumps to save the Ship of State. Our history dotes and repeats itself. If Sassycus (rather than Alcibiades) find a parallel in Beauregard, so Weakwash, as he is called by the brave Lieutenant Lion Gardiner, need not seek far among our own Sachems for his antitype.

With respect,
Your ob't humble servt,
HOMER WILBUR, A. M.

I LOVE to start out arter night 's begun,
An' all the chores about the farm are done,
The critters milked an' foddered, gates shet fast,
Tools cleaned aginst to-morrer, supper past,
An' Nancy darnin' by her ker'sene lamp, —
I love, I say, to start upon a tramp,
To shake the kinkles out o' back an' legs,
An' kind o' rack my life off from the dregs
Thet 's apt to settle in the buttery-hutch
Of folks thet foller in one rut too much :
Hard work is good an' wholesome, past all doubt ;

But 't ain't so, ef the mind gits tuck-
　　ered out.
Now, bein' born in Middlesex, you
　　know,
There 's certin spots where I like best
　　to go :
The Concord road, for instance, (I, for
　　one,
Most gin'lly ollers call it *John Bull's
　　Run*,)
The field o' Lexin'ton where England
　　tried
The fastest colours thet she ever dyed,
An'Concord Bridge, thet Davis, when
　　he came,
Found was the bee-line track to heaven
　　an' fame,
Ez all roads be by natur', ef your soul
Don't sneak thru shun-pikes so 's to
　　save the toll.

They 're 'most too fur away, take too
　　much time
To visit of'en, ef it ain't in rhyme ;
But the 's a walk thet 's hendier, a
　　sight,
An' suits me fust-rate of a winter's
　　night, —
I mean the round whale's-back o' Pros-
　　pect Hill.
I love to p'iter there while night grows
　　still,
An' in the twinklin' villages about,
Fust here, then there, the well-saved
　　lights goes out,
An' nary sound but watch-dogs' false
　　alarms,
Or muffled cock-crows from the drowsy
　　farms,
Where some wise rooster (men act jest
　　thet way)
Stands to 't thet moon-rise is the break
　　o' day ;
(So Mister Seward sticks a three-
　　months' pin
Where the war 'd oughto eend, then
　　tries agin ;
My gran'ther's rule was safer 'n 't is
　　to crow :
*Don't never prophesy, — onless ye
　　know.*)
I love to muse there till it kind o' seems
Ez ef the world went eddyin' off in
　　dreams ;

The northwest wind thet twitches at
　　my baird
Blows out o' sturdier days not easy
　　scared,
An' the same moon thet this Decem-
　　ber shines
Starts out the tents an' booths o' Put-
　　nam's lines ;
The rail-fence posts, acrost the hill thet
　　runs,
Turn ghosts o' sogers should'rin' ghosts
　　o' guns ;
Ez wheels the sentry, glints a flash o'
　　light,
Along the firelock won at Concord
　　Fight,
An', 'twixt the silences, now fur, now
　　nigh,
Rings the sharp chellenge, hums the
　　low reply.

Ez I was settin' so, it warn't long
　　sence,
Mixin' the puffict with the present
　　tense,
I heerd two voices som'ers in the air,
Though, ef I was to die, I can't tell
　　where :
Voices I call 'em : 't was a kind o'
　　sough
Like pine-trees thet the wind 's
　　ageth'rin' through ;
An', fact, I thought it *was* the wind a
　　spell,
Then some misdoubted, could n't fairly
　　tell,
Fust sure, then not, jest as you hold
　　an eel,
I knowed, an' did n't, — fin'lly seemed
　　to feel
'T was Concord Bridge a talkin' off to
　　kill
With the Stone Spike thet 's druv thru
　　Bunker's Hill ;
Whether 't was so, or ef I on'y dreamed,
I could n't say ; I tell it ez it seemed.

THE BRIDGE.

Wal, neighbor, tell us wut 's turned up
　　thet 's new ?
You 're younger 'n I be, — nigher Bos-
　　ton, tu :
An' down to Boston, ef you take their
　　showin,

Wut they don't know ain't hardly
    wuth the knowin'.
There's *sunthin'* goin' on, I know:
    las' night
The British sogers killed in our gret
    fight
(Nigh fifty year they hed n't stirred
    nor spoke)
Made sech a coil you'd thought a dam
    hed broke:
Why, one he up an' beat a revellee
With his own crossbones on a holler
    tree,
Till all the graveyards swarmed out
    like a hive
With faces I hain't seen sence Seventy-
    five.
Wut *is* the news? 'T ain't good, or
    they'd be cheerin'.
Speak slow an' clear, for I'm some
    hard o' hearin'.

THE MONIMENT.

I don't know hardly ef it's good or
    bad, ——

THE BRIDGE.

At wust, it can't be wus than wut we've
    had.

THE MONIMENT.

You know them envys thet the Rebbles
    sent,
An' Cap'n Wilkes he borried o' the
    Trent?

THE BRIDGE.

Wut! they ha'n't hanged 'em? Then
    their wits is gone!
Thet's the sure way to make a goose a
    swan!

THE MONIMENT.

No: England she *would* hev 'em, *Fee,
Faw, Fum!*
(Ez though she hed n't fools enough to
    home,)
So they've returned 'em ——

THE BRIDGE.

    Hev they? Wal, by heaven,
Thet's the wust news I've heerd sence
    Seventy-seven!

By George, I meant to say, though I
    declare
It's 'most enough to make a deacon
    swear.

THE MONIMENT.

Now don't go off half-cock: folks never
    gains
By usin' pepper-sarse instid o' brains.
Come, neighbor, you don't under-
    stan' ——

THE BRIDGE.

            How? Hey?
Not understan'? Why, wut's to hen-
    der, pray?
Must I go huntin' round to find a chap
To tell me when my face hez hed a
    slap?

THE MONIMENT.

See here: the British they found out a
    flaw
In Cap'n Wilkes's readin' o' the law:
(They *make* all laws, you know, an' so,
    o' course,
It's nateral they should understan'
    their force:)
He'd oughto took the vessel into port;
An' hed her sot on by a reg'lar court;
She was a mail-ship, an' a steamer, tu,
An' thet, they say, hez changed the
    pint o' view,
Coz the old practice, bein' meant for
    sails,
Ef tried upon a steamer, kind o' fails;
You *may* take out despatches, but you
    mus' n't
Take nary man ——

THE BRIDGE.

    You mean to say, you dus' n't!
Changed pint o' view! No, no, — it's
    overboard
With law an' gospel, when their ox is
    gored!
I tell ye, England's law, on sea an'
    land,
Hez ollers ben, "*I've gut the heaviest
    hand.*"
Take nary man? Fine preachin' from
    her lips!
Why, she hez taken hunderds from our
    ships,

An' would agin, an' swear she had a
right to,
Ef we warn't strong enough to be per-
lite to.
Of all the sarse thet I can call to mind,
England *does* make the most on-
pleasant kind :
It 's you 're the sinner ollers, she 's the
saint ;
Wut 's good 's all English, all thet
is n't ain't ;
Wut profits her is ollers right an' just,
An' ef you don't read Scriptur so, you
must :
She 's praised herself ontil she fairly
thinks
There ain't no light in Natur when she
winks ;
Hain't she the Ten Comman'ments in
her pus ?
Could the world stir 'thout she went,
tu, ez nus ?
She ain't like other mortals, thet 's a
fact :
She never stopped the habus-corpus
act,
Nor specie payments, nor she never yet
Cut down the int'rest on her public
debt ;
She don't put down rebellions, lets 'em
breed,
An' 's ollers willin' Ireland should
secede ;
She 's all thet 's honest, honnable, an'
fair,
An' when the vartoos died they made
her heir.

THE MONIMENT.

Wal, wal, two wrongs don't never make
a right ;
Ef we 're mistaken, own up, an' don't
fight :
For gracious' sake, ha'n't we enough
to du
'Thout gettin' up a fight with England,
tu ?
She thinks we 're rabble-rid——

THE BRIDGE.
        An' so we can't
Distinguish 'twixt *You ought n't* an'
You sha'n't !
She jedges by herself ; she 's no idear

How 't stiddies folks to give 'em their
fair sheer :
The odds 'twixt her an' us is plain 's a
steeple,—
Her People 's turned to Mob, our Mob
's turned People.

THE MONIMENT.

She 's riled jes' now——

THE BRIDGE.

Plain proof her cause ain't strong,—
The one thet fust gits mad 's 'most ollers
wrong.
Why, sence she helped in lickin' Nap
the Fust,
An' pricked a bubble jest agoin' to
bust,
With Rooshy, Prooshy, Austry, all
asistin',
Th' aint nut a face but wut she 's shook
her fist in,
Ez though she done it all, an' ten times
more,
An' nothin' never hed gut done afore,
Nor never could agin', 'thout she wuz
spliced
On to one eend an' gin th' old airth a
hoist.
She *is* some punkins, thet I wun't deny,
(For ain't she some related to you 'n'
I ?)
But there 's a few small intrists here
below
Outside the counter o' John Bull an'
Co,
An', though they can't conceit how 't
should be so,
I guess the Lord druv down Creation's
spiles
'Thout no *gret* helpin' from the British
Isles,
An' could contrive to keep things pooty
stiff
Ef they withdrawed from business in-a
miff ;
I ha'n't no patience with sech swellin'
fellers ez
Think God can't forge 'thout them to
blow the bellerses.

THE MONIMENT.

You 're ollers quick to set your back
aridge,—

Though 't suits a tom-cat more 'n a
    sober bridge :
Don't you git het : they thought the
    thing was planned ;
They 'll cool off when they come to un-
    derstand.

THE BRIDGE.

Ef *thet* 's wut you expect, you 'll *hev*
    to wait :
·Folks never understand the folks they
    hate :
She 'll fin' some other grievance jest ez
    good,
'Fore the month 's out, to git misun-
    derstood.
England cool off!   She 'll do it, ef she
    sees
She 's run her head into a swarm o'
    bees.
I ain't so prejudiced ez wut you spose :
I hev thought England was the best
    thet goes ;
Remember (no, you can't), when *I* was
    reared,
G·od save the King was all the tune you
    heerd ;
But it 's enough to turn Wachuset roun',
This stumpin' fellers when you think
    they 're down.

THE MONIMENT.

But, neighbor, ef they prove their claim
    at law,
The best way is to settle, an' not jaw.
An' don't le' 's mutter 'bout the awfle
    bricks
We 'll give 'em, ef we ketch 'em in a fix :
That 'ere 's most frequently the kin' o'
    talk
Of critters can't be kicked to toe the
    chalk ;
Your "You 'll see *nex'* time !" an'
    "Look out bumby !"
Most ollers ends in eatin' umble-pie.
'T wun't pay to scringe to England :
    will it pay
To fear that meaner bully, old " They 'll
    say " ?
Suppose they *du* say : words are dreffle
    bores,
But they ain't quite so bad ez seventy-
    fours.
Wut England wants is jest a wedge to fit

Where it 'll help to widen out our split :
She 's found her wedge, an' 't ain't for
    us to come
An' lend the beetle thet 's to drive it
    home.
For growed-up folks like us 't would be
    a scandle,
When we git sarsed, to fly right off the
    handle.
England ain't *all* bad, coz she thinks
    us blind :
Ef she can't change her skin, she can
    her mind ;
An' we shall see her change it double-
    quick,
Soon ez we 've proved thet we 're
    a-goin' to lick.
She an' Columby 's gut to be fas'
    friends ;
For the world prospers by their privit
    ends :
'T would put the clock back all o' fifty
    years,
Ef they should fall together by the ears.

THE BRIDGE.

I 'gree to thet ; she s nigh us to wut
    France is ;
But then she 'll hev to make the fust
    advances ;
We 've gut pride, tu, an' gut it by good
    rights,
An' ketch *me* stoopin' to pick up the
    mites
O' condescension she 'll be lettin' fall
When she finds out we ain't dead arter
    all !
I tell ye wut, it takes more 'n one good
    week
Afore *my* nose forgits it 's hed a tweak.

THE MONIMENT.

She 'll come out right bumby, thet I 'll
    engage,
Soon ez she gits to seein' we 're of age ;
This talkin' down o' hers ain't wuth a
    fuss ;
It 's nat'ral ez nut likin' 't is to us ;
Ef we 're agoin' to prove we *be* growed-
    up,
'T wun't be by barkin' like a tarrier
    pup,
But turnin' to an' makin' things ez
    good

Ez wut we 're ollers braggin' that we
    could ;
We 're boun' to be good friends, an' so
    we 'd oughto,
In spite of all the fools both sides the
    water.

THE BRIDGE.

I b'lieve thet 's so ; but hearken in
    your ear, —
I 'm older 'n you, — Peace wun't keep
    house with Fear :
Ef you want peace, the thing you 've
    gut to du
Is jes' to show you 're up to fightin', tu.
I recollect how sailors' rights was won
Yard locked in yard, hot gun-lip kissin'
    gun :
Why, afore thet, John Bull sot up thet
    he
Hed gut a kind o' mortgage on the sea ;
You 'd thought he held by Gran'ther
    Adam's will,
An' ef you knuckle down, *he* 'll think
    so still.
Better thet all our ships an' all their
    crews
Should sink to rot in ocean's dreamless
    ooze,
Each torn flag wavin' challenge ez it
    went,
An' each dumb gun a brave man's
    moniment,
Than seek sech peace ez only cowards
    crave :
Give *me* the peace of dead men or of
    brave !

THE MONIMENT.

I say, ole boy, it ain't the Glorious
    Fourth :
You 'd oughto larned 'fore this wut talk
    wuz worth.
It ain't *our* nose thet gits put out o' jint :
It 's England thet gives up her dearest
    pint.
We 've gut, I tell ye now, enough to du
In our own fem'ly fight, afore we 're
    thru.
I hoped, las' spring, jest arter Sumter's
    shame,
When every flag-staff flapped its teth-
    ered flame,

An' all the people, startled from their
    doubt,
Come must'rin' to the flag with sech a
    shout, —
I hoped to see things settled 'fore this
    fall,
The Rebbles licked, Jeff Davis hanged,
    an' all ;
Then come Bull Run, an' *sence* then
    I 've ben waitin'
Like boys in Jennooary thaw for skatin',
Nothin' to du but watch my shadder's
    trace
Swing, like a ship at anchor, roun' my
    base,
With daylight's flood an' ebb : it 's
    gittin' slow,
An' I 'most think we 'd better let 'em
    go.
I tell ye wut, this war 's a-goin to
    cost ——

THE BRIDGE.

An' I tell *you* it wun't be money lost ;
Taxes milks dry, but, neighbor, you 'll
    allow
Thet havin' things onsettled kills the
    cow :
We 've gut to fix this thing for good
    an' all ;
It 's no use buildin' wut 's a-goin' to
    fall.
I 'm older 'n you, an' I 've seen things
    an' men,
An' *my* experunce, — tell ye wut it 's
    ben :
Folks thet worked thorough was the
    ones thet thriv,
But bad work follers ye ez long 's ye
    live ;
You can't git red on 't ; jest ez sure ez
    sin,
It 's ollers askin' to be done agin :
Ef we should part, it would n't be a
    week
'Fore your soft-soddered peace would
    spring aleak.
We 've turned our cuffs up, but, to put
    her thru,
We must git mad an' off with jackets,
    tu ;
'T wun't du to think thet killin' ain't
    perlite, ——

You 've gut to be in airnest, ef you
   fight ;
Why, two-thirds o' the Rebbles 'ould
   cut dirt,
Ef they once thought thet Guv'ment
   meant to hurt ;
An' I *du* wish our Gin'rals hed in mind
The folks in front more than the folks
   behind ;
You wun't do much ontil you think it 's
   God,
An' not constitoounts, thet holds the
   rod ;
We want some more o' Gideon's sword,
   I jedge,
For proclamations ha'n't no gret of
   edge ;
There 's nothin' for a cancer but the
   knife,
Onless you set by 't more than by your
   life.
I 've seen hard times ; I see a war be-
   gun
Thet folks thet love their bellies never 'd
   won ;
Pharo's lean kine hung on for seven
   long year ;
But when 't was done, we did n't count
   it dear.
Why, law an' order, honor, civil right,
Ef they *ain't* wuth it, wut *is* wuth a
   fight ?
I 'm older 'n you : the plough, the axe,
   the mill,
All kin's o' labor an' all kin's o' skill,
Would be a rabbit in a wile-cat's claw,
Ef 't warn't for thet slow critter, 'stab-
   lished law ;
Onsettle *thet*, an' all the world goes
   whiz,
A screw 's gut loose in everythin' there
   is :
Good buttresses once settled, don't you
   fret
An' stir 'em ; take a bridge's word for
   thet !
Young folks are smart, but all ain't
   good thet 's new ;
I guess the gran'thers they knowed
   sunthin', tu.

THE MONIMENT.

Amen to thet ! build sure in the beginnin',

An' then don't never tech the underpinnin' :
Th' older a guv'ment is, the better 't
   suits ;
New ones hunt folks's corns out like
   new boots :
Change jes' for change, is like them big
   hotels
Where they shift plates, an' let ye live
   on smells.

THE BRIDGE.

Wal, don't give up afore the ship goes
   down :
It 's a stiff gale, but Providence wun't
   drown ;
An' God wun't leave us yit to sink or
   swim,
Ef we don't fail to du wut 's right by
   Him.
This land o' ourn, I tell ye, 's gut to be
A better country than man ever see.
I feel my sperit swellin' with a cry
Thet seems to say, "Break forth an'
   prophesy ! "
O strange New World, thet yit wast
   never young,
Whose youth from thee by gripin' need
   was wrung,
Brown foundlin' o' the woods, whose
   baby-bed
Was prowled roun' by the Injun's crack-
   lin' tread,
An' who grew'st strong thru shifts an'
   wants an' pains,
Nussed by stern men with empires in
   their brains,
Who saw in vision their young Ishmel
   strain
With each hard hand a vassal ocean's
   mane,
Thou, skilled by Freedom an' by gret
   events
To pitch new States ez Old-World men
   pitch tents,
Thou, taught by Fate to know Jehovah's plan
Thet man's devices can't unmake a
   man,
An' whose free latch-string never was
   drawed in
Against the poorest child of Adam's
   kin, —

The grave 's not dug where traitor
    hands shall lay
In fearful haste thy murdered corse
    away !
I see ——

          Jest here some dogs be-
    gun to bark,
So thet I lost old Concord's last re-
    mark :
I listened long, but all I seemed to
    hear
Was dead leaves goss'pin' on some
    birch-trees near ;
But ez they hedn't no gret things to
    say,
An' sed 'em often, I come right away,
An', walkin' home'ards, jest to pass the
    time,
I put some thoughts thet bothered me
    in rhyme ;
I hain't hed time to fairly try 'em on,
But here they be — it 's

JONATHAN TO JOHN.

It don't seem hardly right, John,
    When both my hands was full,
To stump me to a fight, John, —
    Your cousin, tu, John Bull !
        Ole Uncle S. sez he, "I guess
            We know it now," sez he,
" The lion's paw is all the law,
            Accordin' to J. B.,
        Thet 's fit for you an' me ! "

You wonder why we 're hot, John ?
    Your mark wuz on the guns,
The neutral guns, thet shot, John,
    Our brothers an' our sons :
        Ole Uncle S. sez he, "I guess
            There 's human blood," sez he,
" By fits an' starts, in Yankee hearts,
            Though 't may surprise J. B.,
        More 'n it would you an' me."

Ef *I* turned mad dogs loose, John,
    On *your* front-parlor stairs,
Would it jest meet your views, John,
    To wait an' sue their heirs ?
        Ole Uncle S. sez he, " I guess,
            I on'y guess," sez he,
" Thet ef Vattel on *his* toes fell,

'T would kind o' rile J. B.,
        Ez wal ez you an' me ! "

Who made the law thet hurts, John,
    Heads I win, — ditto tails ?
" *J. B.*" was on his shirts, John,
    Onless my memory fails,
        Ole Uncle S. sez he, " I guess,
            (I 'm good at thet)," sez he,
" Thet sauce for goose ain't *jest* the
            juice
            For ganders with J. B.,
        No more than you or me ! "

When your rights was our wrongs,
        John,
    You did n't stop for fuss, —
Britanny's trident prongs, John,
    Was good 'nough law for us.
        Ole Uncle S. sez he, " I guess,
            Though physic 's good," sez he,
" It does n't foller thet he can swaller
            Prescriptions signed ' *J. B.*,'
        Put up by you an' me ! "

We own the ocean, tu, John :
    You mus' n' take it hard,
Ef we can't think with you, John,
    It 's jest your own back-yard.
        Ole Uncle S. sez he, " I guess,
            Ef *thet* 's his claim," sez he,
" The fencin'-stuff 'll cost enough
            To bust up friend J. B.,
        Ez wal ez you an' me ! "

Why talk so dreffle big, John,
    Of honor when it meant
You did n't care a fig, John,
    But jest for *ten per cent ?*
        Ole Uncle S. sez he, " I guess
            He 's like the rest," sez he :
" When all is done, it 's number one
            Thet 's nearest to J. B.,
        Ez wal ez you an' me ! "

We give the critters back, John,
    Cos Abram thought 't was right ;
It warn't your bullyin' clack, John,
    Provokin' us to fight.
        Ole Uncle S. sez he, " I guess
            We 've a hard row," sez he,
" To hoe jest now ; but thet somehow
            May happen to J. B.,
        Ez wal ez you an' me ! "

We ain't so weak an' poor, John,
  With twenty million people,
An' close to every door, John,
  A school-house an' a steeple.
    Ole Uncle S. sez he, "I guess
      It is a fact," sez he,
  "The surest plan to make a Man
      Is, think him so, J. B.,
    Ez much ez you or me !"

Our folks believe in Law, John ;
  An' it 's for her sake, now,
They 've left the axe an' saw, John,
  The anvil an' the plough.
    Ole Uncle S. sez he, "I guess,
      Ef 't warn't for law," sez he,
  "There 'd be one shindy from here to
        Indy ;
      An' thet don't suit J. B.
    (When 't ain't 'twixt you an' me !)"

We know we 've got a cause, John,
  Thet 's honest, just, an' true ;
We thought 't would win applause,
        John,
  Ef nowheres else, from you.
    Ole Uncle S. sez he, "I guess
      His love of right," sez he,
  "Hangs by a rotten fibre o' cotton :
      There 's natur' in J. B.,
    Ez wal 'z in you an' me !"

The South says, "*Poor folks down !*"
        John,
  An' "*All men up !*" say we, —
White, yaller, black, an' brown, John :
  Now which is your idee ?
    Ole Uncle S. sez he, "I guess,
      John preaches wal," sez he ;
  "But, sermon thru, an' come to *du,*
      Why, there 's the old J. B.
    A crowdin' you an' me !"

Shall it be love, or hate, John ?
  It 's you thet 's to decide ;
Ain't *your* bonds held by Fate, John,
  Like all the world's beside ?
    Ole Uncle S. sez he, "I guess
      Wise men forgive," sez he,
  "But not forgit ; an' some time yet
      Thet truth may strike J. B.,
    Ez wal ez you an' me !"

God means to make this land, John,
  Clear thru, from sea to sea,

Believe an' understand, John,
  The *wuth* o' bein' free.
    Ole Uncle S. sez he, "I guess,
      God's price is high," sez he ·
  "But nothin' else than wut He sells
      Wears long, an' thet J. B.
    May larn, like you an' me !"

No. III.

BIRDOFREDUM SAWIN, ESQ., TO MR. HOSEA BIGLOW.

With the following Letter from the REVEREND HOMER WILBUR, A. M.

TO THE EDITORS OF THE ATLANTIC
MONTHLY.

JAALAM, 7th Feb., 1862.

RESPECTED FRIENDS, — If I know
myself, — and surely a man can hardly
be supposed to have overpassed the
limit of fourscore years without attain-
ing to some proficiency in that most
useful branch of learning (*e cælo de-
scendit*, says the pagan poet), — I have
no great smack of that weakness which
would press upon the publick attention
any matter pertaining to my private
affairs.   But since the following letter
of Mr. Sawin contains not only a direct
allusion to myself, but that in connection
with a topick of interest to all those engaged in the publick ministrations of
the sanctuary, I may be pardoned for
touching briefly thereupon.   Mr. Sawin
was never a stated attendant upon my
preaching, — never, as I believe, even
an occasional one, since the erection of
the new house (where we now worship)
in 1845.   He did, indeed, for a time,
supply a not unacceptable bass in the
choir ; but, whether on some umbrage
(*omnibus hoc vitium est cantoribus*)
taken against the bass-viol, then, and
till his decease in 1850 (*æt.* 77,) under
the charge of Mr. Asaph Perley, or, as
was reported by others, on account of
an imminent subscription for a new
bell, he thenceforth absented himself

from all outward and visible communion. Yet he seems to have preserved (*altâ mente repostum*), as it were, in the pickle of a mind soured by prejudice, a lasting *scunner*, as he would call it, against our staid and decent form of worship ; for I would rather in that wise interpret his fling, than suppose that any chance tares sown by my pulpit discourses should survive so long, while good seed too often fails to root itself. I humbly trust that I have no personal feeling in the matter ; though I know that, if we sound any man deep enough, our lead shall bring up the mud of human nature at last. The Bretons believe in an evil spirit which they call *ar c'houskezik*, whose office it is to make the congregation drowsy ; and though I have never had reason to think that he was specially busy among my flock, yet have I seen enough to make me sometimes regret the hinged seats of the ancient meeting-house, whose lively clatter, not unwillingly intensified by boys beyond eyeshot of the tithing-man, served at intervals as a wholesome *réveil*. It is true, I have numbered among my parishioners some who are proof against the prophylactick fennel, nay, whose gift of somnolence rivalled that of the Cretan Rip Van Winkle, Epimenides, and who, nevertheless, complained not so much of the substance as of the length of my (by them unheard) discourses. Some ingenious persons of a philosophick turn have assured us that our pulpits were set too high, and that the soporifick tendency increased with the ratio of the angle in which the hearer's eye was constrained to seek the preacher. This were a curious topick for investigation. There can be no doubt that some sermons are pitched too high, and I remember many struggles with the drowsy fiend in my youth. Happy Saint Anthony of Padua, whose finny acolytes, however they might profit, could never murmur ! *Quare fremuerunt gentes?* Who is he that can twice a week be inspired, or has eloquence (*ut ita dicum*) always on tap? A good man, and, next to David, a sacred poet (himself, haply,

not inexpert of evil in this particular), has said, —

"The worst speak something good: if all
    want sense,
God takes a text and preacheth patience."

There are one or two other points in Mr. Sawin's letter which I would also briefly animadvert upon. And first, concerning the claim he sets up to a certain superiority of blood and lineage in the people of our Southern States, now unhappily in rebellion against lawful authority and their own better interests. There is a sort of opinions, anachronisms at once and anachorisms, foreign both to the age and the country, that maintain a feeble and buzzing existence, scarce to be called life, like winter flies, which in mild weather crawl out from obscure nooks and crannies to expatiate in the sun, and sometimes acquire vigor enough to disturb with their enforced familiarity the studious hours of the scholar. One of the most stupid and pertinacious of these is the theory that the Southern States were settled by a class of emigrants from the Old World socially superior to those who founded the institutions of New England. The Virginians especially lay claim to this generosity of lineage, which were of no possible account, were it not for the fact that such superstitions are sometimes not without their effect on the course of human affairs. The early adventurers to Massachusetts at least paid their passages ; no felons were ever shipped thither ; and though it be true that many deboshed younger brothers of what are called good families may have sought refuge in Virginia, it is equally certain that a great part of the early deportations thither were the sweepings of the London streets and the leavings of the London stews. It was this my Lord Bacon had in mind when he wrote "It is a shameful and unblessed thing to take the scum of people and wicked condemned men to be the people with whom you plant." That certain names are found there is nothing to the purpose, for, even had an *alias* been beyond the invention of the knaves of that generation, it is known that servants were often called by their masters' names, as slaves are now. On what the heralds call the spindle side, some, at least, of the oldest Virginian families are descended from matrons who were exported and sold for so many hogsheads of tobacco the head. So notorious was this, that it became one of the jokes of contemporary playwrights, not only that men bankrupt in purse and character were "food for the Plantations" (and this before the settlement of New England), but also that any drab would suffice to wive such pitiful adventurers. "Never choose a wife as if you were going to Virginia," says Middleton in one of his comedies. The mule is apt to forget all but the equine side of his pedigree. How early the counterfeit nobility of the Old Dominion became a topick of ridicule in the Mother Country may be learned from a play of Mrs. Behn's, founded on the Rebellion of Bacon: for even these kennels of literature may yield a fact or two to pay the raking. Mrs. Flirt, the keeper of a Virginia ordinary, calls herself the daughter of a baronet "undone in the late rebellion," — her father having in truth been a tailor, — and three of the Council, assuming to themselves an equal splendour of origin, are shown to have been, one "a broken exciseman who came over a poor servant," another a tinker transported for theft, and the third "a common pickpocket often flogged at the cart's tail." The ancestry of South Carolina will as little pass muster at the Herald's Visitation, though I hold them to have been more reputable, inasmuch as many of them were honest tradesmen and artisans, in some measure exiles for conscience' sake, who would have smiled at the high-flying nonsense of their descendants. Some of the more respectable were Jews. The absurdity of supposing a population of eight millions all sprung from gentle loins in the course of a century and a half is too manifest for confutation. But of what use to discuss the matter? An expert genealogist will provide any solvent man with a *genus et proavos* to order. My

Lord Burleigh used to say, with Aristotle and the Emperor Frederick II. to back him, that "nobility was ancient riches," whence also the Spanish were wont to call their nobles *ricos hombres*, and the aristocracy of America are the descendants of those who first became wealthy, by whatever means. Petroleum will in this wise be the source of much good blood among our posterity. The aristocracy of the South, such as it is, has the shallowest of all foundations, for it is only skindeep, — the most odious of all, for, while affecting to despise trade, it traces its origin to a successful traffick in men, women, and children, and still draws its chief revenues thence. And though, as Doctor Chamberlayne consolingly says in his *Present State of England,* "to become a Merchant of Foreign Commerce, without serving any Apprentisage, hath been allowed no disparagement to a Gentleman born, especially to a younger Brother," yet I conceive that he would hardly have made a like exception in favour of the particular trade in question. Oddly enough this trade reverses the ordinary standards of social respectability no less than of morals, for the retail and domestick is as creditable as the wholesale and foreign is degrading to him who follows it. Are our morals, then, no better than *mores* after all? I do not believe that such aristocracy as exists at the South (for I hold with Marius, *fortissimum quemque generosissimum*) will be found an element of anything like persistent strength in war, — thinking the saying of Lord Bacon (whom one quaintly called *inductionis dominus et Verulamii*) as true as it is pithy, that "the more gentlemen, ever the lower books of subsidies." It is odd enough as an historical precedent, that, while the fathers of New England were laying deep in religion, education, and freedom the basis of a polity which has substantially outlasted any then existing, the first work of the founders of Virginia, as may be seen in Wingfield's *Memorial,* was conspiracy and rebellion, — odder yet, as showing the changes which are wrought by circum stance, that the first insurrection in South Carolina was against the aristocratical scheme of the Proprietary Government. I do not find that the cuticular aristocracy of the South has added anything to the refinements of civilization except the carrying of bowie-knives and the chewing of tobacco, — a high-toned Southern gentleman being commonly not only *quadrumanous*, but *quidruminant*.

I confess that the present letter of Mr. Sawin increases my doubts as to the sincerity of the convictions which he professes, and I am inclined to think that the triumph of the legitimate Government, sure sooner or later to take place, will find him and a large majority of his newly adopted fellow-citizens (who hold with Dædalus, the primal sitter-on-the-fence, that *medium tenere tutissimum*) original Union men. The criticisms towards the close of his letter on certain of our failings are worthy to be seriously perpended; for he is not, as I think, without a spice of vulgar shrewdness. *Fas est et ab hoste doceri*: there is no reckoning without your host. As to the good-nature in us which he seems to gird at, while I would not consecrate a chapel, as they have not scrupled to do in France, to *Nôtre Dame de la Haine* (Our Lady of Hate), yet I cannot forget that the corruption of good-nature is the generation of laxity of principle. Good-nature is our national characteristick; and though it be, perhaps, nothing more than a culpable weakness or cowardice, when it leads us to put up tamely with manifold impositions and breaches of implied contracts, (as too frequently in our publick conveyances,) it becomes a positive crime, when it leads us to look unresentfully on peculation, and to regard treason to the best Government that ever existed as something with which a gentleman may shake hands without soiling his fingers. I do not think the gallows-tree the most profitable member of our *Sylva*; but, since it continues to be planted, I would fain see a Northern limb ingrafted on it, that it may bear some other fruit than loyal Tennesseeans.

A relick has recently been discovered on the east bank of Bushy Brook in North Jaalam, which I conceive to be an inscription in Runick characters relating to the early expedition of the Northmen to this continent. I shall make fuller investigations, and communicate the result in due season.

Respectfully,

Your obedient servant,

HOMER WILBUR, A. M.

P. S. — I inclose a year's subscription from Deacon Tinkham.

I HED it on my min' las' time, when I
   to write ye started,
To tech the leadin' featurs o' my gittin'
   me converted;
But, ez my letters hez to go clearn roun'
   by way o' Cuby,
'T wun't seem no staler now than then,
   by th' time it gits where you be.
You know up North, though secs an'
   things air plenty ez you please,
Ther' warn't nut one on 'em thet come
   jes' square with my idees:
They all on 'em wuz too much mixed
   with Covenants o' Works,
An' would hev answered jest ez wal for
   Afrikins an' Turks,
Fer where 's a Christian's privilige an'
   his rewards ensuin',
Ef 't ain't perfessin' right an eend 'thout
   nary need o' doin'?
I dessay they suit workin'-folks thet
   ain't noways pertic'lar,
But nut your Southun gen'leman thet
   keeps his parpendic'lar;
I don't blame nary man thet casts his
   lot along o' *his* folks,
But ef you cal'late to save *me*, 't must
   be with folks thet *is* folks;
Cov'nants o' works go 'ginst my grain,
   but down here I 've found ou'.
The true fus'-fem'ly A 1 plan, — here 's
   how it come about.
When I fus' sot up with Miss S., sez she
   to me, sez she,
"Without you git religion, Sir, the
   thing can't never be;
Nut but wut I respeck," sez she, "your
   intellectle part,
But you wun't noways du for me athout
   a change o' heart:

Nothun religion works wal North, but
   it 's ez soft ez spruce,
Compared to ourn, for keepin' sound,"
   sez she, " upon the goose ;
A day's experunce 'd prove to ye, ez
   easy 'z pull a trigger,
It takes the Southun pint o' view to
   raise ten bales a nigger ;
You 'll fin' thet human natur, South,
   ain't wholesome more 'n skin-deep,
An' once 't a darkie 's took with it, he
   wun't be wuth his keep."
" How *shell* I git it, Ma'am ? " sez I.
   "Attend the nex' camp-meetin',"
Sez she, " an' it 'll come to ye ez cheap
   ez onbleached sheetin',"

Wal, so I went along an' hearn most
   an impressive sarmon
About besprinklin' Afriky with fourth-
   proof dew o' Harmon :
He did n' put no weaknin' in, but gin it
   tu us hot,
'Z ef he an' Satan 'd ben two bulls in
   one five-acre lot :
I don't purtend to foller him, but give
   ye jes' the heads ;
For pulpit ellerkence, you know, 'most
   ollers kin' o' spreads.
Ham's seed wuz gin to us in chairge,
   an' should n't we be li'ble
In Kingdom Come, ef we kep' back
   their priv'lege in the Bible ?
The cusses an' the promerses make one
   gret chain, an' ef
You snake one link out here, one there,
   how much on 't ud be lef' ?
All things wuz gin to man for 's use,
   his sarvice, an' delight ;
An' don't the Greek an' Hebrew words
   thet mean a Man mean White ?
Ain't it belittlin' the Good Book in all
   its proudes' featurs
To think 't wuz wrote for black an'
   brown an' 'lasses-colored creaturs,
Thet could n' read it, ef they would, nor
   ain't by lor allowed to,
But ough' to take wut we think suits
   their naturs, an' be proud to?
Warn't it more prof'table to bring your
   raw materil thru
Where you can work it inta grace an'
   inta cotton tu,

Than sendin' missionaries out where
   fevers might defeat 'em,
An' ef the butcher did n' call, their
   p'rishioners might eat 'em ?
An' then, agin, wut airthly use? Nor
   't warn't our fault, in so fur
Ez Yankee skippers would keep on
   a-totin' on 'em over.
'T improved the whites by savin' 'em
   from ary need o' wurkin',
An' kep' the blacks from bein' lost thru
   idleness an' shirkin' ;
We took to 'em ez nat'ral ez a barn-owl
   doos to mice,
An' hed our hull time on our hands to
   keep us out o' vice ;
It made us feel ez pop'lar ez a hen doos
   with one chicken,
An' fill our place in Natur's scale by
   givin' 'em a lickin' :
For why should Cæsar git his dues
   more 'n Juno, Pomp, an' Cuffy ?
It's justifyin' Ham to spare a nigger
   when he 's stuffy.
Where 'd their soles go tu, like to
   know, ef we should let 'em ketch
Freeknowledgism an' Fourierism an'
   Speritoolism an' sech ?
When Satan sets himself to work to
   raise his very bes' muss,
He scatters roun' onscriptur'l views
   relatin' to Ones'mus.
You 'd ough' to seen, though, how his
   facs an' argymunce an' figgers
Drawed tears o' real conviction from a
   lot o' pen'tent niggers !
It warn't like Wilbur's meetin', where
   you 're shet up in a pew,
Your dickeys sorrin' off your ears, an'
   bilin' to be thru ;
Ther' wuz a tent clost by thet hed a
   kag o' sunthin' in it,
Where you could go, ef you wuz dry,
   an' damp ye in a minute ;
An' ef you did dror off a spell, ther'
   wuz n't no occasion
To lose the thread, because, ye see, he
   bellered like all Bashan.
It's dry work follerin' argymunce an'
   so, 'twix' this an' thet,
I felt conviction weighin' down somehow inside my hat ;
It growed an' growed like Jonah's
   gourd, a kin' o' whirlin' ketched me,

Ontil I fin'lly clean giv out an' owned
    up thet he 'd fetched me ;
An' when nine tenths o' th' perrish took
    to tumblin' roun' an' hollerin',
I did n' fin' no gret in th' way o' turn-
    in' tu an' follerin'.
Soon ez Miss S. see thet, sez she,
    " Thet 's wut I call wuth seein' !
Thet 's actin' like a reas'nable an' in-
    tellectle bein' ! "
An' so we fin'lly made it up, concluded
    to hitch hosses,
An' here I be 'n my ellermunt among
    creation's bosses ;
Arter I 'd drawed sech heaps o' blanks,
    Fortin at last hez sent a prize,
An' chose me for a shinin' light o' mis-
    sionary entaprise.

This leads me to another pint on
    which I 've changed my plan
O' thinkin' so 's 't I might become a
    straight-out Southun man.
Miss S. (her maiden name wuz Higgs,
    o' the fus' fem'ly here)
On her Ma's side 's all Juggernot, on
    Pa's all Cavileer,
An' sence I 've married into her an'
    stept into her shoes,
It ain't more 'n naternal thet I should
    modderfy my views :
I 've ben a-readin' in Debow ontil I 've
    fairly gut
So 'nlightened thet I 'd full ez lives
    ha' ben a Dook ez nut ;
An' when we 've laid ye all out stiff,
    an' Jeff hez gut his crown,
An' comes to pick his nobles out,
    wun't this child be in town !
We 'll hev an Age o' Chivverlry sur-
    passin' Mister Burke's,
Where every fem'ly is fus'-best an'
    nary white man works :
Our system 's sech, the thing 'll root ez
    easy ez a tater ;
For while your lords in furrin parts
    ain't noways marked by natur',
Nor sot apart from ornery folks in
    features nor in figgers,
Ef ourn 'll keep their faces washed,
    you 'll know 'em from their niggers.
Ain't *sech* things wuth secedin' for, an'
    gittin'

Thet waller in your low idees, an' will
    tell all is blue ?
Fact is, we *air* a diff'rent race, an' I,
    for one, don't see,
Sech havin' ollers ben the case, how
    w' ever *did* agree.
It 's sunthin' thet you lab'rin'-folks up
    North hed ough' to think on,
Thet Higgses can't bemean themselves
    to rulin' by a Lincoln, —
Thet men, (an' guv'nors, tu,) thet hez
    sech Normal names ez Pickens,
Accustomed to no kin' o' work, 'thout
    't is to givin' lickins,
Can't masure votes with folks thet get
    their livins from their farms,
An' prob'ly think thet Law 's ez good
    ez hevin' coats o' arms.
Sence I 've ben here, I 've hired a chap
    to look about for me
To git me a transplantable an' thrifty
    fem'ly-tree,
An' he tells *me* the Sawins is ez much
    o' Normal blood
Ez Pickens an' the rest on 'em, an'
    older 'n Noah's flood.
Your Normal schools wun't turn ye
    into Normals, for it 's clear,
Ef eddykatin' done the thing, they 'd
    be some skurcer here.
Pickenses, Boggses, Pettuses, Magof-
    fins, Letchers, Polks, —
Where can you scare up names like
    them among your mudsill folks ?
Ther' 's nothin' to compare with 'em,
    you 'd fin', ef you should glance,
Among the tip-top femerlies in Englan',
    nor in France !
I 've hearn from 'sponsible men whose
    word wuz full ez good 's their note,
Men thet can run their face for drinks,
    an' keep a Sunday coat,
Thet they wuz all on 'em come down,
    and come down pooty fur,
From folks thet, 'thout their crowns wuz
    on, ou' doors would n' never stir,
Nor thet ther' warn't a Southun man
    but wut wuz *primy fashy*
O the bes' blood in Europe, yis, an'
    Afriky an' Ashy :
Sech bein' the case, is 't likely we should
    bend like cotton-wickin',
Or set down under anythin' so low-lived
    ez a lickin' ?

More 'n this, —hain't we the literatoor
   an' science, tu, by gorry?
Hain't we them intellectle twins, them
   giants, Simms an' Maury,
Each with full twice the ushle brains,
   like nothin' thet I know,
'Thout 't wuz a double-headed calf I see
   once to a show?

For all thet, I warn't jest at fust in
   favor o' secedin';
I wuz for layin' low a spell to find out
   where 't wuz leadin',
For hevin' South-Carliny try her hand
   at sepritnationin',
She takin' resks an' findin' funds, an'
   we co-operationin', —
I mean a kin' o' hangin' roun' an' set-
   tin' on the fence,
Till Prov'dunce pinted how to jump
   an' save the most expense;
I recollected thet 'ere mine o' lead to
   Shiraz Centre
Thet bust up Jabez Pettibone, an' did
   n't want to ventur'
'Fore I wuz sartin wut come out ud
   pay for wut went in,
For swappin' silver off for lead ain't
   the sure way to win ;
(An', fact, it *does* look now ez though —
   but folks must live an' larn —
We should git lead, an' more 'n we
   want, out o' the Old Consarn ;)
But when I see a man so wise an' hon-
   est ez Buchanan
A-lettin' us hev all the forts an' all the
   arms an' cannon,
Admittin' we wuz nat'lly right an you
   wuz nat'lly wrong,
Coz you wuz lab'rin'-folks an' we wuz
   wut they call *bong-tong*,
An' coz there warn't no fight in ye
   more 'n in a mashed potater,
While two o' *us* can't skurcely meet
   but wut we fight by natur',
An' th' ain't a bar-room here would
   pay for openin' on 't a night,
Without it giv the priverlege o' bein'
   shot at sight,
Which proves we 're Natur's noblemen,
   with whom it don't surprise
The British aristoxy should feel boun'
   to sympathize, —
Seein' all this, an' seein', tu, the thing
   wuz strikin' roots

While Uncle Sam sot still in hopes thet
   some one 'd bring his boots,
I thought th' ole Union's hoops wuz
   off, an' let myself be sucked in
To rise a peg an' jine the crowd thet
   went for reconstructin'.
Thet is, to hev the pardnership under
   th' ole name continner
Jest ez it wuz, we drorrin' pay, you
   findin' bone an' sinner, —
On'y to put it in the bond, an' enter 't
   in the journals,
Thet you 're the nat'ral rank an' file,
   an' we the nat'ral kurnels.

Now this I thought a fees'ble plan, thet
   'ud work smooth ez grease,
Suitin' the Nineteenth Century an'
   Upper Ten idees,
An' there I meant to stick, an' so did
   most o' th' leaders, tu,
Coz we all thought the chance wuz good
   o' puttin' on it thru ;
But Jeff he hit upon a way o' helpin'
   on us forrard
By bein' unannermous, — a trick you
   ain't quite up to, Norrard.
A baldin hain't no more 'f a chance
   with them new apple-corers
Than folks's oppersition views aginst
   the Ringtail Roarers ;
They 'll take 'em out on him 'bout
   east, — one canter on a rail
Makes a man feel unannermous ez Jo-
   nah in the whale ;
Or ef he 's a slow-moulded cuss thet
   can't seem quite t' agree,
He gits the noose by tellergraph upon
   the nighes' tree :
Their mission-work with Afrikins hez
   put 'em up, thet 's sartin,
To all the mos' across-lot ways o'
   preachin' an' convartin' ;
I 'll bet my hat th' ain't nary priest, nor
   all on 'em together,
Thet cairs conviction to the min' like
   Reveren' Taranfeather ;
Why, he sot up with me one night, an'
   labored to sech purpose,
Thet (ez an owl by daylight 'mongst a
   flock o' teazin' chirpers
Sees clearer 'n mud the wickedness o'
   eatin' little birds)
I see my error an' agreed to shen it
   arterwurds ;

An' I should say, (to jedge our folks by
    facs in my possession,)
Thet three 's Unannermous where one 's
    a 'Riginal Secession ;
So it 's a thing you fellers North may
    safely bet your chink on,
Thet we 're all water-proofed agin th'
    usurpin' reign o' Lincoln.

Jeff's _some_. He 's gut another plan
    thet hez pertic'lar merits,
In givin' things a cherfle look an' stiff-
    nin' loose-hung sperits ;
For while your million papers, wut with
    lyin' an' discussin',
Keep folks's tempers all on eend a-fu-
    min' an' a-fussin',
A-wondrin' this an' guessin' thet, an'
    dreadin' every night,
The breechin' o' the Univarse 'll break
    afore it 's light,
Our papers don't purtend to print on'y
    wut Guv'ment choose,
An' thet insures us all to git the very
    best o' noose :
Jeff hez it of all sorts an' kines, an'
    sarves it out ez wanted,
So 's 't every man gits wut he likes an'
    nobody ain't scanted.
Sometimes it 's vict'ries, (they 're 'bout
    all ther' is thet 's cheap down here,)
Sometimes it 's France an' England on
    the jump to interfere.
Fact is, the less the people know o' wut
    ther' is a-doin',
The hendier 't is for Guv'ment, sence
    it henders trouble brewin' ;
An' noose is like a shinplaster, — it 's
    good, ef you believe it,
Or, wut 's all same, the other man thet
    's goin' to receive it :
Ef you 've a son in th' army, wy, it 's
    comfortin' to hear
He 'll hev no gretter resk to run than
    seein' th' in'my's rear,
Coz, ef an F. F. looks at 'em, they
    ollers break an' run,
Or wilt right down ez debtors will thet
    stumble on a dun
(An' this, ef an'thin', proves the wuth o'
    proper fem'ly pride,
Fer sech mean shucks ez creditors are
    all on Lincoln's side) :
Ef I hev scrip thet wun't go off no
    more 'n a Beigin rifle,

An' read thet it 's at par on 'Change, it
    makes me feel deli'fle ;
It 's cheerin', tu, where every man mus'
    fortify his bed,
To hear thet Freedom 's the one thing
    our darkies mos'ly dread,
An' thet experunce, time 'n' agin, to
    Dixie's Land hez shown
Ther' 's nothin' like a powder-cask f'r
    a stiddy corner-stone ;
Ain't it ez good ez nuts, when salt is
    sellin' by the ounce
For its own weight in Treash'ry-bons,
    (ef bought in small amounts,)
When even whiskey 's gittin' skurce
    an' sugar can't be found,
To know thet all the ellerments o' lux-
    ury abound ?
An' don't it glorify sal'-pork, to come
    to understand
It 's wut the Richmon' editors call fat-
    ness o' the land !
Nex' thing to knowin' you 're well off
    is _nut_ to know when y' ain't ;
An' ef Jeff says all 's goin' wal, who 'll
    ventur' t' say it ain't?

This cairn the Constitooshun roun' ez
    Jeff doos in his hat
Is hendier a dreffle sight, an' comes
    more kin' o' pat.
I tell ye wut, my jedgment is you 're
    pooty sure to fail,
Ez long 'z the head keeps turnin' back
    for counsel to the tail :
Th' advantiges of our consarn for bein'
    prompt air gret,
While, 'long o' Congress, you can't
    strike, 'f you git an iron het ;
They bother roun' with argooin', an'
    var'ous sorts o' foolin',
To make sure ef it 's leg'lly het, an' all
    the while it 's coolin',
So 's 't when you come to strike, it ain't
    no gret to wish ye j'y on,
An' hurts the hammer 'z much or more
    ez wut it doos the iron,
Jeff don't allow no jawin'-sprees for
    three months at a stretch,
Knowin' the ears long speeches suits
    air mostly made to metch ;
He jes' ropes in your tonguey chaps
    an' reg'lar ten-inch bores
An' lets 'em play at Congress, ef they 'll
    du it with closed doors :

So they ain't no more bothersome than
    ef we 'd took an' sunk 'em,
An' yit enj'y th' exclusive right to one
    another's Buncombe
'Thout doin' nobody no hurt, an' 'thout
    its costin' nothin',
Their pay bein' jes' Confedrit funds,
    they findin' keep an' clothin' ;
They taste the sweets o' public life, an'
    plan their little jobs,
An' suck the Treash'ry, (no gret harm,
    for it 's ez dry ez cobs,)
An' go thru all the motions jest ez safe
    ez in a prison,
An' hev their business to themselves,
    while Buregard hez hisn :
Ez long 'z he gives the Hessians fits,
    committees can't make bother
'Bout whether 't 's done the legle way
    or whether 't 's done the tother.
An' *I* tell *you* 'you 've gut to larn thet
    War ain't one long teeter
Betwixt *I wan' to* an' *'T wun't du*, de-
    batin' like a skeetur
Afore he lights, — all is, to give the
    other side a millin',
An' arter thet 's done, th' ain't no resk
    but wut the lor 'll be willin' ;
No metter wut the guv'ment is, ez
    nigh ez I can hit it,
A lickin' 's constitooshunal, pervidin'
    We don't git it.
Jeff don't stan' dilly-dallyin', afore he
    takes a fort,
(With no one in,) to git the leave o'
    the nex' Soopreme Court,
Nor don't want forty-'leven weeks o'
    jawin' an' expoundin'
To prove a nigger hez a right to save
    him, ef he 's drowndin' ;
Whereas ole Abe 'ud sink afore he 'd
    let a darkie boost him,
Ef Taney should n't come along an'
    hed n't interdooced him.
It ain't your twenty millions thet 'll
    ever block Jeff's game,
But one Man thet wun't let 'em jog
    jest ez he 's takin' aim :
Your numbers they may strengthen ye
    or weaken ye, ez 't heppens
They 're willin' to be helpin' bands or
    wuss'n-nothin' cap'ns.

I 've chose my side, an' 't ain't no odds
    ef I wuz drawed with magnets,

Or ef I thought it prudenter to jine the
    nighes' bagnets ;
I 've made my ch'ice, an' ciphered out,
    from all I see an' heard,
Th' ole Constitooshun never 'd git her
    decks for action cleared,
Long 'z you elect for Congressmen poor
    shotes thet want to go
Coz they can't seem to git their grub no
    otherways than so,
An' let your bes' men stay to home coz
    they wun't show ez talkers,
Nor can't be hired to fool ye an' sof'-
    soap ye at a caucus, —
Long 'z ye set by Rotashun more 'n ye
    do by folks's merits,
Ez though experunce thriv by change
    o' sile, like corn an' kerrits, —
Long 'z you allow a critter's "claims"
    coz, spite o' shoves an' tippins,
He 's kep' his private pan jest where 't
    would ketch mos' public drip-
    pins, —
Long 'z A. 'll turn tu an' grin' B.'s exe,
    ef B. 'll help him grin' hisn,
(An' thet 's the main idee by which
    your leadin' men hev risen,) —
Long 'z you let *ary* exe be groun', 'less
    't is to cut the weasan'
O' sneaks thet dunno till they 're told
    wut is an' wut ain't Treason, —
Long 'z ye give out commissions to a
    lot o' peddlin' drones
Thet trade in whiskey with their men
    an' skin 'em to their bones, —
Long 'z ye sift out "safe" canderdates
    thet no one ain't afeared on
Coz they 're so thund'rin' eminent for
    bein' never heard on,
An' hain't no record, ez it 's called, for
    folks to pick a hole in,
Ez ef it hurt a man to hev a body with
    a soul in,
An' it wuz ostentashun to be showin'
    on 't about,
When half his feller-citizens contrive to
    do without,
Long 'z you suppose your votes can
    turn biled kebbage into brain,
An' ary man thet 's pop'lar 's fit to drive
    a lightnin'-train, —
Long 'z you believe democracy means
    I 'm ez good ez you be,
An' that a feller from the ranks can't
    be a knave or booby, —

Long 'z Congress seems purvided, like
    yer street-cars an' yer 'busses,
With ollers room for jes' one more o'
    your spiled-in-bakin' cusses,
Dough 'thout the emptins of a soul, an'
    yit with means about 'em
(Like essence-peddlers *) thet 'll make
    folks long to be without 'em,
Jest heavy 'nough to turn a scale thet 's
    doubtfle the wrong way,
An' make their nat'ral arsenal o' bein'
    nasty pay, —
Long 'z them things last, (an' *I* don't
    see no gret signs of improvin',)
I sha'n't up stakes, not hardly yit, nor 't
    would n't pay for movin'.
For, 'fore you lick us, it 'll be the
    long'st day ever *you* see.
    Yourn, (ez I 'xpec' to be nex' spring,)
        B., Markiss o' Big Boosy.

No. IV.

A MESSAGE OF JEFF DAVIS IN SECRET SESSION.

Confecturally reported by H. Biglow.

TO THE EDITORS OF THE ATLANTIC
                MONTHLY.

    Jaalam, 10th March, 1862.

Gentlemen, — My leisure has been
so entirely occupied with the hitherto
fruitless endeavour to decypher the Runick inscription whose fortunate discovery I mentioned in my last communication, that I have not found time to discuss, as I had intended, the great problem of what we are to do with slavery,
— a topick on which the publick mind in
this place is at present more than ever
agitated. What my wishes and hopes
are I need not say, but for safe conclusions I do not conceive that we are yet
in possession of facts enough on which
to bottom them with certainty. Acknowledging the hand of Providence,
as I do, in all events, I am sometimes
inclined to think that they are wiser

* A rustic euphemism for the American
variety of the *Mephitis.*   H. W.

than we, and am willing to wait till we
have made this continent once more a
place where freemen can live in security and honour, before assuming any
further responsibility. This is the view
taken by my neighbour Habakkuk Slo-
ansure, Esq., the president of our bank,
whose opinion in the practical affairs
of life has great weight with me, as I
have generally found it to be justified
by the event, and whose counsel, had I
followed it, would have saved me from
an unfortunate investment of a considerable part of the painful economies of
half a century in the Northwest-Pas-
sage Tunnel. After a somewhat animated discussion with this gentleman,
a few days since, I expanded, on the
audi alteram partem principle, something which he happened to say by way
of illustration, into the following fable.

FESTINA LENTE.

Once on a time there was a pool
Fringed all about with flag-leaves cool
And spotted with cow-lilies garish,
Of frogs and pouts the ancient parish.
Alders the creaking redwings sink on,
Tussocks that house blithe Bob o' Lincoln
Hedged round the unassailed seclusion,
Where muskrats piled their cells Carthusian ;
And many a moss-embroidered log,
The watering-place of summer frog,
Slept and decayed with patient skill,
As watering-places sometimes will.

Now in this Abbey of Theleme,
Which realized the fairest dream
That ever dozing bull-frog had,
Sunned on a half-sunk lily-pad,
There rose a party with a mission
To mend the polliwogs' condition,
Who notified the selectmen
To call a meeting there and then.
" Some kind of steps," they said, " are
    needed " ;
They don't come on so fast as we did :
Let 's dock their tails ; if that don't make 'em
Frogs by brevet, the Old One take 'em !
That boy, that came the other day
To dig some flag-root down this way,
His jack-knife left, and 't is a sign
That Heaven approves of our design :
'T were wicked not to urge the step on,
When Providence has sent the weapon."

Old croakers, deacons of the mire,
That led the deep batrachian choir,
Uk ! Uk ! Caronk ! with bass that might

Have left Lablache's out of sight,
Shook nobby heads, and said, "No go!
You 'd better let 'em try to grow:
Old Doctor Time is slow, but still
He does know how to make a pill."

But vain was all their hoarsest bass,
Their old experience out of place,
And spite of croaking and entreating,
The vote was carried in marsh-meeting.

"Lord knows," protest the polliwogs,
"We 're anxious to be grown-up frogs;
But don't push in to do the work
Of Nature till she prove a shirk;
'T is not by jumps that she advances,
But wins her way by circumstances:
Pray, wait awhile, until you know
We 're so contrived as not to grow;
Let Nature take her own direction,
And she 'll absorb our imperfection;
You might n't like 'em to appear with,
But we must have the things to steer with."

"No," piped the party of reform,
"All great results are ta'en by storm;
Fate holds her best gifts till we show
We 've strength to make her let them go;
The Providence that works in history,
And seems to some folks such a mystery,
Does not creep slowly on *incog.*,
But moves by jumps, a mighty frog;
No more reject the Age's chrism,
Your queues are an anachronism;
No more the Future's promise mock,
But lay your tails upon the block,
Thankful that we the means have voted
To have you thus to frogs promoted."

The thing was done, the tails were cropped,
And home each philotadpole hopped,
In faith rewarded to exult,
And wait the beautiful result.
Too soon it came; our pool, so long
The theme of patriot bull-frog's song,
Next day was reeking, fit to smother,
With heads and tails that missed each other,—
Here snoutless tails, there tailless snouts;
The only gainers were the pouts.

MORAL.

From lower to the higher next,
Not to the top, is Nature's text;
And embryo Good, to reach full stature,
Absorbs the Evil in its nature.

I think that nothing will ever give
permanent peace and security to this
continent but the extirpation of Slavery
therefrom, and that the occasion is
nigh; but I would do nothing hastily
or vindictively, nor presume to jog the
elbow of Providence. No desperate
measures for me till we are sure that all
others are hopeless, — *flectere si nequeo
superos, Acheronta movebo.* To make
Emancipation a reform instead of a
revolution is worth a little patience,
that we may have the Border States
first, and then the non-slaveholders of
the Cotton States, with us in principle,
— a consummation that seems to be
nearer than many imagine. *Fiat justi-
tia, ruat cœlum,* is not to be taken in a
literal sense by statesmen, whose problem is to get justice done with as little
jar as possible to existing order, which
has at least so much of heaven in it that
it is not chaos. Our first duty toward
our enslaved brother is to educate him,
whether he be white or black. The
first need of the free black is to elevate
himself according to the standard of
this material generation. So soon as
the Ethiopian goes in his chariot, he
will find not only Apostles, but Chief
Priests and Scribes and Pharisees willing to ride with him.

Nil habet infelix paupertas durius in se
Quam quod ridiculos homines facit.

I rejoice in the President's late Message, which at last proclaims the Government on the side of freedom, justice,
and sound policy.

As I write, comes the news of our
disaster at Hampton Roads. I do not
understand the supineness which, after
fair warning, leaves wood to an unequal
conflict with iron. It is not enough
merely to have the right on our side, if
we stick to the old flint-lock of tradition.
I have observed in my parochial experience (*haud ignarus mali*) that the
Devil is prompt to adopt the latest inventions of destructive warfare, and
may thus take even such a three-decker
as Bishop Butler at an advantage. It
is curious, that, as gunpowder made
armour useless on shore, so armour is
having its revenge by baffling its old
enemy at sea, — and that, while gunpowder robbed land warfare of nearly
all its picturesqueness to give even
greater stateliness and sublimity to a
sea-fight, armour bids fair to degrade the

latter into a squabble between two iron-shelled turtles.

Yours, with esteem and respect,
HOMER WILBUR, A. M.

P. S. — I had wellnigh forgotten to say that the object of this letter is to enclose a communication from the gifted pen of Mr. Biglow.

I SENT you a messige, my friens, t'other day,
To tell you I 'd nothin' pertickler to say :
'T wuz the day our new nation gut kin' o' stillborn,
So 't wuz my pleasant dooty t' acknowl-edge the corn,
An' I see clearly then, ef I did n't be-fore,
Thet the *augur* in inauguration means *bore*.
I need n't tell *you* thet my messige wuz written
To diffuse correc' notions in France an' Gret Britten,
An' agin to impress on the poppylar mind
The comfort an' wisdom o' goin' it blind, —
To say thet I did n't abate not a hooter
O' my faith in a happy an' glorious futur',
Ez rich in each soshle an' p'liticle blessin'
Ez them thet we now hed the joy o' possessin'.
With a people united, an' longin' to die
For wut *we* call their country, without askin' why,
An' all the gret things we concluded to slope for
Ez much within reach now ez ever — to hope for.
We 've gut all the ellerments, this very hour,
Thet make up a fus'-class, self-govern-in' power :
We 've a war, an' a debt, an' a flag ; an' ef this
Ain't to be inderpendunt, why, wut on airth is ?
An' nothin' now henders our takin' our station

Ez the freest, enlightenedest, civerlized nation,
Built up on our bran'-new politickle thesis
Thet a Gov'ment's fust right is to tum-ble to pieces, —
I say nothin' henders our takin' our place
Ez the very fus'-best o' the whole human race,
A spittin' tobacker ez proud ez you please
On Victory's bes' carpets, or loafin' at ease
In the Tool'ries front-parlor, discussin affairs
With our heels on the backs o' Na-poleon's new chairs,
An' princes a-mixin' our cocktails an' slings, —
Excep', wal, excep' jest a very few things,
Sech ez navies an' armies an' where-with to pay,
An' gittin' our sogers to run t'other way,
An' not be too over-pertickler in tryin'
To hunt up the very las' ditches to die in.

Ther' are critters so base thet they want it explained,
Jes' wut is the totle amount thet we 've gained,
Ez ef we could maysure stupenjious events
By the low Yankee stan'ard o' dollars an' cents :
They seem to forgit, thet, sence last year revolved,
We 've succeeded in gittin' seceshed an' dissolved,
An' thet no one can't hope to git thru dissolootion
'Thout some kin' o' strain on the best Constitootion.
Who asks for a prospec' more flettrin' an' bright,
When from here clean to Texas it 's all one free fight ?
Hain't we rescued from Seward the gret leadin' featurs
Thet makes it wuth while to be reasonin' creaturs ?

Hain't we saved Habus Coppers, im-
proved it in fact,
By suspendin' the Unionists 'stid o' the
Act ?
Ain't the laws free to all ? Where on
airth else d' ye see
Every freeman improvin' his own rope
an' tree ?
Ain't our piety sech (in our speeches an'
messiges)
Ez t' astonish ourselves in the bes'-
composed pessiges,
An' to make folks that knowed us in th'
ole state o' things
Think convarsion ez easy ez drinkin'
gin-slings ?

It 's ne'ssary to take a good confident
tone
With the public ; but here, jest amongst
us, I own
Things look blacker 'n thunder. Ther'
's no use denyin'
We 're clean out o' money, an' 'most
out o' lyin', —
Two things a young nation can't men-
nage without,
Ef she wants to look wal at her fust
comin' out ;
For the fust supplies physickle strength,
while the second
Gives a morril edvantage thet 's hard to
be reckoned :
For this latter I 'm willin' to du wut I
can ;
For the former you 'll hev to consult on
a plan, —
Though our *fust* want (an' this pint I
want your best views on)
Is plausible paper to print I. O. U.s on.
Some gennlemen think it would cure
all our cankers
In the way o' finance, ef we jes' hanged
the bankers ;
An' I own the proposle 'ud square with
my views,
Ef their lives wuz n't all thet we'd left
'em to lose.
Some say thet more confidence might
be inspired,
Ef we voted our cities an' towns to be
fired, —
A pian thet 'ud suttenly tax our endurance,

Coz 't would be our own bills we
should git for th' insurance ;
But cinders, no metter how sacred we
think 'em,
Might n't strike furrin minds ez good
sources of income,
Nor the people, perhaps, would n't
like the eclaw
O' bein' all turned into paytriots by
law.
Some want we should buy all the cotton
an' burn it,
On a pledge, when we 've gut thru the
war, to return it, —
Then to take the proceeds an' hold
them ez security
For an issue o' bonds to be met at
maturity
With an issue o' notes to be paid in
hard cash
On the fus' Monday follerin' the 'tarnal
Allsmash :
This hez a safe air, an', once hold o' the
gold,
'Ud leave our vile plunderers out in the
cold,
An' *might* temp' John Bull, ef it warn't
for the dip he
Once gut from the banks o' my own
Mississippi.
Some think we could make, by arrangin'
the figgers,
A hendy home-currency out of our
niggers,
But it wun't du to lean much on ary
sech staff,
For they 're gittin' tu current a'ready,
by half.
One gennleman says, ef we lef' our
loan out
Where Floyd could git hold on 't, *he* 'd
take it, no doubt ;
But 't ain't jes' the takin', though 't
hez a good look,
We mus' git sunthin' out on it arter
it 's took,
An' we need now more 'n ever, with
sorrer I own,
Thet some one another should let us
a loan,
Sence a soger wun't fight, on'y jes'
while he draws his
Pay down on the nail, for the best ol
all causes,

'Thout askin' to know wut the quarrel 's
    about, —
An' once come to thet, why, our game
    is played out.
It 's ez true ez though I should n't
    never hev said it,
Thet a hitch hez took place in our
    system o' credit ;
I swear it 's all right in my speeches an'
    messiges,
But ther' 's idees afloat, ez ther' is
    about sessiges :
Folks wun't take a bond ez a basis to
    trade on,
Without nosin' round to find out wut
    it 's made on,
An' the thought more an' more thru
    the public min' crosses
Thet our Treshry hez gut 'mos' too
    many dead hosses.
Wut 's called credit, you see, is some
    like a balloon,
Thet looks while it 's up 'most ez harn-
    some 'z a moon,
But once git a leak in 't an' wut looked
    so grand
Caves righ' down in a jiffy ez flat ez
    your hand.
Now the world is a dreffle mean place,
    for our sins,
Where ther' ollus is critters about with
    long pins
A-prickin' the bubbles we 've blowed
    with sech care,
An' provin' ther' 's nothin' inside but
    bad air :
They 're all Stuart Millses, poor-white
    trash, an' sneaks,
Without no more chivverlry 'n Choc-
    taws or Creeks,
Who think a real gennleman's promise
    to pay
Is meant to be took in trade's ornery way :
Them fellers an' I could n' never agree ;
They 're the naterial foes o' the Southun
    Idee ;
I 'd gladly take all of our other resks on
    me
To be red o' this low-lived politikle
    'con'my !

Now a dastardly notion is gittin' about
Thet our bladder is bust an' the gas
    oozin' out,

An' onless we can mennage in some
    way to stop it,
Why, the thing 's a gone coon, an' we
    might ez wal drop it.
Brag works wal at fust, but it ain't jes'
    the thing
For a stiddy inves'ment the shiners to
    bring,
An' votin' we 're prosp'rous a hundred
    times over
Wun't change bein' starved into livin'
    on clover.
Manassas done sunthin' tow'rds drawin'
    the wool
O'er the green, antislavery eyes o'
    John Bull :
Oh, *warn't* it a godsend, jes' when
    sech tight fixes
Wuz crowdin' us mourners, to throw
    double-sixes !
I wuz tempted to think, an' it wuz n't
    no wonder,
Ther' wuz reely a Providence, — over
    or under, —
When, all packed for Nashville, I fust
    ascertained
From the papers up North wut a
    victory we 'd gained.
'T wuz the time for diffusin' correc'
    views abroad
Of our union an' strength an' relyin' on
    God ;
An', fact, when I 'd gut thru my fust
    big surprise,
I much ez half b'lieved in my own
    tallest lies,
An' conveyed the idee thet the whole
    Southun popperlace
Wuz Spartans all on the keen jump for
    Thermopperlies,
Thet set on the Lincolnites' bombs till
    they bust,
An' fight for the priv'lege o' dyin' the
    fust ;
But Roanoke, Bufort, Millspring, an'
    the rest
Of our recent starn-foremost successes
    out West,
Hain't left us a foot for our swellin' to
    stand on, —
We 've showed *too* much o' wut Bure-
    gard calls *abandon*,
For all our Thermopperlies (**an'** it 's a
    marcy

We hain't hed no more) hev ben clean
    vicy-varsy,
An' wut Spartans wuz lef' when the
    battle wuz done
Wuz them thet wuz too unambitious to
    run.

Oh, ef we hed ou'y jes' gut Reecog-
    nition,
Things now would ha' ben in a different
    position !
You'd ha' hed all you wanted : the
    paper blockade
Smashed up into toothpicks, — un-
    limited trade
In the one thing thet 's needfle, till
    niggers, I swow,
Hed ben thicker 'n provisional shin-
    plasters now,
Quinine by the ton 'ginst the shakes
    when they seize ye, —
Nice paper to coin into C. S. A. specie ;
The voice of the driver 'd be heerd in
    our land,
An' the univarse scringe, ef we lifted
    our hand :
Would n't *thet* be some like a fulfillin'
    the prophecies,
With all the fus' fem'lies in all the fust
    offices ?
'T wuz a beautiful dream, an' all sorrer
    is idle, —
But *ef* Lincoln *would* ha' hanged Ma-
    son an' Slidell !
For would n't the Yankees hev found
    they 'd ketcned Tartars,
Ef they 'd raised two sech critters as
    them into martyrs ?
Mason *wuz* F. F. V., though a cheap
    card to win on,
But t'other was jes' New York trash to
    begin on ;
They ain't o' no good in Európean
    pellices,
But think wut a help they 'd ha' ben
    on their gallowses !
They 'd ha' felt they wuz truly fulfillin'
    their mission,
An', oh, how dog-cheap we 'd ha' gut
    Reecognition !

But somehow another, wutever we 've
    tried,
Though the the'ry 's fust-rate, the facs
    wun't coincide :

Facs are contrary 'z mules, an' ez hard
    in the mouth,
An' they allus hev showed a mean spite
    to the South.
Sech bein' the case, we hed best look
    about
For some kin' o' way to slip *our* necks
    out :
Le' 's vote our las' dollar, ef one can be
    found,
(An', at any rate, votin' it hez a good
    sound,) —
Le' 's swear thet to arms all our people
    is flyin',
(The critters can't read, an' wun't know
    how we 're lyin',) —
Thet Toombs is advancin' to sack Cin-
    cinnater,
With a rovin' commission to pillage an'
    slahter, —
Thet we 've throwed to the winds all
    regard for wut 's lawfle,
An' gone in for sunthin' promiscu'sly
    awfle.
Ye see, hitherto, it 's our own knaves
    an' fools
Thet we 've used, (those for whetstones,
    an' t'others ez tools,)
An' now our las' chance is in puttin' to
    test
The same kin' o' cattle up North an'
    out West, —
Your Belmonts, Vallandighams, Woods-
    es, an' sech,
Poor shotes thet ye could n't persuade
    us to tech,
Not in ornery times, though we 're
    willin' to feed 'em
With a nod now an' then, when we
    happen to need 'em ;
Why, for my part, I 'd ruther shake
    hands with a nigger
Than with cusses that load an' don t
    darst dror a trigger ;
They 're the wust wooden nutmegs the
    Yankees produce,
Shaky everywhere else, an' jes' sound
    on the goose ;
They ain't wuth a cuss, an' I set noth-
    in' by 'em,
But we 're in sech a fix thet I s'pose we
    mus' try 'em.
I—— But, Gennlemen, here 's a de-
    spatch jes' come in

Which shows thet the tide's begun turnin' agin, —
Gret Cornfedrit success ! C'lumbus
  eevacooated !
I mus' run down an' hev the thing properly stated,
An' show wut a triumph it is, an' how
  lucky
To fin'lly git red o' thet cussed Ken-
  tucky, —
An' how, sence Fort Donelson, winnin'
  the day
Consists in triumphantly gittin' away.

No. V.

SPEECH OF HONOURABLE
PRESERVED DOE IN SE-
CRET CAUCUS.

TO THE EDITORS OF THE ATLANTIC
MONTHLY.

JAALAM, 12th April, 1862.

GENTLEMEN, — As I cannot but
hope that the ultimate, if not speedy,
success of the national arms is now
sufficiently ascertained, sure as I am
of the righteousness of our cause and
its consequent claim on the blessing of
God, (for I would not show a faith inferior to that of the pagan historian with
his *Facile evenit quod Dîs cordi est,*)
it seems to me a suitable occasion to
withdraw our minds a moment from the
confusing din of battle to objects of
peaceful and permanent interest. Let
us not neglect the monuments of preterite history because what shall be history is so diligently making under our
eyes. *Cras ingens iterabimus æquor ;*
to-morrow will be time enough for that
stormy sea ; to-day let me engage the
attention of your readers with the Runick inscription to whose fortunate discovery I have heretofore alluded. Well
may we say with the poet, *Multa re-
nascuntur quæ jam cecidere.* And I
would premise, that, although I can no
longer resist the evidence of my own
senses from the stone before me to the

ante-Columbian discovery of this continent by the Northmen, *gens inclytis-
sima,* as they are called in a Palermi-
tan inscription, written fortunately in a
less debatable character than that which
I am about to decipher, yet I would by
no means be understood as wishing to
vilipend the merits of the great Geno-
ese, whose name will never be forgotten so long as the inspiring strains of
" Hail Columbia " shall continue to be
heard. Though he must be stripped
also of whatever praise may belong to
the experiment of the egg, which I find
proverbially attributed by Castilian
authors to a certain Juanito or Jack,
(perhaps an offshoot of our giant-killing
mythus,) his name will still remain one
of the most illustrious of modern times.
But the impartial historian owes a duty
likewise to obscure merit, and my so-
licitude to render a tardy justice is perhaps quickened by my having known
those who, had their own field of labour
been less secluded, might have found a
readier acceptance with the reading
publick. I could give an example, but
I forbear : *forsitan nostris ex ossibus
oritur ultor.*

Touching Runick inscriptions, I find
that they may be classed under three
general heads : 1°. Those which are
understood by the Danish Royal Society of Northern Antiquaries, and
Professor Rafn, their Secretary ; 2°.
Those which are comprehensible only
by Mr. Rafn ; and 3°. Those which
neither the Society, Mr. Rafn, nor anybody else can be said in any definite
sense to understand, and which accordingly offer peculiar temptations to
enucleating sagacity. These last are
naturally deemed the most valuable by
intelligent antiquaries, and to this class
the stone now in my possession fortunately belongs. Such give a picturesque variety to ancient events, because
susceptible oftentimes of as many interpretations as there are individual
archæologists ; and since facts are only
the pulp in which the Idea or event-
seed is softly imbedded till it ripen, it
is of little consequence what colour or
flavour we attribute to them, provided

it be agreeable. Availing myself of the obliging assistance of Mr. Arphaxad Bowers, an ingenious photographick artist, whose house-on-wheels has now stood for three years on our Meeting-House Green, with the somewhat contradictory inscription, — "*our motto is onward*," — I have sent accurate copies of my treasure to many learned men and societies, both native and European. I may hereafter communicate their different and (*me judice*) equally erroneous solutions. I solicit also, Messrs. Editors, your own acceptance of the copy herewith inclosed. I need only premise further, that the stone itself is a goodly block of metamorphick sandstone, and that the Runes resemble very nearly the ornithichnites or fossil bird-tracks of Dr. Hitchcock, but with less regularity or apparent design than is displayed by those remarkable geological monuments. These are rather the *non bene junctarum discordia semina rerum*. Resolved to leave no door open to cavil, I first of all attempted the elucidation of this remarkable example of lithick literature by the ordinary modes, but with no adequate return for my labour. I then considered myself amply justified in resorting to that heroick treatment the felicity of which, as applied by the great Bentley to Milton, had long ago enlisted my admiration. Indeed, I had already made up my mind, that, in case good fortune should throw any such invaluable record in my way, I would proceed with it in the following simple and satisfactory method. After a cursory examination, merely sufficing for an approximative estimate of its length, I would write down a hypothetical inscription based upon antecedent probabilities, and then proceed to extract from the characters engraven on the stone a meaning as nearly as possible conformed to this *a priori* product of my own ingenuity. The result more than justified my hopes, inasmuch as the two inscriptions were made without any great violence to tally in all essential particulars. I then proceeded, not without some anxiety to my second

test, which was, to read the Runick letters diagonally, and again with the same success. With an excitement pardonable under the circumstances, yet tempered with thankful humility, I now applied my last and severest trial, my *experimentum crucis*. I turned the stone, now doubly precious in my eyes, with scrupulous exactness upside down. The physical exertion so far displaced my spectacles as to derange for a moment the focus of vision. I confess that it was with some tremulousness that I readjusted them upon my nose, and prepared my mind to bear with calmness any disappointment that might ensue. But, *O albo dies notanda lapillo!* what was my delight to find that the change of position had effected none in the sense of the writing, even by so much as a single letter! I was now, and justly, as I think, satisfied of the conscientious exactness of my interpretation. It is as follows:—

> HERE
> BJARNA GRÍMOLFSSON
> FIRST DRANK CLOUD-BROTHER
> THROUGH CHILD-OF-LAND-AND-
> WATER:

that is, drew smoke through a reed stem. In other words, we have here a record of the first smoking of the herb *Nicotiana Tabacum* by an European on this continent. The probable results of this discovery are so vast as to baffle conjecture. If it be objected, that the smoking of a pipe would hardly justify the setting up of a memorial stone, I answer, that even now the Moquis Indian, ere he takes his first whiff, bows reverently toward the four quarters of the sky in succession, and that the loftiest monuments have been reared to perpetuate fame, which is the dream of the shadow of smoke. The *Saga*, it will be remembered, leaves this Bjarna to a fate something like that of Sir Humphrey Gilbert, on board a sinking ship in the "wormy sea," having generously given up his place in the boat to a certain Icelander. It is doubly pleasant, therefore, to meet with this proof that the brave old man arrived safely in Vinland. and that his declining years were cheered by the respectful attentions of the dusky denizens of our then uninvaded forests. Most of all was I gratified, however, in this linking forever the name of my native town with one of the most momentous occurrences of modern times. Hitherto Jaalam, though in soil, climate, and geographical position as highly qualified to be the theatre of remarkable historical incidents as any spot on the earth's surface, has been, if I may say it without seeming to question the wisdom of Providence, almost maliciously neglected, as it might appear, by occurrences of world-wide interest in want of a situation. And in matters of this nature it must be confessed that adequate events are as necessary as the *vates sacer* to record them. Jaalam stood always modestly ready, but circumstances made no fitting response to her generous intentions. Now, however, she assumes her place on the historick roll. I have hitherto been a zealous opponent of the Circean herb, but I shall now re-examine the question without bias.

I am aware that the Rev. Jonas Tutchel, in a recent communication to the Bogus Four Corners Weekly Meridian, has endeavoured to show that this is the sepulchral inscription of Thorwald Eriksson, who, as is well known, was slain in Vinland by the natives. But I think he has been misled by a preconceived theory, and cannot but feel that he has thus made an ungracious return for my allowing him to inspect the stone with the aid of my own glasses (he having by accident left his at home) and in my own study. The heathen ancients might have instructed this Christian minister in the rites of hospitality; but much is to be pardoned to the spirit of self-love. He must indeed be ingenious who can make out the words *hèr hvílir* from any characters in the inscription in question, which, whatever else it may be, is certainly not mortuary. And even should the reverend gentleman succeed in persuading some fantastical

wits of the soundness of his views, I do not see what useful end he will have gained. For if the English Courts of Law hold the testimony of grave-stones from the burial-grounds of Protestant dissenters to be questionable, even where it is essential in proving a descent, I cannot conceive that the epitaphial assertions of heathens should be esteemed of more authority by any man of orthodox sentiments.

At this moment, happening to cast my eyes upon the stone, on which a transverse light from my southern window brings out the characters with singular distinctness, another interpretation has occurred to me, promising even more interesting results. I hasten to close my letter in order to follow at once the clew thus providentially suggested.

I inclose, as usual, a contribution from Mr. Biglow, and remain,

Gentlemen, with esteem and respect,
Your Obedient Humble Servant,
HOMER WILBUR, A. M.

I THANK ye, my friens, for the warmth
   o' your greetin':
Ther' 's few airthly blessins but wut 's
   vain an' fleetin';
But ef ther' is one thet hain't *no* cracks
   an' flaws,
An' is wuth goin' in for, it 's pop'lar
   applause ;
It sends up the sperits ez lively ez
   rockets,
An' I feel it — wal, down to the eend o'
   my pockets.
Jes' lovin' the people is Canaan in
   view,
But it 's Canaan paid quarterly t' hev
   'em love you ;
It 's a blessin' thet 's breakin' out ollus
   in fresh spots ;
It 's a-follerin' Moses 'thout losin' the
   flesh-pots.
But, Gennlemen, 'scuse me, I ain't
   sech a raw cus
Ez to go luggin' ellerkence into a
   caucus, —
Thet is, into one where the call com-
   prehends

Nut the People in person, but on'y
  their friends;
I 'm so kin' o' used to convincin' the
  masses
Of th' edvantage o' bein' self-governin'
  asses,
I forgut thet *we* 're all o' the sort thet
  pull wires
An' arrange for the public their wants
  an' desires,
An' thet wut we hed met for wuz jes' to
  agree
Wut the People's opinions in futur'
  should be.

Now, to come to the nub, we 've ben
  all disappinted,
An' our leadin' idees are a kind o' dis-
  jinted, —
Though, fur ez the nateral man could
  discern,
Things ough' to ha' took most an op-
  persite turn.
But The'ry is jes' like a train on the
  rail,
Thet, weather or no, puts her thru without fail,
While Fac 's the ole stage thet gits
  sloughed in the ruts,
An' hez to allow for your darned efs an'
  buts,
An' so, nut intendin' no pers'nal reflections,
They don't — don't nut allus, thet is, —
  make connections:
Sometimes, when it really doos seem
  thet they 'd oughter
Combine jest ez kindly ez new rum an'
  water,
Both 'll be jest ez sot in their ways ez a
  bagnet,
Ez otherwise-minded ez th' eends of a
  magnet,
An' folks like you 'n' me, thet ain't ept
  to be sold,
Git somehow or 'nother left out in the
  cold.

I expected 'fore this, 'thout no gret of a
  row,
Jeff D. would ha' ben where A. Lincoln
  is now,
With Taney to say 't wuz all legle an'
  fair,

An' a jury o' Deemocrats ready to
  swear
Thet the ingin o' State gut throwed into
  the ditch
By the fault o' the North in misplacin'
  the switch.
Things wuz ripenin' fust-rate with
  Buchanan to nuss 'em;
But the People they would n't be Mex-
  icans, cuss 'em!
Ain't the safeguards o' freedom upsot,
  'z you may say,
Ef the right o' rev'lution is took clean
  away?
An' doos n't the right primy-fashy in-
  clude
The bein' entitled to nut be subdued?
The fact is, we 'd gone for the Union so
  strong,
When Union meant South ollus right
  an' North wrong,
Thet the people gut fooled into thinkin'
  it might
Worry on middlin' wal with the North
  in the right.
We might ha' ben now jest ez pros-
  p'rous ez France,
Where p'litikle enterprise hez a fair
  chance,
An' the people is heppy an' proud et
  this hour,
Long ez they hev the votes, to let Nap
  hev the power;
But *our* folks they went an' believed
  wut we 'd told 'em,
An', the flag once insulted, no mortle
  could hold 'em.
'T wuz pervokin' jest when we wuz
  cert'in to win, —
An' I, for one, wun't trust the masses
  agin:
For a people thet knows much ain't fit
  to be free
In the self-cockin', back-action style o'
  J. D.

I can't believe now but wut half on 't is
  lies;
For who 'd thought the North wuz
  a-goin' to rise,
Or take the pervokin'est kin' of a
  stump,
'Thout 't wuz sunthin' ez pressin' ez
  Gabr'el's las' trump?

Or who 'd ha' supposed, arter *sech* swell
　　an' bluster
'Bout the lick-ary-ten-on-ye fighters
　　they 'd muster,
Raised by hand on briled lightnin', ez
　　op'lent 'z you please
In a primitive furrest o' femmily-
　　trees, —
Who 'd ha' thought thet them South-
　　uners ever 'ud show
Starns with pedigrees to 'em like theirn
　　to the foe,
Or, when the vamosin' come, ever to
　　find
Nat'ral masters in front an' mean white
　　folks behind?
By ginger, ef I 'd ha' known half I know
　　now,
When I wuz to Congress, I wouldn't, I
　　swow,
Hev let 'em cair on so high-minded an'
　　sarsy,
'Thout *some* show o' wut you may call
　　vicy-varsy.
To be sure, we wuz under a contrac' jes'
　　then
To be dreffle forbearin' towards South-
　　un men;
We hed to go sheers in preservin' the
　　bellance:
An' ez they seemed to feel they wuz
　　wastin' their tellents
'Thout some un to kick, 't warn't
　　more 'n proper, you know,
Each should funnish his part; an' sence
　　they found the toe,
An' we wuz n't cherubs — wal, we found
　　the buffer,
For fear thet the Compromise System
　　should suffer.

I wun't say the plan hed n't onpleasant
　　featurs, —
For men are perverse an' onreasonin'
　　creaturs,
An' forgit thet in this life 't ain't likely
　　to heppen
Their own privit fancy should ollus be
　　cappen,
But it worked jest ez smooth ez the key
　　of a safe,
An' the gret Union bearins played free
　　from all chafe.
They warn't hard to suit, ef they hed
　　their own way;

An' we (thet is, some on us) made the
　　thing pay:
'T wuz a fair give-an'-take out of Uncle
　　Sam's heap;
Ef they took wut warn't theirn, wut we
　　give come ez cheap:
The elect gut the offices down to tide-
　　waiter,
The people took skinnin' ez mild ez a
　　tater,
Seemed to choose who they wanted tu,
　　footed the bills,
An' felt kind o' 'z though they wuz
　　havin' their wills,
Which kep' 'em ez harmless an' cherfle
　　ez crickets,
While all we invested wuz names on
　　the tickets:
Wal, ther' 's nothin', for folks fond o'
　　lib'ral consumption
Free o' charge, like democ'acy tem-
　　pered with gumption!

Now warn't thet a system wuth pains
　　in presarvin',
Where the people found jints an' their
　　friens done the carvin', —
Where the many done all o' their
　　thinkin' by proxy,
An' were proud on 't ez long ez 't wuz
　　christened Democ'cy, —
Where the few let us sap all o' Free-
　　dom's foundations,
Ef you call it reformin' with prudence
　　an' patience,
An' were willin' Jeff's snake-egg should
　　hetch with the rest,
Ef you writ "Constitootional" over the
　　nest?
But it's all out o' kilter, ('twuz too good
　　to last,)
An' all jes' by J. D.'s perceedin' too
　　fast;
Ef he 'd on'y hung on for a month or
　　two more,
We 'd ha' gut things fixed nicer 'n they
　　hed ben before:
Afore he drawed off an' lef' all in con-
　　fusion,
We wuz safely entrenched in the ole
　　Constitootion,
With an outlyin', heavy-gun, casemated
　　fort
To rake all assailants, — I mean th'
　　S. J. Court.

Now I never 'll acknowledge (nut ef
   you should skin me)
'T wuz wise to abandon sech works to
   the in'my,
An' let him fin' out thet wut scared him
   so long,
Our whole line of argyments, lookin'
   so strong,
All our Scriptur' an' law, every 'ry
   an' fac',
Wuz Quaker-guns daubed with Pro-
   slavery black.
Why, ef the Republicans ever should
   git
Andy Johnson or some one to lend 'em
   the wit
An' the spunk ies' to mount Constitootion an' Court
With Columbiad guns, your real ekle-
   rights sort,
Or drill out the spike from the ole Declaration
Thet can kerry a solid shot clearn roun'
   creation,
We 'd better take maysures for shettin'
   up shop,
An' put off our stock by a vendoo or
   swop.

But they wun't never dare tu; you 'll
   see 'em in Edom
'Fore they ventur' to go where their
   doctrines 'ud lead 'em :
They 've ben takin' our princerples up
   ez we dropt 'em,
An' thought it wuz terrible 'cute to
   adopt 'em ;
But they 'll fin' out 'fore long thet their
   hope 's ben deceivin' 'em,
An' thet princerples ain't o' no good,
   ef you b'lieve in 'em ;
It makes 'em tu stiff for a party to use,
Where they 'd ough' to be easy 'z an
   ole pair o' shoes.
If *we* say 'n our pletform thet all men
   are brothers,
We don't mean thet some folks ain't
   more so 'n some others ;
An' it 's wal understood thet we make
   a selection,
An' thet brotherhood kin' o' subsides
   arter 'lection.
The fust thing for sound politicians to
   larn is,

Thet Truth, to dror kindly in all sorts
   o' harness,
Mus' be kep' in the abstract, — for,
   come to apply it,
You 're ept to hurt some folks's inter-
   ists by it.
Wal, these 'ere Republicans (some on
   'em) ects
Ez though gineral mexims 'ud suit
   speshle facts ;
An' there 's where we 'll nick 'em,
   there 's where they 'll be lost :
For applyin' your princerple 's wut
   makes it cost,
An' folks don't want Fourth o' July t'
   interfere
With the business-consarns o' the rest
   o' the year,
No more 'n they want Sunday to pry
   an' to peek
Into wut they are doin' the rest o' the
   week.

A ginooine statesman should be on his
   guard,
Ef he *must* hev beliefs, nut to b'lieve
   'em tu hard ;
For, ez sure ez he does, he 'll be blar-
   tin' 'em out
'Thout regardin' the natur' o' man
   more 'n a spout,
Nor it don't ask much gumption to
   pick out a flaw
In a party whose leaders are loose in
   the jaw ;
An' so in our own case I ventur' to hint
Thet we 'd better nut air our 'perceedins in print,
Nor pass resserlootions ez long ez your
   arm
Thet may, ez things heppen to turn, do
   us harm ;
For when you 've done all your real
   meanin' to smother,
The darned things 'll up an' mean
   sunthin' or 'nother.
Jeff'son prob'ly meant wal with his
   " born free an' ekle,"
But it 's turned out a real crooked stick
   in the sekle :
It 's taken full eighty-odd year — don't
   you see ? —
From the pop'lar belief to root out thet
   idee,

An', arter all, suckers on 't keep buddin'
   forth
In the nat'lly onprincipled mind o' the
   North.
No, never say nothin' without you 're
   compelled tu,
An' then don't say nothin' thet you can
   be held tu,
Nor don't leave no friction-idees layin'
   loose
For the ign'ant to put to incend'ary use.

You know I 'm a feller thet keeps a
   skinned eye
On the leetle events thet go skurryin'
   by,
Coz it 's of'ner by them than by gret
   ones you 'll see
Wut the p'litickle weather is likely to
   be.
Now I don't think the South 's more 'n
   begun to be licked,
But I *du* think, ez Jeff says, the wind-
   bag 's gut pricked;
It 'll blow for a spell an' keep puffin'
   an' wheezin',
The tighter our army an' navy keep
   squeezin', —
For they can't help spread-eaglein' long
   'z ther' 's a mouth
To blow Enfield's Speaker thru lef' at
   the South.
But it 's high time for us to be settin'
   our faces
Towards reconstructin' the national
   basis,
With an eye to beginnin' agin on the
   jolly ticks
We used to chalk up 'hind the back-
   door o' politics;
An' the fus' thing 's to save wut of
   Slav'ry ther' 's lef'
Arter this (I mus' call it) imprudence
   o' Jeff:
For a real good Abuse, with its roots
   fur an' wide,
Is the kin' o' thing *I* like to hev on my
   side ;
A Scriptur' name makes it ez sweet ez
   a rose,
An' it 's tougher the older an' uglier it
   grows —
(I ain't speakin' now o' the righteous-
   ness of it,

But the p'litickle purchase It gives an'
   the profit).

Things look pooty squally, it must be
   allowed,
An' I don't see much signs of a bow in
   the cloud :
Ther' 's too many Deemocrats — lead-
   ers wut 's wuss —
Thet go for the Union 'thout carin' a cuss
Ef it helps ary party thet ever wuz
   heard on,
So our eagle ain't made a split Austrian
   bird on.
But ther' 's still some consarvative
   signs to be found
Thet shows the gret heart o' the People
   is sound :
(Excuse me for usin' a stump-phrase
   agin,
But, once in the way on 't, they *will*
   stick like sin :)
There 's Phillips, for instance, hez jes'
   ketched a Tartar
In the Law-'n'-Order Party of ole
   Cincinnater ;
An' the Compromise System ain't gone
   out o' reach,
Long 'z you keep the right limits on
   freedom o' speech.
'T warn't none too late, neither, to
   put on the gag,
For he 's dangerous now he goes in for
   the flag
Nut thet I altogether approve o' bad
   eggs,
They 're mos' gin'lly argymunt on its
   las' legs, —
An' their logic is ept to be tu indis-
   criminate,
Nor don't ollus wait the right objecs to
   'liminate ;
But there is a variety on 'em, you 'll
   find,
Jest ez usefle an' more, besides bein'
   refined, —
I mean o' the sort that are laid by the
   dictionary,
Sech ez sophisms an' cant, thet 'll
   kerry conviction ary
Way thet you want to the right class o'
   men,
An' are staler than all 't ever come
   from a hen :

"Disunion" done wal till our resh
  Southun friends
Took the savor all out on 't for national
  ends ;
But I guess "Abolition" 'll work a
  spell yit,
When the war 's done, an' so will
  "Forgive-an'-forgit."
Times mus' be pooty thoroughly out o'
  all jint,
Ef we can't make a good constitootional
  pint ;
An' the good time 'll come to be
  grindin' our exes,
When the war goes to seed in the nettle
  o' texes :
Ef Jon'than don't squirm, with sech
  helps to assist him,
I give up my faith in the free-suffrage
  system ;
Democ'cy wun't be nut a mite in-
  terestin',
Nor p'litikle capital much wuth in-
  vestin' ;
An' my notion is, to keep dark an' lay
  low
Till we see the right minute to put in
  our blow. —

But I 've talked longer now 'n I hed
  any idee,
An' ther' 's others you want to hear
  more 'n you du me ;
So I 'll set down an' give thet 'ere
  bottle a skrimmage,
For I 've spoke till I 'm dry ez a real
  graven image.

No. VI.

SUNTHIN' IN THE PASTORAL
LINE.

TO THE EDITORS OF THE ATLANTIC
MONTHLY.

JAALAM, 17th May, 1862.

GENTLEMEN, — At the special request of Mr. Biglow, I intended to inclose, together with his own contribution, (into which, at my suggestion, he

has thrown a little more of pastoral
sentiment than usual,) some passages
from my sermon on the day of the National Fast, from the text, "Remember
them that are in bonds, as bound with
them," *Heb.* xiii. 3. But I have not
leisure sufficient at present for the copying of them, even were I altogether satisfied with the production as it stands.
I should prefer, I confess, to contribute
the entire discourse to the pages of
your respectable miscellany, if it should
be found acceptable upon perusal, especially as I find the difficulty in selection of greater magnitude than I had
anticipated. What passes without
challenge in the fervour of oral delivery,
cannot always stand the colder criticism
of the closet. I am not so great an enemy of Eloquence as my friend Mr.
Biglow would appear to be from some
passages in his contribution for the current month. I would not, indeed,
hastily suspect him of covertly glancing
at myself in his somewhat caustick animadversions, albeit some of the phrases
he girds at are not entire strangers
to my lips. I am a more hearty ad-
mirer of the Puritans than seems now
to be the fashion, and believe, that, if
they Hebraized a little too much in
their speech, they showed remarkable
practical sagacity as statesmen and
founders. But such phenomena as Puritanism are the results rather of great
religious then of merely social convul-
sions, and do not long survive them.
So soon as an earnest conviction has
cooled into a phrase, its work is over,
and the best that can be done with it is
to bury it. *Ite, missa est.* I am inclined to agree with Mr. Biglow that
we cannot settle the great political
questions which are now presenting
themselves to the nation by the opinions of Jeremiah or Ezekiel as to the
wants and duties of the Jews in their
time, nor do I believe that an entire
community with their feelings and
views would be practicable or even
agreeable at the present day. At the
same time I could wish that their habit
of subordinating the actual to the
moral, the flesh to the spirit, and this

world to the other, were more common.
They had found out, at least, the great
military secret that soul weighs more
than body. — But I am suddenly called
to a sick-bed in the household of a valued parishioner.

With esteem and respect,
Your obedient servant,
HOMER WILBUR.

ONCE git a smell o' musk into a draw,
An' it clings hold like precerdents in
    law :
Your gra'ma'am put it there, — when,
    goodness knows, —
To jes' this-worldify her Sunday-clo'es ;
But the old chist wun't sarve her gran'-
    son's wife,
(For, 'thout new funnitoor, wut good in
    life ?)
An' so ole clawfoot, from the precinks
    dread
O' the spare chamber, slinks into the
    shed,
Where, dim with dust, it fust or last
    subsides
To holdin' seeds an' fifty things be-
    sides ;
But better days stick fast in heart an'
    husk,
An' all you keep in 't gits a scent o'
    musk.

Jes' so with poets : wut they 've airly
    read
Gits kind o' worked into their heart an'
    head,
So 's 't they can't seem to write but jest
    on sheers
With furrin countries or pfayed-out
    ideers,
Nor hev a feelin', ef it doos n't smack
O' wut some critter chose to feel 'way
    back :
This makes 'em talk o' daisies, larks,
    an' things,
Ez though we 'd nothin' here that
    blows an' sings, —
(Why, I 'd give more for one live bobo-
    link
Than a square mile o' larks in printer's
    ink,) —

This makes 'em think our fust o' May
    is May,
Which 't ain't, for all the almanicks can
    say.

O little city-gals, don't never go it
Blind on the word o' noospaper or poet !
They 're apt to puff, an' May-day sel-
    dom looks
Up in the country ez it doos in books ;
They 're no more like than hornets'-
    nests an' hives,
Or printed sarmons be to holy lives.
I, with my trouses perched on cow-
    hide boots,
Tuggin' my foundered feet out by the
    roots,
Hev seen ye come to fling on April's
    hearse
Your muslin nosegays from the mil-
    liner's,
Puzzlin' to find dry ground your queen
    to choose,
An' dance your throats sore in morock-
    er shoes :
I 've seen ye an' felt proud, thet, come
    wut would,
Our Pilgrim stock wuz pethed with
    hardihood.
Pleasure doos make us Yankees kind
    o' winch,
Ez though 't wuz sunthin' paid for by
    the inch ;
But yit we du contrive to worry thru,
Ef Dooty tells us thet the thing 's to
    du,
An' kerry a hollerday, ef we set out,
Ez stiddily ez though 't wuz a redoubt.

I, country-born an' bred, know where
    to find
Some blooms thet make the season suit
    the mind,
An' seem to metch the doubtin' blue-
    bird's notes, —
Half-vent'rin' liverworts in furry coats,
Bloodroots, whose rolled-up leaves ef
    you oncurl,
Each on 'em 's cradle to a baby-pearl, —
But these are jes' Spring's pickets ;
    sure ez sin,
The rebble frosts 'll try to drive 'em in ;
For half our May 's so awfully like
    May n't,

'T would rile a Shaker or an evrige
    saint;
Though I own up I like our back'ard
    springs
Thet kind o' haggle with their greens
    an' things,
An' when you 'most give up, 'thout
    more words
Toss the fields full o' blossoms, leaves,
    an' birds:
Thet 's Northun natur', slow an' apt to
    doubt,
But when it *does* git stirred, ther' 's no
    gin-out!

Fust come the blackbirds clatt'rin' in
    tall trees,
An' settlin' things in windy Congress-
    es, —
Queer politicians, though, for I 'll be
    skinned
Ef all on 'em don't head against the
    wind.
'Fore long the trees begin to show be-
    lief, —
The maple crimsons to a coral-reef,
Then saffern swarms swing off from all
    the willers
So plump they look like yaller caterpil-
    lars,
Then gray hossches'nuts leetle hands
    unfold
Softer 'n a baby's be at three days old:
Thet 's robin-redbreast's almanick; he
    knows
Thet arter this ther' 's only blossom-
    snows;
So, choosin' out a handy crotch an'
    spouse,
He goes to plast'rin' his adobë house.

Then seems to come a hitch, — things
    lag behind,
Till some fine mornin' Spring makes
    up her mind,
An' ez, when snow-swelled rivers cresh
    their dams
Heaped-up with ice thet dovetails in
    an' jams,
A leak comes spirtin' thru some pin-
    hole cleft,
Grows stronger, fercer, tears out right
    an' left,

Then all the waters bow themselves
    an' come,
Suddin, in one gret slope o' shedderin'
    foam,
Jes' so our Spring gits everythin' in
    tune
An' gives one leap from Aperl into June:
Then all comes crowdin' in; afore you
    think,
Young oak-leaves mist the side-hill
    woods with pink;
The catbird in the laylock-bush is loud;
The orchards turn to heaps o' rosy
    cloud;
Red-cedars blossom tu, though few
    folks know it,
An' look all dipt in sunshine like a
    poet;
The lime-trees pile their solid stacks o'
    shade
An' drows'ly simmer with the bees'
    sweet trade;
In ellum-shrouds the flashin' hangbird
    clings
An' for the summer vy'ge his ham-
    mock slings;
All down the loose-walled lanes in
    archin' bowers
The barb'ry droops its strings o' golden
    flowers,
Whose shrinkin' hearts the school-gals
    love to try
With pins, — they 'll worry yourn so,
    boys, bimeby!
But I don't love your cat'logue style, —
    do you? —
Ez ef to sell off Natur' by vendoo;
One word with blood in 't 's twice ez
    good ez two:
'Nuff sed, June's bridesman, poet o'
    the year,
Gladness on wings, the bobolink, is
    here;
Half-hid in tip-top apple-blooms he
    swings,
Or climbs aginst the breeze with quiv-
    erin' wings,
Or, givin' way to 't in a mock despair,
Runs down, a brook o' laughter, thru
    the air.

I ollus feel the sap start in my veins
In Spring, with curus heats an' prickly
    pains,

Thet drive me, when I git a chance, to
    walk
Off by myself to hev a privit talk
With a queer critter thet can't seem to
    'gree
Along o' me like most folks, — Mister
    Me.
Ther' 's times when I 'm unsoshle ez a
    stone,
An' sort o' suffercate to be alone, —
I 'm crowded jes' to think thet folks are
    nigh,
An' can't bear nothin' closer than the
    sky :
Now the wind 's full ez shifty in the
    mind
Ez wut it is ou'-doors, ef I ain't blind,
An' sometimes, in the fairest sou'west
    weather,
My innard vane pints east for weeks
    together,
My natur' gits all goose-flesh, an' my
    sins
Come drizzlin' on my conscience sharp
    ez pins :
Wal, et sech times I jes' slip out o'
    sight
An' take it out in a fair stan'-up fight
With the one cuss I can't lay on the
    shelf,
The crook'dest stick in all the heap, —
    Myself.

'T wuz so las' Sabbath arter meetin'-
    time :
Findin' my feelin's would n't noways
    rhyme
With nobody's, but off the hendle flew
An' took things from an east-wind pint
    o' view,
I started off to lose me in the hills
Where the pines be, up back o' 'Siah's
    Mills :
Pines, ef you 're blue, are the best friends
    I know,
They mope an' sigh an' sheer your feel-
    in's so, —
They hesh the ground beneath so, tu, I
    swan,
You half-forgit you 've gut a body on.
Ther' 's a small school'us' there where
    four roads meet,
The door-steps hollered out by little
    feet,

An' side-posts carved with names whose
    owners grew
To gret men, some on 'em, an' deacons,
    tu ;
'T ain't used no longer, coz the town
    hez gut
A high-school, where they teach the
    Lord knows wut :
Three-story larnin' 's pop'lar now ; I
    guess
We thriv' ez wal on jes' two stories
    less,
For it strikes me ther' 's sech a thing
    ez sinnin'
By overloadin' children's underpin-
    nin' :
Wal, here it wuz I larned my A B C,
An' it 's a kind o' favorite spot with
    me.

We 're curus critters : Now ain't jes'
    the minute
Thet ever fits us easy while we 're in
    it ;
Long ez 't wuz futur', 't would be per-
    fect bliss,
Soon ez it 's past, *thet* time 's wuth ten
    o' this ;
An' yit there ain't a man thet need be
    told
Thet Now 's the only bird lays eggs o'
    gold.
A knee-high lad, I used to plot an' plan
An' think 't wuz life's cap-sheaf to be a
    man ;
Now, gittin' gray, there 's nothin' I
    enjoy
Like dreamin' back along into a boy :
So the ole school'us' is a place I choose
Afore all others, ef I want to muse ;
I set down where I used to set, an' git
My boyhood back, an' better things
    with it, —
Faith, Hope, an' sunthin', ef it is n't
    Cherrity,
It 's want o' guile, an thet 's ez gret a
    rerrity, —
While Fancy's Cushin', free to Prince
    and Clown,
Makes the hard bench ez soft ez milk-
    weed-down.

Now, 'fore I knowed, thet Sabbath
    afternoon

When I sot out to tramp myself in tune,
I found me in the school'us' on my
 seat,
Drummin' the march to No-wheres with
 my feet.
Thinkin' o' nothin', I 've heerd ole
 folks say
Is a hard kind o' dooty in its way :
It 's thinkin' everythin' you ever knew,
Or ever hearn, to make your feelin's
 blue.
I sot there tryin' thet on for a spell :
I thought o' the Rebellion, then o'
 Hell,
Which some folks tell ye now is jest a
 metterfor
(A the'ry, p'raps, it wun't *feel* none the
 better for) ;
I thought o' Reconstruction, wut we 'd
 win
Patchin' our patent self-blow-up agin :
I thought ef this 'ere milkin' o' the
 wits,
So much a month, warn't givin' Natur'
 fits, —
Ef folks warn't druv, findin' their own
 milk fail,
To work the cow thet hez an iron tail,
An' ef idees 'thout ripenin' in the pan
Would send up cream to humor ary
 man :
From this to thet I let my worryin'
 creep,
Till finally I must ha' fell asleep.

Our lives in sleep are some like streams
 thet glide
'Twixt flesh an' sperrit boundin' on each
 side,
Where both shores' shadders kind o'
 mix an' mingle
In sunthin' thet ain't jes' like either
 single ;
An' when you cast off moorin's from
 To-day,
An' down towards To-morrer drift
 away,
The imiges thet tengle on the stream
Make a new upside-down'ard world o'
 dream :
Sometimes they seem like sunrise-
 streaks an' warnin's
D' wut 'll be in Heaven on Sabbath-
 mornin's,

An', mixed right in ez ef jest out o
 spite,
Sunthin' thet says your supper ain't
 gone right.
I 'm gret on dreams, an' often when I
 wake,
I 've lived so much it makes my mem'ry
 ache,
An' can't skurce take a cat-nap in my
 cheer
'Thout hevin' 'em, some good, some
 bad, all queer.

Now I wuz settin' where I 'd ben, it
 seemed,
An' ain't sure yit whether I r'ally
 dreamed,
Nor, ef I did, how long I might ha'
 slep',
When I hearn some un stompin' up the
 step,
An' lookin' round, ef two an' two make
 four,
I see a Pilgrim Father in the door.
He wore a steeple-hat, tall boots, an'
 spurs
With rowels to 'em big ez ches'nut-
 burrs,
An' his gret sword behind him sloped
 away
Long 'z a man's speech thet dunno wut
 to say. —
" Ef your name 's Biglow, an' your
 given-name
Hosee," sez he, " it 's arter you I came ;
I 'm your gret-gran'ther multiplied by
 three." —
" My *wut ?* " sez I. — " Your gret-gret-
 gret," sez he :
" You would n't ha' never ben here but
 for me.
Two hundred an' three year ago this
 May
The ship I come in sailed up Boston
 Bay ;
I 'd been a cunnle in our Civil War, —
But wut on airth hev *you* gut up one
 for ?
Coz we du things in England, 't ain't for
 you
To git a notion you can du 'em tu :
I 'm told you write in public prints : ef
 true,

't 's nateral you should know a thing
   or two." —
"Thet air 's an argymunt I can't endorse, —
'T would prove, coz you wear spurs,
   you kep' a horse:
For brains," sez I, "wutever you may
   think,
Ain't boun' to cash the drafs o' pen-an'-
   ink, —
Though mos' folks write ez ef they
   hoped jes' quickenin'
The churn would argoo skim-milk into
   thickenin';
But skim-milk ain't a thing to change
   its view
O' wut it 's meant for more 'n a smoky
   flue.
But du pray tell me, 'fore we furder
   go,
How in all Natur' did you come to
   know
'Bout our affairs," sez I, "in Kingdom-
   Come?" —
"Wal, I worked round at sperrit-rap-
   pin' some,
An' danced the tables till their legs
   wuz gone,
In hopes o' larnin' wut wuz goin' on,"
Sez he, "but mejums lie so like all-
   split
Thet I concluded it wuz best to quit.
But, come now, ef you wun't confess
   to knowin',
You 've some conjectures how the
   thing 's a-goin'." —
"Gran'ther," sez I, "a vane warn't
   never known
Nor asked to hev a jedgment of its
   own;
An' yit, ef 't ain't gut rusty in the jints,
It 's safe to trust its say on certin pints:
It knows the wind's opinions to a T,
An' the wind settles wut the weather 'll
   be."
"I never thought a scion of our stock
Could grow the wood to make a
   weathercock;
When I wuz younger 'n you, skurce
   more 'n a shaver,
No airthly wind," sez he, "could make
   me waver!"
(Ez he said this, he clinched his jaw an'
   forehead,

Hitchin' his belt to bring his sword-
   hilt forrard.) —
"Jes' so it wuz with me," sez I, "I
   swow,
When I wuz younger 'n wut you see
   me now, —
Nothin' from Adam's fall to Huldy's
   bonnet,
Thet I warn't full-cocked with my jedg-
   ment on it;
But now I 'm gittin' on in life, I find
It 's a sight harder to make up my
   mind, —
Nor I don't often try tu, when events
Will du it for me free of all expense.
The moral question 's ollus plain
   enough, —
It 's jes' the human-natur' side thet 's
   tough;
Wut 's best to think may n't puzzle me
   nor you, —
The pinch comes in decidin' wut to
   du;
Ef you read History, all runs smooth
   ez grease,
Coz there the men ain't nothin' more 'n
   idees, —
But come to make it, ez we must to-
   day,
Th' idees hev arms an' legs an' stop
   the way:
It 's easy fixin' things in facts an' fig-
   gers, —
They can't resist, nor warn't brought
   up with niggers;
But come to try your the'ry on, — why,
   then
Your facts an' figgers change to ign'ant
   men
Actin' ez ugly —" — "Smite 'em hip
   an' thigh!"
Sez gran'ther, "and let every man-
   child die!
Oh for three weeks o' Cromwle an' the
   Lord!
Up, Isr'el, to your tents an' grind the
   sword!" —
"Thet kind o' thing worked wal in ole
   Judee,
But you forgit how long it 's ben A. D.;
You think thet 's ellerkence, — I call it
   shoddy,
A thing," sez I, "wun't cover soul nor
   body;

I like the plain afl-wool o' common-
sense,
Thet warms ye now, an' will a twelve-
month hence.
You took to follerin' where the Proph-
ets beckoned,
An', fust you knowed on, back come
Charles the Second ;
Now wut I want 's to hev all *we* gain
stick,
An' not to start Millennium too quick ;
We hain't to punish only, but to keep,
An' the cure 's gut to go a cent'ry
deep."
"Wal, milk-an'-water ain't the best o'
glue,"
Sez he, " an' so you'll find before you
're thru ;
Ef reshness venters sunthin', shilly-
shally
Loses ez often wut 's ten times the
vally.
Thet exe of ourn, when Charles's neck
gut split,
Opened a gap thet ain't bridged over
yit :
Slav'ry 's your Charles, the Lord hez
gin the exe — "
"Our Charles," sez I, " hez gut eight
million necks.
The hardest question ain't the black
man's right,
The trouble is to 'mancipate the white ;
One 's chained in body an' can be sot
free,
But t'other 's chained in soul to an
idee :
It 's a long job, but we shall worry thru
it ;
Ef bagnets fail, the spellin'-book must
du it."
"Hosee," sez he, " I think you 're
goin' to fail :
The rettlesnake ain't dangerous in the
tail ;
This 'ere rebellion 's nothin' but the
rettle,
You 'll stomp on thet an' think you 've
won the bettle ;
It 's Slavery thet 's the fangs an' thinkin' head,
An' ef you want selvation, cresh it
dead, —
An' cresh it suddin, or you 'll larn by
waitin'

Thet Chance wun't stop to listen te
debatin' ! —
"God's truth !" sez I, — "an' ef *I*
held the club,
An' knowed jes' where to strike, —
but there 's the rub ! " —
"Strike soon," sez he, " or you 'll be
deadly ailin', —
Folks thet 's afeared to fail are sure o'
failin' ;
God hates your sneakin' creturs thet
believe
He 'll settle things they run away an'
leave ! "
He brought his foot down fercely, ez
he spoke,
An' give me sech a startle thet I woke.

No. VII.

LATEST VIEWS OF MR. BIG-
LOW.

PRELIMINARY NOTE.

[IT is with feelings of the liveliest
pain that we inform our readers of the
death of the Reverend Homer Wilbur,
A. M., which took place suddenly, by
an apoplectic stroke, on the afternoon
of Christmas day, 1862. Our venerable friend (for so we may venture to
call him, though we never enjoyed the
high privilege of his personal acquaintance) was in his eighty-fourth year,
having been born June 12, 1779, at
Pigsgusset Precinct (now West Jeru-
sha) in the then District of Maine
Graduated with distinction at Hubville
College in 1805, he pursued his theological studies with the late Reverend
Preserved Thacker, D. D., and was
called to the charge of the First Society in Jaalam in 1809, where he remained till his death.

"As an antiquary he has probably
left no superior, if, indeed, an equal,"
writes his friend and colleague, the
Reverend Jeduthun Hitchcock, to
whom we are indebted for the above
facts ; "in proof of which I need only
allude to his 'History of Jaalam,
Genealogical, Topographical, and Ec-

clesiastical,' 1849, which has won him an eminent and enduring place in our more solid and useful literature. It is only to be regretted that his intense application to historical studies should have so entirely withdrawn him from the pursuit of poetical composition, for which he was endowed by Nature with a remarkable aptitude. His well-known hymn, beginning, ' With clouds of care encompassed round,' has been attributed in some collections to the late President Dwight, and it is hardly presumptuous to affirm that the simile of the rainbow in the eighth stanza would do no discredit to that polished pen."

We regret that we have not room at present for the whole of Mr. Hitchcock's exceedingly valuable communication. We hope to lay more liberal extracts from it before our readers at an early day. A summary of its contents will give some notion of its importance and interest. It contains: 1st, A biographical sketch of Mr. Wilbur, with notices of his predecessors in the pastoral office, and of eminent clerical contemporaries ; 2d, An obituary of deceased, from the Punkin-Falls " Weekly Parallel " ; 3d, A list of his printed and manuscript productions and of projected works ; 4th, Personal anecdotes and recollections, with specimens of table-talk ; 5th, A tribute to his relict, Mrs. Dorcas (Pilcox) Wilbur ; 6th, A list of graduates fitted for different colleges by Mr. Wilbur, with biographical memoranda touching the more distinguished ; 7th, Concerning learned, charitable, and other societies, of which Mr. Wilbur was a member, and of those with which, had his life been prolonged, he would doubtless have been associated, with a complete catalogue of such Americans as have been Fellows of the Royal Society ; 8th, A brief summary of Mr. Wilbur's latest conclusions concerning the Tenth Horn of the Beast in its special application to recent events for which the public, as Mr. Hitchcock assures us, have been waiting with feelings of lively anticipation ; 9th, Mr. Hitchcock's own views on the same topic ; and,

10th, A brief essay on the importance of local histories. It will be apparent that the duty of preparing Mr. Wilbur's biography could not have fallen into more sympathetic hands.

In a private letter with which the reverend gentleman has since favored us, he expresses the opinion that Mr. Wilbur's life was shortened by our unhappy civil war. It disturbed his studies, dislocated all his habitual associations and trains of thought, and unsettled the foundations of a faith, rather the result of habit than conviction, in the capacity of man for self-government. " Such has been the felicity of my life," he said to Mr. Hitchcock, on the very morning of the day he died, "that, through the divine mercy, I could always say, *Summum nec metuo diem, nec opto.* It has been my habit, as you know, on every recurrence of this blessed anniversary, to read Milton's ' Hymn of the Nativity' till its sublime harmonies so dilated my soul and quickened its spiritual sense that I seemed to hear that other song which gave assurance to the shepherds that there was One who would lead them also in green pastures and beside the still waters. But to-day I have been unable to think of anything but that mournful text, 'I came not to send peace, but a sword,' and, did it not smack of pagan presumptuousness, could almost wish I had never lived to see this day."

Mr. Hitchcock also informs us that his friend "lies buried in the Jaalam graveyard, under a large red-cedar which he specially admired. A neat and substantial monument is to be erected over his remains, with a Latin epitaph written by himself ; for he was accustomed to say, pleasantly, 'that there was at least one occasion in a scholar's life when he might show the advantages of a classical training.'"

The following fragment of a letter addressed to us, and apparently intended to accompany Mr. Biglow's contribution to the present number, was found upon his table after his decease. — EDITORS ATLANTIC MONTHLY.]

TO THE EDITORS OF THE ATLANTIC
MONTHLY.

JAALAM, 24th Dec., 1862.

RESPECTED SIRS, — The infirm state
of my bodily health would be a sufficient apology for not taking up the pen
at this time, wholesome as I deem it for
the mind to apricate in the shelter of
epistolary confidence, were it not that a
considerable, I might even say a large,
number of individuals in this parish expect from their pastor some publick expression of sentiment at this crisis.
Moreover, *Qui tacitus ardet magis
uritur.* In trying times like these, the
besetting sin of undisciplined minds is
to seek refuge from inexplicable realities in the dangerous stimulant of angry partisanship or the indolent narcot-
ick of vague and hopeful vaticination :
fortunamque suo temperat arbitrio.
Both by reason of my age and my natural temperament, I am unfitted for
either. Unable to penetrate the in-
scrutable judgments of God, I am more
than ever thankful that my life has been
prolonged till I could in some small
measure comprehend His mercy. As
there is no man who does not at some
time render himself amenable to the
one, — *quum vix justus sit securus,* —
so there is none that does not feel himself in daily need of the other.

I confess, I cannot feel, as some do,
a personal consolation for the manifest
evils of this war in any remote or con-
tingent advantages that may spring
from it. I am old and weak, I can bear
little, and can scarce hope to see better
days ; nor is it any adequate compensation to know that Nature is young and
strong and can bear much. Old men
philosophize over the past, but the
present is only a burthen and a weariness. The one lies before them like a
placid evening landscape ; the other is
full of the vexations and anxieties of
housekeeping. It may be true enough
that *miscet hæc illis, prohibetque Clotho fortunam stare,* but he who said it
was fain at last to call in Atropos with
her shears before her time ; and I cannot help selfishly mourning that the

fortune of our Republick could not at
least stay till my days were numbered.

Tibullus would find the origin of wars
in the great exaggeration of riches, and
does not stick to say that in the days
of the beechen trencher there was
peace. But averse as I am by nature
from all wars, the more as they have
been especially fatal to libraries, I
would have this one go on till we are
reduced to wooden platters again, rather
than surrender the principle to defend
which it was undertaken. Though I
believe Slavery to have been the cause
of it, by so thoroughly demoralizing
Northern politicks for its own purposes
as to give opportunity and hope to treason, yet I would not have our thought
and purpose diverted from their true
object, — the maintenance of the idea of
Government. We are not merely sup-
pressing an enormous riot, but contending for the possibility of permanent
order coexisting with democratical fick-
leness ; and while I would not super-
stitiously venerate form to the sacrifice
of substance, neither would I forget
that an adherence to precedent and
prescription can alone give that continuity and coherence under a democratical constitution which are inherent
in the person of a despotick monarch
and the selfishness of an aristocratical
class. *Stet pro ratione voluntas* is as
dangerous in a majority as in a tyrant.

I cannot allow the present production
of my young friend to go out without a
protest from me against a certain ex-
tremeness in his views, more pardonable in the poet than in the philosopher.
While I agree with him, that the only
cure for rebellion is suppression by
force, yet I must animadvert upon
certain phrases where I seem to see a
coincidence with a popular fallacy on
the subject of compromise. On the one
hand there are those who do not see
that the vital principle of Government
and the seminal principle of Law cannot properly be made a subject of compromise at all, and on the other those
who are equally blind to the truth that
without a compromise of individual

opinions, interests, and even rights, no
society would be possible. *In medio
tutissimus.* For my own part, I would
gladly ——

——

Ef I a song or two could n make
    Like rockets druv by their own burn-
        in',
All leap an' light, to leave a wake
    Men's hearts an' faces skyward turn-
        in'! —
But, it strikes me, 't ain't jest the time
    Fer stringin' words with settisfaction:
Wut 's wanted now 's the silent rhyme
    'Twixt upright Will an' downright
        Action.

Words, ef you keep 'em, pay their keep,
    But gabble 's the short cut to ruin;
It 's gratis, (gals half-price,) but cheap
    At no rate, ef it henders doin';
Ther' 's nothin' wuss, 'less 't is to set
    A martyr-prem'um upon jawrin':
Teapots git dangerous, ef you shet
    Their lids down on 'em with Fort
        Warren.

'Bout long enough it 's ben discussed
    Who sot the magazine afire,
An' whether, ef Bob Wickliffe bust,
    'T would scare us more or blow us
        higher.
D' ye s'pose the Gret Foreseer's plan
    Wuz settled fer him in town-meetin'?
Or thet ther' 'd ben no Fall o' Man,
    Ef Adam 'd on'y bit a sweetin'?

Oh, Jon'than, ef you want to be
    A rugged chap agin an' hearty,
Go fer wutever 'll hurt Jeff D.,
    Nut wut 'll boost up ary party.
Here 's hell broke loose, an' we lay flat
    With half the univarse a-singein',
Till Sen'tor This an' Gov'nor Thet
    Stop squabblin' fer the garding-ingin.

It 's war we 're in, not politics;
    It 's systems wrastlin' now, not
        parties;
An' victory in the eend 'll fix
    Where longest will an' truest heart is.

An' wut 's the Guv'ment folks about?
    Tryin' to hope ther' 's nothin' doin',
An' look ez though they did n't doubt
    Sunthin' pertickler wuz a-brewin'.

Ther' 's critters yit thet talk an' act
    Fer wut they call Conciliation;
They 'd hand a buff'lo-drove a tract
    When they wuz madder than all
        Bashan.
Conciliate? it jest means *be kicked*,
    No metter how they phrase an' tone
        it;
It means thet we 're to set down licked,
    Thet we 're poor shotes an' glad to
        own it!

A war on tick 's ez dear 'z the deuce,
    But it wun't leave no lastin' traces,
Ez 't would to make a sneakin' truce
    Without no moral specie-basis:
Ef green-backs ain't nut jest the cheese,
    I guess ther' 's evils thet 's ex-
        tremer, —
Fer instance, — shinplaster idees
    Like them put out by Gov'nor Sey-
        mour.

Last year, the Nation, at a word,
    When tremblin' Freedom cried to
        shield her,
Flamed weldin' into one keen sword
    Waitin' an' longin' fer a wielder:
A splendid flash! — but how 'd the
        grasp
    With sech a chance ez thet wuz tally?
Ther' warn't no meanin' in our clasp, —
    Half this, half thet, all shilly-shally.

More men? More Man! It 's there
        we fail,
    Weak plans grow weaker yit by
        lengthenin':
Wut use in addin' to the tail,
    When it 's the head 's in need o'
        strengthenin'?
We wanted one thet felt all Chief
    From roots o' hair to sole o' stockin',
Square-sot with thousan'-ton belief
    In him an' us, ef earth went rockin'!

Ole Hick'ry would n't ha' stood see-
        saw
    'Bout doin' things till they wuz done
        with, —

He'd smashed the tables o' the Law
   In time o' need to load his gun with;
He could n't see but jest one side, —
   Ef his, 't wuz God's, an' thet wuz
      plenty;
An' so his "*Forrards!*" multiplied
   An army's fightin' weight by twenty.

But this 'ere histin', creak, creak, creak,
   Your cappen's heart up with a der-
      rick,
This tryin' to coax a lightnin'-streak
   Out of a half-discouraged hay-rick,
This hangin' on mont' arter mont'
   Fer one sharp purpose 'mongst the
      twitter, —
I tell ye, it doos kind o' stunt
   The peth and sperit of a critter.

In six months where'll the People be,
   Ef leaders look on revolution
Ez though it wuz a cup o' tea,
   Jest social el'ments in solution?
This weighin' things doos wal enough
   When war cools down, an' comes to
      writin';
But while it 's makin', the true stuff
   Is pison-mad, pig-headed fightin'.

Democ'acy gives every man
   A right to be his own oppressor;
But a loose Gov'ment ain't the plan,
   Helpless ez spilled beans on a dres-
      ser:
I tell ye one thing we might larn
   From them smart critters, the Seced-
      ers, —
Ef bein' right 's the fust consarn,
   The 'fore-the-fust 's cast-iron leaders.

But 'pears to me I see some signs
   Thet we 're a-goin' to use our senses:
Jeff druv us into these hard lines,
   An' ough' to bear his half th' ex-
      penses;
Slavery 's Secession's heart an' will,
   South, North, East, West, where'er
      you find it,
An' ef it drors into War's mill,
   D' ye say them thunder-stones sha'
      n't grind it?

D' ye s'pose, ef Jeff giv *him* a lick,
   Ole Hick'ry 'd tried his head to sof'n

So 's 't would n't hurt thet ebony stick
   Thet 's made our side see stars so
      of'n?
"No!" he 'd ha' thundered, "on your
      knees,
   An' own one flag, one road to glory!
Soft-heartedness, in times like these,
   Shows sof'ness in the upper story!"

An' why should we kick up a muss
   About the Pres'dunt's proclamation?
It ain't a-goin' to lib'rate us,
   Ef we don't like emancipation:
The right to be a cussed fool
   Is safe from all devices human,
It 's common (ez a gin'l rule)
   To every critter born o' woman.

So *we* 're all right, an' I, fer one,
   Don't think our cause 'll lose in vally
By rammin' Scriptur' in our gun,
   An' gittin' Natur' fer an ally:
Thank God, say I, fer even a plan
   To lift one human bein's level,
Give one more chance to make a man,
   Or, anyhow, to spile a devil!

Not thet I 'm one thet much expec'
   Millennium by express to-morrer;
They *will* miscarry, — I rec'lec'
   Tu many on 'em, to my sorrer:
Men ain't made angels in a day,
   No matter how you mould an' labor
      'em,
Nor 'riginal ones, I guess, don't stay
   With Abe so of'n ez with Abraham.

The'ry thinks Fact a pooty thing,
   An' wants the banns read right en-
      suin';
But fact wun't noways wear the ring
   'Thout years o' settin' up an' wooin':
Though, arter all, Time's dial-plate
   Marks cent'ries with the minute-
      finger,
An' Good can't never come tu late,
   Though it doos seem to try an' linger.

An' come wut will, I think it 's grand
   Abe 's gut his will et last bloom-fur-
      naced
In trial-flames till it 'll stand
   The strain o' bein' in deadly earnest:

Thet 's wut we want, — we want to
know
The folks on our side hez the bravery
To b'lieve ez hard, come weal, come
woe,
In Freedom ez Jeff doos in Slavery.

Set the two forces foot to foot,
An' every man knows who 'll be win-
ner,
Whose faith in God hez ary root
Thet goes down deeper than his din-
ner:
Then 't will be felt from pole to pole,
Without no need o' proclamation,
Earth's Biggest Country 's gut her soul
An' risen up Earth's Greatest Na-
tion!

No. VIII.

KETELOPOTOMACHIA.

PRELIMINARY NOTE.

In the month of February, 1866, the
editors of the "Atlantic Monthly"
received from the Rev. Mr. Hitchcock
of Jaalam a letter enclosing the maca-
ronic verses which follow, and promising to send more, if more should be
communicated. "They were rapped
out on the evening of Thursday last
past," he says, "by what claimed to
be the spirit of my late predecessor in
the ministry here, the Rev. Dr. Wilbur, through the medium of a young
man at present domiciled in my family.
As to the possibility of such spiritual
manifestations, or whether they be properly so entitled, I express no opinion, as
there is a division of sentiment on that
subject in the parish, and many persons
of the highest respectability in social
standing entertain opposing views.
The young man who was improved as
a medium submitted himself to the experiment with manifest reluctance, and
is still unprepared to believe in the
authenticity of the manifestations.
During his residence with me his de-

portment has always been exemplary;
he has been constant in his attendance
upon our family devotions and the public ministrations of the Word, and has
more than once privately stated to me,
that the latter had often brought him
under deep concern of mind. The
table is an ordinary quadrupedal one,
weighing about thirty pounds, three
feet seven inches and a half in height,
four feet square on the top, and of
beech or maple, I am not definitely prepared to say which. It had once belonged to my respected predecessor,
and had been, so far as I can learn upon
careful inquiry, of perfectly regular and
correct habits up to the evening in
question. On that occasion the young
man previously alluded to had been
sitting with his hands resting carelessly
upon it, while I read over to him at his
request certain portions of my last
Sabbath's discourse. On a sudden the
rappings, as they are called, commenced
to render themselves audible, at first
faintly, but in process of time more
distinctly and with violent agitation of
the table. The young man expressed
himself both surprised and pained by
the wholly unexpected, and, so far as
he was concerned, unprecedented occurrence. At the earnest solicitation,
however, of several who happened to
be present, he consented to go on with
the experiment, and with the assistance
of the alphabet commonly employed in
similar emergencies, the following communication was obtained and written
down immediately by myself. Whether
any, and if so, how much weight should
be attached to it, I venture no decision.
That Dr. Wilbur had sometimes employed his leisure in Latin versification
I have ascertained to be the case, though
all that has been discovered of that nature among his papers consists of some
fragmentary passages of a version into
hexameters of portions of the Song of
Solomon. These I had communicated
about a week or ten days previous [ly]
to the young gentleman who officiated
as medium in the communication afterwards received. I have thus, I believe,
stated all the material facts that have

any elucidative bearing upon this mysterious occurrence."

So far Mr. Hitchcock, who seems perfectly master of Webster's unabridged quarto, and whose flowing style leads him into certain further expatiations for which we have not room. We have since learned that the young man he speaks of was a sophomore, put under his care during a sentence of rustication from —— College, where he had distinguished himself rather by physical experiments on the comparative power of resistance in window-glass to various solid substances, than in the more regular studies of the place. In answer to a letter of inquiry, the professor of Latin says, "There was no harm in the boy that I know of beyond his loving mischief more than Latin, nor can I think of any spirits likely to possess him except those commonly called animal. He was certainly not remarkable for his Latinity, but I see nothing in verses you enclose that would lead me to think them beyond his capacity, or the result of any special inspiration whether of beech or maple. Had that of *birch* been tried upon him earlier and more faithfully, the verses would perhaps have been better in quality and certainly in quantity." This exact and thorough scholar then goes on to point out many false quantities and barbarisms. It is but fair to say, however, that the author, whoever he was, seems not to have been unaware of some of them himself, as is shown by a great many notes appended to the verses as we received them, and purporting to be by Scaliger, Bentley and others, — among them the *Esprit de Voltaire!* These we have omitted as clearly meant to be humorous and altogether failing therein.

Though entirely satisfied that the verses are altogether unworthy of Mr. Wilbur, who seems to have been a tolerable Latin scholar after the fashion of his day, yet we have determined to print them here partly as belonging to the *res gestæ* of this collection, and partly as a warning to their putative author which may keep him from such indecorous pranks for the future.

KETTELOPOTOMACHIA.

P. Ovidii Nasonis carmen heroicum macaronicum perplexametrum, inter Getas getice more compostum, denuo per medium ardentispiritualem, adjuvante mensa diabolicæ obsessâ, recuperatum, curâque Jo. Conradi Schwarzii umbræ, aliis necnon plurimis adjuvantibus, restitutum.

LIBER I.

Punctorum garretos colens et cellara
  Quinque,
Gutteribus quæ et gaudes sundayam
  abstingere frontem,
Plerumque insidos solita fluitare liquore
Tanglepedem quem homines appellant
  Di quoque rotgut,
Pimpliidis, rubicundaque, Musa, O,   5
  bourbonolensque,
Fenianas rixas procul, alma, brogipotentis
Patricii cyathos iterantis et horrida
  bella,
Backos dum virides viridis Brigitta
  remittit,
Linquens, eximios celebrem, da, Virginienses
Rowdes, præcipue et Te, heros alte,   10
  Polarde!
Insignes juvenesque, illo certamine
  lictos,
Colemane, Tylere, nec vos oblivione
  relinquam.

Ampla aquilæ invictæ fausto est sub
  tegmine terra,
Backyfer, ooiskeo pollens, ebenoque
  bipede,
Socors præsidum et altrix (denique   15
  quidruminantium),
Duplefveorum uberrima; illis et integre
  cordi est
Deplere assidue et sine proprio incommodo fiscum;
Nunc etiam placidum hoc opus invictiue secuti,
Goosam aureos ni eggos voluissent immo necare
Quæ peperit, saltem ac de illis meliora   20
  merentem.
  Condidit hanc Smithius Dux, Captinus inclytus ille
Regis Ulyssæ instar, docti arcum in
  tendere longum.

Condidit ille Johnsmith, Virginiamque
   vocavit,
Settledit autem Jacobus rex, nomine
   primus,
Rascalis implens ruptis, blagardisque
   deboshtis,   25
Militibusque ex Falstaffi legione fugatis
Wenchisque illi quas poterant seducere
   nuptas ;
Virgineum, ah, littus matronis talibus
   impar !
Progeniem stirpe ex hoc non sine stig-
   mate ducunt
Multi sese qui jactant regum esse ne-
   potes :   30
Haud omnes, Mater, genitos quæ nu-
   per habebas
Bello fortes, consilio cautos, virtute
   decoros,
Jamque et habes, sparso si patrio in
   sanguine virtus,
Mostrabisque iterum, antiquis sub as-
   tris reducta !
De illis qui upkikitant, dicebam, rum-
   pora tanta,   35
Letcheris et Floydis magnisque Extra
   ordine Billis ;
Est his prisca fides jurare et breakere
   wordum ;
Poppere fellerum a tergo, aut stickere
   clam bowiknifo,
Haud sane facinus, dignum sed victrice
   lauro ;
Larrupere et nigerum, factum præstan-
   tius ullo :   40
Ast chlamydem piciplumatam, Icariam,
   flito et ineptam,
Yanko gratis induere, illum et valido
   railo
Insuper acri equitare docere est hos-
   pitio uti.
Nescio an ille Polardus duplefveori-
   bus ortus,
Sed reputo potius de radice poorwite-
   manorum ;   45
Fortuiti proles, ni fallor, Tylerus erat
Præsidis, omnibus ab Whiggis nomi-
   natus a poor cuss ;
Et nobilem tertium evincit venerabile
   nomen.
Ast animosi omnes bellique ad tympana
   ha ! ha !
Vociferant læti, procul et si proelia,
   sive   50

Hostem incautum atsito possint shoot-
   ere salvi ;
Imperiique capaces, esset si stylus
   agmen,
Pro dulci spoliabant et sine dangere
   fito.
Præ ceterisque Polardus : si Secessia
   licta,
Se nunquam licturum jurat, res et un-
   heardof,   55
Verbo hæsit, similisque audaci roosteri
   invicto,
Dunghilli solitus rex pullos whoppere
   molles,
Grantum, hirelingos stripes quique et
   splendida tollunt
Sidera, et Yankos, territum et omnem
   sarsuit orbem.
Usque dabant operam isti omnes,
   noctesque diesque,   60
Samuelem demulgere avunculum, id
   vero siccum ;
Uberibus sed ejus, et horum est culpa,
   remotis,
Parvam domi vaccam, nec mora mini-
   ma, quærunt,
Lacticarentem autem et droppam vix
   in die dantem ;
Reddite avunculi, et exclamabant, reddite pappam !   65
Polko sane consule, gemens, Billy im-
   murmurat Extra ;
Echo respondit, thesauro ex vacuo,
   pappam !
Frustra explorant pocketa, ruber nare
   repertum ;
Officia expulsi aspiciunt rapta, et Para-
   disum
Occlusum, viridesque haud illis nascere
   backos ;   70
Stupent tunc oculis madidis spittantque
   silenter.
Adhibere usu ast longo vires prorsus
   inepti,
Si non ut qui grindeat axve trabemve
   revolvat,
Virginiam excruciant totis nunc might-
   ibu' matrem :
Non melius, puta, nono panis dimid-
   iumne est ?   75
Readere ibi non posse est casus commoner ullo ;
Tanto intentius imprimere est opus erge
   statuta :

Nemo propterea pejor, melior, sine
   doubto,
Obtineat qui contractum, si et postea
   rhino ;
Ergo Polardus, si quis, inexsuperabilis
   heros,   80
Colemanus impavidus nondum, atque
   in purpure natus
Tylerus Iohanides celerisque in flito
   Nathaniel,
Quisque optans digitos in tantum stick-
   ere pium,
Adstant accincti imprimere aut perrum-
   pere leges :
Quales a miserum rabidi tres ægre
   molossi,   85
Quales aut dubium textum atra in veste
   ministri,
Tales circumstabant nunc nostri inopes
   hoc job.
   Hisque Polardus voce canoro talia
   fatus :
Primum autem, veluti est mos, præceps
   quisque liquorat,
Quisque et Nicotianum ingens quid
   inserit atrum,   90
Heroûm nitidum decus et solamen avi-
   tum,
Masticat ac simul altisonans, spittatque
   profuse :
Quis de Virginia meruit præstantius
   unquam ?
Quis se pro patria curavit impigre tu-
   tum ?
Speechisque articulisque hominum quis
   fortior ullus,   95
Ingeminans pennæ lickos et vulnera
   vocis ?
Quisnam putidius (hic) sarsuit Yanki-
   nimicos,
Sæpius aut dedit ultro datam et broke
   his parolam ?
Mente inquassatus solidaque, tyranno
   minante,
Horrisonis (hic) bombis mœnia et alta
   quatente,   100
Sese promptum (hic) jactans Yankos
   lickere centum,
Atque ad lastum invictus non surrendi-
   dit unquam ?
Ergo haud meddlite, posco, mique re-
   linquite (hic) hoc job,
Si non —— knifunque enormem mos-
   trat spittatque tremendus.

Dixerat : ast alii reliquorant et sin
   pauso   105
Pluggos incumbunt maxillis, uterque
   vicissim
Certamine innocuo valde madidam
   inquinit assem :
Tylerus autem, dumque liquorat aridus
   hostis,
Mirum aspicit duplumque bibentem,
   astante Lyæo ;
Ardens impavidusque edidit tamen im-
   pia verba ;   110
Duplum quamvis te aspicio, esses atque
   viginti,
Mendacem dicerem totumque (hic)
   thrasherem acervum ;
Nempe et thrasham, doggonatus (hic)
   sim nisi faxem ;
Lambastabo omnes catawompositer-
   (hic)-que chawam !
Dixit et impulsus Ryeo ruitur bene ti-
   tus,   115
Illi nam gravidum caput et laterem
   habet in hatto.
   Hunc inhiat titubansque Polardus,
   optat et illum
Stickere inermem, protegit autem rite
   Lyæus,
Et pronos geminos, oculis dubitantibus,
   heros
Cernit et irritus hostes, dumque excogi-
   tat utrum   120
Primum inpitchere, corruit, inter utros-
   que recumbit,
Magno asino similis nimio sub pondere
   quassus :
Colemanus hos mœstus, triste ruminans-
   que solamen,
Inspicit hiccans, circumspittat terque
   cubantes ;
Funereisque his ritibus humidis inde
   solutis,   125
Sternitur, invalidusque illis superincidit
   infans :
Hos sepelit somnus et snorunt corniso-
   nantes,
Watchmanus inscios ast calybooso
   deinde reponit.

No. IX.

[THE Editors of the "Atlantic" have
received so many letters of inquiry con-

cerning the literary remains of the late Mr. Wilbur, mentioned by his colleague and successor, Rev. Jeduthan Hitchcock, in a communication from which we made some extracts in our number for February, 1863, and have been so repeatedly urged to print some part of them for the gratification of the public, that they felt it their duty at least to make some effort to satisfy so urgent a demand. They have accordingly carefully examined the papers intrusted to them, but find most of the productions of Mr. Wilbur's pen so fragmentary, and even chaotic, written as they are on the backs of letters in an exceedingly cramped chirography, — here a memorandum for a sermon ; there an observation of the weather ; now the measurement of an extraordinary head of cabbage, and then of the cerebral capacity of some reverend brother deceased ; a calm inquiry into the state of modern literature, ending in a method of detecting if milk be impoverished with water, and the amount thereof ; one leaf beginning with a genealogy, to be interrupted half-way down with an entry that the brindle cow had calved, — that any attempts at selection seemed desperate. His only complete work, "An Enquiry concerning the Tenth Horn of the Beast," even in the abstract of it given by Mr. Hitchcock, would, by a rough computation of the printers, fill five entire numbers of our journal, and as he attempts, by a new application of decimal fractions, to identify it with the Emperor Julian, seems hardly of immediate concern to the general reader. Even the Table-Talk, though doubtless originally highly interesting in the domestic circle, is so largely made up of theological discussion and matters of local or preterite interest, that we have found it hard to extract anything that would at all satisfy expectation. But, in order to silence further inquiry, we subjoin a few passages as illustrations of its general character.]

I think I could go near to be a perfect Christian if I were always a visitor, as I have sometimes been, at the house of some hospitable friend. I can show a great deal of self-denial where the best of everything is urged upon me with kindly importunity. It is not so very hard to turn the other cheek for a kiss. And when I meditate upon the pains taken for our entertainment in this life, on the endless variety of seasons, of human character and fortune, on the costliness of the hangings and furniture of our dwelling here, I sometimes feel a singular joy in looking upon myself as God's guest, and cannot but believe that we should all be wiser and happier, because more grateful, if we were always mindful of our privilege in this regard. And should we not rate more cheaply any honor that men could pay us, if we remembered that every day we sat at the table of the Great King? Yet must we not forget that we are in strictest bonds His servants also ; for there is no impiety so abject as that which expects to be *dead-headed* (*ut ita dicam*) through life, and which, calling itself trust in Providence, is in reality asking Providence to trust us and taking up all our goods on false pretences. It is a wise rule to take the world as we find it, not always to leave it so.

It has often set me thinking when I find that I can always pick up plenty of empty nuts under my shagbark-tree. The squirrels know them by their lightness, and I have seldom seen one with the marks of their teeth in it. What a school-house is the world, if our wits would only not play truant ! For I observe that men set most store by forms and symbols in proportion as they are mere shells. It is the outside they want and not the kernel. What stores of such do not many, who in material things are as shrewd as the squirrels, lay up for the spiritual winter-supply of themselves and their children ! I have seen churches that seemed to me garners of these withered nuts, for it is wonderful how prosaic is the apprehension of symbols by the minds of most men. It is not one sect nor another, but all, who, like the dog of the fable, have let drop the spiritual substance of symbols for their material shadow. If one attribute miraculous virtues to mere holy water, that beautiful emblem of inward purification at the door of God's house, another cannot comprehend the significance of baptism without being ducked over head and ears in the liquid vehicle thereof.

[Perhaps a word of historical comment may be permitted here. My late revered predecessor was, I would humbly affirm, as free from prejudice as falls to the lot of the most highly favored individuals of our species. To be sure, I have heard him say that, "what were called strong prejudices, were in fact only the repulsion of sensitive organizations from that moral and even physical effluvium through which some natures by providential appointment, like certain unsavory quadrupeds, gave warning of their neighborhood. Better ten mistaken suspicions of this kind than one close encounter." This he said somewhat in heat, on being questioned as to his motives for always refusing his pulpit to those itinerant professors of vicarious benevolence who end their discourses by taking up a collection. But at another time I remember his saying, "that there was one large thing which small minds always found room for, and that was great prejudices." This, however, by the way. The statement which I purposed to make was simply this. Down to A. D. 1830, Jaalam had consisted of a single parish, with one house set apart for religious services. In that year the foundations of a Baptist Society were laid by the labors of Elder Joash Q. Balcom, 2d. As the members of the new body were drawn from the First Parish, Mr. Wilbur was for a time considerably exercised in mind. He even went so far as on one occasion to follow the reprehensible practice of the earlier Puritan divines in choosing a punning text, and preached from Hebrews xiii. 9: "Be not carried about with *divers* and strange doctrines." He afterwards, in accordance with one of his own maxims, — "to get a dead injury out of the mind as soon as is decent, bury it, and then ventilate," — in accordance with this maxim, I say, he lived on very friendly terms with Rev. Shearjashub Scrimgour, present pastor of the Baptist Society in Jaalam. Yet I think it was never unpleasing to him that the church edifice of that society (though otherwise a creditable specimen of architecture) remained without a bell, as indeed it does to this day. So much seemed necessary to do away with any appearance of acerbity toward a respectable community of professing Christians, which might be suspected in the conclusion of the above paragraph. — J. H.]

In lighter moods he was not averse from an innocent play upon words. Looking up from his newspaper one morning as I entered his study he said, "When I read a debate in Congress, I feel as if I were sitting at the feet of Zeno in the shadow of the Portico." On my expressing a natural surprise, he added, smiling, "Why, at such times the only view which honorable members give me of what goes on in the world is through their intercalumniations." I smiled at this after a moment's reflection, and he added gravely, "The most punctilious refinement of manners is the only salt that will keep a democracy from stinking; and what are we to expect from the people, if their representatives set them such lessons? Mr. Everett's whole life has been a sermon from this text. There was, at least, this advantage in duelling, that it set a certain limit on the tongue." When Society laid by the rapier, it buckled on the more subtle blade of etiquette wherewith to keep obtrusive vulgarity at bay. In this connection, I may be permitted to recall a playful remark of his upon another occasion. The painful divisions in the First Parish, A. D. 1844, occasioned by the wild notions in respect to the rights of (what Mr. Wilbur, so far as concerned the reasoning faculty, always called) the unfairer part of creation, put forth by Miss Parthenia Almira Fitz, are too well known to need more than a passing allusion. It was during these heats, long since happily allayed, that Mr. Wilbur remarked that "the Church had more trouble in dealing with one *she*resiarch than with twenty *here*siarchs," and that the men's *conscia recti*, or certainty of being right, was nothing to the women's.

When I once asked his opinion of a poetical composition on which I had expended no little pains, he read it attentively, and then remarked, "Unless one's thought pack more neatly in verse than in prose, it is wiser to refrain. Commonplace gains nothing by being translated into rhyme, for it is something which no hocus-pocus can transubstantiate with the real presence of living thought. You entitle your piece, 'My Mother's Grave,' and expend four pages of useful paper in detailing your emotions there. But, my dear sir, watering does not improve the quality of ink, even though you should do it with tears. To publish a sorrow to Tom, Dick, and Harry is in some sort to advertise its unreality, for I have observed in my intercourse with the afflicted that the deepest grief instinctively hides its face with its hands and is silent. If your piece were printed, I have no doubt it would be popular, for people like to fancy that they feel much better than the trouble of feeling. I would put all poets on oath whether they have striven to say everything they possibly could think of, or to leave out all they could not help saying. In your own case, my worthy young friend, what you have written is merely a deliberate exercise, the gymnastic of sentiment. For your excellent maternal relative is still alive, and is to take tea with me this evening, D. V. Beware of simulated feeling; it is hypocrisy's first cousin; it is especially dangerous to a preacher; for he who says one day, 'Go to, let me seem to be pathetic,' may be nearer than he thinks to saying, 'Go to, let me seem to be virtuous, or earnest, or under sorrow for sin.' Depend upon it, Sappho loved her verses more sincerely than she did Phaon, and Petrarch his sonnets better than

Laura, who was indeed but his poetical stalking-horse. After you shall have once heard that muffled rattle of the clods on the coffin-lid of an irreparable loss, you will grow acquainted with a pathos that will make all elegies hateful. When I was of your age, I also for a time mistook my desire to write verses for an authentic call of my nature in that direction. But one day as I was going forth for a walk, with my head full of an 'Elegy on the Death of Flirtilla,' and vainly groping after a rhyme for *lily* that should not be *silly* or *chilly*, I saw my eldest boy Homer busy over the rain-water hogshead, in that childish experiment at parthenogenesis, the changing a horse-hair into a water-snake. An immersion of six weeks showed no change in the obstinate filament. Here was a stroke of unintended sarcasm. Had I not been doing in my study precisely what my boy was doing out of doors? Had my thoughts any more chance of coming to life by being submerged in rhyme than his hair by soaking in water? I burned my elegy and took a course of Edwards on the Will. People do not make poetry; it is made out of *them* by a process for which I do not find myself fitted. Nevertheless, the writing of verses is a good rhetorical exercitation, as teaching us what to shun most carefully in prose. For prose bewitched is like window-glass with bubbles in it, distorting what it should show with pellucid veracity."

It is unwise to insist on doctrinal points as vital to religion. The Bread of Life is wholesome and sufficing in itself, but gulped down with these kickshaws cooked up by theologians, it is apt to produce an indigestion, nay, even at last an incurable dyspepsia of scepticism.

One of the most inexcusable weaknesses of Americans is in signing their names to what are called credentials. But for my interposition, a person who shall be nameless would have taken from this town a recommendation for an office of trust subscribed by the selectmen and all the voters of both parties, ascribing to him as many good qualities as if it had been his tombstone. The excuse was that it would be well for the town to be rid of him, as it would erelong be obliged to maintain him. I would not refuse my name to modest merit, but I would be as cautious as in signing a bond. [I trust I shall be subjected to no imputation of unbecoming vanity, if I mention the fact that Mr. W. indorsed my own qualifications as teacher of the high-school at Pequash Junction. J. H.] When I see a certificate of character with everybody's name to it, I regard it as a letter of introduction from the Devil. Never give a man your name unless you are willing to trust him with your reputation.

There seem now-a-days to be two sources of literary inspiration, — fulness of mind and emptiness of pocket.

I am often struck, especially in reading Montaigne, with the obviousness and familiarity of a great writer's thoughts, and the freshness they gain because said by him. The truth is, we mix their greatness with all they say and give it our best attention. Johannes Faber sic cogitavit, would be no enticing preface to a book, but an accredited name gives credit like the signature to a note of hand. It is the advantage of fame that it is always privileged to take the world by the button, and a thing is weightier for Shakespeare's uttering it by the whole amount of his personality.

It is singular how impatient men are with overpraise of others, how patient with overpraise of themselves; and yet the one does them no injury, while the other may be their ruin.

People are apt to confound mere alertness of mind with attention. The one is but the flying abroad of all the faculties to the open doors and windows at every passing rumor; the other is the concentration of every one of them in a single focus, as in the alchemist over his alembic at the moment of expected projection. Attention is the stuff that memory is made of, and memory is accumulated genius.

Do not look for the Millennium as imminent. One generation is apt to get all the wear it can out of the cast clothes of the last, and is always sure to use up every paling of the old fence that will hold a nail in building the new.

You suspect a kind of vanity in my genealogical enthusiasm. Perhaps you are right; but it is a universal foible. Where it does not show itself in a personal and private way, it becomes public and gregarious. We flatter ourselves in the Pilgrim Fathers, and the Virginian offshoot of a transported convict swells with the fancy of a cavalier ancestry. Pride of birth, I have noticed, takes two forms. One complacently traces himself up to a coronet; another, defiantly, to a lapstone. The sentiment is precisely the same in both cases, only that one is the positive and the other the negative pole of it.

Seeing a goat the other day kneeling in order to graze with less trouble, it seemed to me a type of the common notion of prayer. Most people are ready enough to go down on their knees for material blessings, but how few for those spiritual gifts which alone are an answer to our orisons, if we but knew it!

Some people, now-a-days, seem to have hit upon a new moralization of the moth and the candle. They would lock up the light of Truth, lest poor Psyche should put it out in her effort to draw nigh to it.

<hr />

No. X.

MR. HOSEA BIGLOW TO THE EDITOR OF THE ATLANTIC MONTHLY.

Dear Sir, — Your letter come to han';
Requestin' me to please be funny;

But I ain't made upon a plan
   Thet knows wut's comin', gall or
      honey:
Ther' 's times the world doos look so
     queer,
   Odd fancies come afore I call 'em;
An' then agin, for half a year,
   No preacher 'thout a call 's more
     solemn.

You're 'n want o' sunthin' light an'
     cute,
   Rattlin' an' shrewd an' kin' o' jingle-
     ish,
An' wish, pervidin' it 'ould suit,
   I'd take an' citify my English.
I *ken* write long-tailed, ef I please, —
   But when I'm jokin', no, I thankee;
Then, 'fore I know it, my idees
   Run helter-skelter into Yankee.

Sence I begun to scribble rhyme,
   I tell ye wut, I hain't ben foolin';
The parson's books, life, death, an'
     time
   Hev took some trouble with my
     schoolin';
Nor th' airth don't git put out with me,
   Thet love her 'z though she wuz a
     woman;
Why, th' ain't a bird upon the tree
   But half forgives my bein' human.

An' yit I love th' unhighschooled way
   Ol' farmers hed when I wuz younger;
Their talk wuz meatier, an' 'ould stay,
   While book-froth seems to whet your
     hunger;
For puttin' in a downright lick
   'Twixt Humbug's eyes, ther' 's few
     can metch it,
An' then it helves my thoughts ez slick
   Ez stret-grained hickory doos a
     hetchet.

But when I can't, I can't, thet 's all,
   For Natur' won't put up with gullin'.
Idees you hev to shove an' haul
Like a druv pig ain't wuth a mullein':
Live thoughts ain't sent for; thru all
     rifts
   O' sense they pour an' resh ye on-
     wards,

Like rivers when south-lyin' drifts
   Feel thet th' old airth 's a-wheelin'
     sunwards.

Time wuz, the rhymes come crowdin
     thick
   Ez office-seekers arter 'lection,
An' into ary place 'ould stick
   Without no bother nor objection;
But sence the war my thoughts hang
     back
   Ez though I wanted to enlist 'em,
An' subs'tutes, — *they* don't never lack,
   But then they ll slope afore you 've
     mist 'em.

Nothin' don't seem like wut it wuz;
   I can't see wut there is to hender,
An' yit my brains jes' go buzz, buzz,
   Like bumblebees agin a winder;
'Fore these times come, in all airth's
     row,
   Ther' wuz one quiet place, my head
     in,
Where I could hide an' think, — but
     now
   It 's all one teeter, hopin', dreadin'.

Where 's Peace? I start, some clear-
     blown night,
   When gaunt stone walls grow numb
     an' number,
An', creakin' 'cross the snow-crus'
     white,
   Walk the col' starlight into summer;
Up grows the moon, an' swell by swell
   Thru the pale pasturs silvers dimmer
Than the last smile thet strives to tell
   O' love gone heavenward in its shim-
     mer.

I hev ben gladder o' sech things
   Than cocks o' spring or bees o' clover,
They filled my heart with livin' springs,
   But now they seem to freeze 'em
     over;
Sights innercent ez babes on knee,
   Peaceful ez eyes o' pastur'd cattle,
Jes' coz they be so, seem to me
   To rile me more with thoughts o'
     battle.

In-doors an' out by spells I try;
   Ma'am Natur' keeps her spin-wheel
     goin',

But leaves my natur' stiff and dry
  Ez fiel's o' clover arter mowin';
An' her jes' keepin' on the same,
  Calmer 'n a clock, an' never carin',
An' findin' nary thing to blame,
  Is wus than ef she took to swearin'.

Snow-flakes come whisperin' on the
    pane
  The charm makes blazin' logs so
    pleasant,
But I can't hark to wut they 're say'n',
  With Grant or Sherman ollers pres-
    ent;
The chimbleys shudder in the gale,
  Thet lulls, then suddin takes to flap-
    pin'
Like a shot hawk, but all 's ez stale
  To me ez so much sperit-rappin'.

Under the yaller-pines I house,
  When sunshine makes 'em all sweet-
    scented,
An' hear among their furry boughs
  The baskin' west-wind purr con-
    tented,
While 'way o'erhead, ez sweet an' low
  Ez distant bells thet ring for meetin',
The wedged wil' geese their bugles blow,
  Further an' further South retreatin'.

Or up the slippery knob I strain
  An' see a hundred hills like islan's
Lift their blue woods in broken chain
  Out o' the sea o' snowy silence;
The farm-smokes, sweetes' sight on
    airth,
  Slow thru the winter air a-shrinkin'
Seem kin' o' sad, an' roun' the hearth
  Of empty places set me thinkin'.

Beaver roars hoarse with meltin' snows,
  An' rattles di'mon's from his granite;
Time wuz, he snatched away my prose,
  An' into psalms or satires ran it;
But he, nor all the rest thet once
  Started my blood to country-dances,
Can't set me goin' more 'n a dunce
  Thet hain't no use for dreams an'
    fancies.

Rat-tat-tat-tattle thru the street
  I hear the drummers makin' riot,

An' I set thinkin' o' the feet
  Thet follered once an' now are
    quiet, —
White feet ez snowdrops innercent,
  Thet never knowed the paths o'
    Satan,
Whose comin' step ther' 's ears thet
    won't,
  No, not lifelong, leave off awaitin'.

Why, hain't I held 'em on my knee?
  Did n't I love to see 'em growin',
Three likely lads ez wal could be,
  Hahnsome an' brave an' not tu
    knowin'?
I set an' look into the blaze
  Whose natur', jes' like theirn, keeps
    climbin',
Ez long 'z it lives, in shinin' ways,
  An' half despise myself for rhymin'.

Wut 's words to them whose faith an'
    truth
  On War's red techstone rang true
    metal,
Who ventered life an' love an' youth
  For the gret prize o' death in battle?
To him who, deadly hurt, agen
  Flashed on afore the charge's thun-
    der,
Tippin' with fire the bolt of men
  Thet rived the Rebel line asunder?
'T ain't right to hev the young go fust,
  All throbbin' full o' gifts an' graces,
Leavin' life's paupers dry ez dust
  To try an' make b'lieve fill their
    places:
Nothin' but tells us wut we miss,
  Ther' 's gaps our lives can't never
    fay in,
An' *thet* world seems so fur from this
  Lef' for us loafers to grow gray in!

My eyes cloud up for rain; my mouth
  Will take to twitchin' roun' the cor-
    ners;
I pity mothers, tu, down South,
  For all they sot among the scorners:
I 'd sooner take my chance to stan'
  At Jedgment where your meanest
    slave is,
Than at God's bar hol' up a han'
  Ez drippin' red ez yourn, Jeff Davis!

Come, Peace! not like a mourner
 bowed
 For honor lost an' dear ones wasted,
But proud, to meet a people proud,
 With eyes thet tell o' triumph tasted!
Come, with han' grippin' on the hilt,
 An' step thet proves ye Victory's
 daughter!
Longin' for you, our sperits wilt
 Like shipwrecked men's on raf's for
 water.

Come, while our country feels the lift
 Of a gret instinct shoutin' forwards,
An' knows thet freedom ain't a gift
 Thet tarries long in han's o' cowards!
Come, sech ez mothers prayed for, when
 They kissed their cross with lips thet
 quivered,
An' bring fair wages for brave men,
 A nation saved, a race delivered!

No. XI.

MR. HOSEA BIGLOW'S SPEECH
IN MARCH MEETING.

TO THE EDITOR OF THE ATLANTIC
MONTHLY.

JAALAM, April 5, 1866.

MY DEAR SIR, —

(an' noticin' by your kiver thet you 're
some dearer than wut you wuz, I enclose the deffrence) I dunno ez I know
jest how to interdroce this las' perduc-
tion of my mews, ez Parson Willber
allus called 'em, which is goin' to be
the last an' stay the last onless sunthin'
pertikler sh'd interfear which I don't
expec' ner I wun't yield tu ef it wuz ez
pressin' ez a deppity Shiriff. Sence
Mr. Wilbur's disease I hev n't hed no
one thet could dror out my talons. He
ust to kind o' wine me up an' set the
penderlum agoin' an' then somehow I
seemed to go on tick as it wear tell I
run down, but the noo minister ain't
of the same brewin' nor I can't seem
to git ahold of no kine of huming nater

in him but sort of slide rite off as you
du on the eedge of a mow. Minny-
steeril natur is wal enough an' a site
better 'n most other kines I know on,
but the other sort sech as Welbor hed
wuz of the Lord's makin' an' naterally
more wonderfle an' sweet tastin' leastways to me so fur as heerd from. He
used to interdooce 'em smooth ez ile
athout sayin' nothin' in pertickler an' I
misdoubt he did n't set so much by the
sec'nd Ceres as wut he done by the
Fust, fact, he let on onct thet his mine
misgive him of a sort of fallin' off in
spots. He wuz as outspoken as a nor-
wester he wuz, but I tole him I hoped
the fall wuz from so high up thet a feller could ketch a good many times fust
afore comin' bunt onto the ground as I
see Jethro C. Swett from the meetin'
house steeple up to th' old perrish, an'
took up for dead but he 's alive now an'
spry as wut you be. Turnin' of it over
I recclected how they ust to put wut
they called Argymunce onto the frunts
of poymns, like poorches afore housen
whare you could rest ye a spell whilst
you wuz concludin' whether you 'd go
in or nut espeshully ware tha wuz dar-
ters, though I most allus found it the
best plen to go in fust an' think afterwards an' the gals likes it best tu. I
dno as speechis ever hez any argimunts
to 'em, I never see none thet hed an' I
guess they never du but tha must allus
be a B'ginnin' to everythin' athout it is
Eternity so I 'll begin rite away an'
anybody may put it afore any of his
speeches ef it soots an' welcome. I
don't claim no paytent.

THE ARGYMUNT.

Interducshin, w'ich may be skipt.
Begins by talkin' about himself : thet 's
jest natur an' most gin'ally allus pleasin', I b'leeve I 've notist, to one of the
cumpany, an' thet 's more than wut you
can say of most speshes of talkin'.
Nex' comes the gittin' the goodwill of
the orjunce by lettin' 'em gether from
wut you kind of ex'dentally let drop
thet they air about East, A one, an' no
mistaik, skare 'em up an' take 'em as

they rise. Spring interdooced with a fiew approput flours. Speach finally begins witch nobuddy need n't feel obolygated to read as I never read 'em an' never shell this one ag'in. Subjick staited; expanded; delayted; extended. Pump lively. Subjick staited ag'in so 's to avide all mistaiks. Ginnle remarks; continooed; kerried on; pushed furder; kind o' gin out. Subjick *re-*staited; dielooted; stirred up permiscoous. Pump ag'in. Gits back to where he sot out. Can't seem to stay thair. Ketches into Mr. Seaward's hair. Breaks loose ag'in an' staits his subjick; stretches it; turns it; folds it; onfolds it; folds it ag'in so 's 't no one can't find it. Argoos with an imedginary bean thet ain't aloud to say nothin' in repleye. Gives him a real good dressin' an' is settysfide he 's rite. Gits into Johnson's hair. No use tryin' to git into his head. Gives it up. Hez to stait his subjick ag'in; doos it back-'ards, sideways, eendways, criss-cross, bevellin', noways. Gits finally red on it. Concloods. Concloods more. Reads some xtrax. Sees his subjick a-nosin' round arter him ag'in. Tries to avide it. Wun't du. *Mis*states it. Can't conjectur' no other plawsable way of staytin' on it. Tries pump. No fx. Finely concloods to conclood. Yeels the flore.

You kin spall an' punctooate thet as you please. I allus do, it kind of puts a noo soot of close onto a word, thisere funattick spellin' doos an' takes 'em out of the prissen dress they wair ir the Dixonary. Ef I squeeze the cents out of 'em it 's the main thing, an' wut they wuz made for; wut 's left 's jest pummis.

Mistur Wilbur sez he to me onct, sez he, "Hosee," sez he, "in litterytoor the only good thing is Natur. It 's amazin' hard to come at," sez he, "but onct git it an' you 've gut everythin'. Wut 's the sweetest small on airth?" sez he. "Noomone hay," sez I, pooty bresk, for he wuz allus hankerin' round in hayin. "Nawthin' of the kine," sez he. "My leetle Huldy's breath," sez I ag'in. "You 're a good lad," sez

he, his eyes sort of ripplin' like, for he lost a babe onct nigh about her age, — "You 're a good lad; but 't ain't thet nuther," sez he. "Ef you want to know," sez he, "open your winder of a mornin' et ary season, and you 'll larn thet the best of perfooms is jest fresh air, *fresh air*," sez he, emphysizin', "athout no mixtur. Thet 's wut *I* call natur in writin', and it bathes my lungs and washes 'em sweet whenever I git a whiff on 't," sez he. I offen think o' thet when I set down to write, but the winders air *so* ept to git stuck, an' breakin' a pane costs sunthin'.

Yourn for the last time,
 Nut to be continooed,
  HOSEA BIGLOW.

I DON'T much s'pose, hows'ever I should
    plen it,
I could git boosted into th' House or
    Sennit, —
Nut while the twolegged gab-machine 's
    so plenty,
'Nablin' one man to du the talk o'
    twenty;
I 'm one o' them thet finds it ruther
    hard
To mannyfactur' wisdom by the yard,
An' maysure off, accordin' to demand,
The piece-goods el'kence that I keep
    on hand,
The same ole pattern runnin' thru an'
    thru,
An' nothin' but the customer thet 's
    new.
I sometimes think, the furder on I go,
Thet it gits harder to feel sure I know,
An' when I 've settled my idees, I find
'T warn't I sheered most in makin' up
    my mind;
'T wuz this an' thet an' t' other thing
    thet done it,
Sunthin' in th' air, I could n' seek nor
    shun it.
Mos' folks go off so quick now in dis-
    cussion,
All th' ole flint locks seems altered tc
    percussion,
Whilst I in ag'in' sometimes git a hint

Thet I'm percussion changin' back to
   flint;
Wal, ef it's so, I ain't agoin' to werrit,
For th' ole Queen's-arm hez this per-
   tickler merit, —
It gives the mind a hahnsome wedth o'
   margin
To kin' o' make its will afore dischargin'
   in':
I can't make out but jest one ginnle
   rule, —
No man need go an' *make* himself a
   fool,
Nor jedgment ain't like mutton, thet
   can't bear
Cookin' tu long, nor be took up tu rare.

Ez I wuz say'n', I hain't no chance to
   speak
So 's 't all the country dreads me onct a
   week,
But I 've consid'ble o' thet sort o' head
Thet sets to home an' thinks wut *might*
   be said,
The sense thet grows an' werrits under-
   neath,
Comin' belated like your wisdom-teeth,
An' git so el'kent, sometimes, to my
   gardin
Thet I don' vally public life a fardin'.
Our Parson Wilbur (blessin's on his
   head!)
'Mongst other stories of ole times he
   hed,
Talked of a feller thet rehearsed his
   spreads
Beforehan' to his rows o' kebbige-
   heads,
(Ef 't war n't Demossenes, I guess 't
   wuz Sisro,)
Appealin' fust to thet an' then to this
   row,
Accordin' ez he thought thet his idees
Their diff'runt ev'riges o' brains 'ould
   please;
"An'," sez the Parson, "to hit right,
   you must
Git used to maysurin' your hearers fust;
For, take my word for 't, when all 's
   come an' past,
The kebbige-heads 'll cair the day et
   last;
Th' ain't ben a meetin' sence the worl'
   begun

But they made (raw or biled ones) ten
   to one."

I 've allus foun' 'em, I allow, sence
   then
About ez good for talkin' to ez men;
They 'll take edvice, like other folks, to
   keep,
(To use it 'ould be holdin' on 't tu
   cheap,)
They listen wal, don' kick up when you
   scold 'em,
An' ef they 've tongues, hev sense
   enough to hold 'em;
Though th' ain't no denger we shall
   lose the breed,
I gin'lly keep a score or so for seed,
An' when my sappiness gits spry in
   spring,
So 's 't my tongue itches to run on full
   swing,
I fin' 'em ready-planted in March-
   meetin',
Warm ez a ly'ceum-audience in their
   greetin',
An' pleased to hear my spoutin' frum
   the fence, —
Comin', ez 't doos, entirely free 'f ex-
   pense.
This year I made the follerin' observa-
   tions
Extrump'ry, like most other tri'ls o'
   patience,
An', no reporters bein' sent express
To work their abstrac's up into a mess
Ez like th' oridg'nal ez a woodcut
   pictur'
Thet chokes the life out like a boy-
   constrictor,
I 've writ 'em out, an' so avide all
   jeal'sies
'Twixt nonsense o' my own an' some
   one's else's.

(N. B. Reporters gin'lly git a hint
To make dull orjunces seem 'live in
   print,
An', ez I hev t' report myself, I vum,
I 'll put th' applauses where they 'd
   ough' to come!)

MY FELLER KEBBIGE-HEADS, who look
   so green,
I vow to gracious thet ef I could dreen

The world of all its hearers but jest you,
'T would leave 'bout all tha' is wuth
    talkin' to,
An' you, my ven'able ol' frien's, thet
    show
Upon your crowns a sprinklin' o' March
    snow,
Ez ef mild Time had christened every
    sense
For wisdom's church o' second inno-
    cence,
Nut Age's winter, no, no sech a thing,
But jest a kin' o' slippin'-back o'
    spring, —   [Sev'ril noses blowed.]
We 've gathered here, ez ushle, to de-
    cide
Which is the Lord's an' which is Sa-
    tan's side,
Coz all the good or evil thet can heppen
Is 'long o' which on 'em you choose for
    Cappen.   [Cries o' " Thet 's so ! "]

Aprul 's come back ; the swellin' buds
    of oak
Dim the fur hillsides with a purplish
    smoke ;
The brooks are loose an', singing to be
    seen,
(Like gals,) make all the hollers soft
    an' green ;
The birds are here, for all the season 's
    late ;
They take the sun's height an' don'
    never wait ;
Soon 'z he officially declares it 's spring
Their light hearts lift 'em on a north-
    'ard wing,
An' th' ain't an acre, fur ez you can hear,
Can't by the music tell the time o' year ;
But thet white dove Carliny scared
    away,
Five year ago, jes' sech an Aprul day ;
Peace, that we hoped 'ould come an'
    build last year
An' coo by every housedoor, is n't
    here, —
No, nor wun't never be, for all our jaw,
Till we 're ez brave in pol'tics ez in war !
O Lord, ef folks wuz made so 's 't they
    could see
The begnet-pint there is to an idee !
                              [Sensation.]
Ten times the danger in 'em th' is in
    steel ;

They run your soul thru an' you never
    feel,
But crawl about an' seem to think
    you 're livin',
Poor shells o' men, nut wuth the Lord's
    forgivin',
Tell you come bust ag'in a real live fect,
An' go to pieces when you 'd ough' to
    ect !
Thet kin' o' begnet 's wut we 're cross-
    in' now,
An' no man, fit to nevvigate a scow,
'Ould stan' expectin' help from King-
    dom Come,
While t' other side druv their cold iron
    home.

My frien's, you never gethered from my
    mouth,
No, nut one word ag'in the South ez
    South,
Nor th' ain't a livin' man, white, brown,
    nor black,
Gladder 'n wut I should be to take 'em
    back ;
But all I ask of Uncle Sam is fust
To write up on his door, " No goods on
    trust " ;
                       [Cries of " Thet 's the ticket ! "]
Give us cash down in ekle laws for all,
An' they 'll be snug inside afore nex'
    fall.
Give wut they ask, an' we shell hev
    Jamaker,
Wuth minus some consid'able an acre ;
Give wut they need, an' we shell git
    'fore long
A nation all one piece, rich, peacefle,
    strong ;
Make 'em Amerikin, an' they 'll begin
To love their country ez they loved
    their sin ;
Let 'em stay Southun, an' you 've kep'
    a sore
Ready to fester ez it done afore.
No mortle man can boast of perfic'
    vision,
But the one moleblin' thing is Indecis-
    ion,
An' th' ain't no futur' for the man nor
    state
Thet out of j-u-s-t can't spell great.
Some folks 'ould call thet reddikle ; do
    you?

T was commonsense afore the war wuz
    thru :
Thet loaded all our guns an' made 'em
    speak
So 's 't Europe heared 'em clearn acrost
    the creek ;
"They 're drivin' o' their spiles down
    now," sez she,
"To the hard grennit o' God's fust
    idee :
Ef they reach thet, Democ'cy need n't
    fear
The tallest airthquakes *we* can git up
    here."
Some call 't insultin' to ask *ary* pledge,
An' say 't will only set their teeth on
    edge,
But folks you 've jest licked, fur 'z I
    ever see,
Are 'bout ez mad 'z they wal know how
    to be ;
It 's better than the Rebs themselves
    expected
'Fore they see Uncle Sam wilt down
    henpecked ;
Be kind 'z you please, but fustly make
    things fast,
For plain Truth 's all the kindness thet
    'll last ;
Ef treason is a crime, ez *some* folks
    say,
How could we punish it a milder way
Than sayin' to 'em, " Brethren, lookee
    here,
We 'll jes' divide things with ye, sheer
    an' sheer,
An sence both come o' pooty strong-
    backed daddies,
You take the Darkies, ez we 've took
    the Paddies ;
Ign'ant an' poor we took 'em by the
    hand,
An' they 're the bones an' sinners o'
    the land."
I ain't o' them that fancy there 's a loss
    on
Every inves'ment thet don't start from
    Bos'on ;
But I know this : our money 's safest
    trusted
In sunthin', come wut will, thet *can't*
    be busted,
An' thet 's the old Amerikin idee,
To make a man a Man an' let him be.
         [Gret applause.]

Ez for their l'yalty, don't take a goad
    to 't,
But I do' want to block their only road
    to 't
By lettin' 'em believe thet they can git
Mor'n wut they lost, out of our little
    wit :
I tell ye wut, I 'm 'fraid we 'll drif' to
    leeward
'Thout we can put more stiffenin' into
    Seward ;
He seems to think Columby 'd better
    ect
Like a scared widder with a boy stiff-
    necked
Thet stomps an' swears he wun't come
    in to supper ;
She mus' set up for him, ez weak ez
    Tupper,
Keepin' the Constitootion on to warm,
Tell he 'll eccept her 'pologies in form :
The neighbors tell her he 's a cross-
    grained cuss
Thet needs a hidin' 'fore he comes to
    wus :
" No," sez Ma Seward, " he 's ez good
    'z the best,
All he wants now is sugar-plums an'
    rest " ;
" He sarsed my Pa," sez one ; " He
    stoned my son,"
Another edds. " O, wal, 't wuz jest
    his fun."
" He tried to shoot our Uncle Samwell
    dead."
" 'T wuz only tryin' a noo gun he hed."
" Wal, all we ask 's to hev it under-
    stood
You 'll take his gun away from him for
    good ;
We don't, wal, nut exac'ly, like his
    play,
Seein' he allus kin' o' shoots our way.
You kill your fatted calves to no good
    eend,
'Thout his fust sayin', ' Mother, I hev
    sinned ! ' "
        (" Amen ! " frum Deac'n Greenleaf.)

The Pres'dunt *he* thinks thet the slick-
    est plan
'Ould be t' allow thet he 's our on'y
    man,
An' thet we fit thru all thet dreffle war
Jes' for his private glory an' eclor ;

"Nobody ain't a Union man," sez he,
"'Thout he agrees, thru thick an' thin,
  with me ;
War n't Andrew Jackson's 'nitials jes'
  like mine ?
An' ain't thet sunthin' like a right
  divine
To cut up ez kentenkerous ez I please,
An' treat your Congress like a nest o'
  fleas ? "

Wal, I expec' the People would n'
  care, if
The question now wuz techin' bank or
  tariff,
But I conclude they 've 'bout made up
  their mind
This ain't the fittest time to go it blind,
Nor these ain't metters thet with
  pol'tics swings,
But goes 'way down amongst the roots
  o' things ;
Coz Sumner talked o' whitewashin'
  one day
They wun't let four years' war be
  throwed away.
"Let the South hev her rights ?" They
  say, "Thet 's you !
But nut greb hold of other folks's tu."
Who owns this country, is it they or
  Andy ?
Leastways it ough' to be the People
  and he ;
Let him be senior pardner, ef he 's so,
But let them kin' o' smuggle in ez Co ;
               [Laughter.]
Did he diskiver it? Consid'ble num-
  bers
Think thet the job wuz taken by Co-
  lumbus.
Did he set tu an' make it wut it is ?
Ef so, I guess the One-Man-power *hez*
  riz.
Did he put thru the rebbles, clear the
  docket,
An' pay th' expenses out of his own
  pocket ?
Ef thet 's the case, then everythin' I
  exes
Is t' hev him come an' pay my ennooal
  texes.   [Profound sensation.]
Was 't he thet shou'dered all them
  million guns?
Did he lose all the fathers, brothers,
  sons ?

Is this ere pop'lar gov'ment thet we
  run
A kin' o' sulky, made to kerry one ?
An' is the country goin' to knuckle
  down
To hev Smith sort their letters 'stid o'
  Brown ?
Who wuz the 'Nited States 'fore Rich-
  mon' fell ?
Wuz the South needfle their full name
  to spell ?
An' can't we spell it in thet short-han'
  way
Till th' underpinnin' 's settled so 's to
  stay ?
Who cares for the Resolves of '61,
Thet tried to coax an airthquake with
  a bun ?
Hez act'ly nothin' taken place sence
  then
To larn folks they must hendle fects
  like men ?
Ain't *this* the true p'int? Did the
  Rebs accep' 'em ?
Ef nut, whose fault is 't thet we hev n't
  kep' 'em ?
War n't there *two* sides? an' don't it
  stend to reason
Thet this week's 'Nited States ain't
  las' week's treason ?
When all these sums is done, with
  nothin' missed,
An' nut afore, this school 'll be dis-
  missed.

I knowed ez wal ez though I 'd seen 't
  with eyes
Thet when the war wuz over copper 'd
  rise,
An' thet we 'd hev a rile-up in our
  kettle
'T would need Leviathan's whole skin
  to settle :
I thought 't would take about a generation
'Fore we could wal begin to be a nation,
But I allow I never did imegine
'T would be our Pres'dunt thet 'ould
  drive a wedge in
To keep the split from closin' ef it
  could,
An' healin' over with new wholesome
  wood ;

For th' ain't no chance o' healin' while
   they think
Thet law an' gov'ment 's only printer's
   ink ;
I mus' confess I thank him for dis-
   coverin'
The curus way in which the States are
   sovereign ;
They ain't nut *quite* enough so to rebel,
But, when they fin' it 's costly to raise
   h —,   [A groan from Deac'n G.]
Why, then, for jes' the same superl'-
   tive reason,
They 're 'most too much so to be tetched
   for treason ;
They *can't* go out, but ef they somehow
   du,
Their sovereignty don't noways go out
   tu ;
The State goes out, the sovereignty
   don't stir,
But stays to keep the door ajar for her.
He thinks secession never took 'em out,
An' mebby he 's correc', but I mis-
   doubt ;
Ef they war n't out, then why, 'n the
   name o' sin,
Make all this row 'bout lettin' of 'em
   in ?
In law, p'r'aps nut ; but there 's a dif-
   furence, ruther,
Betwixt your mother-'n-law an' real
   mother,   [Derisive cheers.]
An' I, for one, shall wish they 'd all
   been *som'eres*,
Long 'z U. S. Texes are sech reg'lar
   comers.
But, O my patience ! must we wriggle
   back
Into th' ole crooked, pettyfoggin' track,
When our artil'ry-wheels a road hev
   cut
Stret to our purpose ef we keep the rut ?
War 's jes' dead waste excep' to wipe
   the slate
Clean for the cyph'rin' of some nobler
   fate.   [Applause.]

Ez for dependin' on their oaths an' thet,
'T wun't bind 'em mor 'n the ribbin
   roun' my het ;
I heared a fable once from Othniel
   Starns,

That pints it slick ez weathercocks do
   barns :
Onct on a time the wolves hed certing
   rights
Inside the fold ; they used to sleep there
   nights.
An', bein' cousins o' the dogs, they
   took
Their turns et watchin', reg'lar ez a
   book ;
But somehow, when the dogs hed gut
   asleep,
Their love o' mutton beat their love o'
   sheep,
Till gradilly the shepherds come to see
Things war n't agoin' ez they 'd ough'
   to be ;
So they sent off a deacon to remonstrate
Along 'th the wolves an' urge 'em to
   go on straight ;
They did n' seem to set much by the
   deacon,
Nor preachin' did n' cow 'em, nut to
   speak on ;
Fin'ly they swore thet they 'd go out
   an' stay,
An' hev their fill o' mutton every day ;
Then dogs an' shepherds, after much
   hard dammin',
               [Groan from Deac'n G.]
Turned tu an' give 'em a tormented
   lammin',
An' sez, "Ye sha' n't go out, the mur-
   rain rot ye,
To keep us wastin' half our time to
   watch ye !"
But then the question come, How live
   together
'Thout losin' sleep, nor nary yew nor
   wether ?
Now there wuz some dogs (noways
   wuth their keep)
Thet sheered their cousins' tastes an'
   sheered the sheep ;
They sez, "Be gin'rous, let 'em swear
   right in,
An', ef they backslide, let 'em swear
   ag'in ;
Jes' let 'em put on sheep-skins whilst
   they 're swearin' ;
To ask for more 'ould be beyond all
   bearin'."
"Be gin'rous for yourselves, where *you*
   're to pay,

Thet 's the best prectice," sez a shep-
    herd gray ;
" Ez for their oaths they wun't be wuth
    a button,
Long 'z you don't cure 'em o' their
    taste for mutton ;
Th' ain't but one solid way, howe'er
    you puzzle :
Tell they 're converted, let 'em wear a
    muzzle."
              [Cries of "Bully for you !"]

I 've noticed thet each half-baked
    scheme's abetters
Are in the hebbit o' producin' letters
Writ by all sorts o' never-heared-on
    fellers,
'Bout ez oridge'nal ez the wind in
    bellers ;
I 've noticed, tu, it 's the quack med'-
    cines gits
(An' needs) the grettest heaps o' stiffy-
    kits ;
         [Two apothekeries goes out.]

Now, sence I lef' off creepin' on all
    fours,
I hain't ast no man to endorse my
    course ;
It 's full ez cheap to be your own en-
    dorser,
An' ef I 've made a cup, I 'll fin' the
    saucer ;
But I 've some letters here from t' other
    side,
An' them 's the sort thet helps me to
    decide ;
Tell me for wut the copper-comp'nies
    hanker,
An' I 'll tell you jest where it 's safe to
    anchor.   [Faint hiss.]
Fus'ly the Hon'ble B. O. Sawin writes
Thet for a spell he could 'n sleep o'
    nights,
Puzzlin' which side wuz preudentest to
    pin to,
Which way th' ole homestead, which
    the temp'ry leanto ;
Et fust he jedged 't would right-side-up
    his pan
To come out ez a 'ridge'nal Union
    man,
"But now," he sez, " I ain't nut quite
    so fresh ;
The winnin' horse is goin' to be Secesh ;

You might, las' spring, hev eas'ly
    walked the course,
'Fore we contrived to doctor th' Union
    horse ;
Now *we* 're the ones to walk aroun' the
    nex' track ;
Jest you take hold an' read the follerin
    extrac',
Out of a letter I received last week
From an ole frien' thet never sprung a
    leak,
A Nothun Dem'crat *o'* th' ole Jarsey
    blue,
Born copper-sheathed an' copper-fast-
    ened tu."

" These four years past it hez been
    tough
To say which side a feller went for ;
Guideposts all gone, roads muddy 'n'
    rough,
An' nothin' duin' wut 't wuz meant for :
Pickets a-firin' left an' right,
Both sides a lettin' rip et sight, —
Life war n't wuth hardly payin' rent for.

" Columby gut her back up so,
It war n't no use a-tryin' to stop her, —
War 's emptin's riled her very dough
An' made it rise an' act improper ;
'T wuz full ez much ez I could du
To jes' lay low an' worry thru,
'Thout hevin' to sell out my copper.

" Afore the war your mod'rit men
Could set an' sun 'em on the fences,
Cyph'rin' the chances up, an' then
Jump off which way bes' paid expenses ;
Sence, 't wus so resky ary way,
I did n't hardly darst to say
I 'greed with Paley's Evidences.
         [Groan from Deac'n G.

" Ask Mac ef tryin' to set the fence
War n't like bein' rid upon a rail on 't,
Headin' your party with a sense
O' bein' tipjint in the tail on 't,
An' tryin' to think thet, on the whole,
You kin' o' quasi own your soul
When Belmont 's gut a bill o' sale on 't.
      [Three cheers for Grant and Sherman.

" Come peace, I sposed thet folks 'ould
    like
Their pol'tics done ag'in by proxy,

Give their noo loves the bag an' strike
A fresh trade with their reg'lar doxy;
But the drag 's broke, now slavery 's
   gone,
An' there 's gret resk they 'll blunder on,
Ef they ain't stopped, to real Democ'cy.

"We 've gut an awful row to hoe
In this 'ere job o' reconstructin';
Folks dunno skurce which way to go,
Where th' ain't some boghole to be
   ducked in;
But one thing 's clear; there *is* a crack,
Ef we pry hard, 'twixt white an' black,
Where the ole makebate can be tucked
   in.

"No white man sets in airth's broad
   aisle
Thet I ain't willin' t' own ez brother,
An' ef he 's heppened to strike ile,
I dunno, fin'ly, but I 'd ruther;
An' Paddies, long 'z they vote all right,
Though they ain't jest a nat'ral white,
I hold one 'em good 'z another.
           [Applause.]

"Wut *is* there lef' I 'd like to know,
Ef 't ain't the difference o' color,
To keep up self-respec' an' show
The human natur' of a fullah?
Wut good in bein' white, onless
It 's fixed by law, nut lef' to guess,
That we are smarter an' they duller?

"Ef we 're to hev our ekle rights,
'T wun't du to 'low no competition;
Th' ole debt doo us for bein' whites
Ain't safe onless we stop th' emission
O' these noo notes, whose specie base
Is human natur', 'thout no trace
O' shape, nor color, nor condition.
          [Continood applause.]

"So fur I 'd writ an' could n' jedge
Aboard wut boat I 'd best take pessige,
My brains all mincemeat, 'thout no
   edge
Upon 'em more than tu a sessige,
But now it seems ez though I see
Sunthin' resemblin' an idee,
Sence Johnson's speech an' veto mes-
   sage.

"I like the speech best, I confess,
The logic, preudence, an' good taste
   on 't,
An' it 's so mad, I ruther guess
There 's some dependence to be placed
   on 't;   [Laughter.]
It 's narrer, but 'twixt you an' me,
Out o' the allies o' J. D.
A temp'ry party can be based on 't.

"Jes' to hold on till Johnson 's thru
An' dug his Presidential grave is,
An' *then!* — who knows but we could
   slew
The country roun' to put in ——?
Wun't some folks rare up when we
   pull
Out o' their eyes our Union wool
An' larn 'em wut a p'lit'cle shave is!

"O, did it seem 'z ef Providence
Could ever send a second Tyler?
To see the South all back to once,
Reapin' the spiles o' the Freesiler,
Is cute ez though an ingineer
Should claim th' old iron for his sheer
Coz 't was himself that bust the biler!"
          [Gret laughter.]

Thet tells the story! Thet 's wut we
   shall git
By tryin' squirtguns on the burnin'
   Pit;
For the day never comes when it 'l.
   du
To kick off Dooty like a worn-out shoe.
I seem to hear a whisperin' in the air,
A sighin' like, of unconsoled despair,
Thet comes from nowhere an' from
   everywhere,
An' seems to say, "Why died we?
   war n't it, then,
To settle, once for all, thet men wuz
   men?
O, airth's sweet cup snetched from us
   barely tasted,
The grave's real chill is feelin' life wuz
   wasted!
O, you we lef', long-lingerin' et the
   door,
Lovin' you best, coz we loved Her the
   more,
Thet Death, not we, had conquered,
   we should feel

Ef she upon our memory turned her
    heel,
An' unregretful throwed us all away
To flaunt it in a Blind Man's Holi-
    day!"

My frien's, I 've talked nigh on to long
    enough.
I hain't no call to bore ye coz ye 're
    tough ;

My lungs are sound, an' our own v'ice
    delights
Our ears, but even kebbige-heads hez
    rights.
It 's the las' time thet I shell e'er ad-
    dress ye,
But you 'll soon fin' some new torment-
    or : bless ye !

[Tumult'ous applause and cries of " Go on ! "
    " Don't stop ! "]

GLOSSARY.

A.

Act'lly, *actually.*
Air, *are.*
Airth, *earth.*
Airy, *area.*
Aree, *area.*
Arter, *after.*
Ax, *ask.*

B.

Beller, *bellow.*
Bellowses, *lungs.*
Ben, *been.*
Bile, *boil.*
Bimeby, *by and by.*
Blurt out, *to speak bluntly.*
Bust, *burst.*
Buster, *a roistering blade;* used also as a general superlative.

C.

Caird, *carried.*
Cairn, *carrying.*
Caleb, *a turncoat.*
Cal'late, *calculate.*
Cass, *a person with two lives.*
Close, *clothes.*
Cockerel, *a young cock.*
Cocktail, *a kind of drink;* also, *an ornament peculiar to soldiers.*
Convention, *a place where people are imposed on; a juggler's show.*
Coons, *a cant term, for a now defunct party;* derived, perhaps, from the fact of their being commonly *up a tree.*
Cornwallis, *a sort of muster in masquerade;* supposed to have had its origin soon after the Revolution, and to commemorate the surrender of Lord Cornwallis. It took the place of the old Guy Fawkes procession.
Crooked stick, *a perverse, froward person.*
Cunnle, *a colonel.*
Cus, *a curse;* also, *a pitiful fellow.*

D.

Darsn't, used indiscriminately, either in singular or plural number, for *dare not, dares not,* and *dared not.*
Deacon off, *to give the cue to;* derived from a custom, once universal, but now extinct, in our New England Congregational churches. An important part of the office of deacon was to read aloud the hymns *given out* by the minister, one line at a time, the congregation singing each line as soon as read.
Demmercrat, leadin', *one in favor of extending slavery; a free-trade lecturer maintained in the custom-house.*
Desput, *desperate.*
Doos, *does.*
Doughface, *a contented lick-spittle;* a common variety of Northern politician.
Dror, *draw.*
Du, *do.*
Dunno, dno, *do not* or *does not know.*
Dut, *dirt.*

E.

Eend, *end.*
Ef, *if.*
Emptins, *yeast.*
Env'y, *envoy.*
Everlasting, an intensive, without reference to duration.
Ev'y, *every.*
Ez, *as.*

F.

Fence, *on the* ; said of one who halts between two opinions; a trimmer.

Fer, *for.*

Ferfle, ferful, *fearful* ; also an intensive.

Fin', *find.*

Fish-skin, used in New England to clarify coffee.

Fix, *a difficulty, a nonplus.*

Foller, folly, *to follow.*

Forrerd, *forward.*

Frum, *from.*

Fur, *far.*

Furder, *farther.*

Furrer, *furrow.* Metaphorically, *to draw a straight furrow* is to live uprightly or decorously.

Fust, *first.*

G.

Gin, *gave.*

Git, *get.*

Gret, *great.*

Grit, *spirit, energy, pluck.*

Grout, *to sulk.*

Grouty, *crabbed, surly.*

Gum, *to impose on.*

Gump, *a foolish fellow, a dullard.*

Gut, *got.*

H.

Hed, *had.*

Heern, *heard.*

Hellum, *helm.*

Hendy, *handy.*

Het, *heated.*

Hev, *have.*

Hez, *has.*

Holl, *whole.*

Holt, *hold.*

Huf, *hoof.*

Hull, *whole.*

Hum, *home.*

Humbug, *General Taylor's anti-slavery.*

Hut, *hurt.*

I.

Idno, *I do not know.*

In'my, *enemy.*

Insines, *ensigns;* used to designate both the officer who carries the standard, and the standard itself.

Inter, intu, *into.*

J.

Jedge, *judge.*

Jest, *just.*

Jine, *join.*

Jint, *joint.*

Junk, *a fragment of any solid substance.*

K.

Keer, *care.*

Kep', *kept.*

Killock, *a small anchor.*

Kin', kin' o', kinder, *kind, kind of.*

L.

Lawth, *loath.*

Less, *let's, let us.*

Let daylight into, *to shoot.*

Let on, *to hint, to confess, to own.*

Lick, *to beat, to overcome.*

Lights, *the bowels.*

Lily-pads, *leaves of the water-lily.*

Long-sweetening, *molasses.*

M.

Mash, *marsh.*

Mean, *stingy, ill-natured.*

Min', *mind.*

N.

Nimepunce, *ninepence, twelve and a half cents.*

Nowers, *nowhere.*

O.

Offen, *often.*

Ole, *old.*

Ollers, olluz, *always.*

On, *of;* used before *it* or *them*, or at the end of a sentence, as *on't, on'em, nut ez ever I heerd on.*

On'y, *only.*

Ossifer, *officer*, (seldom heard).

P.

Peaked, *pointed*.
Peek, *to peep*.
Pickerel, *the pike, a fish*.
Pint, *point*.
Pocket full of rocks, *plenty of money*.
Pooty, *pretty*.
Pop'ler, *conceited, popular*.
Pus, *purse*.
Put out, *troubled, vexed*.

Q.

Quarter, *a quarter-dollar*.
Queen's-arm, *a musket*.

R.

Resh, *rush*.
Revelee, *the réveille*.
Rile, *to trouble*.
Riled, *angry ; disturbed*, as the sediment in any liquid.
Riz, *risen*.
Row, a long row to hoe, *a difficult task*.
Rugged, *robust*.

S.

Sarse, *abuse, impertinence*.
Sartin, *certain*.
Saxon, *sacristan, sexton*.
Scaliest, *worst*.
Scringe, *cringe*.
Scrouge, *to crowd*.
Sech, *such*.
Set by, *valued*.
Shakes, great, *of considerable consequence*.
Shappoes, *chapeaux, cocked-hats*.
Sheer, *share*.
Shet, *shut*.
Shut, *shirt*.
Skeered, *scared*.
Skeeter, *mosquito*.
Skooting, *running*, or *moving swiftly*.
Slarterin', *slaughtering*.
Slim, *contemptible*.
Snaked, *crawled like a snake ;* but *to snake any one out* is to track him to his hiding-place ; *to snake a thing out* is to snatch it out.

Soffies, *sofas*.
Sogerin', *soldiering ;* a barbarous amusement common among men in the savage state.
Som'ers, *somewhere*.
So'st, *so as that*.
Sot, *set, obstinate, resolute*.
Spiles, *spoils ; objects of political ambition*.
Spry, *active*.
Staddles, *stout stakes driven into the salt marshes*, on which the hay-ricks are set, and thus raised out of the reach of high tides.
Streaked, *uncomfortable, discomfited*.
Suckle, *circle*.
Sutthin', *something*.
Suttin, *certain*.

T.

Take on, *to sorrow*.
Talents, *talons*.
Taters, *potatoes*.
Tell, *till*.
Tetch, *touch*.
Tetch tu, *to be able ;* used always after a negative in this sense.
Tollable, *tolerable*.
Toot, used derisively for *playing on any wind instrument*.
Thru, *through*.
Thundering, a euphemism common in New England, for the profane English expression *devilish*. Perhaps derived from the belief, common formerly, that thunder was caused by the Prince of the Air, for some of whose accomplishments consult Cotton Mather.
Tu, *to, too ;* commonly has this sound when used emphatically, or at the end of a sentence. At other times it has the sound of *t* in *tough*, as, *Ware ye goin' tu? Goin' ta Boston*.

U.

Ugly, *ill-tempered, intractable*.
Uncle Sam, *United States ;* the largest boaster of liberty and owner of slaves.

Unrizzest, applied to dough or bread; *heavy, most unrisen,* or *most incapable of rising.*

V.

V-spot, *a five-dollar bill.*
Vally, *value.*

W.

Wake snakes, *to get into trouble.*
Wal, *well;* spoken with great deliberation, and sometimes with the *a* very much flattened, sometimes (but more seldom) very much broadened.
Wannut, *walnut,* (*hickory.*)
Ware, *where.*
Ware, *were.*
Whopper, *an uncommonly large lie;* as, that General Taylor is in favor of the Wilmot Proviso.

Wig, *Whig;* a party now dissolved.
Wunt, *will not.*
Wus, *worse.*
Wut, *what.*
Wuth, *worth;* as, *Antislavery perfessions 'fore 'lection aint wuth a Bungtown copper.*
Wuz, *was,* sometimes *were.*

Y.

Yaller, *yellow.*
Yeller, *yellow.*
Yellers, *a disease of peach-trees.*

Z.

Zach, Ole, *a second Washington, an antislavery slaveholder, a humane buyer and seller of men and women, a Christian hero generally.*

INDEX.

A.

A. wants his axe ground, 282.

A. B., information wanted concerning, 207.

Abraham (Lincoln), his constitutional scruples, 282.

Abuse, an, its usefulness, 295.

Adam, eldest son of, respected, 185 — his fall, 301 — how if he had bitten a sweet apple? 304.

Adam, Grandfather, forged will of, 271.

Æneas goes to hell, 214.

Æolus, a seller of money, as is supposed by some, 215.

Æschylus, a saying of, 199, *note*.

Alligator, a decent one conjectured to be, in some sort, humane, 220.

Allsmash, the eternal, 286.

Alphonso the Sixth of Portugal, tyrannical act of, 221.

Ambrose, Saint, excellent (but rationalistic) sentiment of, 193.

"American Citizen," new compost so called, 215.

American Eagle, a source of inspiration, 196 — hitherto wrongly classed, 199 — long bill of, *ib.*

Americans bebrothered, 265.

Amos cited, 193.

Anakim, that they formerly existed, shown, 221.

Angels providentially speak French, 189 — conjectured to be skilled in all tongues, *ib.*

Anglo-Saxondom, its idea, what, 188.

Anglo-Saxon mask, 188.

Anglo-Saxon race, 187.

Anglo-Saxon verse, by whom carried to perfection, 186.

Antiquaries, Royal Society of Northern, 289.

Antonius, a speech of, 194 — by whom best reported, *ib.*

Antony of Padua, Saint, happy in his hearers, 275.

Apocalypse, beast in, magnetic to theologians, 209.

Apollo, confessed mortal by his own oracle, 209.

Apollyon, his tragedies popular, 206.

Appian, an Alexandrian, not equal to Shakespeare as an orator, 194.

Applause, popular, the *summum bonum*, 291.

Ararat, ignorance of foreign tongues is an, 200.

Arcadian background, 216.

Ar c'houskezik, an evil spirit, 275.

Ardennes, Wild Boar of, an ancestor of Rev. Mr. Wilbur, 254.

Aristocracy, British, their natural sympathies, 280.

Aristophanes, 192.

Arms, profession of, once esteemed, especially that of gentlemen, 185.

Arnold, 195.

Ashland, 216.

Astor, Jacob, a rich man, 211.

Astræa, nineteenth century forsaken by, 215.

Athenians, ancient, an institution of, 195.

Atherton, Senator, envies the loon, 202.

"Atlantic," editors of. See *Neptune.*

Atropos, a lady skilful with the scissors, 304.

Austin, Saint, profane wish of, 195; *note* — prayer of, 254.

Austrian eagle split, 295.

Aye-Aye, the, an African animal, America supposed to be settled by, 190.

B.

B., a Congressman, *vide A.*

Babel, probably the first Congress, 200 — a gabble-mill, *ib.*

THE UNHAPPY LOT OF MR. KNOTT.

1850.

THE UNHAPPY LOT OF MR. KNOTT.

PART I.

SHOWING HOW HE BUILT HIS HOUSE
AND HIS WIFE MOVED INTO IT.

MY worthy friend, A. Gordon Knott,
　From business snug withdrawn,
Was much contented with a lot
That would contain a Tudor cot
'Twixt twelve feet square of garden-
　　plot,
　And twelve feet more of lawn.

He had laid business on the shelf
　To give his taste expansion,
And, since no man, retired with pelf,
The building mania can shun,
Knott, being middle-aged himself,
Resolved to build (unhappy elf !)
　A mediæval mansion.

He called an architect in counsel ;
　" I want," said he, " a — you know
　　what,
(You are a builder, I am Knott,)
　A thing complete from chimney-pot
Down to the very grounsel ;
　Here 's a half-acre of good land ;
　Just have it nicely mapped and
　　planned
And make your workmen drive on ;
　Meadow there is, and upland too,
　And I should like a water-view,
　D' you think you could contrive one ?
　(Perhaps the pump and trough would
　　do,
　　If painted a judicious blue ?)
　The woodland I 've attended to :
　(He meant three pines stuck up
　　askew,
Two dead ones and a live one.)
　" A pocket-full of rocks 't would take
To build a house of free-stone,
　But then it is not hard to make

What nowadays is *the* stone ;
　The cunning painter in a trice
　Your house's outside petrifies,
　And people think it very gneiss
Without inquiring deeper ;
　My money never shall be thrown
　Away on such a deal of stone,
When stone of deal is cheaper."

And so the greenest of antiques
　Was reared for Knott to dwell in :
The architect worked hard for weeks
In venting all his private peaks
Upon the roof, whose crop of leaks
　Had satisfied Fluellen ;
Whatever anybody had
Out of the common, good or bad,
　Knott had it all worked well in,
A donjon-keep, where clothes might
　　dry,
A porter's lodge that was a sty,
A campanile slim and high,
　Too small to hang a bell in ;
All up and down and here and there,
With Lord-knows-whats of round and
　　square
Stuck on at random everywhere, —
It was a house to make one stare,
　All corners and all gables ;
Like dogs let loose upon a bear,
Ten emulous styles *staboyed* with care,
The whole among them seemed to tear,
And all the oddities to spare
　Were set upon the stables.

Knott was delighted with a pile
　Approved by fashion's leaders :
(Only he made the builder smile,
By asking, every little while,
Why that was called the Twodoor style,
　Which certainly had *three* doors ?)
Yet better for this luckless man
If he had put a downright ban
　Upon the thing *in limine* ;

For, though to quit affairs his plan,
　Ere many days, poor Knott began
Perforce accepting draughts, that ran
　All ways — except up chimney;
The house, though painted stone to
　　mock,
With nice white lines round every block
　Some trepidation stood in,
When tempests (with petrific shock,
So to speak,) made it really rock,
　Though not a whit less wooden;
And painted stone, howe'er well done,
Will not take in the prodigal sun
Whose beams are never quite at one
　With our terrestrial lumber;
So the wood shrank around the knots,
And gaped in disconcerting spots,
And there were lots of dots and rots
　And crannies without number,
Wherethrough, as you may well pre-
　　sume,
The wind, like water through a flume,
　Came rushing in ecstatic,
Leaving, in all three floors, no room
　That was not a rheumatic;
And, what with points and squares and
　　rounds
Grown shaky on their poises,
The house at nights was full of pounds,
Thumps, bumps, creaks, scratchings,
　raps — till — "Zounds!"
Cried Knott, "this all goes beyond
　　bounds;
I do not deal in tongues and sounds,
Nor have I let my house and grounds
　To a family of Noyeses!"

But, though Knott's house was full of
　　airs,
He had but one — a daughter;
And, as he owned much stocks and
　　shares,
Many who wished to render theirs
Such vain, unsatisfying cares,
And needed wives to sew their tears,
　In matrimony sought her;
They vowed her gold they wanted not,
　Their faith would never falter,
They longed to tie this single Knott
　In the Hymenæal halter;
So daily at the door they rang,
　Cards for the belle delivering,
Or in the choir at her they sang,
Achieving such a rapturous twang
　As set her nerves ashivering.

Now Knott had quite made up his
　　mind
　That Colonel Jones should have her;
No beauty he, but oft we find
Sweet kernels 'neath a roughish rind,
So hoped his Jenny 'd be resigned
　And make no more palaver;
Glanced at the fact that love was blind,
That girls were ratherish inclined
　To pet their little crosses,
Then nosologically defined
The rate at which the system pined
In those unfortunates who dined
Upon that metaphoric kind
　Of dish — their own proboscis.

But she, with many tears and moans,
　Besought him not to mock her,
Said 't was too much for flesh and
　　bones
To marry mortgages and loans,
That fathers' hearts were stocks and
　　stones,
And that she 'd go, when Mrs. Jones,
　To Davy Jones's locker;
Then gave her head a little toss
That said as plain as ever was,
　If men are always at a loss
　　Mere womankind to bridle —
To try the thing on woman cross
　Were fifty times as idle;
For she a strict resolve had made
　And registered in private,
That either she would die a maid,
Or else be Mrs. Doctor Slade,
　If woman could contrive it;
And, though the wedding-day was set,
　Jenny was more so, rather,
Declaring, in a pretty pet,
That, howsoe'er they spread their net,
She would out-Jennyral them yet,
　The colonel and her father.

Just at this time the Public's eyes
　Were keenly on the watch, a stir
Beginning slowly to arise
About those questions and replies,
Those raps that unwrapped mysteries
　So rapidly at Rochester,
And Knott, already nervous grown
By lying much awake alone,
And listening, sometimes to a moan,
　And sometimes to a clatter,
Whene'er the wind at night would rouse
The gingerbread-work on his house,
Or when some hasty-tempered mouse,

Behind the plastering, made a towse
  About a family matter,
Began to wonder if his wife,
A paralytic half her life,
Which made it more surprising,
Might not to rule him from her urn,
Have taken a peripatetic turn
  For want of exorcising.

This thought, once nestled in his head,
Erelong contagious grew, and spread
Infecting all his mind with dread,
Until at last he lay in bed
  And heard his wife, with well-known
    tread,
Entering the kitchen through the shed,
  (Or was 't his fancy, mocking?)
Opening the pantry, cutting bread,
And then (she 'd been some ten years
    dead)
  Closets and drawers unlocking;
Or, in his room (his breath grew thick)
He heard the long-familiar click
Of slender needles flying quick,
  As if she knit a stocking;
For whom? — he prayed that years
    might first
  With pains rheumatic shooting,
Before those ghostly things she knit
Upon his unfleshed sole might fit,
He did not fancy it a bit,
  To stand upon that footing;
At other times, his frightened hairs
Above the bedclothes trusting,
He heard her, full of household cares,
  (No dream entrapped in supper's
    snares,
The foal of horrible nightmares,
  But broad awake, as he declares,)
Go bustling up and down the stairs,
Or setting back last evening's chairs,
  Or with the poker thrusting
The raked-up sea-coal's hardened
    crust —
And — what! impossible! it must!
He knew she had returned to dust,
And yet could scarce his senses trust,
Hearing her as she poked and fussed
  About the parlor, dusting!

Night after night he strove to sleep
  And take his ease in spite of it;
But still his flesh would chill and creep,
And, though two night-lamps he might
    keep,

He could not so make light of it.
At last, quite desperate, he goes
And tells his neighbors all his woes,
  Which did but their amount enhance;
They made such mockery of his fears
That soon his days were of all jeers,
  His nights of the rueful countenance:
"I thought most folks," one neighbor
    said,
"Gave up the ghost when they were
    dead,"
Another gravely shook his head,
  Adding, "from all we hear, it 's
Quite plain poor Knott is going mad —
For how can he at once be sad
  And think he 's full of spirits?"
A third declared he knew a knife
  Would cut this Knott much quicker,
"The surest way to end all strife,
And lay the spirit of a wife,
  Is just to take and lick her!"
A temperance man caught up the word,
"Ah, yes," he groaned, "I 've always
    heard
  Our poor friend somewhat slanted
Tow'rd taking liquor overmuch;
I fear these spirits may be Dutch,
  (A sort of gins, or something such,)
  With which his house is haunted;
I see the thing as clear as light, —
If Knott would give up getting tight,
  Naught farther would be wanted":
So all his neighbors stood aloof
And, that the spirits 'neath his roof
Were not entirely up to proof,
  Unanimously granted.

Knott knew that cocks and sprites were
    foes,
And so bought up, Heaven only knows
How many, for he wanted crows
To give ghosts caws, as I suppose,
  To think that day was breaking;
Moreover what he called his park,
He turned into a kind of ark
For dogs, because a little bark
  Is a good tonic in the dark,
  If one is given to waking;
But things went on from bad to worse,
His curs were nothing but a curse,
  And, what was still more shocking,
Foul ghosts of living fowl made scoff
And would not think of going off
  In spite of all his cocking.

23

Shanghais, Bucks-counties, Domini-
　　ques,
Malays (that did n't lay for weeks,)
Polanders, Bantams, Dorkings,
(Waiving the cost, no trifling ill,
Since each brought in his little bill,)
By day or night were never still,
But every thought of rest would kill
　With cacklings and with quorkings;
Henry the Eighth of wives got free
　By a way he had of axing;
But poor Knott's Tudor henery
　Was not so fortunate, and he
　Still found his trouble waxing;
As for the dogs, the rows they made,
And how they howled, snarled, barked
　　and bayed,
Beyond all human knowledge is;
All night, as wide awake as gnats,
The terriers rumpused after rats,
Or, just for practice, taught their brats
　To worry cast-off shoes and hats,
The bull-dogs settled private spats,
All chased imaginary cats,
Or raved behind the fence's slats
At real ones, or, from their mats,
With friends, miles off, held pleasant
　　chats,
Or, like some folks in white cravats,
Contemptuous of sharps and flats,
　Sat up and sang dogsologies.
Meanwhile the cats set up a squall,
And, safe upon the garden-wall,
　All night kept cat-a-walling,
As if the feline race were all,
In one wild cataleptic sprawl,
　Into love's tortures falling.

PART II.

SHOWING WHAT IS MEANT BY A FLOW
OF SPIRITS.

At first the ghosts were somewhat shy,
Coming when none but Knott was nigh,
And people said 't was all their eye,
(Or rather his) a flam, the sly
　Digestion's machination;
Some recommended a wet sheet,
Some a nice broth of pounded peat,
Some a cold flat-iron to the feet,
Some a decoction of lamb's-bleat.

Some a southwesterly grain of wheat;
Meat was by some pronounced unmeet,
Others thought fish most indiscreet,
And that 't was worse than all to eat
Of vegetables, sour or sweet,
(Except, perhaps, the skin of beet,)
　In such a concatenation:
One quack his button gently plucks
And murmurs "biliary ducks!"
　Says Knott, "I never ate one";
But all, though brimming full of wrath,
Homœo, Allo, Hydropath,
Concurred in this — that t'other's path
　To death's door was the straight one.
Still, spite of medical advice,
The ghosts came thicker, and a spice
　Of mischief grew apparent;
Nor did they only come at night,
But seemed to fancy broad daylight,
Till Knott, in horror and affright,
　His unoffending hair rent;
Whene'er with handkerchief on lap,
He made his elbow-chair a trap,
To catch an after-dinner nap,
The spirits, always on the tap,
Would make a sudden *rap, rap, rap,*
The half-spun cord of sleep to snap,
(And what is life without its nap
But threadbareness and mere mishap?)
As 't were with a percussion cap
　The trouble's climax capping;
It seemed a party dried and grim
Of mummies had come to visit him,
Each getting off from every limb
　Its multitudinous wrapping;
Scratchings sometimes the walls ran
　　round,
The merest penny-weights of sound;
Sometimes 't was only by the pound
　They carried on their dealing,
A thumping 'neath the parlor floor,
Thump-bump-thump-bumping o'er and
　　o'er,
As if the vegetables in store
　(Quiet and orderly before)
　Were all together pealing;
You would have thought the thing was
　　done
By the spirit of some son of a gun,
And that a forty-two-pounder,
Or that the ghost which made such
　　sounds
Could be none other than John Pounds,
　Of Ragged Schools the founder.

Through three gradations of affright,
The awful noises reached their height ;
  At first they knocked nocturnally,
Then, for some reason, changing quite,
(As mourners, after six months' flight,
Turn suddenly from dark to light,)
  Began to knock diurnally,
And last, combining all their stocks,
  (Scotland was ne'er so full of Knox,)
Into one Chaos (father of Nox,)
Nocte pluit — they showered knocks,
  And knocked, knocked, knocked, knocked,
          eternally ;
Ever upon the go, like buoys,
(Wooden sea-urchins,) all Knott's joys,
They turned to troubles and a noise
  That preyed on him internally.

Soon they grew wider in their scope ;
Whenever Knott a door would ope,
  It would ope not, or else elope
And fly back (curbless as a trope
Once started down a stanza's slope
By a bard that gave it too much rope —)
  Like a clap of thunder slamming ;
And, when kind Jenny brought his hat,
(She always, when he walked, did that,)
Just as upon his head it sat,
  Submitting to his settling pat —
Some unseen hand would jam it flat,
Or give it such a furious bat
  That eyes and nose went cramming
Up out of sight, and consequently,
As when in life it paddled free,
  His beaver caused much damning ;
If these things seem o'er-strained to be,
Read the account of Doctor Dee,
'T is in our college library ;
Read Wesley's circumstantial plea,
And Mrs. Crowe, more like a bee,
Sucking the nightshade's honeyed fee,
And Stilling's Pneumatology ;
Consult Scot, Glanvil, grave Wie-
  rus, and both Mathers ; further see,
Webster, Casaubon, James First's trea-
  tise, a right royal Q. E. D.
Writ with the moon in perigee,
Bodin de Demonomanie —
(Accent that last line gingerly)
All full of learning as the sea
Of fishes, and all disagree,
Save in *Sathanas apage !*
Or, what will surely put a flea
In unbelieving ears — with glee,

Out of a paper (sent to me
By some friend who forgot to P...
A...Y... — I use cryptography
Lest I his vengeful pen should dree —
His P...O...S...T...A...G...E...)
  Things to the same effect I cut,
About the tantrums of a ghost,
Not more than three weeks since, at
          most,
      Near Stratford, in Connecticut.

Knott's Upas daily spread its roots,
Sent up on all sides livelier shoots,
And bore more pestilential fruits ;
  The ghosts behaved like downright
          brutes,
They snipped holes in his Sunday suits,
Practised all night on octave flutes,
Put peas (not peace) into his boots,
  Whereof grew corns in season,
They scotched his sheets, and, what
          was worse,
Stuck his silk nightcap full of burrs,
Till he, in language plain and terse,
(But much unlike a Bible verse,)
  Swore he should lose his reason.

The tables took to spinning, too,
Perpetual yarns, and arm-chairs grew
  To prophets and apostles ;
One footstool vowed that only he
Of law and gospel held the key,
That teachers of whate'er degree
To whom opinion bows the knee
Wern't fit to teach Truth's a. b. c.
And were (the whole lot) to a T
  Mere fogies all and fossils ;
A teapoy, late the property
  Of Knox's Aunt Keziah,
(Whom Jenny most irreverently
Had nicknamed her aunt-tipathy)
With tips emphatic claimed to be
  The prophet Jeremiah ;
The tins upon the kitchen-wall,
Turned tintinnabulators all,
And things that used to come at call
  For simple household services
Began to hop and whirl and prance,
Fit to put out of countenance
The *Commis* and *Grisettes* of France
  Or Turkey's dancing Dervises.

Of course such doings, far and wide,
With rumors filled the country-side,

And (as it is our nation's pride
To think a Truth not verified
Till with majorities allied,)
Parties sprung up, affirmed, denied,
And candidates with questions plied,
Who, like the circus-riders, tried
At once both hobbies to bestride,
And each with his opponent vied
     In being inexplicit.

Earnest inquirers multiplied ;
Folks, whose tenth cousins lately died,
Wrote letters long, and Knott replied ;
All who could either walk or ride
Gathered to wonder or deride,
     And paid the house a visit ;
Horses were at his pine-trees tied,
Mourners in every corner sighed,
Widows brought children there that
     cried,
Swarms of lean Seekers, eager-eyed,
(People Knott never could abide,)
Into each hole and cranny pried
With strings of questions cut and dried
From the Devout Inquirer's Guide,
For the wise spirits to decide —
     As, for example, is it
True that the damned are fried or
     boiled ?
Was the Earth's axis greased or oiled ?
Who cleaned the moon when it was
     soiled ?
How baldness might be cured or foiled ?
     How heal diseased potatoes ?
Did spirits have the sense of smell ?
Where would departed spinsters dwell ?
If the late Zenas Smith were well ?
If Earth were solid or a shell ?
Were spirits fond of Doctor Fell ?
Did the bull toll Cock-Robin's knell ?
What remedy would bugs expel ?
If Paine's invention were a sell ?
Did spirits by Webster's system spell ?
Was it a sin to be a belle ?
Did dancing sentence folks to hell ?
If so, then where most torture fell —
     On little toes or great toes ?
If life's true seat were in the brain ?
Did Ensign mean to marry Jane ?
By whom, in fact, was Morgan slain ?
Could matter ever suffer pain ?
What would take out a cherry-stain ?
Who picked the pocket of Seth Crane,
Of Waldo precinct, State of Maine ?
Was Sir John Franklin sought in vain ?

Did primitive Christians ever train ?
What was the family-name of Cain ?
Them spoons, were they by Betty
     ta'en ?
Would earth-worm poultice cure a
     sprain ?
Was Socrates so dreadful plain ?
What teamster guided Charles's wain ?
Was Uncle Ethan mad or sane,
And could his will in force remain ?
If not, what counsel to retain ?
Did Le Sage steal Gil Blas from Spain ?
Was Junius writ by Thomas Paine ?
Were ducks discomforted by rain ?
How did Britannia rule the main ?
Was Jonas coming back again ?
Was vital truth upon the wane ?
Did ghosts, to scare folks, drag a chain ?
Who was our Huldah's chosen swain ?
Did none have teeth pulled without
     payin',
     Ere ether was invented ?
Whether mankind would not agree,
If the universe were tuned in C. ?
What was it ailed Lucindy's knee ?
Whether folks eat folks in Feejee ?
Whether *his* name would end with T. ?
If Saturn's rings were two or three,
And what bump in Phrenology
     They truly represented ?
These problems dark, wherein they
     groped,
Wherewith man's reason vainly coped,
Now that the spirit-world was oped,
In all humility they hoped
     Would be resolved *instanter* ;
Each of the miscellaneous rout
Brought his, or her, own little doubt,
And wished to pump the spirits out,
Through his, or her, own private spout,
     Into his or her decanter.

PART III.

WHEREIN IT IS SHOWN THAT THE
MOST ARDENT SPIRITS ARE MORE
ORNAMENTAL THAN USEFUL.

Many a speculating wight
Came by express-trains, day and night,
To see if Knott would "sell his right,"
Meaning to make the ghosts a sight —
     What they called a "meenaygerie" ;

One threatened, if he would not
    "trade,"
His run of custom to invade,
(He could not these sharp folks per-
    suade
That he was not, in some way, paid,)
    And stamp him as a plagiary,
By coming down, at one fell swoop,
With THE ORIGINAL KNOCKING
    TROUPE,
Come recently from Hades,
Who (for a quarter-dollar heard)
Would ne'er rap out a hasty word
Whence any blame might be incurred
    From the most fastidious ladies;
The late lamented Jesse Soule
To stir the ghosts up with a pole
And be director of the whole,
    Who was engaged the rather
For the rare merits he'd combine,
Having been in the spirit line,
Which trade he only did resign,
    With general applause, to shine,
Awful in mail of cotton fine,
    As ghost of Hamlet's father!
Another a fair plan reveals
Never yet hit on, which, he feels,
To Knott's religious sense appeals—
"We'll have your house set up on
    wheels,
    A speculation pious;
For music, we can shortly find
A barrel-organ that will grind
Psalm-tunes,—an instrument designed
For the New England tour—refined
From secular drosses, and inclined
To an unworldly turn, (combined
    With no sectarian bias;)
Then, travelling by stages slow,
Under the style of Knott & Co.,
I would accompany the show
As moral lecturer, the foe
Of Rationalism; you could throw
The rappings in, and make them go
Strict Puritan principles, you know,
(How *do* you make 'em? with your
    toe?)
And the receipts which thence might
    flow,
    We could divide between us;
Still more attractions to combine,
Beside these services of mine,
I will throw in a very fine
(It would do nicely for a sign)

    Original Titian's Venus."
Another offered handsome fees
If Knott would get Demosthenes
(Nay, his mere knuckles, for more ease)
To rap a few short sentences;
Or if, for want of proper keys,
    His Greek might make confusion,
Then just to get a rap from Burke,
To recommend a little work
    On Public Elocution.
Meanwhile, the spirits made replies
To all the reverent *whats* and *whys*,
Resolving doubts of every size,
And giving seekers grave and wise,
Who came to know their destinies,
    A rap-turous reception;
When unbelievers void of grace
Came to investigate the place,
(Creatures of Sadducistic race,
    With grovelling intellects and base,)
They could not find the slightest trace
    To indicate deception;
Indeed, it is declared by some
That spirits (of this sort) are glum,
Almost, or wholly, deaf and dumb,
And (out of self-respect) quite mum
To sceptic natures cold and numb,
Who of *this* kind of Kingdom Come
    Have not a just conception;
True, there were people who demurred
That, though the raps no doubt were
    heard
    Both under them and o'er them,
Yet, somehow, when a search they made,
They found Miss Jenny sore afraid,
Or Jenny's lover, Doctor Slade,
Equally awe-struck and dismayed,
Or Deborah, the chamber-maid,
Whose terrors not to be gainsaid,
In laughs hysteric were displayed,
    Was always there before them;
This had its due effect with some
Who straight departed, muttering,
    Hum!
    Transparent hoax! and Gammon!
But these were few: believing souls
Came, day by day, in larger shoals,
As the ancients to the windy holes
'Neath Delphi's tripod brought their
    doles,
    Or to the shrine of Ammon.

The spirits seemed exceeding tame,
Call whom you fancied, and he came;

The shades august of eldest fame
    You summoned with an awful ease ;
As grosser spirits gurgled out
From chair and table with a spout,
In Auerbach's cellar once, to flout
The senses of the rabble rout,
Where'er the gimlet twirled about
    Of cunning Mephistophiles —
So did these spirits seem in store,
Behind the wainscot or the door,
Ready to thrill the being's core
Of every enterprising bore
    With their astounding glamour ;
Whatever ghost one wished to hear,
By strange coincidence, was near
To make the past or future clear
    (Sometimes in shocking grammar)
By raps and taps, now there, now
        here —
It seemed as if the spirit queer
Of some departed auctioneer
Were doomed to practise by the year
    With the spirit of his hammer ;
Whate'er you asked was answered, yet
One could not very deeply get
Into the obliging spirits' debt,
Because they used the alphabet
    In all communications,
And new revealings (though sublime)
Rapped out, one letter at a time,
    With boggles, hesitations,
Stoppings, beginnings o'er again,
And getting matters into train,
Could hardly overload the brain
    With too excessive rations,
Since just to ask *if two and two
Really make four ?* or, *How d' ye
    do ?*
And get the fit replies thereto
In the tramundane rat-tat-too,
    Might ask a whole day's patience.

'T was strange ('mongst other things) to
        find
In what odd sets the ghosts combined,
    Happy forthwith to thump any
Piece of intelligence inspired,
The truth whereof had been inquired
    By some one of the company ;
For instance, Fielding, Mirabeau,
Orator Henley, Cicero,
Paley, John Zisca, Marivaux,
Melancthon, Robertson, Junot,
Scaliger, Chesterfield, Rousseau,

Hakluyt, Boccaccio, South, De Foe,
Diaz, Josephus, Richard Roe,
Odin, Arminius, Charles *le gros*,
Tiresias, the late James Crow,
Casabianca, Grose, Prideaux,
Old Grimes, Young Norval, Swift,
        Brissot,
Maimonides, the Chevalier D'O,
Socrates, Fenelon, Job, Stow,
The inventor of *Elixir pro*,
Euripides, Spinoza, Poe,
Confucius, Hiram Smith, and Fo,
Came (as it seemed, somewhat *de trop*)
With a disembodied Esquimaux,
To say that it was so and so,
    With Franklin's expedition ;
One testified to ice and snow,
One that the mercury was low,
One that his progress was quite slow,
One that he much desired to go,
One that the cook had frozen his toe,
(Dissented from by Dandolo,
Wordsworth, Cynaegirus, Boileau,
La Hontan, and Sir Thomas Roe,)
One saw twelve white bears in a row,
One saw eleven and a crow,
With other things we could not know
(Of great statistic value, though)
    By our mere mortal vision.

Sometimes the spirits made mistakes,
And seemed to play at ducks and drakes
With bold inquiry's hardiest stakes
    In science or in mystery ;
They knew so little (and that wrong)
Yet rapped it out so bold and strong,
One would have said the entire throng
    Had been Professors of History ;
What made it odder was, that those
Who, you would naturally suppose,
Could solve a question, if they chose,
As easily as count their toes,
    Were just the ones that blundered ;
One day, Ulysses happening down,
A reader of Sir Thomas Browne
    And who (with him) had wondered
What song it was the Sirens sang,
Asked the shrewd Ithacan — *bang !
    bang !*
With this response the chamber rang,
    " I guess it was Old Hundred."
And Franklin, being asked to name
The reason why the lightning came,
    Replied, " Because it thundered."

On one sole point the ghosts agreed,
One fearful point, than which, indeed,
  Nothing could seem absurder;
Poor Colonel Jones they all abused,
And finally downright accused
  The poor old man of murder;
'T was thus; by dreadful raps was
    shown
Some spirit's longing to make known
A bloody fact, which he alone
Was privy to, (such ghosts more prone
  In Earth's affairs to meddle are;)
Who are you? with awe-stricken looks,
All ask: his airy knuckles he crooks,
And raps, "I *was* Eliab Snooks,
  That used to be a pedler;
Some on ye still are on my books!"
Whereat, to inconspicuous nooks,
(More fearing this than common
    spooks,)
  Shrank each indebted meddler;
Further the vengeful ghost declared
That while his earthly life was spared,
About the country he had fared,
  A duly licensed follower
Of that much-wandering trade that wins
Slow profit from the sale of tins
  And various kinds of hollow-ware;
That Colonel Jones enticed him in,
Pretending that he wanted tin,
There slew him with a rolling-pin,
Hid him in a potato-bin,
  And (the same night) him ferried
Across Great Pond to t'other shore,
And there, on land of Widow Moore,
Just where you turn to Larkin's store,
  Under a rock him buried;
Some friends (who happened to be by)
He called upon to testify
That what he said was not a lie,
  And that he did not stir this
Foul matter, out of any spite
But from a simple love of right;—
  Which statements the Nine Wor-
    thies,
Rabbi Akiba, Charlemagne,
Seth, Colley Cibber, General Wayne,
Cambyses, Tasso, Tubal-Cain,
The owner of a castle in Spain,
Jehanghire, and the Widow of Nain,
(The friends aforesaid,) made more plain
  And by loud raps attested;
To the same purport testified
Plato, John Wilkes, and Colonel Pride

Who knew said Snooks before he died,
  Had in his wares invested,
Thought him entitled to belief
And freely could concur, in brief,
  In everything the rest did.

Eliab this occasion seized,
(Distinctly here the spirit sneezed,)
To say that he should ne'er be eased
Till Jenny married whom she pleased,
  Free from all checks and urgin's,
(This spirit dropt his final g's)
And that, unless Knott quickly sees
This done, the spirits to appease,
They would come back his life to tease,
As thick as mites in ancient cheese,
And let his house on an endless lease
To the ghosts (terrific rappers these
And veritable Eumenides)
  Of the Eleven Thousand Virgins!

Knott was perplexed and shook his
    head,
He did not wish his child to wed
  With a suspected murderer,
(For, true or false, the rumor spread,)
But as for this roiled life he led,
"It would not answer," so he said,
  "To have it go no furderer."
At last, scarce knowing what it meant,
Reluctantly he gave consent
That Jenny, since 't was evident
That she *would* follow her own bent,
  Should make her own election;
For that appeared the only way
These frightful noises to allay
Which had already turned him gray
  And plunged him in dejection.

Accordingly, this artless maid
Her father's ordinance obeyed,
And, all in whitest crape arrayed,
(Miss Pulsifer the dresses made
And wishes here the fact displayed
That she still carries on the trade,
The third door south from Bagg's Ar-
    cade,)
A very faint "I do" essayed
And gave her hand to Hiram Slade,
From which time forth, the ghosts were
    laid,
  And ne'er gave trouble after;
But the Selectmen, be it known,

Dug underneath the aforesaid stone,
Where the poor pedler's corpse was
   thrown,
And found thereunder a jaw-bone,
Though, when the crowner sat thereon,
He nothing hatched, except alone
   Successive broods of laughter;
It was a frail and dingy thing,
In which a grinder or two did cling,
   In color like molasses,
Which surgeons, called from far and
   wide,
Upon the horror to decide,
Having put on their glasses,
Reported thus — " To judge by looks,
These bones, by some queer hooks or
   crooks,
May have belonged to Mr. Snooks,
But, as men deepest-read in books
   Are perfectly aware, bones,
If buried fifty years or so,
Lose their identity and grow
   From human bones to bare bones."

Still, if to Jaalam you go down,
You 'll find two parties in the town,
One headed by Benaiah Brown;
   And one by Perez Tinkham ;
The first believe the ghosts all through
And vow that they shall never rue
The happy chance by which they knew
That people in Jupiter are blue,
And very fond of Irish stew,

Two curious facts which Prince Lee
   Boo
Rapped clearly to a chosen few —
   Whereas the others think 'em
A trick got up by Doctor Slade
With Deborah the chamber-maid
   And that sly cretur Jinny.
That all the revelations wise,
At which the Brownites made big eyes,
Might have been given by Jared Keyes,
   A natural fool and ninny,
And, last week, did n't Eliab Snooks
Come back with never better looks,
As sharp as new-bought mackerel
   hooks,
   And bright as a new pin, eh?
Good Parson Wilbur, too, avers
(Though to be mixed in parish stirs
Is worse than handling chestnut-burrs)
That no case to his mind occurs
Where spirits ever did converse
Save in a kind of guttural Erse,
   (So say the best authorities ;)
And that a charge by raps conveyed,
Should be most scrupulously weighed
   And searched into, before it is
Made public, since it may give pain
That cannot soon be cured again,
And one word may infix a stain
   Which ten cannot gloss over,
Though speaking for his private part,
He is rejoiced with all his heart
   Miss Knott missed not her lover.

AN ORIENTAL APOLOGUE.

AN ORIENTAL APOLOGUE.

I.

SOMEWHERE in India, upon a time,
(Read it not Injah, or you spoil the
verse,)
  There dwelt two saints whose privi-
  lege sublime
It was to sit and watch the world grow
worse,
  Their only care (in that delicious
  clime)
At proper intervals to pray and curse;
  Pracrit the dialect each prudent
  brother
Used for himself, Damnonian for the
other.

II.

One half the time of each was spent
in praying
For blessings on his own unworthy head,
  The other half in fearfully portraying
Where certain folks would go when
they were dead;
  This system of exchanges — there 's
  no saying
To what more solid barter 't would have
led,
  But that a river, vext with boils and
  swellings
At rainy times, kept peace between
their dwellings.

III.

So they two played at wordy battle-
dore
And kept a curse forever in the air,
  Flying this way or that from shore to
  shore;
No other labor did this holy pair,
  Clothed and supported from the lav-
  ish store
Which crowds lanigerous brought with
daily care;

They toiled not neither did they spin;
their bias
Was tow'rd the harder task of being
pious.

IV.

Each from his hut rushed six score
times a day,
  Like a great canon of the Church full-
  rammed
With cartridge theologic, (so to say,)
  Touched himself off, and then, recoil-
  ing, slammed
His hovel's door behind him in a way
  That to his foe said plainly, — you'll
  be damned;
And so like Potts and Wainwright,
shrill and strong
The two D—D'd each other all day
long.

V.

One was a dancing Dervise, a Mo-
hammedan,
  The other was a Hindoo, a gymnoso-
  phist;
One kept his whatd'yecallit and his
Ramadan,
  Laughing to scorn the sacred rites and
  laws of his
Transfluvial rival, who, in turn, called
Ahmed an
  Old top, and, as a clincher, shook across
  a fist
With nails six inches long, yet lifted
not
His eyes from off his navel's mystic
knot.

VI.

"Who whirls not round six thousand
times an hour
  Will go," screamed Ahmed, "to the
  evil place:

May he eat dirt, and may the dog and
　　Giaour
Defile the graves of him and all his
　　race ;
Allah loves faithful souls and gives
　　them power
To spin till they are purple in the face ;
　　Some folks get you know what, but
　　　he that pure is
Earns Paradise and ninety thousand
　　houries."

VII.

"Upon the silver mountain, South
　　by East,
Sits Brahma fed upon the sacred bean ;
　　He loves those men whose nails are
　　　still increased,
Who all their lives keep ugly, foul, and
　　lean ;
　　'T is of his grace that not a bird or
　　　beast
Adorned with claws like mine was ever
　　seen ;
　　The suns and stars are Brahma's
　　　thoughts divine
Even as these trees I seem to see are
　　mine."

VIII.

"Thou seem'st to see, indeed !"
　　roared Ahmed back ;
"Were I but once across this plaguy
　　stream,
　　With a stout sapling in my hand, one
　　　whack
On those lank ribs would rid thee of
　　that Dream !
　　Thy Brahma-blasphemy is ipecac
To my soul's stomach ; couldst thou
　　grasp the scheme
　　Of true redemption, thou wouldst
　　　know that Deity
Whirls by a kind of blessed sponta-
　　neity.

IX.

"And this it is which keeps our earth
　　here going
With all the stars."—"O, vile ! but
　　there 's a place
　Prepared for such ; to think of Brah-
　　ma throwing

Worlds like a juggler's balls up into
　　Space !
Why, not so much as a smooth lotos
　　blowing
Is e'er allowed that silence to efface
　　Which broods around Brahma, and
　　　our earth, 't is known,
Rests on a tortoise, moveless as this
　　stone."

X.

So they kept up their banning amœ-
　　bean,
When suddenly came floating down the
　　stream
　A youth whose face like an incarnate
　　　pæan
Glowed, 't was so full of grandeur and
　　of gleam ;
　" If there *be* gods, then, doubtless,
　　　this must be one,"
Thought both at once, and then began
　　to scream,
　" Surely, whate'er immortals know,
　　　thou knowest,
Decide between us twain before thou
　　goest ! "

XI.

The youth was drifting in a slim ca-
　　noe
Most like a huge white waterlily's petal,
　　But neither of our theologians knew
Whereof 't was made ; whether of
　　heavenly metal
　Seldseen, or of a vast pearl split in
　　　two
And hallowed, was a point they could
　　not settle ;
　'T was good debate-seed, though,
　　　and bore large fruit
In after years of many a tart dispute.

XII.

There were no wings upon the stran-
　　ger's shoulders
And yet he seemed so capable of rising
　　That, had he soared like thistledown,
　　　beholders
Had thought the circumstance noways
　　surprising ;
　Enough that he remained, and, when
　　　the scolders

Hailed him as umpire in their vocal
　　prize-ring,
　The painter of his boat he lightly
　　　threw
　Around a lotos-stem, and brought
　　　her to.

XIII.

The strange youth had a look as if
　　he might
Have trod far planets where the atmos-
　　phere
　(Of nobler temper) steeps the face
　　　with light,
Just as our skins are tanned and freck-
　　led here;
　His air was that of a cosmopolite
In the wide universe from sphere to
　　sphere;
　Perhaps he was (his face had such
　　　grave beauty)
　An officer of Saturn's guards off duty.

XIV.

Both saints began to unfold their tales
　　at once,
Both wished their tales, like simial ones,
　　prehensile,
　That they might seize his ear; *fool!
　　　knave!* and *dunce!*
Flew zigzag back and forth, like strokes
　　of pencil
　In a child's fingers; voluble as duns,
They jabbered like the stones on that
　　immense hill
　In the *Arabian Nights*; until the
　　　stranger
　Began to think his ear-drums in some
　　　danger.

XV.

In general those who nothing have to
　　say
Contrive to spend the longest time in
　　doing it;
　They turn and vary it in every way,
Hashing it, stewing it, mincing it, *ra-
　　gouting* it;
　Sometimes they keep it purposely at
　　　bay,
Then let it slip to be again pursuing it;
　They drone it, groan it, whisper it
　　　and shout it,

Refute it, flout it, swear to 't, prove
　　it, doubt it.

XVI.

Our saints had practised for some
　　thirty years;
Their talk, beginning with a single stem,
　Spread like a banyan, sending down
　　　live piers,
　Colonies of digression, and, in them,
　Germs of yet new migrations; once
　　　by the ears,
They could convey damnation in a hem,
　And blow the pinch of premise-prim-
　　　ing off
　Long syllogistic batteries, with a
　　　cough.

XVII.

Each had a theory that the human
　　ear
A providential tunnel was, which led
　To a huge vacuüm (and surely here
They showed some knowledge of the
　　general head),
　For cant to be decanted through, a
　　　mere
Auricular canal or raceway to be fed
　All day and night, in sunshine and in
　　　shower,
　From their vast heads of milk-and-
　　　water-power.

XVIII.

The present being a peculiar case,
Each with unwonted zeal the other
　　scouted,
　Put his spurred hobby through its
　　　every pace,
Pished, pshawed, poohed, horribled,
　　bahed, jeered, sneered, flouted,
Sniffed, nonsensed, infideled, fudged,
　　with his face
Looked scorn too nicely shaded to be
　　shouted,
　And, with each inch of person and of
　　　vesture,
　Contrived to hint some most disdain-
　　　ful gesture.

XIX.

At length, when their breath's end
　　was come about,

And both could, now and then, just
　　gasp "impostor!"
　　Holding their heads thrust menacing-
　　　ly out,
As staggering cocks keep up their fight-
　　ing posture,
　　The stranger smiled and said, "Be-
　　　yond a doubt
'T is fortunate, my friends, that you
　　have lost your
　　United parts of speech, or it had been
　　Impossible for me to get between.

XX.

"Produce! says Nature,—what have
　　you produced?
A new strait-waistcoat for the human
　　mind;
　　Are you not limbed, nerved, jointed,
　　　arteried, juiced
As other men? yet, faithless to your
　　kind,
　　Rather like noxious insects you are
　　　used
To puncture life's fair fruit, beneath
　　the rind
　　Laying your creed-eggs whence in
　　　time there spring
　　Consumers new to eat and buzz and
　　　sting.

XXI.

"Work! you have no conception
　　how 't will sweeten
Your views of Life and Nature, God
　　and Man;
　　Had you been forced to earn what
　　　you have eaten,
Your heaven had shown a less dyspep-
　　tic plan;
　　At present your whole function is to
　　　eat ten
And talk ten times as rapidly as you
　　can;
　　Were your shape true to cosmogonic
　　　laws,
　　You would be nothing but a pair of
　　　jaws.

XXII.

"Of all the useless beings in creation
The earth could spare most easily you
　　bakers

Of little clay gods, formed in shape
　　and fashion
Precisely in the image of their makers;
　　Why, it would almost move a saint
　　　to passion,
To see these blind and deaf, the hourly
　　breakers
　　Of God's own image in their brother
　　　men,
　　Set themselves up to tell the how,
　　　where, when,

XXIII.

"Of God's existence; one's diges-
　　tion's worse—
So makes a god of vengeance and of
　　blood;
　　Another,—but no matter, they re-
　　　verse
Creation's plan, out of their own vile
　　mud
　　Pat up a god, and burn, drown, hang,
　　　or curse
Whoever worships not; each keeps his
　　stud
　　Of texts which wait with saddle on
　　　and bridle
　　To hunt down atheists to their ugly
　　　idol.

XXIV.

"This, I perceive, has been your oc-
　　cupation;
You should have been more usefully
　　employed;
　　All men are bound to earn their daily
　　　ration,
Where States make not that primal
　　contract void
　　By cramps and limits; simple devas-
　　　tation
Is the worm's task, and what he has
　　destroyed
　　His monument; creating is man's
　　　work
　　And that, too, something more than
　　　mist and murk."

XXV.

So having said, the youth was seen
　　no more,
And straightway our sage Brahmin, the
　　philosopher,

Cried, "That was aimed at thee, thou
 endless bore,
Idle and useless as the growth of moss
 over
A rotting tree-trunk!" "I would
 square that score
Full soon," replied the Dervise, "could
 I cross over
And catch thee by the beard. Thy
 nails I'd twin
And make thee work, as was advised
 by him."

XXVI.

"Work? Am I not at work from
 morn till night
Sounding the deeps of oracles umbilical
Which for man's guidance never
 come to light,
With all their various aptitudes, until
 I call?"
"And I, do I not twirl from left to
 right
For conscience' sake? Is that no work?
 Thou silly gull,
He had thee in his eye; 't was Ga-
 briel
Sent to reward my faith, I know him
 well."

XXVII.

"'T was Vishnu, thou vile whirligig!"
 and so
The good old quarrel was begun anew;
One would have sworn the sky was
 black as sloe,
Had but the other dared to call it blue;
Nor were the followers who fed them
 slow
To treat each other with their curses,
 too,
 Each hating t'other (moves it tears
  or laughter?)
 Because he thought him sure of hell
  hereafter.

XXVIII.

At last some genius built a bridge of
 boats
Over the stream, and Ahmed's zealots
 filed
Across, upon a mission to (cut throats
And) spread religion pure and unde-
 filed;

They sowed the propagandist's wildest oats,
Cutting off all, down to the smallest
 child,
 And came back, giving thanks for
  such fat mercies,
 To find their harvest gone past prayers or curses.

XXIX.

All gone except their saint's religious
 hops,
Which he kept up with more than com-
 mon flourish;
But these, however satisfying crops
For the inner man, were not enough to
 nourish
The body politic, which quickly drops
Reserve in such sad junctures, and
 turns currish;
 So Ahmed soon got cursed for all the
  famine
 Where'er the popular voice could
  edge a damn in.

XXX.

At first he pledged a miracle quite
 boldly,
And, for a day or two, they growled
 and waited;
But, finding that this kind of manna
 coldly
Sat on their stomachs, they erelong be-
 rated
The saint for still persisting in that
 old lie,
Till soon the whole machine of saint-
 ship grated,
 Ran slow, creaked, stopped, and,
  wishing him in Tophet,
 They gathered strength enough to
  stone the prophet.

XXXI.

Some stronger ones contrived (by
 eating leather,
Their weaker friends, and one thing or
 another)
The winter months of scarcity to
 weather;
Among these was the late saint's
 younger brother,
 Who, in the spring, collecting them
  together,

Persuaded them that Ahmed's holy
    pother
Had wrought in their behalf, and that
    the place
Of Saint should be continued to his
    race.

XXXII.

Accordingly, 't was settled on the spot
That Allah favored that peculiar breed ;

Beside, as all were satisfied, 't would
    not
Be quite respectable to have the need
    Of public spiritual food forgot ;
And so the tribe, with proper forms de-
    creed
That he, and, failing him, his next
    of kin,
Forever for the people's good should
    spin.

UNDER THE WILLOWS,

AND

OTHER POEMS.

UNDER THE WILLOWS.

TO CHARLES ELIOT NORTON.

AGRO DOLCE.

THE wind is roistering out of doors,
My windows shake and my chimney
    roars;
My Elmwood chimneys seem crooning
    to me,
As of old, in their moody, minor key,
And out of the past the hoarse wind
    blows,
As I sit in my arm-chair, and toast my
    toes.

"Ho! ho! nine-and-forty," they seem
    to sing,
"We saw you a little toddling thing.
We knew you child and youth and man,
A wonderful fellow to dream and plan,
With a great thing always to come, —
    who knows?
Well, well! 't is some comfort to toast
    one's toes.

"How many times have you sat at gaze
Till the mouldering fire forgot to blaze,
Shaping among the whimsical coals
Fancies and figures and shining goals!
What matters the ashes that cover
    those?
While hickory lasts you can toast your
    toes.

"O dream-ship-builder! where are they
    all,
Your grand three-deckers, deep-chested
    and tall,
That should crush the waves under
    canvas piles,
And anchor at last by the Fortunate
    Isles?
There 's gray in your beard, the years
    turn foes,
While you muse in your arm-chair and
    toast your toes."

I sit and dream that I hear, as of yore,
My Elmwood chimneys' deep-throated
    roar;
If much be gone, there is much re-
    mains;
By the embers of loss I count my
    gains,
You and yours with the best, till the
    old hope glows
In the fanciful flame, as I toast my toes.

Instead of a fleet of broad-browed
    ships,
To send a child's armada of chips!
Instead of the great guns, tier on tier,
A freight of pebbles and grass-blades
    sere!
"Well, maybe more love with the less
    gift goes,"
I growl, as, half moody, I toast my toes.

UNDER THE WILLOWS.

FRANK-HEARTED hostess of the field
    and wood,
Gypsy, whose roof is every spreading
    tree,
June is the pearl of our New England
    year.
Still a surprisal, though expected long,
Her coming startles. Long she lies in
    wait,
Makes many a feint, peeps forth, draws
    coyly back,
Then, from some southern ambush in
    the sky,
With one great gush of blossom storms
    the world.
A week ago the sparrow was divine:

The bluebird, shifting his light load of
    song
From post to post along the cheerless
    fence,
Was as a rhymer ere the poet come ;
But now, O rapture ! sunshine winged
    and voiced,
Pipe blown through by the warm wild
    breath of the West
Shepherding his soft droves of fleecy
    cloud,
Gladness of woods, skies, waters, all in
    one,
The bobolink has come, and, like the
    soul
Of the sweet season vocal in a bird,
Gurgles in ecstasy we know not what
Save *June ! Dear June ! Now God
    be praised for June.*

May is a pious fraud of the almanac,
A ghastly parody of real Spring
Shaped out of snow and breathed with
    eastern wind ;
Or if, o'er-confident, she trust the date,
And, with her handful of anemones,
Herself as shivery, steal into the sun,
The season need but turn his hourglass
    round,
And Winter suddenly, like crazy Lear,
Reels back, and brings the dead May
    in his arms,
Her budding breasts and wan dislustred
    front
With frosty streaks and drifts of his
    white beard
All overblown. Then, warmly walled
    with books,
While my wood-fire supplies the sun's
    defect,
Whispering old forest-sagas in its
    dreams,
I take my May down from the happy
    shelf
Where perch the world's rare song-
    birds in a row,
Waiting my choice to open with full
    breast,
And beg an alms of spring-time, ne'er
    denied
In-doors by vernal Chaucer, whose
    fresh woods
Throb thick with merle and mavis all
    the year.

July breathes hot, sallows the crispy
    fields,
Curls up the wan leaves of the lilac-
    hedge,
And every eve cheats us with show of
    clouds
That braze the horizon's western rim,
    or hang
Motionless, with heaped canvas droop-
    ing idly,
Like a dim fleet by starving men be-
    sieged,
Conjectured half, and half descried
    afar,
Helpless of wind, and seeming to slip
    back
Adown the smooth curve of the oily
    sea.

But June is full of invitations sweet,
Forth from the chimney's yawn and
    thrice-read tomes
To leisurely delights and sauntering
    thoughts
That brook no ceiling narrower than the
    blue.
The cherry, drest for bridal, at my
    pane
Brushes, then listens, *Will he come?*
    The bee,
All dusty as a miller, takes his toll
Of powdery gold, and grumbles. What
    a day
To sun me and do nothing ! Nay, I
    think
Merely to bask and ripen is sometimes
The student's wiser business ; the
    brain
That forages all climes to line its cells,
Ranging both worlds on lightest wings
    of wish,
Will not distil the juices it has sucked
To the sweet substance of pellucid
    thought,
Except for him who hath the secret
    learned
To mix his blood with sunshine, and to
    take
The winds into his pulses. Hush !
    'T is he !
My oriole, my glance of summer fire,
Is come at last, and, ever on the watch,
Twitches the pack-thread I had lightly
    wound

About the bough to help his housekeep-
    ing, —
Twitches and scouts by turns, blessing
    his luck,
Yet fearing me who laid it in his way,
Nor, more than wiser we in our affairs,
Divines the providence that hides and
    helps.
Heave, ho! Heave, ho! he whistles
    as the twine
Slackens its hold; *once more, now!*
    and a flash
Lightens across the sunlight to the
    elm
Where his mate dangles at her cup of
    felt.
Nor all his booty is the thread; he
    trails
My loosened thought with it along the
    air,
And I must follow, would I ever find
The inward rhyme to all this wealth of
    life.

I care not how men trace their ances-
    try,
To ape or Adam; let them please their
    whim;
But I in June am midway to believe
A tree among my far progenitors,
Such sympathy is mine with all the
    race,
Such mutual recognition vaguely sweet
There is between us. Surely there are
    times
When they consent to own me of their
    kin,
And condescend to me, and call me
    cousin,
Murmuring faint lullabies of eldest
    time,
Forgotten, and yet dumbly felt with
    thrills
Moving the lips, though fruitless of all
    words.
And I have many a lifelong leafy
    friend,
Never estranged nor careful of my
    soul,
That knows I hate the axe, and wel-
    comes me
Within his tent as if I were a bird,
Or other free companion of the earth,
Yet undegenerate to the shifts of men.

Among them one, an ancient willow,
    spreads
Eight balanced limbs, springing at once
    all round
His deep-ridged trunk with upward
    slant diverse,
In outline like enormous beaker, fit
For hand of Jotun, where 'mid snow
    and mist
He holds unwieldly revel. This tree,
    spared,
I know not by what grace, — for in the
    blood
Of our New World subduers lingers yet
Hereditary feud with trees, they being
(They and the red-man most) our
    fathers' foes, —
Is one of six, a willow Pleiades,
The seventh fallen, that lean along the
    brink
Where the steep upland dips into the
    marsh,
Their roots, like molten metal cooled
    in flowing,
Stiffened in coils and runnels down the
    bank.
The friend of all the winds, wide-armed
    he towers
And glints his steely aglets in the sun,
Or whitens fitfully with sudden bloom
Of leaves breeze-lifted, much as when
    a shoal
Of devious minnows wheel from where
    a pike
Lurks balanced 'neath the lily-pads,
    and whirl
A rood of silver bellies to the day.

Alas! no acorn from the British oak
'Neath which slim fairies tripping
    wrought those rings
Of greenest emerald, wherewith fireside
    life
Did with the invisible spirit of Nature
    wed,
Was ever planted here! No darnel
    fancy
Might choke one useful blade in Puri-
    tan fields;
With horn and hoof the good old Devil
    came,
The witch's broomstick was not contra-
    band,
But all that superstition had of fair.

Or piety of native sweet, was doomed.
And if there be who nurse unholy faiths,
Fearing their god as if he were a wolf
That snuffed round every home and
    was not seen,
There should be some to watch and
    keep alive
All beautiful beliefs. And such was
    that, —
By solitary shepherd first surmised
Under Thessalian oaks, loved by some
    maid
Of royal stirp, that silent came and
    vanished,
As near her nest the hermit thrush, nor
    dared
Confess a mortal name, — that faith
    which gave
A Hamadryad to each tree; and I
Will hold it true that in this willow
    dwells
The open-handed spirit, frank and
    blithe,
Of ancient Hospitality, long since,
With ceremonious thrift, bowed out of
    doors.

In June 't is good to lie beneath a tree
While the blithe season comforts every
    sense,
Steeps all the brain in rest, and heals
    the heart,
Brimming it o'er with sweetness una-
    wares,
Fragrant and silent as that rosy snow
Wherewith the pitying apple-tree fills up
And tenderly lines some last-year rob-
    in's nest.
There muse I of old times, old hopes,
    old friends,
Old friends! The writing of those
    words has borne
My fancy backward to the gracious past,
The generous past, when all was pos-
    sible,
For all was then untried; the years be-
    tween
Have taught some sweet, some bitter
    lessons, none
Wiser than this, — to spend in all things
    else,
But of old friends to be most miserly.
Each year to ancient friendships adds
    a ring,

As to an oak, and precious more and
    more,
Without deservingness or help of ours,
They grow, and, silent, wider spread,
    each year,
Their unbought ring of shelter or of
    shade.
Sacred to me the lichens on the bark,
Which Nature's milliners would scrape
    away;
Most dear and sacred every withered
    limb!
'T is good to set them early, for our
    faith
Pines as we age, and, after wrinkles
    come,
Few plant, but water dead ones with
    vain tears.

This willow is as old to me as life;
And under it full often have I stretched,
Feeling the warm earth like a thing
    alive,
And gathering virtue in at every pore
Till it possessed me wholly, and
    thought ceased,
Or was transfused in something to
    which thought
Is coarse and dull of sense. Myself
    was lost,
Gone from me like an ache, and what
    remained
Become a part of the universal joy.
My soul went forth, and, mingling with
    the tree,
Danced in the leaves; or, floating in
    the cloud,
Saw its white double in the stream be-
    low;
Or else, sublimed to purer ecstasy,
Dilated in the broad blue over all.
I was the wind that dappled the lush
    grass,
The tide that crept with coolness to its
    roots,
The thin-winged swallow skating on the
    air;
The life that gladdened everything was
    mine.
Was I then truly all that I beheld?
Or is this stream of being but a glass
Where the mind sees its visionary self,
As, when the kingfisher flits o'er his
    bay,

Across the river's hollow heaven below
His picture flits, — another, yet the same?
But suddenly the sound of human voice
Or footfall, like the drop a chemist pours,
Doth in opacous cloud precipitate
The consciousness that seemed but now dissolved
Into an essence rarer than its own,
And I am narrowed to myself once more.

For here not long is solitude secure,
Nor Fantasy left vacant to her spell.
Here, sometimes, in this paradise of shade,
Rippled with western winds, the dusty Tramp,
Seeing the treeless causey burn beyond,
Halts to unroll his bundle of strange food
And munch an unearned meal. I cannot help
Liking this creature, lavish Summer's bedesman,
Who from the almshouse steals when nights grow warm,
Himself his large estate and only charge,
To be the guest of haystack or of hedge,
Nobly superior to the household gear
That forfeits us our privilege of nature.
I bait him with my match-box and my pouch,
Nor grudge the uncostly sympathy of smoke,
His equal now, divinely unemployed.
Some smack of Robin Hood is in the man,
Some secret league with wild wood-wandering things;
He is our ragged Duke, our barefoot Earl,
By right of birth exonerate from toil,
Who levies rent from us his tenants all,
And serves the state by merely being. Here
The Scissors-grinder, pausing, doffs his hat,
And lets the kind breeze, with its delicate fan,
Winnow the heat from out his dank gray hair, —
A grimy Ulysses, a much-wandered man,
Whose feet are known to all the populous ways,
And many men and manners he hath seen,
Not without fruit of solitary thought.
He, as the habit is of lonely men, —
Unused to try the temper of their mind
In fence with others, — positive and shy,
Yet knows to put an edge upon his speech,
Pithily Saxon in unwilling talk.
Him I entrap with my long-suffering knife,
And, while its poor blade hums away in sparks,
Sharpen my wit upon his gritty mind,
In motion set obsequious to his wheel,
And in its quality not much unlike.

Nor wants my tree more punctual visitors.
The children, they who are the only rich,
Creating for the moment, and possessing
Whate'er they choose to feign, — for still with them
Kind Fancy plays the fairy godmother,
Strewing their lives with cheap material
For wingèd horses and Aladdin's lamps,
Pure elfin-gold, by manhood's touch profane
To dead leaves disenchanted, — long ago
Between the branches of the tree fixed seats,
Making an o'erturned box their table. Oft
The shrilling girls sit here between school hours,
And play at *What's my thought like?* while the boys,
With whom the age chivalric ever bides,
Pricked on by knightly spur of female eyes,
Climb high to swing and shout on perilous boughs,
Or, from the willow's armory equipped
With musket dumb, green banner, edgeless sword,
Make good the rampart of their tree-redoubt
'Gainst eager British storming from below,
And keep alive the tale of Bunker's Hill.

Here, too, the men that mend our vil-
    lage ways,
Vexing Macadam's ghost with pounded
    slate,
Their nooning take; much noisy talk
    they spend
On horses and their ills; and, as John
    Bull
Tells of Lord This or That, who was
    his friend,
So these make boast of intimacies long
With famous teams, and add large esti-
    mates,
By competition swelled from mouth to
    mouth,
Of how much they could draw, till one,
    ill pleased
To have his legend overbid, retorts:
"You take and stretch truck-horses in
    a string
From here to Long Wharf end, one
    thing I know,
Not heavy neither, they could never
    draw, —
Ensign's long bow!" Then laughter
    loud and long.
So they in their leaf-shadowed micro-
    cosm
Image the larger world; for wheresoe'er
Ten men are gathered, the observant
    eye
Will find mankind in little, as the stars
Glide up and set. and all the heavens
    revolve
In the small welkin of a drop of dew.

I love to enter pleasure by a postern,
Not the broad popular gate that gulps
    the mob;
To find my theatres in roadside nooks,
Where men are actors, and suspect it
    not;
Where Nature all unconscious works
    her will,
And every passion moves with easy
    gait,
Unhampered by the buskin or the train.
Hating the crowd, where we gregarious
    men
Lead lonely lives, I love society,
Nor seldom find the best with simple
    souls
Unswerved by culture from their native
    bent,

The ground we meet on being primal
    man
And nearer the deep bases of our lives.

But O, half heavenly, earthly half, my
    soul,
Canst thou from those late ecstasies
    descend,
Thy lips still wet with the miraculous
    wine
That transubstantiates all thy baser
    stuff
To such divinity that soul and sense,
Once more commingled in their source,
    are lost, —
Canst thou descend to quench a vulgar
    thirst
With the mere dregs and rinsings of
    the world?
Well, if my nature find her pleasure so,
I am content, nor need to blush; I take
My little gift of being clean from God,
Not haggling for a better, holding it
Good as was ever any in the world,
My days as good and full of miracle.
I pluck my nutriment from any bush,
Finding out poison as the first men did
By tasting and then suffering, if I must.
Sometimes my bush burns, and some-
    times it is
A leafless wilding shivering by the wall;
But I have known when winter barberries
Pricked the effeminate palate with sur-
    prise
Of savor whose mere harshness seemed
    divine.

O, benediction of the higher mood
And human-kindness of the lower! for
    both
I will be grateful while I live, nor ques-
    tion
The wisdom that hath made us what
    we are,
With such large range as from the ale-
    house bench
Can reach the stars and be with both at
    home.
They tell us we have fallen on prosy
    days,
Condemned to glean the leavings of
    earth's feast
Where gods and heroes took delight of
    old;

But though our lives, moving in one
    dull round
Of repetition infinite, become
Stale as a newspaper once read, and
    though
History herself, seen in her workshop,
    seem
To have lost the art that dyed those
    glorious panes,
Rich with memorial shapes of saint and
    sage,
That pave with splendor the Past's
    dusky aisles, —
Panes that enchant the light of common
    day
With colors costly as the blood of kings,
Until it edge our thought with hues
    ideal, —
Yet while the world is left, while nature
    lasts
And man the best of nature, there shall
    be
Somewhere contentment for these hu-
    man hearts,
Some freshness, some unused material
For wonder and for song. I lose my-
    self
In other ways where solemn guide-
    posts say,
*This way to Knowledge, This way to
    Repose,*
But here, here only, I am ne'er be-
    trayed,
For every by-path leads me to my love.

God's passionless reformers, influences,
That purify and heal and are not seen,
Shall man say whence your virtue is,
    or how
Ye make medicinal the wayside weed?
I know that sunshine, through what-
    ever rift
How shaped it matters not, upon my
    walls
Paints discs as perfect-rounded as its
    source,
And, like its antitype, the ray divine,
However finding entrance, perfect still,
Repeats the image unimpaired of God.

We, who by shipwreck only find the
    shores
Of divine wisdom, can but kneel at
    first ;

Can but exult to feel beneath our feet,
That long stretched vainly down the
    yielding deeps,
The shock and sustenance of solid earth;
Inland afar we see what temples gleam
Through immemorial stems of sacred
    groves,
And we conjecture shining shapes
    therein ;
Yet for a space we love to wonder here
Among the shells and sea-weed of the
    beach.

So mused I once within my willow-tent
One brave June morning, when the
    bluff northwest,
Thrusting aside a dank and snuffling
    day
That made us bitter at our neighbors'
    sins,
Brimmed the great cup of heaven with
    sparkling cheer
And roared a lusty stave ; the sliding
    Charles,
Blue toward the west, and bluer and
    more blue,
Living and lustrous as a woman's
    eyes
Look once and look no more, with
    southward curve
Ran crinkling sunniness, like Helen's
    hair
Glimpsed in Elysium, insubstantial
    gold ;
From blossom-clouded orchards, far
    away
The bobolink tinkled ; the deep mead-
    ows flowed
With multitudinous pulse of light and
    shade
Against the bases of the southern
    hills,
While here and there a drowsy island
    rick
Slept and its shadow slept ; the wood-
    en bridge
Thundered, and then was silent ; on
    the roofs
The sun-warped shingles rippled with
    the heat ;
Summer on field and hill, in heart and
    brain,
All life washed clean in this high tide
    of June.

DARA.

WHEN Persia's sceptre trembled in a
    hand
Wilted with harem-heats, and all the
    land
Was hovered over by those vulture ills
That snuff decaying empire from afar,
Then, with a nature balanced as a star,
Dara arose, a shepherd of the hills.

He who had governed fleecy subjects
    well
Made his own village by the selfsame
    spell
Secure and quiet as a guarded fold ;
Then, gathering strength by slow and
    wise degrees
Under his sway, to neighbor villages
Order returned, and faith and justice
    old.

Now when it fortuned that a king more
    wise
Endued the realm with brain and hands
    and eyes,
He sought on every side men brave
    and just ;
And having heard our mountain shep-
    herd's praise,
How he refilled the mould of elder
    days,
To Dara gave a satrapy in trust.

So Dara shepherded a province wide,
Nor in his viceroy's sceptre took more
    pride
Than in his crook before ; but envy
    finds
More food in cities than on mountains
    bare ;
And the frank sun of natures clear and
    rare
Breeds poisonous fogs in low and mar-
    ish minds.

Soon it was hissed into the royal ear,
That, though wise Dara's province, year
    by year,
Like a great sponge, sucked wealth and
    plenty up,
Yet, when he squeezed it at the king's
    behest,

Some yellow drops, more rich than all
    the rest.
Went to the filling of his private cup.

For proof, they said, that, wheresoe'er
    he went,
A chest, beneath whose weight the
    camel bent,
Went with him ; and no mortal eye had
    seen
What was therein, save only Dara's
    own ;
But, when 't was opened, all his tent
    was known
To glow and lighten with heaped jewels'
    sheen.

The King set forth for Dara's province
    straight ;
There, as was fit, outside the city's
    gate,
The viceroy met him with a stately
    train,
And there, with archers circled, close
    at hand,
A camel with the chest was seen to
    stand :
The King's brow reddened, for the guilt
    was plain.

"Open me here," he cried, " this
    treasure-chest ! "
'T was done ; and only a worn shep-
    herd's vest
Was found therein.   Some blushed and
    hung the head ;
Not Dara ; open as the sky's blue roof
He stood, and "O my lord, behold the
    proof
That I was faithful to my trust," he
    said.

"To govern men, lo all the spell I had !
My soul in these rude vestments ever
    clad
Still to the unstained past kept true and
    leal,
Still on these plains could breathe her
    mountain air,
And fortune's heaviest gifts serenely
    bear,
Which bend men from their truth and
    make them reel.

" For ruling wisely I should have small
     skill,
Were I not lord of simple Dara still;
That sceptre kept, I could not lose my
     way."
Strange dew in royal eyes grew round
     and bright,
And strained the throbbing lids; be-
     fore 't was night
Two added provinces blest Dara's
     sway.

THE FIRST SNOW-FALL.

THE snow had begun in the gloaming,
     And busily all the night
Had been heaping field and highway
     With a silence deep and white.

Every pine and fir and hemlock
     Wore ermine too dear for an earl,
And the poorest twig on the elm-tree
     Was ridged inch deep with pearl.

From sheds new-roofed with Carrara
     Came Chanticleer's muffled crow,
The stiff rails softened to swan's-
     down,
     And still fluttered down the snow.

I stood and watched by the window
     The noiseless work of the sky,
And the sudden flurries of snow-birds,
     Like brown leaves whirling by.

I thought of a mound in sweet Auburn
     Where a little headstone stood;
How the flakes were folding it gently,
     As did robins the babes in the wood.

Up spoke our own little Mabel,
     Saying, "Father, who makes it
     snow?"
And I told of the good All-father
     Who cares for us here below.

Again I looked at the snow-fall,
     And thought of the leaden sky
That arched o'er our first great sorrow,
     When that mound was heaped so
     high.

I remembered the gradual patience
     That fell from that cloud like snow,
Flake by flake, healing and hiding
     The scar that renewed our woe. .

And again to the child I whispered,
     "The snow that husheth all,
Darling, the merciful Father
     Alone can make it fall!"

Then, with eyes that saw not, I kissed
     her;
     And she, kissing back, could not
     know
That *my* kiss was given to her sister,
     Folded close under deepening snow.

THE SINGING LEAVES.

A BALLAD.

I.

" WHAT fairings will ye that I bring?"
     Said the King to his daughters three;
" For I to Vanity Fair am boun,
     Now say what shall they be?"

Then up and spake the eldest daughter,
     That lady tall and grand:
" O, bring me pearls and diamonds
     great,
     And gold rings for my hand."

Thereafter spake the second daughter,
     That was both white and red:
" For me bring silks that will stand
     alone,
     And a gold comb for my head."

Then came the turn of the least daugh-
     ter,
     That was whiter than thistle-down,
And among the gold of her blithesome
     hair
     Dim shone the golden crown.

" There came a bird this morning,
     And sang 'neath my bower eaves,
Till I dreamed, as his music made me,
     'Ask thou for the Singing Leaves.'"

Then the brow of the King swelled crimson
  With a flush of angry scorn:
"Well have ye spoken, my two eldest,
  And chosen as ye were born;

"But she like a thing of peasant race,
  That is happy binding the sheaves";
Then he saw her dead mother in her face,
  And said, "Thou shalt have thy leaves."

II.

He mounted and rode three days and nights
  Till he came to Vanity Fair,
And 't was easy to buy the gems and the silk,
  But no Singing Leaves were there.

Then deep in the greenwood rode he,
  And asked of every tree,
"O, if you have ever a Singing Leaf,
  I pray you give it me!"

But the trees all kept their counsel,
  And never a word said they,
Only there sighed from the pine-tops
  A music of seas far away.

Only the pattering aspen
  Made a sound of growing rain,
That fell ever faster and faster,
  Then faltered to silence again.

"O, where shall I find a little foot-page
  That would win both hose and shoon,
And will bring to me the Singing Leaves
  If they grow under the moon?"

Then lightly turned him Walter the page,
  By the stirrup as he ran:
"Now pledge ye me the truesome word
  Of a king and gentleman,

"That you will give me the first, first thing
  You meet at your castle-gate,
And the Princess shall get the Singing Leaves,
  Or mine be a traitor's fate."

The King's head dropt upon his breast
  A moment, as it might be;
'T will be my dog, he thought, and said,
  "My faith I plight to thee."

Then Walter took from next his heart
  A packet small and thin,
"Now give you this to the Princess Anne,
  The Singing Leaves are therein."

III.

As the King rode in at his castle-gate,
  A maiden to meet him ran,
And "Welcome, father!" she laughed and cried
  Together, the Princess Anne.

"Lo, here the Singing Leaves," quoth he,
  "And woe, but they cost me dear!"
She took the packet, and the smile
  Deepened down beneath the tear.

It deepened down till it reached her heart,
  And then gushed up again,
And lighted her tears as the sudden sun
  Transfigures the summer rain.

And the first Leaf, when it was opened,
  Sang: "I am Walter the page,
And the songs I sing 'neath thy window
  Are my only heritage."

And the second Leaf sang: "But in the land
  That is neither on earth or sea,
My lute and I are lords of more
  Than thrice this kingdom's fee."

And the third Leaf sang, "Be mine! Be mine!"
  And ever it sang, "Be mine!"
Then sweeter it sang and ever sweeter,
  And said, "I am thine, thine, thine!"

At the first Leaf she grew pale enough,
  At the second she turned aside,
At the third, 't was as if a lily flushed
  With a rose's red heart's tide.

"Good counsel gave the bird," said she,
  "I have my hope thrice o'er,

For they sing to my very heart," she
  said,
"And it sings to them evermore."

She brought to him her beauty and
  truth,
But and broad earldoms three,
And he made her queen of the broader
  lands
He held of his lute in fee.

SEA-WEED.

Not always unimpeded can I pray,
Nor, pitying saint, thine intercession
  claim :
Too closely clings the burden of the
  day,
And all the mint and anise that I pay
But swells my debt and deepens my
  self-blame.

Shall I less patience have than Thou,
  who know
That Thou revisit'st all who wait for
  thee,
Nor only fill'st the unsounded deeps
  below,
But dost refresh with punctual overflow
The rifts where unregarded mosses be ?

The drooping sea-weed hears, in night
  abyssed,
Far and more far the wave's receding
  shocks,
Nor doubts, for all the darkness and
  the mist,
That the pale shepherdess will keep her
  tryst,
And shoreward lead again her foam-
  fleeced flocks.

For the same wave that rims the Carib
  shore
With momentary brede of pearl and
  gold,
Goes hurrying thence to gladden with
  its roar
Lorn weeds bound fast on rocks of Labrador,
By love divine on one sweet errand
  rolled.

And, though Thy healing waters far
  withdraw,
I, too, can wait and feed on hope of
  Thee
And of the dear recurrence of Thy law,
Sure that the parting grace that morn-
  ing saw
Abides its time to come in search of me.

THE FINDING OF THE LYRE.

There lay upon the ocean's shore
What once a tortoise served to cover.
A year and more, with rush and roar,
The surf had rolled it over,
Had played with it, and flung it by,
As wind and weather might decide it,
Then tossed it high where sand-drifts
  dry
Cheap burial might provide it.

It rested there to bleach or tan,
The rains had soaked, the suns had
  burned it :
With many a ban the fisherman
Had stumbled o'er and spurned it ;
And there the fisher-girl would stay,
Conjecturing with her brother
How in their play the poor estray
Might serve some use or other.

So there it lay, through wet and dry,
As empty as the last new sonnet,
Till by and by came Mercury,
And, having mused upon it,
"Why, here," cried he, "the thing of
  things
In shape, material, and dimension !
Give it but strings, and, lo, it sings,
A wonderful invention !"

So said, so done ; the chords he strained,
And, as his fingers o'er them hovered,
The shell disdained a soul had gained,
The lyre had been discovered.
O empty world that round us lies,
Dead shell, of soul and thought for-
  saken,
Brought we but eyes like Mercury's,
In thee what songs should waken !

NEW YEAR'S EVE. 1850.

This is the midnight of the century, —
hark!
Through aisle and arch of Godminster
have gone
Twelve throbs that tolled the zenith of
the dark,
And mornward now the starry hands
move on;
"Mornward!" the angelic watchers
say,
" Passed is the sorest trial;
No plot of man can stay
The hand upon the dial;
Night is the dark stem of the lily Day."

If we, who watched in valleys here be-
low,
Toward streaks, misdeemed of morn,
our faces turned
When volcan glares set all the east
aglow, —
We are not poorer that we wept and
yearned;
Though earth swing wide from God's
intent,
And though no man nor nation
Will move with full consent
In heavenly gravitation,
Yet by one Sun is every orbit bent.

FOR AN AUTOGRAPH.

Though old the thought and oft ex-
prest,
'T is his at last who says it best, —
I 'll try my fortune with the rest.

Life is a leaf of paper white
Whereon each one of us may write
His word or two, and then comes night.

"Lo, time and space enough," we cry,
"To write an epic!" so we try
Our nibs upon the edge, and die.

Muse not which way the pen to hold,
Luck hates the slow and loves the bold,
Soon come the darkness and the cold.

Greatly begin! though thou have time
But for a line, be that sublime, —
Not failure, but low aim, is crime.

Ah, with what lofty hope we came!
But we forget it, dream of fame,
And scrawl, as I do here, a name.

AL FRESCO.

The dandelions and buttercups
Gild all the lawn: the drowsy bee
Stumbles among the clover-tops,
And summer sweetens all but me:
Away, unfruitful lore of books,
For whose vain idiom we reject
The soul's more native dialect,
Aliens among the birds and brooks,
Dull to interpret or conceive
What gospels lost the woods retrieve!
Away, ye critics, city-bred,
Who springes set of thus and so,
And in the first man's footsteps tread,
Like those who toil through drifted
snow!
Away, my poets, whose sweet spell
Can make a garden of a cell!
I need ye not, for I to-day
Will make one long sweet verse of play.

Snap, chord of manhood's tenser
strain!
To-day I will be a boy again;
The mind's pursuing element,
Like a bow slackened and unbent,
In some dark corner shall be leant.
The robin sings, as of old, from the
limb!
The cat-bird croons in the lilac-bush!
Through the dim arbor, himself more
dim,
Silently hops the hermit-thrush,
The withered leaves keep dumb for him;
The irreverent buccaneering bee
Hath stormed and rifled the nunnery
Of the lily, and scattered the sacred floor
With haste-dropt gold from shrine to
door;
There, as of yore,
The rich, milk-tingeing buttercup
Its tiny polished urn holds up,
Filled with ripe summer to the edge,

The sun in his own wine to pledge;
And our tall elm, this hundredth year
Doge of our leafy Venice here,
Who, with an annual ring, doth wed
The blue Adriatic overhead,
Shadows with his palatial mass
The deep canals of flowing grass.

O unestranged birds and bees!
O face of Nature always true!
O never-unsympathizing trees!
O never-rejecting roof of blue,
Whose rash disherison never falls
On us unthinking prodigals,
Yet who convictest all our ill,
So grand and unappeasable!
Methinks my heart from each of these
Plucks part of childhood back again,
Long there imprisoned, as the breeze
Doth every hidden odor seize
Of wood and water, hill and plain.
Once more am I admitted peer
In the upper house of Nature here,
And feel through all my pulses run
The royal blood of breeze and sun.

Upon these elm-arched solitudes
No hum of neighbor toil intrudes;
The only hammer that I hear
Is wielded by the woodpecker,
The single noisy calling his
In all our leaf-hid Sybaris;
The good old time, close-hidden here,
Persists, a loyal cavalier,
While Roundheads prim, with point of fox,
Probe wainscot-chink and empty box;
Here no hoarse-voiced iconoclast
Insults thy statues, royal Past;
Myself too prone the axe to wield,
I touch the silver side of the shield
With lance reversed, and challenge peace,
A willing convert of the trees.

How chanced it that so long I tost
A cable's length from this rich coast,
With foolish anchors hugging close
The beckoning weeds and lazy ooze,
Nor had the wit to wreck before
On this enchanted island's shore,
Whither the current of the sea,
With wiser drift, persuaded me?

O, might we but of such rare days
Build up the spirit's dwelling-place!
A temple of so Parian stone
Would brook a marble god alone,
The statue of a perfect life,
Far-shrined from earth's bestaining strife,
Alas! though such felicity
In our vext world here may not be,
Yet, as sometimes the peasant's hut
Shows stones which old religion cut
With text inspired, or mystic sign
Of the Eternal and Divine,
Torn from the consecration deep
Of some fallen nunnery's mossy sleep,
So, from the ruins of this day
Crumbling in golden dust away,
The soul one gracious block may draw,
Carved with some fragment of the law,
Which, set in life's prosaic wall,
Old benedictions may recall,
And lure some nunlike thoughts to take
Their dwelling here for memory's sake.

MASACCIO.

(IN THE BRANCACCI CHAPEL.)

HE came to Florence long ago,
And painted here these walls, that shone
For Raphael and for Angelo,
With secrets deeper than his own,
Then shrank into the dark again,
And died, we know not how or when.

The shadows deepened, and I turned
Half sadly from the fresco grand;
"And is this," mused I, "all ye earned,
High-vaulted brain and cunning hand,
That ye to greater men could teach
The skill yourselves could never reach?"

"And who were they," I mused, "that wrought
Through pathless wilds, with labor long,
The highways of our daily thought?
Who reared those towers of earliest song
That lift us from the crowd to peace
Remote in sunny silences?"

Out clanged the Ave Mary bells,
And to my heart this message came:
Each clamorous throat among them tells

What strong-souled martyrs died in
      flame
To make it possible that thou
Shouldst here with brother sinners bow.

Thoughts that great hearts once broke
      for, we
Breathe cheaply in the common air;
The dust we trample heedlessly
Throbbed once in saints and heroes rare,
Who perished, opening for their race
New pathways to the commonplace.

Henceforth, when rings the health to
      those
Who live in story and in song,
O nameless dead, who now repose
Safe in Oblivion's chambers strong,
One cup of recognition true
Shall silently be drained to you!

WITHOUT AND WITHIN.

My coachman, in the moonlight there,
   Looks through the side-light of the
      door;
I hear him with his brethren swear,
   As I could do,—but only more.

Flattening his nose against the pane,
   He envies me my brilliant lot,
Breathes on his aching fists in vain,
   And dooms me to a place more hot.

He sees me in to supper go,
   A silken wonder by my side,
Bare arms, bare shoulders, and a row
   Of flounces, for the door too wide.

He thinks how happy is my arm
   'Neath its white-gloved and jewelled
      load;
And wishes me some dreadful harm,
   Hearing the merry corks explode.

Meanwhile I inly curse the bore
   Of hunting still the same old coon,
And envy him, outside the door,
   In golden quiets of the moon.

The winter wind is not so cold
   As the bright smile he sees me win,
Nor the host's oldest wine so old
   As our poor gabble sour and thin.

I envy him the ungyved prance
   With which his freezing feet he
      warms,
And drag my lady's-chains and dance
   The galley-slave of dreary forms.

O, could he have my share of din,
   And I his quiet!—past a doubt
'T would still be one man bored within,
   And just another bored without.

Nay, when, once paid my mortal fee,
   Some idler on my headstone grim
Traces the moss-blurred name, will he
   Think me the happier, or I him?

GODMINSTER CHIMES.

WRITTEN IN AID OF A CHIME OF BELLS
FOR CHRIST CHURCH, CAMBRIDGE.

GODMINSTER? Is it Fancy's play?
   I know not, but the word
Sings in my heart, nor can I say
   Whether 't was dreamed or heard;
Yet fragrant in my mind it clings
   As blossoms after rain,
And builds of half-remembered things
   This vision in my brain.

Through aisles of long-drawn centuries
   My spirit walks in thought,
And to that symbol lifts its eyes
   Which God's own pity wrought:
From Calvary shines the altar's gleam,
   The Church's East is there,
The Ages one great minster seem,
   That throbs with praise and prayer.

And all the way from Calvary down
   The carven pavement shows
Their graves who won the martyr's
      crown
   And safe in God repose;
The saints of many a warring creed
   Who now in heaven have learned
That all paths to the Father lead
   Where Self the feet have spurned.

And, as the mystic aisles I pace,
   By aureoled workmen built,
Lives ending at the Cross I trace
   Alike through grace and guilt;

One Mary bathes the blessed feet
  With ointment from her eyes,
With spikenard one, and both are sweet,
  For both are sacrifice.

Moravian hymn and Roman chant
  In one devotion blend,
To speak the soul's eternal want
  Of Him, the inmost friend ;
One prayer soars cleansed with martyr
    fire,
  One choked with sinner's tears,
In heaven both meet in one desire,
  And God one music hears.

Whilst thus I dream, the bells clash out
  Upon the Sabbath air,
Each seems a hostile faith to shout,
  A selfish form of prayer ;
My dream is shattered, yet who knows
  But in that heaven so near
These discords find harmonious close
  In God's atoning ear ?

O chime of sweet Saint Charity,
  Peal soon that Easter morn
When Christ for all shall risen be,
  And in all hearts new-born !
That Pentecost when utterance clear
  To all men shall be given,
When all shall say *My Brother* here,
  And hear *My Son* in heaven !

THE PARTING OF THE WAYS.

Who hath not been a poet? Who hath
    not,
With life's new quiver full of wingèd
    years,
Shot at a venture, and then, following
    on,
Stood doubtful at the Parting of the
    Ways?

There once I stood in dream, and as I
    paused,
Looking this way and that, came forth
    to me
The figure of a woman veiled, that said,
"My name is Duty, turn and follow
    me";
Something there was that chilled me in
    her voice ;

I felt Youth's hand grow slack and cold
    in mine,
As if to be withdrawn, and I exclaimed :
"O, leave the hot wild heart within my
    breast !
Duty comes soon enough, too soon
    comes Death ;
This slippery globe of life whirls of it-
    self,
Hasting our youth away into the dark ;
These senses, quivering with electric
    heats,
Too soon will show, like nests on win-
    try boughs
Obtrusive emptiness, too palpable
    wreck,
Which whistling northwinds line with
    downy snow
Sometimes, or fringe with foliaged
    rime, in vain,
Thither the singing birds no more re-
    turn."

Then glowed to me a maiden from the
    left,
With bosom half disclosed, and naked
    arms
More white and undulant than necks
    of swans ;
And all before her steps an influence ran
Warm as the whispering South that
    opens buds
And swells the laggard sails of North-
    ern May.
"I am called Pleasure, come with me !"
    she said,
Then laughed, and shook out sunshine
    from her hair,
Nor only that, but, so it seemed, shook
    out
All memory too, and all the moonlit
    past,
Old loves, old aspirations, and old
    dreams,
More beautiful for being old and gone.

So we two went together ; downward
    sloped
The path through yellow meads, or so
    I dreamed,
Yellow with sunshine and young green,
    but I
Saw naught nor heard, shut up in one
    close joy ;

I only felt the hand within my own,
Transmuting all my blood to golden fire,
Dissolving all my brain in throbbing
    mist.

Suddenly shrank the hand; suddenly
    burst
A cry that split the torpor of my brain,
And as the first sharp thrust of light-
    ning loosens
From the heaped cloud its rain, loos-
    ened my sense:
"Save me!" it thrilled; "O, hide me!
    there is Death!
Death the divider, the unmerciful,
That digs his pitfalls under Love and
    Youth
And covers Beauty up in the cold
    ground;
Horrible Death! bringer of endless
    dark;
Let him not see me! hide me in thy
    breast!"
Thereat I strove to clasp her, but my
    arms
Met only what slipped crumbling down,
    and fell,
A handful of gray ashes, at my feet.

I would have fled, I would have fol-
    lowed back
That pleasant path we came, but all
    was changed;
Rocky the way, abrupt, and hard to find;
Yet I toiled on, and, toiling on, I
    thought,
"That way lies Youth, and Wisdom,
    and all Good;
For only by unlearning Wisdom comes
And climbing backward to diviner
    Youth;
What the world teaches profits to the
    world,
What the soul teaches profits to the
    soul,
Which then first stands erect with God-
    ward face,
When she lets fall her pack of withered
    facts,
The gleanings of the outward eye and
    ear,
And looks and listens with her finer
    sense;
Nor Truth nor Knowledge cometh
    from without."

After long weary days I stood again
And waited at the Parting of the Ways;
Again the figure of a woman veiled
Stood forth and beckoned, and I fol-
    lowed now:
Down to no bower of roses led the path.
But through the streets of towns where
    chattering Cold
Hewed wood for fires whose glow was
    owned and fenced,
Where Nakedness wove garments of
    warm wool
Not for itself; — or through the fields
    it led
Where Hunger reaped the unattaina-
    ble grain,
Where Idleness enforced saw idle lands,
Leagues of unpeopled soil, the common
    earth,
Walled round with paper against God
    and Man.
"I cannot look," I groaned, "at only
    these;
The heart grows hardened with perpet-
    ual wont,
And palters with a feigned necessity,
Bargaining with itself to be content;
Let me behold thy face."
              The Form replied:
"Men follow Duty, never overtake;
Duty nor lifts her veil nor looks be-
    hind."
But, as she spake, a loosened lock of
    hair
Slipped from beneath her hood, and I,
    who looked
To see it gray and thin, saw amplest
    gold;
Not that dull metal dug from sordid
    earth,
But such as the retiring sunset flood
Leaves heaped on bays and capes of
    island cloud.
"O Guide divine," I prayed, "although
    not yet
I may repair the virtue which I feel
Gone out at touch of untuned things
    and foul
With draughts of Beauty, yet declare
    how soon!"

"Faithless and faint of heart," the
    voice returned,
"Thou see'st no beauty save thou make
    it first;

Man, Woman, Nature, each is but a
    glass
Where the soul sees the image of her-
    self,
Visible echoes, offsprings of herself.
But, since thou need'st assurance of how
    soon,
Wait till that angel comes who opens
    all,
The reconciler, he who lifts the veil,
The reuniter, the rest-bringer, Death."

I waited, and methought he came ; but
    how,
Or in what shape, I doubted, for no
    sign,
By touch or mark, he gave me as he
    passed :
Only I know a lily that I held
Snapt short below the head and shriv-
    elled up ;
Then turned my Guide and looked at
    me unveiled,
And I beheld no face of matron stern,
But that enchantment I had followed
    erst,
Only more fair, more clear to eye and
    brain,
Heightened and chastened by a house-
    hold charm ;
She smiled, and "Which is fairer," said
    her eyes,
"The hag's unreal Florimel or mine?"

ALADDIN.

WHEN I was a beggarly boy,
    And lived in a cellar damp,
I had not a friend nor a toy,
    But I had Aladdin's lamp ;
When I could not sleep for the cold,
    I had fire enough in my brain,
And builded, with roofs of gold,
    My beautiful castles in Spain !

Since then I have toiled day and night,
    I have money and power good store,
But I 'd give all my lamps of silver
    bright,
For the one that is mine no more ;
Take, Fortune, whatever you choose,
    You gave, and may snatch again ;

I have nothing 't would pain me to lose,
For I own no more castles in Spain !

AN INVITATION.

TO J. F. H.

NINE years have slipt like hour-glass
    sand
From life's still-emptying globe away,
Since last, dear friend, I clasped your
    hand,
And stood upon the impoverished land,
Watching the steamer down the bay.

I held the token which you gave,
While slowly the smoke-pennon curled
O'er the vague rim 'tween sky and wave,
And shut the distance like a grave,
Leaving me in the colder world.

The old worn world of hurry and heat,
The young, fresh world of thought and
    scope,
While you, where beckoning billows
    fleet
Climb far sky-beaches still and sweet,
Sank wavering down the ocean-slope.

You sought the new world in the old,
I found the old world in the new,
All that our human hearts can hold,
The inward world of deathless mould,
The same that Father Adam knew.

He needs no ship to cross the tide,
Who, in the lives about him, sees
Fair window-prospects opening wide
O'er history's fields on every side,
To Ind and Egypt, Rome and Greece.

Whatever moulds of various brain
E'er shaped the world to weal or woe,
Whatever empires' wax and wane,
To him that hath not eyes in vain,
Our village-microcosm can show.

Come back our ancient walks to tread,
Dear haunts of lost or scattered friends,
Old Harvard's scholar-factories red,
Where song and smoke and laughter
    sped
The nights to proctor-haunted ends.

Constant are all our former loves,
Unchanged the icehouse-girdled pond,
Its hemlock glooms, its shadowy coves,
Where floats the coot and never moves,
Its slopes of long-tamed green beyond.

Our old familiars are not laid,
Though snapt our wands and sunk our
    books ;
They beckon, not to be gainsaid,
Where, round broad meads that mowers
    wade,
The Charles his steel-blue sickle crooks.

Where, as the cloudbergs eastward
    blow,
From glow to gloom the hillsides shift
Their plumps of orchard-trees arow,
Their lakes of rye that wave and flow,
Their snowy whiteweed's summer drift.

There have we watched the West un-
    furl
A cloud Byzantium newly born,
With flickering spires and domes of
    pearl,
And vapory surfs that crowd and curl
Into the sunset's Golden Horn.

There, as the flaming occident
Burned slowly down to ashes gray,
Night pitched o'erhead her silent tent,
And glimmering gold from Hesper
    sprent
Upon the darkened river lay,

Where a twin sky but just before
Deepened, and double swallows
    skimmed,
And, from a visionary shore,
Hung visioned trees, that, more and
    more
Grew dusk as those above were dimmed.

Then eastward saw we slowly grow
Clear-edged the lines of roof and spire,
While great elm-masses blacken slow,
And linden-ricks their round heads
    show
Against a flush of widening fire.

Doubtful at first and far away,
The moon-flood creeps more wide and
    wide ;

Up a ridged beach of cloudy gray,
Curved round the east as round a bay,
It slips and spreads its gradual tide.

Then suddenly, in lurid mood,
The moon looms large o'er town and
    field
As upon Adam, red like blood,
'Tween him and Eden's happy wood,
Glared the commissioned angel's shield.

Or let us seek the seaside, there
To wander idly as we list,
Whether, on rocky headlands bare,
Sharp cedar-horns, like breakers, tear
The trailing fringes of gray mist,

Or whether, under skies full flown,
The brightening surfs, with foamy din,
Their breeze-caught forelocks backward
    blown,
Against the beach's yellow zone,
Curl slow, and plunge forever in.

And, as we watch those canvas towers
That lean along the horizon's rim,
"Sail on," I'll say ; "may sunniest
    hours
Convoy you from this land of ours,
Since from my side you bear not him ! "

For years thrice three, wise Horace
    said,
A poem rare let silence bind ;
And love may ripen in the shade,
Like ours, for nine long seasons laid
In deepest arches of the mind.

Come back ! Not ours the Old World's
    good,
The Old World's ill, thank God, not
    ours ;
But here, far better understood,
The days enforce our native mood,
And challenge all our manlier powers.

Kindlier to me the place of birth
That first my tottering footsteps trod ;
There may be fairer spots of earth,
But all their glories are not worth
The virtue in the native sod.

Thence climbs an influence more benign
Through pulse and nerve, through heart
    and brain ;

Sacred to me those fibres fine
That first clasped earth.   O, ne'er be
    mine
The alien sun and alien rain !

These nourish not like homelier glows
Or waterings of familiar skies,
And nature fairer blooms bestows
On the heaped hush of wintry snows,
In pastures dear to childhood's eyes,

Than where Italian earth receives
The partial sunshine's ampler boons,
Where vines carve friezes 'neath the
    eaves,
And, in dark firmaments of leaves,
The orange lifts its golden moons.

THE NOMADES.

WHAT Nature makes in any mood
To me is warranted for good,
Though long before I learned to see
She did not set us moral theses,
And scorned to have her sweet caprices
Strait-waistcoated in you or me.

I, who take root and firmly cling,
Thought fixedness the only thing ;
Why Nature made the butterflies,
(Those dreams of wings that float and
    hover
At noon the slumberous poppies over,)
Was something hidden from mine eyes,

Till once, upon a rock's brown bosom,
Bright as a thorny cactus-blossom,
I saw a butterfly at rest ;
Then first of both I felt the beauty ;
The airy whim, the grim-set duty,
Each from the other took its best.

Clearer it grew than winter sky
That Nature still had reasons why ;
And, shifting sudden as a breeze,
My fancy found no satisfaction,
No antithetic sweet attraction,
So great as in the Nomades.

Scythians, with Nature not at strife,
Light Arabs of our complex life,

They build no houses, plant no mills
To utilize Time's sliding river,
Content that it flow waste forever,
If they, like it, may have their wills.

An hour they pitch their shifting tents
In thoughts, in feelings, and events ;
Beneath the palm-trees, on the grass,
They sing, they dance, make love, and
    chatter,
Vex the grim temples with their clatter,
And make Truth's fount their looking-
    glass.

A picnic life ; from love to love,
From faith to faith they lightly move,
And yet, hard-eyed philosopher,
The flightiest maid that ever hovered
To me your thought-webs fine discov-
    ered,
No lens to see them through like her.

So witchingly her finger-tips
To Wisdom, as away she trips,
She kisses, waves such sweet farewells
To Duty, as she laughs " To-morrow ! "
That both from that mad contrast bor-
    row
A perfectness found nowhere else.

The beach-bird on its pearly verge
Follows and flies the whispering surge,
While, in his tent, the rock-stayed shell
Awaits the flood's star-timed vibrations,
And both, the flutter and the patience,
The sauntering poet loves them well.

Fulfil so much of God's decree
As works its problem out in thee,
Nor dream that in thy breast alone
The conscience of the changeful sea-
    sons,
The Will that in the planets reasons
With Space-wide logic, has its throne.

Thy virtue makes not vice of mine,
Unlike, but none the less divine ;
Thy toil adorns, not chides, my play ;
Nature of sameness is so chary,
With such wild whim the freakish fairy
Picks presents for the christening-day.

SELF-STUDY.

A PRESENCE both by night and day,
That made my life seem just begun,
Yet scarce a presence, rather say
The warning aureole of one.

And yet I felt it everywhere;
Walked I the woodland's aisles along,
It seemed to brush me with its hair;
Bathed I, I heard a mermaid's song.

How sweet it was! A buttercup
Could hold for me a day's delight,
A bird could lift my fancy up
To ether free from cloud or blight.

Who was the nymph? Nay, I will see,
Methought, and I will know her near;
If such, divined, her charm can be,
Seen and possessed, how triply dear!

So every magic art I tried,
And spells as numberless as sand,
Until, one evening, by my side
I saw her glowing fulness stand.

I turned to clasp her, but "Farewell,"
Parting she sighed, "we meet no more;
Not by my hand the curtain fell
That leaves you conscious, wise, and
    poor.

"Since you have found me out, I go;
Another lover I must find,
Content his happiness to know,
Nor strive its secret to unwind."

PICTURES FROM APPLEDORE.

I.

A HEAP of bare and splintery crags
Tumbled about by lightning and frost,
With rifts and chasms and storm-
    bleached jags,
That wait and growl for a ship to be
    lost;
No island, but rather the skeleton
Of a wrecked and vengeance-smitten
    one,
Where, æons ago, with half-shut eye,
The sluggish saurian crawled to die,

Gasping under titanic ferns;
Ribs of rock that seaward jut,
Granite shoulders and boulders and
    snags,
Round which, though the winds in
    heaven be shut,
The nightmared ocean murmurs and
    yearns,
Welters, and swashes, and tosses, and
    turns,
And the dreary black sea-weed lolls and
    wags;
Only rock from shore to shore,
Only a moan through the bleak clefts
    blown,
With sobs in the rifts where the coarse
    kelp shifts,
Falling and lifting, tossing and drifting,
And under all a deep, dull roar,
Dying and swelling, forevermore, —
Rock and moan and roar alone,
And the dread of some nameless thing
    unknown,
These make Appledore.

These make Appledore by night:
Then there are monsters left and right;
Every rock is a different monster;
All you have read of, fancied, dreamed,
When you waked at night because you
    screamed,
There they lie for half a mile,
Jumbled together in a pile,
And (though you know they never once
    stir),
If you look long, they seem to be
    moving
Just as plainly as plain can be,
Crushing and crowding, wading and
    shoving
Out into the awful sea,
Where you can hear them snort and
    spout
With pauses between, as if they were
    listening,
Then tumult anon when the surf breaks
    glistening
In the blackness where they wallow
    about.

II.

All this you would scarcely comprehend,
Should you see the isle on a sunny day;
Then it is simple enough in its way, —

Two rocky bulges, one at each end,
With a smaller bulge and a hollow be-
    tween;
Patches of whortleberry and bay;
Accidents of open green;
Sprinkled with loose slabs square and
    gray,
Like graveyards for ages deserted; a
    few
Unsocial thistles; an elder or two,
Foamed over with blossoms white as
    spray;
And on the whole island never a tree
Save a score of sumachs, high as your
    knee,
That crouch in hollows where they may,
(The cellars where once stood a village,
    men say,)
Huddling for warmth, and never grew
Tall enough for a peep at the sea;
A general dazzle of open blue;
A breeze always blowing and playing
    rat-tat
With the bow of the ribbon round your
    hat;
A score of sheep that do nothing but
    stare
Up or down at you everywhere;
Three or four cattle that chew the cud
Lying about in a listless despair;
A medrick that makes you look over-
    head
With short, sharp scream, as he sights
    his prey,
And, dropping straight and swift as
    lead,
Splits the water with sudden thud; —
This is Appledore by day.

A common island, you will say;
But stay a moment: only climb
Up to the highest rock of the isle,
Stand there alone for a little while,
And with gentle approaches it grows
    sublime.
Dilating slowly as you win
A sense from the silence to take it in.
So wide the loneness, so lucid the air,
The granite beneath you so savagely
    bare,
You well might think you were looking
    down
From some sky-silenced mountain's
    crown,

Whose waist-belt of pines is wont to
    tear
Locks of wool from the topmost cloud.
Only be sure you go alone,
For Grandeur is inaccessibly proud,
And never yet has backward thrown
Her veil to feed the stare of a crowd;
To more than one was never shown
That awful front, nor is it fit
That she, Cothurnus-shod, stand bowed
Until the self-approving pit
Enjoy the gust of its own wit
In babbling plaudits cheaply loud;
She hides her mountains and her sea
From the harriers of scenery,
Who hunt down sunsets, and huddle
    and bay,
Mouthing and mumbling the dying day.

Trust me, 't is something to be cast
Face to face with one's Self at last,
To be taken out of the fuss and strife,
The endless clatter of plate and knife,
The bore of books and the bores of the
    street,
From the singular mess we agree to call
    Life,
Where that is best which the most fools
    vote is,
And planted firm on one's own two
    feet
So nigh to the great warm heart of
    God,
You almost seem to feel it beat
Down from the sunshine and up from
    the sod;
To be compelled, as it were, to notice
All the beautiful changes and chances
Through which the landscape flits and
    glances,
And to see how the face of common day
Is written all over with tender histories,
When you study it that intenser way
In which a lover looks at his mistress.

Till now you dreamed not what could
    be done
With a bit of rock and a ray of sun;
But look, how fade the lights and shades
Of keen bare edge and crevice deep!
How doubtfully it fades and fades,
And glows again, yon craggy steep,
O'er which, through color's dreamiest
    grades,

The musing sunbeams pause and creep!
Now pink it blooms, now glimmers
    gray,
Now shadows to a filmy blue,
Tries one, tries all, and will not stay,
But flits from opal hue to hue,
And runs through every tenderest range
Of change that seems not to be change,
So rare the sweep, so nice the art,
That lays no stress on any part,
But shifts and lingers and persuades;
So soft that sun-brush in the west,
That asks no costlier pigments' aids,
But mingling knobs, flaws, angles,
    dints,
Indifferent of worst or best,
Enchants the cliffs with wraiths and
    hints
And gracious preludings of tints,
Where all seems fixed, yet all evades,
And indefinably pervades
Perpetual movement with perpetual
    rest!

III.

Away northeast is Boone Island light;
You might mistake it for a ship,
Only it stands too plumb upright,
And like the others does not slip
Behind the sea's unsteady brink;
Though, if a cloud-shade chance to dip
Upon it a moment, 't will suddenly sink,
Levelled and lost in the darkened main,
Till the sun builds it suddenly up again,
As if with a rub of Aladdin's lamp.
On the main-land you see a misty camp
Of mountains pitched tumultuously:
That one looming so long and large
Is Saddleback, and that point you see
Over yon low and rounded marge,
Like the boss of a sleeping giant's targe
Laid over his breast, is Ossipee;
That shadow there may be Kearsarge;
That must be Great Haystack; I love
    these names,
Wherewith the lonely farmer tames
Nature to mute companionship
With his own mind's domestic mood,
And strives the surly world to clip
In the arms of familiar habitude.
'T is well he could not contrive to make
A Saxon of Agamenticus:
He glowers there to the north of us,
Wrapt in his blanket of blue haze,

Unconvertibly savage, and scorns to
    take
The white man's baptism or his ways.
Him first on shore the coaster divines
Through the early gray, and sees him
    shake
The morning mist from his scalp-lock
    of pines;
Him first the skipper makes out in the
    west,
Ere the earliest sunstreak shoots trem-
    ulous,
Plashing with orange the palpitant lines
Of mutable billow, crest after crest,
And murmurs *Agamenticus!*
As if it were the name of a saint.
But is that a mountain playing cloud,
Or a cloud playing mountain, just there,
    so faint?
Look along over the low right shoulder
Of Agamenticus into that crowd
Of brassy thunderheads behind it;
Now you have caught it, but, ere you
    are older
By half an hour, you will lose it and
    find it
A score of times; while you look 't is
    gone,
And, just as you 've given it up, anon
It is there again, till your weary eyes
Fancy they see it waver and rise,
With its brother clouds; it is Agio-
    chook,
There if you seek not, and gone if you
    look,
Ninety miles off as the eagle flies.

But mountains make not all the shore
The main-land shows to Appledore;
Eight miles the heaving water spreads
To a long low coast with beaches and
    heads
That run through unimagined mazes,
As the lights and shades and magical
    hazes
Put them away or bring them near,
Shimmering, sketched out for thirty
    miles
Between two capes that waver like
    threads,
And sink in the ocean, and reappear,
Crumbled and melted to little isles,
With filmy trees, that seem the mere
Half-fancies of drowsy atmosphere;

And see the beach there, where it is
Flat as a threshing-floor, beaten and
    packed
With the flashing flails of weariless
    seas,
How it lifts and looms to a precipice,
O'er whose square front, a dream, no
    more,
The steepened sand-stripes seem to
    pour,
A murmurless vision of cataract;
You almost fancy you hear a roar,
Fitful and faint from the distance wan-
    dering;
But 't is only the blind old ocean maun-
    dering,
Raking the shingle to and fro,
Aimlessly clutching and letting go
The kelp-haired sedges of Appledore,
Slipping down with a sleepy forgetting,
And anon his ponderous shoulder set-
    ting,
With a deep, hoarse pant against Ap-
    pledore.

IV.

Eastward as far as the eye can see,
Still eastward, eastward, endlessly,
The sparkle and tremor of purple sea
That rises before you, a flickering hill,
On and on to the shut of the sky,
And beyond, you fancy it sloping until
The same multitudinous throb and thrill
That vibrate under your dizzy eye
In ripples of orange and pink are sent
Where the poppied sails doze on the
    yard,
And the clumsy junk and proa lie
Sunk deep with precious woods and
    nard,
'Mid the palmy isles of the Orient.
    Those leaning towers of clouded
        white
On the farthest brink of doubtful ocean,
That shorten and shorten out of sight,
Yet seem on the selfsame spot to stay,
Receding with a motionless motion,
Fading to dubious films of gray,
Lost, dimly found, then vanished
    wholly,
Will rise again, the great world under,
First films, then towers, then high-
    heaped clouds,

Whose nearing outlines sharpen slowly
Into tall ships with cobweb shrouds,
That fill long Mongol eyes with wonder,
Crushing the violet wave to spray
Past some low headland of Cathay;—
What was that sigh which seemed so
    near,
Chilling your fancy to the core?
'T is only the sad old sea you hear,
That seems to seek forevermore
Something it cannot find, and so,
Sighing, seeks on, and tells its woe
To the pitiless breakers of Appledore.

V.

How looks Appledore in a storm?
    I have seen it when its crags seemed
        frantic,
    Butting against the mad Atlantic,
When surge on surge would heap
    enorme,
    Cliffs of emerald topped with snow,
    That lifted and lifted, and then let go
A great white avalanche of thunder,
    A grinding, blinding, deafening ire
Monadnock might have trembled under;
    And the island, whose rock-roots
        pierce below
    To where they are warmed with the
        central fire,
You could feel its granite fibres racked,
    As it seemed to plunge with a shud-
        der and thrill
    Right at the breast of the swooping
        hill,
And to rise again snorting a cataract
Of rage-froth from every cranny and
    ledge,
    While the sea drew its breath in
        hoarse and deep,
And the next vast breaker curled its
    edge,
    Gathering itself for a mightier leap.

North, east, and south there are reefs
    and breakers
    You would never dream of in smooth
        weather,
That toss and gore the sea for acres,
    Bellowing and gnashing and snarling
        together;
Look northward, where Duck Island
    lies,

And over its crown you will see arise,
Against a background of slaty skies,
 A row of pillars still and white,
 That glimmer, and then are gone
  from sight,
As if the moon should suddenly kiss,
 While you crossed the gusty desert
  by night,
The long colonnades of Persepolis;
Look southward for White Island light,
 The lantern stands ninety feet o'er
  the tide;
There is first a half-mile of tumult and
  fight,
Of dash and roar and tumble and fright,
 And surging bewilderment wild and
  wide,
Where the breakers struggle left and
  right,
 Then a mile or more of rushing sea,
And then the light-house slim and lone;
And whenever the weight of ocean is
  thrown
Full and fair on White Island head,
 A great mist-jotun you will see
 Lifting himself up silently
High and huge o'er the light-house top,
With hands of wavering spray out-
  spread,
 Groping after the little tower,
 That seems to shrink and shorten and
  cower,
Till the monster's arms of a sudden
  drop,
 And silently and fruitlessly
He sinks back into the sea.

You, meanwhile, where drenched you
  stand,
 Awaken once more to the rush and
  roar,
And on the rock-point tighten your
  hand,
As you turn and see a valley deep,
 That was not there a moment before,
Suck rattling down between you and a
  heap
 Of toppling billow, whose instant fall
 Must sink the whole island once for
  all,
Or watch the silenter, stealthier seas
 Feeling their way to you more and
  more;
If they once should clutch you high as
  the knees,

They would whirl you down like a sprig
  of kelp,
Beyond all reach of hope or help; —
 And such in a storm is Appledore.

VI.

'T is the sight of a lifetime to behold
The great shorn sun as you see it now,
Across eight miles of undulant gold
That widens landward, weltered and
  rolled,
With freaks of shadow and crimson
  stains;
To see the solid mountain brow
As it notches the disk, and gains and
  gains
Until there comes, you scarce know
  when,
A tremble of fire o'er the parted lips
Of cloud and mountain, which van-
  ishes, — then
From the body of day the sun-soul
  slips
And the face of earth darkens; but now
  the strips
Of western vapor, straight and thin,
From which the horizon's swervings
  win
A grace of contrast, take fire and burn
Like splinters of touchwood, whose
  edges a mould
Of ashes o'erfeathers; northward turn
For an instant, and let your eye grow
  cold
On Agamenticus, and when once more
You look, 't is as if the land-breeze,
  growing,
From the smouldering brands the film
  were blowing,
And brightening them down to the very
  core;
Yet they momently cool and dampen
  and deaden,
The crimson turns golden, the gold
  turns leaden,
Hardening into one black bar
O'er which, from the hollow heaven
  afar,
Shoots a splinter of light like diamond,
Half seen, half fancied; by and by
Beyond whatever is most beyond
In the uttermost waste of desert sky,
Grows a star;
And over it, visible spirit of dew, —

Ah, stir not, speak not, hold your
    breath,
Or surely the miracle vanisheth, —
The new moon, tranced in unspeakable
    blue !
No frail illusion ; this were true,
Rather, to call it the canoe
Hollowed out of a single pearl,
That floats us from the Present's whirl
Back to those beings which were ours,
When wishes were winged things like
    powers !
Call it not light, that mystery tender,
Which broods upon the brooding ocean,
That flush of ecstasied surrender
To indefinable emotion,
That glory, mellower than a mist
Of pearl dissolved with amethyst,
Which rims Square Rock, like what
    they paint
Of mitigated heavenly splendor
Round the stern forehead of a Saint !

No more a vision, reddened, largened,
The moon dips toward her mountain
    nest,
And, fringing it with palest argent,
Slow sheathes herself behind the mar-
    gent
Of that long cloud-bar in the West,
Whose nether edge, erelong, you see
The silvery chrism in turn anoint,
And then the tiniest rosy point
Touched doubtfully and timidly
Into the dark blue's chilly strip,
As some mute, wondering thing below,
Awakened by the thrilling glow,
Might, looking up, see Dian dip
One lucent foot's delaying tip
In Latmian fountains long ago.

Knew you what silence was before?
Here is no startle of dreaming bird
That sings in his sleep, or strives to sing;
Here is no sough of branches stirred,
Nor noise of any living thing,
Such as one hears by night on shore ;
Only, now and then, a sigh,
With fickle intervals between,
Sometimes far, and sometimes nigh,
Such as Andromeda might have heard,
And fancied the huge sea-beast unseen
Turning in sleep ; it is the sea
That welters and wavers uneasily
Round the lonely reefs of Appledore.

THE WIND-HARP.

I TREASURE in secret some long, fine
    hair
    Of tenderest brown, but so inwardly
      golden
I half used to fancy the sunshine there,
So shy, so shifting, so waywardly rare,
    Was only caught for the moment and
      holden
While I could say *Dearest !* and kiss
    it, and then
In pity let go to the summer again.

I twisted this magic in gossamer strings
    Over a wind-harp's Delphian hollow ;
Then called to the idle breeze that
    swings
All day in the pine-tops, and clings, and
    sings
    'Mid the musical leaves, and said, "O,
    follow
The will of those tears that deepen my
    words,
And fly to my window to waken these
    chords."

So they trembled to life, and, doubt-
    fully
    Feeling their way to my sense, sang,
      "Say whether
They sit all day by the greenwood tree,
The lover and loved, as it wont to be,
    When we " —— but grief con-
      quered, and all together
They swelled such weird murmur as
    haunts a shore
Of some planet dispeopled, — "Never-
    more ! "

Then from deep in the past, as seemed
    to me,
The strings gathered sorrow and sang
    forsaken,
"One lover still waits 'neath the green-
    wood tree,
But 't is dark," and they shuddered,
    "where lieth she
    Dark and cold ! Forever must one
    be taken ? "
But I groaned, "O harp of all ruth
    bereft,
This Scripture is sadder, — 'the other
    left' ! "

There murmured, as if one strove to
    speak,
    And tears came instead ; then the sad
        tones wandered
And faltered among the uncertain
        chords
In a troubled doubt between sorrow and
        words ;
    At last with themselves they ques-
        tioned and pondered,
" Hereafter ? — who knoweth ? " and so
        they sighed
Down the long steps that lead to silence
    and died.

AUF WIEDERSEHEN !

SUMMER.

THE little gate was reached at last,
    Half hid in lilacs down the lane ;
She pushed it wide, and, as she past,
A wistful look she backward cast,
    And said, — " *Auf wiedersehen !* "

With hand on latch, a vision white
    Lingered reluctant, and again
Half doubting if she did aright,
Soft as the dews that fell that night,
    She said, — " *Auf wiedersehen !* "

The lamp's clear gleam flits up the stair ;
    I linger in delicious pain ;
Ah, in that chamber, whose rich air
To breathe in thought I scarcely dare,
    Thinks she, — " *Auf wiedersehen !* " ?

'T is thirteen years ; once more I press
    The turf that silences the lane ;
I hear the rustle of her dress,
I smell the lilacs, and — ah, yes,
    I hear " *Auf wiedersehen !* "

Sweet piece of bashful maiden art !
    The English words had seemed too
        fain,
But these — they drew us heart to heart,
Yet held us tenderly apart ;
    She said, " *Auf wiedersehen !* "

PALINODE.

AUTUMN.

STILL thirteen years : 't is autumn now
    On field and hill, in heart and brain ;
The naked trees at evening sough ;
The leaf to the forsaken bough
    Sighs not, — " *Auf wiedersehen !* "

Two watched yon oriole's pendent
        dome,
    That now is void, and dank with rain,
And one, — O, hope more frail than
        foam !
The bird to his deserted home
    Sings not, — " *Auf wiedersehen !* "

The loath gate swings with rusty creak ;
    Once, parting there, we played at
        pain ;
There came a parting, when the weak
And fading lips essayed to speak
    Vainly, — " *Auf wiedersehen !* "

Somewhere is comfort, somewhere faith,
    Though thou in outer dark remain ;
One sweet sad voice ennobles death,
And still, for eighteen centuries saith
    Softly, — " *Auf wiedersehen !* "

If earth another grave must bear,
    Yet heaven hath won a sweeter strain,
And something whispers my despair,
That, from an orient chamber there,
    Floats down, " *Auf wiedersehen !* "

AFTER THE BURIAL.

YES, faith is a goodly anchor ;
    When skies are sweet as a psalm,
At the bows it lolls so stalwart,
    In its bluff, broad-shouldered calm.

And when over breakers to leeward
    The tattered surges are hurled,
It may keep our head to the tempest,
    With its grip on the base of the world.

But, after the shipwreck, tell me
    What help in its iron thews,
Still true to the broken hawser,
    Deep down among sea-weed and ooze

In the breaking gulfs of sorrow,
When the helpless feet stretch out
And find in the deeps of darkness
No footing so solid as doubt,

Then better one spar of Memory,
One broken plank of the Past,
That our human heart may cling to,
Though hopeless of shore at last !

To the spirit its splendid conjectures,
To the flesh its sweet despair,
Its tears o'er the thin-worn locket
With its anguish of deathless hair !

Immortal ? I feel it and know it,
Who doubts it of such as she ?
But that is the pang's very secret, —
Immortal away from me.

There 's a narrow ridge in the grave-
yard
Would scarce stay a child in his race,
But to me and my thought it is wider
Than the star-sown vague of Space.

Your logic, my friend, is perfect,
Your moral most drearily true ;
But, since the earth clashed on *her*
coffin,
I keep hearing that, and not you.

Console if you will, I can bear it ;
'T is a well-meant alms of breath ;
But not all the preaching since Adam
Has made Death other than Death.

It is pagan ; but wait till you feel it, —
That jar of our earth, that dull shock
When the ploughshare of deeper pas-
sion
Tears down to our primitive rock.

Communion in spirit ! Forgive me,
But I, who am earthy and weak,
Would give all my incomes from dream-
land
For a touch of her hand on my cheek.

That little shoe in the corner,
So worn and wrinkled and brown,
With its emptiness confutes you,
And argues your wisdom down.

THE DEAD HOUSE.

HERE once my step was quickened,
  Here beckoned the opening door,
And welcome thrilled from the threshold
  To the foot it had known before.

A glow came forth to meet me
  From the flame that laughed in the
    grate,
And shadows adance on the ceiling,
  Danced blither with mine for a mate.

" I claim you, old friend," yawned the
    arm-chair,
  " This corner, you know, is your
    seat " ;
" Rest your slippers on me," beamed
    the fender,
  " I brighten at touch of your feet."

" We know the practised finger,"
  Said the books, " that seems like
    brain " ;
And the shy page rustled the secret
  It had kept till I came again.

Sang the pillow, " My down once
    quivered
  On nightingales' throats that flew
Through moonlit gardens of Hafiz
  To gather quaint dreams for you."

Ah me, where the Past sowed heart's-
    ease,
  The Present plucks rue for us men !
I come back : that scar unhealing
  Was not in the churchyard then.

But, I think, the house is unaltered,
  I will go and beg to look
At the rooms that were once familiar
  To my life as its bed to a brook.

Unaltered ! Alas for the sameness
  That makes the change but more !
'T is a dead man I see in the mirrors,
  'T is his tread that chills the floor !

To learn such a simple lesson,
  Need I go to Paris and Rome,
That the many make the household,
  But only one the home ?

'T was just a womanly presence,
    An influence unexprest,
But a rose she had worn, on my grave-
        sod
    Were more than long life with the
        rest !

'T was a smile, 't was a garment's
        rustle,
    'T was nothing that I can phrase,
But the whole dumb dwelling grew
        conscious,
    And put on her looks and ways.

Were it mine I would close the shutters,
    Like lids when the life is fled,
And the funeral fire should wind it,
    This corpse of a home that is dead.

For it died that autumn morning
    When she, its soul, was borne
To lie all dark on the hillside
    That looks over woodland and corn.

A MOOD.

Pine in the distance,
Patient through sun or rain,
Meeting with graceful persistence,
With yielding but rooted resistance,
The northwind's wrench and strain,
No memory of past existence
Brings thee pain ;
Right for the zenith heading,
Friendly with heat or cold,
Thine arms to the influence spreading
Of the heavens, just from of old,
Thou only aspirest the more,
Unregretful the old leaves shedding
That fringed thee with music before,
And deeper thy roots embedding
In the grace and the beauty of yore ;
Thou sigh'st not, " Alas, I am older,
The green of last summer is sear ! "
But loftier, hopefuller, bolder,
Wins broader horizons each year.

To me 't is not cheer thou art singing :
There 's a sound of the sea,
O mournful tree,
In thy boughs forever clinging,
And the far-off roar

Of waves on the shore
A shattered vessel flinging.

As thou musest still of the ocean
On which thou must float at last,
And seem'st to foreknow
The shipwreck's woe
And the sailor wrenched from the
        broken mast,
Do I, in this vague emotion,
This sadness that will not pass,
Though the air throb with wings,
And the field laughs and sings,
Do I forebode, alas !
The ship-building longer and wearier,
The voyage's struggle and strife,
And then the darker and drearier
Wreck of a broken life ?

THE VOYAGE TO VINLAND

I.

BIÖRN'S BECKONERS.

Now Biörn, the son of Heriulf, had ill
        days
Because the heart within him seethed
        with blood
That would not be allayed with any
        toil,
Whether of war or hunting or the oar,
But was anhungered for some joy un-
        tried :
For the brain grew not weary with the
        limbs,
But, while they slept, still hammered
        like a Troll,
Building all night a bridge of solid
        dream
Between him and some purpose of his
        soul,
Or will to find a purpose. With the
        dawn
The sleep-laid timbers, crumbled to
        soft mist,
Denied all foothold. But the dream
        remained,
And every night with yellow-bearded
        kings
His sleep was haunted, — mighty men
        of old,

Once young as he, now ancient like the
gods,
And safe as stars in all men's memories.
Strange sagas read he in their sea-blue
eyes
Cold as the sea, grandly compassion-
less ;
Like life, they made him eager and
then mocked.
Nay, broad awake, they would not let
him be ;
They shaped themselves gigantic in the
mist,
They rose far-beckoning in the lamps
of heaven,
They whispered invitation in the winds,
And breath came from them, mightier
than the wind,
To strain the lagging sails of his resolve,
Till that grew passion which before was
wish,
And youth seemed all too costly to be
staked
On the soiled cards wherewith men
played their game,
Letting Time pocket up the larger life,
Lost with base gain of raiment, food,
and roof.
"What helpeth lightness of the feet?"
they said,
"Oblivion runs with swifter foot than
they ;
Or strength of sinew? New men come
as strong,
And those sleep nameless ; or renown
in war ?
Swords grave no name on the long-
memoried rock
But moss shall hide it ; they alone who
wring
Some secret purpose from the unwilling
gods
Survive in song for yet a little while
To vex, like us, the dreams of later men,
Ourselves a dream, and dreamlike all
we did."

II.

THORWALD'S LAY.

So Biörn went comfortless but for his
thought,
And by his thought the more discomforted,

Till Eric Thurlson kept his Yule-tide
feast :
And thither came he, called among the
rest,
Silent, lone-minded, a church-door to
mirth :
But, ere deep draughts forbade such
serious song
As the grave Skald might chant, nor
after blush,
Then Eric looked at Thorwald, where
he sat,
Mute as a cloud amid the stormy hall,
And said : "O Skald, sing now an
olden song,
Such as our fathers heard who led great
lives ;
And, as the bravest on a shield is borne
Along the waving host that shouts him
king,
So rode their thrones upon the throng-
ing seas !"
Then the old man arose ; white-haired
he stood,
White-bearded, and with eyes that
looked afar
From their still region of perpetual
snow,
Beyond the little smokes and stirs of
men :
His head was bowed with gathered
flakes of years,
As winter bends the sea-foreboding
pine,
But something triumphed in his brow
and eye,
Which whoso saw it could not see and
crouch :
Loud rang the emptied beakers as he
mused,
Brooding his eyried thoughts ; then, as
an eagle
Circles smooth-winged above the wind-
vexed woods,
So wheeled his soul into the air of song
High o'er the stormy hall ; and thus he
sang :
"The fletcher for his arrow-shaft picks
out
Wood closest-grained, long-seasoned,
straight as light ;
And from a quiver full of such as these
The wary bowman, matched against his
peers,

Long doubting, singles yet once more
    the best.
Who is it needs such flawless shafts as
    Fate?
What archer of his arrows is so choice,
Or hits the white so surely? They are
    men,
The chosen of her quiver; nor for her
Will every reed suffice, or cross-grained
    stick
At random from life's vulgar fagot
    plucked:
Such answer household ends; but she
    will have
Souls straight and clear, of toughest
    fibre, sound
Down to the heart of heart; from these
    she strips
All needless stuff, all sapwood, seasons
    them,
From circumstance untoward feathers
    plucks
Crumpled and cheap, and barbs with
    iron will:
The hour that passes is her quiver-boy:
When she draws bow, 't is not across
    the wind,
Nor 'gainst the sun her haste-snatched
    arrow sings,
For sun and wind have plighted faith to
    her:
Ere men have heard the sinew twang,
    behold
In the butt's heart her trembling mes-
    senger!

"The song is old and simple that I
    sing;
But old and simple are despised as
    cheap,
Though hardest to achieve of human
    things:
Good were the days of yore, when men
    were tried
By ring of shields, as now by ring of
    words;
But while the gods are left, and hearts
    of men,
And unlocked ocean, still the days are
    good.
Still o'er the earth hastes Opportunity,
Seeking the hardy soul that seeks for
    her.
Be not abroad, nor deaf with household
    cares

That chatter loudest as they mean the
    least;
Swift-willed is thrice-willed; late means
    nevermore;
Impatient is her foot, nor turns again."

He ceased; upon his bosom sank his
    beard
Sadly, as one who oft had seen her pass
Nor stayed her: and forthwith the
    frothy tide
Of interrupted wassail roared along;
But Biörn, the son of Heriulf, sat apart
Musing, and, with his eyes upon the fire,
Saw shapes of arrows, lost as soon as
    seen.
"A ship," he muttered, "is a wingéd
    bridge
That leadeth every way to man's desire,
And ocean the wide gate to manful
    luck";
And then with that resolve his heart
    was bent,
Which, like a humming shaft, through
    many a stripe
Of day and night, across the unpath-
    wayed seas
Shot the brave prow that cut on Vinland
    sands
The first rune in the Saga of the West.

III.

GUDRIDA'S PROPHECY.

Four weeks they sailed, a speck in sky-
    shut seas,
Life, where was never life that knew
    itself,
But tumbled lubber-like in blowing
    whales;
Thought, where the like had never been
    before
Since Thought primeval brooded the
    abyss;
Alone as men were never in the world.
They saw the icy foundlings of the sea,
White cliffs of silence, beautiful by day,
Or looming, sudden-perilous, at night
In monstrous hush; or sometimes in
    the dark
The waves broke ominous with paly
    gleams
Crushed by the prow in sparkles of
    cold fire.

Then came green stripes of sea that
 promised land
But brought it not, and on the thirtieth
 day
Low in the West were wooded shores
 like cloud.
They shouted as men shout with sud-
 den hope;
But Biörn was silent, such strange loss
 there is
Between the dream's fulfilment and the
 dream,
Such sad abatement in the goal attained.
Then Gudrida, that was a prophetess,
Rapt with strange influence from At-
 lantis sang:
Her words: the vision was the dream-
 ing shore's.

 Looms there the New Land:
 Locked in the shadow
 Long the gods shut it,
 Niggards of newness
 They, the o'er-old.

 Little it looks there,
 Slim as a cloud-streak;
 It shall fold peoples
 Even as a shepherd
 Foldeth his flock.

 Silent it sleeps now;
 Great ships shall seek it,
 Swarming as salmon;
 Noise of its numbers
 Two seas shall hear.

 Men from the Northland,
 Men from the Southland,
 Haste empty-handed;
 No more than manhood
 Bring they, and hands.

 Dark hair and fair hair,
 Red blood and blue blood,
 There shall be mingled;
 Force of the ferment
 Makes the New Man.

 Pick of all kindreds,
 King's blood shall theirs be,
 Shoots of the eldest
 Stock upon Midgard,
 Sons of the poor.

 Them waits the New Land;
 They shall subdue it,
 Leaving their sons' sons
 Space for the body,
 Space for the soul.

 Leaving their sons' sons
 All things save song-craft,
 Plant long in growing,
 Thrusting its tap-root
 Deep in the Gone.

 Here men shall grow up
 Strong from self-helping;
 Eyes for the present
 Bring they as eagles',
 Blind to the Past.

 They shall make over
 Creed, law, and custom;
 Driving-men, doughty
 Builders of empire,
 Builders of men.

 Here are no singers;
 What should they sing of?
 They, the unresting?
 Labor is ugly,
 Loathsome is change.

 Those the old gods hate,
 Dwellers in dream-land,
 Drinking delusion
 Out of the empty
 Skull of the Past.

 These hate the old gods,
 Warring against them;
 Fatal to Odin,
 Here the wolf Fenrir
 Lieth in wait.

 Here the gods' Twilight
 Gathers, earth-gulfing;
 Blackness of battle,
 Fierce till the Old World
 Flare up in fire.

 Doubt not, my Northmen;
 Fate loves the fearless;
 Fools, when their roof-tree
 Falls, think it doomsday;
 Firm stands the sky.

26

Over the ruin
See I the promise ;
Crisp waves the cornfield,
Peace-walled, the homestead
Waits open-doored.

There lies the New Land ;
Yours to behold it,
Not to possess it ;
Slowly Fate's perfect
Fulness shall come.

Then from your strong loins
Seed shall be scattered,
Men to the marrow,
Wilderness tamers,
Walkers of waves.

Jealous, the old gods
Shut it in shadow,
Wisely they ward it,
Egg of the serpent,
Bane to them all.

Stronger and sweeter
New gods shall seek it,
Fill it with man-folk
Wise for the future,
Wise from the past.

Here all is all men's,
Save only Wisdom ;
King he that wins her ;
Him hail they helmsman,
Highest of heart.

Might makes no master
Here any longer ;
Sword is not swayer ;
Here e'en the gods are
Selfish no more.

Walking the New Earth,
Lo, a divine One
Greets all men godlike,
Calls them his kindred,
He, the Divine.

Is it Thor's hammer
Rays in his right hand?
Weaponless walks he ;
It is the White Christ,
Stronger than Thor.

Here shall a realm rise
Mighty in manhood ;
Justice and Mercy
Here set a stronghold
Safe without spear.

Weak was the Old World,
Wearily war-fenced ;
Out of its ashes,
Strong as the morning,
Springeth the New.

Beauty of promise,
Promise of beauty,
Safe in the silence
Sleep thou, till cometh
Light to thy lids !

Thee shall awaken
Flame from the furnace,
Bath of all brave ones,
Cleanser of conscience,
Welder of will.

Lowly shall love thee,
Thee, open-handed !
Stalwart shall shield thee,
Thee, worth their best blood,
Waif of the West !

Then shall come singers,
Singing no swan-song,
Birth-carols, rather,
Meet for the man-child
Mighty of bone.

MAHMOOD THE IMAGE-BREAKER.

OLD events have modern meanings
    only that survives
Of past history which finds kindred in
    all hearts and lives.

Mahmood once, the idol-breaker,
    spreader of the Faith,
Was at Sumnat tempted sorely, as the
    legend saith.

In the great pagoda's centre, monstrous
    and abhorred,
Granite on a throne of granite, sat the
    temple's lord.

Mahmood paused a moment, silenced
  by the silent face
That, with eyes of stone unwavering,
  awed the ancient place.

Then the Brahmins knelt before him,
  by his doubt made bold,
Pledging for their idol's ransom countless gems and gold.

Gold was yellow dirt to Mahmood, but
  of precious use,
Since from it the roots of power suck
  a potent juice.

"Were yon stone alone in question,
  this would please me well,"
Mahmood said ; "but, with the block
  there, I my truth must sell.

"Wealth and rule slip down with Fortune, as her wheel turns round ;
He who keeps his faith, he only cannot
  be discrowned.

"Little were a change of station, loss
  of life or crown,
But the wreck were past retrieving if
  the Man fell down."

So his iron mace he lifted, smote with
  might and main,
And the idol, on the pavement tumbling, burst in twain.

Luck obeys the downright striker ;
  from the hollow core,
Fifty times the Brahmins' offer deluged
  all the floor.

INVITA MINERVA.

The Bardling came where by a river
  grew
The pennoned reeds, that, as the west-
  wind blew,
Gleamed and sighed plaintively, as if
  they knew
What music slept enchanted in each
  stem,
Till Pan should choose some happy one
  of them,
And with wise lips enlife it through and
  through.

The Bardling thought, "A pipe is all
  I need ;
Once I have sought me out a clear,
  smooth reed,
And shaped it to my fancy, I proceed
To breathe such strains as, yonder 'mid
  the rocks,
The strange youth blows, that tends
  Admetus' flocks,
And all the maidens will to me pay
  heed."

The summer day he spent in questful
  round,
And many a reed he marred, but never
  found
A conjuring-spell to free the imprisoned
  sound ;
At last his vainly wearied limbs he laid
Beneath a sacred laurel's flickering
  shade,
And sleep about his brain her cobweb
  wound.

Then strode the mighty Mother through
  his dreams,
Saying : "The reeds along a thousand
  streams
Are mine, and who is he that plots and
  schemes
To snare the melodies wherewith my
  breath
Sounds through the double pipes of Life
  and Death,
Atoning what to men mad discord
  seems ?

"He seeks not me, but I seek oft in
  vain
For him who shall my voiceful reeds
  constrain,
And make them utter their melodious
  pain ;
He flies the immortal gift, for well he
  knows
His life of life must with its overflows
Flood the unthankful pipe, nor come
  again.

"Thou fool, who dost my harmless
  subjects wrong,
'T is not the singer's wish that makes
  the song :
The rhythmic beauty wanders dumb,
  how long,

Nor stoops to any daintiest instrument,
Till, found its mated lips, their sweet
    consent
Makes mortal breath than Time and
    Fate more strong."

THE FOUNTAIN OF YOUTH.

I.

'T is a woodland enchanted !
By no sadder spirit
Than blackbirds and thrushes,
That whistle to cheer it
All day in the bushes,
This woodland is haunted :
And in a small clearing,
Beyond sight or hearing
Of human annoyance,
The little fount gushes,
First smoothly, then dashes
And gurgles and flashes,
To the maples and ashes
Confiding its joyance ;
Unconscious confiding,
Then, silent and glossy,
Slips winding and hiding
Through alder-stems mossy,
Through gossamer roots
Fine as nerves,
That tremble, as shoots
Through their magnetized curves
The allurement delicious
Of the water's capricious
Thrills, gushes, and swerves.

II.

'T is a woodland enchanted !
I am writing no fiction ;
And this fount, its sole daughter,
To the woodland was granted
To pour holy water
And win benediction ;
In summer-noon flushes,
When all the wood hushes,
Blue dragon-flies knitting
To and fro in the sun,
With sidelong jerk flitting
Sink down on the rushes,
And, motionless sitting,
Hear it bubble and run,

Hear its low inward singing,
With level wings swinging
On green tasselled rushes,
To dream in the sun.

III.

'T is a woodland enchanted !
The great August noonlight,
Through myriad rifts slanted,
Leaf and bole thickly sprinkles
With flickering gold ;
There, in warm August gloaming,
With quick, silent brightenings,
From meadow-lands roaming,
The firefly twinkles
His fitful heat-lightnings ;
There the magical moonlight
With meek, saintly glory
Steeps summit and wold ;
There whippoorwills plain in the
    solitudes hoary
With lone cries that wander
Now hither, now yonder,
Like souls doomed of old
To a mild purgatory ;
But through noonlight and moonlight
The little fount tinkles
Its silver saints'-bells,
That no sprite ill-boding
May make his abode in
Those innocent dells.

IV.

'T is a woodland enchanted !
When the phebe scarce whistles
Once an hour to his fellow,
And, where red lilies flaunted,
Balloons from the thistles
Tell summer's disasters,
The butterflies yellow,
As caught in an eddy
Of air's silent ocean,
Sink, waver, and steady
O'er goats'-beard and asters,
Like souls of dead flowers,
With aimless emotion
Still lingering unready
To leave their old bowers ;
And the fount is no dumber,
But still gleams and flashes,
And gurgles and plashes,
To the measure of summer ;

The butterflies hear it,
And spell-bound are holden,
Still balancing near it
O'er the goats'-beard so golden.

V.

'T is a woodland enchanted!
A vast silver willow,
I know not how planted,
(This wood is enchanted,
And full of surprises,)
Stands stemming a billow,
A motionless billow
Of ankle-deep mosses;
Two great roots it crosses
To make a round basin,
And there the Fount rises;
Ah, too pure a mirror
For one sick of error
To see his sad face in!
No dew-drop is stiller
In its lupin-leaf setting
Than this water moss-bounded;
But a tiny sand-pillar
From the bottom keeps jetting,
And mermaid ne'er sounded
Through the wreaths of a shell,
Down amid crimson dulses
In some spell of ocean,
A melody, sweeter
Than the delicate pulses,
The soft, noiseless metre
The pause and the swell
Of that musical motion:
I recall it, not see it;
Could vision be clearer?
Half I'm fain to draw nearer
Half tempted to flee it;
The sleeping Past wake not,
Beware!
One forward step take not,
Ah! break not
That quietude rare!
By my step unaffrighted
A thrush hops before it,
And o'er it
A birch hangs delighted,
Dipping, dipping, dipping its tremu-
        lous hair;
Pure as the fountain, once
I came to the place,
(How dare I draw nearer?)
I bent o'er its mirror,

And saw a child's face
'Mid locks of bright gold in it;
Yes, pure as this fountain once, —
Since, how much error!
Too holy a mirror
For the man to behold in it
His harsh, bearded countenance!

VI.

'T is a woodland enchanted!
Ah, fly unreturning!
Yet stay; —
'T is a woodland enchanted,
Where wonderful chances
Have sway;
Luck flees from the cold one
But leaps to the bold one
Half-way;
Why should I be daunted?
Still the smooth mirror glances,
Still the amber sand dances,
One look, — then away!
O magical glass!
Canst keep in thy bosom
Shades of leaf and of blossom
When summer days pass,
So that when thy wave hardens
It shapes as it pleases,
Unharmed by the breezes,
Its fine hanging gardens?
Hast those in thy keeping,
And canst not uncover,
Enchantedly sleeping,
The old shade of thy lover?
It is there! I have found it!
He wakes, the long sleeper!
The pool is grown deeper,
The sand dance is ending,
The white floor sinks, blending
With skies that below me
Are deepening and bending,
And a child's face alone
That seems not to know me,
With hair that fades golden
In the heaven-glow round it,
Looks up at my own;
Ah, glimpse through the portal
That leads to the throne,
That opes the child's olden
Regions Elysian!
Ah, too holy vision
For thy skirts to be holden
By soiled hand of mortal!

It wavers, it scatters,
'T is gone past recalling !
A tear's sudden falling
The magic cup shatters,
Breaks the spell of the waters,
And the sand cone once more,
With a ceaseless renewing,
Its dance is pursuing
On the silvery floor,
O'er and o'er,
With a noiseless and ceaseless renewing.

VII.

'T is a woodland enchanted !
If you ask me, *Where is it ?*
I can but make answer,
" 'T is past my disclosing ; "
Not to choice is it granted
By sure paths to visit
The still pool enclosing
Its blithe little dancer ;
But in some day, the rarest
Of many Septembers,
When the pulses of air rest,
And all things lie dreaming
In drowsy haze steaming
From the wood's glowing embers,
Then, sometimes, unheeding,
And asking not whither,
By a sweet inward leading
My feet are drawn thither,
And, looking with awe in the magical
    mirror,
I see through my tears,
Half doubtful of seeing,
The face unperverted,
The warm golden being
Of a child of five years ;
And spite of the mists and the error,
And the days overcast,
Can feel that I walk undeserted,
But forever attended
By the glad heavens that bended
O'er the innocent past ;
Toward fancy or truth
Doth the sweet vision win me ?
Dare I think that I cast
In the fountain of youth
The fleeting reflection
Of some bygone perfection
That still lingers in me ?

YUSSOUF.

A STRANGER came one night to Yus-
    souf's tent,
Saying, " Behold one outcast and in
    dread,
Against whose life the bow of power is
    bent,
Who flies, and hath not where to lay
    his head ;
I come to thee for shelter and for food,
To Yussouf, called through all our tribes
    ' The Good.' "

" This tent is mine," said Yussouf,
    " but no more
Than it is God's ; come in, and be at
    peace ;
Freely shalt thou partake of all my store
As I of His who buildeth over these
Our tents his glorious roof of night and
    day,
And at whose door none ever yet heard
    Nay."

So Yussouf entertained his guest that
    night,
And, waking him ere day, said : " Here
    is gold,
My swiftest horse is saddled for thy
    flight,
Depart before the prying day grow
    bold."
As one lamp lights another, nor grows
    less,
So nobleness enkindleth nobleness.

That inward light the stranger's face
    made grand,
Which shines from all self-conquest ;
    kneeling low,
He bowed his forehead upon Yussouf's
    hand,
Sobbing : " O Sheik, I cannot leave
    thee so ;
I will repay thee ; all this thou hast
    done
Unto that Ibrahim who slew thy son ! "

" Take thrice the gold," said Yussouf,
    " for with thee
Into the desert, never to return,
My one black thought shall ride away
    from me ;

First-born, for whom by day and night
    I yearn,
Balanced and just are all of God's de-
    crees;
Thou art avenged, my first-born, sleep
    in peace!"

THE DARKENED MIND.

THE fire is burning clear and blithely,
Pleasantly whistles the winter wind;
We are about thee, thy friends and
    kindred,
On us all flickers the firelight kind;
There thou sittest in thy wonted corner
Lone and awful in thy darkened mind.

There thou sittest; now and then thou
    moanest;
Thou dost talk with what we cannot see,
Lookest at us with an eye so doubtful,
It doth put us very far from thee;
There thou sittest; we would fain be
    nigh thee,
But we know that it can never be.

We can touch thee, still we are no
    nearer;
Gather round thee, still thou art alone;
The wide chasm of reason is between us;
Thou confutest kindness with a moan;
We can speak to thee, and thou canst
    answer,
Like two prisoners through a wall of
    stone.

Hardest heart would call it very awful
When thou look'st at us and seest — O
    what?
If we move away, thou sittest gazing
With those vague eyes at the selfsame
    spot,
And thou mutterest, thy hands thou
    wringest,
Seeing something, — us thou seëst not.

Strange it is that, in this open bright-
    ness,
Thou shouldst sit in such a narrow cell;
Strange it is that thou shouldst be so
    lonesome
Where those are who love thee all so
    well;
Not so much of thee is left among us
As the hum outliving the hushed bell.

WHAT RABBI JEHOSHA SAID.

RABBI JEHOSHA used to say
That God made angels every day,
Perfect as Michael and the rest
First brooded in creation's nest,
Whose only office was to cry
Hosanna! once, and then to die;
Or rather, with Life's essence blent,
To be led home from banishment.

Rabbi Jehosha had the skill
To know that Heaven is in God's will;
And doing that, though for a space
One heart-beat long, may win a grace
As full of grandeur and of glow
As Princes of the Chariot know.

'T were glorious, no doubt, to be
One of the strong-winged Hierarchy,
To burn with Seraphs, or to shine
With Cherubs, deathlessly divine;
Yet I, perhaps, poor earthly clod,
Could I forget myself in God,
Could I but find my nature's clew
Simply as birds and blossoms do,
And but for one rapt moment know
'T is Heaven must come, not we must
    go,
Should win my place as near the throne
As the pearl-angel of its zone,
And God would listen 'mid the throng
For my one breath of perfect song,
That, in its simple human way,
Said all the Host of Heaven could say.

ALL-SAINTS.

ONE feast, of holy days the crest,
    I, though no Churchman, love to
    keep,
All-Saints, — the unknown good that
    rest
    In God's still memory folded deep;
The bravely dumb that did their deed,
    And scorned to blot it with a name,
Men of the plain heroic breed,
    That loved Heaven's silence more
    than fame.

Such lived not in the past alone,
    But thread to-day the unheeding
    street,

And stairs to Sin and Famine known
  Sing with the welcome of their feet ;
The den they enter grows a shrine,
  The grimy sash an oriel burns,
Their cup of water warms like wine,
  Their speech is filled from heavenly
    urns.

About their brows to me appears
  An aureole traced in tenderest light,
The rainbow-gleam of smiles through
    tears
  In dying eyes, by them made bright,
Of souls that shivered on the edge
  Of that chill ford repassed no more,
And in their mercy felt the pledge
  And sweetness of the farther shore.

A WINTER-EVENING HYMN
TO MY FIRE.

I.

Beauty on my hearth-stone blazing !
To-night the triple Zoroaster
Shall my prophet be and master :
To-night will I pure Magian be,
Hymns to thy sole honor raising,
While thou leapest fast and faster,
Wild with self-delighted glee,
Or sink'st low and glowest faintly
As an aureole still and saintly,
Keeping cadence to my praising
Thee ! still thee ! and only thee !

II.

Elfish daughter of Apollo !
Thee, from thy father stolen and bound
To serve in Vulcan's clangorous smithy
Prometheus (primal Yankee) found,
And, when he had tampered with thee,
  (Too confiding little maid !)
In a reed's precarious hollow
To our frozen earth conveyed :
For he swore I know not what ;
Endless ease should be thy lot,
Pleasure that should never falter,
Life-long play, and not a duty
Save to hover o'er the altar,
Vision of celestial beauty,
Fed with precious woods and spices,
Then, perfidious ! having got
Thee in the net of his devices,

Sold thee into endless slavery,
Made thee a drudge to boil the pot,
Thee, Helios' daughter, who dost bea
His likeness in thy golden hair ;
Thee, by nature wild and wavery
Palpitating, evanescent
As the shade of Dian's crescent
Life, motion, gladness, everywhere !

III.

Fathom deep men bury thee
In the furnace dark and still,
There, with dreariest mockery,
Making thee eat, against thy will,
Blackest Pennsylvanian stone ;
But thou dost avenge thy doom,
For, from out thy catacomb,
Day and night thy wrath is blown
In a withering simoom,
And, adown that cavern drear,
Thy black pitfall in the floor,
Staggers the lusty antique cheer,
Despairing, and is seen no more !

IV.

Elfish I may rightly name thee ;
We enslave, but cannot tame thee ;
With fierce snatches, now and then,
Thou pluckest at thy right again,
And thy down-trod instincts savage
To stealthy insurrection creep,
While thy wittol masters sleep,
And burst in undiscerning ravage :
Then how thou shak'st thy bacchant
    locks !
While brazen pulses, far and near,
Throb thick and thicker wild with fear
And dread conjecture, till the drear
Disordered clangor every steeple rocks !

V.

But when we make a friend of thee,
And admit thee to the hall
On our nights of festival,
Then, Cinderella, who could see
In thee the kitchen's stunted thrall ?
Once more a Princess lithe and tall,
Thou dancest with a whispering tread,
While the bright marvel of thy head
In crinkling gold floats all abroad,
And gloriously dost vindicate
The legend of thy lineage great,
Earth-exiled daughter of the Pythian
    god !

Now in the ample chimney-place,
To honor thy acknowledged race,
We crown thee high with laurel good,
Thy shining father's sacred wood,
Which, guessing thy ancestral right,
Sparkles and snaps its dumb delight,
And, at thy touch, poor outcast now,
Feels through its gladdened fibres go
The tingle and thrill and vassal glow
Of instincts loyal to the sun.

VI.

O thou of home the guardian Lar,
And, when our earth hath wandered far
Into the cold, and deep snow covers
The walks of our New England lovers,
Their sweet secluded evening-star!
'T was with thy rays the English Muse
Ripened her mild domestic hues;
'T was by thy flicker that she conned
The fireside wisdom that enrings
With light from heaven familiar things;
By thee she found the homely faith
In whose mild eyes thy comfort stay'th,
When Death, extinguishing his torch,
Gropes for the latch-string in the porch;
The love that wanders not beyond
His earliest nest, but sits and sings
While children smooth his patient
        wings;
Therefore with thee I love to read
Our brave old poets: at thy touch how
        stirs
Life in the withered words! how swift
        recede
Time's shadows! and how glows again
Through its dead mass the incandes-
        cent verse,
As when upon the anvils of the brain
It glittering lay, cyclopically wrought
By the fast-throbbing hammers of the
        poet's thought!
Thou murmurest, too, divinely stirred,
The aspirations unattained,
The rhythms so rathe and delicate,
They bent and strained
And broke, beneath the sombre weight
Of any airiest mortal word.

VII.

What warm protection dost thou bend
Round curtained talk of friend with
        friend,
While the gray snow-storm, held aloof,
To softest outline rounds the roof,
Or the rude North with baffled strain
Shoulders the frost-starred window-
        pane!
Now the kind nymph to Bacchus born
By Morpheus' daughter, she that seems
Gifted upon her natal morn
By him with fire, by her with dreams,
Nicotia, dearer to the Muse
Than all the grapes' bewildering juice,
We worship, unforbid of thee;
And, as her incense floats and curls
In airy spires and wayward whirls,
Or poises on its tremulous stalk
A flower of frailest revery,
So winds and loiters, idly free,
The current of unguided talk,
Now laughter-rippled, and now caught
In smooth, dark pools of deeper
        thought.
Meanwhile thou mellowest every word,
A sweetly unobtrusive third;
For thou hast magic beyond wine,
To unlock natures each to each;
The unspoken thought thou canst di-
        vine;
Thou fillest the pauses of the speech
With whispers that to dream-land reach
And frozen fancy-springs unchain
In Arctic outskirts of the brain;
Sun of all inmost confidences!
To thy rays doth the heart unclose
Its formal calyx of pretences,
That close against rude day's offences,
And open its shy midnight rose.

VIII.

Thou holdest not the master key
With which thy Sire sets free the mys-
        tic gates
Of Past and Future: not for common
        fates
Do they wide open fling,
And, with a far-heard ring,
Swing back their willing valves melo-
        diously;
Only to ceremonial days,
And great processions of imperial song
That set the world at gaze,
Doth such high privilege belong:
But thou a postern-door canst ope
To humbler chambers of the selfsame
        palace

Where Memory lodges, and her sister
    Hope,
Whose being is but as a crystal chalice
Which, with her various mood, the
    elder fills
    Of joy or sorrow,
So coloring as she wills
With hues of yesterday the unconscious
    morrow.

IX.

Thou sinkest, and my fancy sinks with
    thee:
For thee I took the idle shell,
And struck the unused chords again,
But they are gone who listened well;
Some are in heaven, and all are far
    from me:
Even as I sing, it turns to pain,
And with vain tears my eyelids throb
    and swell:
Enough; I come not of the race
That hawk their sorrows in the market-
    place.
Earth stops the ears I best had loved
    to please;
Then break, ye untuned chords, or rust
    in peace!
As if a white-haired actor should come
    back
Some midnight to the theatre void and
    black,
And there rehearse his youth's great
    part
'Mid thin applauses of the ghosts,
So seems it now: ye crowd upon my
    heart,
And I bow down in silence, shadowy
    hosts!

FANCY'S CASUISTRY.

How struggles with the tempest's
    swells
That warning of tumultuous bells!
The fire is loose! and frantic knells
    Throb fast and faster,
As tower to tower confusedly tells
    News of disaster.

But on my far-off solitude
No harsh alarums can intrude;

The terror comes to me subdued
    And charmed by distance,
To deepen the habitual mood
    Of my existence.

Are those, I muse, the Easter chimes?
And listen, weaving careless rhymes
While the loud city's griefs and crimes
    Pay gentle allegiance
To the fine quiet that sublimes
    These dreamy regions.

And when the storm o'erwhelms the
    shore,
I watch entranced as, o'er and o'er,
The light revolves amid the roar
    So still and saintly,
Now large and near, now more and
    more
    Withdrawing faintly.

This, too, despairing sailors see
Flash out the breakers 'neath their lee
In sudden snow, then lingeringly
    Wane tow'rd eclipse,
While through the dark the shuddering
    sea
    Gropes for the ships.

And is it right, this mood of mind
That thus, in revery enshrined,
Can in the world mere topics find
    For musing stricture,
Seeing the life of humankind
    Only as picture?

The events in line of battle go;
In vain for me their trumpets blow
As unto him that lieth low
    In death's dark arches,
And through the sod hears throbbing
    slow
    The muffled marches.

O Duty, am I dead to thee
In this my cloistered ecstasy,
In this lone shallop on the sea
    That drifts tow'rd Silence?
And are those visioned shores I see
    But sirens' islands?

My Dante frowns with lip-locked mien,
As who would say, "'T is those, I ween,
Whom lifelong armor-chafe makes lean
    That win the laurel";

But where *is* Truth? What does it
    mean,
    The world-old quarrel?

Such questionings are idle air:
Leave what to do and what to spare
To the inspiring moment's care,
    Nor ask for payment
Of fame or gold, but just to wear
    Unspotted raiment.

TO MR. JOHN BARTLETT,

WHO HAD SENT ME A SEVEN-POUND
TROUT.

FIT for an Abbot of Theleme,
    For the whole Cardinals' College,
      or
The Pope himself to see in dream
Before his lenten vision gleam,
    He lies there, the sogdologer!

His precious flanks with stars besprent,
    Worthy to swim in Castaly!
The friend by whom such gifts are sent,
For him shall bumpers full be spent,
    His health! be Luck his fast ally!

I see him trace the wayward brook
    Amid the forest mysteries,
Where at their shades shy aspens look,
Or where, with many a gurgling crook,
    It croons its woodland histories.

I see leaf-shade and sun-fleck lend
    Their tremulous, sweet vicissitude
To smooth, dark pool, to crinkling
    bend, ——
(O, stew him, Ann, as 't were your
    friend,
    With amorous solicitude!)

I see him step with caution due,
    Soft as if shod with moccasins,
Grave as in church, for who plies you,
Sweet craft, is safe as in a pew
    From all our common stock o' sins.

The unerring fly I see him cast,
    That as a rose-leaf falls as soft,
A flash! a whirl! he has him fast!
We tyros, how that struggle last
    Confuses and appalls us oft.

Unfluttered he: calm as the sky
    Looks on our tragi-comedies,
This way and that he lets him fly,
A sunbeam-shuttle, then to die
    Lands him, with cool *aplomb*, at
      ease.

The friend who gave our board such
    gust,
    Life's care may he o'erstep it half,
And, when Death hooks him, as he
    must,
He 'll do it handsomely, I trust,
    And John H—— write his epi-
      taph!

O, born beneath the Fishes' sign,
    Of constellations happiest,
May he somewhere with Walton dine,
May Horace send him Massic wine,
    And Burns Scotch drink, the nap-
      piest!

And when they come his deeds to
    weigh,
    And how he used the talents his,
One trout-scale in the scales he 'll lay
(If trout had scales), and 't will out-
    sway
    The wrong side of the balances.

ODE TO HAPPINESS.

SPIRIT, that rarely comest now
    And only to contrast my gloom,
    Like rainbow-feathered birds that
      bloom
A moment on some autumn bough
That, with the spurn of their farewell,
Sheds its last leaves, — thou once didst
    dwell
    With me year-long, and make in-
      tense
To boyhood's wisely vacant days
Their fleet but all-sufficing grace
    Of trustful inexperience,
    While soul could still transfigure
      sense,
And thrill, as with love's first caress,
At life's mere unexpectedness.
    Days when my blood would leap and
      run

As full of sunshine as a breeze,
  Or spray tossed up by Summer
      seas
That doubts if it be sea or sun !
Days that flew swiftly like the band
  That played in Grecian games at
      strife,
And passed from eager hand to hand
  The onward-dancing torch of life !

Wing-footed ! thou abid'st with him
  Who asks it not ; but he who hath
Watched o'er the waves thy waning
      path,
Shall nevermore behold returning
Thy high-heaped canvas shoreward
      yearning !
Thou first reveal'st to us thy face
Turned o'er the shoulder's parting
      grace,
  A moment glimpsed, then seen no
      more, —
Thou whose swift footsteps we can
      trace
  Away from every mortal door.

Nymph of the unreturning feet,
  How may I win thee back ? But
      no,
  I do thee wrong to call thee so :
'T is I am changed, not thou art fleet :
The man thy presence feels again,
Not in the blood, but in the brain,
Spirit, that lov'st the upper air
Serene and passionless and rare,
  Such as on mountain heights we
      find
  And wide-viewed uplands of the
      mind ;
Or such as scorns to coil and sing
Round any but the eagle's wing
  Of souls that with long upward beat
  Have won an undisturbed retreat
Where, poised like wingèd victories,
They mirror in relentless eyes
  The life broad-basking 'neath their
      feet, —
Man ever with his Now at strife,
  Pained with first gasps of earthly
      air,
  Then praying Death the last to
      spare,
Still fearful of the ampler life.

Not unto them dost thou consent
  Who, passionless, can lead at ease
A life of unalloyed content
  A life like that of land-locked seas,
That feel no elemental gush
Of tidal forces, no fierce rush
  Of storm deep-grasping scarcely
      spent
'Twixt continent and continent.
Such quiet souls have never known
  Thy truer inspiration, thou
Who lov'st to feel upon thy brow
Spray from the plunging vessel thrown
  Grazing the tuskèd lee shore, the cliff
That o'er the abrupt gorge holds its
      breath,
  Where the frail hair-breadth of an *if*
Is all that sunders life and death :
These, too, are cared-for, and round
      these
Bends her mild crook thy sister Peace ;
  These in unvexed dependence lie,
  Each 'neath his strip of household
      sky ;
O'er these clouds wander, and the blue
Hangs motionless the whole day
      through ;
  Stars rise for them, and moons grow
      large
And lessen in such tranquil wise
As joys and sorrows do that rise
  Within their nature's sheltered
      marge ;
Their hours into each other flit
Like the leaf-shadows of the vine
And fig-tree under which they sit,
  And their still lives to heaven incline
With an unconscious habitude,
  Unhistoried as smokes that rise
From happy hearths and sight elude
  In kindred blue of morning skies.

Wayward ! when once we feel thy lack,
'T is worse than vain to woo thee back !
  Yet there is one who seems to be
Thine elder sister, in whose eyes
A faint far northern light will rise
  Sometimes, and bring a dream of
      thee ;
She is not that for which youth hoped,
  But she hath blessings all her own.
Thoughts pure as lilies newly oped,
  And faith to sorrow given alone ;
Almost I deem that it is thou

Come back with graver matron brow,
　With deepened eyes and bated breath,
　Like one that somewhere hath met
　　Death,
But " No," she answers, " I am she
Whom the gods love, Tranquillity ;
　That other whom you seek forlorn
Half earthly was ; but I am born
Of the immortals, and our race
Wear still some sadness on our face :
　He wins me late, but keeps me long,
Who, dowered with every gift of pas-
　　sion,
In that fierce flame can forge and fash-
　　ion
Of sin and self the anchor strong ;
Can thence compel the driving force
Of daily life's mechanic course,
Nor less the nobler energies
Of needful toil and culture wise ;
Whose soul is worth the tempter's lure
Who can renounce, and yet endure,
To him I come, not lightly wooed,
But won by silent fortitude."

VILLA FRANCA.

1859.

WAIT a little : do *we* not wait?
Louis Napoleon is not Fate,
Francis Joseph is not Time ;
There's One hath swifter feet than
　Crime ;
Cannon-parliaments settle naught ;
Venice is Austria's, — whose is
　Thought?
Minié is good, but, spite of change,
Gutenberg's gun has the longest range.
　Spin, spin, Clotho, spin !
　Lachesis, twist ! and Atropos,
　　sever !
　In the shadow, year out, year in,
　The silent headsman waits forever.

Wait, we say : our years are long ;
Men are weak, but Man is strong ;
Since the stars first curved their rings,
We have looked on many things ;
Great wars come and great wars go,
Wolf-tracks light on polar snow ;
We shall see him come and gone,

This second-hand Napoleon.
　Spin, spin, Clotho, spin !
　Lachesis, twist ! and Atropos,
　　sever !
　In the shadow, year out, year in,
　The silent headsman waits forever.

We saw the elder Corsican,
And Clotho muttered as she span,
While crowned lackeys bore the train,
Of the pinchbeck Charlemagne :
" Sister, stint not length of thread !
Sister, stay the scissors dread !
On Saint Helen's granite bleak,
Hark, the vulture whets his beak ! "
　Spin, spin, Clotho, spin !
　Lachesis, twist ! and Atropos,
　　sever !
　In the shadow, year out, year in,
　The silent headsman waits forever.

The Bonapartes, we know their bees
That wade in honey red to the knees ;
Their patent reaper, its sheaves sleep
　sound
In dreamless garners underground :
We know false glory's spendthrift race
Pawning nations for feathers and lace ;
It may be short, it may be long,
" 'T is reckoning-day ! " sneers unpaid
　　Wrong.
　Spin, spin, Clotho, spin !
　Lachesis, twist ! and Atropos,
　　sever !
　In the shadow, year out, year in,
　The silent headsman waits forever.

The Cock that wears the Eagle's skin
Can promise what he ne'er could win ;
Slavery reaped for fine words sown,
System for all, and rights for none,
Despots atop, a wild clan below,
Such is the Gaul from long ago ;
Wash the black from the Ethiop's
　face,
Wash the past out of man or race !
　Spin, spin, Clotho, spin !
　Lachesis, twist ! and Atropos,
　　sever !
　In the shadow, year out, year in,
　The silent headsman waits forever.

'Neath Gregory's throne a spider
　　swings,
And snares the people for the kings ;

" Luther is dead ; old quarrels pass ;
The stake's black scars are healed with
    grass ";
So dreamers prate ; did man e'er live
Saw priest or woman yet forgive ?
But Luther's broom is left, and eyes
Peep o'er their creeds to where it lies.
    Spin, spin, Clotho, spin !
    Lachesis, twist ! and Atropos,
      sever !
    In the shadow, year out, year in,
    The silent headsman waits forever.

Smooth sails the ship of either realm,
Kaiser and Jesuit at the helm ;
We look down the depths, and mark
Silent workers in the dark
Building slow the sharp-tusked reefs,
Old instincts hardening to new beliefs ;
Patience a little ; learn to wait ;
Hours are long on the clock of Fate.
    Spin, spin, Clotho, spin !
    Lachesis, twist ! and Atropos,
      sever !
    Darkness is strong, and so is Sin,
    But surely God endures forever !

THE MINER.

Down 'mid the tangled roots of things
    That coil about the central fire,
I seek for that which giveth wings
    To stoop, not soar, to my desire.

Sometimes I hear, as 't were a sigh,
    The sea's deep yearning far above,
" Thou hast the secret not," I cry,
    " In deeper deeps is hid my Love."

They think I burrow from the sun,
    In darkness, all alone, and weak ;
Such loss were gain if He were won,
    For 't is the sun's own Sun I seek.

" The earth," they murmur, " is the
      tomb
That vainly sought his life to prison ;
Why grovel longer in the gloom ?
He is not here ; he hath arisen."

More life for me where he hath lain
    Hidden while ye believed him dead,

Than in cathedrals cold and vain,
    Built on loose sands of *It is said.*

My search is for the living gold ;
    Him I desire who dwells recluse,
And not his image worn and old,
    Day-servant of our sordid use.

If him I find not, yet I find
    The ancient joy of cell and church,
The glimpse, the surety undefined,
    The unquenched ardor of the search.

Happier to chase a flying goal
    Than to sit counting laurelled gains,
To guess the Soul within the soul
    Than to be lord of what remains.

Hide still, best Good, in subtile wise,
    Beyond my nature's utmost scope ;
Be ever absent from mine eyes
    To be twice present in my hope !

GOLD EGG: A DREAM-FAN-TASY.

HOW A STUDENT IN SEARCH OF THE
BEAUTIFUL FELL ASLEEP IN DRES-
DEN OVER HERR PROFESSOR DOCTOR
VISCHER'S WISSENSCHAFT DES SCHÖ-
NEN, AND WHAT CAME THEREOF.

I SWAM with undulation soft,
    Adrift on Vischer's ocean,
And, from my cockboat up aloft,
Sent down my mental plummet oft
    In hope to reach a notion.

But from the metaphysic sea
    No bottom was forthcoming,
And all the while (how drearily !)
In one eternal note of B
    My German stove kept humming.

" What 's Beauty ? " mused I ; " is it
      told
    By synthesis ? analysis ?
Have you not made us lead of gold ?
To feed your crucible, not sold
    Our temple's sacred chalices ? "

Then o'er my senses came a change ;
  My book seemed all traditions,
Old legends of profoundest range,
Diablery, and stories strange
  Of goblins, elves, magicians.

Old gods in modern saints I found,
  Old creeds in strange disguises ;
I thought them safely underground,
And here they were, all safe and sound,
  Without a sign of phthisis.

Truth was, my outward eyes were
    closed,
  Although I did not know it ;
Deep into dream-land I had dozed,
And so was happily transposed
  From proser into poet.

So what I read took flesh and blood,
  And turned to living creatures :
The words were but the dingy bud
That bloomed, like Adam, from the
    mud,
  To human forms and features.

I saw how Zeus was lodged once more
  By Baucis and Philemon ;
The text said, " Not alone of yore,
But every day, at every door,
  Knocks still the masking Demon."

DAIMON 't was printed in the book,
  And, as I read it slowly,
The letters stirred and changed, and
    took
Jove's stature, the Olympian look
  Of painless melancholy.

He paused upon the threshold worn :
  " With coin I cannot pay you ;
Yet would I fain make some return ;
The gift for cheapness do not spurn,
  Accept this hen, I pray you.

" Plain feathers wears my Hemera,
  And has from ages olden ;
She makes her nest in common hay,
And yet, of all the birds that lay,
  Her eggs alone are golden."

He turned, and could no more be seen ;
  Old Baucis stared a moment,
Then tossed poor Partlet on the green,
And with a tone, half jest, half spleen,
  Thus made her housewife's comment :

" The stranger had a queerish face,
  His smile was hardly pleasant,
And, though he meant it for a grace,
Yet this old hen of barnyard race
  Was but a stingy present.

" She 's quite too old for laying eggs,
  Nay, even to make a soup of ;
One only needs to see her legs, —
You might as well boil down the pegs
  I made the brood-hen's coop of !

" Some eighteen score of such do I
  Raise every year, her sisters ;
Go, in the woods your fortunes try,
All day for one poor earthworm pry,
  And scratch your toes to blisters ! "

Philemon found the rede was good,
  And, turning on the poor hen,
He clapt his hands, and stamped, and
    shooed,
Hunting the exile tow'rd the wood,
  To house with snipe and moor-hen.

A poet saw and cried : " Hold ! hold !
  What are you doing, madman ?
Spurn you more wealth than can be told,
The fowl that lays the eggs of gold,
  Because she 's plainly clad, man ? "

To him Philemon : " I 'll not balk
  Thy will with any shackle ;
Wilt add a burden to thy walk ?
There ! take her without further talk ;
  You 're both but fit to cackle ! "

But scarce the poet touched the bird,
  It swelled to stature regal ;
And when her cloud-wide wings she
    stirred,
A whisper as of doom was heard,
  'T was Jove's bolt-bearing eagle.

As when from far-off cloud-bergs
    springs
  A crag, and, hurtling under,
From cliff to cliff the rumor flings,
So she from flight-foreboding wings
  Shook out a murmurous thunder.

She gripped the poet to her breast.
  And, ever upward soaring,
Earth seemed a new moon in the west

And then one light among the rest
  Where squadrons lie at mooring.

How tell to what heaven-hallowed seat
  The eagle bent his courses?
The waves that on its bases beat,
The gales that round it weave and fleet,
  Are life's creative forces.

Here was the bird's primeval nest,
  High on a promontory
Star-pharosed, where she takes her rest
To brood new æons 'neath her breast,
  The future's unfledged glory.

I know not how, but I was there
  All feeling, hearing, seeing;
It was not wind that stirred my hair
But living breath, the essence rare
  Of unembodied being.

And in the nest an egg of gold
  Lay soft in self-made lustre,
Gazing whereon, what depths untold
Within, what marvels manifold,
  Seemed silently to muster!

Daily such splendors to confront
  Is still to me and you sent?
It glowed as when Saint Peter's front,
Illumed, forgets its stony wont,
  And seems to throb translucent.

One saw therein the life of man,
  (Or so the poet found it,)
The yolk and white, conceive who can,
Were the glad earth, that, floating, span
  In the glad heaven around it.

I knew this as one knows in dream,
  Where no effects to causes
Are chained as in our work-day scheme,
And then was wakened by a scream
  That seemed to come from Baucis.

"Bless Zeus!" she cried, "I'm safe
    below!"
  First pale, then red as coral;
And I, still drowsy, pondered slow,
And seemed to find, but hardly know,
  Something like this for moral.

Each day the world is born anew
  For him who takes it rightly;

Not fresher that which Adam knew,
Not sweeter that whose moonlit dew
  Entranced Arcadia nightly.

Rightly? That's simply: 'tis to see
  Some substance casts these shadows
Which we call Life and History,
That aimless seem to chase and flee
  Like wind-gleams over meadows.

Simply? That's nobly: 'tis to know
  That God may still be met with,
Nor groweth old, nor doth bestow
These senses fine, this brain aglow,
  To grovel and forget with.

Beauty, Herr Doctor, trust in me,
  No chemistry will win you;
Charis still rises from the sea;
If you can't find her, *might* it be
  Because you seek within you?

A FAMILIAR EPISTLE TO A FRIEND.

ALIKE I hate to be your debtor,
Or write a mere perfunctory letter;
For letters, so it seems to me,
Our careless quintessence should be,
Our real nature's truant play
When Consciousness looks t' other
    way;
Not drop by drop, with watchful skill,
Gathered in Art's deliberate still,
But life's insensible completeness
Got as the ripe grape gets its sweet-
    ness,
As if it had a way to fuse
The golden sunlight into juice.
Hopeless my mental pump I try,
The boxes hiss, the tube is dry;
As those petroleum wells that spout
Awhile like M. C.'s then give out,
My spring, once full as Arethusa,
Is a mere bore as dry's Creusa;
And yet you ask me why I'm glum,
And why my graver Muse is dumb.
Ah me! I've reasons manifold
Condensed in one, — I'm getting old!

When life, once past its fortieth year,
Wheels up its evening hemisphere,

The mind's own shadow, which the boy
Saw onward point to hope and joy,
Shifts round, irrevocably set
Tow'rd morning's loss and vain regret,
And, argue with it as we will,
The clock is unconverted still.

"But count the gains," I hear you say,
"Which far the seeming loss outweigh;
Friendships built firm 'gainst flood and wind
On rock-foundations of the mind;
Knowledge instead of scheming hope;
For wild adventure, settled scope;
Talents, from surface-ore profuse,
Tempered and edged to tools for use;
Judgment, for passion's headlong whirls;
Old sorrows crystalled into pearls;
Losses by patience turned to gains,
Possessions now, that once were pains;
Joy's blossom gone, as go it must,
To ripen seeds of faith and trust;
Why heed a snow-flake on the roof
If fire within keep Age aloof
Though blundering north-winds push and strain
With palms benumbed against the pane?"

My dear old Friend, you 're very wise;
We always are with others' eyes,
And see *so* clear! (our neighbor's deck on)
What reef the idiot 's sure to wreck on;
Folks when they learn how life has quizzed 'em
Are fain to make a shift with Wisdom,
And, finding she nor breaks nor bends,
Give her a letter to their friends.
Draw passion's torrent whoso will
Through sluices smooth to turn a mill,
And, taking solid toll of grist,
Forget the rainbow in the mist,
The exulting leap, the aimless haste
Scattered in iridescent waste;
Prefer who likes the sure esteem
To cheated youth's midsummer dream,
When every friend was more than Damon,

Each quicksand safe to build a fame on;
Believe that prudence snug excels
Youth's gross of verdant spectacles,
Through which earth's withered stubble seen
Looks autumn-proof as painted green, —
I side with Moses 'gainst the masses,
Take you the drudge, give me the glasses!
And, for your talents shaped with practice,
Convince me first that such the fact is;
Let whoso likes be beat, poor fool,
On life's hard stithy to a tool,
Be whoso will a ploughshare made,
Let me remain a jolly blade!

What 's Knowledge, with her stocks and lands,
To gay Conjecture's yellow strands?
What 's watching her slow flocks increase
To ventures for the golden fleece?
What her deep ships, safe under lee,
To youth's light craft, that drinks the sea,
For Flying Islands making sail,
And failing where 't is gain to fail?
Ah me! Experience (so we 're told),
Time's crucible, turns lead to gold;
Yet what 's experience won but dross,
Cloud-gold transmuted to our loss?
What but base coin the best event
To the untried experiment?

'T was an old couple, says the poet,
That lodged the gods and did not know it;
Youth sees and knows them as they were
Before Olympus' top was bare;
From Swampscot's flats his eye divine
Sees Venus rocking on the brine,
With lucent limbs, that somehow scatter a
Charm that turns Doll to Cleopatra;
Bacchus (that now is scarce induced
To give Eld's lagging blood a boost),
With cymbals' clang and pards to draw him,
Divine as Ariadne saw him,
Storms through Youth's pulse with all his train
And wins new Indies in his brain;

Apollo (with the old a trope,
A sort of finer Mister Pope),
Apollo —— but the Muse forbids ;
At his approach cast down thy lids,
And think it joy enough to hear
Far off his arrows singing clear ;
He knows enough who silent knows
The quiver chiming as he goes ;
He tells too much who e'er betrays
The shining Archer's secret ways.

Dear Friend, you 're right and I am
    wrong ;
My quibbles are not worth a song,
And I sophistically tease
My fancy sad to tricks like these.
I could not cheat you if I would ;
You know me and my jesting mood,
Mere surface-foam, for pride concealing
The purpose of my deeper feeling.
I have not spilt one drop of joy
Poured in the senses of the boy,
Nor Nature fails my walks to bless
With all her golden inwardness ;
And as blind nestlings, unafraid,
Stretch wide-mouthed to every shade
By which their downy dream is stirred,
Taking it for the mother-bird,
So, when God's shadow, which is light,
Unheralded, by day or night,
My wakening instincts falls across,
Silent as sunbeams over moss,
In my heart's nest half-conscious things
Stir with a helpless sense of wings,
Lift themselves up, and tremble long
With premonitions sweet of song.

Be patient, and perhaps (who knows ?)
These may be winged one day like
    those ;
If thrushes, close-embowered to sing,
Pierced through with June's delicious
    sting ;
If swallows, their half-hour to run
Star-breasted in the setting sun.
At first they 're but the unfledged
    proem,
Or songless schedule of a poem ;
When from the shell they 're hardly dry
If some folks thrust them forth, must I ?

But let me end with a comparison
Never yet hit upon by e'er a son
Of our American Apollo,

(And there 's where I shall beat them
    hollow,
If he indeed 's no courtly St. John,
But, as West said, a Mohawk Injun.)
A poem 's like a cruise for whales :
Through untried seas the hunter sails,
His prow dividing waters known
To the blue iceberg's hulk alone :
At last, on farthest edge of day,
He marks the smoky puff of spray ;
Then with bent oars the shallop flies
To where the basking quarry lies ;
Then the excitement of the strife,
The crimsoned waves, — ah, this is life !

But, the dead plunder once secured
And safe beside the vessel moored,
All that had stirred the blood before
Is so much blubber, nothing more,
(I mean no pun, nor image so
Mere sentimental verse, you know,)
And all is tedium, smoke, and soil,
In trying-out the noisome oil.

Yes, this *is* life ! And so the bard
Through briny deserts, never scarred
Since Noah's keel, a subject seeks,
And lies upon the watch for weeks ;
That once harpooned and helpless ly-
    ing,
What follows is but weary trying.

Now I 've a notion, if a poet
Beat up for themes, his verse will show
    it ;
I wait for subjects that hunt me,
By day or night won't let me be,
And hang about me like a curse,
Till they have made me into verse,
From line to line my fingers tease
Beyond my knowledge, as the bees
Build no new cell till those before
With limpid summer-sweet run o'er ;
Then, if I neither sing nor shine,
Is it the subject's fault, or mine ?

———

AN EMBER PICTURE.

How strange are the freaks of memory
    The lessons of life we forget,
While a trifle, a trick of color,
    In the wonderful web is set, —

Set by some mordant of fancy,
  And, spite of the wear and tear
Of time or distance or trouble,
  Insists on its right to be there.

A chance had brought us together ;
  Our talk was of matters-of-course ;
We were nothing, one to the other,
  But a short half-hour's resource.

We spoke of French acting and actors,
  And their easy, natural way :
Of the weather, for it was raining
  As we drove home from the play.

We debated the social nothings
  We bore ourselves so to discuss ;
The thunderous rumors of battle
  Were silent the while for us.

Arrived at her door, we left her
  With a drippingly hurried adieu,
And our wheels went crunching the
      gravel
  Of the oak-darkened avenue.

As we drove away through the shadow,
  The candle she held in the door
From rain-varnished tree-trunk to tree-
      trunk
  Flashed fainter, and flashed no
      more ; —

Flashed fainter, then wholly faded
  Before we had passed the wood ;
But the light of the face behind it
  Went with me and stayed for good.

The vision of scarce a moment,
  And hardly marked at the time,
It comes unbidden to haunt me,
  Like a scrap of ballad-rhyme.

Had she beauty? Well, not what they
      call so ;
  You may find a thousand as fair ;
And yet there's her face in my memory
  With no special claim to be there.

As I sit sometimes in the twilight,
  And call back to life in the coals
Old faces and hopes and fancies
  Long buried, (good rest to their
      souls !)

Her face shines out in the embers ;
  I see her holding the light,
And hear the crunch of the gravel
  And the sweep of the rain that night.

'T is a face that can never grow older,
  That never can part with its gleam,
'T is a gracious possession forever,
  For is it not all a dream ?

TO H. W. L.,

ON HIS BIRTHDAY, 27TH FEBRUARY,
1867.

I NEED not praise the sweetness of his
      song,
  Where limpid verse to limpid verse
      succeeds
Smooth as our Charles, when, fearing
      lest he wrong
The new moon's mirrored skiff, he
      slides along,
  Full without noise, and whispers in
      his reeds.

With loving breath of all the winds his
      name
  Is blown about the world, but to his
      friends
A sweeter secret hides behind his fame,
And Love steals shyly through the loud
      acclaim
  To murmur a *God bless you!* and
      there ends.

As I muse backward up the checkered
      years
  Wherein so much was given, so much
      was lost,
Blessings in both kinds, such as cheapen
      tears, —
But hush ! this is not for profaner ears ;
  Let them drink molten pearls nor
      dream the cost.

Some suck up poison from a sorrow's
      core,
  As naught but nightshade grew upon
      earth's ground ;
Love turned all his to heart's-ease, and
      the more

Fate tried his bastions, she but forced
    a door
  Leading to sweeter manhood and
    rcie sound.

Even as a wind-waved fountain's sway-
    ing shade
  Seems of mixed race, a gray wraith
    shot with sun,
So through his trial faith translucent
    rayed
Till darkness, half disnatured so, be-
    trayed
  A heart of sunshine that would fain
    o'errun.

Surely if skill in song the shears may
    stay
  And ot its purpose cheat the charmed
    abyss,
If our poor life be lengthened by a lay,
He shall not go, although his presence
    may,
  And the next age in praise shall
    double this.

Long days be his, and each as lusty-
    sweet
  As gracious natures find his song to
    be ;
May Age steal on with softly-cadenced
    feet
Falling in music, as for him were meet
  Whose choicest verse is harsher-toned
    than he !

THE NIGHTINGALE IN THE
STUDY.

" Come forth ! " my catbird calls to me,
  " And hear me sing a cavatina
That, in this old familiar tree,
  Shall hang a garden of Alcina.

" These buttercups shall brim with wine
  Beyond all Lesbian juice or Massic ;
May not New England be divine ?
  My ode to ripening summer classic ?

" Or, if to me you will not hark,
  By Beaver Brook a thrush is ringing
Till all the alder-coverts dark
  Seem sunshine-dappled with his sing-
    ing.

" Come out beneath the unmastered
    sky,
  With its emancipating spaces,
And learn to sing as well as I,
  Without premeditated graces.

" What boot your many-volumed gains,
  Those withered leaves forever turn-
    ing,
To win, at best, for all your pains,
  A nature mummy-wrapt in learning ?

" The leaves wherein true wisdom lies
  On living trees the sun are drinking ;
Those white clouds, drowsing through
    the skies,
  Grew not so beautiful by thinking.

"'Come out ! ' with me the oriole cries,
  Escape the demon that pursues you !
And, hark, the cuckoo weatherwise,
  Still hiding farther onward, wooes
    you."

" Alas, dear friend, that, all my days,
  Has poured from that syringa thicket
The quaintly discontinuous lays
  To which I hold a season-ticket,

" A season-ticket cheaply bought
  With a dessert of pilfered berries,
And who so oft my soul hast caught
  With morn and evening voluntaries,

" Deem me not faithless, if all day
  Among my dusty books I linger,
No pipe, like thee, for June to play
  With fancy-led, half-conscious finger.

" A bird is singing in my brain
  And bubbling o'er with mingled
    fancies,
Gay, tragic, rapt, right heart of Spain
  Fed with the sap of old romances.

" I ask no ampler skies than those
  His magic music rears above me,
No falser friends, no truer foes, —
  And does not Doña Clara love me?

" Cloaked shapes, a twanging of guitars,
  A rush of feet, and rapiers clashing,
Then silence deep with breathless stars,
  And overhead a white hand flashing.

" O music of all moods and climes,
    Vengeful, forgiving, sensuous, saintly,
Where still, between the Christian
      chimes,
    The moorish cymbal tinkles faintly !

" O life borne lightly in the hand,
    For friend or foe with grace Castilian !
O valley safe in Fancy's land,
    Not tramped to mud yet by the mil-
      lion !

" Bird of to-day, thy songs are stale
    To his, my singer of all weathers,
My Calderon, my nightingale,
    My Arab soul in Spanish feathers.

" Ah, friend, these singers dead so long,
    And still, God knows, in purgatory,
Give its best sweetness to all song,
    To Nature's self her better glory."

IN THE TWILIGHT.

MEN say the sullen instrument,
    That, from the Master's bow,
    With pangs of joy or woe,
Feels music's soul through every fibre
      sent,
    Whispers the ravished strings
More than he knew or meant ;
    Old summers in its memory glow ;
    The secrets of the wind it sings ;
    It hears the April-loosened springs ;
    And mixes with its mood
      All it dreamed when it stood
      In the murmurous pine-wood
        Long ago !

The magical moonlight then
    Steeped every bough and cone ;
The roar of the brook in the glen
    Came dim from the distance blown ;
The wind through its glooms sang low,
    And it swayed to and fro
      With delight as it stood,
      In the wonderful wood,
        Long ago !

O my life, have we not had seasons
    That only said, Live and rejoice?
That asked not for causes and reasons,

    But made us all feeling and voice?
When we went with the winds in their
      blowing,
    When Nature and we were peers,
And we seemed to share in the flowing
    Of the inexhaustible years?
Have we not from the earth drawn
      juices
    Too fine for earth's sordid uses?
    Have I heard, have I seen
      All I feel, all I know?
    Doth my heart overween?
    Or could it have been
        Long ago?

Sometimes a breath floats by me,
    An odor from Dreamland sent,
That makes the ghost seem nigh me
    Of a splendor that came and went,
Of a life lived somewhere, I know
      not
    In what diviner sphere,
Of memories that stay not and go not,
    Like music heard once by an ear
      That cannot forget or reclaim it,
      A something so shy, it would shame
        it
        To make it a show,
      A something too vague, could I
        name it,
        For others to know,
    As if I had lived it or dreamed it,
    As if I had acted or schemed it,
        Long ago !

And yet, could I live it over,
    This life that stirs in my brain,
Could I be both maiden and lover,
Moon and tide, bee and clover,
    As I seem to have been, once again,
Could I but speak it and show it,
    This pleasure more sharp than pain,
    That baffles and lures me so,
The world should once more have a
      poet,
      Such as it had
      In the ages glad,
        Long ago !

THE FOOT-PATH.

IT mounts athwart the windy hill
    Through sallow slopes of upland bare.

And Fancy climbs with foot-fall still
  Its narrowing curves that end in air.

By day, a warmer-hearted blue
  Stoops softly to that topmost swell;
Its thread-like windings seem a clew
  To gracious climes where all is well.

By night, far yonder, I surmise
  An ampler world than clips my ken,
Where the great stars of happier skies
  Commingle nobler fates of men.

I look and long, then haste me home,
  Still master of my secret rare;
Once tried, the path would end in
    Rome,
But now it leads me everywhere.

Forever to the new it guides,
  From former good, old overmuch;
What Nature for her poets hides,
  'T is wiser to divine than clutch.

The bird I list hath never come
  Within the scope of mortal ear;
My prying step would make him dumb,
  And the fair tree, his shelter, sear.

Behind the hill, behind the sky,
  Behind my inmost thought, he sings;
No feet avail; to hear it nigh,
  The song itself must lend the wings.

Sing on, sweet bird, close hid, and raise
  Those angel stairways in my brain,
That climb from these low-vaulted days
  To spacious sunshines far from pain.

Sing when thou wilt, enchantment fleet,
  I leave thy covert haunt untrod,

And envy Science not her feat
  To make a twice-told tale of God.

They said the fairies tript no more,
  And long ago that Pan was dead;
'T was but that fools preferred to bore
  Earth's rind inch-deep for truth in-
    stead.

Pan leaps and pipes all summer long,
  The fairies dance each full-mooned
    night;
Would we but doff our lenses strong,
  And trust our wiser eyes' delight.

City of Elf-land, just without
  Our seeing, marvel ever new,
Glimpsed in fair weather, a sweet doubt
  Sketched-in, mirage-like, on the blue.

I build thee in yon sunset cloud,
  Whose edge allures to climb the
    height;
I hear thy drowned bells, inly-loud,
  From still pools dusk with dreams
    of night.
Thy gates are shut to hardiest will,
  Thy countersign of long-lost speech,—
Those fountained courts, those cham-
    bers still,
  Fronting Time's far East, who shall
    reach?

I know not and will never pry,
  But trust our human heart for all;
Wonders that from the seeker fly
  Into an open sense may fall.

Hide in thine own soul, and surprise
  The password of the unwary elves;
Seek it, thou canst not bribe their
    spies;
  Unsought, they whisper it themselves.

POEMS OF THE WAR.

———◆———

THE WASHERS OF THE SHROUD.

OCTOBER, 1861.

ALONG a river-side, I know not where,
I walked one night in mystery of
    dream;
A chill creeps curdling yet beneath my
    hair,
To think what chanced me by the pallid
    gleam
Of a moon-wraith that waned through
    haunted air.

Pale fireflies pulsed within the meadow-
    mist
Their halos, wavering thistledowns of
    light;
The loon, that seemed to mock some
    goblin tryst,
Laughed; and the echoes, huddling
    in affright,
Like Odin's hounds, fled baying down
    the night.

Then all was silent, till there smote my
    ear
A movement in the stream that checked
    my breath:
Was it the slow plash of a wading deer?
But something said, "This water is of
    Death!
The Sisters wash a shroud,—ill thing
    to hear!"

I, looking then, beheld the ancient
    Three
Known to the Greek's and to the North-
    man's creed,
That sit in shadow of the mystic Tree,

Still crooning, as they weave their end-
    less brede,
One song: "Time was, Time is, and
    Time shall be."

No wrinkled crones were they, as I
    had deemed,
But fair as yesterday, to-day, to-morrow,
To mourner, lover, poet, ever seemed;
Something too high for joy, too deep
    for sorrow,
Thrilled in their tones, and from their
    faces gleamed.

"Still men and nations reap as they
    have strawn,"
So sang they, working at their task the
    while;
"The fatal raiment must be cleansed
    ere dawn:
For Austria? Italy? the Sea-Queen's
    isle?
O'er what quenched grandeur must our
    shroud be drawn?

"Or is it for a younger, fairer corse,
That gathered States for children round
    his knees,
That tamed the wave to be his posting-
    horse,
Feller of forests, linker of the seas,
Bridge-builder, hammerer, youngest
    son of Thor's?

"What make we, murmur'st thou? and
    what are we?
When empires must be wound, we
    bring the shroud,
The time-old web of the implacable
    Three:

Is it too coarse for him, the young and
    proud?
Earth's mightiest deigned to wear it, —
    why not he?"

"Is there no hope?" I moaned, "so
    strong, so fair!
Our Fowler whose proud bird would
    brook erewhile
No rival's swoop in all our western air!
Gather the ravens, then, in funeral file
For him, life's morn yet golden in his
    hair?

"Leave me not hopeless, ye unpitying
    dames!
I see, half seeing. Tell me, ye who
    scanned
The stars, Earth's elders, still must
    noblest aims
Be traced upon oblivious ocean-sands?
Must Hesper join the wailing ghosts
    of names?"

"When grass-blades stiffen with red
    battle-dew,
Ye deem we choose the victor and the
    slain:
Say, choose we them that shall be leal
    and true
To the heart's longing, the high faith
    of brain?
Yet there the victory lies, if ye but
    knew.

"Three roots bear up Dominion:
    Knowledge, Will, —
These twain are strong, but stronger
    yet the third, —
Obedience, — 't is the great tap-root
    that still,
Knit round the rock of Duty, is not
    stirred,
Though Heaven-loosed tempests spend
    their utmost skill.

"Is the doom sealed for Hesper? 'T
    is not we
Denounce it, but the Law before all
    time:
The brave makes danger opportunity;
The waverer, paltering with the chance
    sublime,
Dwarfs it to peril: which shall Hesper
    be?

"Hath he let vultures climb his eagle's
    seat
To make Jove's bolts purveyors of their
    maw?
Hath he the Many's plaudits found
    more sweet
Than Wisdom? held Opinion's wind
    for Law?
Then let him hearken for the doom-
    ster's feet!

"Rough are the steps, slow-hewn in
    flintiest rock,
States climb to power by; slippery
    those with gold
Down which they stumble to eternal
    mock:
No chafferer's hand shall long the scep-
    tre hold,
Who, given a Fate to shape, would sell
    the block.

"We sing old Sagas, songs of weal and
    woe,
Mystic because too cheaply understood;
Dark sayings are not ours; men hear
    and know,
See Evil weak, see strength alone in
    Good,
Yet hope to stem God's fire with walls
    of tow.

"Time Was unlocks the riddle of Time
    Is,
That offers choice of glory or of gloom;
The solver makes Time Shall Be surely
    his.
But hasten, Sisters! for even now the
    tomb
Grates its slow hinge and calls from the
    abyss."

"But not for him," I cried, "not yet
    for him,
Whose large horizon, westering, star by
    star
Wins from the void to where on Ocean's
    rim
The sunset shuts the world with golden
    bar,
Not yet his thews shall fail, his eye
    grow dim!

"His shall be larger manhood, saved
    for those

That walk unblenching through the
    trial-fires;
Not suffering, but faint heart, is worst
    of woes,
And he no base-born son of craven
    sires,
Whose eye need blench confronted with
    his foes.

"Tears may be ours, but proud, for
    those who win
Death's royal purple in the foeman's
    lines;
Peace, too, brings tears; and 'mid the
    battle-din,
The wiser ear some text of God divines,
For the sheathed blade may rust with
    darker sin.

"God, give us peace! not such as lulls
    to sleep,
But sword on thigh, and brow with pur-
    pose knit!
And let our Ship of State to harbor
    sweep,
Her ports all up, her battle-lanterns lit,
And her leashed thunders gathering for
    their leap!"

So cried I with clenched hands and
    passionate pain,
Thinking of dear ones by Potomac's
    side;
Again the loon laughed mocking, and
    again
The echoes bayed far down the night
    and died,
While waking I recalled my wandering
    brain.

TWO SCENES FROM THE LIFE
OF BLONDEL.

AUTUMN, 1863.

SCENE I. — *Near a Castle in Germany.*

'T WERE no hard task, perchance, to
    win
    The popular laurel for my song;
'T were only to comply with sin,
    And own the crown, though snatched
    by wrong:

Rather Truth's chaplet let me wear,
    Though sharp as death its thorns may
    sting;
Loyal to Loyalty, I bear
    No badge but of my rightful king.

Patient by town and tower I wait,
    Or o'er the blustering moorland go;
I buy no praise at cheaper rate,
    Or what faint hearts may fancy so;
For me, no joy in lady's bower,
    Or hall, or tourney, will I sing,
Till the slow stars wheel round the hour
    That crowns my hero and my king.

While all the land runs red with strife,
    And wealth is won by pedler-crimes,
Let who will find content in life
    And tinkle in unmanly rhymes;
I wait and seek; through dark and
    light,
Safe in my heart my hope I bring,
Till I once more my faith may plight
    To him my whole soul owns her king.

When power is filched by drone and
    dolt,
    And, with caught breath and flashing
    eye,
Her knuckles whitening round the bolt,
    Vengeance leans eager from the sky,
While this and that the people guess,
    And to the skirts of praters cling,
Who court the crowd they should com-
    press,
    I turn in scorn to seek my king.

Shut in what tower of darkling chance
    Or dungeon of a narrow doom,
Dream'st thou of battle-axe and lance
    That for the Cross make crashing
    room?
Come! with hushed breath the battle
    waits
    In the wild van thy mace's swing;
While doubters parley with their fates,
    Make thou thine own and ours, my
    king!

O, strong to keep upright the old,
    And wise to buttress with the new,
Prudent, as only are the bold,
    Clear-eyed, as only are the true,
To foes benign, to friendship stern,

Intent to imp Law's broken wing,
Who would not die, if death might earn
  The right to kiss thy hand, my king?

Scene II. — *An Inn near the Château
  of Chalus.*

Well, the whole thing is over, and
      here I sit
  With one arm in a sling and a milk-
      score of gashes,
And this flagon of Cyprus must e'en
      warm my wit,
  Since what's left of youth's flame is a
      head flecked with ashes.

I remember I sat in this very same
      inn, —
  I was young then, and one young man
      thought I was handsome,
I had found out what prison King
      Richard was in,
  And was spurring for England to push
      on the ransom.

How I scorned the dull souls that sat
      guzzling around
  And knew not my secret nor recked
      my derision!
Let the world sink or swim, John or
      Richard be crowned,
  All one, so the beer-tax got lenient
      revision.
How little I dreamed, as I tramped up
      and down,
  That granting our wish one of Fate's
      saddest jokes is!
I had mine with a vengeance, — my
      king got his crown,
  And made his whole business to
      break other folks's.

I might as well join in the safe old *tum,
      tum:*
  A hero's an excellent loadstar, —
      but, bless ye,
What infinite odds 'twixt a hero to come
  And your only too palpable hero *in
      esse!*
Precisely the odds (such examples are
      rife)
  'Twixt the poem conceived and the
      rhyme we make show of,
'Twixt the boy's morning dream and
      the wake-up of life,

'Twixt the Blondel God meant and a
      Blondel I know of!

But the world's better off, I'm con-
      vinced of it now,
  Than if heroes, like buns, could be
      bought for a penny
To regard all mankind as their haltered
      milch-cow,
  And just care for themselves.   Well,
      God cares for the many;
For somehow the poor old Earth blun-
      ders along,
  Each son of hers adding his mite of
      unfitness,
And, choosing the sure way of coming
      out wrong,
  Gets to port as the next generation
      will witness.

You think her old ribs have come all
      crashing through,
  If a whisk of Fate's broom snap your
      cobweb asunder;
But her rivets were clinched by a wiser
      than you,
  And our sins cannot push the Lord's
      right hand from under.
Better one honest man who can wait
      for God's mind
  In our poor shifting scene here,
      though heroes were plenty!
Better one bite, at forty, of Truth's
      bitter rind,
  Than the hot wine that gushed from
      the vintage of twenty!

I see it all now: when I wanted a
      king,
  'T was the kingship that failed in
      myself I was seeking, —
'T is so much less easy to do than to
      sing,
  So much simpler to reign by a proxy
      than *be* king!
Yes, I think I *do* see: after all 's said
      and sung,
  Take this one rule of life and you
      never will rue it,
'T is but do your own duty and hold
      your own tongue
  And Blondel were royal himself, if
      he knew it!

MEMORIÆ POSITUM.

R. G. SHAW.

I.

BENEATH the trees,
My life-long friends in this dear spot,
Sad now for eyes that see them not,
I hear the autumnal breeze
Wake the dry leaves to sigh for glad-
    ness gone,
Whispering vague omens of oblivion, —
    Hear, restless as the seas,
Time's grim feet rustling through the
    withered grace
Of many a spreading realm and strong-
    stemmed race,
    Even as my own through these.

Why make we moan
For loss that doth enrich us yet
With upward yearnings of regret?
    Bleaker than unmossed stone
Our lives were but for this immortal
    gain
Of unstilled longing and inspiring
    pain!
    As thrills of long-hushed tone
Live in the viol, so our souls grow
    fine
With keen vibrations from the touch
    divine
    Of noble natures gone.

'T were indiscreet
To vex the shy and sacred grief
With harsh obtrusions of relief;
    Yet, Verse, with noiseless feet,
Go whisper: "*This* death hath far
    choicer ends
Than slowly to impearl in hearts of
    friends;
    These obsequies 't is meet
Not to seclude in closets of the heart,
But, church-like, with wide doorways,
    to impart
    Even to the heedless street."

II.

Brave, good, and true,
I see him stand before me now,
And read again on that young brow,
    Where every hope was new,
How sweet were life! Yet, by the
    mouth firm-set,
And look made up for Duty's utmost
    debt,
    I could divine he knew
That death within the sulphurous hos-
    tile lines,
In the mere wreck of nobly-pitched
    designs,
    Plucks heart's-ease, and not rue.

Happy their end
Who vanish down life's evening
    stream
Placid as swans that drift in dream
    Round the next river-bend!
Happy long life, with honor at the close,
Friends' painless tears, the softened
    thought of foes!
    And yet, like him, to spend
All at a gush, keeping our first faith
    sure
From mid-life's doubt and eld's con-
    tentment poor, —
    What more could Fortune send?

Right in the van,
On the red rampart's slippery swell,
With heart that beat a charge, he fell
    Foeward, as fits a man;
But the high soul burns on to light
    men's feet
Where death for noble ends makes dy-
    ing sweet;
    His life her crescent's span
Orbs full with share in their undarken-
    ing days
Who ever climbed the battailous steeps
    of praise
    Since valor's praise began.

III.

His life's expense
Hath won him coeternal youth
With the immaculate prime of Truth;
    While we, who make pretence
At living on, and wake and eat and
    sleep,
And life's stale trick by repetition keep,
    Our fickle permanence
(A poor leaf-shadow on a brook, whose
    play
Of busy idlesse ceases with our day)
    Is the mere cheat of sense.

We bide our chance,
Unhappy, and make terms with Fate
A little more to let us wait :
He leads for aye the advance,
Hope's forlorn-hopes that plant the
    desperate good
For nobler Earths and days of manlier
    mood ;
Our wall of circumstance
Cleared at a bound, he flashes o'er the
    fight,
A saintly shape of fame, to cheer the
    right
And steel each wavering glance.

I write of one,
While with dim eyes I think of three ;
Who weeps not others fair and brave
    as he ?
Ah, when the fight is won,
Dear Land, whom triflers now make
    bold to scorn,
(Thee ! from whose forehead Earth
    awaits her morn,)
How nobler shall the sun
Flame in thy sky, how braver breathe
    thy air,
That thou bred'st children who for thee
    could dare
And die as thine have done !

1863.

ON BOARD THE '76.

WRITTEN FOR MR. BRYANT'S SEVEN-
TIETH BIRTHDAY.

NOVEMBER 3, 1864.

OUR ship lay tumbling in an angry sea,
    Her rudder gone, her main-mast
        o'er the side ;
Her scuppers, from the waves' clutch
        staggering free,
    Trailed threads of priceless crimson
        through the tide :
Sails, shrouds, and spars with pirate
        cannon torn,
    We lay, awaiting morn.

Awaiting morn, such morn as mocks
        despair ;
    And she that bore the promise of the
        world

Within her sides, now hopeless, helm-
        less, bare,
    At random o'er the wildering waters
        hurled ;
The reek of battle drifting slow alee
    Not sullener than we.

Morn came at last to peer into our
        woe,
    When lo, a sail ! Now surely help
        was nigh ;
The red cross flames aloft, Christ's
        pledge ; but no,
    Her black guns grinning hate, she
        rushes by
And hails us : — " Gains the leak ! Ay,
        so we thought !
    Sink, then, with curses fraught !"

I leaned against my gun still angry-
        hot,
    And my lids tingled with the tears
        held back ;
This scorn methought was crueller than
        shot :
    The manly death-grip in the battle-
        wrack,
Yard-arm to yard-arm, were more
        friendly far
    Than such fear-smothered war.

There our foe wallowed, like a wounded
        brute
    The fiercer for his hurt. What now
        were best?
Once more tug bravely at the peril's
        root,
    Though death came with it ? Or
        evade the test
If right or wrong in this God's world of
        ours
    Be leagued with mightier powers ?

Some, faintly loyal, felt their pulses
        lag
    With the slow beat that doubts and
        then despairs ;
Some, caitiff, would have struck the
        starry flag
    That knits us with our past, and
        makes us heirs
Of deeds high-hearted as were ever
        done
    'Neath the all-seeing sun.

But there was one, the Singer of our
   crew,
   Upon whose head Age waved his
      peaceful sign,
But whose red heart's-blood no sur-
   render knew;
   And couchant under brows of mas-
      sive line,
The eyes, like guns beneath a parapet,
   Watched, charged with lightnings
      yet.

The voices of the hills did his obey;
   The torrents flashed and tumbled in
      his song;
He brought our native fields from far
      away,
   Or set us 'mid the innumerable
      throng
Of dateless woods, or where we heard
      the calm
   Old homestead's evening psalm.

But now he sang of faith to things un-
      seen,
   Of freedom's birthright given to us in
      trust;
And words of doughty cheer he spoke
      between,
   That made all earthly fortune seem
      as dust,
Matched with that duty, old as Time
      and new,
   Of being brave and true.

We, listening, learned what makes the
      might of words, —
   Manhood to back them, constant as
      a star;
His voice rammed home our cannon,
      edged our swords,
   And sent our boarders shouting;
      shroud and spar
Heard him and stiffened; the sails
      heard, and wooed
   The winds with loftier mood.

In our dark hours he manned our guns
      again;
   Remanned ourselves from his own
      manhood's store;
Pride, honor, country, throbbed through
      all his strain;
   And shall we praise? God's praise
      was his before;

And on our futile laurels he looks
      down,
   Himself our bravest crown.

ODE RECITED AT THE HAR-
VARD COMMEMORATION.

JULY 21, 1865.

I.

WEAK-WINGED is song,
Nor aims at that clear-ethered height
Whither the brave deed climbs for
      light:
   We seem to do them wrong,
Bringing our robin's-leaf to deck their
      hearse
Who in warm life-blood wrote their
      nobler verse,
Our trivial song to honor those who
      come
With ears attuned to strenuous trump
      and drum,
And shaped in squadron-strophes their
      desire,
Live battle-odes whose lines were
      steel and fire:
   Yet sometimes feathered words are
      strong,
A gracious memory to buoy up and
      save
From Lethe's dreamless ooze, the com-
      mon grave
   Of the unventurous throng.

II.

To-day our Reverend Mother welcomes
      back
   Her wisest Scholars, those who un-
      derstood
The deeper teaching of her mystic tome,
   And offered their fresh lives to make
      it good:
   No lore of Greece or Rome,
No science peddling with the names of
      things,
Or reading stars to find inglorious fates,
   Can lift our life with wings
Far from Death's idle gulf that for the
      many waits,

And lengthen out our dates
With that clear fame whose memory
    sings
In manly hearts to come, and nerves
    them and dilates :
Nor such thy teaching, Mother of us
    all !
    Not such the trumpet-call
    Of thy diviner mood,
    That could thy sons entice
From happy homes and toils, the fruit-
    ful nest
Of those half-virtues which the world
    calls best,
    Into War's tumult rude :
But rather far that stern device
The sponsors chose that round thy
    cradle stood
    In the dim, unventured wood,
    The VERITAS that lurks beneath
    The letter's unprolific sheath,
Life of whate'er makes life worth
    living,
Seed-grain of high emprise, immortal
    food,
    One heavenly thing whereof earth
    hath the giving.

III.

Many loved Truth, and lavished life's
    best oil
    Amid the dusk of books to find her,
Content at last, for guerdon of their toil,
    With the cast mantle she hath left
    behind her.
    Many in sad faith sought for her,
    Many with crossed hands sighed
    for her ;
    But these, our brothers, fought for
    her,
    At life's dear peril wrought for her,
    So loved her that they died for her,
    Tasting the raptured fleetness
    Of her divine completeness :
    Their higher instinct knew
Those love her best who to themselves
    are true,
And what they dare to dream of, dare
    to do ;
They followed her and found her
Where all may hope to find,
Not in the ashes of the burnt-out mind,

But beautiful, with danger's sweetness
    round her.
    Where faith made whole with deed
    Breathes its awakening breath
    Into the lifeless creed,
    They saw her plumed and mailed,
    With sweet stern face unveiled,
And all-repaying eyes, look proud on
    them in death.

IV.

Our slender life runs rippling by, and
    glides
    Into the silent hollow of the past ;
    What is there that abides
To make the next age better for the
    last?
    Is earth too poor to give us
    Something to live for here that shall
    outlive us ?
    Some more substantial boon
Than such as flows and ebbs with For-
    tune's fickle moon ?
    The little that we see
    From doubt is never free ;
    The little that we do
    Is but half-nobly true ;
With our laborious hiving
What men call treasure, and the gods
    call dross,
    Life seems a jest of Fate's contriving,
    Only secure in every one's conniving,
A long account of nothings paid with
    loss,
Where we poor puppets, jerked by un-
    seen wires,
    After our little hour of strut and rave,
With all our pasteboard passions and
    desires,
Loves, hates, ambitions, and immortal
    fires,
    Are tossed pell-mell together in the
    grave.
But stay ! no age was e'er degenerate,
Unless men held it at too cheap a rate,
For in our likeness still we shape our
    fate
    Ah, there is something here
Unfathomed by the cynic's sneer,
Something that gives our feeble light
A high immunity from Night,
Something that leaps life's narrow
    bars

To claim its birthright with the hosts
     of heaven ;
   A seed of sunshine that can leaven
Our earthy dulness with the beams
     of stars,
     And glorify our clay
With light from fountains elder than
     the Day ;
   A conscience more divine than we,
   A gladness fed with secret tears,
   A vexing, forward-reaching sense
Of some more noble permanence ;
   A light across the sea,
Which haunts the soul and will not
     let it be,
Still beaconing from the heights of
     undegenerate years.

V.

     Whither leads the path
   To ampler fates that leads ?
   Not down through flowery
     meads,
     To reap an aftermath
   Of youth's vainglorious weeds,
   But up the steep, amid the wrath
And shock of deadly-hostile creeds,
Where the world's best hope and
     stay
By battle's flashes gropes a desperate
     way,
And every turf the fierce foot clings-to
     bleeds.
   Peace hath her not ignoble wreath,
   Ere yet the sharp, decisive word
Light the black lips of cannon, and the
     sword
     Dreams in its easeful sheath ;
But some day the live coal behind the
     thought,
     Whether from Baäl's stone ob-
        scene,
     Or from the shrine serene
Of God's pure altar brought,
Bursts up in flame ; the war of tongue
     and pen
Learns with what deadly purpose it
     was fraught,
And, helpless in the fiery passion
     caught,
Shakes all the pillared state with shock
     of men :
Some day the soft Ideal that we wooed

Confronts us fiercely, foe-beset, pursued,
And cries reproachful : " Was it, then,
     my praise,
And not myself was loved ? Prove now
     thy truth ;
I claim of thee the promise of thy
     youth ;
Give me thy life, or cower in empty
     phrase,
The victim of thy genius, not its mate ! "
   Life may be given in many ways,
   And loyalty to Truth be sealed
As bravely in the closet as the field,
     So bountiful is Fate ;
     But then to stand beside her,
     When craven churls deride her,
To front a lie in arms and not to yield,
        This shows, methinks, God's
           plan
        And measure of a stalwart man,
        Limbed like the old heroic
           breeds,
        Who stand self-poised on man-
           hood's solid earth,
     Not forced to frame excuses for his
        birth,
Fed from within with all the strength
     he needs.

VI.

Such was he, our Martyr-Chief,
     Whom late the Nation he had led,
     With ashes on her head,
Wept with the passion of an angry
     grief :
Forgive me, if from present things I
     turn
To speak what in my heart will beat
     and burn,
And hang my wreath on his world-
     honored urn.
     Nature, they say, doth dote,
     And cannot make a man
     Save on some worn-out plan,
     Repeating us by rote :
For him her Old World moulds aside
     she threw,
     And, choosing sweet clay from the
        breast
     Of the unexhausted West,
With stuff untainted shaped a hero
     new,

Wise, steadfast in the strength of God,
    and true.
        How beautiful to see
Once more a shepherd of mankind in-
    deed,
Who loved his charge, but never loved
    to lead ;
One whose meek flock the people joyed
    to be,
        Not lured by any cheat of birth,
        But by his clear-grained human
            worth,
And brave old wisdom of sincerity !
    They knew that outward grace is
        dust ;
    They could not choose but trust
In that sure-footed mind's unfaltering
        skill,
        And supple-tempered will
That bent like perfect steel to spring
    again and thrust.
        His was no lonely mountain-peak
            of mind,
        Thrusting to thin air o'er our cloudy
            bars,
        A sea-mark now, now lost in vapors
            blind ;
        Broad prairie rather, genial, level-
            lined,
        Fruitful and friendly for all human
            kind,
Yet also nigh to heaven and loved of
        loftiest stars.
        Nothing of Europe here,
Or, then, of Europe fronting mornward
        still,
        Ere any names of Serf and Peer
        Could Nature's equal scheme de-
            face ;
        Here was a type of the true elder
            race,
And one of Plutarch's men talked with
        us face to face.
I praise him not ; it were too late ;
And some innative weakness there must
        be
In him who condescends to victory
Such as the Present gives, and cannot
        wait,
        Safe in himself as in a fate.
        So always firmly he :
        He knew to bide his time,
        And can his fame abide,
Still patient in his simple faith sublime,

        Till the wise years decide.
Great captains, with their guns and
        drums,
        Disturb our judgment for the hour,
        But at last silence comes ;
These all are gone, and, standing
        like a tower,
Our children shall behold his fame,
        The kindly-earnest, brave, foresee-
            ing man,
Sagacious, patient, dreading praise,
        not blame,
    New birth of our new soil, the first
        American.

VII.

Long as man's hope insatiate can
        discern
        Or only guess some more inspir-
            ing goal
        Outside of Self, enduring as the
            pole,
Along whose course the flying axles
        burn
Of spirits bravely-pitched, earth's
        manlier brood ;
    Long as below we cannot find
The meed that stills the inexorable
        mind ;
So long this faith to some ideal Good,
Under whatever mortal names it
        masks,
    Freedom, Law, Country, this ethe-
        real mood
That thanks the Fates for their severer
        tasks,
    Feeling its challenged pulses leap,
    While others skulk in subterfuges
        cheap,
And, set in Danger's van, has all the
        boon it asks,
    Shall win man's praise and woman's
        love,
    Shall be a wisdom that we set above
All other skills and gifts to culture dear,
    A virtue round whose forehead we
        inwreathe
    Laurels that with a living passion
        breathe
When other crowns grow, while we
        twine them, sear.
    What brings us thronging these high
        rites to pay,

And seal these hours the noblest of our
            year,
    Save that our brothers found this
            better way?

VIII.

We sit here in the Promised Land
That flows with Freedom's honey
            and milk ;
But 't was they won it, sword in hand,
Making the nettle danger soft for us as
            silk.
We welcome back our bravest and
            our best ; —
    Ah me ! not all ! some come not with
            the rest,
Who went forth brave and bright as
            any here !
I strive to mix some gladness with my
            strain,
        But the sad strings complain,
        And will not please the ear :
I sweep them for a pæan, but they wane
        Again and yet again
Into a dirge, and die away, in pain.
In these brave ranks I only see the
            gaps,
Thinking of dear ones whom the dumb
            turf wraps,
Dark to the triumph which they died
            to gain :
    Fitlier may others greet the living,
    For me the past is unforgiving ;
        I with uncovered head
        Salute the sacred dead,
Who went, and who return not. — Say
            not so !
'T is not the grapes of Canaan that re-
            pay,
But the high faith that failed not by
            the way ;
Virtue treads paths that end not in the
            grave ;
No bar of endless night exiles the
            brave ;
        And to the saner mind
We rather seem the dead that stayed
            behind.
Blow, trumpets, all your exultations
            blow !
For never shall their aureoled presence
            lack :
I see them muster in a gleaming row,

With ever-youthful brows that nobler
            show ;
We find in our dull road their shining
            track ;
        In every nobler mood
We feel the orient of their spirit glow,
Part of our life's unalterable good,
Of all our saintlier aspiration ;
        They come transfigured back,
Secure from change in their high-
            hearted ways,
Beautiful evermore, and with the rays
Of morn on their white Shields of Ex-
            pectation !

IX.

        But is there hope to save
    Even this ethereal essence from the
            grave ?
    What ever 'scaped Oblivion's subtle
            wrong
    Save a few clarion names, or golden
            threads of song ?
        Before my musing eye
    The mighty ones of old sweep by,
    Disvoicèd now and insubstantial
            things,
    As noisy once as we ; poor ghosts of
            kings,
    Shadows of empire wholly gone to
            dust,
    And many races, nameless long ago,
    To darkness driven by that imperious
            gust
    Of ever-rushing Time that here doth
            blow :
    O visionary world, condition strange,
    Where naught abiding is but only
            Change,
    Where the deep-bolted stars themselves
            still shift and range !
    Shall we to more continuance make
            pretence ?
    Renown builds tombs ; a life-estate is
            Wit ;
        And, bit by bit,
    The cunning years steal all from us but
            woe ;
        Leaves are we, whose decays no har-
            vest sow.
        But, when we vanish hence,
    Shall they lie forceless in the dark
            below,

28

Save to make green their little length
    of sods,
Or deepen pansies for a year or two,
Who now to us are shining-sweet as
    gods?
Was dying all they had the skill to
    do?
That were not fruitless: but the Soul
    resents
Such short-lived service, as if blind
    events
Ruled without her, or earth could so
    endure;
She claims a more divine investiture
Of longer tenure than Fame's airy
    rents;
Whate'er she touches doth her nature
    share;
Her inspiration haunts the ennobled
    air,
    Gives eyes to mountains blind,
Ears to the deaf earth, voices to the
    wind,
And her clear trump sings succor
    everywhere
By lonely bivouacs to the wakeful
    mind;
For soul inherits all that soul could
    dare:
    Yea, Manhood hath a wider span
And larger privilege of life than man.
The single deed, the private sacrifice,
So radiant now through proudly-
    hidden tears,
Is covered up erelong from mortal
    eyes
With thoughtless drift of the decidu-
    ous years;
But that high privilege that makes all
    men peers,
That leap of heart whereby a people
    rise
    Up to a noble anger's height,
And, flamed on by the Fates, not shrink,
    but grow more bright,
    That swift validity in noble veins,
    Of choosing danger and disdaining
    shame,
    Of being set on flame
By the pure fire that flies all contact
    base,
But wraps its chosen with angelic
    might,
    These are imperishable gains,

Sure as the sun, medicinal as light,
These hold great futures in their lusty
    reins
And certify to earth a new imperial
    race.

X.

    Who now shall sneer?
    Who dare again to say we trace
    Our lines to a plebeian race?
    Roundhead and Cavalier!
Dumb are those names erewhile in
    battle loud;
Dream-footed as the shadow of a cloud,
    They flit across the ear:
That is best blood that hath most iron
    in 't
To edge resolve with, pouring without
    stint
    For what makes manhood dear.
    Tell us not of Plantagenets,
Hapsburgs, and Guelfs, whose thin
    bloods crawl
Down from some victor in a border-
    brawl!
    How poor their outworn coronets,
Matched with one leaf of that plain
    civic wreath
Our brave for honor's blazon shall be-
    queath,
    Through whose desert a rescued Na-
    tion sets
Her heel on treason, and the trumpet
    hears
Shout victory, tingling Europe's sullen
    ears
With vain resentments and more vain
    regrets!

XI.

    Not in anger, not in pride,
    Pure from passion's mixture rude
    Ever to base earth allied,
    But with far-heard gratitude,
    Still with heart and voice re-
    newed,
To heroes living and dear martyrs
    dead,
The strain should close that consecrates
    our brave.
    Lift the heart and lift the head!
    Lofty be its mood and grave,

Not without a martial ring,
Not without a prouder tread
And a peal of exultation :
Little right has he to sing
Through whose heart in such an
    hour
Beats no march of conscious
    power,
Sweeps no tumult of elation !
'T is no Man we celebrate,
By his country's victories great,
A hero half, and half the whim of
    Fate,
But the pith and marrow of a
    Nation
Drawing force from all her men,
Highest, humblest, weakest, all,
For her time of need, and then
Pulsing it again through them,
Till the basest can no longer cower,
Feeling his soul spring up divinely tall,
Touched but in passing by her mantle-
    hem.
Come back, then, noble pride, for 't is
    her dower !
    How could poet ever tower,
    If his passions, hopes, and fears,
    If his triumphs and his tears,
    Kept not measure with his peo-
        ple ?
Boom, cannon, boom to all the winds
    and waves !
Clash out, glad bells, from every rock-
    ing steeple !
Banners, adance with triumph, bend
    your staves !
    And from every mountain-peak
    Let beacon-fire to answering bea-
        con speak,
    Katahdin tell Monadnock, White-
        face he,
And so leap on in light from sea to sea,
    Till the glad news be sent
    Across a kindling continent,
Making earth feel more firm and air
    breathe braver :
'Be proud ! for she is saved, and all
    have helped to save her !
    She that lifts up the manhood of
        the poor,
    She of the open soul and open door,
    With room about her hearth for all
        mankind !
    The fire is dreadful in her eyes no
        more ;

From her bold front the helm she
    doth unbind,
Sends all her handmaid armies
    back to spin,
And bids her navies, that so lately
    hurled
Their crashing battle, hold their
    thunders in,
Swimming like birds of calm along
    the unharmful shore.
No challenge sends she to the elder
    world,
That looked askance and hated ; a
    light scorn
Plays o'er her mouth, as round her
    mighty knees
She calls her children back, and
    waits the morn
Of nobler day, enthroned between her
    subject seas.''

XII.

Bow down, dear Land, for thou hast
    found release !
    Thy God, in these distempered
        days,
    Hath taught thee the sure wisdom of
        His ways,
And through thine enemies hath
    wrought thy peace !
    Bow down in prayer and praise !
No poorest in thy borders but may now
Lift to the juster skies a man's enfran-
    chised brow.
O Beautiful ! my Country ! ours once
    more !
Smoothing thy gold of war-dishevelled
    hair
O'er such sweet brows as never other
    wore,
    And letting thy set lips,
    Freed from wrath's pale eclipse,
The rosy edges of their smile lay bare,
What words divine of lover or of poet
Could tell our love and make thee
    know it,
Among the Nations bright beyond
    compare ?
    What were our lives without
        thee ?
    What all our lives to save thee ?
    We reck not what we gave thee ;
    We will not dare to doubt thee,
But ask whatever else, and we will
    dare !

L'ENVOI.

TO THE MUSE.

WHITHER? Albeit I follow fast,
  In all life's circuit I but find,
Not where thou art, but where thou
    wast,
    Sweet beckoner, more fleet than
      wind !
I haunt the pine-dark solitudes,
  With soft brown silence carpeted,
And plot to snare thee in the woods:
    Peace I o'ertake, but thou art fled !
I find the rock where thou didst rest,
The moss thy skimming foot hath
    prest;
    All Nature with thy parting thrills,
Like branches after birds new-flown ;
    Thy passage hill and hollow fills
With hints of virtue not their own ;
  In dimples still the water slips
Where thou hast dipt thy finger-tips ;
  Just, just beyond, forever burn
  Gleams of a grace without return ;
  Upon thy shade I plant my foot,
And through my frame strange rap-
    tures shoot ;
All of thee but thyself I grasp ;
  I seem to fold thy luring shape,
And vague air to my bosom clasp,
  Thou lithe, perpetual Escape !

One mask and then another drops,
And thou art secret as before :
  Sometimes with flooded ear I list,
  And hear thee, wondrous organist,
From mighty continental stops
A thunder of new music pour ;
Through pipes of earth and air and
    stone
Thy inspiration deep is blown ;
Through mountains, forests, open
    downs,
Lakes, railroads, prairies, states, and
    towns,
Thy gathering fugue goes rolling on

From Maine to utmost Oregon ;
The factory-wheels in cadence hum,
From brawling parties concords come;
All this I hear, or seem to hear,
But when, enchanted, I draw near
To mate with words the various theme,
Life seems a whiff of kitchen steam,
History an organ-grinder's thrum,
  For thou hast slipt from it and me
And all thine organ-pipes left dumb,
    Most mutable Perversity !

Not weary yet, I still must seek,
And hope for luck next day, next week ;
I go to see the great man ride,
Shiplike, the swelling human tide
That floods to bear him into port,
Trophied from Senate-hall and Court ;
Thy magnetism, I feel it there.
Thy rhythmic presence fleet and rare,
Making the Mob a moment fine
With glimpses of their own Divine,
As in their demigod they see
    Their cramped ideal soaring free ;
'T was thou didst bear the fire about,
    That, like the springing of a mine
Sent up to heaven the street-long
    shout ;
Full well I know that thou wast here,
It was thy breath that brushed my ear;
But vainly in the stress and whirl
I dive for thee, the moment's pearl.

Through every shape thou well canst
    run,
Proteus, 'twixt rise and set of sun,
Well pleased with logger-camps in
    Maine
  As where Milan's pale Duomo lies
A stranded glacier on the plain,
  Its peaks and pinnacles of ice
  Melted in many a quaint device,
And sees, above the city's din,

Afar its silent Alpine kin :
I track thee over carpets deep
To wealth's and beauty's inmost keep ;
Across the sand of bar-room floors
'Mid the stale reek of boosing boors ;
Where drowse the hay-field's fragrant
　　heats,
Or the flail-heart of Autumn beats ;
I dog thee through the market's throngs
To where the sea with myriad tongues
Laps the green edges of the pier,
And the tall ships that eastward steer,
Curtsey their farewells to the town,
O'er the curved distance lessening
　　down ;
I follow allwhere for thy sake.
Touch thy robe's hem, but ne'er o'er-
　　take,
Find where, scarce yet unmoving, lies,
Warm from thy limbs, thy last disguise ;
But thou another shape hast donned,
And lurest still just, just beyond !

But here a voice, I know not whence,
Thrills clearly through my inward sense,
Saying : " See where she sits at home
While thou in search of her dost roam !
All summer long her ancient wheel
　　Whirls humming by the open door,
Or, when the hickory's social zeal
　　Sets the wide chimney in a roar,
Close-nestled by the tinkling hearth,
It modulates the household mirth
With that sweet serious undertone
Of duty, music all her own ;
Still as of old she sits and spins
Our hopes, our sorrows, and our sins ;
With equal care she twines the fates
Of cottages and mighty states ;
She spins the earth, the air, the sea,
The maiden's unschooled fancy free,
The boy's first love, the man's first grief,
The budding and the fall o' the leaf ;

The piping west-wind's snowy care
For her their cloudy fleeces spare,
Or from the thorns of evil times
She can glean wool to twist her rhymes ;
Morning and noon and eve supply
To her their fairest tints for dye,
But ever through her twirling thread
There spires one line of warmest red,
Tinged from the homestead's genial
　　heart,
The stamp and warrant of her art ;
With this Time's sickle she outwears,
And blunts the Sisters' baffled shears.

" Harass her not : thy heat and stir
But greater coyness breed in her ;
Yet thou mayst bend, ere Age's frost,
Thy long apprenticeship not lost,
Learning at last that Stygian Fate
Unbends to him that knows to wait.
The Muse is womanish, nor deigns
Her love to him that pules and plains,
With proud, averted face she stands
To him that wooes with empty hands.
Make thyself free of Manhood's guild ;
Pull down thy barns and greater build ;
The wood, the mountain, and the plain
Wave breast-deep with the poet's grain ;
Pluck thou the sunset's fruit of gold,
Glean from the heavens and ocean old ;
From fireside lone and trampling street
Let thy life garner daily wheat ;
The epic of a man rehearse,
Be something better than thy verse ;
Make thyself rich, and then the Muse
Shall court thy precious interviews,
Shall take thy head upon her knee,
And such enchantment lilt to thee,
That thou shalt hear the life-blood flow
From farthest stars to grass-blades
　　low,
And find the Listener's science still
Transcends the Singer's deepest skill ! "

To

MR. JAMES T. FIELDS,

———◆———

My dear Fields :

Dr. Johnson's sturdy self-respect led him to invent the Bookseller as a substitute for the Patron. My relations with you have
enabled me to discover how pleasantly the Friend may replace the
Bookseller. Let me record my sense of many thoughtful services
by associating your name with a poem which owes its appearance
in this form to your partiality.

Cordially yours,

J. R. LOWELL.

Cambridge, *November 29, 1869.*

THE CATHEDRAL.

FAR through the memory shines a happy
    day,
Cloudless of care, down-shod to every
    sense,
And simply perfect from its own re-
    source,
As to a bee the new campanula's
Illuminate seclusion swung in air.
Such days are not the prey of setting
    suns,
Nor ever blurred with mist of after-
    thought;
Like words made magical by poets dead,
Wherein the music of all meaning is
The sense hath garnered or the soul di-
    vined,
They mingle with our life's ethereal
    part,
Sweetening and gathering sweetness
    evermore,
By beauty's franchise disenthralled of
    time.

I can recall, nay, they are present still,
Parts of myself, the perfume of my
    mind,
Days that seem farther off than Homer's
    now
Ere yet the child had loudened to the
    boy,
And I, recluse from playmates, found
    perforce
Companionship in things that not de-
    nied
Nor granted wholly; as is Nature's
    wont,
Who, safe in uncontaminate reserve,
Lets us mistake our longing for her love,
And mocks with various echo of our-
    selves.
These first sweet frauds upon our con-
    sciousness,
That blend the sensual with its imaged
    world,

These virginal cognitions, gifts of morn,
Ere life grow noisy, and slower-footed
    thought
Can overtake the rapture of the sense,
To thrust between ourselves and what
    we feel,
Have something in them secretly divine.
Vainly the eye, once schooled to serve
    the brain,
With pains deliberate studies to renew
The ideal vision: second-thoughts are
    prose;
For beauty's acme hath a term as brief
As the wave's poise before it break in
    pearl.
Our own breath dims the mirror of the
    sense,
Looking too long and closely: at a flash
We snatch the essential grace of mean-
    ing out,
And that first passion beggars all be-
    hind,
Heirs of a tamer transport prepossessed.
Who, seeing once, has truly seen again
The gray vague of unsympathizing sea
That dragged his Fancy from her moor-
    ings back
To shores inhospitable of eldest time,
Till blank foreboding of earth-gendered
    powers,
Pitiless seignories in the elements,
Omnipotences blind that darkling
    smite,
Misgave him, and repaganized the
    world?
Yet, by some subtler touch of sympathy,
These primal apprehensions, dimly
    stirred,
Perplex the eye with pictures from with-
    in.
This hath made poets dream of lives
    foregone
In worlds fantastical, more fair than
    ours:

So Memory cheats us, glimpsing half-
    revealed.
Even as I write she tries her wonted
    spell
In that continuous redbreast boding
    rain :
The bird I hear sings not from yonder
    elm ;
But the flown ecstasy my childhood
    heard
Is vocal in my mind, renewed by him,
Haply made sweeter by the accumulate
    thrill
That threads my undivided life and
    steals
A pathos from the years and graves be-
    tween.

I know not how it is with other men,
Whom I but guess, deciphering my-
    self ;
For me, once felt is so felt nevermore.
The fleeting relish at sensation's brim
Had in it the best ferment of the wine.
One spring I knew as never any since :
All night the surges of the warm south-
    west
Boomed intermittent through the wal-
    lowing elms,
And brought a morning from the Gulf
    adrift,
Omnipotent with sunshine, whose quick
    charm
Startled with crocuses the sullen turf
And wiled the bluebird to his whiff of
    song :
One summer hour abides, what time I
    perched,
Dappled with noonday, under simmer-
    ing leaves,
And pulled the pulpy oxhearts, while
    aloof
An oriole clattered and the robins
    shrilled,
Denouncing me an alien and a thief :
One morn of autumn lords it o'er the
    rest,
When in the lane I watched the ash-
    leaves fall,
Balancing softly earthward without
    wind,
Or twirling with directer impulse down
On those fallen yesterday, now barbed
    with frost,

While I grew pensive with the pensive
    year :
And once I learned how marvellous
    winter was,
When past the fence-rails, downy-gray
    with rime,
I creaked adventurous o'er the span-
    gled crust
That made familiar fields seem far and
    strange
As those stark wastes that whiten end-
    lessly
In ghastly solitude about the pole,
And gleam relentless to the unsetting
    sun :
Instant the candid chambers of my brain
Were painted with these sovran images :
And later visions seem but copies pale
From those unfading frescos of the past,
Which I, young savage, in my age of
    flint,
Gazed at, and dimly felt a power in me
Parted from Nature by the joy in her
That doubtfully revealed me to myself.
Thenceforward I must stand outside the
    gate ;
And paradise was paradise the more,
Known once and barred against satiety.

What we call Nature, all outside our-
    selves,
Is but our own conceit of what we see,
Our own reaction upon what we feel ;
The world's a woman to our shifting
    mood,
Feeling with us, or making due pre-
    tence ;
And therefore we the more persuade
    ourselves
To make all things our thought's con-
    federates,
Conniving with us in whate'er we dream.
So when our Fancy seeks analogies,
Though she have hidden what she after
    finds,
She loves to cheat herself with feigned
    surprise.
I find my own complexion everywhere.
No rose, I doubt, was ever, like the first,
A marvel to the bush it dawned upon,
The rapture of its life made visible,
The mystery of its yearning realized,
As the first babe to the first woman
    born

No falcon ever felt delight of wings
As when, an eyas, from the stolid cliff
Loosing himself, he followed his high
heart
To swim on sunshine, masterless as
wind;
And I believe the brown earth takes
delight
In the new snowdrop looking back at her,
To think that by some vernal alchemy
It could transmute her darkness into
pearl;
What is the buxom peony after that,
With its coarse constancy of hoyden
blush?
What the full summer to that wonder
new?

But, if in nothing else, in us there is
A sense fastidious hardly reconciled
To the poor makeshifts of life's scenery,
Where the same slide must double all
its parts,
Shoved in for Tarsus and hitched back
for Tyre.
I blame not in the soul this daintiness,
Rasher of surfeit than a humming-bird,
In things indifferent by sense purveyed;
It argues her an immortality
And dateless incomes of experience,
This unthrift housekeeping that will
not brook
A dish warmed-over at the feast of life,
And finds Twice stale, served with
whatever sauce.
Nor matters much how it may go with
me
Who dwell in Grub Street and am
proud to drudge
Where men, my betters, wet their crust
with tears:
Use can make sweet the peach's shady
side,
That only by reflection tastes of sun.

But she, my Princess, who will sometimes deign
My garret to illumine till the walls,
Narrow and dingy, scrawled with hack-
neyed thought
(Poor Richard slowly elbowing Plato
out),
Dilate and drape themselves with tapes-
tries

Nausikaa might have stooped o'er,
while, between,
Mirrors, effaced in their own clearness,
send
Her only image on through deepening
deeps
With endless repercussion of delight,—
Bringer of life, witching each sense to
soul,
That sometimes almost gives me to
believe
I might have been a poet, gives at least
A brain desaxonized, an ear that makes
Music where none is, and a keener pang
Of exquisite surmise outleaping
thought,—
Her will I pamper in her luxury:
No crumpled rose-leaf of too careless
choice
Shall bring a northern nightmare to her
dreams,
Vexing with sense of exile; hers shall be
The invitiate firstlings of experience,
Vibrations felt but once and felt life-
long:
O, more than half-way turn that Gre-
cian front
Upon me, while with self-rebuke I spell,
On the plain fillet that confines thy
hair
In conscious bounds of seeming uncon-
straint,
The *Naught in overplus*, thy race's
badge!

One feast for her I secretly designed
In that Old World so strangely beautiful
To us the disinherited of eld,—
A day at Chartres, with no soul beside
To roil with pedant prate my joy serene
And make the minster shy of confi-
dence,
I went, and, with the Saxon's pious care,
First ordered dinner at the pea-green
inn,
The flies and I its only customers.
Eluding these, I loitered through the
town,
With hope to take my minster una-
wares
In its grave solitude of memory.
A pretty burgh, and such as Fancy loves
For bygone grandeurs, faintly rumorous
now

Upon the mind's horizon, as of storm
Brooding its dreamy thunders far aloof,
That mingle with our mood, but not
    disturb.
Its once grim bulwarks, tamed to lovers'
    walks,
Look down unwatchful on the sliding
    Eure,
Whose listless leisure suits the quiet
    place,
Lisping among his shallows homelike
    sounds
At Concord and by Bankside heard
    before.
Chance led me to a public pleasure-
    ground,
Where I grew kindly with the merry
    groups,
And blessed the Frenchman for his
    simple art
Of being domestic in the light of day.
His language has no word, we growl,
    for Home ;
But he can find a fireside in the sun,
Play with his child, make love, and
    shriek his mind,
By throngs of strangers undisprivacied.
He makes his life a public gallery,
Nor feels himself till what he feels
    comes back
In manifold reflection from without ;
While we, each pore alert with con-
    sciousness,
Hide our best selves as we had stolen
    them,
And each bystander a detective were,
Keen-eyed for every chink of undisguise.

So, musing o'er the problem which was
    best, —
A life wide-windowed, shining all
    abroad,
Or curtains drawn to shield from sight
    profane
The rites we pay to the mysterious I, —
With outward senses furloughed and
    head bowed
I followed some fine instinct in my
    feet,
Till, to unbend me from the loom of
    thought,
Looking up suddenly, I found mine eyes
Confronted with the minster's vast re-
    pose.

Silent and gray as forest-leaguered cliff
Left inland by the ocean's slow retreat,
That hears afar the breeze-borne rote,
    and longs,
Remembering shocks of surf that clomb
    and fell,
Spume-sliding down the baffled decu-
    man,
It rose before me, patiently remote
From the great tides of life it breasted
    once,
Hearing the noise of men as in a dream.
I stood before the triple northern port,
Where dedicated shapes of saints and
    kings,
Stern faces bleared with immemorial
    watch,
Looked down benignly grave and
    seemed to say,
Ye come and go incessant ; we remain
Safe in thehallowed quiets of the past ;
Be reverent, ye who flit and are forgot,
Of faith so nobly realized as this.
I seem to have heard it said by learned
    folk
Who drench you with æsthetics till you
    feel
As if all beauty were a ghastly bore,
The faucet to let loose a wash of words,
That Gothic is not Grecian, therefore
    worse ;
But, being convinced by much experi-
    ment
How little inventiveness there is in
    man,
Grave copier of copies, I give thanks
For a new relish, careless to inquire
My pleasure's pedigree, if so it please,
Nobly, I mean, nor renegade to art.
The Grecian gluts me with its perfect-
    ness,
Unanswerable as Euclid, self-contained,
The one thing finished in this hasty
    world,
Forever finished, though the barbarous
    pit,
Fanatical on hearsay, stamp and shout
As if a miracle could be encored.
But ah ! this other, this that never ends,
Still climbing, luring fancy still to climb,
As full of morals half-divined as life,
Graceful, grotesque, with ever new
    surprise
Of hazardous caprices sure to please,

Heavy as nightmare, airy-light as fern,
Imagination's very self in stone !
With one long sigh of infinite release
From pedantries past, present, or to
    come,
I looked, and owned myself a happy
    Goth.
Your blood is mine, ye architects of
    dream,
Builders of aspiration incomplete,
So more consummate, souls self-confi-
    dent,
Who felt your own thought worthy of
    record
In monumental pomp ! No Grecian drop
Rebukes these veins that leap with
    kindred thrill,
After long exile, to the mother-tongue.

Ovid in Pontus, puling for his Rome
Of men invirile and disnatured dames
That poison sucked from the Attic
    bloom decayed,
Shrank with a shudder from the blue-
    eyed race
Whose force rough-handed should re-
    new the world,
And from the dregs of Romulus express
Such wine as Dante poured, or he who
    blew
Roland's vain blast, or sang the Cam-
    peador
In verse that clanks like armor in the
    charge, —
Homeric juice, though brimmed in
    Odin's horn.
And they could build, if not the col-
    umned fane
That from the height gleamed seaward
    many-hued,
Something more friendly with their
    ruder skies :
The gray spire, molten now in driving
    mist,
Now lulled with the incommunicable
    blue ;
The carvings touched to meaning new
    with snow,
Or commented with fleeting grace of
    shade ;
The statues, motley as man's memory,
Partial as that, so mixed of true and
    false,
History and legend meeting with a kiss

Across this bound-mark where their
    realms confine ;
The painted windows, frecking gloom
    with glow,
Dusking the sunshine which they seem
    to cheer,
Meet symbol of the senses and the soul ;
And the whole pile, grim with the
    Northman's thought
Of life and death, and doom, life's equal
    fee, —
These were before me : and I gazed
    abashed,
Child of an age that lectures, not creates,
Plastering our swallow - nests on the
    awful Past,
And twittering round the work of larger
    men,
As we had builded what we but deface.
Far up the great bells wallowed in
    delight,
Tossing their clangors o'er the heedless
    town,
To call the worshippers who never
    came,
Or women mostly, in loath twos and
    threes.
I entered, reverent of whatever shrine
Guards piety and solace for my kind
Or gives the soul a moment's truce of
    God,
And shared decorous in the ancient rite
My sterner fathers held idolatrous.
The service over, I was tranced in
    thought :
Solemn the deepening vaults, and most
    to me,
Fresh from the fragile realm of deal and
    paint,
Or brick mock-pious with a marble
    front ;
Solemn the lift of high-embowered roof,
The clustered stems that spread in
    boughs disleaved,
Through which the organ blew a dream
    of storm,
Though not more potent to sublime
    with awe
And shut the heart up in tranquillity,
Than aisles to me familiar that o'erarch
The conscious silences of brooding
    woods,
Centurial shadows, cloisters of the elk :
Yet here was sense of undefined regret,

Irreparable loss, uncertain what:
Was all this grandeur but anachro-
  nism,—
A shell divorced of its informing life,
Where the priest housed him like a
  hermit-crab,
An alien to that faith of elder days
That gathered round it this fair shape
  of stone?
Is old Religion but a spectre now,
Haunting the solitude of darkened
  minds,
Mocked out of memory by the sceptic
  day?
Is there no corner safe from peeping
  Doubt,
Since Gutenberg made thought cosmo-
  polite
And stretched electric threads from
  mind to mind?
Nay, did Faith build this wonder? or
  did Fear,
That makes a fetish and misnames it God
(Blockish or metaphysic, matters not),
Contrive this coop to shut its tyrant in,
Appeased with playthings, that he might
  not harm?

I turned and saw a beldame on her
  knees;
With eyes astray, she told mechanic
  beads
Before some shrine of saintly woman-
  hood,
Bribed intercessor with the far-off
  Judge:
Such my first thought, by kindlier soon
  rebuked,
Pleading for whatsoever touches life
With upward impulse: be He nowhere
  else,
God is in all that liberates and lifts,
In all that humbles, sweetens, and con-
  soles:
Blessèd the natures shored on every side
With landmarks of hereditary thought!
Thrice happy they that wander not life-
  long
Beyond near succor of the household
  faith,
The guarded fold that shelters not con-
  fines!
Their steps find patience in familiar
  paths,

Printed with hope by loved feet gone
  before
Of parent, child, or lover, glorified
By simple magic of dividing Time.
My lids were moistened as the woman
  knelt,
And—was it will, or some vibration
  faint
Of sacred Nature, deeper than the
  will?—
My heart occultly felt itself in hers,
Through mutual intercession gently
  leagued.

Or was it not mere sympathy of brain'
A sweetness intellectually conceived
In simpler creeds to me impossible?
A juggle of that pity for ourselves
In others, which puts on such pretty
  masks
And snares self-love with bait of charity?
Something of all it might be, or of none:
Yet for a moment I was snatched
  away
And had the evidence of things not
  seen;
For one rapt moment; then it all came
  back,
This age that blots out life with ques-
  tion-marks,
This nineteenth century with its knife
  and glass
That make thought physical, and thrust
  far off
The Heaven, so neighborly with man
  of old,
To voids sparse-sown with alienated
  stars.

'T is irrecoverable, that ancient faith,
Homely and wholesome, suited to the
  time,
With rod or candy for child-minded
  men:
No theologic tube, with lens on lens
Of syllogism transparent, brings it
  near,—
At best resolving some new nebula,
Or blurring some fixed-star of hope to
  mist.
Science was Faith once; Faith were
  Science now,
Would she but lay her bow and arrows
  by

And arm her with the weapons of the time.
Nothing that keeps thought out is safe from thought.
For there's no virgin-fort but self-respect,
And Truth defensive hath lost hold on God.
Shall we treat Him as if He were a child
That knew not His own purpose? nor dare trust
The Rock of Ages to their chemic tests,
Lest some day the all-sustaining base divine
Should fail from under us, dissolved in gas?
The arméd eye that with a glance discerns
In a dry blood-speck between ox and man,
Stares helpless at this miracle called life,
This shaping potency behind the egg,
This circulation swift of deity,
Where suns and systems inconspicuous float
As the poor blood-disks in our mortal veins.
Each age must worship its own thought of God,
More or less earthy, clarifying still
With subsidence continuous of the dregs;
Nor saint nor sage could fix immutably
The fluent image of the unstable Best,
Still changing in their very hands that wrought;
To-day's eternal truth To-morrow proved
Frail as frost-landscapes on a window-pane.
Meanwhile Thou smiledst, inaccessible,
At Thought's own substance made a cage for Thought,
And Truth locked fast with her own master-key;
Nor didst Thou reck what image man might make
Of his own shadow on the flowing world;
The climbing instinct was enough for Thee.
Or wast Thou, then, an ebbing tide that left

Strewn with dead miracle those eldest shores,
For men to dry, and dryly lecture on,
Thyself thenceforth incapable of flood?
Idle who hopes with prophets to be snatched
By virtue in their mantles left below;
Shall the soul live on other men's report,
Herself a pleasing fable of herself?
Man cannot be God's outlaw if he would,
Nor so abscond him in the caves of sense
But Nature still shall search some crevice out
With messages of splendor from that Source
Which, dive he, soar he, baffles still and lures.
This life were brutish did we not sometimes
Have intimation clear of wider scope,
Hints of occasion infinite, to keep
The soul alert with noble discontent
And onward yearnings of unstilled desire;
Fruitless, except we now and then divined
A mystery of Purpose, gleaming through
The secular confusions of the world,
Whose will we darkly accomplish, doing ours.
No man can think nor in himself perceive,
Sometimes at waking, in the street sometimes,
Or on the hillside, always unforewarned,
A grace of being, finer than himself,
That beckons and is gone,—a larger life
Upon his own impinging, with swift glimpse
Of spacious circles luminous with mind,
To which the ethereal substance of his own
Seems but gross cloud to make that visible,
Touched to a sudden glory round the edge.
Who that hath known these visitations fleet
Would strive to make them trite and ritual?
I, that still pray at morning and at eve,

Loving those roots that feed us from
   the past,
And prizing more than Plato things I
   learned
At that best academe, a mother's knee,
Thrice in my life perhaps have truly
   prayed,
Thrice, stirred below my conscious self,
   have felt
That perfect disenthralment which is
   God ;
Nor know I which to hold worst
   enemy, —
Him who on speculation's windy waste
Would turn me loose, stript of the rai-
   ment warm
By Faith contrived against our naked-
   ness,
Or him who, cruel-kind, would fain
   obscure,
With painted saints and paraphrase of
   God,
The soul's east-window of divine sur-
   prise.
Where others worship I but look and
   long ;
For, though not recreant to my fathers'
   faith,
Its forms to me are weariness, and most
That drony vacuum of compulsory
   prayer,
Still pumping phrases for the Ineffable,
Though all the valves of memory gasp
   and wheeze.
Words that have drawn transcendent
   meanings up
From the best passion of all bygone
   time,
Steeped through with tears of triumph
   and remorse,
Sweet with all sainthood, cleansed in
   martyr-fires,
Can they, so consecrate and so inspired,
By repetition wane to vexing wind ?
Alas ! we cannot draw habitual breath
In the thin air of life's supremer heights,
We cannot make each meal a sacra-
   ment,
Nor with our tailors be disbodied
   souls, —
We men, too conscious of earth's
   comedy,
Who see two sides, with our posed
   selves debate,

And only for great stakes can be sub-
   lime !
Let us be thankful when, as I do here,
We can read Bethel on a pile of stones,
And, seeing where God *has* been, trust
   in Him.

Brave Peter Fischer there in Nurem-
   berg,
Moulding Saint Sebald's miracles in
   bronze,
Put saint and stander-by in that quaint
   garb
Familiar to him in his daily walk,
Not doubting God could grant a
   miracle
Then and in Nuremberg, if so He
   would ;
But never artist for three hundred years
Hath dared the contradiction ludicrous
Of supernatural in modern clothes.
Perhaps the deeper faith that is to come
Will see God rather in the strenuous
   doubt,
Than in the creed held as an infant's
   hand
Holds purposeless whatso is placed
   therein.

Say it is drift, not progress, none the less
With the old sextant of the fathers'
   creed,
We shape our courses by new-risen
   stars,
And, still lip-loyal to what once was
   truth,
Smuggle new meanings under ancient
   names,
Unconscious perverts of the Jesuit,
   Time.
Change is the mask that all Continu-
   ance wears
To keep us youngsters harmlessly
   amused ;
Meanwhile some ailing or more watch-
   ful child,
Sitting apart, sees the old eyes gleam
   out,
Stern, and yet soft with humorous pity
   too.
Whilere, men burnt men for a doubtful
   point,
As if the mind were quenchable with
   fire,

The form of building or the creed pro-
    fessed,
The Cross, bold type of shame to hom-
    age turned,
Of an unfinished life that sways the
    world,
Shall tower as sovereign emblem over
    all.

The kobold Thought moves with us
    when we shift
Our dwelling to escape him ; perched
    aloft
On the first load of household-stuff he
    went ;
For, where the mind goes, goes old fur-
    niture.
I, who to Chartres came to feed my
    eye
And give to Fancy one clear holiday,
Scarce saw the minster for the thoughts
    it stirred
Buzzing o'er past and future with vain
    quest.
Here once there stood a homely wood-
    en church,
Which slow devotion nobly changed
    for this
That echoes vaguely to my modern
    steps.
By suffrage universal it was built,
As practised then, for all the country
    came
From far as Rouen, to give votes for
    God,
Each vote a block of stone securely laid
Obedient to the master's deep-mused
    plan.
Will what our ballots rear, responsible
To no grave forethought, stand so long
    as this,—
Delight like this the eye of after days
Brightening with pride that here, at
    least, were men
Who meant and did the noblest thing
    they knew ?
Can our religion cope with deeds like
    this ?
We, too, build Gothic contract-shams,
    because
Our deacons have discovered that it
    pays,
And pews sell better under vaulted
    roofs

Of plaster painted like an Indian squa
Shall not that Western Goth, of who
    we spoke,
So fiercely practical, so keen of eye,
Find out, some day, that nothing pays
    but God,
Served whether on the smoke-shut
    battle-field,
In work obscure done honestly, or vote
For truth unpopular, or faith maintained
To ruinous convictions, or good deeds
Wrought for good's sake, mindless of
    heaven or hell ?
Shall he not learn that all prosperity,
Whose bases stretch not deeper than
    the sense,
Is but a trick of this world's atmosphere,
A desert-born mirage of spire and dome,
Or find too late, the Past's long lesson
    missed,
That dust the prophets shake from off
    their feet
Grows heavy to drag down both tower
    and wall ?
I know not ; but, sustained by sure
    belief
That man still rises level with the
    height
Of noblest opportunities, or makes
Such, if the time supply not, I can
    wait.
I gaze round on the windows, pride of
    France,
Each the bright gift of some mechanic
    guild
Who loved their city and thought gold
    well spent
To make her beautiful with piety ;
I pause, transfigured by some stripe of
    bloom,
And my mind throngs with shining
    auguries,
Circle on circle, bright as seraphim,
With golden trumpets, silent, that await
The signal to blow news of good to
    men.

Then the revulsion came that always
    comes
After these dizzy elations of the mind :
And with a passionate pang of doubt I
    cried,
" O mountain-born, sweet with snow-
    filtered air

rom uncontaminate wells of ether
  drawn
And never-broken secrecies of sky,
Freedom, with anguish won, misprized
  till lost,
They keep thee not who from thy sacred
  eyes
Catch the consuming lust of sensual
  good
And the brute's license of unfettered
  will.
Far from the popular shout and venal
  breath
Of Cleon blowing the mob's baser mind
To bubbles of wind-piloted conceit,
Thou shrinkest, gathering up thy skirts,
  to hide
In fortresses of solitary thought
And private virtue strong in self-re-
  straint.

Must we too forfeit thee misunderstood,
Content with names, nor inly wise to
  know
That best things perish of their own
  excess,
And quality o'er-driven becomes defect?
Nay, is it thou indeed that we have
  glimpsed,
Or rather such illusion as of old
Through Athens glided menadlike and
  Rome,
A shape of vapor, mother of vain dreams
And mutinous traditions, specious plea
Of the glaived tyrant and long-memoried
  priest?"

I walked forth saddened; for all
  thought is sad,
And leaves a bitterish savor in the
  brain,—
Tonic, it may be, not delectable,—
And turned, reluctant, for a parting
  look
At those old weather-pitted images
Of bygone struggle, now so sternly
  calm.
About their shoulders sparrows had
  built nests,
And fluttered, chirping, from gray
  perch to perch,
Now on a mitre poising, now a crown,
Irreverently happy.   While I thought
How confident they were, what careless
  hearts

Flew on those lightsome wings and
  shared the sun,
A larger shadow crossed; and, looking
  up,
I saw where, nesting in the hoary
  towers,
The sparrow-hawk slid forth on noise-
  less air,
With sidelong head that watched the
  joy below,
Grim Norman baron o'er this clan of
  Kelts.
Enduring Nature, force conservative,
Indifferent to our noisy whims! Men
  prate
Of all heads to an equal grade cashiered
On level with the dullest, and expect
(Sick of no worse distemper than them-
  selves)
A wondrous cure-all in equality;
They reason that To-morrow must be
  wise
Because To-day was not, nor Yester-
  day,
As if good days were shapen of them-
  selves,
Not of the very lifeblood of men's
  souls;
Meanwhile, long-suffering, imperturb-
  able,
Thou quietly complet'st thy syllogism,
And from the premise sparrow here
  below
Draw'st sure conclusion of the hawk
  above,
Pleased with the soft-billed songster,
  pleased no less
With the fierce beak of natures aquiline.

Thou beautiful Old Time, now hid
  away
In the Past's valley of Avilion,
Haply, like Arthur, till thy wound be
  healed,
Then to reclaim the sword and crown
  again!
Thrice beautiful to us; perchance less
  fair
To who possessed thee, as a mountain
  seems
To dwellers round its bases but a heap
Of barren obstacle that lairs the storm
And the avalanche's silent bolt holds
  back

Leashed with a hair, — meanwhile
  some far-off clown,
Hereditary delver of the plain,
Sees it an unmoved vision of repose,
Nest of the morning, and conjectures
  there
The dance of streams to idle shepherds'
  pipes,
And fairer habitations softly hung
On breezy slopes, or hid in valleys cool,
For happier men. No mortal ever
  dreams
That the scant isthmus he encamps
  upon
Between two oceans, one, the Stormy,
  passed,
And one, the Peaceful, yet to venture on,
Has been that future whereto prophets
  yearned
For the fulfilment of Earth's cheated
  hope,
Shall be that past which nerveless
  poets moan
As the lost opportunity of song.

O Power, more near my life than life
  itself
(Or what seems life to us in sense
  immured),
Even as the roots, shut in the darksome
  earth,
Share in the tree-top's joyance, and
  conceive
Of sunshine and wide air and wingèd
  things
By sympathy of nature, so do I
Have evidence of Thee so far above,
Yet in and of me! Rather Thou the
  root
Invisibly sustaining, hid in light,
Not darkness, or in darkness made by
  us.
If sometimes I must hear good men
  debate
Of other witness of Thyself than Thou,
As if there needed any help of ours
To nurse Thy flickering life, that else
  must cease,
Blown out, as 't were a candle, by men's
  breath,
My soul shall not be taken in their snare,
To change her inward surety for their
  doubt
Muffled from sight in formal robes of
  proof:
While she can only feel herself through
  Thee,
I fear not Thy withdrawal; more I
  fear,
Seeing, to know Thee not, hoodwinked
  with dreams
Of signs and wonders, while, unnoticed,
  Thou,
Walking Thy garden still, commun'st
  with men,
Missed in the commonplace of miracle.

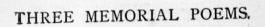

THREE MEMORIAL POEMS.

> "Coscïenza fusca
> O della propria o dell' altrui vergogna
> Pur sentirà la tua parola brusca."

If I let fall a word of bitter mirth
When public shames more shameful pardon won,
Some have misjudged me, and my service done,
If small, yet faithful, deemed of little worth:
Through veins that drew their life from Western earth
Two hundred years and more my blood hath run
In no polluted course from sire to son;
And thus was I predestined ere my birth
To love the soil wherewith my fibres own
Instinctive sympathies; yet love it so
As honor would, nor lightly to dethrone
Judgment, the stamp of manhood, nor forego
The son's right to a mother dearer grown
With growing knowledge and more chaste than snow.

THREE MEMORIAL POEMS.

⁎ Readers, it is hoped, will remember that, by his Ode at the Harvard Commemoration, the author had precluded himself from many of the natural outlets of
thought and feeling common to such occasions as are celebrated in these poems.

ODE

READ AT THE ONE HUNDREDTH ANNI-
VERSARY OF THE FIGHT AT CONCORD
BRIDGE.

19TH APRIL, 1875.

I.

Who cometh over the hills,
Her garments with morning sweet,
The dance of a thousand rills
Making music before her feet?
Her presence freshens the air;
Sunshine steals light from her face;
The leaden footstep of Care
Leaps to the tune of her pace,
Fairness of all that is fair,
Grace at the heart of all grace,
Sweetener of hut and of hall,
Bringer of life out of naught,
Freedom, O, fairest of all
The daughters of Time and Thought!

II.

She cometh, cometh to-day:
Hark! hear ye not her tread,
Sending a thrill through your clay,
Under the sod there, ye dead,
Her nurslings and champions?
Do ye not hear, as she comes,
The bay of the deep-mouthed guns,
The gathering buzz of the drums?
The bells that called ye to prayer,
How wildly they clamor on her,
Crying, "She cometh! prepare
Her to praise and her to honor,
That a hundred years ago
Scattered here in blood and tears
Potent seeds wherefrom should grow
Gladness for a hundred years!"

III.

Tell me, young men, have ye seen,
Creature of diviner mien
For true hearts to long and cry for,

Manly hearts to live and die for?
What hath she that others want?
Brows that all endearments haunt,
Eyes that make it sweet to dare,
Smiles that cheer untimely death,
Looks that fortify despair,
Tones more brave than trumpet's
    breath:
Tell me, maidens, have ye known
Household charm more sweetly rare,
Grace of woman ampler blown,
Modesty more debonair,
Younger heart with wit full grown?
O for an hour of my prime,
The pulse of my hotter years,
That I might praise her in rhyme
Would tingle your eyelids to tears,
Our sweetness, our strength, and our
    star,
Our hope, our joy, and our trust,
Who lifted us out of the dust,
And made us whatever we are!

IV.

Whiter than moonshine upon snow
Her raiment is, but round the hem
Crimson stained; and, as to and fro
Her sandals flash, we see on them,
And on her instep veined with blue,
Flecks of crimson, on those fair feet,
High-arched, Diana-like, and fleet,
Fit for no grosser stain than dew:
O, call them rather chrisms than stains,
Sacred and from heroic veins!
For, in the glory-guarded pass,
Her haughty and far-shining head
She bowed to shrive Leonidas
With his imperishable dead;
Her, too, Morgarten saw,
Where the Swiss lion fleshed his icy
    paw;
She followed Cromwell's quenchless
    star
Where the grim Puritan tread
Shook Marston, Naseby, and Dunbar:
Yea, on her feet are dearer dyes
Yet fresh, nor looked on with untearful
    eyes.

V.

Our fathers found her in the woods
Where Nature meditates and broods,
The seeds of unexampled things
Which Time to consummation brings

Through life and death and man's un-
    stable moods;
They met her here, not recognized,
A sylvan huntress clothed in furs,
To whose chaste wants her bow sufficed,
Nor dreamed what destinies were hers:
She taught them bee-like to create
Their simpler forms of Church and
    State:
She taught them to endue
The past with other functions than it
    knew,
And turn in channels strange the uncer-
    tain stream of Fate;
Better than all, she fenced them in their
    need
With iron-handed Duty's sternest creed,
'Gainst Self's lean wolf that ravens word
    and deed.

VI.

Why cometh she hither to-day
To this low village of the plain
Far from the Present's loud highway,
From Trade's cool heart and seething
    brain?
Why cometh she? She was not far
    away.
Since the soul touched it, not in vain,
With pathos of immortal gain,
'T is here her fondest memories stay.
She loves yon pine-bemurmured ridge
Where now our broad-browed poet
    sleeps,
Dear to both Englands; near him he
Who wore the ring of Canace;
But most her heart to rapture leaps
Where stood that era-parting bridge,
O'er which, with footfall still as dew,
The Old Time passed into the New;
Where, as your stealthy river creeps,
He whispers to his listening weeds
Tales of sublimest homespun deeds.
Here English law and English thought
'Gainst the self-will of England fought;
And here were men (coequal with their
    fate),
Who did great things, unconscious they
    were great.
They dreamed not what a die was cast
With that first answering shot; what
    then?
There was their duty; they were men
Schooled the soul's inward gospel to
    obey,

Though leading to the lion's den.
They felt the habit-hallowed world give
    way
Beneath their lives, and on went they,
    Unhappy who was last.
When Buttrick gave the word,
That awful idol of the unchallenged
    Past,
Strong in their love, and in their lineage
    strong,
Fell crashing : if they heard it not,
Yet the earth heard,
Nor ever hath forgot,
As on from startled throne to throne,
Where Superstition sate or conscious
    Wrong,
A shudder ran of some dread birth un-
    known.
Thrice venerable spot !
River more fateful than the Rubicon !
O'er those red planks, to snatch her dia-
    dem,
Man's Hope, star-girdled, sprang with
    them,
And over ways untried the feet of Doom
    strode on.

VII.

Think you these felt no charms
  In their gray homesteads and em-
    bowered farms ?
In household faces waiting at the door
Their evening step should lighten up no
    more ?
In fields their boyish feet had known ?
In trees their fathers' hands had set,
And which with them had grown,
Widening each year their leafy coronet ?
Felt they no pang of passionate regret
For those unsolid goods that seem so
    much our own ?
These things are dear to every man that
    lives,
And life prized more for what it lends
    than gives.
Yea, many a tie, through iteration sweet,
Strove to detain their fatal feet ;
And yet the enduring half they chose,
Whose choice decides a man life's slave
    or king,
The invisible things of God before the
    seen and known :
Therefore their memory inspiration
    blows

With echoes gathering on from zone to
    zone ;
For manhood is the one immortal thing
Beneath Time's chargeful sky,
And, where it lightened once, from age
    to age,
Men come to learn, in grateful pilgrim-
    age,
That length of days is knowing when to
    die.

VIII.

What marvellous change of things and
    men !
She, a world-wandering orphan then,
So mighty now ! Those are her streams
That whirl the myriad, myriad wheels
Of all that does, and all that dreams,
Of all that thinks, and all that feels,
Through spaces stretched from sea to
    sea ;
By idle tongues and busy brains,
By who doth right, and who refrains,
Hers are our losses and our gains ;
Our maker and our victim she.

IX.

Maiden half mortal, half divine,
We triumphed in thy coming ; to the
    brinks
Our hearts were filled with pride's tu-
    multuous wine ;
Better to-day who rather feels than
    thinks.
Yet will some graver thoughts intrude,
And cares of sterner mood ;
They won thee : who shall keep thee ?
    From the deeps
Where discrowned empires o'er their
    ruins brood,
And many a thwarted hope wrings its
    weak hands and weeps,
I hear the voice as of a mighty wind
From all heaven's caverns rushing un-
    confined,
" I, Freedom, dwell with Knowledge :
    I abide
With men whom dust of faction cannot
    blind
To the slow tracings of the Eternal
    Mind ;
With men by culture trained and for-
    tified,
Who bitter duty to sweet lusts prefer,

Fearless to counsel and obey.
Conscience my sceptre is, and law my
    sword,
Not to be drawn in passion or in play,
But terrible to punish and deter ;
Implacable as God's word,
Like it, a shepherd's crook to them that
    blindly err.
Your firm-pulsed sires, my martyrs and
    my saints,
Offshoots of that one stock whose pa-
    tient sense
Hath known to mingle flux with per-
    manence,
Rated my chaste denials and restraints
Above the moment's dear-paid para-
    dise :
Beware lest, shifting with Time's grad-
    ual creep,
The light that guided shine into your
    eyes.
The envious Powers of ill nor wink nor
    sleep :
Be therefore timely wise,
Nor laugh when this one steals, and that
    one lies,
As if your luck could cheat those sleep-
    less spies,
Till the deaf Fury comes your house to
    sweep !"
I hear the voice, and unaffrighted bow ;
Ye shall not be prophetic now,
Heralds of ill, that darkening fly
Between my vision and the rainbowed
    sky,
Or on the left your hoarse forebodings
    croak
From many a blasted bough
On Yggdrasil's storm-sinewed oak,
That once was green, Hope of the West,
    as thou :
Yet pardon if I tremble while I boast ;
For I have loved as those who pardon
    most.

X.

Away, ungrateful doubt, away !
At least she is our own to-day.
Break into rapture, my song,
Verses, leap forth in the sun,
Bearing the joyance along
Like a tide of fire as ye run !
Pause not for choosing of words,
Let them but blossom and sing
Blithe as the orchards and birds

With the new coming of spring !
Dance in your jollity, bells ;
Shout, cannon ; cease not, ye drums ;
Answer, ye hillside and dells ;
Bow, all ye people ! She comes,
Radiant, calm-fronted, as when
She hallowed that April day.
Stay with us ! Yes, thou shalt stay,
Softener and strengthener of men,
Freedom, not won by the vain,
Not to be courted in play,
Not to be kept without pain.
Stay with us ! Yes, thou wilt stay,
Handmaid and mistress of all,
Kindler of deed and of thought,
Thou that to hut and to hall
Equal deliverance brought !
Souls of her martyrs, draw near,
Touch our dull lips with your fire,
That we may praise without fear
Her our delight, our desire,
Our faith's inextinguishable star,
Our hope, our remembrance, our trust,
Our present, our past, our to be,
Who will mingle her life with our dust
And makes us deserve to be free !

UNDER THE OLD ELM.

POEM READ AT CAMBRIDGE ON THE
HUNDREDTH ANNIVERSARY OF WASH-
INGTON'S TAKING COMMAND OF THE
AMERICAN ARMY, 3D JULY, 1775.

I.

1.

WORDS pass as wind, but where great
    deeds were done
A power abides transfused from sire to
    son :
The boy feels deeper meanings thrill his
    ear,
That tingling through his pulse life-long
    shall run,
With sure impulsion to keep honor
    clear,
When, pointing down, his father whis-
    pers, "Here,
Here, where we stand, stood he, the
    purely Great,
Whose soul no siren passion could un-
    sphere,

Then nameless, now a power and mixed
  with fate."
Historic town, thou holdest sacred dust,
Once known to men as pious, learnëd,
  just,
And one memorial pile that dares to
  last ;
But Memory greets with reverential kiss
No spot in all thy circuit sweet as this,
Touched by that modest glory as it past,
O'er which yon elm hath piously dis-
  played
These hundred years its monumental
  shade.

2.

Of our swift passage through this scen-
  ery
Of life and death, more durable than we,
What landmark so congenial as a tree
Repeating its green legend every spring,
And, with a yearly ring,
Recording the fair seasons as they flee,
Type of our brief but still-renewed
  mortality?
We fall as leaves : the immortal trunk
  remains,
Builded with costly juice of hearts and
  brains
Gone to the mould now, whither all that
  be
Vanish returnless, yet are procreant
  still
In human lives to come of good or ill,
And feed unseen the roots of Destiny.

II.

1.

MEN'S monuments, grown old, forget
  their names
They should eternize, but the place
Where shining souls have passed im-
  bibes a grace
Beyond mere earth ; some sweetness of
  their fames
Leaves in the soil its unextinguished
  trace,
Pungent, pathetic, sad with nobler aims,
That penetrates our lives and heightens
  them or shames.
This insubstantial world and fleet
Seems solid for a moment when we
  stand

On dust ennobled by heroic feet
Once mighty to sustain a tottering
  land,
And mighty still such burthen to up-
  bear,
Nor doomed to tread the path of things
  that merely were :
Our sense, refined with virtue of the
  spot,
Across the mists of Lethe's sleepy
  stream
Recalls him, the sole chief without a
  blot,
No more a pallid image and a dream,
But as he dwelt with men decorously
  supreme.

2.

Our grosser minds need this terrestrial
  hint
To raise long-buried days from tombs
  of print :
" Here stood he," softly we repeat,
And lo, the statue shrined and still
In that gray minster-front we call the
  Past,
Feels in its frozen veins our pulses
  thrill,
Breathes living air and mocks at
  Death's deceit.
It warms, it stirs, comes down to us at
  last,
Its features human with familiar light,
A man, beyond the historian's art to
  kill,
Or sculptor's to efface with patient
  chisel-blight.

3.

Sure the dumb earth hath memory, nor
  for naught
Was Fancy given, on whose enchanted
  loom
Present and Past commingle, fruit and
  bloom
Of one fair bough, inseparably wrought
Into the seamless tapestry of thought.
So charmed, with undeluded eye we see
In history's fragmentary tale
Bright clews of continuity,
Learn that high natures over Time pre-
  vail,
And feel ourselves a link in that entail
That binds all ages past with all that
  are to be.

III.

1.

BENEATH our consecrated elm
A century ago he stood,
Famed vaguely for that old fight in the
    wood
Whose red surge sought, but could not
    overwhelm
The life foredoomed to wield our rough-
    hewn helm : —
From colleges, where now the gown
To arms had yielded, from the town,
Our rude self-summoned levies flocked
    to see
The new-come chiefs and wonder
    which was he.
No need to question long ; close-lipped
    and tall,
Long trained in murder-brooding for-
    ests lone
To bridle others' clamors and his own,
Firmly erect, he towered above them
    all,
The incarnate discipline that was to
    free
With iron curb that armed democracy.

2.

A motley rout was that which came to
    stare,
In raiment tanned by years of sun and
    storm,
Of every shape that was not uniform,
Dotted with regimentals here and
    there ;
An army all of captains, used to pray
And stiff in fight, but serious drill's
    despair,
Skilled to debate their orders, not
    obey ;
Deacons were there, selectmen, men
    of note
In half-tamed hamlets ambushed round
    with woods,
Ready to settle Freewill by a vote,
But largely liberal to its private moods ;
Prompt to assert by manners, voice, or
    pen,
Or ruder arms, their rights as English-
    men,
Nor much fastidious as to how and
    when :

Yet seasoned stuff and fittest to create
A thought-staid army or a lasting
    state :
Haughty they said he was, at first :
    severe :
But owned, as all men own, the steady
    hand
Upon the bridle, patient to command,
Prized, as all prize, the justice pure
    from fear,
And learned to honor first, then love
    him, then revere.
Such power there is in clear-eyed self-
    restraint
And purpose clean as light from every
    selfish taint.

3.

Musing beneath the legendary tree,
The years between furl off : I seem to
    see
The sun-flecks, shaken the stirred foli-
    age through,
Dapple with gold his sober buff and
    blue
And weave prophetic aureoles round
    the head
That shines our beacon now nor dark-
    ens with the dead.
O, man of silent mood,
A stranger among strangers then,
How art thou since renowned the Great,
    the Good,
Familiar as the day in all the homes of
    men !
The wingèd years, that winnow praise
    and blame,
Blow many names out : they but fan
    to flame
The self-renewing splendors of thy
    fame.

IV.

1.

How many subtlest influences unite,
With spiritual touch of joy or pain,
Invisible as air and soft as light,
To body forth that image of the brain
We call our Country, visionary shape,
Loved more than woman, fuller of fire
    than wine,
Whose charm can none define,
Nor any, though he flee it, can escape !

All party-colored threads the weaver Time
Sets in his web, now trivial, now sublime,
All memories, all forebodings, hopes and fears,
Mountain and river, forest, prairie, sea,
A hill, a rock, a homestead, field, or tree,
The casual gleanings of unreckoned years,
Take goddess-shape at last and there is She,
Old at our birth, new as the springing hours,
Shrine of our weakness, fortress of our powers,
Consoler, kindler, peerless mid her peers,
A force that 'neath our conscious being stirs,
A life to give ours permanence, when we
Are borne to mingle our poor earth with hers,
And all this glowing world goes with us on our biers.

2.

Nations are long results, by ruder ways
Gathering the might that warrants length of days;
They may be pieced of half-reluctant shares
Welded by hammer-strokes of broad-brained kings,
Or from a doughty people grow, the heirs
Of wise traditions widening cautious rings;
At best they are computable things,
A strength behind us making us feel bold
In right, or, as may chance, in wrong;
Whose force by figures may be summed and told,
So many soldiers, ships, and dollars strong,
And we but drops that bear compulsory part
In the dumb throb of a mechanic heart;
But Country is a shape of each man's mind
Sacred from definition, unconfined
By the cramped walls where daily drudgeries grind;
An inward vision, yet an outward birth
Of sweet familiar heaven and earth;
A brooding Presence that stirs motions blind
Of wings within our embryo being's shell
That wait but her completer spell
To make us eagle-natured, fit to dare
Life's nobler spaces and untarnished air.

3.

You, who hold dear this self-conceived ideal,
Whose faith and works alone can make it real,
Bring all your fairest gifts to deck her shrine
Who lifts our lives away from Thine and Mine
And feeds the lamp of manhood more divine
With fragrant oils of quenchless constancy.
When all have done their utmost, surely he
Hath given the best who gives a character
Erect and constant, which nor any shock
Of loosened elements, nor the forceful sea
Of flowing or of ebbing fates, can stir
From its deep bases in the living rock
Of ancient manhood's sweet security:
And this he gave, serenely far from pride
As baseness, boon with prosperous stars allied,
Part of what nobler seed shall in our loins abide.

4.

No bond of men as common pride so strong,
In names time-filtered for the lips of song,
Still operant, with the primal Forces bound
Whose currents, on their spiritual round,
Transfuse our mortal will nor are gainsaid:

These are their arsenals, these the exhaustless mines
That give a constant heart in great
   designs;
These are the stuff whereof such
   dreams are made
As make heroic men: thus surely he
Still holds in place the massy blocks he
   laid
'Neath our new frame, enforcing soberly
The self-control that makes and keeps
   a people free.

V.

1.

O, FOR a drop of that Cornelian ink
Which gave Agricola dateless length
   of days,
To celebrate him fitly, neither swerve
To phrase unkempt, nor pass discre-
   tion's brink,
With him so statue-like in sad reserve,
So diffident to claim, so forward to de-
   serve!
Nor need I shun due influence of his
   fame
Who, mortal among mortals, seemed
   as now
The equestrian shape with unimpas-
   sioned brow,
That paces silent on through vistas of
   acclaim.

2.

What figure more immovably august
Than that grave strength so patient
   and so pure,
Calm in good fortune, when it wavered,
   sure,
That mind serene, impenetrably just,
Modelled on classic lines so simple
   they endure?
That soul so softly radiant and so
   white
The track it left seems less of fire than
   light,
Cold but to such as love distempera-
   ture?
And if pure light, as some deem, be
   the force
That drives rejoicing planets on their
   course,

Why for his power benign seek an im-
   purer source?
His was the true enthusiasm that burns
   long,
Domestically bright,
Fed from itself and shy of human sight,
The hidden force that makes a lifetime
   strong,
And not the short-lived fuel of a song.
Passionless, say you? What is passion
   for
But to sublime our natures and control
To front heroic toils with late return,
Or none, or such as shames the con-
   queror?
That fire was fed with substance of the
   soul
And not with holiday stubble, that
   could burn,
Unpraised of men who after bonfires
   run,
Through seven slow years of unadvan-
   cing war,
Equal when fields were lost or fields
   were won,
With breath of popular applause or
   blame,
Nor fanned nor damped, unquench-
   ably the same,
Too inward to be reached by flaws of
   idle fame.

3.

Soldier and statesman, rarest unison;
High-poised example of great duties
   done
Simply as breathing, a world's honors
   worn
As life's indifferent gifts to all men
   born;
Dumb for himself, unless it were to
   God,
But for his barefoot soldiers eloquent,
Tramping the snow to coral where they
   trod,
Held by his awe in hollow-eyed con-
   tent;
Modest, yet firm as Nature's self; un-
   blamed
Save by the men his nobler temper
   shamed;
Never seduced through show of present
   good
By other than unsetting lights to steer

New-trimmed in Heaven, nor than his
    steadfast mood
More steadfast, far from rashness as
    from fear;
Rigid, but with himself first, grasping
    still
In swerveless poise the wave-beat
    helm of will;
Not honored then or now because he
    wooed
The popular voice, but that he still
    withstood;
Broad-minded, higher-souled, there is
    but one
Who was all this and ours, and all
    men's — WASHINGTON.

4.

Minds strong by fits, irregularly great,
That flash and darken like revolving
    lights,
Catch more the vulgar eye unschooled
    to wait
On the long curve of patient days and
    nights
Rounding a whole life to the circle fair
Of orbed fulfilment; and this balanced
    soul,
So simple in its grandeur, coldly bare
Of draperies theatric, standing there
In perfect symmetry of self-control,
Seems not so great at first, but greater
    grows
Still as we look, and by experience
    learn
How grand this quiet is, how nobly
    stern
The discipline that wrought through
    lifelong throes
That energetic passion of repose.

5.

A nature too decorous and severe,
Too self-respectful in its griefs and
    joys,
For ardent girls and boys
Who find no genius in a mind so clear
That its grave depths seem obvious and
    near,
Nor a soul great that made so little
    noise.
They feel no force in that calm-cadenced
    phrase,

The habitual full-dress of his well-bred
    mind,
That seems to pace the minuet's courtly
    maze
And tell of ampler leisures, roomier
    length of days.
His firm-based brain, to self so little
    kind
That no tumultuary blood could blind,
Formed to control men, not amaze,
Looms not like those that borrow
    height of haze:
It was a world of statelier movement
    then
Than this we fret in, he a denizen
Of that ideal Rome that made a man
    for men.

VI.

I.

THE longer on this earth we live
And weigh the various qualities of men,
Seeing how most are fugitive,
Or fitful gifts, at best, of now and then,
Wind-wavered corpse-lights, daughters
    of the fen,
The more we feel the high stern-
    featured beauty
Of plain devotedness to duty,
Steadfast and still, nor paid with mortal
    praise,
But finding amplest recompense
For life's ungarlanded expense
In work done squarely and unwasted
    days.
For this we honor him, that he could
    know
How sweet the service and how free
Of her, God's eldest daughter here be-
    low,
And choose in meanest raiment which
    was she.

2.

Placid completeness, life without a fall
From faith or highest aims, truth's
    breachless wall,
Surely if any fame can bear the touch,
His will say "Here!" at the last trum-
    pet's call,
The unexpressive man whose life ex-
    pressed so much.

VII.

1.

NEVER to see a nation born
Hath been given to mortal man,
Unless to those who, on that summer
    morn,
Gazed silent when the great Virginian
Unsheathed the sword whose fatal flash
Shot union through the incoherent clash
Of our loose atoms, crystallizing them
Around a single will's unpliant stem,
And making purpose of emotion rash.
Out of that scabbard sprang, as from its
    womb,
Nebulous at first but hardening to a star,
Through mutual share of sunburst and
    of gloom,
The common faith that made us what
    we are.

2.

That lifted blade transformed our jan-
    gling clans,
Till then provincial, to Americans,
And made a unity of wildering plans;
Here was the doom fixed: here is
    marked the date
When this New World awoke to man's
    estate,
Burnt its last ship and ceased to look
    behind:
Nor thoughtless was the choice; no love
    or hate
Could from its poise move that deliber-
    ate mind,
Weighing between too early and too late
Those pitfalls of the man refused by
    Fate:
His was the impartial vision of the great
Who see not as they wish, but as they
    find.
He saw the dangers of defeat, nor less
The incomputable perils of success;
The sacred past thrown by, an empty
    rind;
The future, cloud-land, snare of proph-
    ets blind;
The waste of war, the ignominy of
    peace;
On either hand a sullen rear of woes,
Whose garnered lightnings none could
    guess,
Piling its thunder-heads and muttering
    "Cease!"

Yet drew not back his hand, but gravely
    chose
The seeming-desperate task whence our
    new nation rose.

3.

A noble choice and of immortal seed!
Nor deem that acts heroic wait on
    chance
Or easy were as in a boy's romance;
The man's whole life preludes the single
    deed
That shall decide if his inheritance
Be with the sifted few of matchless
    breed,
Our race's sap and sustenance,
Or with the unmotived herd that only
    sleep and feed.
Choice seems a thing indifferent; thus
    or so,
What matters it? The Fates with
    mocking face
Look on inexorable, nor seem to know
Where the lot lurks that gives life's
    foremost place.
Yet Duty's leaden casket holds it still,
And but two ways are offered to our will,
Toil with rare triumph, ease with safe
    disgrace,
The problem still for us and all of hu-
    man race.
He chose, as men choose, where most
    danger showed,
Nor ever faltered 'neath the load
Of petty cares, that gall great hearts the
    most,
But kept right on the strenuous up-hill
    road,
Strong to the end, above complaint or
    boast:
The popular tempest on his rock-mailed
    coast
Wasted its wind-borne spray,
The noisy marvel of a day;
His soul sate still in its unstormed
    abode.

VIII.

VIRGINIA gave us this imperial man
Cast in the massive mould
Of those high-statured ages old
Which into grander forms our mortal
    metal ran;

She gave us this unblemished gentle-
    man :
What shall we give her back but love
    and praise
As in the dear old unestrangëd days
Before the inevitable wrong began ?
Mother of States and undiminished
    men,
Thou gavest us a country, giving him,
And we owe alway what we owed thee
    then :
The boon thou wouldst have snatched
    from us agen
Shines as before with no abatement dim.
A great man's memory is the only thing
With influence to outlast the present
    whim
And bind us as when here he knit our
    golden ring.
All of him that was subject to the hours
Lies in thy soil and makes it part of
    ours :
Across more recent graves,
Where unresentful Nature waves
Her pennons o'er the shot-ploughed
    sod,
Proclaiming the sweet Truce of God,
We from this consecrated plain stretch
    out
Our hands as free from afterthought or
    doubt
As here the united North
Poured her embrownëd manhood forth
In welcome of our savior and thy son.
Through battle we have better learned
    thy worth,
The long-breathed valor and undaunted
    will,
Which, like his own, the day's disaster
    done,
Could, safe in manhood, suffer and be
    still.
Both thine and ours the victory hardly
    won ;
If ever with distempered voice or pen
We have misdeemed thee, here we take
    it back,
And for the dead of both don common
    black.
Be to us evermore as thou wast then,
As we forget thou hast not always been,
Mother of States and unpolluted men,
Virginia, fitly named from England's
    manly queen !

AN ODE

FOR THE FOURTH OF JULY, 1876.

I.

1.

ENTRANCED I saw a vision in the cloud
That loitered dreaming in yon sunset
    sky,
Full of fair shapes, half creatures of the
    eye,
Half chance-evoked by the wind's fan-
    tasy
In golden mist, an ever-shifting crowd :
There, mid unreal forms that came and
    went
In air-spun robes, of evanescent dye,
A woman's semblance shone pre-emi-
    nent ;
Not armed like Pallas, not like Hera
    proud,
But, as on household diligence intent,
Beside her visionary wheel she bent
Like Aretë or Bertha, nor than they
Less queenly in her port : about her
    knee
Glad children clustered confident in
    play :
Placid her pose, the calm of energy ;
And over her broad brow in many a
    round
(That loosened would have gilt her gar-
    ment's hem),
Succinct, as toil prescribes, the hair was
    wound
In lustrous coils, a natural diadem.
The cloud changed shape, obsequious
    to the whim
Of some transmuting influence felt in
    me,
And, looking now, a wolf I seemed to
    see
Limned in that vapor, gaunt and hun-
    ger-bold,
Threatening her charge : resolve in
    every limb,
Erect she flamed in mail of sun-wove
    gold,
Penthesilea's self for battle dight ;
One arm uplifted braced a flickering
    spear,
And one her adamantine shield made
    light ;

Her face, helm-shadowed, grew a thing
    to fear,
And her fierce eyes, by danger chal-
    lenged, took
Her trident-sceptred mother's dauntless
    look.
" I know thee now, O goddess-born ! "
    I cried,
And turned with loftier brow and firmer
    stride ;
For in that spectral cloud-work I had
    seen
Her image, bodied forth by love and
    pride,
The fearless, the benign, the mother-
    eyed,
The fairer world's toil-consecrated
    queen.

2.

What shape by exile dreamed elates
    the mind
Like hers whose hand, a fortress of
    the poor,
No blood in vengeance spilt, though
    lawful, stains ?
Who never turned a suppliant from
    her door ?
Whose conquests are the gains of all
    mankind ?
To-day her thanks shall fly on every
    wind,
Unstinted, unrebuked, from shore to
    shore,
One love, one hope, and not a doubt
    behind !
Cannon to cannon shall repeat her
    praise,
Banner to banner flap it forth in flame ;
Her children shall rise up to bless her
    name,
And wish her harmless length of days,
The mighty mother of a mighty brood,
Blessed in all tongues and dear to every
    blood,
The beautiful, the strong, and, best of
    all, the good !

3.

Seven years long was the bow
Of battle bent, and the heightening
Storm-heaps convulsed with the throe
Of their uncontainable lightening ;
Seven years long heard the sea

Crash of navies and wave-borne thun-
    der ;
Then drifted the cloud-rack a-lee,
And new stars were seen, a world's
    wonder ;
Each by her sisters made bright,
All binding all to their stations,
Cluster of manifold light
Startling the old constellations :
Men looked up and grew pale :
Was it a comet or star,
Omen of blessing or bale,
Hung o'er the ocean afar ?

4.

Stormy the day of her birth :
Was she not born of the strong,
She, the last ripeness of earth,
Beautiful, prophesied long ?
Stormy the days of her prime :
Hers are the pulses that beat
Higher for perils sublime,
Making them fawn at her feet.
Was she not born of the strong ?
Was she not born of the wise ?
Daring and counsel belong
Of right to her confident eyes :
Human and motherly they,
Careless of station or race :
Hearken ! her children to-day
Shout for the joy of her face.

II.

1.

No praises of the past are hers,
No fanes by hallowing time caressed,
No broken arch that ministers
To Time's sad instinct in the breast :
She has not gathered from the years
Grandeur of tragedies and tears,
Nor from long leisure the unrest
That finds repose in forms of classic
    grace :
These may delight the coming race
Who haply shall not count it to our
    crime
That we who fain would sing are here
    before our time.
She also hath her monuments ;
Not such as stand decrepitly resigned
To ruin-mark the path of dead events

That left no seed of better days be-
   hind,
The tourist's pensioners that show their
   scars
And maunder of forgotten wars ;
She builds not on the ground, but in
   the mind,
Her open-hearted palaces
For larger-thoughted men with heaven
   and earth at ease :
Her march the plump mow marks, the
   sleepless wheel,
The golden sheaf, the self-swayed com-
   monweal ;
The happy homesteads hid in orchard
   trees
Whose sacrificial smokes through
   peaceful air
Rise lost in heaven, the household's
   silent prayer ;
What architect hath bettered these ?
With softened eye the westward trav-
   eller sees
A thousand miles of neighbors side by
   side,
Holding by toil-won titles fresh from
   God
The lands no serf or seigneur ever trod,
With manhood latent in the very sod,
Where the long billow of the wheat-
   field's tide
Flows to the sky across the prairie
   wide,
A sweeter vision than the castled
   Rhine,
Kindly with thoughts of Ruth and
   Bible-days benign.

2.

O ancient commonwealths, that we
   revere
Haply because we could not know you
   near,
Your deeds like statues down the
   aisles of Time
Shine peerless in memorial calm sub-
   lime,
And Athens is a trumpet still, and
   Rome ;
Yet which of your achievements is not
   foam
Weighed with this one of hers (below
   you far

In fame, and born beneath a milder
   star),
That to Earth's orphans, far as curves
   the dome,
Of death-deaf sky, the bounteous West
   means home,
With dear precedency of natural ties
That stretch from roof to roof and make
   men gently wise ?
And if the nobler passions wane,
Distorted to base use, if the near goal
Of insubstantial gain
Tempt from the proper race-course of
   the soul
That crowns their patient breath
Whose feet, song-sandaled, are too fleet
   for Death,
Yet may she claim one privilege urbane
And haply first upon the civic roll,
That none can breathe her air nor grow
   humane.

3.

O, better far the briefest hour
Of Athens self-consumed, whose plastic
   power
Hid Beauty safe from Death in words
   or stone ;
Of Rome, fair quarry where those eagles
   crowd
Whose fulgurous vans about the world
   had blown
Triumphant storm and seeds of polity ;
Of Venice, fading o'er her shipless sea,
Last iridescence of a sunset cloud ;
Than this inert prosperity,
This bovine comfort in the sense alone !
Yet art came slowly even to such as
   those,
Whom no past genius cheated of their
   own
With prudence of o'ermastering prece-
   dent ;
Petal by petal spreads the perfect rose,
Secure of the divine event ;
And only children rend the bud half-
   blown
To forestall Nature in her calm intent:
Time hath a quiver full of purposes
Which miss not of their aim, to us un-
   known,
And brings about the impossible with
   ease :
Haply for us the ideal dawn shall break

From where in legend-tinted line
The peaks of Hellas drink the morn-
    ing's wine,
To tremble on our lids with mystic
    sign
Till the drowsed ichor in our veins
    awake
And set our pulse in tune with moods
    divine :
Long the day lingered in its sea-fringed
    nest,
Then touched the Tuscan hills with
    golden lance
And paused ; then on to Spain and
    France
The splendor flew, and Albion's misty
    crest :
Shall Ocean bar him from his destined
    West?
Or are we, then, arrived too late,
Doomed with the rest to grope discon-
    solate,
Foreclosed of Beauty by our modern
    date?

III.

1.

POETS, as their heads grow gray,
Look from too far behind the eyes,
Too long-experienced to be wise
In guileless youth's diviner way ;
Life sings not now, but prophesies ;
Time's shadows they no more behold,
But, under them, the riddle old
That mocks, bewilders, and defies :
In childhood's face the seed of shame,
In the green tree an ambushed flame,
In Phosphor a vaunt-guard of Night,
They, though against their will, divine,
And dread the care-dispelling wine
Stored from the Muse's vintage bright,
By age imbued with second-sight.
From Faith's own eyelids there peeps
    out,
Even as they look, the leer of doubt ;
The festal wreath their fancy loads
With care that whispers and forebodes :
Nor this our triumph-day can blunt
    Megæra's goads.

2.

Murmur of many voices in the air
Denounces us degenerate,

Unfaithful guardians of a noble fate,
And prompts indifference or despair :
Is this the country that we dreamed in
    youth,
Where wisdom and not numbers should
    have weight,
Seed-field of simpler manners, braver
    truth,
Where shams should cease to dominate
In household, church, and state?
Is this Atlantis? This the unpoisoned
    soil,
Sea-whelmed for ages and recovered
    late,
Where parasitic greed no more should
    coil
Round Freedom's stem to bend awry
    and blight
What grew so fair, sole plant of love
    and light?
Who sit where once in crowned seclu-
    sion sate
The long-proved athletes of debate
Trained from their youth, as none
    thinks needful now?
Is this debating-club where boys dis-
    pute,
And wrangle o'er their stolen fruit,
The Senate, erewhile cloister of the
    few,
Where Clay once flashed and Webster's
    cloudy brow
Brooded those bolts of thought that all
    the horizon knew?

3.

O, as this pensive moonlight blurs my
    pines,
Here while I sit and meditate these lines
To gray-green dreams of what they are
    by day,
So would some light, not reason's sharp-
    edged ray,
Trance me in moonshine as before the
    flight
Of years had won me this unwelcome
    right
To see things as they are, or shall be
    soon,
In the frank prose of undissembling
    noon !

4

Back to my breast, ungrateful sigh !
Whoever fails, whoever errs,

The penalty be ours, not hers !
The present still seems vulgar, seen too
    nigh ;
The golden age is still the age that 's
    past :
I ask no drowsy opiate
To dull my vision of that only state
Founded on faith in man, and therefore
    sure to last.
For, O, my country, touched by thee,
The gray hairs gather back their gold ;
Thy thought sets all my pulses free ;
The heart refuses to be old ;
The love is all that I can see.
Not to thy natal-day belong
Time's prudent doubt or age's wrong,
But gifts of gratitude and song ;
Unsummoned crowd the thankful words,
As sap in spring-time floods the tree,
Foreboding the return of birds,
For all that thou hast been to me !

IV.

1.

FLAWLESS his heart and tempered to
    the core
Who, beckoned by the forward-leaning
    wave,
First left behind him the firm-footed
    shore,
And, urged by every nerve of sail and
    oar,
Steered for the Unknown which gods to
    mortals gave,
Of thought and action the mysterious
    door,
Bugbear of fools, a summons to the
    brave :
Strength found he in the unsympathiz-
    ing sun,
And strange stars from beneath the
    horizon won,
And the dumb ocean pitilessly grave :
High-hearted surely he ;
But bolder they who first off-cast
Their moorings from the habitable Past
And ventured chartless on the sea
Of storm-engendering Liberty :
For all earth's width of waters is a span,
And their convulsed existence mere re-
    pose,
Matched with the unstable heart of man,

Shoreless in wants, mist-girt in all it
    knows,
Open to every wind of sect or clan,
And sudden-passionate in ebbs and
    flows.

2.

They steered by stars the elder shipmen
    knew,
And laid their courses where the cur-
    rents draw
Of ancient wisdom channelled deep in
    law,
The undaunted few
Who changed the Old World for the
    New,
And more devoutly prized
Than all perfection theorized
The more imperfect that had roots and
    grew.
They founded deep and well,
Those danger-chosen chiefs of men
Who still believed in Heaven and Hell,
Nor hoped to find a spell,
In some fine flourish of a pen,
To make a better man
Than long-considering Nature will or
    can,
Secure against his own mistakes,
Content with what life gives or takes,
And acting still on some fore-ordered
    plan,
A cog of iron in an iron wheel,
Too nicely poised to think or feel,
Dumb motor in a clock-like common-
    weal.
They wasted not their brain in schemes
Of what man might be in some bubble-
    sphere,
As if he must be other than he seems
Because he was not what he should be
    here,
Postponing Time's slow proof to petu-
    lant dreams :
Yet herein they were great
Beyond the incredulous lawgivers of
    yore,
And wiser than the wisdom of the shelf,
That they conceived a deeper-rooted
    state,
Of hardier growth, alive from rind to
    core,
By making man sole sponsor of him-
    self.

3.

God of our fathers, Thou who wast,
Art, and shalt be when those eye-wise
  who flout
Thy secret presence shall be lost
In the great light that dazzles them to
  doubt,
We, sprung from loins of stalwart
  men
Whose strength was in their trust

That Thou wouldst make thy dwelling
  in their dust
And walk with those a fellow-citizen
Who build a city of the just,
We, who believe Life's bases rest
Beyond the probe of chemic test,
Still, like our fathers, feel Thee near,
Sure that, while lasts the immutable
  decree,
The land to Human Nature dear
Shall not be unbeloved of Thee.

HEARTSEASE AND RUE.

Along the wayside where we pass bloom few
Gay plants of heartsease, more of saddening rue;
So life is mingled; so should poems be
That speak a conscious word to you and me.

I. FRIENDSHIP.

AGASSIZ.

Come
Dicesti *egli ebbe?* non viv' egli ancora?
Non fiere gli occhi suoi lo dolce lome?

I. I.

The electric nerve, whose instanta-
neous thrill
Makes next-door góssips of the anti-
podes,
Confutes poor Hope's last fallacy of
ease, —
The distance that divided her from ill:
Earth sentient seems again as when of
old
    The horny foot of Pan
Stamped, and the conscious horror
ran
Beneath men's feet through all her
fibres cold:
Space's blue walls are mined; we feel
the throe
From underground of our night-man-
tled foe:
    The flame-winged feet
Of Trade's new Mercury, that dry-shod
run
Through briny abysses dreamless of the
sun,
    Are mercilessly fleet,
And at a bound annihilate
Ocean's prerogative of short reprieve;
    Surely ill news might wait,
And man be patient of delay to grieve:
    Letters have sympathies
And tell-tale faces that reveal,
To senses finer than the eyes,
Their errand's purport ere we break
the seal;

They wind a sorrow round with circumstance
To stay its feet, nor all unwarned dis-
place
The veil that darkened from our sidelong glance
    The inexorable face:
    But now Fate stuns as with a
mace;
The savage of the skies, that men have
caught
    And some scant use of language
taught,
    Tells only what he must, —
The steel-cold fact in one laconic
thrust.

2.

So thought I, as, with vague, mechanic
eyes,
I scanned the festering news we half
despise
    Yet scramble for no less,
And read of public scandal, private
fraud,
Crime flaunting scot-free while the mob
applaud,
Office made vile to bribe unworthiness,
    And all the unwholesome mess
The Land of Honest Abraham serves
of late
    To teach the Old World how to
wait,
    When suddenly,
As happens if the brain, from over-
weight
    Of blood, infect the eye,
Three tiny words grew lurid as I read,
And reeled commingling: *Agassiz is
dead.*

As when, beneath the street's familiar
        jar,
An earthquake's alien omen rumbles
        far,
Men listen and forebode, I hung my
        head,
    And strove the present to recall,
As if the blow that stunned were yet to
        fall.

3.

Uprooted is our mountain oak,
That promised long security of shade
And brooding-place for many a wingèd
        thought;
    Not by Time's softly warning
        stroke
With pauses of relenting pity stayed,
But ere a root seemed sapt, a bough
        decayed,
From sudden ambush by the whirlwind
        caught
And in his broad maturity betrayed!

4.

Well might I, as of old, appeal to you,
    O mountains, woods and streams,
To help us mourn him, for ye loved
        him too;
    But simpler moods befit our mod-
        ern themes,
And no less perfect birth of nature can,
Though ye yearn tow'rd him, sympa-
        thize with man,
Save as dumb fellow-prisoners through
        a wall;
    Answer ye rather to my call,
Strong poets of a more unconscious
        day,
When Nature spake nor sought nice
        reasons why;
Too much for softer arts forgotten
        since
That teach our forthright tongue to
        lisp and mince,
And drown in music the heart's bitter
        cry!
Lead me some steps in your directer
        way,
Teach me those words that strike a
        solid root
    Within the ears of men;
Ye chiefly, virile both to think and feel,

Deep-chested Chapman and firm-footed
        Ben,—
For he was masculine from head to
        heel.
Nay, let himself stand undiminished by
With those clear parts of him that will
        not die.
Himself from out the recent dark I
        claim
To hear, and, if I flatter him, to
        blame;
To show himself, as still I seem to see,
A mortal, built upon the antique plan,
Brimful of lusty blood as ever ran,
And taking life as simply as a tree!
To claim my foiled good-bye let him
        appear,
Large-limbed and human as I saw him
        near,
Loosed from the stiffening uniform of
        fame:
And let me treat him largely: I should
        fear
(If with too prying lens I chanced to
        err,
Mistaking catalogue for character)
His wise forefinger raised in smiling
        blame.
Nor would I scant him with judicial
        breath
And turn mere critic in an epitaph;
I choose the wheat, incurious of the
        chaff
That swells fame living, chokes it after
        death,
And would but memorize the shining
        half
Of his large nature that was turned to
        me:
Fain had I joined with those that hon-
        ored him
With eyes that darkened because his
        were dim,
And now been silent: but it might not
        be.

II. I.

In some the genius is a thing apart,
    A pillared hermit of the brain,
Hoarding with incommunicable art
        Its intellectual gain;
    Man's web of circumstance and
        fate

They from their perch of self ob-
    serve,
Indifferent as the figures on a slate
    Are to the planet's sun - swung
      curve
    Whose bright returns they calcu-
      late ;
    Their nice adjustment, part to
      part,
Were shaken from its serviceable
    mood
By unpremeditated stirs of heart
    Or jar of human neighborhood :
Some find their natural selves, and only
    then,
In furloughs of divine escape from
    men,
And when, by that brief ecstasy left
    bare,
Driven by some instinct of desire,
They wander worldward, 't is to blink
    and stare,
Like wild things of the wood about a
    fire,
Dazed by the social glow they cannot
    share;
    His nature brooked no lonely lair,
But basked and bourgeoned in copart-
    nery,
Companionship, and open-windowed
    glee :
    He knew, for he had tried,
    Those speculative heights that lure
The unpractised foot, impatient of a
    guide,
Tow'rd ether too attenuately pure
For sweet unconscious breath, though
    dear to pride,
    But better loved the foothold sure
Of paths that wind by old abodes of
    men
Who hope at last the churchyard's
    peace secure,
And follow time-worn rules, that them
    suffice,
Learned from their sires, traditionally
    wise,
Careful of honest custom's how and
    when ;
His mind, too brave to look on Truth
    askance,
No more those habitudes of faith could
    share,
But, tinged with sweetness of the old
    Swiss manse,

Lingered around them still and fain
    would spare.
Patient to spy a sullen egg for weeks,
The enigma of creation to surprise,
His truer instinct sought the life that
    speaks
Without a mystery from kindly eyes;
In no self-spun cocoon of prudence
    wound,
He by the touch of men was best in-
    spired,
And caught his native greatness at re-
    bound
From generosities itself had fired ;
Then how the heat through every fibre
    ran,
Felt in the gathering presence of the
    man,
While the apt word and gesture came
    unbid !
Virtues and faults it to one metal
    wrought,
    Fined all his blood to thought,
And ran the molten man in all he said
    or did.
All Tully's rules and all Quintilian's
    too
He by the light of listening faces knew,
And his rapt audience all unconscious
    lent
Their own roused force to make him
    eloquent ;
Persuasion fondled in his look and
    tone ;
Our speech (with strangers prudish)
    he could bring
To find new charm in accents not her
    own ;
Her coy constraints and icy hindran-
    ces
Melted upon his lips to natural ease,
As a brook's fetters swell the dance of
    spring.
Nor yet all sweetness : not in vain he
    wore,
Nor in the sheath of ceremony, con-
    trolled
By velvet courtesy or caution cold,
That sword of honest anger prized of
    old,
    But, with two-handed wrath,
If baseness or pretension crossed his
    path,
    Struck once nor needed to strike
    more.

2.

His magic was not far to seek, —
He was so human! Whether strong
    or weak,
Far from his kind he neither sank nor
    soared,
But sate an equal guest at every board:
No beggar ever felt him condescend,
No prince presume; for still himself
    he bare
At manhood's simple level, and where-
    e'er
He met a stranger, there he left a
    friend.
How large an aspect! nobly unsevere,
With freshness round him of Olympian
    cheer,
Like visits of those earthly gods he
    came;
His look, wherever its good-fortune
    fell,
Doubled the feast without a miracle,
And on the hearthstone danced a hap-
    pier flame;
Philemon's crabbed vintage grew be-
    nign;
Amphitryon's gold-juice humanized to
    wine.

III. I.

The garrulous memories
Gather again from all their far-flown
    nooks,
Singly at first, and then by twos and
    threes,
Then in a throng innumerable, as the
    rooks
    Thicken their twilight files
Tow'rd Tintern's gray repose of roofless
    aisles:
Once more I see him at the table's
    head
When Saturday her monthly banquet
    spread
    To scholars, poets, wits,
All choice, some famous, loving things,
    not names,
And so without a twinge at others'
    fames;
Such company as wisest moods befits,
Yet with no pedant blindness to the
    worth
    Of undeliberate mirth,

Natures benignly mixed of air and
    earth,
Now with the stars and now with equal
    zest
Tracing the eccentric orbit of a jest.

2.

I see in vision the warm-lighted hall,
The living and the dead I see again,
And but my chair is empty; 'mid them
    all
'T is I that seem the dead: they all re-
    main
Immortal, changeless creatures of the
    brain:
Wellnigh I doubt which world is real
    most,
Of sense or spirit, to the truly sane;
In this abstraction it were light to
    deem
Myself the figment of some stronger
    dream;
They are the real things, and I the
    ghost
That glide unhindered through the
    solid door,
Vainly for recognition seek from chair
    to chair,
And strive to speak and am but futile
    air,
As truly most of us are little more.

3.

Him most I see whom we most dearly
    miss,
    The latest parted thence,
His features poised in genial armistice
And armed neutrality of self-defence
Beneath the forehead's walled preëmi-
    nence,
While Tyro, plucking facts with care-
    less reach,
Settles off-hand our human how and
    whence;
The long-trained veteran scarcely win-
    cing hears
The infallible strategy of volunteers
Making through Nature's walls its
    easy breach,
And seems to learn where he alone
    could teach.
Ample and ruddy, the board's end he
    fills

As he our fireside were, our light and
    heat,
Centre where minds diverse and various
    skills
Find their warm nook and stretch un-
    hampered feet;
I see the firm benignity of face,
Wide-smiling champaign, without tame-
    ness sweet,
The mass Teutonic toned to Gallic
    grace,
The eyes whose sunshine runs before
    the lips
While Holmes's rockets curve their
    long ellipse,
And burst in seeds of fire that burst
    again
      To drop in scintillating rain.

4.

There too the face half-rustic, half-
    divine,
Self-poised, sagacious, freaked with
    humor fine,
Of him who taught us not to mow
    and mope
About our fancied selves, but seek
    our scope
In Nature's world and Man's, nor fade
    to hollow trope,
Content with our New World and
    timely bold
To challenge the o'ermastery of the
    Old;
Listening with eyes averse I see
    him sit
Pricked with the cider of the Judge's
    wit
(Ripe-hearted homebrew, fresh and
    fresh again),
While the wise nose's firm-built
    aquiline
    Curves sharper to restrain
The merriment whose most unruly
    moods
Pass not the dumb laugh learned
    in listening woods
    Of silence-shedding pine:
Hard by is he whose art's consoling
    spell
Hath given both worlds a whiff of
    asphodel,
His look still vernal 'mid the wintry
    ring

Of petals that remember, not fore-
    tell,
The paler primrose of a second
    spring.

5.

And more there are: but other forms
    arise
And seen as clear, albeit with dimmer
    eyes:
First he from sympathy still held
    apart
By shrinking over-eagerness of heart,
Cloud charged with searching fire,
    whose shadow's sweep
Heightened mean things with sense of
    brooding ill,
And steeped in doom familiar field and
    hill, —
New England's poet, soul reserved and
    deep,
November nature with a name of May,
Whom high o'er Concord plains we
    laid to sleep,
While the orchards mocked us in their
    white array
And building robins wondered at our
    tears,
Snatched in his prime, the shape au-
    gust
That should have stood unbent 'neath
    fourscore years,
The noble head, the eyes of furtive trust,
    All gone to speechless dust.
    And he our passing guest,
Shy nature, too, and stung with life's
    unrest,
Whom we too briefly had but could not
    hold,
Who brought ripe Oxford's culture to
    our board,
    The Past's incalculable hoard,
Mellowed by scutcheoned panes in
    cloisters old,
Seclusions ivy-hushed, and pavements
    sweet
With immemorial lisp of musing feet;
Young head time-tonsured smoother
    than a friar's,
Boy face, but grave with answerless
    desires,
Poet in all that poets have of best,
But foiled with riddles dark and cloudy
    aims,
    Who now hath found sure rest,

Not by still Isis or historic Thames,
Nor by the Charles he tried to love
    with me,
  But, not misplaced, by Arno's hal-
    lowed brim,
Nor scorned by Santa Croce's neigh-
    boring fames,
    Haply not mindless, wheresoe'er
    he be,
  Of violets that to-day I scattered
    over him ;
    He, too, is there,
After the good centurion fitly named,
Whom learning dulled not, nor con-
    vention tamed,
Shaking with burly mirth his hyacin-
    thine hair,
  Our hearty Grecian of Homeric
    ways,
Still found the surer friend where
    least he hoped the praise.

6.

  Yea truly, as the sallowing years
Fall from us faster, like frost-loos-
    ened leaves
Pushed by the misty touch of shorten-
    ing days,
  And that unwakened winter nears,
'T is the void chair our surest guest
    receives,
'T is lips long cold that give the
    warmest kiss,
'T is the lost voice comes oftenest to
    our ears ;
We count our rosary by the beads
    we miss :
  To me, at least, it seemeth so,
An exile in the land once found di-
    vine,
  While my starved fire burns low,
And homeless winds at the loose
    casement whine
Shrill ditties of the snow-roofed
    Apennine.

IV. 1.

Now forth into the darkness all are
    gone,
But memory, still unsated, follows
    on,
Retracing step by step our homeward
    walk,

With many a laugh among our serious
    talk,
Across the bridge where, on the dim-
    pling tide,
The long red streamers from the win-
    dows glide,
    Or the dim western moon
Rocks her skiff's image on the broad
    lagoon,
And Boston shows a soft Venetian
    side
In that Arcadian light when roof and
    tree,
Hard prose by daylight, dream in
    Italy ;
Or haply in the sky's cold chambers
    wide
Shivered the winter stars, while all
    below,
As if an end were come of human ill,
The world was wrapt in innocence of
    snow
And the cast-iron bay was blind and
    still ;
These were our poetry ; in him per-
    haps
Science had barred the gate that lets
    in dream,
And he would rather count the perch
    and bream
Than with the current's idle fancy
    lapse ;
And yet he had the poet's open eye
That takes a frank delight in all it
    sees,
Nor was earth voiceless, nor the mys-
    tic sky,
To him the life-long friend of fields
    and trees :
Then came the prose of the suburban
    street,
Its silence deepened by our echoing
    feet,
And converse such as rambling haz-
    ard finds ;
Then he who many cities knew and
    many minds,
And men once world-noised, now mere
    Ossian forms
Of misty memory, bade them live
    anew
As when they shared earth's manifold
    delight,
In shape, in gait, in voice, in gesture
    true,

And, with an accent brightening as he
    warms,
Would stop forgetful of the shortening
    night,
Drop my confining arm, and pour pro-
    fuse
Much worldly wisdom kept for others'
    use,
Not for his own, for he was rash and
    free,
His purse or knowledge all men's, like
    the sea.
Still can I hear his voice's shrilling
    might
(With pauses broken, while the fitful
    spark
He blew more hotly rounded on the
    dark
To hint his features with a Rembrandt
    light)
Call Oken back, or Humboldt, or La-
    marck,
Or Cuvier's taller shade, and many
    more
Whom he had seen, or knew from oth-
    ers' sight,
And make them men to me as ne'er
    before :
Not seldom, as the undeadened fibre
    stirred
Of noble friendships knit beyond the
    sea,
German or French thrust by the lag-
    ging word,
For a good leash of mother-tongues
    had he.
At last, arrived at where our paths di-
    vide,
" Good night ! " and, ere the distance
    grew too wide,
" Good night ! " again ; and now with
    cheated ear
I half hear his who mine shall never
    hear.

2.

Sometimes it seemed as if New Eng-
    land air
For his large lungs too parsimonious
    were,
As if those empty rooms of dogma
    drear
Where the ghost shivers of a faith
    austere

Counting the horns o'er of the
    Beast,
Still scaring those whose faith in it is
    least,
As if those snaps o' th' moral atmos-
    phere
That sharpen all the needles of the
    East,
Had been to him like death,
Accustomed to draw Europe's freer
    breath
    In a more stable element ;
Nay, even our landscape, half the
    year morose,
Our practical horizon grimly pent,
Our air, sincere of ceremonious haze,
Forcing hard outlines mercilessly
    close,
Our social monotone of level days,
    Might make our best seem banish-
    ment ;
        But it was nothing so ;
Haply his instinct might divine,
Beneath our drift of puritan snow,
    The marvel sensitive and fine
Of sanguinaria over-rash to blow
And trust its shyness to an air ma-
    lign ;
Well might he prize truth's warranty
    and pledge
In the grim outcrop of our granite
    edge,
Or Hebrew fervor flashing forth at
    need
In the gaunt sons of Calvin's iron
    breed,
As prompt to give as skilled to win
    and keep ;
But, though such intuitions might
    not cheer,
Yet life was good to him, and, there
    or here,
With that sufficing joy, the day was
    never cheap ;
Thereto his mind was its own ample
    sphere,
And, like those buildings great that
    through the year
Carry one temperature, his nature
    large
Made its own climate, nor could any
    marge
Traced by convention stay him from
    his bent :
He had a habitude of mountain air ;

He brought wide outlook where he
    went,
    And could on sunny uplands dwell
Of prospect sweeter than the pastures
    fair
High-hung of viny Neufchâtel;
    Nor, surely, did he miss
      Some pale, imaginary bliss
Of earlier sights whose inner landscape
    still was Swiss.

v. 1.

I cannot think he wished so soon to
    die
With all his senses full of eager heat,
And rosy years that stood expectant
    by
To buckle the winged sandals on
    their feet,
He that was friends with earth, and
    all her sweet
Took with both hands unsparingly:
Truly this life is precious to the
    root,
And good the feel of grass beneath
    the foot;
To lie in buttercups and clover-
    bloom,
    Tenants in common with the bees,
And watch the white clouds drift
    through gulfs of trees,
Is better than long waiting in the
    tomb;
Only once more to feel the coming
    spring
As the birds feel it when it bids them
    sing,
Only once more to see the moon
Through leaf-fringed abbey-arches of
    the elms
Curve her mild sickle in the West
Sweet with the breath of hay-cocks,
    were a boon
Worth any promise of soothsayer
    realms
Or casual hope of being elsewhere
    blest;
    To take December by the beard
And crush the creaking snow with
    springy foot,
While overhead the North's dumb
    streamers shoot,
Till Winter fawn upon the cheek en-
    deared,

    Then the long evening-ends
Lingered by cosy chimney-nooks,
With high companionship of books
    Or slippered talk of friends
      And sweet habitual looks,
Is better than to stop the ears with
    dust:
Too soon the spectre comes to say,
    "Thou must!"

2.

When toil-crooked hands are crost
    upon the breast,
    They comfort us with sense of
    rest;
They must be glad to lie forever
    still;
    Their work is ended with their
    day;
Another fills their room; 't is the
    World's ancient way,
    Whether for good or ill;
But the deft spinners of the brain,
Who love each added day and find
    it gain,
    Them overtakes the doom
To snap the half-grown flower upon
    the loom
(Trophy that was to be of life-long
    pain),
The thread no other skill can ever
    knit again.
    'T was so with him, for he was
    glad to live,
    'T was doubly so, for he left work
    begun;
Could not this eagerness of Fate
    forgive
Till all the allotted flax were spun?
It matters not; for, go at night or
    noon,
A friend, whene'er he dies, has died
    too soon,
And, once we hear the hopeless *He is
    dead*,
So far as flesh hath knowledge, all is
    said.

VI. 1.

I seem to see the black procession
    go:
    That crawling prose of death too
    well I know,

The vulgar paraphrase of glorious
  woe;
I see it wind through that unsightly
  grove,
Once beautiful, but long defaced
With granite permanence of cockney
  taste
And all those grim disfigurements we
  love:
There, then, we leave him: Him?
  such costly waste
Nature rebels at: and it is not true
Of those most precious parts of him we
  knew:
Could we be conscious but as dream-
  ers be,
'T were sweet to leave this shifting
  life of tents
Sunk in the changeless calm of
  Deity;
Nay, to be mingled with the elements,
The fellow-servant of creative
  powers,
Partaker in the solemn year's
  events,
To share the work of busy-fingered
  hours,
To be night's silent almoner of dew,
To rise again in plants and breathe
  and grow,
To stream as tides the ocean caverns
  through,
Or with the rapture of great winds to
  blow
About earth's shaken coignes, were
  not a fate
To leave us all-disconsolate;
Even endless slumber in the sweeten-
  ing sod
  Of charitable earth
That takes out all our mortal stains,
And makes us cleanlier neighbors of
  the clod,
Methinks were better worth
Than the poor fruit of most men's
  wakeful pains,
  The heart's insatiable ache:
But such was not his faith,
Nor mine: it may be he had trod
Outside the plain old path of *God thus
  spake,*
  But God to him was very God,
  And not a visionary wraith
Skulking in murky corners of the
  mind,

And he was sure to be
Somehow, somewhere, imperishable as
  He,
Not with His essence mystically com-
  bined,
As some high spirits long, but whole
  and free,
  A perfected and conscious Agassiz.
And such I figure him: the wise of
  old
Welcome and own him of their peace-
  ful fold,
  Not truly with the guild enrolled
Of him who seeking inward guessed
Diviner riddles than the rest,
And groping in the darks of thought
Touched the Great Hand and knew
  it not;
Rather he shares the daily light,
From reason's charier fountains won,
Of his great chief, the slow-paced
  Stagyrite,
And Cuvier clasps once more his long-
  lost son.

2.

The shape erect is prone: forever
  stilled
The winning tongue; the forehead's
  high-piled heap,
A cairn which every science helped to
  build,
Unvalued will its golden secrets keep:
He knows at last if Life or Death be
  best:
Wherever he be flown, whatever vest
The being hath put on which lately
  here
So many-friended was, so full of cheer
To make men feel the Seeker's noble
  zest,
We have not lost him all; he is not
  gone
To the dumb herd of them that wholly
  die;
The beauty of his better self lives on
In minds he touched with fire, in many
  an eye
He trained to Truth's exact severity;
He was a Teacher: why be grieved for
  him
Whose living word still stimulates the
  air?
In endless file shall loving scholars
  come

The glow of his transmitted touch to
  share,
And trace his features with an eye less
  dim
Than ours whose sense familiar wont
  makes numb.

FLORENCE, ITALY, *February,* 1874.

TO HOLMES

ON HIS SEVENTY-FIFTH BIRTHDAY.

DEAR Wendell, why need count the
    years
  Since first your genius made me
    thrill,
If what moved then to smiles or tears,
  Or both contending, move me still?

What has the Calendar to do
  With poets? What Time's fruitless
    tooth
With gay immortals such as you
  Whose years but emphasize your
    youth?

One air gave both their lease of
    breath;
  The same paths lured our boyish
    feet;
One earth will hold us safe in death,
  With dust of saints and scholars
    sweet.

Our legends from one source were
    drawn,
  I scarce distinguish yours from mine,
And *don't* we make the Gentiles yawn
  With " You remembers?" o'er our
    wine!

If I, with too senescent air,
  Invade your elder memory's pale,
You snub me with a pitying " Where
  Were you in the September Gale?"

Both stared entranced at Lafayette,
  Saw Jackson dubbed with LL. D.
What Cambridge saw not strikes us yet
  As scarcely worth one's while to see.

Ten years my senior, when my name
  In Harvard's entrance-book was
    writ,

Her halls still echoed with the fame
  Of you, her poet and her wit.

'T is fifty years from then to now:
  But your Last Leaf renews its green,
Though, for the laurels on your brow
  (So thick they crowd), 't is hardly
    seen.

The oriole's fledglings fifty times
  Have flown from our familiar elms;
As many poets with their rhymes
  Oblivion's darkling dust o'erwhelms.

The birds are hushed, the poets gone
  Where no harsh critic's lash can
    reach,
And still your wingèd brood sing on
  To all who love our English speech.

Nay, let the foolish records be
  That make believe you 're seventy-
    five;
You 're the old Wendell still to me, —
  And that 's the youngest man alive.

The gray-blue eyes, I see them still,
  The gallant front with brown o'er-
    hung,
The shape alert, the wit at will,
  The phrase that stuck, but never
    stung.

You keep your youth as yon Scotch
    firs,
  Whose gaunt line my horizon hems,
Though twilight all the lowland blurs,
  Hold sunset in their ruddy stems.

You with the elders? Yes, 't is true,
  But in no sadly literal sense,
With elders and coevals too,
  Whose verb admits no preterite tense.

Master alike in speech and song
  Of fame's great antiseptic — Style,
You with the classic few belong
  Who tempered wisdom with a smile.

Outlive us all! Who else like you
  Could sift the seedcorn from our
    chaff,
And make us with the pen we knew
  Deathless at least in epitaph?

WOLLASTON, *August* 29, 1884.

IN A COPY OF OMAR KHAY-YÁM.

These pearls of thought in Persian
    gulfs were bred,
Each softly lucent as a rounded moon;
The diver Omar plucked them from
    their bed,
Fitzgerald strung them on an English
    thread.

Fit rosary for a queen, in shape and
    hue,
When Contemplation tells her pensive
    beads
Of mortal thoughts, forever old and
    new.
Fit for a queen? Why, surely then for
    you!

The moral? Where Doubt's eddies
    toss and twirl
Faith's slender shallop till her footing
    reel,
Plunge: if you find not peace beneath
    the whirl,
Groping, you may like Omar grasp a
    pearl.

ON RECEIVING A COPY OF MR. AUSTIN DOBSON'S "OLD WORLD IDYLLS."

I.

At length arrived, your book I take
To read in for the author's sake.
Too gray for new sensations grown,
Can charm to Art or Nature known
This torpor from my senses shake?

Hush! my parched ears what runnels
    slake?
Is a thrush gurgling from the brake?
Has Spring, on all the breezes blown,
At length arrived?

Long may you live such songs to
    make,
And I to listen while you wake,
With skill of late disused, each tone
Of the *Lesboum barbiton*,
At mastery, through long finger-ache,
At length arrived.

II.

As I read on, what changes steal
O'er me and through, from head to
    heel?
A rapier thrusts coat-skirt aside,
My rough Tweeds bloom to silken
    pride,
Who was it laughed? Your hand, Dick
    Steele!

Down vistas long of clipt *charmille*
Watteau as Pierrot leads the reel;
Tabor and pipe the dancers guide
As I read on.

While in and out the verses wheel
The wind-caught robes trim feet reveal,
Lithe ankles that to music glide,
But chastely and by chance descried;
Art? Nature? Which do I most feel
As I read on?

TO C. F. BRADFORD

ON THE GIFT OF A MEERSCHAUM PIPE.

The pipe came safe, and welcome too,
As anything must be from you;
A meerschaum pure, 't would float as
    light
As she the girls call Amphitrite.
Mixture divine of foam and clay,
From both it stole the best away:
Its foam is such as crowns the glow
Of beakers brimmed by Veuve Clic-
    quot;
Its clay is but congested lymph
Jove chose to make some choicer
    nymph;
And here combined, — why, this must
    be
The birth of some enchanted sea,
Shaped to immortal form, the type
And very Venus of a pipe.

When high I heap it with the weed
From Lethe wharf, whose potent seed
Nicotia, big from Bacchus, bore
And cast upon Virginia's shore,
I 'll think, — So fill the fairer bowl
And wise alembic of thy soul,
With herbs far-sought that shall distil,
Not fumes to slacken thought and
    will,

But bracing essences that nerve
To wait, to dare, to strive, to serve.

When curls the smoke in eddies soft,
And hangs a shifting dream aloft,
That gives and takes, though chance-
    designed,
The impress of the dreamer's mind,
I 'll think, — So let the vapors bred
By Passion, in the heart or head,
Pass off and upward into space,
Waving farewells of tenderest grace,
Remembered in some happier time,
To blend their beauty with my rhyme.

While slowly o'er its candid bowl
The color deepens (as the soul
That burns in mortals leaves its trace
Of bale or beauty on the face),
I 'll think, — So let the essence rare
Of years consuming make me fair;
So, 'gainst the ills of life profuse,
Steep me in some narcotic juice;
And if my soul must part with all
That whiteness which we greenness
    call,
Smooth back, O Fortune, half thy
    frown,
And make me beautifully brown!

Dream-forger, I refill thy cup
With reverie's wasteful pittance up,
And while the fire burns slow away,
Hiding itself in ashes gray,
I 'll think, — As inward Youth re-
    treats,
Compelled to spare his wasting heats,
When Life's Ash-Wednesday comes
    about,
And my head 's gray with fires burnt out,
While stays one spark to light the eye,
With the last flash of memory,
'T will leap to welcome C. F. B.,
Who sent my favorite pipe to me.

BANKSIDE.

(HOME OF EDMUND QUINCY.)

DEDHAM, MAY 21, 1877.

I.

I CHRISTENED you in happier days,
    before
These gray forebodings on my brow
    were seen;

You are still lovely in your new-leaved
    green;
The brimming river soothes his grassy
    shore;
The bridge is there; the rock with
    lichens hoar;
And the same shadows on the water
    lean,
Outlasting us. How many graves be-
    tween
That day and this! How many shad-
    ows more
Darken my heart, their substance from
    these eyes
Hidden forever! So our world is
    made
Of life and death commingled; and the
    sighs
Outweigh the smiles, in equal balance
    laid:
What compensation? None, save that
    the Allwise
So schools us to love things that can-
    not fade.

II.

Thank God, he saw you last in pomp
    of May,
Ere any leaf had felt the year's regret;
Your latest image in his memory set
Was fair as when your landscape's
    peaceful sway
Charmed dearer eyes with his to make
    delay
On Hope's long prospect, — as if
    They forget
The happy, They, the unspeakable
    Three, whose debt,
Like the hawk's shadow, blots our
    brightest day:
Better it is that ye should look so
    fair,
Slopes that he loved, and ever-mur-
    muring pines
That make a music out of silent air,
And bloom-heaped orchard-trees in
    prosperous lines;
In you the heart some sweeter hints
    divines,
And wiser, than in winter's dull despair.

III.

Old Friend, farewell! Your kindly
    door again
I enter, but the master's hand in mine

No more clasps welcome, and the tem-
   perate wine,
That cheered our long nights, other
   lips must stain:
All is unchanged, but I expect in vain
The face alert, the manners free and
   fine,
The seventy years borne lightly as the
   pine
Wears its first down of snow in green
   disdain:
Much did he, and much well; yet most
   of all
I prized his skill in leisure and the ease
Of a life flowing full without a plan;
For most are idly busy; him I call
Thrice fortunate who knew himself to
   please,
Learned in those arts that make a
   gentleman.

IV.

Nor deem he lived unto himself alone;
His was the public spirit of his sire,
And in those eyes, soft with domestic
   fire,
A quenchless light of fiercer temper
   shone
What time about the world our shame
   was blown
On every wind; his soul would not
   conspire
With selfish men to soothe the mob's
   desire,
Veiling with garlands Moloch's bloody
   stone;
The high-bred instincts of a better day
Ruled in his blood, when to be citizen
Rang Roman yet, and a Free People's
   sway
Was not the exchequer of impoverished
   men,
Nor statesmanship with loaded votes
   to play,
Nor public office a tramps' boosing-
   ken.

JOSEPH WINLOCK.

DIED JUNE 11, 1875.

SHY soul and stalwart, man of patient
   will
Through years one hair's-breadth on
   our Dark to gain,

Who, from the stars he studied not in
   vain,
Had learned their secret to be strong
   and still,
Careless of fames that earth's tin trum-
   pets fill;
Born under Leo, broad of build and
   brain,
While others slept, he watched in that
   hushed fane
Of Science, only witness of his skill:
Sudden as falls a shooting-star he fell,
But inextinguishable his luminous trace
In mind and heart of all that knew him
   well.
Happy man's doom! To him the Fates
   were known
Of orbs dim hovering on the skirts of
   space,
Unprescient, through God's mercy, of
   his own!

SONNET.

TO FANNY ALEXANDER.

UNCONSCIOUS as the sunshine, simply
   sweet
And generous as that, thou dost not
   close
Thyself in art, as life were but a rose
To rumple bee-like with luxurious
   feet;
Thy higher mind therein finds sure
   retreat,
But not from care of common hopes
   and woes;
Thee the dark chamber, thee the un-
   friended, knows,
Although no babbling crowds thy praise
   repeat:
Consummate artist, who life's landscape bleak
Hast brimmed with sun to many a
   clouded eye,
Touched to a brighter hue the beggar's
   cheek,
Hung over orphaned lives a gracious
   sky,
And traced for eyes, that else would
   vainly seek,
Fair pictures of an angel drawing
   nigh!

FLORENCE, 1873.

JEFFRIES WYMAN.

DIED SEPTEMBER 4, 1874.

THE wisest man could ask no more of
  Fate
Than to be simple, modest, manly,
  true,
Safe from the Many, honored by the
  Few ;
To count as naught in World, or
  Church, or State,
But inwardly in secret to be great ;
To feel mysterious Nature ever new ;
To touch, if not to grasp, her endless
  clue,
And learn by each discovery how to
  wait.
He widened knowledge and escaped the
  praise ;
He wisely taught, because more wise to
  learn ;
He toiled for Science, not to draw
  men's gaze,
But for her lore of self-denial stern.
That such a man could spring from our
  decays
Fans the soul's nobler faith until it
  burn.

TO A FRIEND

WHO GAVE ME A GROUP OF WEEDS
  AND GRASSES, AFTER A DRAWING
  OF DÜRER.

TRUE as the sun's own work, but more
  refined,
It tells of love behind the artist's eye,
Of sweet companionships with earth
  and sky,
And summers stored, the sunshine of
  the mind.
What peace ! Sure, ere you breathe,
  the fickle wind
Will break its truce and bend that
  grass-plume high,
Scarcely yet quiet from the gilded fly
That flits a more luxurious perch to
  find.
Thanks for a pleasure that can never
  pall,
A serene moment, deftly caught and
  kept

To make immortal summer on my
  wall.
Had he who drew such gladness ever
  wept ?
Ask rather could he else have seen at
  all,
Or grown in Nature's mysteries an
  adept ?

WITH AN ARMCHAIR.

I.

ABOUT the oak that framed this chair,
  of old
The seasons danced their round ; de-
  lighted wings
Brought music to its boughs ; shy
  woodland things
Shared its broad roof, 'neath whose
  green glooms grown bold,
Lovers, more shy than they, their secret
  told ;
The resurrection of a thousand springs
Swelled in its veins, and dim imagin-
  ings
Teased them, perchance, of life more
  manifold.
Such shall it know when its proud
  arms enclose
My Lady Goshawk, musing here at
  rest,
Careless of him who into exile goes,
Yet, while his gift by those fair limbs is
  prest,
Through some fine sympathy of nature
  knows
That, seas between us, she is still his
  guest.

II.

Yet sometimes, let me dream, the conscious wood
A momentary vision may renew
Of him who counts it treasure that he
  knew,
Though but in passing, such a priceless
  good,
And, like an elder brother, felt his
  mood
Uplifted by the spell that kept her
  true,
Amid her lightsome compeers, to the
  few

That wear the crown of serious woman-
hood:
Were he so happy, think of him as one
Who in the Louvre or Pitti feels his
soul
Rapt by some dead face which, till then
unseen,
Moves like a memory and, till life outrun,
Is vexed with vague misgiving, past
control,
Of nameless loss and thwarted might-
have-been.

E. G. DE R.

WHY should I seek her spell to decom-
pose
Or to its source each rill of influence
trace
That feeds the brimming river of her
grace?
The petals numbered but degrade to
prose
Summer's triumphant poem of the
rose:
Enough for me to watch the wavering
chase,
Like wind o'er grass, of moods across
her face,
Fairest in motion, fairer in repose.
Steeped in her sunshine, let me, while
I may,
Partake the bounty: ample 't is for me
That her mirth cheats my temples of
their gray,
Her charm makes years long spent
seem yet to be.
Wit, goodness, grace, swift flash from
grave to gay, —
All these are good, but better far is she.

BON VOYAGE!

SHIP, blest to bear such freight across
the blue,
May stormless stars control thy horo-
scope;
In keel and hull, in every spar and
rope,
Be night and day to thy dear office
true!
Ocean, men's path and their divider
too,
No fairer shrine of memory and hope

To the underworld adown thy wester-
ing slope
E'er vanished, or whom such regrets
pursue:
Smooth all thy surges as when Jove to
Crete
Swam with less costly burthen, and
prepare
A pathway meet for her home-coming
soon
With golden undulations such as greet
The printless summer-sandals of the
moon
And tempt the Nautilus his cruise to
dare!

TO WHITTIER.

ON HIS SEVENTY-FIFTH BIRTHDAY.

NEW ENGLAND's poet, rich in love as
years,
Her hills and valleys praise thee, her
swift brooks
Dance in thy verse; to her grave
sylvan nooks
Thy steps allure us, which the wood-
thrush hears
As maids their lovers', and no treason
fears;
Through thee her Merrimacs and Agio-
chooks
And many a name uncouth win gracious
looks,
Sweetly familiar to both Englands'
ears:
Peaceful by birthright as a virgin lake,
The lily's anchorage, which no eyes
behold
Save those of stars, yet for thy brother's sake
That lay in bonds, thou blewst a blast
as bold
As that wherewith the heart of Roland
brake,
Far heard across the New World and
the Old.

ON AN AUTUMN SKETCH OF
H. G. WILD.

THANKS to the artist, ever on my wall
The sunset stays: that hill in glory
rolled,

Those trees and clouds in crimson and
    in gold,
Burn on, nor cool when evening's
    shadows fall.
Not round *these* splendors Midnight
    wraps her pall;
These leaves the flush of Autumn's
    vintage hold
In Winter's spite, nor can the North-
    wind bold
Deface my chapel's western window
    small:
On one, ah me! October struck his
    frost,
But not repaid him with those Tyrian
    hues;
His naked boughs but tell him what is
    lost,
And parting comforts of the sun re-
    fuse:
His heaven is bare, — ah, were its hol-
    low crost
Even with a cloud whose light were
    yet to lose!

April, 1854.

TO MISS D. T.

ON HER GIVING ME A DRAWING OF LITTLE STREET ARABS.

As, cleansed of Tiber's and Oblivion's
    slime,
Glow Farnesina's vaults with shapes
    again
That dreamed some exiled artist from
    his pain
Back to his Athens and the Muse's
    clime,
So these world-orphaned waifs of Want
    and Crime,
Purged by Art's absolution from the
    stain
Of the polluting city-flood, regain
Ideal grace secure from taint of time.
An Attic frieze you give, a pictured
    song;
For as with words the poet paints, for
    you
The happy pencil at its labor sings,
Stealing his privilege, nor does him
    wrong,
Beneath the false discovering the true,
And Beauty's best in unregarded things.

WITH A COPY OF AUCASSIN AND NICOLETE.

LEAVES fit to have been poor Juliet's
    cradle-rhyme,
With gladness of a heart long quenched
    in mould
They vibrate still, a nest not yet grown
    cold
From its fledged burthen. The numb
    hand of Time
Vainly his glass turns; here is endless
    prime;
Here lips their roses keep and locks
    their gold;
Here Love in pristine innocency bold
Speaks what our grosser conscience
    makes a crime.
Because it tells the dream that all have
    known
Once in their lives, and to life's end the
    few;
Because its seeds o'er Memory's desert
    blown
Spring up in heartsease such as Eden
    knew;
Because it hath a beauty all its own,
Dear Friend, I plucked this herb of
    grace for you.

ON PLANTING A TREE AT IN-VERARAY.

WHO does his duty is a question
Too complex to be solved by me,
But he, I venture the suggestion,
Does part of his that plants a tree.

For after he is dead and buried,
And epitaphed, and well forgot,
Nay, even his shade by Charon fer-
    ried
To — let us not inquire to what,

His deed, its author long outliving,
By Nature's mother-care increased,
Shall stand, his verdant almoner, giv-
    ing
A kindly dole to man and beast.

The wayfarer, at noon reposing,
Shall bless its shadow on the grass,
Or sheep beneath it huddle, dozing
Until the thundergust o'erpass.

The owl, belated in his plundering,
Shall here await the friendly night,
Blinking whene'er he wakes, and won-
    dering
What fool it was invented light.

Hither the busy birds shall flutter,
With the light timber for their nests,
And, pausing from their labor, utter
The morning sunshine in their breasts.

What though his memory shall have
    vanished,
Since the good deed he did survives?
It is not wholly to be banished
Thus to be part of many lives.

Grow, then, my foster-child, and
    strengthen,
Bough over bough, a murmurous pile,
And as your stately stem shall lengthen,
So may the statelier of Argyll!

1880.

AN EPISTLE TO GEORGE WIL-
LIAM CURTIS.

" De prodome,
Des qu'il s'atorne a grant bonte
Ja n'iert tot dit ne tot conte,
Que leingue ne puet pas retraire
Tant d'enor com prodom set faire."
            CRESTIEN DE TROIES,
Li Romans dou Chevalier au Lyon, 784-788.

1874.

CURTIS, whose Wit, with Fancy arm in
    arm,
Masks half its muscle in its skill to
    charm,
And who so gently can the Wrong ex-
    pose
As sometimes to make converts, never
    foes,
Or only such as good men must ex-
    pect,
Knaves sore with conscience of their
    own defect,
I come with mild remonstrance. Ere I
    start,
A kindlier errand interrupts my heart,
And I must utter, though it vex your
    ears,
The love, the honor, felt so many years.

Curtis, skilled equally with voice and
    pen
To stir the hearts or mould the minds
    of men, —
That voice whose music, for I 've heard
    you sing
Sweet as Casella, can with passion
    ring,
That pen whose rapid ease ne'er trips
    with haste,
Nor scrapes nor sputters, pointed with
    good taste,
First Steele's, then Goldsmith's, next it
    came to you,
Whom Thackeray rated best of all our
    crew, —
Had letters kept you, every wreath were
    yours;
Had the World tempted, all its chariest
    doors
Had swung on flattered hinges to ad-
    mit
Such high-bred manners, such good-
    natured wit;
At courts, in senates, who so fit to
    serve?
And both invited, but you would not
    swerve,
All meaner prizes waiving that you might
In civic duty spend your heat and light,
Unpaid, untrammelled, with a sweet
    disdain
Refusing posts men grovel to attain.
Good Man all own you; what is left
    me, then,
To heighten praise with but Good
    Citizen?

But why this praise to make you blush
    and stare,
And give a backache to your Easy-
    Chair?
Old Crestien rightly says no language
    can
Express the worth of a true Gentle-
    man,
And I agree; but other thoughts deride
My first intent, and lure my pen aside.
Thinking of you, I see my firelight
    glow
On other faces, loved from long ago,
Dear to us both, and all these loves
    combine
With this I send and crowd in every
    line;

Fortune with me was in such gener-
ous mood
That all my friends were yours, and all
were good;
Three generations come where one I
call,
And the fair grandame, youngest of
them all,
In her own Florida who found and sips
The fount that fled from Ponce's long-
ing lips.
How bright they rise and wreathe my
hearthstone round,
Divine my thoughts, reply without a
sound,
And with them many a shape that mem-
ory sees,
As dear as they, but crowned with au-
reoles these!
What wonder if, with protest in my
thought,
Arrived, I find 't was only love I
brought?
I came with protest; Memory barred
the road
Till I repaid you half the debt I owed.

No, 't was not to bring laurels that I
came,
Nor would you wish it, daily seeing
fame,
(Or our cheap substitute, unknown of
yore,)
Dumped like a load of coal at every
door,
Mime and hetæra getting equal weight
With him whose toils heroic saved the
State.
But praise can harm not who so calmly
met
Slander's worst word, nor treasured up
the debt,
Knowing, what all experience serves to
show,
No mud can soil us but the mud we
throw.
You have heard harsher voices and
more loud,
As all must, not sworn liegemen of the
crowd,
And far aloof your silent mind could
keep
As when, in heavens with winter-mid-
night deep,

The perfect moon hangs thoughtful, nor
can know
What hounds her lucent calm drives
mad below.

But to my business, while you rub your
eyes
And wonder how you ever thought me
wise.
Dear friend and old, they say you shake
your head
And wish some bitter words of mine un-
said:
I wish they might be, — there we are
agreed;
I hate to speak, still more what makes
the need;
But I must utter what the voice within
Dictates, for acquiescence dumb were
sin;
I blurt ungrateful truths, if so they
be,
That none may need to say them after
me.
'T were my felicity could I attain
The temperate zeal that balances your
brain;
But nature still o'erleaps reflection's
plan,
And one must do his service as he
can.
Think you it were not pleasanter to
speak
Smooth words that leave unflushed the
brow and cheek?
To sit well-dined, with cynic smile, un-
seen
In private box, spectator of the scene
Where men the comedy of life re-
hearse,
Idly to judge which better and which
worse
Each hireling actor spoiled his worth-
less part?
Were it not sweeter with a careless
heart,
In happy commune with the untainted
brooks,
To dream all day, or, walled with silent
books,
To hear nor heed the World's unmean-
ing noise,
Safe in my fortress stored with lifelong
joys?

I love too well the pleasures of retreat
Safe from the crowd and cloistered from
  the street;
The fire that whispers its domestic joy,
Flickering on walls that knew me still a
  boy,
And knew my saintly father; the full
  days,
Not careworn from the world's soul-
  squandering ways,
Calm days that loiter with snow-silent
  tread,
Nor break my commune with the undy-
  ing dead;
Truants of Time, to-morrow like to-
  day,
That come unbid, and claimless glide
  away
By shelves that sun them in the indul-
  gent Past,
Where Spanish castles, even, were
  built to last,
Where saint and sage their silent vigil
  keep,
And wrong hath ceased or sung itself to
  sleep.
Dear were my walks, too, gathering fra-
  grant store
Of Mother Nature's simple-minded
  lore;
I learned all weather-signs of day or
  night;
No bird but I could name him by his
  flight,
No distant tree but by his shape was
  known,
Or, near at hand, by leaf or bark alone.
This learning won by loving looks I
  hived
As sweeter lore than all from books derived.
I know the charm of hillside, field, and
  wood,
Of lake and stream, and the sky's downy
  brood,
Of roads sequestered rimmed with sallow sod,
But friends with hardhack, aster, gold-
  enrod,
Or succory keeping summer long its
  trust
Of heaven-blue fleckless from the eddying dust:
These were my earliest friends, and
  latest too,

Still unestranged, whatever fate may do.
For years I had these treasures, knew
  their worth,
Estate most real man can have on earth.
I sank too deep in this soft-stuffed re-
  pose
That hears but rumors of earth's wrongs
  and woes;
Too well these Capuas could my mus-
  cles waste,
Not void of toils, but toils of choice and
  taste;
These still had kept me could I but have
  quelled
The Puritan drop that in my veins re-
  belled.
But there were times when silent were
  my books
As jailers are, and gave me sullen looks,
When verses palled, and even the wood-
  land path,
By innocent contrast, fed my heart with
  wrath,
And I must twist my little gift of words
Into a scourge of rough and knotted
  cords
Unmusical, that whistle as they swing
To leave on shameless backs their
  purple sting.

How slow Time comes! Gone, who so
  swift as he?
Add but a year, 't is half a century
Since the slave's stifled moaning broke
  my sleep,
Heard 'gainst my will in that seclusion
  deep,
Haply heard louder for the silence
  there,
And so my fancied safeguard made my
  snare.
After that moan had sharpened to a
  cry,
And the cloud, hand-broad then, heaped
  all our sky
With its stored vengeance, and such
  thunders stirred
As heaven's and earth's remotest cham-
  bers heard,
I looked to see an ampler atmosphere
By that electric passion-gust blown
  clear.
I looked for this; consider what I see —
But I forbear, 't would please nor you
  nor me

To check the items in the bitter list
Of all I counted on and all I mist.
Only three instances I choose from all,
And each enough to stir a pigeon's gall:
Office a fund for ballot-brokers made
To pay the drudges of their gainful
    trade;
Our cities taught what conquered cities
    feel
By ædiles chosen that they might safely
    steal;
And gold, however got, a title fair
To such respect as only gold can bear.
I seem to see this; how shall I gainsay
What all our journals tell me every
    day?
Poured our young martyrs their high-
    hearted blood
That we might trample to congenial
    mud
The soil with such a legacy sublimed?
Methinks an angry scorn is here well-
    timed:
Where find retreat? How keep re-
    proach at bay?
Where'er I turn some scandal fouls the
    way.

Dear friend, if any man I wished to
    please,
'T were surely you whose humor's
    honied ease
Flows flecked with gold of thought,
    whose generous mind
Sees Paradise regained by all mankind,
Whose brave example still to vanward
    shines,
Checks the retreat, and spurs our lag-
    ging lines.
Was I too bitter? Who his phrase can
    choose
That sees the life-blood of his dearest
    ooze?
I loved my Country so as only they
Who love a mother fit to die for may;
I loved her old renown, her stainless
    fame,—
What better proof than that I loathed
    her shame?
That many blamed me could not irk me
    long,
But, if you doubted, must I not be
    wrong?
'T is not for me to answer: this I
    know,

That man or race so prosperously low
Sunk in success that wrath they cannot
    feel,
Shall taste the spurn of parting For-
    tune's heel;
For never land long lease of empire
    won
Whose sons sate silent when base deeds
    were done.

POSTSCRIPT, 1887.

Curtis, so wrote I thirteen years ago,
Tost it unfinished by, and left it so;
Found lately, I have pieced it out, or
    tried,
Since time for callid juncture was de-
    nied.
Some of the verses pleased me, it is
    true,
And still were pertinent,—those honor-
    ing you.
These now I offer: take them, if you
    will,
Like the old hand-grasp, when at Shady
    Hill
We met, or Staten Island, in the days
When life was its own spur, nor needed
    praise.
If once you thought me rash, no longer
    fear;
Past my next milestone waits my seven-
    tieth year.
I mount no longer when the trumpets
    call;
My battle-harness idles on the wall,
The spider's castle, camping-ground of
    dust,
Not without dints, and all in front, I
    trust,
Shivering sometimes it calls me as it
    hears
Afar the charge's tramp and clash of
    spears;
But 't is such murmur only as might
    be
The sea-shell's lost tradition of the
    sea,
That makes me muse and wonder
    Where? and When?
While from my cliff I watch the waves
    of men
That climb to break midway their seem-
    ing gain,

And think it triumph if they shake their
   chain.
Little I ask of Fate; will she refuse
Some days of reconcilement with the
   Muse?
I take my reed again and blow it free
Of dusty silence, murmuring, " Sing to
   me ! "
And, as its stops my curious touch re-
   tries,
The stir of earlier instincts I sur-
   prise, —
Instincts, if less imperious, yet more
   strong,
And happy in the toil that ends with
   song.

Home am I come: not, as I hoped
   might be,
To the old haunts, too full of ghosts
   for me,
But to the olden dreams that time en-
   dears,
And the loved books that younger
   grow with years;
To country rambles, timing with my
   tread
Some happier verse that carols in my
   head,
Yet all with sense of something vainly
   mist,
Of something lost, but when I never
   wist.
How empty seems to me the populous
   street,
One figure gone I daily loved to
   meet, —
The clear, sweet singer with the crown
   of snow

Not whiter than the thoughts that
   housed below!
And, ah, what absence feel I at my
   side,
Like Dante when he missed his lau-
   relled guide,
What sense of diminution in the air
Once so inspiring, Emerson not there!
But life is sweet, though all that makes
   it sweet
Lessen like sound of friends' departing
   feet,
And Death is beautiful as feet of
   friend
Coming with welcome at our journey's
   end;
For me Fate gave, whate'er she else
   denied,
A nature sloping to the southern side;
I thank her for it, though when clouds
   arise
Such natures double-darken gloomy
   skies.
I muse upon the margin of the sea,
Our common pathway to the new To
   Be,
Watching the sails, that lessen more
   and more,
Of good and beautiful embarked be-
   fore;
With bits of wreck I patch the boat
   shall bear
Me to that unexhausted Otherwhere,
Whose friendly-peopled shore I some-
   times see,
By soft mirage uplifted, beckon me,
Nor sadly hear, as lower sinks the sun,
My moorings to the past snap one by
   one.

II. SENTIMENT.

ENDYMION.

A MYSTICAL COMMENT ON TITIAN'S
"SACRED AND PROFANE LOVE."

I.

My day began not till the twilight fell,
And, lo, in ether from heaven's sweetest
    well,
The New Moon swam divinely isolate
In maiden silence, she that makes my
    fate
Haply not knowing it, or only so
As · I the secrets of my sheep may
    know;
Nor ask I more, entirely blest if she,
In letting me adore, ennoble me
To height of what the Gods meant mak-
    ing man,
As only she and her best beauty can.
Mine be the love that in itself can
    find
Seed of white thoughts, the lilies of the
    mind,
Seed of that glad surrender of the will
That finds in service self's true purpose
    still;
Love that in outward fairness sees the
    tent
Pitched for an inmate far more excel-
    lent;
Love with a light irradiate to the core,
Lit at her lamp, but fed from inborn
    store;
Love thrice-requited with the single
    joy
Of an immaculate vision naught could
    cloy,
Dearer because, so high beyond my
    scope,

My life grew rich with her, unbribed by
    hope
Of other guerdon save to think she
    knew
One grateful votary paid her all her
    due ;
Happy if she, high-radiant there, re-
    signed
To his sure trust her image in his
    mind.
O fairer even than Peace is when she
    comes
Hushing War's tumult, and retreating
    drums
Fade to a murmur like the sough of
    bees
Hidden among the noon-stilled linden-
    trees,
Bringer of quiet, thou that canst allay
The dust and din and travail of the
    day,
Strewer of Silence, Giver of the dew
That doth our pastures and our souls
    renew,
Still dwell remote, still on thy shoreless
    sea
Float unattained in silent empery,
Still light my thoughts, nor listen to a
    prayer
Would make thee less imperishably
    fair !

II.

Can, then, my twofold nature find con-
    tent
In vain conceits of airy blandishment ?
Ask I no more ? Since yesterday I
    task
My storm-strewn thoughts to tell me
    what I ask :

Faint premonitions of mutation strange
Steal o'er my perfect orb, and, with
the change,
Myself am changed; the shadow of my
earth
Darkens the disc of that celestial
worth
Which only yesterday could still suffice
Upwards to waft my thoughts in sacri-
fice;
My heightened fancy with its touches
warm
Moulds to a woman's that ideal form;
Nor yet a woman's wholly, but divine
With awe her purer essence bred in
mine.
Was it long brooding on their own sur-
mise,
Which, of the eyes engendered, fools
the eyes,
Or have I seen through that translu-
cent air
A Presence shaped in its seclusions
bare,
My Goddess looking on me from above
As look our russet maidens when they
love,
But high-uplifted o'er our human heat
And passion-paths too rough for her
pearl feet?

Slowly the Shape took outline as I
gazed
At her full-orbed or crescent, till, be-
dazed
With wonder-working light that subtly
wrought
My brain to its own substance, steeping
thought
In trances such as poppies give, I
saw
Things shut from vision by sight's sober
law,
Amorphous, changeful, but defined at
last
Into the peerless Shape mine eyes hold
fast.
This, too, at first I worship: soon,
like wine,
Her eyes, in mine poured, frenzy-phil-
tred mine;
Passion put Worship's priestly raiment
on
And to the woman knelt, the Goddess
gone.

Was I, then, more than mortal made?
or she
Less than divine that she might mate
with me?
If mortal merely, could my nature cope
With such o'ermastery of maddening
hope?
If Goddess, could she feel the blissful
woe
That women in their self-surrender
know?

III.

Long she abode aloof there in her
heaven,
Far as the grape-bunch of the Pleiad
seven
Beyond my madness' utmost leap; but
here
Mine eyes have feigned of late her rapture near,
Moulded of mind-mist that broad day
dispels,
Here in these shadowy woods and
brook-lulled dells.

Have no heaven-habitants e'er felt a
void
In hearts sublimed with ichor unal-
loyed?
E'er longed to mingle with a mortal
fate
Intense with pathos of its briefer date?
Could she partake, and live, our human
stains?
Even with the thought there tingles
through my veins
Sense of unwarned renewal; I, the
dead,
Receive and house again the ardor
fled,
As once Alcestis; to the ruddy brim
Feel masculine virtue flooding every
limb,
And life, like Spring returning, brings
the key
That sets my senses from their winter
free,
Dancing like naked fauns too glad for
shame.
Her passion, purified to palest flame,
Can it thus kindle? Is her purpose
this?
I will not argue, lest I lose a bliss

That makes me dream Tithonus' for-
　　tune mine,
(Or what of it was palpably divine
Ere came the fruitlessly immortal
　　gift ;)
I cannot curb my hope's imperious
　　drift
That wings with fire my dull mor-
　　tality ;
Though fancy-forged, 't is all I feel or
　　see.

IV.

My Goddess sinks ; round Latmos'
　　darkening brow
Trembles the parting of her presence
　　now,
Faint as the perfume left upon the
　　grass
By her limbs' pressure or her feet that
　　pass
By me conjectured, but conjectured so
As things I touch far fainter substance
　　show.
Was it mine eyes' imposture I have
　　seen
Flit with the moonbeams on from
　　shade to sheen
Through the wood-openings ? Nay, I
　　see her now
Out of her heaven new-lighted, from
　　her brow
The hair breeze-scattered, like loose
　　mists that blow
Across her crescent, goldening as they
　　go,
High-kirtled for the chase, and what
　　was shown,
Of maiden rondure, like the rose half-
　　blown.
If dream, turn real ! If a vision, stay !
Take mortal shape, my philtre's spell
　　obey !
If hags compel thee from thy secret
　　sky
With gruesome incantations, why
　　not I,
Whose only magic is that I distil
A potion, blent of passion, thought,
　　and will,
Deeper in reach, in force of fate more
　　rich,
Than e'er was juice wrung by Thessa-
　　lian witch

From moon-enchanted herbs, — a po-
　　tion brewed
Of my best life in each diviner mood ?
Myself the elixir am, myself the bowl
Seething and mantling with my soul of
　　soul.
Taste and be humanized : what though
　　the cup,
With thy lips frenzied, shatter ? Drink
　　it up !
If but these arms may clasp, o'er-
　　quited so,
My world, thy heaven, all life means I
　　shall know.

V.

Sure she hath heard my prayer and
　　granted half,
As Gods do who at mortal madness
　　laugh.
Yet if life's solid things illusion seem,
Why may not substance wear the mask
　　of dream ?
In sleep she comes ; she visits me in
　　dreams,
And, as her image in a thousand
　　streams,
So in my veins, that her obey, she
　　sees,
Floating and flaming there, her im-
　　ages
Bear to my little world's remotest zone
Glad messages of her, and her alone.
With silence-sandalled Sleep she comes
　　to me,
(But softer-footed, sweeter-browed,
　　than she,)
In motion gracious as a seagull's wing,
And all her bright limbs, moving,
　　seem to sing.
Let me believe so, then, if so I may
With the night's bounty feed my beg-
　　gared day.
In dreams I see her lay the goddess
　　down
With bow and quiver, and her crescent
　　crown
Flicker and fade away to dull eclipse
As down to mine she deigns her longed
　　for lips ;
And as her neck my happy arms en-
　　fold,
Flooded and lustred with her loosened
　　gold,

She whispers words each sweeter than
    a kiss:
Then, wakened with the shock of sud-
    den bliss,
My arms are empty, my awakener
    fled,
And, silent in the silent sky o'erhead,
But coldly as on ice-plated snow, she
    gleams,
Herself the mother and the child of
    dreams.

VI.

Gone is the time when phantasms could
    appease
My quest phantasmal and bring cheated
    ease;
When, if she glorified my dreams, I
    felt
Through all my limbs a change im-
    mortal melt
At touch of hers illuminate with soul.
Not long could I be stilled with Fancy's
    dole;
Too soon the mortal mixture in me
    caught
Red fire from her celestial flame, and
    fought
For tyrannous control in all my
    veins:
My fool's prayer was accepted; what
    remains?
Or was it some eidolon merely, sent
By her who rules the shades in banish-
    ment,
To mock me with her semblance?
    Were it thus,
How 'scape I shame, whose will was
    traitorous?
What shall compensate an ideal
    dimmed?
How blanch again my statue virgin-
    limbed,
Soiled with the incense-smoke her
    chosen priest
Poured more profusely as within de-
    creased
The fire unearthly, fed with coals from
    far
Within the soul's shrine? Could my
    fallen star
Be set in heaven again by prayers and
    tears
And quenchless sacrifice of all my
    years,

How would the victim to the flamen
    leap,
And life for life's redemption paid hold
    cheap!

But what resource when she herself de-
    scends
From her blue throne, and o'er her vas-
    sal bends
That shape thrice-deified by love, those
    eyes
Wherein the Lethe of all others lies?
When my white queen of heaven's re-
    moteness tires,
Herself against her other self conspires,
Takes woman's nature, walks in mortal
    ways,
And finds in my remorse her beauty's
    praise?
Yet all would I renounce to dream
    again
The dream in dreams fulfilled that made
    my pain,
My noble pain that heightened all my
    years
With crowns to win and prowess-breed-
    ing tears;
Nay, would that dream renounce once
    more to see
Her from her sky there looking down at
    me!

VII.

Goddess, reclimb thy heaven, and be
    once more
An inaccessible splendor to adore,
A faith, a hope of such transcendent
    worth
As bred ennobling discontent with
    earth;
Give back the longing, back the elated
    mood
That, fed with thee, spurned every
    meaner good;
Give even the spur of impotent despair
That, without hope, still bade aspire and
    dare;
Give back the need to worship, that
    still pours
Down to the soul the virtue it adores!

Nay, brightest and most beautiful, deem
    naught
These frantic words, the reckless wind
    of thought;

Still stoop, still grant, — I live but in
    thy will;
Be what thou wilt, but be a woman
    still!
Vainly I cried, nor could myself believe
That what I prayed for I would fain re-
    ceive.
My moon is set; my vision set with
    her;
No more can worship vain my pulses
    stir.
Goddess Triform, I own thy triple
    spell,
My heaven's queen, — queen, too, of
    my earth and hell!

THE BLACK PREACHER.

A BRETON LEGEND.

AT Carnac in Brittany, close on the
    bay,
They show you a church, or rather the
    gray
Ribs of a dead one, left there to bleach
With the wreck lying near on the crest
    of the beach,
Roofless and splintered with thunder-
    stone,
'Mid lichen - blurred gravestones all
    alone;
'T is the kind of ruin strange sights to
    see
That may have their teaching for you
    and me.

Something like this, then, my guide had
    to tell,
Perched on a saint cracked across when
    he fell;
But since I might chance give his mean-
    ing a wrench,
He talking his *patois* and I English-
    French,
I 'll put what he told me, preserving the
    tone,
In a rhymed prose that makes it half
    his, half my own.

An abbey-church stood here, once on a
    time,
Built as a death-bed atonement for
    crime:

'T was for somebody's sins, I know not
    whose;
But sinners are plenty, and you can
    choose.
Though a cloister now of the dusk-
    winged bat,
'T was rich enough once, and the
    brothers grew fat,
Looser in girdle and purpler in jowl,
Singing good rest to the founder's lost
    soul.
But one day came Northmen, and lithe
    tongues of fire
Lapped up the chapter-house, licked off
    the spire,
And left all a rubbish-heap, black and
    dreary,
Where only the wind sings *miserere*.

No priest has kneeled since at the altar's
    foot,
Whose crannies are searched by the
    nightshade's root,
Nor sound of service is ever heard,
Except from throat of the unclean bird,
Hooting to unassoiled shapes as they
    pass
In midnights unholy his witches' mass,
Or shouting "Ho! ho!" from the bel-
    fry high
As the Devil's sabbath-train whirls by.

But once a year, on the eve of All-
    Souls,
Through these arches dishallowed the
    organ rolls,
Fingers long fleshless the bell-ropes
    work,
The chimes peal muffled with sea-mists
    mirk,
The skeleton windows are traced anew
On the baleful flicker of corpse-lights
    blue,
And the ghosts must come, so the legend
    saith,
To a preaching of Reverend Doctor
    Death.

Abbots, monks, barons, and ladies fair
Hear the dull summons and gather
    there:
No rustle of silk now, no clink of
    mail,
Nor ever a one greets his church-mate
    pale;

No knight whispers love in the *châte-
laine's* ear,
His next-door neighbor this five hun-
dred year;
No monk has a sleek *benedicite*
For the great lord shadowy now as he;
Nor needeth any to hold his breath,
Lest he lose the least word of Doctor
Death.

He chooses his text in the Book Divine,
Tenth verse of the Preacher in chapter
nine : —
" ' Whatsoever thy hand shall find thee
to do,
That do with thy whole might, or thou
shalt rue;
For no man is wealthy, or wise, or
brave,
In that quencher of might - be's and
would-be's, the grave.'
Bid by the Bridegroom, ' To-morrow,'
ye said,
And To-morrow was digging a trench
for your bed ;
Ye said ' God can wait ; let us finish our
wine ; '
Ye had wearied Him, fools, and that
last knock was mine! "

But I can't pretend to give you the
sermon,
Or say if the tongue were French,
Latin, or German;
Whatever he preached in, I give you my
word
The meaning was easy to all that
heard ;
Famous preachers there have been and
be,
But never was one so convincing as he ;
So blunt was never a begging friar,
No Jesuit's tongue so barbed with fire,
Cameronian never, nor Methodist,
Wrung gall out of Scripture with such a
twist.

And would you know who his hearers
must be ?
I tell you just what my guide told
me :
Excellent teaching men have, day and
night,
From two earnest friars, a black and a
white,

The Dominican Death and the Carmel-
ite Life ;
And between these two there is never
strife,
For each has his separate office and
station,
And each his own work in the congrega-
tion ;
Whoso to the white brother deafens his
ears,
And cannot be wrought on by blessings
or tears,
Awake in his coffin must wait and
wait,
In that blackness of darkness that
means *too late,*
And come once a year, when the ghost-
bells tolls,
As till Doomsday it shall on the eve of
All-Souls,
To hear Doctor Death, whose words
smart with the brine
Of the Preacher, the tenth verse of
chapter nine.

ARCADIA REDIVIVA.

I, WALKING the familiar street,
    While a crammed horse-car jingled
        through it,
Was lifted from my prosy feet
    And in Arcadia ere I knew it.

Fresh sward for gravel soothed my
        tread,
    And shepherd's pipes my ear de-
        lighted;
The riddle may be lightly read :
    I met two lovers newly plighted.

They murmured by in happy care,
    New plans for Paradise devising,
Just as the moon, with pensive stare,
    O'er Mistress Craigie's pines was
        rising.

Astarte, known nigh threescore years,
    Me to no speechless rapture urges;
Them in Elysium she enspheres,
    Queen, from of old, of thaumaturges.

The railings put forth bud and bloom,
    The house-fronts all with myrtles
        twine them,

And light-winged Loves in every room
    Make nests, and then with kisses line
        them.

O sweetness of untasted life!
    O dream, its own supreme fulfilment!
O hours with all illusion rife,
    As ere the heart divined what ill
        meant!

"Et ego," sighed I to myself,
    And strove some vain regrets to bri-
        dle,
"Though now laid dusty on the shelf,
    Was hero once of such an idyl!

An idyl ever newly sweet,
    Although since Adam's day recited,
Whose measures time them to Love's
        feet,
    Whose sense is every ill requited."

Maiden, if I may counsel, drain
    Each drop of this enchanted season,
For even our honeymoons must wane,
    Convicted of green cheese by Rea-
        son.

And none will seem so safe from change,
    Nor in such skies benignant hover,
As this, beneath whose witchery strange
    You tread on rose-leaves with your
        lover.

The glass unfilled all tastes can fit,
    As round its brim Conjecture dances;
For not Mephisto's self hath wit
    To draw such vintages as Fancy's.

When our pulse beats its minor key,
    When play-time halves and school-
        time doubles,
Age fills the cup with serious tea,
    Which once Dame Clicquot starred
        with bubbles.

"Fie, Mr. Graybeard! Is this wise?
    Is this the moral of a poet,
Who, when the plant of Eden dies,
    Is privileged once more to sow it?

"That herb of clay-disdaining root,
    From stars secreting what it feeds on,
Is burnt-out passion's slag and soot
    Fit soil to strew its dainty seeds on?

"Pray, why, if in Arcadia once,
    Need one so soon forget the way
        there?
Or why, once there, be such a dunce
    As not contentedly to stay there?"

Dear child, 't was but a sorry jest,
    And from my heart I hate the cynic
Who makes the Book of Life a nest
    For comments staler than rabbinic.

If Love his simple spell but keep,
    Life with ideal eyes to flatter,
The Grail itself were crockery cheap
    To Every-day's communion-platter.

One Darby is to me well known,
    Who, as the hearth between them
        blazes,
Sees the old moonlight shine on Joan,
    And float her youthward in its hazes.

He rubs his spectacles, he stares, —
    'T is the same face that witched him
        early!
He gropes for his remaining hairs, —
    Is this a fleece that feels so curly?

"Good heavens! but now 't was win-
        ter gray,
    And I of years had more than plenty;
The almanac 's a fool! 'T is May!
    Hang family Bibles! I am twenty!

"Come, Joan, your arm; we 'll walk
        the room —
    The lane, I mean — do you remem-
        ber?
How confident the roses bloom,
    As if it ne'er could be December!

"Nor more it shall, while in your eyes
    My heart its summer heat recovers,
And you, howe'er your mirror lies,
    Find your old beauty in your lover's."

THE NEST.

MAY.

WHEN oaken woods with buds are pink,
    And new-come birds each morning
        sing,
When fickle May on Summer's brink
    Pauses, and knows not which to fling,

Whether fresh bud and bloom again,
Or hoar-frost silvering hill and plain,

Then from the honeysuckle gray
　The oriole with experienced quest
Twitches the fibrous bark away,
　The cordage of his hammock-nest,
Cheering his labor with a note
Rich as the orange of his throat.

High o'er the loud and dusty road
　The soft gray cup in safety swings,
To brim ere August with its load
　Of downy breasts and throbbing
　　wings,
O'er which the friendly elm-tree heaves
An emerald roof with sculptured eaves.

Below, the noisy World drags by
　In the old way, because it must,
The bride with heartbreak in her eye,
　The mourner following hated dust:
Thy duty, wingèd flame of Spring,
Is but to love, and fly, and sing.

Oh, happy life, to soar and sway
　Above the life by mortals led,
Singing the merry months away,
　Master, not slave of daily bread,
And, when the Autumn comes, to flee
Wherever sunshine beckons thee!

PALINODE. — DECEMBER.

Like some lorn abbey now, the wood
　Stands roofless in the bitter air;
In ruins on its floor is strewed
　The carven foliage quaint and rare,
And homeless winds complain along
The columned choir once thrilled with
　　song.

And thou, dear nest, whence joy and
　　praise
　The thankful oriole used to pour,
Swing'st empty while the north winds
　　chase
　Their snowy swarms from Labrador:
But, loyal to the happy past,
I love thee still for what thou wast.

Ah, when the Summer graces flee
　From other nests more dear than
　　thou,

And, where June crowded once, I see
　Only bare trunk and disleaved bough;
When springs of life that gleamed and
　　gushed
Run chilled, and slower, and are
　　hushed;

When our own branches, naked long,
　The vacant nests of Spring betray,
Nurseries of passion, love, and song
　That vanished as our year grew gray;
When Life drones o'er a tale twice
　　told
O'er embers pleading with the cold, —

I'll trust, that, like the birds of Spring,
　Our good goes not without repair,
But only flies to soar and sing
　Far off in some diviner air,
Where we shall find it in the calms
Of that fair garden 'neath the palms.

A YOUTHFUL EXPERIMENT IN ENGLISH HEXAMETERS.

IMPRESSIONS OF HOMER.

SOMETIMES come pauses of calm, when
　　the rapt bard, holding his heart
　　back,
Over his deep mind muses, as when o'er
　　awestricken ocean
Poises a heapt cloud luridly, ripening
　　the gale and the thunder;
Slow rolls onward the verse with a long
　　swell heaving and swinging,
Seeming to wait till, gradually wid'ning
　　from far-off horizons,
Piling the deeps up, heaping the glad-
　　hearted surges before it,
Gathers the thought as a strong wind
　　darkening and cresting the tu-
　　mult.
Then every pause, every heave, each
　　trough in the waves, has its mean-
　　ing;
Full-sailed, forth like a tall ship steadies
　　the theme, and around it,
Leaping beside it in glad strength, run-
　　ning in wild glee beyond it
Harmonies billow exulting and floating
　　the soul where it lists them,
Swaying the listener's fantasy hither
　　and thither like driftweed.

BIRTHDAY VERSES.

WRITTEN IN A CHILD'S ALBUM.

'T WAS sung of old in hut and hall
How once a king in evil hour
Hung musing o'er his castle wall,
And, lost in idle dreams, let fall
Into the sea his ring of power.

Then, let him sorrow as he might,
And pledge his daughter and his throne
To who restored the jewel bright,
The broken spell would ne'er unite;
The grim old ocean held its own.

Those awful powers on man that wait,
On man, the beggar or the king,
To hovel bare or hall of state
A magic ring that masters fate
With each succeeding birthday bring.

Therein are set four jewels rare:
Pearl winter, summer's ruby blaze,
Spring's emerald, and, than all more
    fair,
Fall's pensive opal, doomed to bear
A heart of fire bedreamed with haze.

To him the simple spell who knows
The spirits of the ring to sway,
Fresh power with every sunrise flows,
And royal pursuivants are those
That fly his mandates to obey.

But he that with a slackened will
Dreams of things past or things to be,
From him the charm is slipping still,
And drops, ere he suspect the ill,
Into the inexorable sea.

ESTRANGEMENT.

THE path from me to you that led,
    Untrodden long, with grass is grown,
Mute carpet that his lieges spread
    Before the Prince Oblivion
When he goes visiting the dead.

And who are they but who forget?
    You, who my coming could surmise
Ere any hint of me as yet
    Warned other ears and other eyes,
See the path blurred without regret.

But when I trace its windings sweet
    With saddened steps, at every spot
That feels the memory in my feet,
    Each grass-blade turns forget-me-
        not,
Where murmuring bees your name re-
    peat.

PHŒBE.

ERE pales in Heaven the morning star,
A bird, the loneliest of its kind,
Hears Dawn's faint footfall from afar
While all its mates are dumb and blind

It is a wee sad-colored thing,
As shy and secret as a maid,
That, ere in choir the robins ring,
Pipes its own name like one afraid.

It seems pain-prompted to repeat
The story of some ancient ill,
But *Phœbe! Phœbe!* sadly sweet
Is all it says, and then is still.

It calls and listens. Earth and sky,
Hushed by the pathos of its fate,
Listen: no whisper of reply
Comes from its doom-dissevered mate.

Phœbe! it calls and calls again,
And Ovid, could he but have heard,
Had hung a legendary pain
About the memory of the bird;

A pain articulate so long
In penance of some mouldered crime
Whose ghost still flies the Furies'
        thong
Down the waste solitudes of time.

Waif of the young World's wonder
        hour,
When gods found mortal maidens fair,
And will malign was joined with power
Love's kindly laws to overbear,

Like Progne, did it feel the stress
And coil of the prevailing words
Close round its being, and compress
Man's ampler nature to a bird's?

One only memory left of all
The motley crowd of vanished scenes

Hers, and vain impulse to recall
By repetition what it means.

Phœbe ! is all it has to say
In plaintive cadence o'er and o'er,
Like children that have lost their
    way,
And know their names, but nothing
    more.

Is it a type, since Nature's Lyre
Vibrates to every note in man,
Of that insatiable desire,
Meant to be so since life began ?

I, in strange lands at gray of dawn,
Wakeful, have heard that fruitless
    plaint,
Through Memory's chambers deep
Renew its iterations faint.

So nigh ! yet from remotest years
It summons back its magic, rife
With longings unappeased, and tears
Drawn from the very source of life.

DAS EWIG-WEIBLICHE.

How was I worthy so divine a loss,
    Deepening my midnights, kindling all
        my morns ?
Why waste such precious wood to make
        my cross,
    Such far-sought roses for my crown of
        thorns ?

And when she came, how earned I such
        a gift ?
    Why spend on me, a poor earth-delv-
        ing mole,
The fireside sweetnesses, the heaven-
        ward lift,
    The hourly mercy, of a woman's
        soul ?

Ah, did we know to give her all her
        right,
    What wonders even in our poor clay
        were done !
It is not Woman leaves us to our
        night,
    But our brute earth that grovels from
        her sun.

Our nobler cultured fields and gracious
        domes
    We whirl too oft from her who still
        shines on
To light in vain our caves and clefts,
        the homes
    Of night-bird instincts pained till she
        be gone.

Still must this body starve our souls
        with shade ;
    But when Death makes us what we
        were before,
Then shall her sunshine all our depths
        invade,
    And not a shadow stain heaven's crys-
        tal floor.

THE RECALL.

Come back before the birds are flown,
Before the leaves desert the tree,
And, through the lonely alleys blown,
Whisper their vain regrets to me
Who drive before a blast more rude,
The plaything of my gusty mood,
In vain pursuing and pursued !

Nay, come although the boughs be bare,
Though snowflakes fledge the summer's
        nest
And in some far Ausonian air
The thrush, your minstrel, warm his
        breast.
Come, sunshine's treasurer, and bring
To doubting flowers their faith in
        spring,
To birds and me the need to sing !

ABSENCE.

Sleep is death's image, — poets tell us
        so ;
But Absence is the bitter self of Death.
And, you away, Life's lips their red
        forego,
Parched in an air unfreshened by your
        breath.

Light of those eyes that made the
        light of mine,
Where shine you ? On what happier
        fields and flowers ?

Heaven's lamps renew their lustre less
    divine,
But only serve to count my darkened
    hours.

If with your presence went your image
    too,
That brain-born ghost my path would
    never cross
Which meets me now where'er I once
    met you,
Then vanishes, to multiply my loss.

MONNA LISA.

She gave me all that woman can,
Nor her soul's nunnery forego,
A confidence that man to man
Without remorse can never show.

Rare art, that can the sense refine
Till not a pulse rebellious stirs,
And, since she never can be mine,
Makes it seem sweeter to be hers!

THE OPTIMIST.

Turbid from London's noise and
    smoke,
Here I find air and quiet too:
Air filtered through the beech and
    oak,
Quiet by nothing harsher broke
Than wood-dove's meditative coo.

The Truce of God is here: the breeze
Sighs as men sigh relieved from care,
Or tilts as lightly in the trees
As might a robin: all is ease,
With pledge of ampler ease to spare.

Time, leaning on his scythe, forgets
To turn the hourglass in his hand,
And all life's petty cares and frets,
Its teasing hopes and weak regrets,
Are still as that oblivious sand.

Repose fills all the generous space
Of undulant plain; the rook and crow
Hush; 't is as if a silent grace,
By Nature murmured, calmed the
    face
Of Heaven above and Earth below.

From past and future toils I rest,
One Sabbath pacifies my year;
I am the halcyon, this my nest;
And all is safely for the best
While the World 's there and I am
    here.

So I turn tory for the nonce,
And think the radical a bore,
Who cannot see, thick-witted dunce,
That what was good for people once
Must be as good forevermore.

Sun, sink no deeper down the sky;
Earth, never change this summer
    mood;
Breeze, loiter thus forever by,
Stir the dead leaf or let it lie:
Since I am happy, all is good.
    Middleton, *August*, 1884.

ON BURNING SOME OLD
LETTERS.

With what odorous woods and spices
Spared for royal sacrifices,
With what costly gums seld-seen,
Hoarded to embalm a queen,
With what frankincense and myrrh,
Burn these precious parts of her,
Full of life and light and sweetness
As a summer day's completeness,
Joy of sun and song of bird
Running wild in every word,
Full of all the superhuman
Grace and winsomeness of woman?

O'er these leaves her wrist has slid,
Thrilled with veins where fire is hid
'Neath the skin's pellucid veil,
Like the opal's passion pale;
This her breath hath sweetened; this
Still seems trembling with the kiss
She half-ventured on my name,
Brow and cheek and throat aflame;
Over all caressing lies
Sunshine left there by her eyes;
From them all an effluence rare
With her nearness fills the air,
Till the murmur I half-hear
Of her light feet drawing near.

Rarest woods were coarse and rough,
Sweetest spice not sweet enough,

Too impure all earthly fire
For this sacred funeral-pyre ;
These rich relics must suffice
For their own dear sacrifice.
Seek we first an altar fit
For such victims laid on it ;
It shall be this slab, brought home
In old happy days from Rome, —
Lazuli, once blest to line
Dian's inmost cell and shrine.
Gently now I lay them there,
Pure as Dian's forehead bare,
Yet suffused with warmer hue,
Such as only Latmos knew.

Fire I gather from the sun
In a virgin lens : 't is done !
Mount the flames, red, yellow, blue,
As her moods were shining through,
Of the moment's impulse born, —
Moods of sweetness, playful scorn,
Half defiance, half surrender,
More than cruel, more than ten-
    der,
Flouts, caresses, sunshine, shade,
Gracious doublings of a maid
Infinite in guileless art,
Playing hide-seek with her heart.

On the altar now, alas,
There they lie a crinkling mass,
Writhing still, as if with grief
Went the life from every leaf ;
Then (heart-breaking palimpsest !)
Vanishing ere wholly guessed,
Suddenly some lines flash back,
Traced in lightning on the black,
And confess, till now denied,
All the fire they strove to hide.
What they told me, sacred trust,
Stays to glorify my dust,
There to burn through dust and damp
Like a mage's deathless lamp,
While an atom of this frame
Lasts to feed the dainty flame.

All is ashes now, but they
In my soul are laid away,
And their radiance round me hov-
    ers
Soft as moonlight over lovers,
Shutting her and me alone
In dream-Edens of our own ;
First of lovers to invent
Love, and teach men what it meant.

THE PROTEST.

I could not bear to see those eyes
On all with wasteful largess shine,
And that delight of welcome rise
Like sunshine strained through amber
    wine,
But that a glow from deeper skies,
From conscious fountains more divine,
Is (is it ?) mine.

Be beautiful to all mankind,
As Nature fashioned thee to be ;
'T would anger me did all not find
The sweet perfection that 's in thee :
Yet keep one charm of charms be-
    hind, —
Nay, thou 'rt so rich, keep two or
    three
For (is it ?) me !

THE PETITION.

Oh, tell me less or tell me more,
Soft eyes with mystery at the core,
That always seem to meet my own
Frankly as pansies fully blown,
Yet waver still 'tween no and yes !

So swift to cavil and deny,
Then parley with concessions shy,
Dear eyes, that make their youth be
    mine
And through my inmost shadows shine,
Oh, tell me more or tell me less !

FACT OR FANCY?

In town I hear, scarce wakened yet,
My neighbor's clock behind the wall
Record the day's increasing debt,
And *Cuckoo ! Cuckoo !* faintly call.

Our senses run in deepening grooves,
Thrown out of which they lose their
    tact,
And consciousness with effort moves
From habit past to present fact.

So, in the country waked to-day,
I hear, unwitting of the change,
A cuckoo's throb from far away
Begin to strike, nor think it strange.

The sound creates its wonted frame:
My bed at home, the songster hid
Behind the wainscoting, — all came
As long association bid.

Then, half-aroused, ere yet Sleep's
    mist
From the mind's uplands furl away,
To the familiar sound I list,
Disputed for by Night and Day.

I count to learn how late it is,
Until, arrived at thirty-four,
I question, "What strange world is
    this
Whose lavish hours would make me
    poor?"

Cuckoo! Cuckoo! Still on it went,
With hints of mockery in its tone;
How could such hoards of time be
    spent
By one poor mortal's wit alone?

I have it! Grant, ye kindly Powers,
I from this spot may never stir,
If only these uncounted hours
May pass, and seem too short, with
    Her!

But who She is, her form and face,
These to the world of dream belong;
She moves through fancy's visioned
    space,
Unbodied, like the cuckoo's song.

AGRO-DOLCE.

ONE kiss from all others prevents me,
And sets all my pulses astir,
And burns on my lips and torments
    me:
'T is the kiss that I fain would give
    her.

One kiss for all others requites me,
Although it is never to be,
And sweetens my dreams and invites
    me:
'T is the kiss that she dare not give
    me.

Ah, could it be mine, it were sweeter
Than honey bees garner in dream,

Though its bliss on my lips were fleeter
Than a swallow's dip to the stream.

And yet, thus denied, it can never
In the prose of life vanish away;
O'er my lips it must hover forever,
The sunshine and shade of my day.

THE BROKEN TRYST.

WALKING alone where we walked to-
    gether,
When June was breezy and blue,
I watch in the gray autumnal weather
The leaves fall inconstant as you.

If a dead leaf startle behind me,
I think 't is your garment's hem,
And, oh, where no memory could find
    me,
Might I whirl away with them!

CASA SIN ALMA.

RECUERDO DE MADRID.

SILENCIOSO por la puerta
Voy de su casa desierta
Do siempre feliz entré,
Y la encuentro en vano abierta
Cual la boca de una muerta
Despues que el alma se fué.

A CHRISTMAS CAROL.

FOR THE SUNDAY-SCHOOL CHILDREN
OF THE CHURCH OF THE DISCIPLES.

"WHAT means this glory round our
    feet,"
    The Magi mused, "more bright than
        morn?"
And voices chanted clear and sweet,
    "To-day the Prince of Peace is
        born!"

"What means that star," the Shep-
    herds said,
    "That brightens through the rocky
        glen?"
And angels, answering overhead,
    Sang, "Peace on earth, good-will to
        men!"

'T is eighteen hundred years and more
  Since those sweet oracles were
    dumb;
We wait for Him, like them of yore;
  Alas, He seems so slow to come!

But it was said, in words of gold
  No time or sorrow e'er shall dim,
That little children might be bold
  In perfect trust to come to Him.

All round about our feet shall shine
  A light like that the wise men saw,
If we our loving smiles incline
  To that sweet Life which is the Law.

So shall we learn to understand
  The simple faith of shepherds then,
And, clasping kindly hand in hand,
  Sing, " Peace on earth, good-will to
    men ! "

And they who do their souls no wrong,
  But keep at eve the faith of morn,
Shall daily hear the angel-song,
  " To-day the Prince of Peace is
    born ! "

MY PORTRAIT GALLERY.

Oft round my hall of portraiture I
    gaze,
By Memory reared, the artist wise and
    holy,
From stainless quarries of deep-buried
    days.
There, as I muse in soothing melan-
    choly,
Your faces glow in more than mortal
    youth,
Companions of my prime, now van-
    ished wholly,
The loud, impetuous boy, the low-
    voiced maiden,
Now for the first time seen in flawless
    truth.
Ah, never master that drew mortal
    breath
Can match thy portraits, just and gen-
    erous Death,
Whose brush with sweet regretful tints
    is laden !
Thou paintest that which struggled
    here below

Half understood, or understood for woe,
And with a sweet forewarning
Mak'st round the sacred front an
    aureole glow
Woven of that light that rose on Easter
    morning.

PAOLO TO FRANCESCA.

I was with thee in Heaven : I cannot
    tell
If years or moments, so the sudden
    bliss,
When first we found, then lost, us in a
    kiss,
Abolished Time, abolished Earth and
    Hell,
Left only Heaven. Then from our
    blue there fell
The dagger's flash, and did not fall
    amiss,
For nothing now can rob my life of
    this, —
That once with thee in Heaven, all else
    is well.
Us, undivided when man's vengeance
    came,
God's half-forgives that doth not here
    divide ;
And, were this bitter whirl-blast fanged
    with flame,
To me 't were summer, we being side
    by side :
This granted, I God's mercy will not
    blame,
For, given thy nearness, nothing is de-
    nied.

SONNET.

Scottish Border.

As sinks the sun behind yon alien hills
Whose heather - purpled slopes, in
    glory rolled,
Flush all my thought with momentary
    gold,
What pang of vague regret my fancy
    thrills?
Here 't is enchanted ground the peas-
    ant tills,
Where the shy ballad dared its blooms
    unfold,
And memory's glamour makes new
    sights seem old,

As when our life some vanished dream
  fulfils.
Yet not to thee belong these painless
  tears,
Land loved ere seen : before my darkened eyes,
From far beyond the waters and the
  years,
Horizons mute that wait their poet rise ;
The stream before me fades and disappears,
And in the Charles the western splendor
  dies.

SONNET.

*On being asked for an Autograph in
Venice.*

AMID these fragments of heroic days
When thought met deed with mutual
  passion's leap,
There sits a Fame whose silent trump
  makes cheap
What short-lived rumor of ourselves
  we raise.
They had far other estimate of praise
Who stamped the signet of their souls
  so deep
In art and action, and whose memories
  keep
Their height like stars above our misty
  ways :
In this grave presence to record my
  name
Something within me hangs the head
  and shrinks.
Dull were the soul without some joy in
  fame ;
Yet here to claim remembrance were,
  methinks,
Like him who, in the desert's awful
  frame,
Notches his cockney initials on the
  Sphinx.

THE DANCING BEAR.

FAR over Elf-land poets stretch their
  sway,
And win their dearest crowns beyond
  the goal
Of their own conscious purpose ; they
  control
With gossamer threads wide-flown our
  fancy's play,

And so our action. On my walk to-
  day,
A wallowing bear begged clumsily his
  toll,
When straight a vision rose of Atta
  Troll,
And scenes ideal witched mine eyes
  away.
"*Merci, Mossieu!*" the astonished
  bear-ward cried,
Grateful for thrice his hope to me, the
  slave
Of partial memory, seeing at his side
A bear immortal. The glad dole I gave
Was none of mine ; poor Heine o'er the
  wide
Atlantic welter stretched it from his
  grave.

THE MAPLE.

THE Maple puts her corals on in May,
While loitering frosts about the low-
  lands cling,
To be in tune with what the robins
  sing,
Plastering new log-huts 'mid her
  branches gray ;
But when the Autumn southward turns
  away,
Then in her veins burns most the blood
  of Spring,
And every leaf, intensely blossoming,
Makes the year's sunset pale the set of
  day.
O Youth unprescient, were it only so
With trees you plant, and in whose
  shade reclined,
Thinking their drifting blooms Fate's
  coldest snow,
You carve dear names upon the faithful
  rind,
Nor in that vernal stem the cross fore-
  know
That Age shall bear, silent, yet unre-
  signed !

NIGHTWATCHES.

WHILE the slow clock, as they were miser's gold,
Counts and recounts the mornward
  steps of Time,

The darkness thrills with conscience of
    each crime
By Death committed, daily grown more
    bold.
Once more the list of all my wrongs is
    told,
And ghostly hands stretch to me from
    my prime
Helpless farewells, as from an alien
    clime ;
For each new loss redoubles all the
    old.
This morn 't was May ; the blossoms
    were astir
With southern wind ; but now the
    boughs are bent
With snow instead of birds, and all
    things freeze.
How much of all my past is dumb with
    her,
And of my future, too, for with her
    went
Half of that world I ever cared to
    please !

DEATH OF QUEEN MERCEDES.

Hers all that Earth could promise or
    bestow, —
Youth, Beauty, Love, a crown, the
    beckoning years,
Lids never wet, unless with joyous
    tears,
A life remote from every sordid woe,
And by a nation's swelled to lordlier
    flow.
What lurking-place, thought we, for
    doubts or fears,
When, the day's swan, she swam along
    the cheers
Of the Alcalá, five happy months
    ago ?
The guns were shouting Io Hymen
    then
That, on her birthday, now denounce
    her doom ;
The same white steeds that tossed their
    scorn of men
To-day as proudly drag her to the
    tomb.
Grim jest of fate ! Yet who dare call it
    blind,
Knowing what life is, what our human-
    kind ?

PRISON OF CERVANTES.

Seat of all woes ? Though Nature's
    firm decree
The narrowing soul with narrowing
    dungeon bind,
Yet was his free of motion as the wind,
And held both worlds, of spirit and
    sense, in fee.
In charmed communion with his dual
    mind
He wandered Spain, himself both
    knight and hind,
Redressing wrongs he knew must ever
    be.
His humor wise could see life's long
    deceit,
Man's baffled aims, nor therefore both
    despise ;
His knightly nature could ill fortune
    greet
Like an old friend. Whose ever such
    kind eyes
That pierced so deep, such scope, save
    his whose feet
By Avon ceased 'neath the same April's
    skies ?

TO A LADY PLAYING ON THE
CITHERN.

So dreamy-soft the notes, so far away
They seem to fall, the horns of Oberon
Blow their faint Hunt's-up from the
    good-time gone ;
Or, on a morning of long-withered May,
Larks tinkle unseen o'er Claudian
    arches gray,
That Romeward crawl from Dream-
    land ; and anon
My fancy flings her cloak of Darkness
    on,
To vanish from the dungeon of To-day.
In happier times and scenes I seem to
    be,
And, as her fingers flutter o'er the
    strings,
The days return when I was young as
    she,
And my fledged thoughts began to feel
    their wings
With all Heaven's blue before them :
    Memory
Or Music is it such enchantment sings ?

THE EYE'S TREASURY.

GOLD of the reddening sunset, back-
    ward thrown
In largess on my tall paternal trees,
Thou with false hope or fear didst
    never tease
His heart that hoards thee ; nor is child-
    hood flown
From him whose life no fairer boon hath
    known
Than that what pleased him earliest
    still should please.
And who hath incomes safe from chance
    as these,
Gone in a moment, yet for life his
    own ?
All other gold is slave of earthward
    laws ;
This to the deeps of ether takes its
    flight,
And on the topmost leaves makes glori-
    ous pause
Of parting pathos ere it yield to night :
So linger, as from me earth's light with-
    draws,
Dear touch of Nature, tremulously
    bright !

PESSIMOPTIMISM.

YE little think what toil it was to
    build
A world of men imperfect even as
    this,
Where we conceive of Good by what
    we miss,
Of Ill by that wherewith best days are
    filled ;
A world whose every atom is self-
    willed,
Whose corner-stone is propt on arti-
    fice,
Whose joy is shorter-lived than woman's
    kiss,
Whose wisdom hoarded is but to be
    spilled.
Yet this is better than a life of caves,
Whose highest art was scratching on a
    bone,
Or chipping toilsome arrowheads of
    flint ;
Better, though doomed to hear while
    Cleon raves,

To see wit's want eterned in paint or
    stone,
And wade the drain-drenched shoals of
    daily print.

THE BRAKES.

WHAT countless years and wealth of
    brain were spent
To bring us hither from our caves and
    huts,
And trace through pathless wilds the
    deep-worn ruts
Of faith and habit, by whose deep in-
    dent
Prudence may guide if genius be not
    lent, —
Genius, not always happy when it shuts
Its ears against the plodder's ifs and
    buts,
Hoping in one rash leap to snatch the
    event.
The coursers of the sun, whose hoofs of
    flame
Consume morn's misty threshold, are
    exact
As bankers' clerks, and all this star-
    poised frame,
One swerve allowed, were with convul-
    sion rackt ;
This world were doomed, should Dul-
    ness fail, to tame
Wit's feathered heels in the stern stocks
    of fact.

A FOREBODING.

WHAT were the whole void world, if
    thou wert dead,
Whose briefest absence can eclipse my
    day,
And make the hours that danced with
    Time away
Drag their funereal steps with muffled
    head ?
Through thee, meseems, the very rose
    is red,
From thee the violet steals its breath in
    May,
From thee draw life all things that grow
    not gray,
And by thy force the happy stars are
    sped.

Thou near, the hope of thee to overflow
Fills all my earth and heaven, as when
  in Spring,
Ere April come, the birds and blossoms
  know,

And grasses brighten round her feet to
  cling;
Nay, and this hope delights all nature
  so
That the dumb turf I tread on seems to
  sing.

III. FANCY.

UNDER THE OCTOBER MAPLES.

WHAT mean these banners spread,
These paths with royal red
So gaily carpeted?
Comes there a prince to-day?
Such footing were too fine
For feet less argentine
Than Dian's own or thine,
Queen whom my tides obey.

Surely for thee are meant
These hues so orient
That with a sultan's tent
Each tree invites the sun;
Our Earth such homage pays,
So decks her dusty ways,
And keeps such holidays,
For one, and only one.

My brain shapes form and face,
Throbs with the rhythmic grace
And cadence of her pace
To all fine instincts true;
Her footsteps, as they pass,
Than moonbeams over grass
Fall lighter, — and, alas,
More insubstantial too!

LOVE'S CLOCK.

A PASTORAL.

DAPHNIS *waiting*.

" O DRYAD feet,
Be doubly fleet,
Timed to my heart's expectant beat
While I await her!

' At four,' vowed she;
'T is scarcely three,
Yet by *my* time it seems to be
A good hour later!"

CHLOE.

" Bid me not stay!
Hear reason, pray!
'T is striking six! Sure never day
Was short as this is!"

DAPHNIS.

" Reason nor rhyme
Is in the chime!
It can't be five; I 've scarce had time
To beg two kisses!"

BOTH.

" Early or late,
When lovers wait,
And Love's watch gains, if Time a gait
So snail-like chooses,
Why should his feet
Become more fleet
Than cowards' are, when lovers meet
And Love's watch loses?"

ELEANOR MAKES MACAROONS.

LIGHT of triumph in her eyes,
Eleanor her apron ties;
As she pushes back her sleeves,
High resolve her bosom heaves.
Hasten, cook! impel the fire

To the pace of her desire;
As you hope to save your soul,
Bring a virgin casserole,
Brightest bring of silver spoons, —
Eleanor makes macaroons!

Almond-blossoms, now adance
In the smile of Southern France,
Leave your sport with sun and breeze,
Think of duty, not of ease;
Fashion, 'neath their jerkins brown,
Kernels white as thistledown,
Tiny cheeses made with cream
From the Galaxy's mid-stream,
Blanched in light of honeymoons, —
Eleanor makes macaroons!

Now for sugar, — nay, our plan
Tolerates no work of man.
Hurry, then, ye golden bees;
Fetch your clearest honey, please,
Garnered on a Yorkshire moor,
While the last larks sing and soar,
From the heather-blossoms sweet,
Where sea-breeze and sunshine meet,
And the Augusts mask as Junes, —
Eleanor makes macaroons!

Next the pestle and mortar find,
Pure rock-crystal, — these to grind
Into paste more smooth than silk,
Whiter than the milkweed's milk:
Spread it on a rose-leaf, thus,
Cate to please Theocritus;
Then the fire with spices swell,
While, for her completer spell,
Mystic canticles she croons, —
Eleanor makes macaroons!

Perfect! and all this to waste
On a graybeard's palsied taste!
Poets so their verses write,
Heap them full of life and light,
And then fling them to the rude
Mumbling of the multitude.
Not so dire her fate as theirs,
Since her friend this gift declares
Choicest of his birthday boons, —
Eleanor's dear macaroons!

February 22, 1884.

TELEPATHY.

"AND how could you dream of meeting?"
　　Nay, how can you ask me, sweet?

All day my pulse had been beating
　　The tune of your coming feet.

And as nearer and ever nearer
　　I felt the throb of your tread,
To be in the world grew dearer,
　　And my blood ran rosier red.

Love called, and I could not linger,
　　But sought the forbidden tryst,
As music follows the finger
　　Of the dreaming lutanist.

And though you had said it and said it,
　　"We must not be happy to-day,"
Was I not wiser to credit
　　The fire in my feet than your Nay?

SCHERZO.

WHEN the down is on the chin
And the gold-gleam in the hair,
When the birds their sweethearts win
And champagne is in the air,
Love is here, and Love is there,
Love is welcome everywhere.

Summer's cheek too soon turns thin,
Days grow briefer, sunshine rare;
Autumn from his cannikin
Blows the froth to chase Despair:
Love is met with frosty stare,
Cannot house 'neath branches bare.

When new life is in the leaf
And new red is in the rose,
Though Love's Maytime be as brief
As a dragon-fly's repose,
Never moments come like those,
Be they Heaven or Hell: who knows?

All too soon comes Winter's grief,
Spendthrift Love's false friends turn
　　foes;
Softly comes Old Age, the thief,
Steals the rapture, leaves the throes:
Love his mantle round him throws, —
"Time to say Good-bye; it snows."

"FRANCISCUS DE VERULA-
MIO SIC COGITAVIT."

THAT's a rather bold speech, my Lord
　　Bacon,
　　For, indeed, is 't so easy to know

Just how much we from others have
    taken,
  And how much our own natural
    flow?

Since your mind bubbled up at its
    fountain,
  How many streams made it elate,
While it calmed to the plain from the
    mountain,
  As every mind must that grows
    great?

While you thought 't was You think-
    ing as newly
  As Adam still wet with God's dew,
You forgot in your self-pride that
    truly
  The whole Past was thinking through
    you.

Greece, Rome, nay, your namesake,
    old Roger,
  With Truth's nameless delvers who
    wrought
In the dark mines of Truth, helped to
    prod your
  Fine brain with the goad of their
    thought.

As mummy was prized for a rich hue
  The painter no elsewhere could find,
So 't was buried men's thinking with
    which you
  Gave the ripe mellow tone to your
    mind.

I heard the proud strawberry saying,
  "Only look what a ruby I 've
    made!"
It forgot how the bees in their may-
    ing
  Had brought it the stuff for its
    trade.

And yet there 's the half of a truth
    in it,
  And my Lord might his copyright
    sue;
For a thought 's his who kindles new
    youth in it,
  Or so puts it as makes it more true.

The birds but repeat without ending
  The same old traditional notes,

Which some, by more happily blend-
    ing,
  Seem to make over new in their
    throats;

And we men through our old bit of
    song run,
  Until one just improves on the rest,
And we call a thing his, in the long
    run,
  Who utters it clearest and best.

AUSPEX.

My heart, I cannot still it,
  Nest that had song-birds in it;
And when the last shall go,
  The dreary days, to fill it,
Instead of lark or linnet,
  Shall whirl dead leaves and snow.

Had they been swallows only,
  Without the passion stronger
That skyward longs and sings, —
  Woe 's me, I shall be lonely
When I can feel no longer
  The impatience of their wings!

A moment, sweet delusion,
  Like birds the brown leaves hover;
But it will not be long
  Before their wild confusion
Fall wavering down to cover
  The poet and his song.

THE PREGNANT COMMENT.

OPENING one day a book of mine,
I absent, Hester found a line
Praised with a pencil-mark, and this
She left transfigured with a kiss.

When next upon the page I chance,
Like Poussin's nymphs my pulses
    dance,
And whirl my fancy where it sees
Pan piping 'neath Arcadian trees,
Whose leaves no winter - scenes re-
    hearse,
Still young and glad as Homer's
    verse,
"What mean," I ask, "these sudden
    joys?

This feeling fresher than a boy's?
What makes this line, familiar long,
New as the first bird's April song?
I could, with sense illumined thus,
Clear doubtful texts in Æschylus!"

Laughing, one day she gave the key,
My riddle's open-sesame;
Then added, with a smile demure,
Whose downcast lids veiled triumph
    sure,
" If what I left there give you pain,
You — you — can take it off again;
'T was for *my* poet, not for him,
Your Doctor Donne there!"

           Earth grew dim
And wavered in a golden mist,
As rose, not paper, I kissed.
Donne, you forgive? I let you keep
Her precious comment, poet deep.

THE LESSON.

I SAT and watched the walls of night
With cracks of sudden lightning glow,
And listened while with clumsy might
The thunder wallowed to and fro.

The rain fell softly now; the squall,
That to a torrent drove the trees,
Had whirled beyond us to let fall
Its tumult on the whitening seas.

But still the lightning crinkled keen,
Or fluttered fitful from behind
The leaden drifts, then only seen,
That rumbled eastward on the wind.

Still as gloom followed after glare,
While bated breath the pine-trees drew,
Tiny Salmoneus of the air,
His mimic bolts the firefly threw.

He thought, no doubt, "Those flashes
    grand,
That light for leagues the shuddering
    sky,
Are made, a fool could understand,
By some superior kind of fly.

" He 's of our race's elder branch,
His family-arms the same as ours,

Both born the twy-forked flame to
    launch,
Of kindred, if unequal, powers."

And is man wiser? Man who takes
His consciousness the law to be
Of all beyond his ken, and makes
God but a bigger kind of Me?

SCIENCE AND POETRY.

HE who first stretched his nerves of
    subtile wire
Over the land and through the sea-
    depths still,
Thought only of the flame-winged mes-
    senger
As a dull drudge that should encircle
    earth
With sordid messages of Trade, and
    tame
Blithe Ariel to a bagman. But the Muse
Not long will be defrauded. From her
    foe
Her misused wand she snatches; at a
    touch
The Age of Wonder is renewed again,
And to our disenchanted day restores
The Shoes of Swiftness that give odds
    to Thought,
The Cloak that makes invisible; and
    with these
I glide, an airy fire, from shore to
    shore,
Or from my Cambridge whisper to Ca-
    thay.

A NEW YEAR'S GREETING.

THE century numbers fourscore years;
You, fortressed in your teens,
To Time's alarums close your ears,
And, while he devastates your peers,
Conceive not what he means.

If e'er life's winter fleck with snow
Your hair's deep shadowed bowers,
That winsome head an art would know
To make it charm, and wear it so
As 't were a wreath of flowers.

If to such fairies years must come,
May yours fall soft and slow

As, shaken by a bee's low hum,
The rose-leaves waver, sweetly dumb,
Down to their mates below!

THE DISCOVERY.

I WATCHED a moorland torrent run
Down through the rift itself had
    made,
Golden as honey in the sun,
Of darkest amber in the shade.

In this wild glen at last, methought,
The magic's secret I surprise;
Here Celia's guardian fairy caught
The changeful splendors of her eyes.

All else grows tame, the sky's one
    blue,
The one long languish of the rose,
But these, beyond prevision new,
Shall charm and startle to the close.

WITH A SEASHELL.

SHELL, whose lips, than mine more
    cold,
Might with Dian's ear make bold,
Seek my Lady's; if thou win
To that portal, shut from sin,
Where commissioned angels' swords
Startle back unholy words,
Thou a miracle shalt see
Wrought by it and wrought in thee;
Thou, the dumb one, shalt recover
Speech of poet, speech of lover.
If she deign to lift you there,
Murmur what I may not dare:
In that archway, pearly-pink
As the Dawn's untrodden brink,
Murmur, " Excellent and good,
Beauty's best in every mood.
Never common, never tame,

Changeful fair as windwaved flame"
Nay, I maunder; this she hears
Every day with mocking ears,
With a brow not sudden-stained
With the flush of bliss restrained,
With no tremor of the pulse
More than feels the dreaming dulse
In the midmost ocean's caves,
When a tempest heaps the waves.
Thou must woo her in a phrase
Mystic as the opal's blaze,
Which pure maids alone can see
When their lovers constant be.
I with thee a secret share,
Half a hope, and half a prayer,
Though no reach of mortal skill
Ever told it all, or will;
Say, " He bids me — nothing more —
Tell you what you guessed before! "

THE SECRET.

I HAVE a fancy: how shall I bring it
Home to all mortals wherever they be?
Say it or sing it? Shoe it or wing it,
So it may outrun or outfly ME,
Merest cocoon-web whence it broke
    free?

Only one secret can save from dis-
    aster,
Only one magic is that of the Master:
Set it to music; give it a tune, —
Tune the brook sings you, tune the
    breeze brings you,
Tune the wild columbines nod to in
    June!

This is the secret: so simple, you see!
Easy as loving, easy as kissing,
Easy as — well, let me ponder — as
    missing,
Known, since the world was, by scarce
    two or three.

IV. HUMOR AND SATIRE.

FITZ ADAM'S STORY.

[The greater part of this poem was written many years ago as part of a larger one, to be called "The Nooning," made up of tales in verse, some of them grave, some comic. It gives me a sad pleasure to remember that I was encouraged in this project by my friend the late Arthur Hugh Clough.]

THE next whose fortune 't was a tale to
        tell
Was one whom men, before they
        thought, loved well,
And after thinking wondered why they
        did,
For half he seemed to let them, half
        forbid,
And wrapped him so in humors, sheath
        on sheath,
'T was hard to guess the mellow soul
        beneath;
But, once divined, you took him to your
        heart,
While he appeared to bear with you as
        part
Of life's impertinence, and once a year
Betrayed his true self by a smile or
        tear,
Or rather something sweetly-shy and
        loath,
Withdrawn ere fully shown, and mixed
        of both.
A cynic? Not precisely: one who
        thrust
Against a heart too prone to love and
        trust,
Who so despised false sentiment he
        knew
Scarce in himself to part the false and
        true,

And strove to hide, by roughening-o'er
        the skin,
Those cobweb nerves he could not dull
        within.
Gentle by birth, but of a stem decayed,
He shunned life's rivalries and hated
        trade;
On a small patrimony and larger pride,
He lived uneaseful on the Other Side
(So he called Europe), only coming
        West
To give his Old-World appetite new
        zest;
Yet still the New World spooked it in
        his veins,
A ghost he could not lay with all his
        pains;
For never Pilgrims' offshoot scapes
        control
Of those old instincts that have shaped
        his soul.
A radical in thought, he puffed away
With shrewd contempt the dust of usage
        gray,
Yet loathed democracy as one who saw,
In what he longed to love, some vulgar
        flaw,
And, shocked through all his delicate
        reserves,
Remained a Tory by his taste and
        nerves.
His fancy's thrall, he drew all ergoes
        thence,
And thought himself the type of com-
        mon sense;
Misliking women, not from cross or
        whim,
But that his mother shared too much in
        him,
And he half felt that what in them was
        grace

Made the unlucky weakness of his race.
What powers he had he hardly cared to
    know,
But sauntered through the world as
    through a show;
A critic fine in his haphazard way,
A sort of mild La Bruyère on half-
    pay.
For comic weaknesses he had an eye
Keen as an acid for an alkali,
Yet you could feel, through his sardonic
    tone,
He loved them all, unless they were his
    own.
You might have called him, with his
    humorous twist,
A kind of human entomologist;
As these bring home, from every walk
    they take,
Their hat-crowns stuck with bugs of
    curious make,
So he filled all the lining of his head
With characters impaled and ticketed,
And had a cabinet behind his eyes
For all they caught of mortal oddities.
He might have been a poet — many
    worse —
But that he had, or feigned, contempt
    of verse;
Called it tattooing language, and held
    rhymes
The young world's lullaby of ruder
    times.
Bitter in words, too indolent for gall,
He satirized himself the first of all,
In men and their affairs could find no
    law,
And was the ill logic that he thought
    he saw.

Scratching a match to light his pipe
    anew,
With eyes half shut some musing whiffs
    he drew,
And thus began: "I give you all my
    word,
I think this mock-Decameron absurd;
Boccaccio's garden! how bring that to
    pass
In our bleak clime save under double
    glass?
The moral east-wind of New-England
    life
Would snip its gay luxuriance like a
    knife;

Mile-deep the glaciers brooded here,
    they say,
Through æons numb; we feel their
    chill to-day.
These foreign plants are but half-hardy
    still,
Die on a south, and on a north wall
    chill.
Had we stayed Puritans! *They* had
    some heat
(Though whence derived I have my own
    conceit),
But you have long ago raked up their
    fires;
Where they had faith, you 've ten
    sham-Gothic spires.
Why more exotics? Try your native
    vines,
And in some thousand years you *may*
    have wines;
Your present grapes are harsh, all pulps
    and skins,
And want traditions of ancestral bins
That saved for evenings round the pol-
    ished board
Old lava-fires, the sun-steeped hillside's
    hoard.
Without a Past, you lack that southern
    wall
O'er which the vines of Poesy should
    crawl;
Still they 're your only hope; no mid-
    night oil
Makes up for virtue wanting in the
    soil;
Manure them well and prune them;
    't won't be France,
Nor Spain, nor Italy, but there 's your
    chance.
You have one story-teller worth a
    score
Of dead Boccaccios, — nay, add twenty
    more, —
A hawthorn asking spring's most dainty
    breath,
And him you 're freezing pretty well to
    death.
However, since you say so, I will tease
My memory for a story by degrees,
Though you will cry, 'Enough!' I 'm
    wellnigh sure,
Ere I have dreamed through half my
    overture.
Stories were good for men who had no
    books

(Fortunate race !) and built their nests
    like rooks
In lonely towers, to which the Jongleur
    brought
His pedler's box of cheap and tawdry
    thought,
With here and there a fancy fit to
    see
Wrought to quaint grace in golden
    filigree, —
Some ring that with the Muse's finger
    yet
Is warm, like Aucassin and Nicolete ;
The morning newspaper has spoilt his
    trade,
(For better or for worse, I leave un-
    said,)
And stories now, to suit a public nice,
Must be half epigram, half pleasant
    vice.

"All tourists know Shebagog Coun-
    ty : there
The summer idlers take their yearly
    stare,
Dress to see Nature in a well-bred
    way,
As 't were Italian opera, or play,
Encore the sunrise (if they 're out of
    bed),
And pat the Mighty Mother on the
    head :
These have I seen, — all things are
    good to see, —
And wondered much at their compla-
    cency.
This world's great show, that took in
    getting-up
Millions of years, they finish ere they
    sup ;
Sights that God gleams through with
    soul-tingling force
They glance approvingly as things of
    course,
Say, 'That 's a grand rock,' 'This a
    pretty fall,'
Not thinking, 'Are we worthy ?' What
    if all
The scornful landscape should turn
    round and say,
'This is a fool, and that a popinjay'?
I often wonder what the Mountain
    thinks
Of French boots creaking o'er his
    breathless brinks,

Or how the Sun would scare the chat-
    tering crowd,
If some fine day he chanced to think
    aloud.
I, who love Nature much as sinners
    can,
Love her where she most grandeur
    shows, — in man :
Here find I mountain, forest, cloud,
    and sun,
River and sea, and glows when day is
    done ;
Nay, where she makes grotesques, and
    moulds in jest
The clown's cheap clay, I find unfad-
    ing zest.
The natural instincts year by year
    retire,
As deer shrink northward from the
    settler's fire,
And he who loves the wild game-flavor
    more
Than city-feasts, where every man 's a
    bore
To every other man, must seek it
    where
The steamer's throb and railway's iron
    blare
Have not yet startled with their punc-
    tual stir
The shy, wood - wandering brood of
    Character.

"There is a village, once the county
    town,
Through which the weekly mail rolled
    dustily down,
Where the courts sat, it may be, twice
    a year,
And the one tavern reeked with rustic
    cheer ;
Cheeshogquesumscot erst, now Jethro
    hight,
Red-man and pale-face bore it equal
    spite.
The railway ruined it, the natives
    say,
That passed unwisely fifteen miles
    away,
And made a drain to which, with steady
    ooze,
Filtered away law, stage-coach, trade,
    and news.
The railway saved it ; so at least think
    those

Who love old ways, old houses, old
    repose.
Of course the Tavern stayed: its
    genial host
Thought not of flitting more than did
    the post
On which high-hung the fading sign-
    board creaks,
Inscribed, 'The Eagle Inn, by Ezra
    Weeks.'

    " If in life's journey you should ever
        find
An inn medicinal for body and mind,
'T is sure to be some drowsy-looking
    house
Whose easy landlord has a bustling
    spouse:
He, if he like you, will not long forego
Some bottle deep in cobwebbed dust
    laid low,
That, since the War we used to call the
    'Last,'
Has dozed and held its lang-syne mem-
    ories fast;
From him exhales that Indian-summer
    air
Of hazy, lazy welcome everywhere,
While with her toil the napery is white,
The china dustless, the keen knife-
    blades bright,
Salt dry as sand, and bread that seems
    as though
'T were rather sea-foam baked than
    vulgar dough.

    " In our swift country, houses trim
        and white
Are pitched like tents, the lodging of a
    night;
Each on its bank of baked turf mounted
    high
Perches impatient o'er the roadside
    dry,
While the wronged landscape coldly
    stands aloof,
Refusing friendship with the upstart
    roof.
Not so the Eagle; on a grass-green
    swell
That toward the south with sweet con-
    cessions fell
It dwelt retired, and half had grown
    to be
As aboriginal as rock or tree.

It nestled close to earth, and seemed to
    brood
O'er homely thoughts in a half-con-
    scious mood,
As by the peat that rather fades than
    burns
The smouldering grandam nods and
    knits by turns,
Happy, although her newest news were
    old
Ere the first hostile drum at Concord
    rolled.
If paint it e'er had known, it knew no
    more
Than yellow lichens spattered thickly
    o'er
That soft lead-gray, less dark beneath
    the eaves
Which the slow brush of wind and
    weather leaves.
The ample roof sloped backward to the
    ground,
And vassal lean-tos gathered thickly
    round,
Patched on, as sire or son had felt the
    need,
Like chance growths sprouting from
    the old roof's seed,
Just as about a yellow - pine - tree
    spring
Its rough-barked darlings in a filial
    ring.
But the great chimney was the central
    thought
Whose gravitation through the cluster
    wrought;
For 't is not styles far-fetched from
    Greece or Rome,
But just the Fireside, that can make a
    home;
None of your spindling things of mod-
    ern style,
Like pins stuck through to stay the
    card-built pile,
It rose broad-shouldered, kindly, deb-
    onair,
Its warm breath whitening in the Octo-
    ber air,
While on its front a heart in outline
    showed
The place it filled in that serene abode.

    " When first I chanced the Eagle to
        explore,
Ezra sat listless by the open door;

One chair careened him at an angle
    meet,
Another nursed his hugely - slippered
    feet ;
Upon a third reposed a shirt-sleeved
    arm,
And the whole man diffused tobacco's
    charm.
'Are you the landlord?' 'Wahl, I
    guess I be,'
Watching the smoke, he answered lei-
    surely.
He was a stoutish man, and through
    the breast
Of his loose shirt there showed a
    brambly chest ;
Streaked redly as a wind-foreboding
    morn,
His tanned cheeks curved to temples
    closely shorn ;
Clean-shaved he was, save where a
    hedge of gray
Upon his brawny throat leaned every
    way
About an Adam's-apple, that beneath
Bulged like a boulder from a brambly
    heath.
The Western World's true child and
    nursling he,
Equipt with aptitudes enough for
    three :
No eye like his to value horse or
    cow,
Or gauge the contents of a stack or
    mow ;
He could foretell the weather at a
    word,
He knew the haunt of every beast and
    bird,
Or where a two-pound trout was sure
    to lie,
Waiting the flutter of his home-made
    fly ;
Nay, once in autumns five, he had the
    luck
To drop at fair-play range a ten-tined
    buck ;
Of sportsmen true he favored every
    whim,
But never cockney found a guide in
    him ;
A natural man, with all his instincts
    fresh,
Not buzzing helpless in Reflection's
    mesh,

Firm on its feet stood his broad-shoul-
    dered mind,
As bluffly honest as a northwest wind;
Hard-headed and soft-hearted, you 'd
    scarce meet
A kindlier mixture of the shrewd and
    sweet ;
Generous by birth, and ill at saying
    ' No,'
Yet in a bargain he was all men's foe,
Would yield no inch of vantage in a
    trade,
And give away ere nightfall all he
    made.

" 'Can I have lodging here ?' once
    more I said.
He blew a whiff, and, leaning back his
    head,
'You come a piece through Bailey's
    woods, I s'pose,
Acrost a bridge where a big swamp-oak
    grows ?
It don't grow, neither ; it 's ben dead
    ten year,
Nor th' ain't a livin' creetur, fur nor
    near,
Can tell wut killed it ; but I some mis-
    doubt
'T was borers, there 's sech heaps on
    'em about.
You did n' chance to run ag'inst my
    son,
A long, slab-sided youngster with a
    gun ?
He 'd oughto ben back more 'n an
    hour ago,
An' brought some birds to dress for
    supper — sho !
There he comes now. 'Say, Obed, wut
    ye got?
(He 'll hev some upland plover like as
    not.)
Wal, them 's real nice uns, an 'll eat A 1,
Ef I can stop their bein' over-done ;
Nothin' riles *me* (I pledge my fastin'
    word)
Like cookin' out the natur' of a bird ;
(Obed, you pick 'em out o' sight an'
    sound,
Your ma'am don't love no feathers
    cluttrin' round ;)
Jes' scare 'em with the coals, — thet 's
    my idee.'
Then, turning suddenly about on me,

'Wal, Square, I guess so. Callilate to stay?
I 'll ask Mis' Weeks; 'bout *thet* it 's hern to say.'

"Well, there I lingered all October through,
In that sweet atmosphere of hazy blue,
So leisurely, so soothing, so forgiving,
That sometimes makes New England fit for living.
I watched the landscape, erst so granite glum,
Bloom like the south side of a ripening plum,
And each rock-maple on the hillside make
His ten days' sunset doubled in the lake;
The very stone walls draggling up the hills
Seemed touched, and wavered in their roundhead wills.
Ah! there 's a deal of sugar in the sun!
Tap me in Indian summer, I should run
A juice to make rock-candy of, — but then
We get such weather scarce one year in ten.

"There was a parlor in the house, a room
To make you shudder with its prudish gloom.
The furniture stood round with such an air,
There seemed an old maid's ghost in every chair
Which looked as it had scuttled to its place
And pulled extempore a Sunday face,
Too smugly proper for a world of sin,
Like boys on whom the minister comes in.
The table, fronting you with icy stare,
Strove to look witless that its legs were bare,
While the black sofa with its horse-hair pall
Gloomed like a bier for Comfort's funeral.
Each piece appeared to do its chilly best
To seem an utter stranger to the rest,

As if acquaintanceship were deadly sin,
Like Britons meeting in a foreign inn.
Two portraits graced the wall in grimmest truth,
Mister and Mistress W. in their youth, —
New England youth, that seems a sort of pill,
Half wish-I-dared, half Edwards on the Will,
Bitter to swallow, and which leaves a trace
Of Calvinistic colic on the face.
Between them, o'er the mantel, hung in state
Solomon's temple, done in copper-plate;
Invention pure, but meant, we may presume,
To give some Scripture sanction to the room.
Facing this last, two samplers you might see,
Each, with its urn and stiffly-weeping tree,
Devoted to some memory long ago
More faded than their lines of worsted woe;
Cut paper decked their frames against the flies
Though none e'er dared an entrance who were wise,
And bushed asparagus in fading green
Added its shiver to the franklin clean.

"When first arrived, I chilled a half-hour there,
Nor dared deflower with use a single chair;
I caught no cold, yet flying pains could find
For weeks in me, — a rheumatism of mind.
One thing alone imprisoned there had power
To hold me in the place that long half-hour:
A scutcheon this, a helm-surmounted shield,
Three griffins argent on a sable field;
A relic of the shipwrecked past was here,
And Ezra held some Old-World lumber dear.

Nay, do not smile; I love this kind of
    thing,
These cooped traditions with a broken
    wing,
This freehold nook in Fancy's pipe-
    blown ball,
This less than nothing that is more than
    all!
Have I not seen sweet natures kept
    alive
Amid the humdrum of your business
    hive,
Undowered spinsters shielded from all
    harms,
By airy incomes from a coat of arms?"

He paused a moment, and his fea-
    tures took
The flitting sweetness of that inward
    look
I hinted at before; but, scarcely seen,
It shrank for shelter 'neath his harder
    mien,
And, rapping his black pipe of ashes
    clear,
He went on with a self-derisive sneer:
"No doubt we make a part of God's
    design,
And break the forest-path for feet di-
    vine;
To furnish foothold for this grand pre-
    vision
Is good, and yet — to be the mere tran-
    sition,
That, you will say, is also good,
    though I
Scarce like to feed the ogre By-and-
    by.
Raw edges rasp my nerves; my taste
    is wooed
By things that are, not going to be,
    good,
Though were I what I dreamed two
    lustres gone,
I 'd stay to help the Consummation
    on,
Whether a new Rome than the old
    more fair,
Or a deadflat of rascal-ruled despair;
But *my* skull somehow never closed the
    suture
That seems to knit yours firmly with
    the future,
So you 'll excuse me if I 'm sometimes
    fain

To tie the past's warm nightcap o'er
    my brain;
I 'm quite aware 't is not in fashion
    here,
But then your northeast winds are *so*
    severe !

"But to my story: though 't is truly
    naught
But a few hints in Memory's sketchbook
    caught,
And which may claim a value on the
    score
Of calling back some scenery now no
    more.
Shall I confess? The tavern's only
    Lar
Seemed (be not shocked!) its homely-
    featured bar.
Here dozed a fire of beechen logs, that
    bred
Strange fancies in its embers golden-red,
And nursed the loggerhead whose his-
    sing dip,
Timed by nice instinct, creamed the
    mug of flip
That made from mouth to mouth its
    genial round,
Nor left one nature wholly winter-
    bound;
Hence dropt the tinkling coal all mel-
    low-ripe
For Uncle Reuben's talk-extinguished
    pipe;
Hence rayed the heat, as from an in-
    door sun,
That wooed forth many a shoot of
    rustic fun.
Here Ezra ruled as king by right
    divine;
No other face had such a wholesome
    shine,
No laugh like his so full of honest
    cheer;
Above the rest it crowed like Chanti-
    cleer.

"In this one room his dame you
    never saw,
Where reigned, by custom old a Salic
    law;
Here coatless lolled he on his throne of
    oak,
And every tongue paused midway if he
    spoke.

Due mirth he loved, yet was his sway
 severe:
No blear-eyed driveller got his stagger
 here;
'Measure was happiness; who wanted
 more,
Must buy his ruin at the Deacon's
 store;'
None but his lodgers after ten could
 stay,
Nor after nine on eves of Sabbath-
 day.
He had his favorites and his pension-
 ers,
The same that gypsy Nature owns for
 hers:
Loose-ended souls, whose skills bring
 scanty gold,
And whom the poor - house catches
 when they 're old :
Rude country-minstrels, men who doc-
 tor kine,
Or graft, and, out of scions ten, save
 nine;
Creatures of genius they, but never
 meant
To keep step with the civic regiment.
These Ezra welcomed, feeling in his
 mind
Perhaps some motions of the vagrant
 kind;
These paid no money, yet for them he
 drew
Special Jamaica from a tap they knew,
And, for their feelings, chalked behind
 the door
With solemn face a visionary score.
This thawed to life in Uncle Reuben's
 throat
A torpid shoal of jest and anecdote,
Like those queer fish that doze the
 droughts away,
And wait for moisture, wrapt in sun-
 baked clay;
This warmed the one-eyed fiddler to
 his task,
Perched in the corner on an empty
 cask,
By whose shrill art rapt suddenly, some
 boor
Rattled a double-shuffle on the floor;
'Hull's Victory' was, indeed, the fa-
 vorite air,
Though 'Yankee Doodle' claimed its
 proper share.

"'T was there I caught from Uncle
 Reuben's lips,
In dribbling monologue 'twixt whiffs
 and sips,
The story I so long have tried to tell;
The humor coarse, the persons com-
 mon, — well,
From Nature only do I love to paint,
Whether she send a satyr or a saint;
To me Sincerity 's the one thing good,
Soiled though she be and lost to maid-
 enhood.
Quompegan is a town some ten miles
 south
From Jethro, at Nagumscot river-
 mouth,
A seaport town, and makes its title
 good
With lumber and dried fish and eastern
 wood.
Here Deacon Bitters dwelt and kept
 the Store,
The richest man for many a mile of
 shore;
In little less than everything dealt he,
From meeting-houses to a chest of tea;
So dextrous therewithal a flint to skin,
He could make profit on a single pin;
In business strict, to bring the balance
 true
He had been known to bite a fig in
 two,
And change a board-nail for a shingle-
 nail.
All that he had he ready held for sale,
His house, his tomb, whate'er the law
 allows,
And he had gladly parted with his
 spouse.
His one ambition still to get and get,
He would arrest your very ghost for
 debt.
His store looked righteous, should the
 Parson come,
But in a dark back-room he peddled
 rum,
And eased Ma'am Conscience, if she
 e'er would scold,
By christening it with water ere he
 sold.
A small, dry man he was, who wore a
 queue,
And one white neckcloth all the week-
 days through, —
On Monday white, by Saturday as dun

As that worn homeward by the prodigal
    son.
His frosted earlocks, striped with foxy
    brown,
Were braided up to hide a desert
    crown;
His coat was brownish, black perhaps
    of yore;
In summer-time a banyan loose he
    wore;
His trousers short, through many a sea-
    son true,
Made no pretence to hide his stockings
    blue;
A waistcoat buff his chief adornment
    was,
Its porcelain buttons rimmed with
    dusky brass.
A deacon he, you saw it in each limb,
And well he knew to deacon-off a
    hymn,
Or lead the choir through all its wander-
    ing woes
With voice that gathered unction in his
    nose,
Wherein a constant snuffle you might
    hear,
As if with him 't were winter all the
    year.
At pew-head sat he with decorous
    pains,
In sermon-time could foot his weekly
    gains,
Or, with closed eyes and heaven-ab-
    stracted air,
Could plan a new investment in long-
    prayer.
A pious man, and thrifty too, he made
The psalms and prophets partners in
    his trade,
And in his orthodoxy straitened more
As it enlarged the business at his store;
He honored Moses, but, when gain he
    planned,
Had his own notion of the Promised
    Land.

    " Soon as the winter made the sled-
    ding good,
From far around the farmers hauled
    him wood,
For all the trade had gathered 'neath
    his thumb,
He paid in groceries and New England
    rum,

Making two profits with a conscience
    clear, —
Cheap all he bought, and all he paid
    with dear.
With his own mete-wand measuring
    every load,
Each somehow had diminished on the
    road;
An honest cord in Jethro still would fail
By a good foot upon the Deacon's
    scale,
And, more to abate the price, his gimlet
    eye
Would pierce to cat-sticks that none
    else could spy;
Yet none dared grumble, for no farmer
    yet
But New Year found him in the Dea-
    con's debt.

    " While the first snow was mealy un-
    der feet,
A team drawled creaking down Quom-
    pegan street.
Two cords of oak weighed down the
    grinding sled,
And cornstalk fodder rustled over-
    head;
The oxen's muzzles, as they shouldered
    through,
Were silver-fringed; the driver's own
    was blue
As the coarse frock that swung below
    his knee.
Behind his load for shelter waded he;
His mittened hands now on his chest
    he beat,
Now stamped the stiffened cowhides of
    his feet,
Hushed as a ghost's; his armpit scarce
    could hold
The walnut whipstock slippery-bright
    with cold.
What wonder if, the tavern as he past,
He looked and longed, and stayed his
    beasts at last,
Who patient stood and veiled them-
    selves in steam
While he explored the bar-room's
    ruddy gleam?

    " Before the fire, in want of thought
    profound,
There sat a brother-townsman weather-
    bound

A sturdy churl, crisp-headed, bristly-
  eared,
Red as a pepper; 'twixt coarse brows
  and beard
His eyes lay ambushed, on the watch
  for fools,
Clear, gray, and glittering like two bay-
  edged pools;
A shifty creature, with a turn for fun,
Could swap a poor horse for a better
  one, —
He 'd a high-stepper always in his
  stall;
Liked far and near, and dreaded there-
  withal.
To him the in-comer, 'Perez, how d'
  ye do?'
'Jest as I 'm mind to, Obed; how do
  you?'
Then his eyes twinkling such swift
  gleams as run
Along the levelled barrel of a gun
Brought to his shoulder by a man you
  know
Will bring his game down, he con-
  tinued, ' So,
I s'pose you 're haulin' wood? But
  you 're too late;
The Deacon 's off; Old Splitfoot
  could n't wait;
He made a bee-line las' night in the
  storm
To where he won't need wood to keep
  him warm.
'Fore this he 's treasurer of a fund to
  train
Young imps as missionaries; hopes to
  gain
That way a contract that he has in
  view
For fireproof pitchforks of a pattern
  new.
It must have tickled him, all drawbacks
  weighed,
To think he stuck the Old One in a
  trade;
His soul, to start with, was n't worth a
  carrot,
And all he 'd left 'ould hardly serve to
  swear at.'

"By this time Obed had his wits
  thawed out,
And, looking at the other half in
  doubt,

Took off his fox-skin cap to scratch his
  head,
Donned it again, and drawled forth,
  'Mean he 's dead?'
'Jesso; he 's dead and t' other *d* that
  follers
With folks that never love a thing but
  dollars.
He pulled up stakes last evening, fair
  and square,
And ever since there 's been a row
  Down There.
The minute the old chap arrived, you
  see,
Comes the Boss-devil to him, and says
  he,
"What are you good at? Little enough
  I fear;
We callilate to make folks useful here."
"Well," says old Bitters, "I expect I
  can
Scale a fair load of wood with e'er a
  man."
"Wood we don't deal in; but perhaps
  you'll suit,
Because we buy our brimstone by the
  foot:
Here, take this measurin' rod, as
  smooth as sin,
And keep a reckonin' of what loads
  comes in.
You 'll not want business, for we need
  a lot
To keep the Yankees that you send us
  hot;
At firin' up they 're barely half as spry
As Spaniards or Italians, though they 're
  dry;
At first we have to let the draught on
  stronger,
But, heat 'em through, they seem to
  hold it longer."

"'Bitters he took the rod, and pretty
  soon
A teamster comes, whistling an ex-psalm
  tune.
A likelier chap you would n't ask to
  see,
No different, but his limp, from you or
  me' —
'No different, Perez! Don't your
  memory fail?
Why, where in thunder was his horns
  and tail?'

'They 're only worn by some old-fash-
ioned pokes!
They mostly aim at looking just like
folks.
Sech things are scarce as queues and
top-boots here;
'T would spoil their usefulness to look
too queer.
Ef you could always know 'em when
they come,
They 'd get no purchase on you: now
be mum.
On come the teamster, smart as Davy
Crockett,
Jinglin' the red-hot coppers in his
pocket,
And clost behind, ('t was gold-dust,
you 'd ha' sworn,)
A load of sulphur yallower 'n seed-
corn;
To see it wasted as it is Down There
Would make a Friction-Match Co. tear
its hair!
"Hold on!" says Bitters, "stop right
where you be;
You can't go in athout a pass from
me."
"All right," says 't other, " only step
round smart;
I must be home by noon-time with the
cart."
Bitters goes round it sharp-eyed as a
rat,
Then with a scrap of paper on his hat
Pretends to cipher. " By the public
staff,
That load scarce rises twelve foot and
a half."
"There 's fourteen foot and over," says
the driver,
"Worth twenty dollars, ef it 's worth a
stiver;
Good fourth-proof brimstone, that 'll
make 'em squirm, —
I leave it to the Headman of the Firm;
After we masure it, we always lay
Some on to allow for settlin' by the
way.
Imp and full-grown, I 've carted sulphur
here,
And gi'n fair satisfaction, thirty year."
With that they fell to quarrellin' so
loud
That in five minutes they had drawed a
crowd,

And afore long the Boss, who heard the
row,
Comes elbowin' in with " What's to pay
here now ? "
Both parties heard, the measurin'-rod
he takes,
And of the load a careful survey makes.
" Sence I have bossed the business
here," says he,
" No fairer load was ever seen by me."
Then, turnin' to the Deacon, " You
mean cuss,
None of your old Quompegan tricks
with us!
They won't do here: we 're plain old-
fashioned folks,
And don't quite understand that kind o
jokes.
I know this teamster, and his pa afore
him,
And the hard working Mrs. D. that
bore him;
He would n't soil his conscience with a
lie,
Though he might get the custom-house
thereby.
Here, constable, take Bitters by the
queue,
And clap him into furnace ninety-two.
And try this brimstone on him; if he's
bright,
He 'll find the masure honest afore
night.
He is n't worth his fuel, and I 'll bet
The parish oven has to take him yet ! " '

" This is my tale, heard twenty years
ago
From Uncle Reuben, as the logs burned
low,
Touching the wall and ceiling with that
bloom
That makes a rose's calyx of a room.
I could not give his language, where-
through ran
The gamy flavor of the bookless man
Who shapes a word before the fancy
cools,
As lonely Crusoe improvised his tools.
I liked the tale, — 't was like so many
told
By Rutebeuf and his brother Trouvères
bold;
Nor were the hearers much unlike to
theirs,

Men unsophisticate, rude-nerved as
   bears.
Ezra is gone and his large-hearted
   kind,
The landlords of the hospitable mind;
Good Warriner of Springfield was the
   last;
An inn is now a vision of the past;
One yet-surviving host my mind re-
   calls, —
You 'll find him if you go to Trenton
   Falls."

THE ORIGIN OF DIDACTIC
POETRY.

WHEN wise Minerva still was young
   And just the least romantic,
Soon after from Jove's head she flung
   That preternatural antic,
'T is said, to keep from idleness
   Or flirting, those twin curses,
She spent her leisure, more or less,
   In writing po——, no, verses.

How nice they were! to rhyme with
   far
   A kind *star* did not tarry;
The metre, too, was regular
   As schoolboy's dot and carry;
And full they were of pious plums,
   So extra-super-moral, —
For sucking Virtue's tender gums
   Most tooth-enticing coral.

A clean, fair copy she prepares,
   Makes sure of moods and tenses,
With her own hand, — for prudence
   spares
   A man- (or woman-) -uensis;
Complete, and tied with ribbons proud,
   She hinted soon how cosy a
Treat it would be to read them loud
   After next day's Ambrosia.

The Gods thought not it would amuse
   So much as Homer's Odyssees,
But could not very well refuse
   The properest of Goddesses:
So all sat round in attitudes
   Of various dejection,
As with a *hem !* the queen of prudes
   Began her grave prelection.

At the first pause Zeus said, "Well
   sung! —
I mean — ask Phœbus, — *he* knows."
Says Phœbus, "Zounds! a wolf's
   among
Admetus's merinos!
Fine! very fine! but I must go;
   They stand in need of me there:
Excuse me!" snatched his stick, and so
   Plunged down the gladdened ether.

With the next gap, Mars said, "For me
   Don't wait, — naught could be finer,
But I 'm engaged at half past three, —
   A fight in Asia Minor !"
Then Venus lisped, "I 'm sorely tried,
   These duty-calls are vip'rous;
But I *must* go; I have a bride
   To see about in Cyprus."

Then Bacchus, — "I must say good
   bye,
Although my peace it jeopards;
I meet a man at four, to try
   A well-broke pair of leopards."
His words woke Hermes. "Ah!" he
   said,
   "I *so* love moral theses!"
Then winked at Hebe, who turned red
   And smoothed her apron's creases.

Just then Zeus snored, — the Eagle
   drew
   His head the wing from under;
Zeus snored, — o'er startled Greece
   there flew
   The many-volumed thunder.
Some augurs counted nine, some ten;
   Some said 't was war, some, famine,
And all, that other-minded men
   Would get a precious ——.

Proud Pallas sighed, "It will not do;
   Against the Muse I 've sinned, oh !"
And her torn rhymes sent flying through
   Olympus's back window.
Then, packing up a peplus clean,
   She took the shortest path thence,
And opened, with a mind serene,
   A Sunday-school in Athens.

The verses? Some in ocean swilled,
   Killed every fish that bit to 'em;
Some Galen caught, and, when distilled,
   Found morphine the residuum;

But some that rotted on the earth
Sprang up again in copies,
And gave two strong narcotics birth,
Didactic verse and poppies.

Years after, when a poet asked
The Goddess's opinion,
As one whose soul its wings had tasked
In Art's clear-aired dominion,
"Discriminate," she said, "betimes;
The Muse is unforgiving;
Put all your beauty in your rhymes,
Your morals in your living."

THE FLYING DUTCHMAN.

DON'T believe in the Flying Dutch-
man?
I 've known the fellow for years;
My button I 've wrenched from his
clutch, man :
I shudder whenever he nears !

He 's a Rip van Winkle skipper,
A wandering Jew of the sea,
Who sails his bedevilled old clipper
In the wind's eye, straight as a bee.

Back topsails! you can't escape him ;
The man-ropes stretch with his
weight,
And the queerest old toggeries drape
him,
The Lord knows how long out of
date !

Like a long-disembodied idea,
(A kind of ghost plentiful now,)
He stands there ; you fancy you see a
Coeval of Teniers or Douw.

He greets you ; would have you take
letters :
You scan the addresses with dread,
While he mutters his *donners* and *wet-
ters,* —
They 're all from the dead to the
dead !

You seem taking time for reflection,
But the heart fills your throat with a
jam,
As you spell in each faded direction
An ominous ending in *dam.*

Am I tagging my rhymes to a legend ?
That were changing green turtle to
mock :
No, thank you !   I 've found out which
wedge-end
Is meant for the head of a block.

The fellow I have in my mind's eye
Plays the old skipper's part here on
shore,
And sticks like a burr, tills he finds I
Have got just the gauge of his bore.

This postman 'twixt one ghost and t'
other,
With last dates that smell of the
mould,
I have met him (O man and brother,
Forgive me!) in azure and gold.

In the pulpit I 've known of his preach-
ing,
Out of hearing behind the time,
Some statement of Balaam's impeach-
ing,
Giving Eve a due sense of her crime.

I have seen him some poor ancient
thrashing
Into something (God save us !) more
dry,
With the Water of Life itself washing
The life out of earth, sea, and sky.

O dread fellow-mortal, get newer
Despatches to carry, or none !
We 're as quick as the Greek and the
Jew were
At knowing a loaf from a stone.

Till the couriers of God fail in duty,
We sha'n't ask a mummy for news,
Nor sate the soul's hunger for beauty
With your drawings from casts of a
Muse.

CREDIDIMUS JOVEM REG-
NARE.

O DAYS endeared to every Muse,
When nobody had any Views,
Nor, while the cloudscape of his mind
By every breeze was new designed,
Insisted all the world should see

Camels or whales where none there be!
O happy days, when men received
From sire to son what all believed,
And left the other world in bliss,
Too busy with bedevilling this!

Beset by doubts of every breed
In the last bastion of my creed,
With shot and shell for Sabbath-chime,
I watch the storming-party climb,
Panting (their prey in easy reach),
To pour triumphant through the breach
In walls that shed like snowflakes tons
Of missiles from old-fashioned guns,
But crumble 'neath the storm that
        pours
All day and night from bigger bores.
There, as I hopeless watch and wait
The last life-crushing coil of Fate,
Despair finds solace in the praise
Of those serene dawn-rosy days
Ere microscopes had made us heirs
To large estates of doubts and snares,
By proving that the title-deeds,
Once all-sufficient for men's needs,
Are palimpsests that scarce disguise
The tracings of still earlier lies,
Themselves as surely written o'er
An older fib erased before.

So from these days I fly to those
That in the landlocked Past repose,
Where no rude wind of doctrine
        shakes
From bloom-flushed boughs untimely
        flakes ;
Where morning's eyes see nothing
        strange,
No crude perplexity of change,
And morrows trip along their ways
Secure as happy yesterdays.
Then there were rulers who could
        trace
Through heroes up to gods their race,
Pledged to fair fame and noble use
By veins from Odin filled or Zeus,
And under bonds to keep divine
The praise of a celestial line.
Then priests could pile the altar's
        sods,
With whom gods spake as they with
        gods,
And everywhere from haunted earth
Broke springs of wonder, that had
        birth

In depths divine beyond the ken
And fatal scrutiny of men ;
Then hills and groves and streams and
        seas
Thrilled with immortal presences,
Not too ethereal for the scope
Of human passion's dream or hope.

Now Pan at last is surely dead,
And King No-Credit reigns instead,
Whose officers, morosely strict,
Poor Fancy's tenantry evict,
Chase the last Genius from the door,
And nothing dances any more.
Nothing ? Ah, yes, our tables do,
Drumming the Old One's own tattoo,
And, if the oracles are dumb,
Have we not mediums ? Why be
        glum ?

Fly thither ? Why, the very air
Is full of hindrance and despair !
Fly thither ? But I cannot fly ;
My doubts enmesh me if I try, —
Each Lilliputian, but, combined,
Potent a giant's limbs to bind.
This world and that are growing
        dark ;
A huge interrogation mark,
The Devil's crook episcopal,
Still borne before him since the Fall,
Blackens with its ill-omened sign
The old blue heaven of faith benign.
Whence ? Whither ? Wherefore ? How ?
        Which ? Why ?
All ask at once, all wait reply.
Men feel old systems cracking under
        'em ;
Life saddens to a mere conundrum
Which once Religion solved, but she
Has lost — has Science found ?— the
        key.

What was snow-bearded Odin, trow,
The mighty hunter long ago,
Whose horn and hounds the peasant
        hears
Still when the Northlights shake their
        spears ?
Science hath answers twain, I 've
        heard ;
Choose which you will, nor hope a
        third ;
Whichever box the truth be stowed in,
There 's not a sliver left of Odin.

Either he was a pinchbrowed thing,
With scarcely wit a stone to fling,
A creature both in size and shape
Nearer than we are to the ape,
Who hung sublime with brat and
    spouse
By tail prehensile from the boughs,
And, happier than his maimed de-
    scendants,
The culture curtailed *in*dependents,
Could pluck his cherries with both
    paws,
And stuff with both his big-boned
    jaws;
Or else the core his name enveloped
Was from a solar myth developed,
Which, hunted to its primal shoot,
Takes refuge in a Sanskrit root,
Thereby to instant death explaining
The little poetry remaining.

Try it with Zeus, 't is just the same;
The thing evades, we hug a name;
Nay, scarcely that, — perhaps a vapor
Born of some atmospheric caper.
All Lempriere's fables blur together
In cloudy symbols of the weather,
And Aphrodite rose from frothy seas
But to illustrate such hypotheses.
With years enough behind his back,
Lincoln will take the selfsame track,
And prove, hulled fairly to the cob,
A mere vagary of Old Prob.
Give the right man a solar myth,
And he 'll confute the sun therewith.

They make things admirably plain,
But one hard question *will* remain:
If one hypothesis you lose,
Another is its place you choose,
But, your faith gone, O man and
    brother,
Whose shop shall furnish you an-
    other?
One that will wash, I mean, and wear,
And wrap us warmly from despair?
While they are clearing up our puzzles,
And clapping prophylactic muzzles
On the Actæon's hounds that sniff
Our devious track through But and If,
Would they 'd explain away the Devil
And other facts that won't keep level,
But rise beneath our feet or fail,
A reeling ship's deck in a gale!
God vanished long ago, iwis,

A mere subjective synthesis;
A doll, stuffed out with hopes and
    fears,
Too homely for us pretty dears,
Who want one that conviction carries,
Last make of London or of Paris.
He gone, I felt a moment's spasm,
But calmed myself with Protoplasm,
A finer name, and, what is more,
As enigmatic as before;
Greek, too, and sure to fill with ease
Minds caught in the Symplegades
Of soul and sense, life's two condi-
    tions,
Each baffled with its own omni-
    science.
The men who labor to revise
Our Bibles will, I hope, be wise,
And print it without foolish qualms
Instead of God in David's psalms:
Noll had been more effective far
Could he have shouted at Dunbar,
"Rise, Protoplasm!" No dourest
    Scot
Had waited for another shot.

And yet I frankly must confess
A secret unforgivingness,
And shudder at the saving chrism
Whose best New Birth is Pessimism;
My soul — I mean the bit of phos-
    phorus,
That fills the place of what that was
    for us —
Can't bid its inward bores defiance
With the new nursery-tales of science.
What profits me, though doubt by
    doubt,
As nail by nail, be driven out,
When every new one, like the last,
Still holds my coffin-lid as fast?
Would I find thought a moment's
    truce,
Give me the young world's Mother
    Goose
With life and joy in every limb,
The chimney-corner tales of Grimm!
Our dear and admirable Huxley
Cannot explain to me why ducks lay,
Or rather, how into their eggs
Blunder potential wings and legs
With will to move them and decide
Whether in air or lymph to glide.
Who gets a hair's-breadth on by show-
    ing

That Something Else set all agoing?
Farther and farther back we push
From Moses and his burning bush;
Cry, "Art Thou there?" Above,
    below,
All Nature mutters *yes* and *no!*
'T is the old answer : we 're agreed
Being from Being must proceed,
Life be Life's source. I might as
    well
Obey the meeting-house's bell,
And listen while Old Hundred pours
Forth through the summer - opened
    doors,
From old and young. I hear it yet,
Swelled by bass-viol and clarinet,
While the gray minister, with face
Radiant, let loose his noble bass.
If Heaven it reached not, yet its roll
Waked all the echoes of the soul,
And in it many a life found wings
To soar away from sordid things.
Church gone and singers too, the
    song
Sings to me voiceless all night long,
Till my soul beckons me afar,
Glowing and trembling like a star.
Will any scientific touch
With my worn strings achieve as much?

I don't object, not I, to know
My sires were monkeys, if 't was so;
I touch my ear's collusive tip
And own the poor-relationship.
That apes of various shapes and sizes
Contained their germs that all the
    prizes
Of senate, pulpit, camp, and bar win
May give us hopes that sweeten
    Darwin.
Who knows but from our loins may
    spring
(Long hence) some winged sweet-
    throated thing
As much superior to us
As we to Cynocephalus?

This is consoling, but, alas,
It wipes no dimness from the glass
Where I am flattening my poor nose,
In hope to see beyond my toes.
Though I accept my pedigree,
Yet where, pray tell me, is the key
That should unlock a private door
To the Great Mystery, such no more?

Each offers his, but one nor all
Are much persuasive with the wall
That rises now, as long ago,
Between I wonder and I know,
Nor will vouchsafe a pin-hole peep
At the veiled Isis in its keep.
Where is no door, I but produce
My key to find it of no use.
Yet better keep it, after all,
Since Nature 's economical,
And who can tell but some fine day
(If it occur to her) she may,
In her good-will to you and me,
Make door and lock to match the key?

TEMPORA MUTANTUR.

THE world turns mild; democracy,
    they say,
Rounds the sharp knobs of character
    away,
And no great harm, unless at grave
    expense
Of what needs edge of proof, the moral
    sense;
For man or race is on the downward
    path
Whose fibre grows too soft for honest
    wrath,
And there 's a subtle influence that
    springs
From words to modify our sense of
    things
A plain distinction grows obscure of
    late:
Man, if he will, may pardon; but the
    State
Forgets its function if not fixed as
    Fate.
So thought our sires: a hundred years
    ago,
If men were knaves, why, people called
    them so,
And crime could see the prison-portal
    bend
Its brow severe at no long vista's end.
In those days for plain things plain
    words would serve;
Men had not learned to admire the
    graceful swerve
Wherewith the Æsthetic Nature's gen-
    ial mood
Makes public duty slope to private
    good;

No muddled conscience raised the saving doubt :
A soldier proved unworthy was drummed out ;
An officer cashiered, a civil servant
(No matter though his piety were fervent)
Disgracefully dismissed, and through the land
Each bore for life a stigma from the brand
Whose far-heard hiss made others more averse
To take the facile step from bad to worse.
The Ten Commandments had a meaning then
Felt in their bones by least considerate men,
Because behind them Public Conscience stood,
And without wincing made their mandates good.
But now that " Statesmanship " is just a way
To dodge the primal curse and make it pay,
Since office means a kind of patent drill
To force an entrance to the Nation's till,
And peculation something rather less
Risky than if you spelt it with an *s* ;
Now that to steal by law is grown an art,
Whom rogues the sires, their milder sons call smart,
And " slightly irregular " dilutes the shame
Of what had once a somewhat blunter name,
With generous curve we draw the moral line :
Our swindlers are permitted to resign ;
Their guilt is wrapped in deferential names,
And twenty sympathize for one that blames.
Add national disgrace to private crime,
Confront mankind with brazen front sublime,
Steal but enough, the world is unsevere, —
Tweed is a statesman, Fisk a financier :
Invent a mine, and be — the Lord knows what ;

Secure, at any rate, with what you 've got.
The public servant who has stolen or lied,
If called on, may resign with honest pride :
As unjust favor put him in, why doubt
Disfavor as unjust has turned him out ?
Even if indicted, what is that but fudge
To him who counted-in the elective judge ?
Whitewashed, he quits the politician's strife
At ease in mind, with pockets filled for life :
His " lady " glares with gems whose vulgar blaze
The poor man through his heightened taxes pays,
Himself content if one huge Kohinoor
Bulge from a shirt-front ampler than before,
But not too candid, lest it haply tend
To rouse suspicion of the People's Friend.
A public meeting, treated at his cost,
Resolves him back more virtue than he lost ;
With character regilt he counts his gains ;
What 's gone was air, the solid good remains ;
For what is good, except what friend and foe
Seem quite unanimous in thinking so,
The stocks and bonds which, in our age of loans,
Replace the stupid pagan's stocks and stones ?
With choker white, wherein no cynic eye
Dares see idealized a hempen tie,
At parish - meetings he conducts in prayer,
And pays for missions to be sent elsewhere ;
On 'Change respected, to his friends endeared,
Add but a Sunday-school-class, he 's revered,
And his too early tomb will not be dumb
To point a moral for our youth to come.

1872.

IN THE HALF-WAY HOUSE.

I.

At twenty we fancied the blest Middle
　　Ages
A spirited cross of romantic and grand,
All templars and minstrels and ladies
　　and pages,
　　And love and adventure in Outre-
　　　Mer land ;
But ah, where the youth dreamed of
　　building a minster,
　　The man takes a pew and sits reck-
　　　oning his pelf,
And the Graces wear fronts, the Muse
　　thins to a spinster
　　When Middle-Age stares from one's
　　　glass at oneself !

II.

Do you twit me with days when I had
　　an Ideal,
　　And saw the sear future through
　　　spectacles green ?
Then find me some charm, while I
　　look round and see all
　　These fat friends of forty, shall keep
　　　me nineteen ;
Should we go on pining for chaplets of
　　laurel
　　Who 've paid a perruquier for mend-
　　　ing our thatch,
Or, our feet swathed in baize, with
　　our Fate pick a quarrel,
　　If, instead of cheap bay-leaves, she
　　　sent a dear scratch ?

III.

We called it our Eden, that small
　　patent-baker,
　　When life was half moonshine and
　　　half Mary Jane ;
But the butcher, the baker, the candle-
　　stick maker ! —
　　Did Adam have duns and slip down
　　　a back-lane ?
Nay, after the Fall did the modiste
　　keep coming
　　With last styles of fig-leaf to Madam
　　　Eve's bower ?
Did Jubal, or whoever taught the girls
　　thrumming,
　　Make the patriarchs deaf at a dollar
　　　the hour ?

IV.

As I think what I was, I sigh *Desunt
　　nonnulla !*
Years are creditors Sheridan's self
　　could not bilk ;
But then, as my boy says, " What
　　right has a fullah
　　To ask for the cream, when himself
　　　spilt the milk ? "
Perhaps when you 're older, my lad,
　　you 'll discover
　　The secret with which Auld Lang
　　　Syne there is gilt, —
Superstition of old man, maid, poet, and
　　lover,
　　That cream rises thickest on milk that
　　　was spilt !

V.

We sailed for the moon, but, in sad
　　disillusion,
　　Snug under Point Comfort are glad to
　　　make fast,
And strive (sans our glasses) to make a
　　confusion
　　'Twixt our rind of green cheese and
　　　the moon of the past.
Ah, Might-have-been, Could-have-been,
　　Would-have-been ! rascals,
　　He 's a genius or fool whom ye cheat
　　　at twoscore,
And the man whose boy-promise was
　　likened to Pascal's
　　Is thankful at forty they don't call him
　　　bore !

VI.

With what fumes of fame was each con-
　　fident pate full !
　　How rates of insurance should rise on
　　　the Charles !
And which of us now would not feel
　　wisely grateful,
　　If his rhymes sold as fast as the Em-
　　　blems of Quarles ?
E'en if won, what 's the good of Life's
　　medals and prizes ?
　　The rapture 's in what never was or is
　　　gone ;
That we missed them makes Helens
　　of plain Ann Elizys,
　　For the goose of To-day still is Mem-
　　　ory's swan.

VII.

And yet who would change the old
    dream for new treasure?
Make not youth's sourest grapes the
    best wine of our life?
Need he reckon his date by the Alma-
    nac's measure
Who is twenty life-long in the eyes of
    his wife?
Ah, Fate, should I live to be nonagena-
    rian,
    Let me still take Hope's frail I. O.
    U.'s upon trust,
Still talk of a trip to the Islands Ma-
    carian,
    And still climb the dream-tree for —
    ashes and dust!

AT THE BURNS CENTEN-
NIAL.

JANUARY, 1859.

I.

A HUNDRED years! they 're quickly
    fled
    With all their joy and sorrow;
Their dead leaves shed upon the dead,
    Their fresh ones sprung by morrow!
And still the patient seasons bring
    Their change of sun and shadow;
New birds still sing with every spring,
    New violets spot the meadow.

II.

A hundred years! and Nature's powers
    No greater grown nor lessened!
They saw no flowers more sweet than
    ours,
    No fairer new moon's crescent.
Would she but treat us poets so,
    So from our winter free us,
And set our slow old sap aflow
    To sprout in fresh ideas!

III.

Alas, think I, what worth or parts
    Have brought me here competing
To speak what starts in myriad hearts
    With Burns's memory beating!

Himself had loved a theme like this;
    Must I be its entomber?
No pen save his but 's sure to miss
    Its pathos or its humor.

IV.

As I sat musing what to say,
    And how my verse to number,
Some elf in play passed by that way,
    And sank my lids in slumber;
And on my sleep a vision stole,
    Which I will put in metre,
Of Burns's soul at the wicket-hole
    Where sits the good Saint Peter.

V.

The saint, methought, had left his post
    That day to Holy Willie,
Who swore, " Each ghost that comes
    shall toast
    In brunstane, will he, nill he;
There 's nane need hope with phrases
    fine
    Their score to wipe a sin frae;
I 'll chalk a sign, to save their tryin',—
    A hand (☞) and ' *Vide infra !*'"

VI.

Alas! no soil 's too cold or dry
    For spiritual small potatoes,
Scrimped natures, spry the trade to
    ply
    Of *diaboli advocatus;*
Who lay bent pins in the penance-
    stool
    Where Mercy plumps a cushion,
Who 've just one rule for knave and
    fool,
    It saves so much confusion!

VII.

So when Burns knocked, Will knit his
    brows,
    His window gap made scanter,
And said, " Go rouse the other house;
    We lodge no Tam O' Shanter!"
" *We* lodge!" laughed Burns. " Now
    well I see
    Death cannot kill old nature;
No human flea but thinks that he
    May speak for his Creator!

VIII.

'But, Willie, friend, don't turn me
        forth,
    Auld Clootie needs no gauger:
And if on earth I had small worth,
    You've let in worse, I'se wager!"
"Na, nane has knockit at the yett
    But found me hard as whunstane;
There's chances yet your bread to get
    Wi Auld Nick, gaugin' brunstane."

IX.

Meanwhile, the Unco' Guid had ta'en
    Their place to watch the process,
Flattening in vain on many a pane
    Their disembodied noses.
Remember, please, 't is all a dream;
    One can't control the fancies
Through sleep that stream with way-
        ward gleam,
    Like midnight's boreal dances.

X.

Old Willie's tone grew sharp 's a
        knife;
    "*In primis*, I indite ye,
For makin' strife wi' the water o' life,
    And preferrin' *aqua vitæ!*"
Then roared a voice with lusty din,
    Like a skipper's when 't is blowy,
"If that's a sin, *I*'d ne'er got in,
    As sure as my name 's Noah!"

XI.

Baulked, Willie turned another leaf, —
    "There's many here have heard ye,
To the pain and grief o' true belief,
    Say hard things o' the clergy!"
Then rang a clear tone over all, —
    "One plea for him allow me:
I once heard call from o'er me, 'Saul,
    Why persecutest thou me?'"

XII.

To the next charge vexed Willie
        turned,
    And, sighing, wiped his glasses:
"I'm much concerned to find ye
        yearned
    O'er-warmly tow'rd the lasses!"

Here David sighed; poor Willie's face
    Lost all its self-possession:
"I leave this case to God's own grace:
    It baffles *my* discretion!"

XIII.

Then sudden glory round me broke,
    And low melodious surges
Of wings whose stroke to splendor
        woke
    Creation's farthest verges;
A cross stretched, ladder-like, secure
    From earth to heaven's own portal,
Whereby God's poor, with footing
        sure,
    Climbed up to peace immortal.

XIV.

I heard a voice serene and low
    (With my heart I seemed to hear it)
Fall soft and slow as snow on snow,
    Like grace of the heavenly spirit;
As sweet as over new-born son
    The croon of new-made mother,
The voice begun, "Sore tempted
        one!"
    Then, pausing, sighed, "Our bro-
        ther!

XV.

"If not a sparrow fall, unless
    The Father sees and knows it,
Think! recks He less His form express,
    The soul His own deposit?
If only dear to Him the strong,
    That never trip nor wander,
Where were the throng whose morn-
        ing song
    Thrills His blue arches yonder?

XVI.

"Do souls alone clear-eyed, strong-
        kneed,
    To Him true service render,
And they who need His hand to lead,
    Find they His heart untender?
Through all your various ranks and
        fates
    He opens doors to duty,
And he that waits there at your gates
    Was servant of His Beauty.

XVII.

" The Earth must richer sap secrete,
  (Could ye in time but know it !)
Must juice concrete with fiercer heat,
  Ere she can make her poet ;
Long generations go and come,
  At last she bears a singer,
For ages dumb of senses numb
  The compensation-bringer !

XVIII.

" Her cheaper broods in palaces
  She raises under glasses,
But souls like these, heav'n's hostages,
  Spring shelterless as grasses :
They share Earth's blessing and her
    bane,
  The common sun and shower ;
What makes your pain to them is gain,
  Your weakness is their power.

XIX.

" These larger hearts must feel the
    rolls
  Of stormier-waved temptation ;
These star-wide souls between their
    poles
  Bear zones of tropic passion.
He loved much ! — that is gospel good,
  Howe'er the text you handle ;
From common wood the cross was
    hewed,
  By love turned priceless sandal.

XX.

" If scant his service at the kirk,
  He *paters* heard and *aves*
From choirs that lurk in hedge and
    birk,
  From blackbird and from mavis ;
The cowering mouse, poor unroofed
    thing,
  In him found Mercy's angel ;
The daisy's ring brought every spring
  To him Love's fresh evangel !

XXI.

" Not he the threatening texts who
    deals
  Is highest 'mong the preachers,
But he who feels the woes and weals
  Of all God's wandering creatures.

He doth good work whose heart can
    find
  The spirit 'neath the letter ;
Who makes his kind of happier mind,
  Leaves wiser men and better.

XXII.

" They make Religion be abhorred
  Who round with darkness gulf her,
And think no word can please the
    Lord
  Unless it smell of sulphur.
Dear Poet-heart, that childlike guessed
  The Father's loving kindness,
Come now to rest ! Thou didst His
    hest,
  If haply 't was in blindness ! "

XXIII.

Then leapt heaven's portals wide
    apart,
  And at their golden thunder
With sudden start I woke, my heart
  Still throbbing-full of wonder.
" Father," I said, " 't is known to
    Thee
  How Thou thy Saints preparest ;
But this I see, — Saint Charity
  Is still the first and fairest ! "

XXIV.

Dear Bard and Brother ! let who may
  Against thy faults be railing,
(Though far, I pray, from us be they
  That never had a failing !)
One toast I 'll give, and that not
    long,
  Which thou wouldst pledge if pres-
    ent, —
To him whose song, in nature strong,
  Makes man of prince and peasant !

IN AN ALBUM.

THE misspelt scrawl, upon the wall
  By some Pompeian idler traced,
In ashes packed (ironic fact !)
  Lies eighteen centuries uneffaced,
While many a page of bard and sage,
  Deemed once mankind's immortal gain,

Lost from Time's ark, leaves no more
　　mark
Than a keel's furrow through the main.

O Chance and Change! our buzz's
　　range
Is scarcely wider than a fly's;
Then let us play at fame to-day,
To-morrow be unknown and wise;
And while the fair beg locks of hair,
And autographs, and Lord knows what,
Quick! let us scratch our moment's
　　match,
Make our brief blaze, and be forgot!

Too pressed to wait, upon her slate
Fame writes a name or two in doubt;
Scarce written, these no longer please,
And her own finger rubs them out:
It may ensue, fair girl, that you
Years hence this yellowing leaf may see,
And put to task, your memory ask
In vain, "This Lowell, who was he?"

AT THE COMMENCEMENT DINNER, 1866.

IN ACKNOWLEDGING A TOAST TO THE SMITH PROFESSOR.

I RISE, Mr. Chairman, as both of us
　　know,
With the impromptu I promised you
　　three weeks ago,
Dragged up to my doom by your might
　　and my mane,
To do what I vowed I'd do never
　　again;
And I feel like your good honest dough
　　when possest
By a stirring, impertinent devil of
　　yeast.
"You must rise," says the leaven.
　　"I can't," says the dough:
"Just examine my bumps and you'll
　　see it's no go."
"But you must," the tormentor in-
　　sists, "'t is all right;
You must rise when I bid you, and,
　　what's more, be light."
'T is a dreadful oppression, this mak-
　　ing men speak
What they're sure to be sorry for all
　　the next week;

Some poor stick requesting, like Aar-
　　on's, to bud
Into eloquence, pathos, or wit in cold
　　blood,
As if the dull brain that you vented
　　your spite on
Could be got, like an ox, by mere pok-
　　ing, to Brighton.

They say it is wholesome to rise with
　　the sun,
And I dare say it may be if not over-
　　done;
(I think it was Thomson who made the
　　remark
'T was an excellent thing in its way —
　　for a lark;)
But to rise after dinner and look down
　　the meeting
On a distant (as Gray calls it) prospect
　　of Eating,
With a stomach half full and a cere-
　　brum hollow
As the tortoise-shell ere it was strung
　　for Apollo,
Under contract to raise anerithmon
　　gelasma
With rhymes so hard hunted they
　　gasp with the asthma,
And jokes not much younger than
　　Jethro's phylacteries,
Is something I leave you yourselves to
　　characterize.

I've a notion, I think, of a good dinner
　　speech,
Tripping light as a sandpiper over the
　　beach,
Swerving this way and that as the
　　wave of the moment
Washes out its slight trace with a
　　dash of whim's foam on 't,
And leaving on memory's rim just a
　　sense
Something graceful had gone by, a live
　　present tense;
Not poetry, — no, not quite that, but
　　as good,
A kind of winged prose that could fly
　　if it would.

'T is a time for gay fancies as fleeting
　　and vain
As the whisper of foam-beads on fresh
　　poured champagne,

Since dinners were not perhaps strictly
designed
For manœuvring the heavy dragoons
of the mind.
When I hear your set speeches that
start with a pop,
Then wander and maunder, too feeble
to stop,
With a vague apprehension from popu-
lar rumor
There used to be something by mortals
called humor,
Beginning again when you thought
they were done,
Respectable, sensible, weighing a ton,
And as near to the present occasions
of men
As a Fast Day discourse of the year
eighteen ten,
I — well, I sit still, and my sentiments
smother,
For am I not also a bore and a brother?

And a toast, — what should that be?
Light, airy, and free,
The foam - Aphrodite of Bacchus's
sea,
A fancy-tinged bubble, an orbed rain-
bow-stain,
That floats for an instant 'twixt goblet
and brain ;
A breath-born perfection, half some-
thing, half naught,
And breaks if it strike the hard edge of
a thought.
Do you ask me to make such? Ah no,
not so simple ;
Ask Apelles to paint you the ravishing
dimple
Whose shifting enchantment lights Ve-
nus's cheek,
And the artist will tell you his skill is
to seek ;
Once fix it, 't is naught, for the charm
of it rises
From the sudden bopeeps of its smiling surprises.

I 've tried to define it, but what mother's son
Could ever yet do what he knows
should be done?
My rocket has burst, and I watch in
the air
Its fast-fading heart's-blood drop back
in despair ;

Yet one chance is left me, and, if I am
quick,
I can palm off, before you suspect me,
the stick.
Now since I 've succeeded — I pray
do not frown —
To Ticknor's and Longfellow's classical gown,
And profess four strange languages,
which, luckless elf,
I speak like a native (of Cambridge)
myself,
Let me beg, Mr. President, leave to
propose
A sentiment treading on nobody's toes,
And give, in such ale as with pump-
handles *we* brew,
Their memory who saved us from all
talking Hebrew, —
A toast that to deluge with water is
good,
For in Scripture they come in just after
the flood :
I give you the men but for whom, as I
guess, sir,
Modern languages ne'er could have
had a professor,
The builders of Babel, to whose zeal
the lungs
Of the children of men owe confusion
of tongues ;
And a name all-embracing I couple
therewith,
Which is that of my founder — the
late Mr Smith.

A PARABLE.

AN ass munched thistles, while a nightingale
From passion's fountain flooded all the
vale.
" Hee-haw ! " cried he, " I hearken,"
as who knew
For such ear-largess humble thanks
were due.
" Friend," said the wingèd pain, " in
vain you bray,
Who tunnels bring, not cisterns, for my
lay ;
None but his peers the poet rightly
hear,
Nor mete we listeners by their length
of ear."

COLONNA, ITALY, 1852.

V. EPIGRAMS.

SAYINGS.

I.

In life's small things be resolute and great
To keep thy muscle trained : know'st thou when Fate
Thy measure takes, or when she 'll say to thee,
" I find thee worthy ; do this deed for me "?

2.

A camel-driver, angry with his drudge,
Beating him, called him hunchback ; to the hind
Thus spake a dervish : " Friend, the Eternal Judge
Dooms not His work, but ours, the crooked mind."

3.

Swiftly the politic goes : is it dark ? — he borrows a lantern ;
Slowly the statesman and sure, guiding his steps by the stars.

4.

" Where lies the capital, pilgrim, seat of who governs the Faithful?"
"Thither my footsteps are bent : it is where Saadi is lodged."

INSCRIPTIONS.

FOR A BELL AT CORNELL UNIVERSITY.

I call as fly the irrevocable hours,
  Futile as air or strong as fate to make
Your lives of sand or granite ; awful powers,
  Even as men choose, they either give or take

FOR A MEMORIAL WINDOW TO SIR WALTER RALEIGH, SET UP IN ST. MARGARET'S, WESTMINSTER, BY AMERICAN CONTRIBUTORS.

The New World's sons, from England's breasts we drew
  Such milk as bids remember whence we came ;
Proud of her Past wherefrom our Present grew,
  This window we inscribe with Raleigh's name.

PROPOSED FOR A SOLDIERS' AND SAILORS' MONUMENT IN BOSTON.

To those who died for her on land and sea,
That she might have a country great and free,
Boston builds this : build ye her monument
In lives like theirs, at duty's summons spent.

A MISCONCEPTION.

B, taught by Pope to do his good by stealth,
'Twixt participle and noun no difference feeling,

In office placed to serve the Commonwealth,
Does himself all the good he can by stealing.

THE BOSS.

SKILLED to pull wires, he baffles Nature's hope,
Who sure intended him to stretch a rope.

SUN-WORSHIP.

IF I were the rose at your window,
Happiest rose of its crew,
Every blossom I bore would bend inward,
They 'd know where the sunshine grew.

CHANGED PERSPECTIVE.

FULL oft the pathway to her door
I 've measured by the selfsame track,
Yet doubt the distance more and more,
'T is so much longer coming back!

WITH A PAIR OF GLOVES LOST IN A WAGER.

WE wagered, she for sunshine, I for rain,
And I should hint sharp practice if I dared;
For was not she beforehand sure to gain
Who made the sunshine we together shared?

SIXTY-EIGHTH BIRTHDAY.

As life runs on, the road grows strange
With faces new, and near the end
The milestones into headstones change,
'Neath every one a friend.

INTERNATIONAL COPYRIGHT.

IN vain we call old notions fudge,
And bend our conscience to our dealing;
The Ten Commandments will not budge,
And stealing will continue stealing.

LETTER FROM BOSTON.

December, 1846.

DEAR M. —— *

By way of saving time,
I 'll do this letter up in rhyme,
Whose slim stream through four pages
    flows
Ere one is packed with tight-screwed
    prose,
Threading the tube of an epistle,
Smooth as a child's breath through a
    whistle.

The great attraction now of all
Is the " Bazaar " at Faneuil Hall,
Where swarm the anti-slavery folks
As thick, dear Miller, as your jokes.
There 's GARRISON, his features very
Benign for an incendiary,
Beaming forth sunshine through his
    glasses
On the surrounding lads and lasses,
(No bee could blither be, or brisker,)—
A Pickwick somehow turned John
    Ziska,
His bump of firmness swelling up
Like a rye cupcake from its cup.
And there, too, was his English tea-
    set,
Which in his ear a kind of flea set,
His Uncle Samuel for its beauty
Demanding sixty dollars duty,
['T was natural Sam should serve his
    trunk ill,
For G., you know, has cut his uncle,)
Whereas, had he but once made tea
    in 't,
His uncle's ear had had the flea in 't,
There being not a cent of duty
On any pot that ever drew tea.†

There was MARIA CHAPMAN, too.
With her swift eyes of clear steel-
    blue,
The coiled-up mainspring of the Fair,
Originating everywhere
The expansive force without a sound
That whirls a hundred wheels around,
Herself meanwhile as calm and still
As the bare crown of Prospect Hill;
A nobl woman, brave and apt,
Cumæan sibyl not more rapt,
Who might, with those fair tresses
    shorn,
The Maid of Orleans' casque have
    worn,
Herself the Joan of our Ark,
For every shaft a shining mark.

And there, too, was ELIZA FOLLEN,
Who scatters fruit-creating pollen
Where'er a blossom she can find
Hardy enough for Truth's north wind,
Each several point of all her face
Tremblingly bright with the inward
    grace,
As if all motion gave it light
Like phosphorescent seas at night.

There jokes our EDMUND,‡ plainly son
Of him who bearded Jefferson,
A non-resistant by conviction,

in 1846, a handsome silver tea-set was presented to him by his friends in that city.
On the arrival of this gift at the Boston
custom -house, it was charged with an
enormous entrance duty, which would have
been remitted if the articles had ever been
used. It was supposed that if the owner
had not been the leader of the unpopular
abolitionists, this heavy impost would not
have been laid on a friendly British tribute
to an eminent American.

* Mr. James Miller McKim.
† When Mr. Garrison visited Edinburgh
‡ Edmund Quincy.

But with a bump in contradiction,
So that whene'er it gets a chance
His pen delights to play the lance,
And — you may doubt it, or believe it —
Full at the head of Joshua Leavitt
The very calumet he 'd launch,
And scourge him with the olive branch.
A master with the foils of wit,
'T is natural he should love a hit;
A gentleman, withal, and scholar,
Only base things excite his choler,
And then his satire 's keen and thin
As the lithe blade of Saladin.
Good letters are a gift apart,
And his are gems of Flemish art,
True offspring of the fireside Muse,
Not a rag-gathering of news
Like a new hopfield which is all poles,
But of one blood with Horace Walpole's.

There, with one hand behind his back,
Stands PHILLIPS buttoned in a sack,
Our Attic orator, our Chatham;
Old fogies, when he lightens at 'em,
Shrivel like leaves; to him 't is granted
Always to say the word that 's wanted,
So that he seems but speaking clearer
The tiptop thought of every hearer;
Each flash his brooding heart lets fall
Fires what 's combustible in all,
And sends the applauses bursting in
Like an exploded magazine.
His eloquence no frothy show,
The gutter's street-polluted flow,
No Mississippi's yellow flood
Whose shoalness can't be seen for mud; —
So simply clear, serenely deep,
So silent-strong its graceful sweep,
None measures its unrippling force
Who has not striven to stem its course;
How fare their barques who think to play
With smooth Niagara's mane of spray,
Let Austin's total shipwreck say.*
He never spoke a word too much —
Except of Story, or some such,

* On the occasion of the murder of Rev. Elijah P. Lovejoy, editor of an anti-slavery newspaper at Alton, Illinois, an indignation meeting was held in Boston, at which Mr. Austin, Attorney-General of Massachusetts, made a violent pro-slavery speech, which called forth a crushing reply from Wendell Phillips, who thenceforth became a main pillar of abolitionism.

Whom, though condemned by ethics strict,
The heart refuses to convict.

Beyond, a crater in each eye,
Sways brown, broad-shouldered PILLSBURY,
Who tears up words like trees by the roots,
A Theseus in stout cow-hide boots.
The wager of eternal war
Against that loathsome Minotaur
To whom we sacrifice each year
The best blood of our Athens here,
(Dear M., pray brush up your Lempriere).
A terrible denouncer he,
Old Sinai burns unquenchably
Upon his lips; he well might be a
Hot-blazing soul from fierce Judea,
Habakkuk, Ezra, or Hosea.
His words are red-hot iron searers,
And nightmare - like he mounts his hearers,
Spurring them like avenging Fate, or
As Waterton his alligator.

Hard by, as calm as summer even,
Smiles the reviled and pelted STEPHEN,†
The unappeasable Boanerges
To all the Churches and the Clergies,
The grim *savant* who, to complete
His own peculiar cabinet,
Contrived to label 'mong his kicks
One from the followers of Hicks;
Who studied mineralogy
Not with soft book upon the knee,
But learned the properties of stones
By contact sharp of flesh and bones,
And made the *experimentum crucis*
With his own body's vital juices;
A man with caoutchouc endurance,
A perfect gem for life insurance,
A kind of maddened John the Baptist,
To whom the harshest word comes aptest,
Who, struck by stone or brick ill starred,
Hurls back an epithet as hard,
Which, deadlier than stone or brick,
Has a propensity to stick.
His oratory is like the scream

† Stephen S. Foster.

Of the iron-horse's frenzied steam
Which warns the world to leave wide
   space
For the black engine's swerveless race.
Ye men with neckcloths white, I warn
   you —
Habet a whole haymow *in cornu.*

A Judith there, turned Quakeress,
Sits ABBY in her modest dress,*
Serving a table quietly,
As if that mild and downcast eye
Flashed never, with its scorn intense,
More than Medea's eloquence.
So the same force which shakes its
   dread
Far-blazing locks o'er Ætna's head,
Along the wires in silence fares
And messages of commerce bears.
No nobler gift of heart and brain,
No life more white from spot or
   stain,
Was e'er on Freedom's altar laid
Than hers, the simple Quaker maid.

These last three (leaving in the lurch
Some other themes) assault the Church,
Who therefore writes them in her lists
As Satan's limbs and atheists;
For each sect has one argument
Whereby the rest to hell are sent,
Which serves them like the Graiæ's
   tooth,
Passed round in turn from mouth to
   mouth; —
If any *ism* should arise,
They look on it with constable's eyes,
Tie round its neck a heavy *athe-*,
And give it kittens' hydropathy.
This trick with other (useful very)
   tricks
Is laid to the Babylonian *meretrix,*
But 't was in vogue before her day
Wherever priesthoods had their way,

   * Abby Kelley.

And Buddha's Popes with this struck
   dumb
The followers of Fi and Fum.
Well, if the world, with prudent fear,
Pay God a seventh of the year,
And as a Farmer, who would pack
All his religion in one stack,
For this world works six days in seven
And idles on the seventh for Heaven,
Expecting, for his Sunday's sowing,
In the next world to go a-mowing
The crop of all his meeting-going; —
If the poor Church, by power enticed,
Finds none so infidel as Christ,
Quite backward reads his Gospel meek,
(As 't were in Hebrew writ, not
   Greek,)
Fencing the gallows and the sword
With conscripts drafted from his word,
And makes one gate of Heaven so wide
That the rich orthodox might ride
Through on their camels, while the
   poor
Squirm through the scant, unyielding
   door,
Which, of the Gospel's straitest size,
Is narrower than bead-needles' eyes,
What wonder World and Church
   should call
The true faith atheistical?

Yet after all, 'twixt you and me,
Dear Miller, I could never see
That Sin's and Error's ugly smirch
Stained the walls only of the Church;
There are good priests, and men who
   take
Freedom's torn cloak for lucre's sake;
I can't believe the Church so strong,
As some men do, for Right or Wrong.
But, for this subject (long and vext)
I must refer you to my next,
As also for a list exact
Of goods with which the Hall was
   packed.

FRAGMENTS OF AN UNFINISHED POEM.

I AM a man of forty, sirs, a native of
    East Haddam,
And have some reason to surmise that
    I descend from Adam;
But what 's my pedigree to you? That
    I will soon unravel;
I 've sucked my Haddam-Eden dry,
    therefore desire to travel,
And, as a natural consequence, pre-
    sume I need n't say,
I wish to write some letters home and
    have those letters p—
[I spare the word suggestive of those
    grim Next Morns that mount
Clump, clump, the stairways of the
    brain with — "*Sir, my small
    account,*"
And, after every good we gain — Love,
    Fame, Wealth, Wisdom — still,
As punctual as a cuckoo clock, hold up
    their little bill,
The *garçons* in our Café of Life, by
    dreaming us forgot—
Sitting, like Homer's heroes, full and
    musing God knows what, —
Till they say, bowing, *S'il vous plaît,
    voila, Messieurs, la note !*]
I would not hint at this so soon, but in
    our callous day,
The tollman Debt, who drops his bar
    across the world's highway,
Great Cæsar in mid-march would stop,
    if Cæsar could not pay;
Pilgriming 's dearer than it was: men
    cannot travel now
Scot-free from Dan to Beersheba upon
    a simple vow;
Nay, as long back as Bess's time, when
    Walsingham went over
Ambassador to Cousin France, at Can-
    terbury and Dover

He was so fleeced by innkeepers that,
    ere he quitted land,
He wrote to the Prime Minister to take
    the knaves in hand.
If I with staff and scallop-shell should
    try my way to win,
Would Bonifaces quarrel as to who
    should take me in?
Or would my pilgrim's progress end
    where Bunyan started his on,
And my grand tour be round and round
    the back-yard of a prison?
I give you here a saying deep and
    therefore, haply, tru
'T is out of Merlin's pr ecies, but
    quite as good as new
The question boath for men and meates
    longe voyages yt beginne
Lyes in a notshell, rather saye lyes in a
    case of tinne.
But, though men may not travel now,
    as in the Middle Ages,
With self-sustaining retinues of little
    gilt-edged pages,
Yet one may manage pleasantly, wher-
    e'er he likes to roam,
By sending his small pages (at so much
    per small page) home;
And if a staff and scallop-shell won't
    serve so well as then,
Our outlay is about as small — just
    paper, ink, and pen.
Be thankful! Humbugs never die,
    more than the wandering Jew;
Bankrupt, they publish their own
    deaths, slink for a while from
    view,
Then take an *alias,* change the sign,
    and the old trade renew;
Indeed, 't is wondrous how each Age,
    though laughing at the Past,

Insists on having its tight shoe made
    on the same old last ;
How it is sure its system would break
    up at once without
The bunion which it *will* believe
    hereditary gout :
How it takes all its swans for geese,
    nay, stranger yet and sadder,
Sees in its treadmill's fruitless jog a
    heavenward Jacob's-ladder,
Shouts, *Lo, the Shining Heights are*
    reached ! One moment more
    aspire !
Trots into cramps its poor, dear legs,
    gets never an inch the higher,
And, like the others, ends with pipe and
    mug beside the fire.
There, 'tween each doze, it whiffs and
    sips and watches with a sneer
The green recruits that trudge and
    sweat where it had swinked
    whilere,
And sighs to think this soon spent zeal
    should be in simple truth
The only interval between old Fogy-
    hood and Youth :
" Well," thus it muses, " well, what
    odds ? 'T is not for us to warn ;
'T will be the same when we are dead,
    and was ere we were born ;
Without the Treadmill, too, how grind
    our store of winter's corn ?
Had we no stock, nor twelve per cent.
    received from Treadmill shares,
We might . . . but these poor devils
    at last will get our easy-chairs.
High aims and hopes have great re-
    wards, they, too, serene and
    snug,
Shall one day have their soothing pipe
    and their enlivening mug ;
From Adam, empty- handed Youth
    hath always heard the hum
Of Good Times Coming, and will hear
    until the last day come ;
Young ears hear forward, old ones back,
    and, while the earth rolls on,
Full-handed Eld shall hear recede the
    steps of Good Times Gone ;
Ah what a cackle we set up whene'er
    an egg was laid !
Cack-cack-cack-cackle ! rang around,
    the scratch for worms was stayed,
Cut-cut-ca-dah-cut ! from *this* egg the
    coming cock shall stalk !

The great New Era dawns, the age of
    Deeds and not of Talk !
And every stupid hen of us hugged
    close his egg of chalk.
Thought, — sure, I feel life stir within,
    each day with greater strength,
When, lo, the chick ! from former
    chicks he differed not a jot,
But grew and crew and scratched and
    went, like those before, to pot ! "
So muse the dim *Emeriti*, and, mourn-
    ful though it be,
I must confess a kindred thought hath
    sometimes come to me,
Who, though but just of forty turned,
    have heard the rumorous fame
Of nine and ninety Coming Men, all —
    coming till they came.
Pure Mephistopheles all this ? the
    vulgar nature jeers ;
Good friend, while I was writing it, my
    eyes were dim with tears ;
Thrice happy he who cannot see, or
    who his eyes can shut,
Life's deepest sorrow is contained in
    that small word there — But !

. . . .

We 're pretty nearly crazy here with
    change and go ahead,
With flinging our caught bird away for
    two i' th' bush instead,
With butting 'gainst the wall which we
    declare *shall* be a portal,
And questioning Deeps that never yet
    have oped their lips to mortal ;
We 're growing pale and hollow-eyed,
    and out of all condition,
With *mediums* and prophetic chairs,
    and crickets with a mission,
(The most astounding oracles since
    Balaam's donkey spoke, —
'T would seem our furniture was all of
    Dodonean oak.)
Make but the public laugh, be sure
    't will take you to be somebody ;
'T will wrench its button from your
    clutch, my densely earnest glum
    body ;
'T is good, this noble earnestness, good
    in its place, but why
Make great Achilles' shield the pan to
    bake a penny pie ?
Why, when we have a kitchen-range,
    insist that we shall stop,

And bore clear down to central fires to
broil our daily chop?
Excalibur and Durandart are swords of
price, but then
Why draw them sternly when you wish
to trim your nails or pen?
Small gulf between the ape and man;
you bridge it with your staff;
But it will be impassable until the ape
can laugh; —
No, no, be common now and then, be
sensible, be funny,
And, as Siberians bait their traps for
bears with pots of honey,
From which, ere they 'll withdraw their
snouts, they 'll suffer many a
club-lick,
So bait your moral figure-of-fours to
catch the Orson public.
Look how the dead leaves melt their
way down through deep-drifted
snow;
They take the sun-warmth down with
them — pearls could not conquer
so;
There *is* a moral here, you see; if you
would preach, you must
Steep all your truths in sunshine would
you have them pierce the crust;
Brave Jeremiah, you are grand and
terrible, a sign
And wonder, but were never quite a
popular divine;
Fancy the figure you would cut among
the nuts and wine!
I, on occasion, too, could preach, but
hold it wiser far
To give the public sermons it will take
with its cigar,
And morals fugitive, and vague as are
these smoke-wreaths light
In which . . . I trace . . . a . . . let
me see — bless me! 't is out of
sight.

* * * * *

There are some goodish things at sea;
for instance, one can feel
A grandeur in the silent man forever at
the wheel,
That bit of two-legged intellect, that
particle of drill,
Who the huge floundering hulk in-
spires with reason, brain, and
will,

And makes the ship, though skies **are**
black and headwinds whistle
loud,
Obey her conscience there which feels
the loadstar through the cloud;
And when by lusty western gales the
full-sailed barque is hurled
Towards the great moon which, setting
on the silent underworld,
Rounds luridly up to look on ours, and
shoots a broadening line,
Of palpitant light from crest to crest
across the ridgy brine,
Then from the bows look back and feel
a thrill that never stales,
In that full-bosomed, swan-white pomp
of onward-yearning sails;
Ah, when dear cousin Bull laments
that you can't make a poem,
Take him aboard a clipper-ship, young
Jonathan, and show him
A work of art that in its grace and
grandeur may compare
With any thing that any race has fash-
ioned any where;
'T is not a statue, grumbles John; nay,
if you come to that,
We think of Hyde Park Corner, and
concede you beat us flat
With your equestrian statue to a Nose
and a Cocked-hat;
But 't is not a cathedral; well, e'en
that we will allow,
Both statues and cathedrals are ana-
chronistic now;
Your minsters, coz, the monuments of
men who conquered you,
You 'd sell a bargain, if we 'd take the
deans and chapters too;
No; mortal men build nowadays, as
always heretofore,
Good temples to the gods which they
in very truth adore;
The shepherds of this Broker Age, with
all their willing flocks,
Although they bow to stones no more,
do bend the knee to stocks,
And churches can't be beautiful though
crowded, floor and gallery,
If people worship preacher, and if
preacher worship salary;
'T is well to look things in the face, the
god o' the modern universe,
Hermes, cares naught for halls of art
and libraries of puny verse,

If they don't sell, he notes them thus
    upon his ledger — say, *per*
Contra to a loss of so much stone, best
    Russia duck and paper ;
And, after all, about this Art men talk
    a deal of fudge,
Each nation has its path marked out,
    from which it must not budge ;
The Romans had as little art as Noah
    in his ark,
Yet somehow on this globe contrived
    to make an epic mark ;
Religion, painting, sculpture, song, —
    for these they ran up jolly ticks
With Greece and Egypt, but they were
    great artists in their politics,
And if we make no minsters, John, nor
    epics, yet the Fates
Are not entirely deaf to men who *can*
    build ships and states ;
The arts are never pioneers, but men
    have strength and health
Who, called on suddenly, can improvise
    a commonwealth,
Nay, can more easily go on and frame
    them by the dozen,
Than you can make a dinner-speech,
    dear sympathizing cousin :
And, though our restless Jonathan have
    not your graver bent, sure he
Does represent this hand-to-mouth,
    pert, rapid, nineteenth century ;

This is the Age of Scramble ; men
    move faster than they did
When they pried up the imperial
    Past's deep-dusted coffin-lid,
Searching for scrolls of precedent ; the
    wire-leashed lightning now
Replaces Delphos — men don't leave
    the steamer for the scow ;
What public, were they new to-day,
    would ever stop to read
The Iliad, the Shanàmeh, or the Nibe-
    lungenlied ?
Their public 's gone, the artist Greek,
    the lettered Shah, the hairy
    Graf —
Folio and plesiosaur sleep well ; *we*
    weary o'er a paragraph ;
The mind moves planet-like no more,
    it fizzes, cracks, and bustles ;
From end to end with journals dry the
    land o'ershadowed rustles,
As with dead leaves a winter-beech,
    and with their breath - roused
    jars
Amused, we care not if they hide the
    eternal skies and stars ;
Down to the general level of the Board
    of Brokers sinking,
The Age takes in the newspapers, or,
    to say sooth unshrinking,
The newspapers take in the Age, and
    stocks do all the thinking.

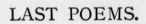

LAST POEMS.

LAST POEMS.

LAST POEMS.

The following note was prefixed to this group when published in 1895 : "This little volume contains those of the poems which Mr. Lowell wrote in his last years which, I believe, he might have wished to preserve. Three of them were published before his death. Of the rest, two appear here for the first time. C. E. N."

HOW I CONSULTED THE ORACLE OF THE GOLDFISHES.

WHAT know we of the world immense
Beyond the narrow ring of sense ?
What should we know, who lounge about
The house we dwell in, nor find out,
Masked by a wall, the secret cell
Where the soul's priests in hiding dwell ?
The winding stair that steals aloof
To chapel-mysteries 'neath the roof ?

It lies about us, yet as far
From sense sequestered as a star
New launched its wake of fire to trace
In secrecies of unprobed space,
Whose beacon's lightning - pinioned
    spears
Might earthward haste a thousand years
Nor reach it. So remote seems this
World undiscovered, yet it is
A neighbor near and dumb as death,
So near, we seem to feel the breath
Of its hushed habitants as they
Pass us unchallenged, night and day.

Never could mortal ear nor eye
By sound or sign suspect them nigh,
Yet why may not some subtler sense
Than those poor two give evidence ?
Transfuse the ferment of their being
Into our own, past hearing, seeing,
As men, if once attempered so,
Far off each other's thought can know ?
As horses with an instant thrill
Measure their rider's strength of will ?

Comes not to all some glimpse that brings
Strange sense of sense-escaping things ?
Wraiths some transfigured nerve divines ?
Approaches, premonitions, signs,
Voices of Ariel that die out
In the dim No Man's Land of Doubt ?

Are these Night's dusky birds ? Are
    these
Phantasmas of the silences
Outer or inner ? — rude heirlooms
From grovellers in the cavern-glooms,
Who in unhuman Nature saw
Misshapen foes with tusk and claw,
And with those night-fears brute and
    blind
Peopled the chaos of their mind,
Which, in ungovernable hours,
Still make their bestial lair in ours ?

Were they, or were they not ? Yes ; no ;
Uncalled they come, unbid they go,
And leave us fumbling in a doubt
Whether within us or without
The spell of this illusion be
That witches us to hear and see
As in a twi-life what it will,
And hath such wonder-working skill
That what we deemed most solid-wrought
Turns a mere figment of our thought,
Which when we grasp at in despair
Our fingers find vain semblance there,
For Psyche seeks a corner-stone
Firmer than aught to matter known.

Is it illusion ? Dream-stuff ? Show
Made of the wish to have it so ?
'T were something, even though this were
    all :
So the poor prisoner, on his wall
Long gazing, from the chance designs
Of crack, mould, weather-stain, refines
New and new pictures without cease,
Landscape, or saint, or altar-piece :

But these are Fancy's common brood
Hatched in the nest of solitude;
This is Dame Wish's hourly trade,
By our rude sires a goddess made.
Could longing, though its heart broke,
        give
Trances in which we chiefly live?
Moments that darken all beside,
Tearfully radiant as a bride?
Beckonings of bright escape, of wings
Purchased with loss of baser things?
Blithe truancies from all control
Of Hylë, outings of the soul?

The worm, by trustful instinct led,
Draws from its womb a slender thread,
And drops, confiding that the breeze
Will waft it to unpastured trees:
So the brain spins itself, and so
Swings boldly off in hope to blow
Across some tree of knowledge, fair
With fruitage new, none else shall
        share:
Sated with wavering in the Void,
It backward climbs, so best employed,
And, where no proof is nor can be,
Seeks refuge under Analogy;
Truth's soft half-sister, she may tell
Where lurks, seld-sought, the other's
        well.

With metaphysic midges sore,
My Thought seeks comfort at her door,
And, at her feet a suppliant cast,
Evokes a spectre of the past.
Not such as shook the knees of Saul,
But winsome, golden-gay withal, —
Two fishes in a globe of glass,
That pass, and waver, and re-pass,
And lighten that way, and then this,
Silent as meditation is.
With a half-humorous smile I see
In this their aimless industry,
These errands nowhere and returns
Grave as a pair of funeral urns,
This ever-seek and never-find,
A mocking image of my mind.
But not for this I bade you climb
Up from the darkening deeps of time:
Help me to tame these wild day-mares
That sudden on me unawares.
Fish, do your duty, as did they
Of the Black Island far away
In life's safe places, — far as you
From all that now I see or do.

You come, embodied flames, as when
I knew you first, nor yet knew men;
Your gold renews my golden days,
Your splendor all my loss repays.

'T is more than sixty years ago
Since first I watched your to-and-fro;
Two generations come and gone
From silence to oblivion,
With all their noisy strife and stress
Lulled in the grave's forgivingness,
While you unquenchably survive
Immortal, almost more alive.
I watched you then a curious boy,
Who in your beauty found full joy,
And, by no problem-debts distrest,
Sate at life's board a welcome guest.
You were my sister's pets, not mine;
But Property's dividing line
No hint of dispossession drew
On any map my simplesse knew;
O golden age, not yet dethroned!
What made me happy, that I owned;
You were my wonders, you my Lars,
In darkling days my sun and stars,
And over you entranced I hung,
Too young to know that I was young.
Gazing with still unsated bliss,
My fancies took some shape like this:
" I have my world, and so have you,
A tiny universe for two,
A bubble by the artist blown,
Scarcely more fragile than our own,
Where you have all a whale could
        wish,
Happy as Eden's primal fish.
Manna is dropt you thrice a day
From some kind heaven not far away,
And still you snatch its softening crumbs,
Nor, more than we, think whence it
        comes.
No toil seems yours but to explore
Your cloistered realm from shore to
        shore;
Sometimes you trace its limits round,
Sometimes its limpid depths you sound,
Or hover motionless midway,
Like gold-red clouds at set of day;
Erelong you whirl with sudden whim
Off to your globe's most distant rim,
Where, greatened by the watery lens,
Methinks no dragon of the fens
Flashed huger scales against the sky,
Roused by Sir Bevis or Sir Guy,

And the one eye that meets my view,
Lidless and strangely largening, too,
Like that of conscience in the dark,
Seems to make me its single mark.
What a benignant lot is yours
That have an own All-out-of-doors,
No words to spell, no sums to do,
No Nepos and no parlyvoo!
How happy you without a thought
Of such cross things as Must and
    Ought, —
I too the happiest of boys
To see and share your golden joys! "

So thought the child, in simpler words,
Of you his finny flocks and herds;
Now, an old man, I bid you rise
To the fine sight behind the eyes,
And, lo, you float and flash again
In the dark cistern of my brain.
But o'er your visioned flames I brood
With other mien, in other mood;
You are no longer there to please,
But to stir argument, and tease
My thought with all the ghostly shapes
From which no moody man escapes.
Diminished creature, I no more
Find Fairyland beside my door,
But for each moment's pleasure pay
With the *quart d'heure* of Rabelais!

I watch you in your crystal sphere,
And wonder if you see and hear
Those shapes and sounds that stir the
    wide
Conjecture of the world outside;
In your pent lives, as we in ours,
Have you surmises dim of powers,
Of presences obscurely shown,
Of lives a riddle to your own,
Just on the senses' outer verge,
Where sense-nerves into soul-nerves
    merge,
Where we conspire our own deceit
Confederate in deft Fancy's feat,
And the fooled brain befools the eyes
With pageants woven of its own lies?
But *are* they lies? Why more than those
Phantoms that startle your repose,
Half seen, half heard, then flit away,
And leave you your prose-bounded day?

The things ye see as shadows I
Know to be substance; tell me why

My visions, like those haunting you,
May not be as substantial too.
Alas, who ever answer heard
From fish, and dream-fish too? Absurd!
Your consciousness I half divine,
But you are wholly deaf to mine.
Go, I dismiss you; ye have done
All that ye could; our silk is spun:
Dive back into the deep of dreams,
Where what is real is what seems!
Yet I shall fancy till my grave
Your lives to mine a lesson gave;
If lesson none, an image, then,
Impeaching self-conceit in men
Who put their confidence alone
In what they call the Seen and Known.
How seen? How known? As through
    your glass
Our wavering apparitions pass
Perplexingly, then subtly wrought
To some quite other thing by thought.
Here shall my resolution be:
The shadow of the mystery
Is haply wholesomer for eyes
That cheat us to be overwise,
And I am happy in my right
To love God's darkness as His light.

TURNER'S OLD TÉMÉRAIRE.

UNDER A FIGURE SYMBOLIZING THE
CHURCH.

THOU wast the fairest of all man-made
    things;
The breath of heaven bore up thy cloudy
    wings,
And, patient in their triple rank,
The thunders crouched about thy flank,
Their black lips silent with the doom of
    kings.

The storm-wind loved to rock him in thy
    pines,
And swell thy vans with breath of great
    designs;
Long-wildered pilgrims of the main
By thee relaid their course again,
Whose prow was guided by celestial
    signs.

How didst thou trample on tumultuous
    seas,

Or, like some basking sea-beast stretched
    at ease,
Let the bull-fronted surges glide
Caressingly along thy side,
Like glad hounds leaping by the hunts-
    man's knees!

Heroic feet, with fire of genius shod,
In battle's ecstasy thy deck have trod,
While from their touch a fulgor ran
Through plank and spar, from man to
    man,
Welding thee to a thunderbolt of God.

Now a black demon, belching fire and
    steam,
Drags thee away, a pale, dismantled
    dream,
And all thy desecrated bulk
Must landlocked lie, a helpless hulk,
To gather weeds in the regardless stream.

Woe 's' me, from Ocean's sky-horizoned
    air
To this! Better, the flame-cross still
    aflare,
Shot-shattered to have met thy doom
Where thy last lightnings cheered the
    gloom,
Than here be safe in dangerless de-
    spair.

Thy drooping symbol to the flagstaff
    clings,
Thy rudder soothes the tide to lazy rings,
Thy thunders now but birthdays greet,
Thy planks forget the martyrs' feet,
Thy masts what challenges the sea-wind
    brings.

Thou a mere hospital, where human
    wrecks,
Like winter-flies, crawl those renownëd
    decks,
Ne'er trodden save by captive foes,
And wonted sternly to impose
God's will and thine on bowed imperial
    necks!

Shall nevermore, engendered of thy fame,
A new sea-eagle heir thy conqueror
    name,
And with commissioned talons wrench
From thy supplanter's grimy clench

His sheath of steel, his wings of smoke
    and flame?

This shall the pleased eyes of our children
    see;
For this the stars of God long even as
    we;
Earth listens for his wings; the Fates
Expectant lean; Faith cross-propt waits,
And the tired waves of Thought's insur-
    gent sea.

ST. MICHAEL THE WEIGHER.

STOOD the tall Archangel weighing
All man's dreaming, doing, saying,
All the failure and the pain,
All the triumph and the gain,
In the unimagined years,
Full of hopes, more full of tears,
Since old Adam's hopeless eyes
Backward searched for Paradise,
And, instead, the flame-blade saw
Of inexorable Law.

Waking, I beheld him there,
With his fire-gold, flickering hair,
In his blinding armor stand,
And the scales were in his hand:
Mighty were they, and full well
They could poise both heaven and hell.
" Angel," asked I humbly then,
" Weighest thou the souls of men?
That thine office is, I know."
" Nay," he answered me, "not so;
But I weigh the hope of Man
Since the power of choice began,
In the world, of good or ill."
Then I waited and was still.

In one scale I saw him place
All the glories of our race,
Cups that lit Belshazzar's feast,
Gems, the lightning of the East,
Kublai's sceptre, Cæsar's sword,
Many a poet's golden word,
Many a skill of science, vain
To make men as gods again.

In the other scale he threw
Things regardless, outcast, few,
Martyr-ash, arena sand,
Of St. Francis' cord a strand,

Beechen cups of men whose need
Fasted that the poor might feed,
Disillusions and despairs
Of young saints with grief-grayed hairs,
Broken hearts that brake for Man.

Marvel through my pulses ran
Seeing then the beam divine
Swiftly on this hand decline,
While Earth's splendor and renown
Mounted light as thistle-down.

A VALENTINE.

Let others wonder what fair face
    Upon their path shall shine,
And, fancying half, half hoping, trace
    Some maiden shape of tenderest grace
        To be their Valentine.

Let other hearts with tremor sweet
    One secret wish enshrine
That Fate may lead their happy feet
    Fair Julia in the lane to meet
        To be their Valentine.

But I, far happier, am secure
    I know the eyes benign,
The face more beautiful and pure
    Than Fancy's fairest portraiture
        That mark my Valentine.

More than when first I singled thee,
    This only prayer is mine, —
That, in the years I yet shall see,
    As, darling, in the past, thou 'lt be
        My happy Valentine.

AN APRIL BIRTHDAY — AT SEA.

On this wild waste, where never blossom
    came,
    Save the white wind-flower in the
        billow's cap,
Or those pale disks of momentary flame,
    Loose petals dropped from Dian's care-
        less lap,
    What far fetched influence all my
        fancy fills,
    With singing birds and dancing daffo-
        dils?

Why, 't is her day whom jocund April
    brought,
    And who brings April with her in her
        eyes;
It is her vision lights my lonely thought,
    Even as a rose that opes its hushed
        surprise
        In sick men's chambers, with its
            glowing breath
        Plants Summer at the glacier edge
            of Death.

Gray sky, sea gray as mossy stones on
    graves; —
    Anon comes April in her jollity;
And dancing down the bleak vales 'tween
    the waves,
    Makes them green glades for all her
        flowers and me.
        The gulls turn thrushes, charmed are
            sea and sky
        By magic of my thought, and know
            not why.

Ah, but I know, for never April's shine,
    Nor passion gust of rain, nor all her
        flowers
Scattered in haste, were seen so sudden
    fine
    As she in various mood, on whom the
        powers
        Of happiest stars in fair conjunction
            smiled
        To bless the birth of April's darling
            child.

LOVE AND THOUGHT.

What hath Love with Thought to
    do?
Still at variance are the two.
Love is sudden, Love is rash,
Love is like the levin flash,
Comes as swift, as swiftly goes,
And his mark as surely knows.

Thought is lumpish, Thought is slow,
Weighing long 'tween yes and no;
When dear Love is dead and gone,
Thought comes creeping in anon,
And, in his deserted nest,
Sits to hold the crowner's quest.

Since we love, what need to think ?
Happiness stands on a brink
Whence too easy 't is to fall
Whither 's no return at all ;
Have a care, half-hearted lover,
Thought would only push her over !

THE NOBLER LOVER.

IF he be a nobler lover, take him !
　You in you I seek, and not myself ;
Love with men 's what women choose to
　　make him,
　Seraph strong to soar, or fawn-eyed elf ;
All I am or can, your beauty gave it,
　Lifting me a moment nigh to you,
And my bit of heaven, I fain would save
　　it —
　Mine I thought it was, I never knew.

What you take of me is yours to serve
　　you,
　All I give, you gave to me before ;
Let him win you ! If I but deserve you,
　I keep all you grant to him and more :
You shall make me dare what others dare
　　not,
　You shall keep my nature pure as snow,
And a light from you that others share not
　Shall transfigure me where'er I go.

Let me be your thrall ! However lowly
　Be the bondsman's service I can do,
Loyalty shall make it high and holy ;
　Naught can be unworthy, done for you.
Men shall say, " A lover of this fashion
　Such an icy mistress well beseems."
Women say, " Could we deserve such
　　passion,
　We might be the marvel that he
　　dreams."

ON HEARING A SONATA OF BEETHOVEN'S PLAYED IN THE NEXT ROOM.

UNSEEN Musician, thou art sure to
　please,
For those same notes in happier days I
　heard
Poured by dear hands that long have
　never stirred

Yet now again for me delight the keys :
Ah me, to strong illusions such as these
What are Life's solid things ? The walls
　　that gird
Our senses, lo, a casual scent or word
Levels, and 't is the soul that hears and
　　sees !

Play on, dear girl, and many be the years
Ere some grayhaired survivor sit like me
And, for thy largess pay a meed of tears
Unto another who, beyond the sea
Of Time and Change, perhaps not sadly
　　hears
A music in this verse undreamed by thee !

VERSES

INTENDED TO GO WITH A POSSET DISH
TO MY DEAR LITTLE GODDAUGHTER,
1882.

It is of interest to know that the goddaughter was a child of Leslie Stephen.

IN good old times, which means, you
　know,
The time men wasted long ago,
And we must blame our brains or mood
If that we squander seems less good,
In those blest days when wish was act
And fancy dreamed itself to fact,
Godfathers used to fill with guineas
The cups they gave their pickaninnies,
Performing functions at the chrism
Not mentioned in the Catechism.
No millioner, poor I fill up
With wishes my more modest cup,
Though had I Amalthea's horn
It should be hers the newly born.
Nay, shudder not ! I should bestow it
So brimming full she could n't blow it.
Wishes are n't horses : true, but still
There are worse roadsters than goodwill.
And so I wish my darling health,
And just to round my couplet, wealth,
With faith enough to bridge the chasm
'Twixt Genesis and Protoplasm,
And bear her o'er life's current vext
From this world to a better next,
Where the full glow of God puts out
Poor reason's farthing candle, Doubt.
I 've wished her healthy, wealthy, wise,
What more can godfather devise ?

But since there's room for countless wishes
In these old-fashioned posset dishes,
I'll wish her from my plenteous store
Of those commodities two more,
Her father's wit, veined through and through
With tenderness that Watts (but whew!
Celia's aflame, I mean no stricture
On his Sir Josh-surpassing picture) —
I wish her next, and 't is the soul
Of all I 've dropt into the bowl,
Her mother's beauty — nay, but two
So fair at once would never do.
Then let her but the half possess,
Troy was besieged ten years for less.
Now if there 's any truth in Darwin,
And we from what was, all we are win,
I simply wish the child to be
A sample of Heredity,
Enjoying to the full extent
Life's best, the Unearned Increment
Which Fate her Godfather to flout
Gave *him* in legacies of gout.
Thus, then, the cup is duly filled;
Walk steady, dear, lest all be spilled.

ON A BUST OF GENERAL GRANT.

"This poem is the last, so far as is known, written by Mr. Lowell. He laid it aside for revision, leaving two of the verses incomplete. In a pencilled fragment of the poem the first verse appears as follows : —

'Strong, simple, silent, such are Nature's Laws.'

In the final copy, from which the poem is now printed, the verse originally stood : —

'Strong, steadfast, silent are the   laws.'

but 'steadfast' is crossed out, and 'simple' written above.

"A similar change is made in the ninth verse of the stanza, where 'simpleness' is substituted for 'steadfastness.' The change from 'steadfast' to 'simple' was not made, probably through oversight, in the first verse of the second stanza. There is nothing to indicate what epithet Mr. Lowell would have chosen to complete the first verse of the third stanza. C. E. N."

STRONG, simple, silent are the [steadfast] laws
That sway this universe, of none withstood,

Unconscious of man's outcries or applause,
Or what man deems his evil or his good ;
And when the Fates ally them with a cause
That wallows in the sea-trough and seems lost,
Drifting in danger of the reefs and sands
Of shallow counsels, this way, that way, tost,
Strength, silence, simpleness, of these three strands
They twist the cable shall the world hold fast
To where its anchors clutch the bed-rock of the Past.

Strong, simple, silent, therefore such was he
Who helped us in our need; the eternal law
That who can saddle Opportunity
Is God's elect, though many a mortal flaw
May minish him in eyes that closely see,
Was verified in him : what need we say
Of one who made success where others failed,
Who, with no light save that of common day,
Struck hard, and still struck on till Fortune quailed,
But that (so sift the Norns) a desperate man
Ne'er fell at last to one who was not wholly man.

A face all prose where Time's [benignant] haze
Softens no raw edge yet, nor makes all fair
With the beguiling light of vanished days;
This is relentless granite, bleak and bare,
Roughhewn, and scornful of æsthetic phrase ;
Nothing is here for fancy, naught for dreams,
The Present's hard uncompromising light
Accents all vulgar outlines, flaws, and seams,
Yet vindicates some pristine natural right
O'ertopping that hereditary grace
Which marks the gain or loss of some time-fondled race.

So Marius looked, methinks, and Crom-
well so,
Not in the purple born, to those they
led
Nearer for that and costlier to the foe,
New moulders of old forms, by nature
bred
The exhaustless life of manhood's seeds
to show,
Let but the ploughshare of portentous
times
Strike deep enough to reach them where
they lie:
Despair and danger are their fostering
climes,
And their best sun bursts from a stormy
sky:
He was our man of men, nor would abate
The utmost due manhood could claim of
fate.

Nothing ideal, a plain-people's man
At the first glance, a more deliberate
ken
Finds type primeval, theirs in whose
veins ran
Such blood as quelled the dragon in his
den,
Made harmless fields, and better worlds
began:

He came grim-silent, saw and did the
deed
That was to do; in his master-grip
Our sword flashed joy; no skill of words
could breed
Such sure conviction as that close-
clamped lip;
He slew our dragon, nor, so seemed it,
knew
He had done more than any simplest man
might do.

Yet did this man, war-tempered, stern as
steel
Where steel opposed, prove soft in civil
sway;
The hand hilt-hardened had lost tact to
feel
The world's base coin, and glozing knaves
made prey
Of him and of the entrusted Common-
weal;
So Truth insists and will not be denied.
We turn our eyes away, and so will Fame,
As if in his last battle he had died
Victor for us and spotless of all blame,
Doer of hopeless tasks which praters
shirk,
One of those still plain men that do the
world's rough work.